Cleanth Brooks and Robert Penn Warren

Cleanth Brooks and Robert Penn Warren

A Literary Correspondence

Edited by James A. Grimshaw, Jr.

University of Missouri Press
Columbia and London

The letters of Robert Penn Warren copyright (c) by Robert Penn Warren.
Reprinted by permission of William Morris Agency, Inc., on behalf of the
Author's estate

The letters of Cleanth Brooks copyright (c) by Cleanth Brooks. Reprinted
by permission of the Cleanth Brooks Estate

All additional material copyright (c) 1998 by
The Curators of the University of Missouri
University of Missouri Press, Columbia, Missouri 65201
Printed and bound in the United States of America
5 4 3 2 1   02 01 00 99 98

Library of Congress Cataloging-in-Publication Data

Brooks, Cleanth, 1906–
    Cleanth Brooks and Robert Penn Warren : a literary correspondence
/ edited by James A. Grimshaw, Jr.
        p. cm.
    Includes bibliographical references and index.
    ISBN 0-8262-1165-8 (alk. paper)
    1. Brooks, Cleanth, 1906–   —Correspondence.   2. Warren, Robert
Penn, 1905–   —Correspondence.   3. Southern States—Intellectual
life—20th century.   4. Authors, American—Southern States—
Correspondence.   5. Authors, American—20th century—
Correspondence.   6. Critics—United States—Correspondence.
I. Warren, Robert Penn, 1905–   . II. Grimshaw, James A.
III. Title.
PS29.B74A4   1998
809—dc21
    [B]   97-46078
                                                              CIP

⊗™ This paper meets the requirements of the
American National Standard for Permanence of Paper
for Printed Library Materials, Z39.48, 1984.

Designer: Stephanie Foley
Typesetter: BOOKCOMP
Printer and binder: Thomson-Shore, Inc.
Typeface: Palatino

To Marisa Bisi Erskine
and
In memory of Albert Russell Erskine, Jr., 1912–1993

Contents

OTHER BOOKS WRITTEN AND EDITED BY JAMES A. GRIMSHAW, JR.

Cleanth Brooks at the United States Air Force Academy

Robert Penn Warren: A Descriptive Bibliography, 1922–1979

The Flannery O'Connor Companion

Robert Penn Warren's Brother to Dragons: *A Discussion*

"Time's Glory": Original Essays on Robert Penn Warren

The Paul Wells Barrus Lectures, 1983–1989

Cleanth Brooks/Robert Penn Warren: Friends of Their Youth

Foreword

by Lewis P. Simpson

THE CORRESPONDENCE SO CAPABLY COLLECTED and edited in this volume by James A. Grimshaw, Jr., affords the most substantial resource we have for recovering the story of the lengthy, indeed almost lifelong, literary collaboration between Cleanth Brooks and Robert Penn Warren. In the most specific sense, the letters here brought together tell the story of the engagement of two college teachers in a particular kind of collaboration: the making, and remaking, of a series of undergraduate textbooks. On the face of it, literary historians may say, the story is hardly worth telling, the production of textbooks being generally recognized, often by those who make them, as a mundane academic activity, which, though it holds forth the prospect of some mercenary reward, may involve, as anyone who reads this correspondence between Brooks and Warren will realize, a good deal of sheer editorial drudgery.

Yet, as anyone who reads this correspondence must also realize, textbook making by Brooks and Warren transcended prosaic academic motives. Grimshaw points to Richard B. Sale's interview with Warren in 1969, in which Warren observed that he and Brooks were redeemed from the drudgery of their work on textbooks by the fact that for them it was a "sociable" activity. The result "of collaborations and argument and teaching in the classroom," the making of each book was, to be sure, "a social event." Yet, Warren immediately added, the process of making a textbook was more than mere sociability: it was "a matter of one's social life in the deepest way." Warren was trying to get at something about his relationship with Brooks he felt but could not easily define. At the same time, Brooks would have surely agreed, Warren was expressing the way Brooks himself felt about his relationship to Warren. This may be summed up as their mutual sense that, in the making of *An Approach to Literature, Understanding Poetry, Understanding Fiction, Modern Rhetoric,* and *American Literature: The Makers and the Making* (a task in which they had the distinguished assistance of their Yale colleague R. W. B. Lewis), they shared not only an unselfish friendship but something even rarer, the experience of a genuine community of vocation. What Warren wrote about his relationship with Brooks in 1976 Brooks might well have said about his relationship with Warren: "I cannot be sure what I most sought, the comfort of his generosity of mind or the rigor of his logic. And, no doubt, he often had to suffer the tension between his natural kindness and a natural love of truth. Both the comfort and the truth have been, over the years, significant . . . , for though we share enough to provide a firm basis for friendship, there are between us vast differences in temperament, character, and the sense of the world." Thus, Warren said, "every agreement [between us] has, in the end, to be regarded in the dramatic context of sometimes hard-won agreement."

Although the analogy is not precise, in thinking about the relationship between Brooks and Warren, I am reminded of the kind of community Melville referred to when he spoke of the "ineffable sociabilities" he felt in his relationship with Hawthorne. As Grimshaw demonstrates, in the context of the literary history of the United States in the twentieth century, and more broadly, of the history of twentieth-century letters generally, the collaboration represented by the textbooks Brooks and Warren planned, published, and afterward carefully revised, keeping some of them in print for many years, represents in a larger sense an intellectual, and not less a spiritual, collaboration that is not only present in their shared efforts but also implicit in the body of eminently distinctive work each man accomplished on his own.

Why the joint work Brooks and Warren did on a series of textbooks transcended the usual rationale of such collaborative endeavors cannot perhaps be comprehended in precise terms. The fact that they had a common cultural inheritance in the small-town world of a South that in the early twentieth century still experienced a dark sense of intimacy with the Civil War; the fact that they both attended Vanderbilt University in the 1920s, when the Fugitive and Agrarian movements made it the most interesting place in the South for youths of serious literary inclinations; the fact that they both became Rhodes Scholars who received the B.Litt. degree from Oxford (Warren in 1930, Brooks in 1932): these facts—plus the hardly incidental one that both refused to enter the Ph.D. mill—provided them with a homogenous background. All this might not have made much difference in the long run, however, save for the fact that, just as they reached the first truly performative stage of their careers, they became colleagues in the English department of the small state university of a state that before secession had been one of the most affluent—and at the same time, one of the most culturally complex—entities in the nation. Now sixty-five years after the Civil War, though its culture remained complex, it was one of the poorest and most backward of the former slave states, with a public education system that was mediocre at best. But in the 1930s education as represented by Louisiana State University and Agricultural and Mechanical College was undergoing a distinct change of fortune. Located in the small city on the Mississippi River that served as the capital of Louisiana (where French could still be heard in the streets), LSU—called by its alumni "The Ole War Skule" in tribute to its origin as a tiny pre–Civil War military academy directed by William Tecumseh Sherman—had been taken under the benevolent wing of a man who wanted to make Louisiana, and the whole nation for that matter, into an affluent populist empire, in which "every man would be king," and he would be the Kingfish.

When he returned to the LSU campus in 1963 for a brief visit, Robert Penn Warren, looking back on the experience of living in the Louisiana of twenty-five years earlier, exclaimed, "After living in Louisiana nothing has been real." I was reminded of this remark one afternoon in the late spring of 1985 when Warren phoned me to ask about the rumor that he reports to Brooks in three letters of that year (see the letters of June 20, July 9, and July 1985). The rumor was to the effect that fifty years earlier, in connection with the publication of the *Southern Review,* he and Brooks had "taken Huey for $100,000." Although I was aware of two or three other rumored intimations that somehow Brooks and Warren had a direct, and somehow shady, connection with Long, I did not know anything about this particular bit of malicious apocrypha. But I knew enough about the origin and publication of the first series of the *Southern Review* (1935–1942) to know that neither Brooks nor Warren ever met the Kingfish or had any contact with him, though Warren saw him once in the flesh when Long spoke briefly at a luncheon on the campus some five months before he was shot down in the halls of the state capitol. Furthermore, I knew that the notion of any direct tie, let alone a conniving one, between Long and two young men who were primarily moved by the conviction of the absolute importance of literature as a way of life was preposterous. Yet those who familiarize themselves with the LSU of the 1930s cannot fail to understand one of the immutable ironies of the time: Brooks and Warren, along with all the other faculty members of that unusual period, no matter how much they may have disliked his authoritarian, manipulative political methods, necessarily had some connection with the man who had taken control of Louisiana after he became governor in 1928 and had made his control virtually absolute after he had taken his seat in the United States Senate in 1932. All of them were inescapably the beneficiaries of this powerful man, who, combining shrewd and ruthless political ambition with a regard for education, advised "the school people" that, since the politicians are going to steal, he would make them "steal for the schools." So it was that, exerting virtual dictatorial control over the state legislators, Long, whose chief personal interest was in the football team and the marching band, saw to it that in the depths of the Great Depression—when universities all over the country were trimming their faculties and allowing their facilities to deteriorate—the Louisiana legislature provided LSU with better funding than it had ever before had. This enabled the institution not only to acquire new buildings but also to do things that had hardly yet been dreamed of at LSU, among them, establish a university press destined to take its place among the best in the country, fund a literary quarterly that from its initial issue was recognized as one of the best of its kind, and, more significantly, enhance the quality of a parochial and undistinguished faculty by infusing it with several "fertile, creative minds."

I am here drawing on the retrospective vision of one of these minds, Robert B. Heilman, whose witness to what happened at LSU in the 1930s—as set forth in a series of rich, memorable essays—is the more arresting because, arriving in Baton Rouge with a fresh Harvard Ph.D. in the late summer of 1935 to be an instructor in the LSU English department, he found himself seated in the visitor's gallery of the Louisiana House of Representatives the night Long was assassinated. Shortly thereafter the head of the English department, William A. Read, told Heilman that in view of Long's death, he was not sure that LSU could reopen for the fall term. "It was my only experience of a situation," Heilman says, "in which the whole life of a state, from its political fabric to its educational system, seemed tied to the life of one man."

LSU did open on time in the fall of 1935; and Heilman remained in Baton Rouge to experience Long's continuing power in the post-assassination years, until it was finally broken by the eruption of the "Louisiana scandals" in 1939. Following this debacle a good many of those who perpetuated Long's regime went to prison, including James Monroe Smith, Long's handpicked president of LSU. Yet, as Heilman observes, Long's influence did not end with the scandals. It was permanent, not because the Kingfish made the Fighting Tigers into a national football power, but because, with no direct hand in it, he was yet responsible for the enlargement of the educational possibilities of LSU, particularly through making possible a "remarkable influx" of talented faculty. In Heilman's opinion the ultimate source of this influx, which included Brooks and Warren, was the "imaginativeness evident in the very complex makeup of the man who ruled Louisiana for a time."

> It was an imaginativeness which could grasp ends beyond profit and power. Huey had it, and I suspect it influenced his appointment of some underlings who had the same quality, notably James Monroe Smith. Smith was a very imaginative man (unlike Huey's statehouse followers, singularly unable to grasp the consequences of conspicuous looting). And aside from that more or less direct channel, the impulse to imaginative leaps could conceivably have been carried more or less unconsciously by lesser university people than Smith, who had some influence on the way things went.

"The impulse to imaginative leaps"—this is what another Rhodes Scholar, Charles W. Pipkin, the youthful political scientist and dean of the LSU Graduate School, responded to when he became interested in LSU's supporting a literary and intellectual journal, and it was surely the impulse Brooks and Warren responded to when they not only seized on the opportunity to serve as the associate editors of the *Southern Review* (with Pipkin as the nominal chief editor) but also boldly made a journal being issued from a deep South institution as provincial as "The Ole War Skule" an important voice in modern letters. Perhaps it may be said that a similar impulse to take the imaginative leap led these two amazingly energetic young teachers and editors, in spite of the heavy burden imposed on them by the combination of teaching and editorial duties, to put their minds to "solving," in Brooks's words, "a serious practical problem," namely, the inability of students to read and understand a poem or a novel. The result was that they not only conceived "an approach to literature" that would involve teachers and students in the act of actually reading a given literary text rather than reading about it but also created the textbooks that would implement their idea.

Initially Brooks and Warren did not realize that the embodiment of their simple idea about focusing on the text in *An Approach to Literature* and *Understanding Poetry* would be so revolutionary in its effect on the literary classroom; and they would always be puzzled by the vehemence of the attacks these books provoked. They were especially vexed by attacks that declared that they had no conception of understanding literature historically, when both of them were so keenly and amply aware that, as Warren put it in a well-known observation, "Historical sense and poetic sense should not, in the end, be contradictory, for if the poetry is the little myth we make, history is the big myth we live, and in our living, constantly remake." When he said this Warren was discussing the rationale of *Brother to Dragons*, his long poem about Thomas Jefferson and the murder of a slave by two of his nephews, in which the relation of history and myth is the basic theme. In fact, it was his effort to understand this relationship that had moved him to write his first book, a biography of John Brown, and that was the fundamental motive for all his poems and novels. Warren's deepening grasp of this theme in the Baton Rouge years enabled him to complete a somewhat uncertain apprenticeship to creative writing by publishing *Thirty-Six Poems*, his first collection of poetry, in 1935, and *Night Rider*, his brilliant first novel, in 1939. The same impulse to the imaginative leap promoted Warren to begin that complex distillation of observation and reflection on the nature of political power embodied in his classic novel *All the King's Men*, which was published four years after he left Louisiana. Although less dramatically in his case, the same impulse to take the imaginative leap moved Brooks to conclude his apprenticeship to criticism in 1939 with *Modern Poetry and the Tradition*, his landmark study of the relation of myth and history.

Acknowledgments

MANY PEOPLE HAVE KINDLY ASSISTED ME over the course of the past ten years, and I am most grateful to each and every one of them. I must begin by thanking Paul Blanchard, Executor of the Cleanth Brooks Estate, and John Michael Walsh, Literary Executor of Cleanth Brooks; John Burt, Literary Executor of Robert Penn Warren, and Rosanna Warren, Gabriel Warren, and the late Eleanor Clark Warren of the Robert Penn Warren Estate; Jill Westmoreland and Owen Laster, William Morris Agency; and the late Cleanth Brooks and the late Robert Penn Warren, both of whom gave early permission and kind encouragement when I first proposed this project.

Of particular help in the early phase of this project were Dr. Patricia C. Willis, Curator, Yale Collection of American Literature, Beinecke Rare Book and Manuscript Library, and staff members Bill Hemmig, Danielle McCellan, and Lori Misure; Dr. Paul Holbrook, Dr. James D. Birchfield, and Ms. Karen T. Ellenberg, King Library Press, University of Kentucky; Boynton Merrill, Jr., Henderson, Kentucky, for his personal interest in this project; and Faye Phillips, Hill Memorial Library, Louisiana State University.

Among the individuals who read the manuscript, listened to ideas, gave moral support, and offered gentle suggestions, I thank the following: Professor Charlotte Beck, Maryville College, Tennessee; Professor Emeritus Joseph Blotner, University of Michigan, and Warren's biographer; Judy Bolton, Public Services, Special Collections, Hill Library, Louisiana State University: Joy Bale Boone, Chair, Robert Penn Warren Committee at the Center for Robert Penn Warren Studies, Western Kentucky University, and Poet Laureate of Kentucky; Professor Emeritus James Byrd, Texas A&M University–Commerce; Professor William Bedford Clark, Texas A&M University at College Station, who is preparing a collection of selected letters of Warren; Carolyn Cole, Graduate Office, University of Iowa; Dr. James Conrad, Archivist, Gee Library, Texas A&M University–Commerce; Dr. Kay Coughenour, Associate Dean, College of Arts and Sciences, Texas A&M University–Commerce; Professor Gerald Duchovnay, Head, Department of Literature and Languages, Texas A&M University–Commerce; Charles East, Baton Rouge, Louisiana; Professor Jonathan R. Eller, Indiana University–Purdue University at Indianapolis; the late Albert Erskine, for his insightful advice and positive encouragement in the early stages of this project, and Marisa Erskine, Westport, Connecticut;

Professor John I. Fischer, Department of English, Louisiana State University; Courtney Fowler and Cody Fowler, Austin, Texas; Tommie Lou Warren Frey and Bob Frey, Clarksville, Tennessee; James A. Grimshaw, IV, and Heather Reese Grimshaw, Boston, Massachusetts; Maurine H. Grimshaw, Greenville, Texas; D. LaRue Haley, Greenville; Dr. Riley Handy, Head, Department of Special Collections, Western Kentucky University; J. J. Hargett and Allene Hargett, Greenville; Professor Emeritus Robert B. Heilman, University of Washington; Professor Emeritus R. W. B. Lewis, Yale University; Robert Sterling Long, Texas A&M University–Commerce; Adele McCarron, Commerce; Professor William E. McCarron, Texas A&M University–Commerce; Dr. Keith McFarland, Dean of Graduate Studies and Research, Texas A&M University–Commerce; Professor Joseph Millichap and Professor Mary Ellen Miller, Western Kentucky University; Dr. Jerry D. Morris, President and CEO, Texas A&M University–Commerce, for his continued and generous support of my Warren work; Professor James A. Perkins, Westminster College, Pennsylvania; Ms. Christa Sammons, Beinecke Rare Book and Manuscript Library, Yale University; Professor Emeritus Lewis P. Simpson, Louisiana State University; the editors of the *Southern Review,* James Olney and Dave Smith; and Dr. Albert Wertheim, Indiana University.

Part of this project was funded by a Texas A&M University–Commerce Faculty Organized Research Grant. Portions of the introduction appeared in different form in *Mississippi Quarterly* 48.1 (winter 1994–1995) and in *Southern Review* 31.2 (spring 1995).

At the University of Missouri Press, Beverly Jarrett, Director and Editor-in-Chief, who believed in the concept, and Jane Lago, Managing Editor, who worked patiently with me, are owed a special thank-you.

Finally, my wife, Darlene H. Grimshaw, assisted in the manuscript preparation and provided moral support during this entire project. She truly has had the patience of Job. The errors are mine, but I have benefited greatly from the many kindnesses of those listed above. If I have omitted others' names, I apologize.

Editorial Notes

WHEN I BEGAN WORKING ON THIS EDITION of the Brooks-Warren literary correspondence around 1987, the letters in their combined collections at the Beinecke Rare Book and Manuscript Library at Yale totaled about 380. Since Brooks's death in 1994, more letters have been deposited; and undoubtedly, additional letters remain at large. For example, letters are missing altogether for the years 1935, 1937, 1938, 1952, 1984, and 1987. A volume this size necessitates selectivity, but the sampling of approximately 372 letters (163 from Brooks and 209 from Warren) contained herein represents fairly their literary correspondence of nearly six decades, gaps notwithstanding. To offer probable explanations for the absence of letters from one or the other correspondent would be pure speculation. At times, one will refer to a prior letter from the other that cannot be located. These missing letters may have been lost or destroyed, or they may simply not have been deposited yet.

This edition of letters does not attempt to reproduce facsimiles of the letters, but it does attempt to provide an accurate reproduction of them. Anyone who has seen the handwriting of Brooks and Warren can readily appreciate the task involved in transcribing these letters. And Warren's typing was not that much of an improvement at times. Consequently, I have tried to make these letters "reader friendly" in terms of format, spelling, and punctuation based on the premise that content counts for more than eccentricities in this edition. However, none of the emendations has altered their style (syntax, diction, and so forth) or their meaning.

The return addresses given at the top of each letter often reflect the letterhead of the stationery on which the letter was written, even if the date indicates that the correspondent was not at that address at that time. Warren often put commas at the end of each line in his return address; those commas have been silently deleted in this edition. The absence of a return address here reflects the absence of one on the original letter. A majority of the letters are dated; however, a few—such as Warren's January 11, 1939, letter—are obviously misdated (it should have been dated 1940). Correct dates have been given in square brackets. When a letter was undated, an estimated date has been provided in square brackets based on the content of the letter.

The originals of all the letters are to be found in the Cleanth Brooks Papers (YCAL MSS 30) and Robert Penn Warren Papers (YCAL MSS 51) in the

Yale Collection of American Literature, Beinecke Rare Book and Manuscript Library, New Haven, Connecticut. The majority of the letters are typed; when they are not, the designation OH, for original holograph, appears to the left of the return address.

In the salutation, Brooks usually used either a comma or a dash following the name; Warren, a colon. In the bodies of the letters, Warren used more dashes than did Brooks. Such punctuation remains undisturbed. Ellipses, unless enclosed in square brackets, appear in the letters. Because so often they were writing in haste, typos occur—for example, "hte" for "the." Corrections of such errors are made silently. More significant corrections are placed in square brackets, [ ]. And in a few instances, illegible words that are supplied based on syntactical meaning are encased in pointed brackets, < >. For those illegibles, scholars, teachers, and serious readers are advised to examine the original document. Capitalization, too, is left as found in the letters unless the need for a capital letter is clear, such as at the beginning of a new sentence. Because these letters were either handwritten or typed, they contain no italic print; words and titles underlined in the originals have been typeset in italics per convention, and italics have occasionally been added to a title for clarity. Also for clarity, commas have been inserted in series, after long introductory clauses, and between compound sentences. The addition of commas, though, has been done discretely and minimally.

Closings are somewhat routine throughout the correspondence: Brooks signed his letters "Cleanth"; Warren signed his "Red." Postscripts appear in all four margins, along with other marginalia. The postscripts have been relegated to a position after the closing. Marginal notes that have been marked for insertion in the body of the letter have been placed at the designated spot and enclosed in braces, { }, with an editorial note in square brackets identifying the original location. Also inserted in square brackets are the page numbers of multipage letters. This otherwise minor interruption in the text is added to facilitate comparison with the originals.

Footnotes provide identification of names referred to but not clarified in the letters as well as some factual information to explain when a pending item was published and to bridge potentially awkward gaps. Additional information related to the correspondence but not included in the letters appears in brackets between the letters. Those notes, however, have been kept at a minimum. Some personal information not related to their literary "conversations" has also been omitted, as have long quotations from other works and lengthy lists of proofreading corrections; such omissions are indicated by seven dots on a line. The personal details are incorporated in their biographies and will surely be part of a more general collection of each man's letters.

Two additional components have been included to aid readers. A chronology shows, in brief, the amount of travel each did (based on their letters) and their major publications. The index, in addition to serving as a guide to names, titles, and subjects mentioned by Brooks and by Warren, will help to match nicknames with individuals: for example, "Tinkum. *See* Brooks, Edith Amy Blanchard."

Chronology

	BROOKS	JOINT	WARREN
1930	Rhodes Scholar from Louisiana, at Oxford		B.Litt., Oxford; fall, Asst. Prof., Southwestern College; Sept. 12, m. Cinina Brescia; "The Briar Patch"
1931			*Prime Leaf*
1932	B.Litt., Oxford; joins LSU faculty in fall		through 1934, Asst. Prof., Vanderbilt
1934	Sept. 12, m. Edith Amy Blanchard		joins LSU faculty
1935	*The Relation of the Alabama-Georgia Dialect to the Provincial Dialects of Great Britain*	July, first issue, *Southern Review*	*Thirty-Six Poems*
1936		*An Approach to Literature* with John Thibaut Purser	
1937			ed., *Southern Harvest: Short Stories by Southern Writers*
1938		*Understanding Poetry*	gives Phi Beta Kappa address at the University of Oklahoma

	BROOKS	JOINT	WARREN
1939	*Modern Poetry and the Tradition*	*An Approach to Literature* (rev. ed.)	Rome, Guggenheim; *Night Rider*
1940			Colorado; Aug., Gambier, Ohio
1941			Apr., Iowa City; July, Mexico
1942		spring, last issue, *Southern Review*	July, Iowa City; Aug., joins faculty at University of Minnesota; *Eleven Poems on the Same Theme*
1943		*Understanding Fiction*	*At Heaven's Gate*
1944	ed., *The Percy Letters*, vol. 1, with David Nichol Smith		Poetry Consultant, Library of Congress; *Selected Poems, 1923–43*
1945	Oct., University of Chicago; *Understanding Drama* with Robert Heilman		July, New London, Conn.
1946	ed., *The Percy Letters*, vol. 2, with Smith		Aug., Gambier, Ohio; *All the King's Men*; *Blackberry Winter*; *The Rime of the Ancient Mariner* introduction
1947	Aug., joins Yale University faculty; *The Well Wrought Urn*		July, Gambier, Ohio; Guggenheim Fellow; Oct., New York City; *The Circus in the Attic and Other Stories*
1948	*Understanding Drama: Twelve Plays*		Feb., Sicily; July, California
1949		*Modern Rhetoric*	Apr., Santa Monica, Calif.; Dec., New York City

	BROOKS	JOINT	WARREN
1950	July, Memphis, Tenn.	*Understanding Poetry* (rev. ed.); *Fundamentals of Good Writing*	Apr., Sewanee, Tenn.; *World Enough and Time;* July Saugatuck, Conn.; joins Yale University faculty; Nov., New York City
1951	*Poems of Mr. John Milton* with John Edward Hardy; ed., *The Percy Letters,* vol. 3, with Smith		May, Grinnell College, Iowa, and Verdi, Nev.; Oct., London; divorces Cinina Brescia
1952		*An Approach to Literature* (3d ed.)	marries Eleanor Clark; "This Very Spot" with David M. Clay (for TV)
1953	Guggenheim Fellow; July, Memphis, Tenn.	*Anthology of Stories from "The Southern Review"*	Mar., New York City; May, Newport, R.I.; Aug., Fairfield, Conn.; *Brother to Dragons*
1954	spring, Italy; July, Memphis, Tenn.; ed., *The Percy Letters,* vol. 4, with Smith		ed., *Short Story Masterpieces* with Albert Erskine
1955	ed., *Tragic Themes in Western Literature*		*Band of Angels;* ed., *Six Centuries of Great Poetry* with Erskine
1956			*Segregation;* Sept., Italy
1957	July, Inglewood, Calif.; *Literary Criticism: A Short History* with William K. Wimsatt; ed., *The Percy Letters,* vol. 5, with Smith		*Promises: Poems, 1954– 1956;* ed., *New Southern Harvest* with Erskine
1958	summer, Inglewood, Calif.	*Modern Rhetoric* (2d ed.)	Apr., Sewanee, Tenn.; *Selected Essays;* Aug., Italy; *Remember the Alamo!*
1959		*Understanding Fiction* (2d ed.)	*How Texas Won Her Freedom; The Cave; The Gods of Mount Olympus*

	BROOKS	JOINT	WARREN
1960	Guggenheim Fellow; July, Inglewood, Calif.	*Understanding Poetry* (3d ed.); *Scope of Fiction*	*All the King's Men (A Play); You, Emperor, and Others: Poems, 1957–1960*
1961	Mar., Europe; ed., *The Percy Letters*, vol. 6, with Smith	*Modern Rhetoric* (shorter ed.); *Conversations on the Craft of Poetry*	rejoins Yale University faculty; *The Legacy of the Civil War; Wilderness*
1963	Breadloaf, Vt.; *The Hidden God; William Faulkner: The Yoknapatawpha Country*		June, Bozeman, Mont.; July, Breadloaf and West Wardsboro, Vt.; ed., *The Selected Poems of Denis Devlin* with Allen Tate
1964	June, Cultural Attaché, London	*An Approach to Literature* (4th ed.)	*Flood*
1965	Oct., lectures at Glasgow; Dec., lectures at Canterbury		*Who Speaks for the Negro?*; May, Texas and Arizona; summer, West Wardsboro, Vt.
1966	Apr., lectures at Leicester; June, returns from London to Northford, Conn.; Oct., Atlanta, Ga.		Feb., lectures at Wesleyan College, Macon, Ga; ed., *Faulkner: A Collection of Critical Essays*; June, France; Oct., back in Fairfield, Conn.; *Selected Poems, 1923–1966*
1967	July, Copenhagen, Denmark, and Italy; Aug., Arizona		ed., *Randall Jarrell, 1914–1965* with Robert Lowell and Peter Taylor
1968	Sept., Austria		summer, West Wardsboro, Vt.; *Incarnations: Poems, 1966–1968*
1969	Feb., Baton Rouge, La.		*Audubon: A Vision*

	BROOKS	JOINT	WARREN
1970		*Modern Rhetoric* (3d ed.)	ed., *Selected Poems of Herman Melville*; summer, West Wardsboro, Vt.
1971	lectures at Newfoundland; *A Shaping Joy*		summer, West Wardsboro, Vt.; *Homage to Theodore Dreiser*; *Meet Me in the Green Glen*; ed., *John Greenleaf Whittier's Poetry*; Aug., "at sea" en route to France; Nov., Rome
1972	Mar., North Carolina and South Carolina; Apr., England and Iran; July, Mississippi	*Modern Rhetoric* (shorter ed.)	May, returns from France; summer, West Wardsboro, Vt.
1973		*American Literature: The Makers and the Making* with R. W. B. Lewis	retires from Yale; summer, West Wardsboro, Vt.
1974	Jan., Baton Rouge, La.		delivers Jefferson Lecture in the Humanities; May, Italy; summer, West Wardsboro, Vt.; *Or Else—Poem/Poems, 1968–1974*
1975	retires from Yale; Feb., Univ. of South Carolina; Aug., Mississippi	*An Approach to Literature* (5th ed.) plus *Notes*	Mar. and summer, West Wardsboro, Vt.; July, *Democracy and Poetry*; Oct.–Dec., Europe
1976	lectures in New Orleans, La.	*Understanding Poetry* (4th ed.)	summer, West Wardsboro, Vt.
1977	ed., *The Percy Letters*, vol. 7, with A. F. Falconer; Nov., Hattiesburg, Miss.		*Selected Poems, 1923–1975*; *A Place to Come To*; May, Greece; summer, West Wardsboro, Vt.

	BROOKS	JOINT	WARREN
1978	Mar., Knoxville, Tenn.; Apr., United States Air Force Academy, Colo.; *William Faulkner: Toward Yoknapatawpha and Beyond*		summer, West Wardsboro, Vt.; *Now and Then: Poems, 1976–1978*
1979	Jan., Chapel Hill, N.C.	*Understanding Fiction* (3d ed.); *Modern Rhetoric* (4th ed.)	ed., *Katherine Anne Porter: A Collection of Critical Essays*
1980		Oct., Lexington, Ky., and Nashville, Tenn.	Apr., Arizona; *Ballad of a Sweet Dream of Peace*; *Jefferson Davis Gets His Citizenship Back*; *Being Here: Poetry, 1977–1980*
1981			*Rumor Verified: Poems, 1979–1980*; Oct., Montana; Nov., North Africa
1982	Apr., lectures at Columbia, Mo.		*Chief Joseph of the Nez Perce*; summer, West Wardsboro, Vt.
1983	*William Faulkner: First Encounters.*		summer, West Wardsboro, Vt.
1985	delivers Jefferson Lecture in the Humanities; moves into New Haven, Conn.; Mar., England; lectures at Athens, Ga.; ed., *The Percy Letters*, vol. 8, with Falconer	Oct., 50th reunion of *Southern Review*, Baton Rouge, La.	*New and Selected Poems, 1923–1985*; summer, West Wardsboro, Vt.; Aug., Boston
1987			*A Robert Penn Warren Reader*
1988	Apr., Roswell, N.M.; ed., *The Percy Letters*, vol. 9, with Falconer		*Portrait of a Father*
1989	lectures at Texas A&M University at College Station		*New and Selected Essays*; dies Sept. 15; Oct., buried in Vermont

Cleanth Brooks and Robert Penn Warren

Introduction

THEY MET IN 1924 IN NASHVILLE. Robert Penn Warren was nineteen; Cleanth Brooks, a freshman, was almost eighteen. For sixty-five years their friendship grew as they collaborated on five textbooks and an anthology— *An Approach to Literature* (1936), *Understanding Poetry* (1938), *Understanding Fiction* (1943), *Modern Rhetoric* (1949), *American Literature: The Makers and the Making* (1973), and *An Anthology of Stories from "The Southern Review"* (1953)— and founded one of the best-regarded literary journals in the first half of this century. In retrospect this pairing seems inspired: Brooks was a versatile critic, meticulously thorough and convincingly lucid in his reading of literature; Warren, a versatile writer, wrote well in every genre and, as their friend and collaborator for *American Literature* has noted, published in every genre except travel. Both Brooks and Warren were also superb teachers to the core.

They were together for varied lengths of time on four campuses—at Vanderbilt in the 1920s; at Oxford in 1930; at Louisiana State University from 1934 to 1942; and at Yale University from the 1950s until their retirements in the 1970s. Yet even when they were on the same campus in the same period of time, they often were not together. Both traveled regularly and frequently— perhaps Warren more than Brooks, to whom, therefore, many publication details fell. When approached, neither thought that their correspondence would be of much interest—a typical response. In *Literary Reflections*, R. W. B. Lewis observes that the great age of letter writing in America ended in 1916 with Henry James's death, a demise Lewis attributes to the advent of the telephone and telegraph.[1] If so, Brooks and Warren may have missed that funeral. Their literary correspondence suggests that the craft, if not the art, of letter writing survived well into the third quarter of this century. These written exchanges reveal insights into their method of approaching literature, into two exceptional and influential minds at work, into the extraordinary details involved in writing a textbook, and into the strength of their friendship under working conditions. Those insights by themselves are instructive and informative to the critical debate currently raging about their part in the New Criticism. Indeed, these letters provide such richly sown ground that

1. *Literary Reflections: A Shoring of Images, 1960–1993* (Boston: Northeastern University Press, 1993), 129.

1

those critics who till them will reap an abundant harvest. Another benefit of these letters may be the entrée they provide into the works of Robert Penn Warren. However, that discussion will require separate development. This introduction will focus on the history of the textbooks as background to the larger concerns mentioned above.

Brooks and Warren have left as their critical legacy a method by which literature may be read and understood, a method found in their textbooks, critical essays and books, and correspondence. Those sources reflect their method in the explication and examples that permeate their criticism. Although their method has been attacked, Christopher Clausen reports "that certain core elements of the New Criticism . . . may be coming around again." Ample evidence is available to suggest that their legacy remains visible and viable today. According to Norman Fruman, "The paradoxical effect of these catastrophic developments [backlashes to the New Criticism] . . . has been a sharply increased respect for what the first generation of New Critics achieved in displacing the ossified hegemony of historical studies: a refocusing of primary interest upon the poem and not the poet, the tale and not the teller, upon the centrality of language in literary studies."[2]

In his 1966 Eugenia Dorothy Blount Lamar Lecture, "A Plea in Mitigation," Warren discusses the end of the era of modern poetry and notes that each age leaves its legacy, which fertilizes the growth of the literature and criticism of the next age. He further states that "every age, as it produces its own poetry, needs to produce its own type of criticism, its own type of exegesis and apology."[3] Not even in his latest poetry, "Altitudes and Extensions, 1980–1984" in *New and Selected Poems, 1923–1985*, does Warren embrace the postmodernism of the San Francisco poets, such as Allen Ginsberg, or the New York School of poets, such as Kenneth Koch—those poets for whom "open form" was a reaction against the new critical mode, that is, against correct grammar, logic, regular meter, rhyme, stanzas, coherence, condensation, polysemy, and control.[4] Those elements are among the poetic functions that Brooks and Warren so meticulously taught students in *Understanding Poetry.* Victor Strandberg has picked up on that animosity and cites Koch, who "makes Warren an explicit object of his contempt in his seven-page satire called 'Fresh Air.' " But Warren says the San Francisco Beats "constitute a footnote to modernism, rather than a radical reaction against it. . . . For example, Ferlinghetti reminds one of Cummings with sauciness somewhat blunted and the language blurred."[5] Nonetheless, the negative responses to

    2. Clausen, "Reading Closely Again," *Commentary,* February 1997, 56; Fruman, "Reconstructing English," *ALSC Newsletter* 3.1 (winter 1997): 9–10.
    3. Robert Penn Warren, *A Plea in Mitigation: Modern Poetry and the End of an Era* (Macon, Ga.: Wesleyan College, 1966), 12, 5.
    4. David Perkins, *A History of Modern Poetry,* vol. 2 (Cambridge: Belknap Press of Harvard University Press, 1987), 490.
    5. Strandberg, *A Colder Fire: The Poetry of Robert Penn Warren* (Lexington: University of Kentucky Press, 1965), 172; Warren, *A Plea in Mitigation,* 13–14.

Brooks and Warren's textbook approach are another form of legacy, if not also a credit to their work.

Textbooks in the first half of this century have not been widely viewed as scholarly enterprises. In fact, some scholars who wrote textbooks were not held in high esteem by their colleagues. Why, then, would Brooks and Warren even have considered doing a textbook? The answer can be found not solely in their correspondence but throughout their writings. In an essay entitled "Forty Years of 'Understanding Poetry,' " Brooks wrote:

> Robert Penn Warren and I found ourselves in the mid-1930s teaching at the Louisiana State University. We had overlapped a year at Vanderbilt in the 1920s and later we had overlapped a year at Oxford. Now in 1934 we had come together again. Among other things, each of us was teaching a section of the department's course in literary forms and types. Granted that Warren and I were young men excited by the new trends in literature—Warren was already a published poet—and granted that our heads were full of literary theory—drawn from the poetry and critical essays of T. S. Eliot and from the then sensational books on theory and practical criticism written by I. A. Richards—nevertheless, our dominant motive was not to implant new fangled ideas in the innocent Louisiana sophomores we faced three times a week. Our motive was to try to solve a serious practical problem.
>
> Our students, many of them bright enough and certainly amiable and charming enough, had no notion of how to read a literary text.[6]

Brooks's essay explains, with a clarity for which he has been known and admired, their concern. He recalls, "Warren, rarely ever at a loss and always bursting with energy, began composing a booklet to distribute to his section of the course. It was mostly on metrics, but he provided some remarks on imagery. He showed the booklet to me and invited comments." It became a mimeographed pamphlet of some 126 pages with "SOPHOMORE POETRY MANUAL" on its cover. Subsequently, LSU Press published the first edition, expanded to include other genres, as *An Approach to Literature* in 1936, "sometimes referred to in the [English] department [by their colleagues] as *The Reproach to Literature*, a witticism" Brooks and Warren picked up and used humorously themselves.[7] F. S. Crofts & Co. purchased the copyright from the LSU Press and published a revised edition of *An Approach to Literature* in 1939. Prentice-Hall, Inc., published the fifth, and last, edition in 1975. Warren offers

6. "Forty Years of 'Understanding Poetry,' " in *Confronting Crisis: Teachers in America*, ed. Ernestine P. Sewell and Billi M. Rogers (Arlington: University of Texas at Arlington Press, 1979), 167–68. A talk by Brooks at East Texas State University in Commerce on March 22, 1990, "Brooks and Warren: Fifty Years after *Understanding Poetry*," provided additional information on this very question.

7. Brooks, "Forty Years of 'Understanding Poetry,' " 169, 170. John Thibaut Purser, a graduate student who also used the sophomore manual, became the third editor in the published version. For more on the origins of this work, see *Notes on "An Approach to Literature," Fifth Edition, 1975* (Englewood Cliffs, N.J.: Prentice-Hall, 1975); for a brief description, see James A. Grimshaw, Jr., *Robert Penn Warren: A Descriptive Bibliography, 1922–1979* (Charlottesville: University Press of Virginia, 1981), B7.a1, n. 2.

yet another reason, in addition to the one Brooks gives, for their writing of textbooks. In a 1969 interview with Richard B. Sale, he explains: "We've done *Understanding Poetry* three times; it's been out thirty-odd years. But the point is, again, that it's a social event. We work together. It's a world of argument, a world of discussion, a world of—the chore aspect is reduced. It's a matter of one's social life in the deepest way."[8]

John Michael Walsh, Brooks's bibliographer, claims that "if we turn to the prefaces to the textbooks we find that Brooks's own view is that his method with different literary forms is, allowing for the differences among the forms themselves, the same method." In *The Achievement of Robert Penn Warren*, James Justus makes a similar observation that "even the ambitious and perceptive later essays reflect [Warren's] primary interest in specific matters . . . and often seem to originate as commissioned lectures or as exploratory byways of more major projects. . . . Even 'Pure and Impure Poetry' is a genial expatiation of certain principles out of *Understanding Poetry*."[9] I would supplement Justus's observation only by saying that most if not all of Warren's essays are part of an intellectual continuum, a continuum that spans and finds expression in virtually every significant genre in literature, a point well demonstrated throughout Joseph Blotner's *Robert Penn Warren: A Biography*. Both claims are substantiated in this correspondence, and readers of these letters will discover an enhanced appreciation of the value of the textbooks as entrées into the literary criticism of Brooks and Warren and into the creative works of Warren.

Such a bold statement bears substantiation. Considering the generally acknowledged influence of *Understanding Poetry*, Walsh can summarize with confidence the belief of others that it "revolutionized the way poetry is taught in this country."[10] John Crowe Ransom's 1939 review identifies it as the first textbook of its kind. Walsh clarifies: "Like all of Brooks's textbooks, *[Understanding Poetry]* stresses the importance of an inductive approach that concentrates on the works themselves and attends to the system of relationships among the parts within each work, and it distinguishes literature and the kind of knowledge it provides from other kinds, especially the scientific, maintaining that literature conveys not practical information but rather attitudes towards, feelings about, and interpretations of human experience." Ransom wrote Allen Tate on July 3, 1950, that "Red supplied the ideas; but now it becomes clear, I think, that Cleanth supplied good stern moral principles." After reading their letters, however, one must reiterate the well-known question

8. In *Robert Penn Warren Talking: Interviews 1950–1978*, ed. Floyd C. Watkins and John T. Hiers (New York: Random House, 1980), 123.
9. Walsh, *Cleanth Brooks: An Annotated Bibliography* (New York: Garland, 1990), xxxi; Justus, *The Achievement of Robert Penn Warren* (Baton Rouge: Louisiana State University Press, 1981), 117.
10. For example, Thomas Daniel Young, "Editors and Critics," in *The History of Southern Literature*, ed. Louis D. Rubin, Jr., et al. (Baton Rouge: Louisiana State University Press, 1985), 411.

asked by Yeats: "Who can separate the dancer from the dance?" The event of writing a textbook, Warren has said repeatedly, was social. Their letters echo the wish that they could sit down together to discuss the issue about which they were writing. One often urged the other to find an excuse to visit. From their letters readers can identify the initial author of a section of a textbook; but after the critiques begin, who can determine the specific contributions of each author? In *The Possibilities of Order: Cleanth Brooks and His Work*, Lewis P. Simpson notes: "What underlies the power of such a text as *Understanding Poetry* is not the sweet unity of doctrine but the tension of agreement based on the reconciliation of often opposing ideas and emotions about poetry."[11] That insight can be applied to each textbook they wrote together.

Warren joined Brooks at LSU in 1934. In *Notes on "An Approach to Literature," Fifth Edition, 1975*, they tell about those early days of teaching large sections of the sophomore course Introduction to Literature. They deduced that students in general and their students in particular were not being taught to read a poem or a story. One day Warren shared with Brooks some notes on teaching poetry, notes from which they published their *Sophomore Poetry Manual*. The purpose of that manual, which grew into their first published textbook, *An Approach to Literature*, was to address how one goes about reading, what one looks for in reading, and how one judges the value of a work. As Brooks stated it: "There is no discrepancy between teaching people to read poetry, to appreciate life by enlarging the imagination, to develop character and responsibility—all of this on the one hand—and what is sometimes called the technical detail, e.g., the way in which rhythm is expressed. Ultimately, we have here a seamless garment." Of one cloth, too, is their technique and philosophy of teaching literature. From the 1936 inception of *An Approach to Literature* to the last collaboration, *American Literature*, their method remained inductive; their mode of working, social. As they say in *Understanding Poetry*, they operated on the principle that "one must teach by contrast and analytical use of concrete examples." In *Understanding Fiction* they offer readers a relationship between meaning and the elements of form. Borrowing from their first three textbooks, they apply constant analyses of specific passages in *Modern Rhetoric*, using example rather than precept but with precept constantly related to example. Notwithstanding today's distracters from the New Criticism and the assertion in the *Yale Alumni Magazine* that at the age of eighty-four Cleanth Brooks was in 1990 still considered a dangerous man in critical circles,[12] Brooks and Warren maintained down to their last textbook a flexibility in their critical approaches to literature. Their overriding interest, observed as late as 1975 by the publisher of *Notes to "An Approach to Literature,"* was in developing ways of bringing the joys of literature to students. As one grateful student, Peter

11. Simpson, *The Possibilities of Order: Cleanth Brooks and His Work* (Baton Rouge: Louisiana State University Press, 1976), xiv; Walsh, *Annotated Bibliography*, xvi.

12. Marc Wortman, "Shattering the Urn," *Yale Alumni Magazine* (December 1990): 32. See also Mark Royden Winchell, *Cleanth Brooks and the Rise of Modern Criticism* (Charlottesville: University Press of Virginia, 1996).

Taylor, reminisces in a small pamphlet entitled *The Fugitives, The Agrarians*, "Looking back, it seems to me that what we were luckiest to observe and be instructed by was the warm, personal friendship that existed and that we knew would continue always to exist between two men who possessed perhaps the best literary minds of our century."[13] Nowhere is that friendship documented more explicitly than in their literary correspondence.

Correspondence on file from the 1930s is sparse but reflects the topics and tone of their letters for nearly six decades. The tone is congenial, friendly, and supportive of each other's work; the topics address details from which aspiring authors of textbooks can learn—keeping current with literary trends and with newcomers in the field; the need for realistic schedules to allow each contributor to complete his portion; criticism of each other's work; negotiating selections of works, permissions, fees, and contracts; and proofing responsibilities, to name only a few of those details. During this period, in February 1935 to be more precise, LSU President James Monroe Smith paid his famous visit to Brooks and Warren to solicit their help in starting what became the *Southern Review*, an accounting of which appears in their introduction to *An Anthology of Stories from "The Southern Review."* What better opportunity could two young assistant professors who were writing textbooks be handed? Carpe diem. And seize the day they did. From Rome, Warren wrote Brooks on January 11, 1940, and praised Brooks's work on the *Southern Review* as well as his reading of modern poetry and his recently published book, *Modern Poetry and the Tradition*. By the end of the 1930s, they had published two textbooks, *Understanding Poetry* in the first edition and *An Approach to Literature* in a revised edition. With their other publications, the editing of a growing literary journal, travel, and a very full teaching schedule, they were approaching a pace that they would maintain well into the 1970s. Consequently, a standard opening throughout their correspondence is the apology for not writing sooner, for not returning a manuscript earlier, or for not sending a chapter for comments—such as Brooks's August 22, 1940, opener: "I'm sorry that I have been no better correspondent, but I can't seem to get ahead of the game." Both were in fact well ahead of the game, as the next ten years would amply demonstrate.[14]

The decade of the 1940s brought forth two more textbooks, *Understanding Fiction* and *Modern Rhetoric*, the latter of which became their albatross. On

13. In *The Fugitives, the Agrarians and Other Twentieth-Century Southern Writers* (Charlottesville: Alderman Library, University of Virginia, 1985), 21.

14. When Brooks was visiting East Texas State University (now Texas A&M University–Commerce) in March 1990, I showed him photocopies of some of these letters. He remarked almost with embarrassment "how often he referred to how busy he thought he was" during those years. Anyone who has looked at his bibliography and at Warren's bibliography knows full well they were extraordinarily busy; and repeatedly in their letters, each acknowledged the other's busy schedule. They were not being pretentious at all; such acknowledgment reflects their genuine professional respect for one another and how much they valued their friendship. Often such acknowledgment also preceded a request that was going to consume a large amount of time and energy.

January 15, 1949, Warren wrote to Brooks: "I got you into this *[Modern Rhetoric]*. Can you ever forgive me?" It was their lightest decade of textbook productivity due to a variety of factors including reallocations, the demise of the *Southern Review*, and other publications (for Warren two poetry volumes and four volumes of fiction, and for Brooks a collaboration with Robert Heilman and a critical work, *The Well Wrought Urn*). Their energy seemed endless, and they were learning from each other, as Warren would reflect in a 1985 article, "Cleanth early led me to see that criticism can be a fundamentally creative act . . . a way to the inwardness of poetry."[15] In a November 11, 1942, letter Warren wrote Brooks about two of their projects. One was *Modern Rhetoric*; about the second he asked: "isn't it possible for us to divide up the reading in terms of periods, and begin to put together an anthology of criticisms of Shakespeare as poet?" It is one of several references Warren made over the years to a book on Shakespeare, one he always wanted to do. But that book was never written.

During these years they continued to share ideas and to elicit each other's opinions about their own work. Brooks, most modest about his own work, would rise to any occasion to defend his friend's work. After Warren's second novel, *At Heaven's Gate*, was published, Brooks wrote in an August 31, 1943, letter a furious rebuke of the "wooden-headed reviews." They accented each other in this and other ways that kept their creative rhythms going. In a July 27, 1944, letter Brooks called upon Warren for his candor: "I am enclosing a MS which I ask you to read carefully—even though I know that you are busy. It's the first piece of verse that I've tried in a long time. Maybe it will be the last, though I've two other poems that I've begun to tinker with." The poem is entitled "The Maelstrom."[16] Even after Warren encouraged him to publish some of his poems, a few of which Brooks did publish, Brooks decided to pursue literary criticism rather than inflict "another third-rate poet on the world." As quick as Brooks was to condemn his own creative work, he was equally quick to praise Warren's critical work. About Warren's essay "A Poem of Pure Imagination: An Experiment in Reading," on *The Rime of the Ancient Mariner*, Brooks had this opening comment in a June 5, 1945, letter: "I have gone over the A.M. paper several times and with a growing admiration. It is easily the finest thing that has ever been done on that poem—and probably the only essay on it that makes entire sense." The respect by this time was mutual. In critiquing Brooks's essay "L'Allegro-Il Penseroso" (later a chapter in *The Well Wrought Urn*), Warren wrote about one month later: "The essay is very finely wrought and subtle. One of your better pieces, certainly. And that is giving it as high praise as it could ask. It really helps me with the poems— gives me a new way of considering them." A real test of their professional

15. "Brooks and Warren," *Humanities*, April 1985, 1–3.
16. Winchell notes the Calument Club publication, *Facets: An Anthology of Verse* (1928), at Vanderbilt, to which Brooks had contributed some poems. Brooks's poems, Winchell claims, "demonstrate the early eclecticism of Cleanth Brooks's poetic sensibility" (*Cleanth Brooks and the Rise of Modern Criticism*, 36).

relationship if not their personal friendship too might have come in Warren's December 4, 1946, letter: "You are going to be surprised when you see the winter *Kenyon Review* to find some of your words appearing there without quotes and not over your name." Warren goes on to explain how it came about that passages by Brooks were included in his essay on Hemingway for the Scribners edition of *A Farewell to Arms,* an essay originally sent to Ransom, who was then editing the *Kenyon Review.* In response, Brooks gives gracious permission and approval for Warren to use the essay without revision by simply adding an acknowledgment.

If the 1940s proved hectic and not conducive to textbook production, the 1950s was one of their most productive periods in collaborative efforts, second only to the 1970s. *Fundamentals of Good Writing* (a shortened version of *Modern Rhetoric*) and *An Anthology of Stories from "The Southern Review"* were new titles albeit reruns of previous work; and their first four textbooks appeared in new editions during this period. Each revision was undertaken with an eye toward improving the textbook for the student, and the candid critiques continued. About a section of the third edition of *Understanding Poetry* that Brooks had sent him, Warren wrote from Minneapolis on February 25, 1950: "I found your piece on ambiguity very good indeed. My only thought is that it needs some talk about how one word charges another sometimes in a complicated context, the sort of thing that Richards does in his comparison of Dryden and Donne-elegies. You might also use some fine examples from *Antony and Cleopatra*—'strong toil of grace'—'knot intrinsicate'—etc." Was Warren simply the "idea man" sending little edicts to Brooks? Never. The dialogue was genuine, and Warren participated both as a man of ideas and as a man of action. On March 17, 1950, Warren wrote about another passage in *Understanding Poetry,* suggesting that in the first line of George Meredith's poem "Lucifer in Starlight" the meter should be read "as a trochee followed by a foot with a hovering accent or a spondee, not as an anapest followed by a monosyllabic foot." Then Warren wrote Brooks on April 24, 1950, that he had yet another "new scansion of 'Lucifer' by Meredith." Their exchanges are filled with such detailed discussions that reflect the genuine enthusiasm they shared in seeking a better understanding of the relationship between literature and life.

Moreover, Warren's addition to *Understanding Poetry,* "How Poems Come About," draws on materials he collected in 1944 while he was Poetry Consultant at the Library of Congress. It is also the harbinger of his 1953 "The Way It Was Written," on *Brother to Dragons.* Some of the content in that section of *Understanding Poetry* appears in interviews with Warren about his own poetry. Although readers should not confuse the life of the poet with the poem, Warren cautions, "What we can learn about the origin of a poem may . . . enlarge our understanding and deepen our appreciation" of poetry. Yet Warren himself remained very private throughout most of his writing career. Not until the late 1980s did he agree to allow his biography to be written.[17]

17. Joseph Blotner, *Robert Penn Warren: A Biography* (New York: Random House, 1997).

In this same section of *Understanding Poetry*, readers can understand better Warren's own sense of the worth of a writer's manuscripts. "The manuscripts and worksheets of a number of poets," he says, "have been preserved. Sometimes from these we can get a fairly good notion of how [a poem came to be] . . . and when we do this we participate in the creative act and sharpen our own capacity for appreciation." That statement explains, perhaps better than any speculations or other theories, why Warren meticulously deposited his manuscripts in the library at the University of Kentucky and at the Beinecke Rare Book and Manuscript Library at Yale. Rather than representing his own sense of self-worth, those deposits serve as a selfless contribution to the study of poetry, that is, an effort to make his manuscripts part of the creative act. Floyd C. Watkins reflects this sentiment in other terms: "No poet in America, perhaps, has made a greater effort than Warren to be a learned practitioner of the devices of his art form and at the same time a knowledgeable scholar aware of the conditions of the world that is his subject."[18]

Their efforts were paying dividends—monetarily, professionally, and personally. After returning from Italy and driving to Memphis to visit friends and family, Brooks reported on the progress of the revision of *Modern Rhetoric*. His July 4, 1954, account implicitly reflects the pleasure that such efforts seemed to bring: "Cheever's piece has just come in. I'll drop a note to him, and I'll write K[atherine] A[nne] P[orter] at once. Harcourt Brace is having Weaver (who has used *Modern Rhetoric* every year) to give MR a reading and his set of suggestions for the revision. Gallagher arranged it before he knew that we were good friends of Weaver's. He wants a meeting with us when Weaver's report is in in the fall. By the bye, Weaver's *Ethics of Rhetoric* is a very able book, with the first really sensible thing ever written on the Scopes trial." Intermingled with their shared joy emerged their shared concerns. In responding to revisions Warren had sent him on *Modern Rhetoric*, Brooks wrote on November 11, 1956: "Even so, I should have acknowledged a long time back [your] fine new poems which simply bowled me over. I hope that that particular spring continues to flow and that you will send us more copies when you can. One of the things that gives me a bad conscience about this whole book is my acute realization that your time ought to be going for something better than a rhetoric. It has been a case of Pegasus at the plow indeed." Were Brooks's responses only praise and concern, however, they might not have been taken seriously. Brooks critiqued with the same candor he requested. About a draft of Warren's preface to *Selected Essays*, Brooks wrote on November 17, 1957: "I like the Preface. I think that it ought to be brief and you have made the main points that ought to be made. I am enclosing a scrappy note on the first few lines. It isn't successful as a re-writing, but it will at least show you what bothers me a bit in the paragraph as it stands." Candor, though, need not be wielded with a meat cleaver. After other comments,

18. *Then and Now: The Personal Past in the Poetry of Robert Penn Warren* (Lexington: University Press of Kentucky, 1982), 3.

Brooks recounted: "One trouble in trying to advise you is that I find that I want to read my own indignations, reservations, and assertions into your Preface, and what might be a necessary preface for a collection of my essays certainly needn't be the proper one for yours. So make all the proper discounts when you read this parcel of suggestions." Such caring is the thing successful working relationships are made of.

In the 1930s, Brooks had helped to bring Warren to LSU; in the 1950s, he helped to bring Warren to Yale. Brooks was also the one to insist that they include Warren's work in their textbooks. After receiving Warren's essay for *Understanding Fiction*, Brooks sent his reaction and advice on September 12, 1958: "Your piece on 'Blackberry Winter' is very, very fine—in your best vein, I think. I immediately had to show it to Tinkum [Brooks's wife], who agrees with me as to its usefulness in our text, but also as to its intrinsic interest and its goodness as a piece of sensitive prose. My only regret is that it may be wasted in UF. (It won't be wasted on the best students, however, and not on the teachers. But you should plan to publish it separately before it goes into our book.)" They shared other ideas and concerns, and the partnership could have slipped quietly into an exchange of platitudes had individuals of lesser dedication and integrity been in their shoes. Their own writing continued to attract attention and spur them on to new heights. Brooks, with William K. Wimsatt, published *Literary Criticism: A Short History;* and Warren ended his poetry hiatus with the publication of his long verse drama, *Brother to Dragons.* They would take advantage of another brief reprieve from textbook deadlines during the 1960s to continue to pursue their own separate writing projects.

In the 1960s, *An Approach to Literature* appeared in a fourth edition; *Understanding Poetry*, in a third edition; and a shortened version of *Understanding Fiction*, retitled *The Scope of Fiction*, was published. This relative calm provided them the opportunity to begin work on a new textbook on American literature, one that would include their friend and colleague R. W. B. Lewis but that would not reach the market until 1973. Their epistolary dialogues served as sounding boards for projects in the making, for concepts still in infancy. For example, Brooks's August 2, 1960, letter includes the following response:

> You ask me in your letter of July 21st, for my meditations on Lee's decision to stay with Virginia and its fundamental appeal to American imagination. I have nothing useful to offer at the moment except that I have been re-reading in the last week Faulkner's *Intruder in the Dust* and remember the same problem arises there. Against the more abstract claims of liberty, justice, etc., there is the concrete claim of the region, the community, the family. I don't know that Faulkner's Gavin Stevens argues those competing claims very well, but surely he is right in arguing that there must be a reconciliation, a true reconciliation, not simply an ironing out of the local claim under the pressures of abstraction. Rereading Faulkner's book and listening to the two platforms via TV have certainly convinced me that the problem of Lee's decision is a very live problem

today. If one had to depend on a conception of the United States from the platforms—thank goodness we don't have to—one would certainly conclude that America was a congeries of competing minorities and classes setting up ground rules to keep from jostling each other. The conception of a living, concrete community simply does not emerge—and maybe for a good many parts of this country it does not exist. Anyway, I hope you will yourself meditate the Lee piece and do it.

Warren was indeed meditating on the Civil War, meditations he would publish as *The Legacy of the Civil War;* and Brooks's example from Faulkner was part of his larger project that would become *William Faulkner: The Yokna-patawpha Country.* Because their literary interests dovetailed with each project, it is almost impossible to discern where one stops and the next one begins. Within that continuum remained critiques and praises for jobs well done. In a March 14, 1962, letter Brooks acknowledged Warren's contribution and confirmed one of the basic concepts of their textbooks: " 'Fiction: Why We Read It' is really a superb job. Both of us know how slippery and difficult the topic is. I think you have handled it with admirable lucidity. Best of all you have given one of the few really *concrete* accounts of the matter, and an account tilted over toward the place of fiction in the human economy, without vulgarizing it or blunting and distorting the other issues. . . . In terms of its concreteness and its simplicity of language—but *simple* in the best sense—it is really a little masterpiece."

Oceans did not impair their collaborations. In fact those separations may have provided for them an even larger audience for their works. In 1965 Brooks was cultural attaché in the American Embassy in London and brought to the attention of the appropriate workers in the United States Information Agency Warren's book on Negro leadership, *Who Speaks for the Negro?* Much of their correspondence during this period focused on the American literature textbook, but Brooks made time to critique Warren's poetry. About *Promises,* Brooks wrote on December 26, 1965, his concern with tone and diction. The problem of tone remained a concern for Brooks throughout his career, and he would monitor the handling of that topic in the various textbooks in which discussion of it was included.

Brooks and Warren had worked together for more than three decades, but they often worked separately on the same topics, even on the same authors. After Brooks's volume on Faulkner was published, Warren edited the Twentieth-Century Views volume on Faulkner. In a March 18, 1966, letter, Warren asked Brooks: "Have you seen Millgate's new book *[The Achievement of William Faulkner]* on F.? If so, what do you think of it? In general I am quite depressed by the general level of the Faulkner criticism. By and large, in a certain way, the French stack up better than we do. DO YOU KNOW of any good pieces done in England—or even interestingly wrong-headed? Particularly if by someone whose name is of interest. PLEASE PLEASE!" Although Brooks did not answer all of Warren's questions, he offered the following comment on March 24, 1966: "Millgate has sent me his new Faulkner and I expect to find it very good, but the wheels spin too fast now—and will until we sail on May 26 [from England]—to allow me to read it."

Among the more mundane yet thoroughly frustrating tasks authors of textbooks and anthologies face is the acquisition of permissions. Because of soaring costs of publication, permissions fees were rising; and some authors simply held out for higher fees. Brooks and Warren each wrote for and negotiated permissions, and each was denied by some potential contributors whose works they had counted on. Permissions for plays and poetry became the most difficult to obtain, but both men were stoic, and refusals were handled quickly with alternate selections inserted. In not one of their letters on file do they seem daunted or distracted from the business at hand; in this arena they maintained remarkable self-control, discipline, and vision.

Those students who are familiar with Brooks and Warren continue to be amazed by the breadth and depth of their knowledge about literature; those readers who come to their works for the first time might be more amazed to learn that neither man completed a Ph.D. In an age that attaches so much importance to formal education, perhaps their professional lives serve as yet another lesson for young students. Both, of course, received numerous honorary doctoral degrees based on their work. The decade of the 1970s, the one in which each officially retired from academic teaching, was their busiest in terms of textbook publications. *American Literature: The Makers and the Making,* appeared in three different sets—in one volume, in two volumes, and in four volumes; and their other four textbooks came out in new editions. Warren turned seventy-four in 1979; Brooks, seventy-three.

The year 1970 saw the release of the third edition of *Modern Rhetoric;* ironically, the fourth edition of their "albatross" would be issued in 1979, the last of the Brooks-Warren textbooks. More of their letters are on file for this decade than for any other. They were busy; their concerns were many. They had begun to deposit materials in libraries, primarily the Beinecke Rare Book and Manuscript Library at Yale and secondarily the King Library at the University of Kentucky. Such actions had legal and tax ramifications. Brooks seems to have taken the initiative on some of those matters as work on *American Literature: The Makers and the Making* forged ahead. The correspondence now included two names in the salutation, Brooks or Warren and Lewis. From their correspondence, a third party does not seem to have presented any problems, other than the minor complication of coordinating three schedules rather than two, a problem that did not seem to hamper work on the book. Three minds enjoyed and participated in "the tension of agreement based on the reconciliation of often opposing ideas and emotions about" literature. In their prefatory remarks to the textbook, they state that "literature clearly does not exist in a vacuum." And their shared discussions of each of the periods covered in the text permit readers to grasp the extended meaning of that earlier declaration. In responding to each other's period introductions, they asked questions they believed students would ask; and they tried to ensure continuity among these introductions. They did such an excellent job that even teachers who did not adopt the text used their introductions to supplement their own class notes. Warren's August 30, 1971, assessment to Brooks from France accurately anticipated that reception: "As for general comment, I want to say—as I am saying to Dick—that after reading the whole volume, I am much happier about it than I had been able to predict. I[t] *does* seem to hang together as a book, and looking carefully at the stuff you two have done, I never detect a sense of strain, of fatigue, or boredom (on your parts)—nothing merely perfunctory. It does feel fresh and freshly considered. And various."

On one of the revisions, things did not go smoothly. Warren wrote Brooks on December 15, 1971, about a letter he had received from Appleton-Century-Crofts about *An Approach to Literature,* the textbook that Mr. Crofts himself had solicited from them some thirty-five years earlier: "I flew into a rage, and am enclosing the typed result. I have *not* sent this to her [Ms. Lumsden]. I did it to relieve my feelings, and to send it to you, with the suggestion that you revise, adapt, or scuttle as seems best." The issue was over the percentage of profit they were offered for the revision. Cleanth's subsequent dealings with this issue indicated that, indeed, new authors were accepting a lower royalty in order to keep ever-increasing book prices down in the hope of boosting sales. The market had been competitive before, but in the 1940s they knew their competitors; in the 1970s, their competition was not always another author. Even Brooks's diplomatic negotiations with Appleton did not prevail; Brooks forwarded a "report" (dated February 10, 1972) of his visit. Ultimately, Prentice-Hall published the fifth edition of *An Approach to Literature* in 1975. Other revision problems arose during this period, and they seemed to be compounded by the number of texts under revision. Nonetheless, Brooks and Warren endured.

They modified strategies and clung to principles. On changes to *Understanding Poetry,* Brooks wrote on March 26, 1972:

> If we are to use in Section II a common factor like birds and perhaps in Sec. III poems of varied form and mood about love, and in IV poems—again of the widest variety—about death, then it will be important to introduce the student early to concepts like dramatic structure, imagery, tone, metrical pattern, and theme. Hence the rather fully worked Sec. I.
>
> Even here, however, there is a common factor: Hardy's "Channel Firing" which is brought back for discussion under every one of the rubrics mentioned above. Obviously one can't give a full treatment of tone, for instance, in the two or three poems as discussed in Sec. I, but then, tone will be discussed in all the rest of the book. What I'm trying to devise is something that will not involve any basic change in our principles or our notions of what literary criticism is, but which will allow us to come at these matters indirectly, in connection with other things, making more use of comparison with other poems, etc. etc.

Five months later, Warren's reply of August 13, 1972, reflects a pessimism uncharacteristic of his earlier days: "I guess I am having the classic reaction of gloom and blankness reported by all victims of my late indisposition.

But anyway I don't have the thing hanging over me. So let's get on with the God-damned textbooks, and let the dead Future bury its half dead." Brooks, however, continued in his customary manner, offering at the end of his correspondence the wonderful summary paragraph, which often began, "To summarize." Warren was participating more vigorously than his response above would indicate. In 1974 he delivered the Jefferson Lecture in the Humanities, subsequently published as *Democracy and Poetry*. Brooks would share that honor in 1985. The end of the decade produced other changes as well. Brooks and Warren retired from Yale. The Brookses sold their eighteenth-century house and accompanying forty acres and moved into town. The Warrens suffered some physical ailments with permanent effects. And their textbook era ended.

The 1980s provided a certain amount of freedom for each of them to pursue his own personal projects. Both remained active in their publishing. Fewer letters have been deposited in the library from this period, though Brooks and Warren continued to correspond about their writing because traveling to see each other in person was more difficult. One letter from this period stands out; Warren wrote it to Brooks on September 16, 1983.

> I want to thank you devoutly for the pains you took with the poetry manuscript. It was very useful to me, and surprising in a few instances. You upgraded poems I was not at all sure about. I only fear that you were too easy on the book—which is like you. But this leads to a broader thought, which I have thought for a long time. You must—you plural—must have known of the dimension of our attachment to Brookses and admiration. I can look back longer than Eleanor, but with no more feeling. But I want to say something more special now. You can't imagine how much I owe you about poetry—on two counts. Our long collaborations always brought something new and eye-opening to me, seminal notions, for me, often couched in some seemingly incidental or casual remark. One of the happiest recollections I have, is that of the long sessions of work on *UP*—not to mention all earlier and later conversations. The other count has to do with the confidence you gave me about my own efforts. I'm sure that you were often over-generous, but even allowing for that, it still meant something fundamental to me. I have often wanted to say something like this to you, but I know how you'd give an embarrassed shrug and disclaimer. Anyway now I can say it without your interruption.

Much of what appears in Warren's 124-page "interview" with Brooks, "A Conversation with Cleanth Brooks," in *The Possibilities of Order: Cleanth Brooks and His Work* summarizes their shared literary views. The evidence, background, and details are provided, in part at least, in their letters. They were two unusual individuals—teachers to the core—who gladly shared their delight in and lessons learned from literature. And as Lewis Simpson aptly notes, that "interview" establishes "an emblem of a remarkable—and in American and modern letters generally, a singular—literary association." Warren died on September 15, 1989; and with Brooks's passing on May 10, 1994, another chapter in American and modern letters was, to use a printing phrase, put to bed.

1930s

Louisiana State University
English Department
<ca. summer 1933>

Dear Red,

I haven't been in Nashville in so long and haven't written to any one or heard from any one in so long that I feel quite exiled. I have heard from Ransom once or twice, though not lately. Are you to be in Vanderbilt this fall? And have you ever finished the novel or the long poem on which you were working when I saw you last?

I managed to get my B.Litt. last year (working under Nichol Smith) and landed—very luckily, I think—in the English Department here last fall. I am teaching this summer, Chaucer and Milton, and trying very hard (with very little success) to find enough breathing spells to do a little writing. In the middle of a very short one, I am taking the time to write you this note.

L.S.U. has undertaken half the editorship of the *Southwest Review*. The other half remains with the Southern Methodists of Dallas. We are hoping to broaden its scope a litt<le> and to improve the quality of the articles. Pipkin,[1] as our generalissimo, has lined up some first rate men, particularly in his field. I am especially interested in pulling up our reviews. What about reviewing some books for us—especially poetry and criticism? (I say 'us,' though I am connected with the magazine in humble enough capacity; but Pipkin has asked me to scout around for some good reviewers.)

[p. 2] If you are willing to do it, I shall send you right away a few books in which I think you would be interested. But I shall be glad for you to do your own selecting, and I will get for you and send you any books you would care to review.

Do you think that McMullan[2] would be interested? I am writing him about

---

1. Charles Wooten ("Pip") Pipkin, an Oxford Ph.D., was chosen by LSU president James Monroe Smith in 1931 to be dean of the Graduate School. He recommended Brooks for a Rhodes scholarship in 1928, according to Thomas W. Cutrer, *Parnassus on the Mississippi: The Southern Review and the Baton Rouge Literary Community, 1935–1942* (Baton Rouge: Louisiana State University Press, 1984), 31. Also, he was one of the founding editors of the *Southern Review* in 1935. Warren refers to Pipkin's death in an August 5, 1941, letter.

2. Hugh McMullan, a graduate of Williams College, was a member of Exeter College, Oxford, while Brooks was there.

15

it at this time, and am taking the liberty of addressing the letter to you, hoping that you know his address and will forward it. I have lost touch with him completely.

Is there any possibility of your coming down into the deep South this summer? If so, I issue a cordial invitation. Baton Rouge has its limitations, but it is very close to New Orleans which I still believe is the best city to live in [in] this country. I manage to get down there every few weeks. There are a great many things I should like to talk to you about. And I have a few things (not poetry) which I should like to show you.

Pipkin sends his regards,
Sincerely,
Cleanth Brooks

R.F.D. 9, Porter Road
Nashville, Tennessee
July 16, 1933

Dear Cleanth:

You honor me. I was delighted to hear from you directly. I felt left out of the jolly scene all last winter, when John R. would read me choice morsels from your epistolary table. And my God, what a man! I said to myself when you outlined all your projects and affairs. How do you ever expect to finish any more of them now since you've dedicated yourself to pimping reviews for a magazine, and in the end probably writing most of them yourself? And you honor me by asking me to do a few myself. I shall be glad to do reviews of books that hold an especial interest for [me], particularly poetry, but other stuff wouldn't be excluded from my interests. I presume that the *Review* doesn't pay. Is that right? I'm not a low and mercenary fellow, at least not any lower than the next one. I merely ask because I am in a position where I have to make most (not all, mind you) of my energies count economically. Or do you pay for articles only, as does that sheet, the *V. Quarterly*? Incidentally, you and Pipkin ought to be able to beat anything else in the South in that line by a long shot, and, in fact, most of the publications out of the South. May I congratulate you on your connection with the project, a connection which, I am sure, you present with too much humility.

No, I shall not be coming into the deep South this summer. But I counter with a left to the chin. Why don't you come up here this summer? There's only one of you and there's two of me. And I'm sure your summer school doesn't run along without any break between it and next term. Ransom will be here in August and Tate[1] is around. The river is almost at my door (I'm living in the country) and my garden exudes beans and potatoes. You ought

---

1. Allen Tate (1899–1979), a member of the Fugitives and the Agrarians, met Warren at Vanderbilt in 1923; he met Brooks in Paris in 1929. He, too, was one of Ransom's students. He was twice married to Caroline Gordon—1924–1945 and 1946–1959.

to come up and talk over [p. 2] things, bringing, of course, those manuscripts you mentioned. And why don't you persuade Pipkin to come with you? We might while away the gloamings as the poet claimed he did:

> Tired the sun with talking
> And sent him down the sky.

(That, my dear Cleanth, is a literary allusion to a damned good poem. Do you know it?)

Life is very busy right now, but we have plenty of time for the modest amenities allowed, of which conversation is chief. I am finishing up a novel this summer, have written two short stories and two reviews, since the first of June, and have hoed many a weary row. I don't know whether the novel is any good or not; you might be able to tell me if you came up here. But if you don't come, please send on a batch of those manuscripts you were talking about. I am very anxious to see them.

Tate was here last week. He is immersed in the present book, which, as far as I can tell, is going to be mighty good. Caroline Tate is in the middle of a novel.

Your note inspired me to write a much delayed letter to Hugh [McMullan]. I hope he will forgive me my damned negligence. As I hope you will.

Again, thanks, write to me soon, and accept my invitation.

As ever,
Red

Vanderbilt University
Nashville, Tennessee
May 20, 1934

Dear Cleanth:

I have been intending to write you a letter for many months, but at last I am doing it for a special and unexpected reason. I understand that there is some chance of a Department of Fine Arts being established at L.S.U., and that Puryear Mims[1] might have a shot at the job of instructing in sculpture. I want to ask you to pass my comment along if you think it might do any good. You probably knew Puryear when you were at Vanderbilt, but I don't remember that you knew him nearly as well as I did. Further, in the last six years I have seen him frequently, and saw him last summer for long sessions many times. Naturally, I am writing this because I like him very much and because I would

---

1. Puryear Mims, a sculptor, was the son of Edwin Mims (1872–1959), who was chairman of the department of English at Vanderbilt (1912–1942) and was an adversary of the Nashville Fugitives and Agrarians. Warren detested Edwin Mims, "who apparently reciprocated the feeling heartily," according to Warren's daughter, Rosanna ("Correcting the Record on Warren and Ransom," *Reckon: The Magazine of Southern Culture* 1.4 [winter 1996]: 12). Yet Warren considered Puryear Mims a friend.

like to have him South again where there would be some more opportunity for seeing him. I make no pretense of being a critic of the fine arts, but I have seen a good deal of his work, which I like. I can, however, express myself on this point: he has developed enormously since he left Vanderbilt in an intellectual way. To a layman, myself for instance, he can define what he is up to . . . and that's a difficult task for an artist when he is talking to a person who does not have a good notion of the technique of the art in question. He has been doing some work in teaching sculpture in the School in New York, but precisely what I don't know. In any case, I feel confident that he would make a good teacher.

At this time I want to congratulate you on the fine piece of work you have done in the thesis.[2] I studied it very carefully, and found little to disagree with and less that I would care to take the responsibility of attacking. I had been doing a bit of reading and thinking along some of the lines you indicate . . . especially on 17th Century criticism, but I fear you have forestalled anything I might have had to say on the point. My only general remark about the thing is this: for book publication it ought to be compressed somewhat and the tone of the writing, here and there, altered a little. Has Ransom mentioned our *Right Wing Series*[3] (unhappy name!) to you? We hope to get some publisher to take a series of short books, say up to one hundred fifty pages, of a critical nature . . . literary criticism, historical interpretation, etc. Naturally, the people contributing [p. 2] to the series would have certain premises, or at least instincts, in common. Ransom and I have thought that your MS., cut a bit, would make an excellent member of such a series. And I am sure Allen [Tate] concurs. I don't know when, if ever, we can put the project through, but we may be able to some time. What do you think of it?

What did you think of the poetry issue of the *A M*?[4] Jarrell[5] is pretty hot, isn't he? He is a sophomore now, the most precocious fellow I ever knew: has read everything, writes polished critical prose, is on the tennis team, and is a damned good fellow besides. I know him extremely well and like him extremely.

I am following my routine for the last three years. I am writing some verse, having done about a dozen poems since last fall. I am almost in the middle of

2. The reference is to Brooks's thesis at Oxford under David Nichol Smith, a noted scholar in seventeenth- and eighteenth-century British literature; later he and Brooks edited *The Percy Letters*.

3. The Right Wing Series was John Crowe Ransom's plan for a series that was modified and published as *Who Owns America?* edited by Allen Tate and Herbert Agar (Boston: Houghton Mifflin, 1936). Brooks's essay is entitled "The Christianity of Modernism"; Warren's, "Literature as Symptom." That collection was followed by the short-lived journal *Free America*, which Brooks and Warren did not support.

4. *A M* was the *American Mercury*, published monthly by Alfred A. Knopf.

5. Randall Jarrell (1914–1965) was another of Ransom's students and was later a contributor to the *Southern Review*. His less-than-favorable review of Stark Young's *Feliciana* and Ellen Glasgow's *Vien of Iron* created strained relations.

another novel,[6] a short one, which I hope to finish this summer. I'm working, and have been working for the last six months, on an essay on Ruskin.[7] I also have a large and flourishing garden, which takes up most of my spare time.

Write and tell me what you are doing. I hear from Corry[8] quite often and from Wecter[9] now and then. I owe Hugh a letter, and have owed him one for six months. Tell Pip hello for me.

And I do hope Puryear gets the job.

As ever,
Red

. . . .

[In February 1934, Warren's left eye was removed due to an injury suffered at his home in Guthrie, Kentucky, in 1921. The attempted collaborations with the other editors at the *Southwest Review* ended in the spring of 1935, about the time Brooks and Warren were appointed managing editors of the *Southern Review* at LSU. Setting up the new journal occupied a great deal of their time during this interim between letters. Warren's first volume of poems, *Thirty-Six Poems*, was published; and Brooks published *The Relation of the Alabama-Georgia Dialect to the Provincial Dialects of Great Britain*.]

August 6, 1936

Dear Red:

A brief note as to how work is progressing.[1] All the biography and history pieces have gone in and will presumably amount to about 100,000 words. All the poetry has gone in, except one or two odd pieces which must be inserted as the proof comes back. Among these is a selection from Whitman. It probably will have to be short to go in the fifth section. I located the poem by Herrick and suppose it should go in the Tone section. As for the other pieces you suggested, the Putnam piece has already gone in. If you think we can't use it, we can snatch it out of galley proof. I took Hart Crane's "Voyages II" and inserted it at the very end of the imagery section—could, of course, go in

6. On a manuscript in the King Library, University of Kentucky, Lexington, Warren wrote: "This untitled & unpublished novel, my second, was written about 1933–34—in Tennessee—R. P. Warren / 1st revised draft." Perhaps the manuscript at Kentucky is what became "God's Own Time"; the working title of his first unpublished novel is "The Apple Tree."

7. Warren's essay on John Ruskin (1819–1900) apparently was not published, and the manuscript has not been located.

8. Andrew Vincent Corry, to whom Warren dedicated *Now and Then: Poems, 1976–1978*, was a Rhodes Scholar with Warren at Oxford.

9. Dixon Wecter, a friend of Corry's, was a member of the department of history at Yale University and is the author of *The Hero in America*. Warren dedicated *World Enough and Time* to him and his wife, Elizabeth.

1. The progress report is on *An Approach to Literature*, their first textbook, which was growing from the pamphlet *Sophomore Poetry Manual* to include all major genres.

Section 7. I took for Emily Dickinson "The Chariot," which Allen thinks is so fine and which is fine, I think, and put it in the seventh section. Allen's "Ode to the Confederate Dead"—second version—has gone in to the seventh section, but on consideration of space I have omitted from that section "Rabbi Ben Ezra." We can put it back in if we find we have room for it. Do you have any other suggestions for Emily Dickinson pieces? They are short, and we might insert one or two more. Same with regard to Hart Crane or other poets, but space is at a premium. So much for the poetry. Essays. I have sent in most of the essays we had selected with the exception of the James piece on DeMaupassant, the piece "On Jargon," "Literature and Science," by Matthew Arnold, and the Aldous Huxley piece. I propose having these typed out and shooting them in if we find that we will have room. All of these, I am certain, ought to be in the book, but I don't think that we can afford to run the book too large, and I think that the essay section can be cut better than can the fiction or poetry or biography. By the way, we were refused permission by the author of "The Cosmic Whirlpool."[2] We must have some comparable essay in order to make the point, and I have written for permission to use a chapter in one of Eddington's[3] books, have rewritten the "essay introduction" to bring it in line with this new piece, and have sent the introduction in. By the way, all introductions are in except the novel introduction, and I think it best for you to send that in direct to the Kingsport Press from Colorado.[4] Also the questions on the short stories and the analysis of one of the short stories which you are to do. I have located the Gold[5] piece, and by tomorrow should have all copy for the short stories sent in except the DeMaupassant. We have sent in *Hedda* [p. 2] *Gabler* and are waiting permission on the Čapek[6] to send it in. Permissions refused on all Barrie[7] plays, and permissions on all Shaw plays must be made to Shaw himself in England. We wouldn't have time to apply, especially since we aren't sure that we could get anything at a reasonable price. I propose *Emperor Jones* as a one-act play as the least of evils. Back to the essays for a moment. I am going to send in a short one by Montaigne. Did you understand that we *had* to send in an Emerson essay? I am working on questions for the history-biography section and for the essays. I am sorry that I seem to be working so slowly, but there have been multitudinous interruptions, and things which we had thought settled with little trouble have taken up days.

2. "The Cosmic Whirlpool," an essay by George W. Gray from his book *New World Picture* (1936), is reprinted in *An Approach to Literature*, rev. ed. (New York: Appleton-Century-Crofts, 1939), 186–92.

3. The book is possibly Sir Arthur Stanley Eddington's *New Pathways in Science* (1935).

4. Warren was attending the University of Colorado Writers' Conference in July, from which he resigned to work on his novel *Night Rider*.

5. Michael Gold's essay "Ring Lardner" was reprinted in *An Approach to Literature*, rev. ed. (1939), 119–20, from *New Masses*.

6. Karl Čapek wrote *R.U.R. (Rossum's Universal Robots)* (1921), a utopian drama.

7. Scottish playwright James M. Barrie (1860–1937), of the "Kailyard School," wrote, for example, *Quality Street* (1901), *What Every Woman Knows* (1908), and *The Twelve-Pound Look* (1910).

For example, there were many questions that had to be written for the poetry section, not only for Section 7, but for Sections 3, 4, etc. Our mimeographed version was very hasty and an incomplete job.

This brief note is to let you know as far as I can what the situation is. Jack[8] is reading proof, and I have been trying to keep copy going off as rapidly as possible to the printer. Write in any suggestions that you have. I am sorry that our letters have no more gossip or conversations, but I must hurry back to work, and I know that you are terribly busy.

Regards from Tinkum[9] and Albert[10] and I to you and Cinina.[11]

Cleanth

August 15 [1936]

Dear Red—

Your wires came in this morning. We are all sorry to hear about Cinina's bad luck,[1] and hope that she will be completely recovered in a few days. Let us know about developments. You ought to have time to get to Kingsport by Saturday week or soon after unless there is further trouble with her foot. But, of course, for goodness' sake don't take any chances.

I am not enclosing any proof right now, for the proof is not the most pressing thing. Rather, I am suggesting that you send in as soon as possible the questions on the short stories and the analysis of one of them. I suggest an analysis of the Wish Book, for in the Introduction to Fiction there is a reference to an analysis of it. If on the other hand, you have in the meantime analyzed some other story, we can very easily change the reference in the Introduction.

I am choosing "La Mere Sauvage" (which I think is damned good) for the Maupassant. We will have a copy of it off to the printer right away.

I am also sending today a carbon of a Glossary which I have been working on for you to see. Cut out some terms which we might omit, add others, and expand those you think necessary. I have prepared the thing merely as a starter and because I knew that we would never get it done at the last minute. We might cut the section on Imagery heavily (I have already made some cuts) since it is dealt with in detail in the "Introduction to Poetry" but there may

---

8. Jack is John Thibaut Purser, the third editor of *An Approach to Literature.*

9. Tinkum—Edith Amy Blanchard—was Brooks's wife for fifty-three years. Variations of that nickname used throughout the letters include Tink, Tinkie, and Tookie.

10. Albert Erskine, one of Ransom's students, was business manager of the original *Southern Review,* editor at Doubleday Doran, and editor at Reynal and Hitchcock before joining Random House in 1947. At Random House he was editor for William Faulkner, James A. Michener, and others as well as for his friend Red. Warren dedicated *Flood* to Albert and his wife, Marisa.

11. Emma Cinina Brescia and Warren met while he was working on his master's degree at Berkeley. They were married in 1930; after an increasingly unhappy relationship—due, perhaps in part, to Cinina's jealousy over Red's career and friends—they divorced in 1951.

1. Cinina's "bad luck" seems to continue with poor health and emotional distress throughout her marriage to Warren.

be some value in retaining it as it is. Moreover, you will notice that as I have prepared it so far, the Glossary tends to become an Index. But that may be a virtue in sending the student back to the Introductions. I have compromised by giving brief definitions for the most part and then referring the student back to the [p. 2] introductions.

All questions on the biography and history sections have been written, and on the essays. They can be attached in the proper places on the Galley proof and rapidly set up. References to Galley will have to be changed to page of course when the rest of the book is paged.

The Ibsen and Čapek plays have gone in to the printer. Publishers want $150 for the Emperor Jones. It's not worth it. We may have to use only two plays after all. If the book does not run too long, and if you think well of it, we might ask Marcus[2] what about using "The Importance of Being Earnest." If we use a one act play as Miss Miller suggested (because she wants three plays and would like to have three even if the third is of only one act) we would have to pay a permission—twenty-five to seventy-five dollars. Why not spend that money on the extra amount it would cost to set up a longer play? It's the money, not the space itself, which has caused us to try to keep down the space of the book. Write what you think of this.

I have not sent in the following essays: Owsley's Foundations, Huxley's Whole Truth, and Emerson. I think that space rules them out. I wish we had the first two, but we can use their space more wisely on a third play perhaps.

Cordial regards from all of us to you and Cinina,

Cleanth

List of stories for your convenience:

Goodbye to Cap'm John	Gentleman from San Francisco	Washerwoman's Day
La Mere Sauvage	Some Like Them Cold	The Wish Book
On the East Side	Kneel to the Rising Sun	I'm a Fool
The Killers	Araby	Lottery Ticket
Jerico	Spotted Horses	The Two Faces

American Express
Rome
November 13, 1939

Dear Cleanth:

It's almost time now for there to be a chance of getting a word from you after your hearing from me that we were going to stay on; and so every day I'm making my little pilgrimage to the American Express. But a letter from Katherine Anne [Porter], dated September 29, did come the other day. I rejoiced to learn that the courts didn't treat Smith's case with complete levity,

2. Marcus M. Wilkerson, a professor of journalism, "was influential in founding the LSU Press [in 1935] and was appointed its first director; also influential were Charles W. Pipkin, the dean of the Graduate School, and . . . Wendell Holmes Stevenson" ("Happy Birthday LSU Press," *LSU Magazine* 61.4 [September 1985]: 43–47).

and that other indictments are coming. And the internal clean-up sounds pretty good. Do let me know exactly what they are doing. Are they really digging into things? And what about the outside academic committee which was hashed over in the AAUP meeting last summer and which, according to your letter of August, Hebert[1] referred to in his speech at the August Commencement? Naturally, I'm consumed with curiosity about all such things—even if they may seem pretty stale to you all now.[2]

I'm also mighty anxious to know what Crofts has done with our text book. Did he make a nice job of manufacturing the new edition; or is it exactly like the other which he brought out, which was nice enough, I suppose? Have you had any line yet on the adoptions? (By the way, we ought to have a little money, shouldn't we, in January? When your check comes will you look about for mine, and ask Mrs. Swallow[3] to deposit it for me? May it be big! And what did the final permission costs come to?) And have you had any word from Holt about the way the poetry book has been going? Is there any chance of royalty in January? Meanwhile, I am doing a little work on the short story book, and expect now to do a good deal, for I now can get at libraries.

For we are now in Rome, for the "duration"—whatever that may be. We hope to be in a little apartment, one which we have already located, within a few days and to escape from the pensione existence which we have been leading now for a couple of weeks. And an apartment is certainly a cheaper way for two people to live than is a pensione. And, naturally, there is a lot more opportunity for work, for the quietest pensione, and the one in which we now are is a good one, is bound to have distractions. I do hope that we can manage to stay on at least until spring or early summer, for I feel that a major move now would disrupt my work damned near completely. In the first place the expense of getting back to America is very great now in comparison with the passage we paid to come over, and I ought to be able to afford that a good deal more easily some months from now. And, again, we can stay under our budget here, but I'm not at all certain that we could in America, especially since Katherine Anne writes that prices are soaring. And again, if we should have to come back now, or soon, where would we go? Our house is rented until next September, and you know what the problem is of finding a place to live. It's a mess, if we do have to come back. But things are very quiet here now, and [p. 2] there seems to be some ground for optimism about Italian neutrality. And in so far as American ships are concerned, the steamer companies here tell me that there will be more American boats than ever coming to Italian ports. I hope that all of this isn't a kind of whistling in the dark. We have had one or two moral collapses, and on such occasions would have sailed within twenty-four hours if there had been a boat.

1. Paul M. Hebert, dean of the LSU School of Law, became acting president of LSU in 1939.
2. James Monroe Smith, president of LSU, was implicated in a scandal involving misappropriation of funds. Warren is, of course, curious. For details of the case, see Cutrer, *Parnassus on the Mississippi*, chap. 8.
3. Mae Swallow (the wife of Alan Swallow) was the secretary for the *Southern Review*.

I have seen our two contributors here. Both of them seem to be, in matters of attitudes and values, very close to us. The younger, especially, who, after his experiences of the last two years, has gone all the way. He has done some fine new work, part of a novel which he hopes to finish by spring and offer to H[oughton] M[ifflin] for a fellowship. By the way, do you have any ideas for any critical article which Praz[4] might do for us?

How did the fall issue pan out? I'm hoping for a copy to come rolling in soon. (By the way, Pier[5] never did get the copy with his story in it—that is, he never did get one from us. Finally, he ordered one from England. I explained to him that at the time his address was indefinite.) And I'm hoping for a batch of MS to come in soon. How is the poetry department? And has much new fiction come in? And has Walter Watkins been published yet? For, you recall, he was trying to bring out his book this winter with the Princeton Press. And what's the dope about the Hardy stuff? And about Blackmur's piece on Hardy and his advance?

I'm getting on with the play, now entering the last stretch. If something doesn't occur now to demoralize me I ought to finish it on schedule. Sometime before long, a batch will come rolling in for you all. I'm doing a little revision and copying now on the part finished to date. I'm very anxious to have a response from you and Albert and your wives. As for the novel, I work a little at that, and begin to get a clearer notion of what my problems are. It's going to be a long pull.[6]

Has your book come out? It must have by this time, but, naturally, I haven't seen any notice of it, and there hasn't been other news. *Please let me hear about this, details in full.* And what are you working on now? And how are your eyes?

Katherine Anne wrote me about the neutrality sessions, which led her to the observation, no doubt a just one, that there seems to be nothing quite so controversial as true neutrality. Well, I wish I could sit in on one of the sessions. For we miss the jawing which constitutes such a large part of our Baton Rouge life. And I especially have been missing football, and look back with nostalgia upon our radio sessions of last fall. Do let me know what the situation is, what kind of team LSU has, etc.

4. Mario Praz was one of several artists and intellectuals with whom the Warrens visited in Italy. Others included Corrado Alvaro, Elio Vittorini, and Alberto Moravia, according to Joseph Blotner, *Robert Penn Warren: A Biography* (New York: Random House, 1997), 247.

5. Pier Marie Pasinetti was a young Italian writer and student of Brooks and Warren's in Baton Rouge; the Warrens visited him on trips to Italy. He later entered the doctoral program at Yale University and became a novelist (Cutrer, *Parnassus on the Mississippi*, 212).

6. The play was *Proud Flesh,* which later became *All the King's Men.* In the copy Warren sent Brooks, the main character's name was Strong, later changed to Talos, and finally Stark. Warren reported on several occasions that while he was working on *All the King's Men* in Rome, he could hear the "boot heels of Benito's Black Shirts clacking on the cobbles of Via Aurelia Safi outside my window" ("Author's Introduction," *All the King's Men* [New York: Harcourt Brace Jovanovich, 1981], xix).

Well, so long, and our best to you both. Tell Albert and Katherine Anne[7] hello for us, and Duncan and Conrad and Imogen and Ken and his wife. Be good.

As ever,
Red

P.S. Our address from now on is American Express, Rome.

American Express
Piazza di Spagna
Rome
December 31, 1939

Dear Cleanth:

Happy New Year to you all: But that is about all of importance which I have for this little bulletin. Last night brought an eight or ten inch fall of snow to Rome, the heaviest since 1848, the great revolutionary year in Europe, and the only snow here, except for a few flakes in 1933 or 1934, since 1919 or thereabouts, the year of the election of the last Pope. So, I am told, people are trying to figure out some mystic significance which will enable them to win lotto or "numbers" or break the bank at Monte Carlo. But there is one little bit of news with us. We have finally received the extension of our passport for six months, that is, until May 25, and we have the promise that it will be extended then for a few weeks, if necessary, unless there is a definite change in the Italian situation. In fact, the whole attitude at the Consulate, that of Mr. Jones, the clean, upstanding, well-dressed boy who handles such matters and whose wife is, we discovered, pregnant, and that of the Consul himself— in fact, to break this sentence down a little, the attitude has become much more carefree and cheerful. I have my friends the Finns, and my friend the Pope, to thank for that, I imagine. The Pope covers all the newspapers here like a tent. And foreign reactions to his recent activities provide the staple of news. (By the way, aren't the Finns raising particular and general hell?)

Your book hasn't come yet. I am terribly anxious to see it, and anxious to have news about the reviews. And I am anxious to hear the report on how the Old Fox Rode Again in New Orleans. Do give me the dope, soon.

Since I began this letter we have been out to a New Years Day dinner at the Pasinetti place—a very fine little party, with the high point bootleg coffee. At least, I suppose that it was bootleg, or maybe they had it left from before the war. Then they gave us a very handsome present, one of the earliest editions of Petrarch, with original binding. Then, God damn it, we left the little valise which contained the book on the street car. Pier and his brother were with

7. Albert Erskine and Katherine Anne Porter, who was twenty-one years his senior, were married from 1938 to 1942, although they were separated for the last two years (Joan Givner, *Katherine Anne Porter: A Life* [New York: Simon and Schuster, 1982], 315, 325–26). Brooks and Warren published five of her short stories in the *Southern Review*.

us, and we were all busily engaged in talking at the time we got off. Almost immediately we realized what we had done, and took a taxi to chase the street car. We overtook several on the line, and searched them. Certainly, one of those we searched was the one. Then we went to the head of the line and got on every car on the line as it passed, with the assistance of the officer in charge there, and made a search, and talked to the conductor. But so far it has all been of no use. Some idiot certainly picked up the bag—some idiot who will use the shoes it contained, an oldish pair, and the bag, and throw away the book as junk. It is all very sickening. There is only the slightest chance that the thing may turn up at lost-and-found office of the company, for we interviewed all of the conductors on the line.

By the way, speaking of the academic life, here is a choice extract from a letter which reached me in the last batch of mail to [be] forwarded from Louisiana. A certain professor at the University of Pennsylvania wrote asking to be put on the MLA program. Here is his proposition: "I have been studying the followers of Dickens in the English novel for some time (15 years) and am doing a book on the subject. I should like to offer a twenty-seven minute paper on the subject at the Christmas meeting if the program has not yet been arranged. I would treat some sixty-odd novels on the following subjects: low life, criminal life, London lodging houses, commercial life, reform, the sailor ashore, tavern life, etc." Well, wouldn't this bird, whose name, incidentally, is T. Ernest M. Bell, get on famously with our Old grey one himself. By the way, too, would the subject "The Sailor Ashore in the English Drama from January 7, 6:30 p.m., 1803 to Saint Luchy's Eve, 1899, or 'Where hare you h'Oscar' or 'Fuggery on the Briny'" be a swell topic for a dissertation at LSU? Or perhaps the old man himself is working on that subject in off moments from his writing of the history of English Literature. You must find out.

Here are one or two SR items which came through to me, since they were addressed to me. You remember that we wrote Edwin Herron, 1360 Webster Street, San Francisco, that we liked and would use his story "Hail Fellow, Well Met," but that we should [p. 2] like to suggest some small revisions. He writes me and asks for the suggestions and, when we send the suggestions, for the MS itself. This he wants sent directly to him at the address given above and not in care of Paul Anderson, who originally submitted the MS to us. Another item is from the father of Walter Watkins, Mr. R. H. Watkins, Superintendent of the City Schools of Laurel, Mississippi. He wants three copies of the issue in which Wattie's piece appears, and promises to remit promptly. Of course, he may have written again, and this may be old stuff to you all. Another matter, which, I trust, you will pass on to Mrs. Swallow is this: Among the rejected manuscripts in the office, in a pile of those to be sent back, was a batch of silly negro poems, by Eleanor Hardee Elder. The manuscript was to be sent to Mrs. Peter Walton Godfrey, Biltmore Apartments, Atlanta, Georgia. This good lady wrote me on September 9 that the manuscript had not been returned. The letter, of course, reached me a few days ago.

Will you kindly ask Mrs. Swallow to send the damned thing back to the burning fountain whence it came, and oblige your old friend and admirer and colleague, Brer Warren?

The mail also brought a letter from Edward Donahoe, a letter written in July, shortly after his marriage. The main part of the letter is taken up with the following story: A drunk staggered into a Catholic church, and went up to the communion rail lifted his foot, and leaned against the thing. To the priest, who was puttering about the altar, he said, "Hey, gimme a straight whiskey!" "Just have a seat," the priest said, not unkindly, "and I'll attend to you in a minute." The drunk obediently sat down. When the whisky didn't come, he staggered, again, to the rail, and called for his whisky. "Just be patient," the priest said, "I'll attend to you shortly." So he sat down again. About this time in came six nuns, moving down the aisle two by two, with their hands folded on their bosoms, and their eyes downcast. The drunk, catching sight of the procession, leaped up and shouted, "Hey, never mind the damned floor show, I want my whisky!" I retell that to you for what it is worth.

I have just had a note from Mr. Crofts to the effect that *An Approach* was going very well—LSU, Auburn, North Dakota, Tufts, Colgate, Cornell (a special class), St. Louis University, and others. He said, in fact, "We are quite pleased. . . ." But by the time this reaches you, you will probably know the cold truth about our returns on this term. Crofts didn't give me any figure on royalty but said that there would probably be one above the advance expense. By the way, in this connection, I had in the last batch of letters from the SR one from Professor John C. Pope, Saybrock College, Yale, asking about the *Approach*. I imagine that you had one, too, for he probably sent the letter in duplicate. Anyway, he said—back in early October—that he had submitted a plan to the Freshman division at Yale, which involved the use of the *Approach, Understanding Poetry,* and Shakespeare's plays for the freshman work at Yale, each for one term. His questions were: What success had we had with actual use in the classroom? and could the format be changed? He also asked about future revisions. He didn't seem very well satisfied with the essay section, and said that a couple of the stories might quickly outlive their usefulness. (But he was high in praise of the thing as a whole.) I wrote him as full an account as I could, mentioning my own experience with the book, and saying that I had been in close contact with you during your use of it. He didn't say that he had seen the new Crofts version, and I am inclined to believe, since he wrote about matters of format (he doesn't like the double columns, but favors something like the Modern Library Giants), that he had only the LSU version. But the decision was taken at least a month ago, so the whole question may now be vindictively academic. He did say that the *Understanding* had strong supporters in the department, but that the *Approach*, which was less well known, was less immediately attractive to *some* of the members. I tried to explain our intention, and to make it plain that we weren't making the cabinet of gems, etc. And I did want him, since he has been so friendly, to understand why he had not received a prompt reply. I do hope that he sent the letter in duplicate, or that you happened to see him at New Orleans. It would be swell to get both books on at Yale. Have you heard definitely about Oklahoma?

I am now working on a copy of the play to send you all. It should be on its way in a day or so. Please let me have very full comments. And I do hope that you all will like it.

I can't think of any more news. But I know that Baton Rouge is teeming with news. And so I await your next with bated breath.

Cinina joins me in love to you all. The same to the Erskines, etc.

We miss you all.

As ever,
Red

1940s

Rome

January 11 [1940][1]

Dear Cleanth:

The new SR came today, and that is something like what a magazine ought to be. I've read it damned near from cover to cover, with pleasure, even if I was acquainted with nearly everything in it. I hadn't seen the Bishop,[2] of course, or the Zabel.[3] I didn't give Bishop a careful reading, and am not entitled to an opinion, but it seemed OK, and the Zabel, which I did read carefully, seems to be exactly what you said it was: the best thing he has done. The job on Millay is not half bad. Has Mrs. Stopher been Vashti-ing round over that little item? And Edna M. herself is going to begin to commence to believe that Louisiana is not a good place for cultural lectures—after the essays by Brooks, Ransom, and Zabel which have been financed by the State University at one time and another. Ransom throttled her with one of her own silk garters; Zabel has choked her with some of her own taffy. I fear that you, my pal, resorted to the homely old cleaver, without compliments. But—as the lady in the old New Yorker cartoon remarked to the psychiatrist—"I have a feeling that my feet are trying to tell me something"—she may be having the feeling that her feet are trying to tell her something—not to take them to Louisiana on any more lecture tours. I forgot—I haven't read the revolution piece. But the issue looks damned good, with less dead wood than we have had for a long time. And the order of the stuff is nice, huh?

I received a few days ago a very handsome volume recently published by the North Carolina Press.[4] For it, both Cinina and I say a large *thank you*. They did do a very nice job of manufacture for you, I feel. And I have reread the

---

1. This letter was dated "1939"; however, as James A. Perkins has noted, the issue of the *Southern Review* that Warren mentions was the winter 1940 issue; thus, he probably typed the incorrect year.

2. John Peale Bishop published a short story, "A Man Who Thought," in *Southern Review* 1 (July 1935): 58–65; and a review essay, "Finnegans Wake," in *Southern Review* 5.3 (winter 1940): 439–52.

3. Morton Dauwen Zabel, editor of *Poetry*, published a review-essay, "Condition of American Criticism: 1939," in *Southern Review* 5.3 (winter 1940): 568–608.

4. Brooks's book from the University of North Carolina Press was *Modern Poetry and the Tradition* (1939).

book. It is all that I thought it was. Certainly, nobody has done a cleaner job of getting at the very central situation in modern poetry. And the individual analyses still strike me as extraordinarily keen. And, may I say again, that I am deeply gratified by your comments on my own stuff. I can make this even more emphatic at this distance than when I said it across the litter of our desk. I only hope that a little amiable perjury didn't creep into the book about that point.

And today the mails brought Mr. Crofts'[5] statement. One hundred and ninety-nine berries. Which, you know, could be a lot worse. And was it welcome news! If he can make a fair success of the book during the next couple of years, so that he has something in the bank on it, I imagine that with another revision, and perhaps a change in format and an enlargement, we can put out the book that will sweep the field. (By the way, I suppose our labors of last spring have paid for the twins which I have heard Purser now has. That ought to be our church-work for the year. And, don't forget to tell me when you write next, did he do the proofs? If he didn't, there ought to be a damned show-down on this whole affair. If he did do the proofs, and if he will do the proofs on the next revision, all right. But if not.) I have been doing a little on the story text book, not much, but something. But I shall get something substantial done this spring, I hope.

I shall have your MS of *Proud Flesh* in the mail next Monday or Tuesday. It has been ready for some days, but I discovered that the copy I had for you all was the only copy left which had in it a number of revisions, and so I had to hang on to it, or try to go back and remake the revisions. So I hung on to it, and made [p. 2] another copy. When you have time, please write me in detail about it, all your suggestions and criticisms. For I don't regard this draft as final. In fact, I am almost certain that if the thing is produced—which, I am sure, is quite unlikely—I shall have to do some heavy cutting in the second and third scenes of the first act. And I imagine that there will be other important revisions to make. But for the time being I am going to lay it by, so that I can have the benefit of the comments of a few people and the benefit of a little perspective.

By the way, I have heard from a reliable source, which you may surmise, that you all may be seeing our friend who is interested in family history much sooner than you ever suspected, and for an indefinite period. He is, I hear from the same most reliable of sources, making desperate efforts to change his whole plan of life. The motives are, I am sure, easily grasped by you, and are motives with which you would have the deepest sympathy. I hear that he simply can't take any more of what he has been taking.

To take up the ever fascinating subject of life in Louisiana, what is the dope about Bryan?[6] Has anything been decided? Lately I've been watching

5. Warren is referring to a royalty statement for *An Approach to Literature*.
6. Adolphus Bryan, a Harvard Ph.D., was Brooks's candidate for chair of the English department at LSU, according to Robert B. Heilman in *The Possibilities of Order: Cleanth*

the mails, day by day, with the hope that the announcement of the great event would appear. I'll draw a deep breath when I do hear that.

And as for our own little fortunes, what is the dope about the promotions? I don't suppose that there is any yet. Hebert, during the talk which I had with him last summer, suggested that I write him in the early spring about the matter, referring to the conversation. I shall do that, say in February. Meanwhile, let me know what you get out of Read.[7] I have the feeling that, if Read doesn't go to the bat this spring, things may be indefinitely postponed. And you are the man to put the burr under that saddle. Let me have word as soon as you know anything.

I'm beginning to feel my way into the new novel. I can't be anything but nervous at this stage—but not as nervous, probably, as I'll be toward the end. And I'm tinkering with some short poems, which I'll send you as soon as there's anything to send. At present they look pretty amorphous.

The weather here has been frightful lately. A terrific snow just after Christmas, the heaviest in nearly a hundred years. And now the weather is damp and cold, with a very nasty wind which, I am told by dolorous natives, is the tramontana.[8] Which name is far too good for it. I can't think of any name which wouldn't be. I am just pulling out of a bad cold, which had me sort of in bed for a couple of days, and now Cinina and the cook seem to be getting it. But the official spring should be here soon. And not too soon.

We still spend a lot of time reading the papers. Now I've found a German beer place, where the Munich beer is still good and only costs eleven cents, American, the stein, and a big one, and where—don't gasp—you get the leading French newspapers only thirty-six hours late, and the Paris edition of the *Herald Tribune*. So I go there about every other day for a little beer—I find that it is only American and Italian beer which disagrees with me, or rather I don't give a damn if the German beer does disagree with me—and there I read the papers. But the reports are almost word for word what we get in the local press. And not as hot on the Finnish and Balkan situation. And occasionally I see the American papers, very late, [p. 3] at the Consulate. Don't you boys let the New Deal get us into the war while I'm here. Or after I get back. But you can sell all the planes you want. And I'm damned near getting to be a big navy man. By the way, I recently saw a very impressive news reel here of American gunnery, coast defense and naval. Very, very interesting, from several points of view.

There isn't any news with us. Which, on the whole, is a comforting thing

Brooks and His Work, ed. Lewis P. Simpson (Baton Rouge: Louisiana State University Press, 1976), 133–34.

7. William A. Read resigned as chairman of the LSU English department in 1940; Hebert, as acting president of the university, appointed Brooks chairman of a special committee to recommend appointment of a new department chairman.

8. The term *tramontana* is said to be used by natives of Colorado. It is a play on the word *tramontane*, suggesting a cold north wind—the opposite of a Chinook wind, which is also prevalent in Colorado.

to remark. There must be a lot with you all. Please give me a full account of New Orleans and the goings-on there during the MLA.[9]

Give our love to Tinkum. And KA and Albert, and the boys and girls. We look forward to the reunion.

As ever,
Red

Rome
January 26, 1940

Dear Cleanth:

The immediate provocation for this letter is provided by a letter, received just this afternoon from John Palmer. He had just written to Dr. Read, he said, asking for some sort of job for next year. He did not ask me to do anything about it—knowing, I suppose, that I couldn't do anything—but my first impulse was to sit down and write to Dr. Read. Then, on a little more reflection, I decided that a letter might not be the thing, that it might be better, if you happened to get a good opportunity and felt so disposed, for you to sound out the Doctor. Or, and this was decisive in my decision not to write to Dr. Read, it might be better to approach the matter through Bryan. In the light of the unsettled condition in the department, I thought it best to write to you about the matter and leave it up to your judgment. For all I know, John may have written to you or Albert already about the business, but just in case he hasn't I'm doing so on my own hook. Here is the way his situation stands. He has, for all intents and purposes, finished the thesis with Nichol Smith's blessing. The blessing must be a very satisfied blessing, for Nichol Smith has agreed to back John strongly for a Carnegie grant for another year in England to pursue the study of the same topic, the history of literary patronage to the end of the 17th century. This was Secretary Allen's idea—John seems to have made a hit with him—and Allen, it seems, is prepared to go to the bat with the Carnegie people to get John the Carnegie grant. In that case, John would pass up the B.Litt, get his status changed, and present the whole job for the D.Phil, even though Nichol Smith tells him, on what grounds I don't know— though this is of mild interest—that the B.Litt is the better degree. But John doesn't want to spend four years in England, especially under the present circumstances; that, it would seem, is easily comprehensible. If he can get a job he is coming on back to America. He is stalling, he says, but trying to burn no bridges behind him, until he knows something about LSU, which, he told me in August, was the place where he would like best to be situated. With the grant suggested to him by Allen, and strongly supported by Nichol Smith, however, it seems that his case for a job, if there is any kind of an opening, is

9. The Modern Language Association of America, the largest professional organization for the disciplines of English and foreign languages, meets the week after Christmas each year in a large, metropolitan city.

extremely strong; and he told me last summer that he would come to LSU on a minimum salary. That's the dope, which I throw into your lap, and which you may be able to do something with. Perhaps John didn't put the full facts about his situation before Read—I mean about the idea of the Carnegie grant being Allen's, and about Nichol Smith's acting against his usual practice in backing up the idea.

John also wrote me that *Night Rider* is out in England, and he enclosed a lot of quotations from the *Times Lit. Sup.* review.[1] He said that it was reviewed as the fiction choice of the week—which, the TLS being what it is, and there being fifty-two weeks in a year, and novels having been written for several hundred years, isn't exactly a thing to inflate the ego excessively. But it is mildly satisfactory. Here, in case you are interested, are some of the remarks from the review: "Once again it may come as a surprise to the reader unversed in the more serious fashion of the American novel at the present time that a subject of this sort tobacco, etc., can be put to high and indeed subtle imaginative purpose." "It is this same awakened or heightened sense of the nation's experience that is at work in the more seriously analytical novel of social economic conditions, whether it deals with the present—like Mr. Steinbeck's *Grapes of Wrath,* for instance—or—like Mr. Warren's novel—with the past. In both instances, the novel [p. 2] takes on an added imaginative strength and urgency as a result." "—his are the story-teller's preoccupations, and the story he tells is full, adventurous, curiously tense and somber, genuine in tragedy." Then there is a reservation about the presentation of Munn's character, which, it says, is not worked out with full clarity: "one observes Munn, as it were, under all sorts of tests of character without feeling one really knows him. Yet the driving sincerity of Mr. Warren's interpretation of events triumphs over such weakness. The story is as distinctively American in spirit as in subject. If an English novelist chose to tackle a comparable theme of English economic history—the dock strike, say, or the rubber boom of almost the same period— what are the chances that he would produce a deeply felt and dramatic story and not an argumentative thesis?" I hope that the sales are satisfactory, though God knows, I get little enough of the royalty after the British Government and Houghton Mifflin have pawed over the sum. My share finally works out to a royalty of about three percent. In other words, a pretty good sale in England wouldn't do more than buy cigarettes for a year.

Speaking of money, I wrote to Holt some time back, asking for word about the *Und. Poetry.* Yesterday I heard that they expect us to clear our indebtedness on the permissions this winter and probably have about $50 each on the black side of the ledger. But we don't get a statement until April. That of course, is an estimate and not a definite fact. By the way, Wilson has left them and gone to Reynal and Hitchcock.

1. *Night Rider* was published in January 1940 by Eyre and Spottiswoode with a second impression in February 1940. The *TLS* review, "Drama in Tobacco," appeared on January 20, 1940, p. 29.

No news with us, except that Tinkum's letter gave us great pleasure, in itself and in the news that she is pretty well off with her insides.

I'm about half through with another longish poem—I've done some fifty lines on it—which I hope will be better than the one I sent the other day. That, certainly, is not a masterpiece.

Sunshine today, at last. And our colds are gone.

Love to you all and to Albert and KA.

As ever,
Red

. . . .

Rome
March 7, 1940

Dear Cleanth:

You remember that, last summer, I told you about my little call on Hebert in regard to the promotion business. I told him the little story of our conversation and of my later conversation with James Monroe; and Hebert then suggested that I write him a summary of the situation this spring and refer him to my conversation of last July. Well, I've finally written him the letter which he suggested, and I am enclosing a carbon for you to glance at. I hope that it looks OK to you in the light of current events, whatever those current events are. And God knows, I hope it doesn't backfire to queer anything. Anyway, let me know what you think, and let me know how matters stand there. What line has Read taken in the matter?

Speaking of department matters, a letter from Mrs. Daggett came yesterday with a postscript to the effect that a faculty committee was appointed to handle the matter of the headship of the English Department, and that Dolph [Bryan] was recommended, but has not yet been appointed officially. For God's sake let me know when the glad news—if it comes off—comes off. She also had some rather nice odds and ends about politics—things which make our life here seem pretty sheltered.

How is the university politicking proceeding. Mrs. Daggett also said that the president of the AAUP had resigned because of "ill health" but that nobody believed that story. What happened? And what happened to Ken? And what is Ken going to do? God, that little item makes me boil every time I think about it.

I had [a] note from John Palmer, a whoop of glee not a note, to the effect that Read had written him that a recommendation for an instructorship had been made. You all must have done some pretty nice work. I do hope that the thing gets approved by the dean. The appointment of John has a double value. First, and more important, it brings a damned good man into the department, and second, it keeps somebody else out. But this second advantage is not negligible.

The only pleasant thing I can think about to tell you is a beer party in Vatican City with two priests and two Associated Press men—one AP man who covered Spain and Bohemia and is now waiting here to bolt for the Balkans when the trouble starts there and the other AP man who is tagging about with Sumner and Myron—or rather, I should say, was tagging about with them. But from their rich experience of men and events the two newshawks had little to offer except amiability.

Write to me when you have a chance. Cinina joins me in love to you all. And give our best to our friends, but don't be too liberal in the interpretation of that last word.

As ever,
Red

[Typed at top of page] I am sending this in duplicate, since I want to have some confidence that you will get the enclosure.

General Delivery
North Bennington, Vermont
June 8, 1940

Dear Cleanth:

I wrote you a card a few days ago just to announce our arrival. We got out by the barest, I suppose, and on no notice at all. The manifestoes were put up on a Saturday; Sunday some of the beating-up occurred; Monday the demonstrations started. Monday morning I called Genoa to try to get our passage moved up to fifteenth of May. But no soap. We decided to go to Genoa and be on the spot if anything broke. So we went to Genoa on Tuesday night. By Thursday noon we had wangled passage, cots, not beds, but we could have scalped those for a mighty big profit if we had had a mind to do so. But I must confess that we didn't stay on the cots very long; on the second night out we both got beds, God knows how. Maybe some of the refugees jumped overboard. But Cinina was in with a gang of women and I was in with a gang of men. We spent the entire voyage listening to horror stories from Norwegians, Belgians, Germans, and French.

Poor Pier Pasinetti had finally managed to wangle his permit to come to America, after working all winter on the proposition. He is the saddest and the bitterest man you ever saw, and if he doesn't learn a little self-control he will shortly end in a concentration camp or with a busted head. He says anything and says it anywhere, in a voice like a fog-horn. The only chance he has for survival is that a lot of other people do the same thing, and I don't suppose they can arrest everybody. (All winter the anti-Fascist sentiment has been increasing, or has at least become more articulate; and the anti-German feeling is absolutely everywhere. We heard a German newsreel roundly hissed in a Roman theater, for instance.) But back to Pier: just a few days before he was supposed to sail, they revoked his permit. He was planning to come here and take out American citizenship.

I suppose we'll be in the war in one way or another before long. I'm confused for the moment, I'm frank to say. I just don't know what we ought to do to save our own skins. But whatever we do, I'm pretty sure of one thing; the things you and I are interested in will come damned near going by the board for some time to come. Even in this little town, which is quite off the main line of activity, you can see the war attitudes pretty well formed. What do you think we ought to do?

Louisiana, I see from the evening paper, still commands some attention in the news. Alexandria this time. And I observe with pleasure that Leche got the rap. What about Maestri?[1] And how are the internal affairs of the University shaping up? Not too well, I imagine. I saw Crofts for a few minutes when I came through NY, and he said that there would, apparently, be a shut-down on money for LSU. What's the dope on that? (By the way, he also said that they had sold right at 800 copies of the *Approach* this spring, which means about seventy-five dollars each for us, in July. And, by the way, did Holt come across this spring? And, if so, for how much?) And Crofts also told me of his talk with you in the spring about our situation there, about promotions, etc. Has anything happened in that line? And if not, was any excuse offered? Crofts also told me of the flirtation which Cornell had begun with you. I have a little flirtation begun, too, but I don't know how far it will go. I'll write you details later. But I hope it will go far enough to give some sort of a stick to bat at the local dog with. I'm pretty damned sore if, after the various promises which have been made us, we don't get some satisfaction pretty soon.

[p. 2] As for news with us, the letter from Cinina to Tinkum, which I mailed a few days before we left Rome, and which was probably on the same boat with us, gave about all the news of the last period in Rome. For the present I'm here working with Francis Fergusson[2] on a revision of my play. (If you have any suggestions I wish you'd spring them now, while I can bring them to bear on the present process of revision.) He is going to put on a couple of scenes experimentally this summer, and talks about doing the whole thing next year, if some of the revisions pan out. I despair of ever getting a commercial production. I hope to get a chunk of the revision done before I go to Colorado to teach two weeks in late July and early August. After that things look pretty vague, though we hope to be able to stop over on the way back for a short visit with John and Robb,[3] and then with my father. He had a touch of flu this

1. Richard Leche was governor of Louisiana; he resigned "due to health" and was subsequently indicted in conjunction with the James Monroe Smith debacle (see Cutrer, *Parnassus on the Mississippi*, 213–30). Apparently Maestri was another player in that corruption.

2. Fergusson, to whom the published version of *All the King's Men* is dedicated, was Warren's "reader" and adviser on the dramatic stage version. He was associate director of the American Laboratory Theatre of the New York School and professor of literature and drama at Bennington College, Vermont.

3. Robb Reavill, Mrs. John Crowe Ransom, was a beautiful and gracious hostess who had that wonderful knack of making her guests feel welcome and at home in their house (see Blotner, *Robert Penn Warren*, 55).

winter, not much, but he is getting on in years now, and since he is simply never ill this seems to have depressed him considerably.

I hope that things are going beautifully with you all, and that Tinkum has finished her walk-building. Have you been keeping the raw material moving up to the point of production? Write and give us the news. Love to you all and to the Erskines, Albrizzios, and Duncan. Cinina joins me in this.

As ever,
Red

Have you heard from John Palmer? I hope he is on the President Roosevelt.

The Southern Review
University, Louisiana
Thursday–Saturday [June 1940]

Dear Red,

We are all very much relieved to know that you all are safely back in this country. Your card was very welcome, and I have waited anxiously for your letter. I certainly look forward to talking with you—about all sorts of things, but certainly about what you found in Europe.

My own mind is pretty well made up and has been for some time. I have thought from the time of the Norwegian invasion that we should send all aid that we could to the allies. I oppose our sending men, and I think that the position can be justified as follows. There are dangers in both positions, but I refuse to let the Demon of the Absolute chase me from one into the other. (That there is a danger that one will lead the country to do the other, I am aware; but I think that a complete German victory is going to put us into war later anyway; and I think that an Allied victory might keep us out.) In the second place, I think that sending aid can be justified on a perfectly selfish basis. I think that one plane sent now and flown by the British and French might save us building ten planes later and fifty Americans in uniform with our own little crop of martinets bossing them. Of course, it may be too late to send them now. If it is, then we are in for it. For a German victory is going to make us arm to the teeth, whether there is ever an invasion [p. 2] or not. Home-made American pie, mother songs, the Ford Sunday evening hour, and home-spun regionalism—all back up arming to the teeth quite as much (and more) as they back up isolation. And the real thing to be dreaded is a militaristic America. I hope the Allies can win quickly. I've thought for months that that was our only chance. (By the way, the Louisiana legislature is preparing to pass a bill to call for 2 years compulsory training in all La. high schools and 2 years in all La. colleges. I am writing a letter to our local state senator asking him to oppose it.)

In general, I think that our intellectuals have, by and large, given a pretty miserable exhibition of unrealistic thinking about the whole business. But I don't include in this our friend Albert, who is a convinced isolationist, and whose position I respect, and who has been a constant help to my thinking in making me keep aware of the other side.

But I didn't begin this letter to blow off on the war situation. Of far more concern is the local situation. I was told several months ago by Dr. Read that our promotions were going through with a measly little raise of two hundred dollars. I've heard no contradiction to this; but I have heard hints in the last few days to indicate that they might not go through after all. Mine has certainly not gone through for the summer session. I have been trying to see Hebert for a week—he's been so busy that I have yet to see him. (Friday) I've got an appointment with Hebert for in the morning. The main matter is to try to jimmy a little money out of him for the S.R. during the summer in order to pay for a proofreader and office helper. By the way, I may as well give the whole story about that help now. Alan Swallow[1] was offered a full-time teaching job at the U. of New Mexico, which I advised him to take. He and [p. 3] his wife left about two weeks ago. That meant getting a new secretary. Albert started interviewing applicants, but P[ipkin] went off his ear in a fit of sudden zeal for Albert and myself—he wanted to give Albert a vacation, and I needed one too—we must have a secretary at once. The upshot was that he offered the secretaryship to one of Ransom's students who has been granted a fellowship here at $125.00 per month for the summer. The boy is undoubtedly an excellent person but can't do shorthand or type. When Albert and I heard of it we blew up and went over and read the riot act. He finally <said> he would call up and cancel the offer, but he was sore as hell. (Notice that he was going to "help" by getting us 1 person in place of 2, and moreover a person who couldn't act as secretary, and even so would have to give up any full-time place about the time that he got the hang of the office.) Well, P. was lucky enough to be saved by the gong. Perhaps before he had time to cancel his offer—I don't know—Ransom indicated that the student had got an offer to help with the K.R.[2] there. He proposed that we might want to consider Robert Lowell and his wife, to whom he has been recently married.[3] A good deal of cross-questioning ensued, and the Lowells arrived yesterday.

[p. 4] She is to be secretary at the regular salary. Robert is to try for a fellowship in the Dept., and this summer I'm going to try to get $30.00 a month for him out of Hebert to help around the office, read proof, and in general help us get things clear. (I probably won't be able to get it.) If he gets a fellowship this fall, we can ask him to be assigned to S.R. work if we like; or we may advise him to work in the department. The nub of the matter is

---

1. Swallow—later a critic, editor, and publisher—had been sponsored by Warren for graduate study at LSU; his wife had worked as secretary for the *Southern Review*.

2. With an inception similar to that of the *Southern Review*, the *Kenyon Review* was instituted by the president of Kenyon College, Gordon Chalmers, who in 1937 asked John Crowe Ransom to start a literary journal of the highest quality (Thomas Daniel Young, *Gentleman in a Dustcoat: A Biography of John Crowe Ransom* [Baton Rouge: Louisiana State University Press, 1976], 297–98).

3. Jean Stafford married Robert Lowell in 1940 after they met at the Writers' Conference in Boulder, Colorado.

his wife, since, as you see, Robert won't necessarily have any connection with the S.R. at all.

I am very favorably impressed with her. She's sharp as a tack, well-read, and ought to be a real help. But there are handicaps. She's got to work up her shorthand. All in all, we've taken a gamble; but Albert and I prayed over the matter, and I believe that it's going to work fine. Robert seems far less the wild-eyed young man than I had thought he might be. He is quiet, even shy, and talks uncommonly good sense. I hope he gets the fellowship.

P. made an unconditional surrender, and has had nothing to do with the Lowell arrangement. He said that anything we did was O.K.

By the way, the disintegration is going on rapidly in that quarter, if I don't miss my guess. We see him very little, but I honestly think that things are coming to a showdown fast. For Pete's sake, stand by; so that if it is necessary to act we can get together and act quickly. Not only is there the internal trouble, but his enemies are after him; and moreover, the Survey Report released a week or so ago bears down noticeably harder on the [p. 5] Graduate School than on anything else.

The department situation is still worrying people like Dolph, Heilman,[4] and your obedient servant. Nothing has happened. But that's part of the trouble. Kirby[5] is now in charge, but no department meetings have been called—no reforms initiated. Perhaps he feels that there is little that he can do as an acting chairman. The chief concern is this, however: we are afraid that the wolf is at work with privy paw. No communiqués are issued from the Uhler[6] camp. But we know him well enough to feel that as long as a permanent head is not appointed, he will still maneuver to get in, or at least to influence the choice. Moreover, the dept. is at work looking to the hiring of three new instructors. (I have yet to be consulted.)

I'm going to try to tell Hebert tomorrow that I wish he would give me a chance to talk with him some evening about the whole situation. Whether he will, or not, I don't know. (And he, moreover, is merely *acting* too. I don't know what his chances of being confirmed are.)

I was talking to Bryan the other day and was impressed by his desire that you should get back. He thinks you could come into Hebert, and with Hebert's admiration for [p. 6] you, and speaking as one who had been away and comes fresh into the troubled situation, could get a very earnest hearing. Maybe so, maybe not. But the more I think of it, the more I'm inclined to agree with him. Of Hebert's esteem of you I have no doubt. He's going to need some

4. Robert B. Heilman, a Harvard Ph.D. in Renaissance drama, joined the LSU faculty in 1935 and became a lifelong friend of Brooks and of Warren.

5. Thomas Kirby, a Johns Hopkins Ph.D., also joined the LSU faculty in 1935; he became chair in 1940 and served in that capacity for nearly forty years.

6. John Earle Uhler, another Johns Hopkins Ph.D., joined the LSU faculty in 1928; in 1931 his controversial novel *Cane Juice* temporarily cost him his job. Uhler was a member of the department of English "reactionary right," according to Cutrer (*Parnassus on the Mississippi*, 232). He was a member of the committee that Brooks chaired regarding the appointment of a new department chairman.

pressure, I believe, if we are to hope to get a really good man from the outside to head the department; or indeed, get the right man here. All this is said with no malice toward Kirby, with whom I am cordial and whose mind I respect. He, by the way, looks on his appointment as temporary; but he would be something other than flesh and blood if he did not climb up on the mount occasionally and take a peep at the glories of the world.

I imagine from your letter that you and C[inina] are not planning to come through here on your way to Colorado. But I wish that you would. It would be mighty fine to be able to see you all for even a little while, and have some talk. But besides this selfish consideration—I think that reasons of state dictate it too, if you possibly can. Won't the summer fares be on which allow you to wander out of your direct course, for only a trifle? I don't mean to urge unduly, but ponder these things in your heart. (If the S.R. situation breaks, I won't stand on ceremony—I'll send a wire!)

The S.R. situation is fair to middling. We've got some fine stuff lined up for the next two issues—if we can get it in. But MSS. have piled up; and there are lots of special things I want to talk with you about. One thing I'll take up now. We've got so much good—and goodish poetry [p. 7] submitted that I suggest that we represent about five or six young poets in the next number with perhaps a couple of poems apiece. We could start them out in a group but it would take a year or more to publish all of them and then the other poets—young ones, former contributors, and established ones—would have four or five more groups ready—we'd still be a year behind. Since we are drawing submissions from so many talented young writers, I think that we give a truer picture of the literary scene, and discharge our proper function best, by giving the interested reader brief samples of a number of writers? What do you think of this? Be candid. But it seems to me a way to catch up with ourselves. If you think well of the plan, I want to send you some MSS. for your judgment—groups of poems by a number of poets with my notes on them. (I hate to break into your work with the play and the novel. But I hesitate undertaking the decisions alone.)

Saturday—

Well, I saw Hebert today at least with a request for $30 a month for the summer to pay Lowell to serve as office-boy and proof-reader. I put it up to him as a [p. 8] temporary help to aid us through this summer. I think that he will come through with it—Lord knows, it was a small request. He was most cordial, and so we went on to talk about other things. I asked whether our promotions went through. He said no; that we had both been recommended by Dr. Read, but that the committee he had appointed on promotions, headed by Dean Frey,[7] had not reported on them favorably. They had reported that they regarded us highly, our publications, etc., etc., but money was tight, a permanent head was not yet appointed, et cetera, et cetera.

7. Fred C. Frey, then LSU Dean of Men, served LSU from 1922 to 1962. During that time he became dean of the university and was considered for the presidency.

Hebert did not associate himself with their findings or arguments. We talked around and around. I get the distinct impression that he regards us highly and would like to do something, if he can. He did say specifically that he was not altogether satisfied with his promotions committee and that he had thus far recommended no promotions at all to the Board. He also suggested specifically that the matter was not closed and that we might have some more talk about it this summer. Another reason for your coming by this summer if you can possibly make it!

I told him that you were back, and he asked when you were coming back to B[aton] R[ouge]. I told him that you had stated that some school was nibbling at you—that I did not know which one. He misunderstood and thought I was speaking of myself, and answered, Cornell. I corrected him, saying that it was true that friends had told me and continued to hint that Cornell was considering me; that I didn't know directly from them, but be that as may, I was speaking of you; that naturally I was very much interested in my own case, but that I was also highly anxious that no other school snake you away; [p. 9] that I knew nothing more about the matter, but hoped that L.S.U. would remain on the alert.

We talked of other things, and talked pretty frankly. Most of them had better wait for a rendition by word of mouth. All that I've said, obviously, is to be kept secret as the grave. For he is in a tight spot, and I am sure would not have been so frank had he not trusted that I would be thoroughly discreet.

I believe that if you could see him this summer, something might be done. {[Handwritten in margin] Nobody ought to know better than you that you can't checkmate with one knight. We need a rook and you're the piece.} I shall try again, but I don't know just how soon I shall have an opportunity. By the way, if you and Cinina can come, it goes without saying that we shall expect you to stay with us. It would be a pure pleasure.

This letter will have to stop—it rapidly approaches the proportions of a tome. And what I have written will indicate why it includes no further comment on your play. I'm mighty interested. Right now things are spinning so fast that I've given every minute of time to them.

Write again soon. Best regards to Cinina from all of us here. Her letter that you refer to hasn't arrived yet. Maybe it will tomorrow.

Cleanth

The Southern Review
University, Louisiana
June 24, 1940

Dear Red,

I am sending you a raft of poems to see what you think of them. What I have especially in mind in this: the publication of one or two poems from five or six poets—the proposition which I mentioned to you in my last letter. On the other hand, I am hoping that you will be candid in saying nix on those that ought to be weeded out and in vetoing the whole proposition if it isn't sound. I don't mind telling you that it feels mighty good to be able to lean on your judgment again after the last number of months.

Here follow some notes on the MSS I am including:

F. Fletcher	FOR DOMINIQUE ROUQUETTE looks like a possibility. LINES FOR A YOUNG POET has some good stuff but may be too lush.
Helen Goldbaum	EXTRA SENSORY—what about this? THE THREE MOTIONS THE HUMAN TOUCH—perhaps?
Woodridge Spears	PAINTING OF A HUNT OIL STEAM FURNACE CORP. These look like the best prospects here, though I am not sure whether LINCOLN UP JOHNS CREEK is not, after all, the best of the bunch.
Stephen Stepanchev	HERMAN MELVILLE MORNING VIOLETS. I think this poet has a lot of stuff, though the sonnets don't interest me much.
[p. 2] John Theobald	ON A SONG OF BRAHMS (DER TOD IST WIE DIE KUHL DER NACHT). I think that this is his best one though I'm not sure it isn't too cute. I am sure that the TO AUSTIN WARREN is out.
Charles Hudeburg	I like all three of these more and more on subsequent readings. What do you think?
Reuel Denney	THE NIAGRA FRONTIER (2 poems) seems to be the best though I am not sure of it.

I am enclosing also several other batches. I'd like your opinion especially on Katherine Hoskins' poem and on that by Bhain Campbell. The Campbell seems to me to have a lot of good stuff but to thin out into some pretty flat allegory in the middle part. I am also enclosing a set of poems by Arthur Blair about which I have no special conviction, but which, at the least, I think are worth passing on to you. I enclose also a little group by George Woodcock which do not impress me particularly but which have something.

As the enclosed letters will indicate, we have been dangling along with Don Gordon for some time. I think his work is goodish but I simply can't get excited. For one thing, it is too monotonous. But maybe I've become snow-blind in the last months. What do you think?

The other material I am sending doesn't call for any special explanations. The poem by Eleanor Ross has something—she's apparently one of Caroline's old students and we have got one promising story from her which we had to turn down. The story submitted by Nicholson is clearly out but the poetry is interesting though I daresay we can't use it. Ebright looks interesting; for a private in the army, he writes pretty well.

Look over this stuff and see what you think. If you spot some groups or people who ought to be worked along toward groups, fine enough. If you [p. 3] think that my suggestion of bringing out five or six with one or two poems apiece is sound, again that's fine. I am having Mrs. Lowell enclose some stationery and you can drop what you like in the mails, or make your notes and suggestions and ship it on back, and I will get them off. In any case, I'll have another set of MSS. to send you before long, though I'm sending only *sifted* stuff. (As you will see by some of the letter dates, this poetry represents the gleanings of about six or eight months.)

All my best,
Cleanth

P.S. I am also sending you an article by Klaus Mann, an article by George Haines, and I am enclosing a letter from Hamilton Basso.[1] The Haines looks pretty good—I'm just not sure whether it would be quite our meat. As for the Basso, I'm pretty leery of it. I would like to have the documentary material which he mentions—it might be interesting—but I'm not sure of the evaluation. Shall we take a chance? Albert is very skeptical.

The Southern Review
University, Louisiana
June 25, 1940

Dear Red:

I am sending another batch of MSS. which should have gone with the others. With references to the Heywood, I think that the first poem has some real quality. I am not convinced that it's worth publishing, but I could see it as a single poem or possibly as a number of a group. I just can't get excited about the Eberhart. What do you think? As for the MacDiarmid[1]—he's awfully interesting as a writer, but I must say that I'm against the long poem, *In a Cornish Garden*. If I liked it much better than I do, I think we might propose to pay for it at prose rates. Even so, I'm not at all sure. The other two pieces of criticism are definitely goodish, I believe, but I'm not sure. If you feel that they're good enough to take, it suits me. On the other hand, I'm far from urging it.

Regards to Cinina and write to me soon.

As ever,
Cleanth

1. Basso later wrote *Sun in Capricorn* (1942), which draws on the Huey Long days in Louisiana.

1. Hugh McDiarmid's pseudonym is Christopher Murray Grieve; he was a leader of the Scottish literary renaissance.

The Southern Review
University, Louisiana
June 29, 1940

Dear Red:

I am sending three more pieces; Caroline's is obviously a piece out of her next novel. I think it's got some good stuff, though I think that the last detail of the torture doesn't get itself integrated, at least in terms of this context (though it may in the larger context of the novel). It seems to be horror for horror's sake. Frankly, I'm on the fence with regard to this piece and happy to have you check your judgment with me on it. Some months ago, Caroline sent in a story with a Civil War setting which I returned. If you think that this piece is acceptable, it's all right by me, and I would appreciate it if you would reply to Caroline at once, since she says she wants a prompt report. On the other hand, if you feel that it's no go, I certainly can have no quarrel with that decision—I'm not that thoroughly convinced about the piece.

The Barrett piece is a reworking of a longer essay which he sent us a good while back. Delmore Schwartz put him in touch with us, and recommends him very highly. You may have noticed in the Spring number the piece which he contributed on Dewey.[1] As for this work, I'm in disagreement, obviously, with his intimation that Maritain has somehow sold us and the church down the river in making out a case for the Allied cause. But that's neither here nor there. The essay itself, from my little reading of Maritain, seems very sensible and acute. My vote is that we should take it, but you use your judgment.

Third, the Healy piece. I am enclosing with the manuscript Healy's letters to me. I think that he bears all the earmarks of a prime s.o.b., and for that reason, I want to lean over backwards in [p. 2] giving fair account of his essay. I've sent back in succession two or three things earlier by him, and in fairness, this is the best thing he has done to date. I have just been reading it over, and though I think he has a case against Ransom, I don't think he has *the* case. More than that, we have already run a lot of material on this point, including Mizener's essay.[2] See what you think of it and either send it to Healy direct or send it back post haste to me and I will get it off to him promptly.

I hope you are having a pleasant stay in Vermont, and I'm still hoping to write you a *long* letter about the play. As it's been, however, the manuscript pile on the one hand and fifteen hours teaching on the other have kept me busy. By the way, don't take time out for these MSS, if you don't have time for them. I simply want your judgment on every doubtful case when I can get it. But I'm not trying to unload on you while you're at work on your revisions. What about a letter from you?

All my best,
Cleanth

1. William Barrett, "John Dewey in His Eightieth Year," *Southern Review* 5.4 (winter 1940): 700–710.
2. Arthur Mizener, "The Romanticism of W. B. Yeats," *Southern Review* 7.3 (1941–1942): 601–23.

[Handwritten] Tinkum sends love to both of you. Cinina's letter from Italy—which you mentioned—has never arrived. Albert is on a short visit to Memphis—will return on Monday or Tuesday. Greet the Ransoms for us.

Regards,
C.

Gambier, Ohio
August 19, 1940

Dear Cleanth:

Many thanks for your letter concerning my negotiations over the leave for next spring. Your theory makes all the facts fall into place in a way which had not occurred to me. I hope that you are right, but even at that the situation, in its total implications, is not too promising. As for Iowa, I really don't care much, in one sense. The more important thing is on the home ground. I acted on the interpretation which you gave me, and am postponing all decision until I get back and can hear more from you and can have a conference with Hebert—By the way, he said in his letter that I should get in touch with him immediately upon arriving, for he had several things to discuss. And I gathered that these things were not directly involved with the matter of the leave. Naturally, my curiosity is considerable.

There is no news with us of any great consequence. John [Crowe Ransom] is pretty busy working on the article which he is doing for the SR end of the symposium, and I am working on my play. We get a bit of talking done, and play bowls on the lawn. The man next door has a set. John has showed me the essays for the symposium which are on hand, and has suggested that he and I, since I am here, sort out those which are to go in the two magazines. He says that he fears that there will not be time for correspondence on the matter, and so I ask permission of you and Albert to do the job here, as soon as enough are on hand to give an idea. Joe Horrell has a pretty good one, which still needs some rewriting. John Gould Fletcher's essay was terrible, and John rejected it. Edd Parks has an unsolicited one here, which is a pretty obvious sort of thing, water on both shoulders and right as far as it goes, probably. I yet don't know how John feels about it. Sidney Cox's piece is better, but pretty inspirational. The big guns haven't fired a round yet.

I don't know exactly when I'll be coming back. I have to wait for a word from Bennington about the date of my business there, and then for a word from New York, where I may have to go for one day. Meanwhile, if you can let me know here, air mail, the date for registration, I'll be very grateful, very.

Not much to add. I hear 5:45 striking, and want to get this in the post office tonight. So I'll sign off. Cinina joins me in love to you and Tinkum and to Albert.

As ever,
Red

P.S. Tell Albert that the Colorado Conference turned over to me five unsold copies of the Hardy SR, and that I have them safe and sound.

The Southern Review
University, Louisiana
August 22, 1940

Dear Red:

I'm sorry that I have been no better correspondent, but I can't seem to get ahead of the game. The Columbia paper[1] and the symposium effort—both of which must be ready by the first—have got me very badly on the run. But there are a few manuscripts which I shall be sending to you in the next few days; one of them, a story by Peter Taylor,[2] seems to me awfully good. Albert likes it and my vote is for taking it as it is, or possibly with one or two excisions.

I suppose that all the symposium manuscript is going to come in to Kenyon and if you are there on the scene, you might well help John with the sorting and shifting of the material. Certainly you would be in the best position of all of us to help direct the allocation of manuscripts to the two magazines. At any rate, you go ahead with anything of the sort that comes up if the manuscripts begin to come in shortly.

I wish I could write you some news but at the moment there is nothing which I can tell you; that is, there is nothing which can well be written. There is, on the other hand, plenty of rumor and conjecture which I look forward to going over with you. I'll send the manuscripts and I'll try to write again in a few days.

Yours,
Cleanth

[Handwritten] Albert & Tinkum send regards to C. and to all the Ransoms.

[March 1941]

Dear Cleanth:

I did a little quicker job on this batch than on the previous one, but before I could take up the MSS item by item, I want to raise a little question which Francis Fergusson has put to me. He says that if the SR plans to notice Hallie Flannigan's book on the Federal Theatre he'd like to have a shot at it. My feeling is that if we do notice it, Fergusson is probably our man, but I haven't much opinion one way or the other on the basic question of whether or not we should review it. But will you please let me know, if the decision

---

1. See Brooks's essay "The Poem as Organism: Modern Critical Procedure," in *English Institute Annual, 1940* (New York: Columbia University Press, 1941), 20–41.

2. *Southern Review* published three stories by Taylor: "A Spinster's Tale," 6 (autumn 1940): 270–92; "Sky Line," 6 (winter 1941): 489–507; and "The Fancy Woman," 7 (summer 1941): 65–92.

is negative, so that I can write Fergusson, and if the decision is positive, can Mrs. Lowell send him the book. Also, I have just had a note from L. C. Knights, who is happy to do the Yeats piece.[1] I do not recall whether we considered Zabel for a contribution to the Yeats number, but I have recently learned, from James Laughlin, that Zabel is in the middle of a book on Yeats which will be published in Laughlin's "Makers" series. (By the way, he told me he was asking you to do a Hopkins. Are you going to do it?) In my last letter I think I asked you about the matter of Wellek's reviewing the new book on Dostoievsky which is in the office. How about it? I am not positive that we should review it at all, but if we should I imagine Wellek would do a good job.

Now for the MSS:

Eberhart: I like two pieces about well enough to publish, I guess, especially if we had some others to back them up; "I Walked Out to the Graveyard," and "A Man of the Forties." How do you feel about these?

Schumacker: Promising, but nothing we can use, I imagine. I have taken the liberty of attaching a note, which you can jerk off if you don't approve.

Simon: Better, by a lot, than the last Simon story, the prizefight one, but even this is rather thin. Probably publishable in a pinch.

Breuer: Very, very obvious irony, but it may be publishable in a very hard pinch.

Wight: Horrible.

Merton: It may be that we should hold "Dirge for Miami" and "Ariadne" for a group. How do you all feel[?]

Chamberlain: I have written a note to him, to be sent back with the MSS. The stuff is hopeless.

[Handwritten in left margin with x's by Schumacker's and Chamberlain's names] I've written back directly to the authors with letters.

Thielen: No opinion. But it leaves me colder than a dead herring. It's a damned phony piece of work. It seems that I do have an opinion after all.

Watts: It seems sensible as far as it goes, but on the positive side of the question it is awfully vague—or maybe I'm just not use[d] to criticism of painting. I'm opposed to publication, but feel that we might keep in touch with the author.

[p. 2] That winds up the MSS. You will notice, however, that you all included an envelope in this batch addressed to Marguerite Young,[2] but no poems by her. I am enclosing {[Handwritten at top of page] I've sent his book directly to him, too.} the Beaudoin pieces which, by mistake, were left out before. I

1. L. C. Knights, "W. B. Yeats: The Assertion of Values," *Southern Review* 7.3 (1941–1942): 426–41.
2. See Marguerite Young, "Six Poems," *Southern Review* 7.4 (1941–1942): 852–55.

am also enclosing a sheet of an old letter to you, one I wrote some ten days ago, I guess, which somehow wasn't put in its envelope with the rest of the letter. The second part must have been rather puzzling to you without the first page. Or maybe I sent you part of a letter intended for someone else. I'm marking it "cold letter."

The only great news here is that Shirley Forgotson[3] is getting married next week. His wife-to-be is a very nice, prettyish, and extremely intelligent girl from New York, who is a graduate student here. She was engaged to a prosperous doctor in New York, it seems, but found Shirley and went running back to New York to break her engagement. I never figured Shirley as exactly a Lochinvar, but he did the trick of stealing the girl right, as it were, out of the groom's arms.

Oh, yes, less exciting is the fact that Fred Brantley[4] has done what strikes me as a very fine story. It needs revision, and the revision may muff the thing, but as soon as it's ready I'll send it on to you all for an opinion. And Leonard Unger[5] is doing some mighty interesting poems. I took the liberty of suggesting that he hold them until he gets five or six more, so that we might have a chance at them as a group. I'm optimistic about them. It seems that the LSU boys here are setting the pace.

By the way, I just had a note from the Deming girl[6] saying that Kirby had written her that there will be no new appointments of fellows in the English Department next year—the same thing he wrote the Sweetser girl here. You'll let me know about that situation, won't you?

Well, so long and our best all around.

As ever,
Red

March 3, 1941

Dear Cleanth and John [Purser]:

I've spent a good bit of time reading Mr. Muller, who has taken an awful lot of space to say very little. I seem to recall that we gave him a space limit—I'm not sure—but if we did, he certainly didn't pay any attention to it. I hate to see us pay out so much dough for this stuff. It is certainly wrongheaded. The notes on it which you, Cleanth, attached seem to me to be to the point, as polemics and more, but I'd like to suggest another (page 16) on the business of simple eloquence. For example, he cites the line from Dante—"In sua voluntade e nostra pace"—which is indeed simple and eloquent—but not

3. Forgotson was a fellow graduate student at LSU with Alan Swallow.
4. Brantley, another LSU student, earned his master's degree at the State University of Iowa and then went on to edit *American Prefaces* and publish short stories.
5. Unger, also a graduate student at LSU, had been recommended by John Crowe Ransom; he entered the graduate English program in 1937 and wrote his thesis under Brooks.
6. Warren's reference to "the Deming girl" is explained more fully in his August 5, 1941, letter.

eloquent as a motto stuck up on a wall in isolation. Its effect grows out of a very complicated and ironical (in your sense) context. It might be said that the whole Comedy is filled with preparation for such a view, and the preparation frequently is accomplished by tensions—the giving of the full human value to a situation or person (Paolo and Francesca, Brunetto, Latino, Capaneo, Ulysses, etc.) in contrast to the divine judgment. And the other two examples of simple eloquence have very complicated contexts, too—dramatic context of Prospero, for example, which gives a very difficult job to Mr. Muller. He has completely misunderstood, or misrepresented, what you mean by ironic contemplation, it seems to me, and that is central. But off the point of Brooks, and on to other items in the piece—he has given Daiches a very superficial reading, sliding over the basi[c] self-contradiction in Daiches, and when he takes Mann as a stick to beat the bad poets with, he is doing a very dangerous thing, for Mann is full of the kind of irony which Muller disapproves of, and in method is very much like a symbolist poet sometimes. But enough of this, I guess.

I'm sorry, John, you had the tiff with Borth[1] over the check. The question with me was primarily one of knowing *when* or *if* so as to adjust my situation rather than of trying to get it immediately—but I'll be glad enough to see it when it comes. Why was Borth so touchy, anyway? I certainly think that you all took the right line in the statement to Hebert—about the principle that an editor can contribute. But I certainly don't want to do so any more.

I had a long talk last night with Stoddard,[2] Dean of the Graduate School, who was, you remember, one of the people mentioned for the LSU presidency. He's a very plausible guy. We had the subject of education up for a couple of hours, and he's sending me a lot of his speeches. It's barely possible that we might get some ammunition from them for liberalizing the departmental situation at LSU, because he takes crack at the institutions like Duke which, because unsure of themselves, try to lean over backward to be ultra-conservative in their interpretation of scholarship.

I'll sign off. Best all around. I hope that Jean [Lowell] is better.

As ever,
Red

[Handwritten in left margin] I'm anxious to see <Allisy['s]> piece, but don't bother to send it to me. But may I have a proof when it is ready?

[ca. 1941]

Dear Cleanth:

1. Daniel Borth resigned as editor of the *Louisiana Business Review* in 1938 due to political interference; he was the LSU comptroller who refused an early payment to Katherine Anne Porter for her story "The Leaning Tower," which appeared in *Southern Review* 7 (autumn 1941): 219–79.
2. George Dinsmore Stoddard was dean of the Graduate School at the University of Iowa from 1936 to 1942; his academic discipline was psychology.

Many, many thanks for your effort to relieve my mind about the appointment. I do feel a little better about it, but that isn't to say that I'm going the rounds of the local beer parlors and setting up drinks on the house to celebrate. Hodges[1] still has to prove himself. But if the Board tips him off as to his line, he may incline his ear in the right direction. I haven't yet given the SR stuff a thorough going-over, but I'll get off a report to you tomorrow on it. It isn't the most promising lay-out in the world, is it. While we are on the SR, yes, we did accept the piece on NeoPlatonism, according to my recollection. And I have just written to Bishop to say that we did want a crack at his paper on Painting and Poetry, which he read at Princeton, and that we did want him to do the fiction review. Baker[2] has written me that he is going to Mexico for a long stay to write—giving up Harvard, because he can't do two things at once. And he would like to do some more long fiction reviews for us. So that would seem to indicate him for the piece after Bishop's. I shall write him to that effect if you give me the word.

Your name is on every tongue here. Last night we had a radio round-table debate on "Ethical Considerations in Criticism"—Austin Warren, Norman Foerster, myself, and three other members of the Department—Warrens against Humanists. You received high compliments over the air from Foerster, who cited you as one of the four or five stars of the "new criticism"—with which, I must add, he feels ill at ease. Foerster is a genial and cunning Humanist, hard to pin. Baker, one of the other men, is a first-rate bigot with lots of learning. He even wants to deny that literature is an art at all—you can predict the rest. We had another session after the radio, and the hair-pulling reached an acute stage—with Baker referring to Ransom as "that charlatan" etc. Baker also said that any competent professor of English could read a poem—the sort of thing in *Understanding Poetry*—that that approach wasn't criticism, because it didn't give moral evaluation, etc. I finally asked him what he thought about a play like Antony and Cleopatra, in which there were no "good" people. He said he thought that the play was a study in illicit passion—yes, that that was the idea of the play, "guilty love." I said that I thought that Cleopatra was a "good" woman, and he almost went wild—she is good, it seems to me, in the sense that she is trying hard toward the end to establish [subsequent pages of this letter are missing].

[Red]

Iowa City
April 15, 1941

Dear Gents:

I'm going to mail in and set up a batch of questions (some of them not new), the answers to which would be gratefully received.

1. General Campbell Blankshear Hodges was the president of LSU in 1941 when the decision to suspend publication of the *Southern Review* was made.
2. Howard Baker was one of Warren's roommates at Berkeley; the other roommate was Lincoln Fitzell.

1. René Wellek wants to know if he may do a shortish review on the Dostoevski book which we have in the office? He also wants to know if we'd be interested in an article on American Scholarship as illustrated in a number of recent books, technical and nontechnical—sort of [a] study of literary method, not just a running review? He keeps asking me, and I'm hoping to be able to give him an answer. I've written before on the Dostoevski question, but not on the second.

2. Austin Warren is working on a piece of Henry James and Kafka, which, as I hear him talk it, sounds pretty hot to me. How about it?

3. A Henry James Centenary comes up in 1943 (I think that is the right date), and how about taking him for a special issue that year, and beginning to lay the ground for it now? This, incidentally, is a suggestion from Zabel. I certainly don't think that the *Hound and Horn*[1] wore the subject out, and besides, we have a lot of new critics about these days. If so, I suggest a signing up of Zabel who has been working on a book on James for many years. (I hasten to say that Zabel didn't put in this request, or hint at it; it is from me.)

4. But, speaking of Zabel, I do think that it would be a good idea to add him to the Yeats special issue, since he is doing a book on Yeats for Laughlin, and has a lot of stuff which ought to go pretty well. I did take the liberty of saying that he would hear from me on this point.

5. John Bishop writes that he cannot do the fiction review, because he is now busy as director of publications for the Bureau of Cultural Relations among the American Republics. But he wants to send the paper on *Poetry and Painting*. What shall I say to that? It strikes me as a pretty good idea, since Allen, I seem to remember, thought it was a good piece—I say *seem* to remember, since my mind is fuzzy on the point.

6. Baker, as you all may recall from a previous letter, is going to Mexico to write, leaving Harvard permanently, it seems, and wants to take up fiction reviewing again for us. How about switching the Bishop item to him? Let me know something to pass on to him.

7. Are the fellowships in English to remain unchanged for next year? No openings?

8. What was the upshot of the conference on SR policy—number of copies per editor and publication of work by editors, etc. and the matter of my little story? (I'm naturally not averse to having the money, and, I may add, I am decidedly not in a mood to accept the interpretation that I was trying to graft on the University—and that's what it amounts to if they don't cough up. This little blow-off of steam is just intended to relieve my feelings, not to communicate anything to you all.)

9. Muller's review has raised so many points that I am tempted to write a letter to the SR—for which I expect *no* payment—on the matter of "simple eloquence" in [p. 2] poetry—just pointing out that when he takes a "large

1. *Hound and Horn*, a journal considered to have high critical standards, ended publication in 1934; Allen Tate had served as its southern editor.

statement" from Dante or Shakespeare and calls it simple eloquence, he is neglecting the whole matter of the context of that statement—and that the statement only has validity in terms of the tension, ironical and otherwise, in the context, etc. I would use, for example, the quotations which he cites. Would there be a place for this, if I get around to it? I wouldn't take up the question of your book, Cleanth, specifically—just the general point. The question of his distortion of your meaning, though tied to the other question, might be embarrassing to you if I took it up.

I've just been looking over the current SR, and find it very good, by my lights. But we've got [to] hump to catch up on our fiction schedule, with only one story in this issue and a special issue Christmas. But it seems that we simply aren't getting much decent fiction in these days. I have hopes for a piece on which Brantley is now working. I'll get it off to you all soon.

Now for the batch of MS which I am sending herewith. The only sure-fire usable piece, to my mind, is Eudora's *Clytie*—and I wouldn't go to the stake for that if either of you happens to have an objection. {[Handwritten in left margin] I have also returned a story to Charles Smith in Denver, Col.} For other items, see below:

Mathews: Fiction and the Ransom Persona:—some good ideas (naturally I'm inclined to think some of them good since I put them into my piece on Ransom), but I don't know that his treatment of the "persona" would wash. It seems to me a cumbersome way of getting at something which could be handled in simpler and less mystical terms—just questions of rhythm, tone, etc.

Well: Walt Whitman:—on the whole superficial, I feel. We can get better criticism than this.

Johnson: stories:—no sale; I've attached a letter which can be sent on to the author with the rejected stuff if you all think it all right.

Shaw: story:—a full bust.

Mangan: I Want to Live:—I don't take to it.

Raiziss: poems:—Not worth nursing in my opinion.

Mizener: The Quarry:—I have given this very close readings, and don't like it as well as the earlier stuff of hers we had. I've done a note which I offer for your criticism.

Wight: The Cockerel:—very dull to me.

Kelm: Father's Day:—an almost for me; I've attached a note. But if you all happen to like this, I'll string along with pleasure.

Winter: Poor Yorick:—I've attached a note. Obvious, we can't use the thing.

{[Handwritten in left margin with Winter's and Johnson's names circled] I've sent it back [as] desired.}

McLuhan: Keats:—What do you all think of this? I'm inclined to think that there's some good stuff in it, but I think that the thing is unusable in its present form.

Linscott: The Picture:—pretty machine-made, I should say.

[p. 3] McGrath: Time to be Born:—definitely out, to my tastes.

Dreyer: The Hat:—No real point, it seems to me.

Watkins:—poems:—The Maze has a little something, but the other two are terrible. Probably not worth nursing.

Scope:—Episode:—I don't think that this is successful, but I do think that we ought to see what else he has in the locker. I've written a note.

Abbe:—poems:—I have written him a note and sent the things back from here.

Goodman:—Movie piece:—interesting, as you say, Cleanth, but I don't feel that we have room for it. And it may be a little too far off our beat—too technical, in a sense. But I'm open to conviction. If you all don't want it, I've attached a note.

I am also sticking in two new poems of my own for your remarks—not offered, I hasten to say, to the SR. I'd like to send you the new version of my play, but I know that you all are up to the neck in work, and shan't add to your troubles. Later, face to face, I'll worry you all for a reading. But I would like to hear what you think of the poems.

There's no great news with us. We went to Chicago for a day or two for the radio program, and had a pretty good time. We saw Zabel, twice for dinner, and for one evening, and saw the Morgan Blums for a bit. Morgan has been drafted for September but hopes to finish his examinations this summer. He is tinkering with Antony and Cleopatra for a dissertation—a "critical" study. He sends regards to you.

Cleanth, I am working with an analysis of Old Mortality for our text book, and am writing to Harcourt to see what the permission fee would be. I've done a little on the text book, but far less than I expected, and hoped. I've done some, for example, on Turgenieff's Reckless Character, some pretty full notes for an analysis.

I ache for LSU news, if there is any. And God knows, there must be, or times have changed.

Our best to our friends. Love to Tinkum.

As ever,
Red

P.S. You remember our talking last fall about a review of President Norlin's book, *Things in the Saddle,* along with another book, the title of which I forget, which we had there. How about Dixon Wecter for that—a short review?

Iowa City
April 25, 1941

Dear Cleanth and John:

Two more questions which I'd like to put to you all in addition to the gang in my last letter. (1) Is there a prayer of a chance of an opening for Leonard Unger there? He is finishing up now—has taken examinations, etc., and is on the last lap of the dissertation. His recommendations here are extremely high. But you know all this stuff. Still in connection with Leonard, you recall that I mentioned his desire to make a shortish sort of reply to the article on *East Coker*—he says that the author of the article hasn't really placed the piece in relation to Eliot's other work, etc., and has convinced me that he has a case. What about that? (2) Schramm wants to use our Hemingway piece in *American Prefaces*, and the Mizener piece. Did the *American Scholar* turn the pieces down? I imagine that they didn't appeal to the *AS*, since I haven't heard anything on the subject. As far as the *American Prefaces* is concerned, it suits me one way or the other. The only argument in favor of early publication is that Joseph Warren Beach, in his new book on the American novel,[1] has an analysis of Hemingway's style which approaches our own, and if we wait too long for publication, we'll be assumed to have filched from Beach. *But* I really don't have an opinion on the *Prefaces* thing, and certainly have made not the slightest commitment. Obviously, I'd prefer *American Scholar*. And obviously I can't undertake to speak for Mizener. But I did propose the Mizener business—if the thing worked out for the Hemingway piece.

I've done the manuscript which you sent me, with the following responses:

Parsons: 3 stories—very nice writing, taken page by page, but I don't get a real kick out of the pieces, and the first one, Cine Bleu, is really a stinker. I Was Glad When He Died is the best.

Olbrich: Rilke—I don't know enough—in fact, I know practically nothing—about Rilke to have a real opinion of this piece. It may be good as hell and again it may be a mere rehash of a lot of stuff already done on the subject. And again it may be wrong. I'm slightly inclined toward publishing this, but I'd like an OK, if possible, on it.

Lyons: poems—Nothing usable, but the boy seems to have a touch.

Sundgaard: —All Is Calm—really a rather feeble story I think. Out.

Kees: Henry James at Newport—I waver on this, but at the moment am against it; but it does have some good effects and I could be convinced if you all put up a fight. What I don't like about [it] is that the "line" of the poem is too simple, no real kink in it.

DeJong: Snow on the Mountain—Very well done, but essentially trivial, I think.

Noyes: This Matter of Debt—again a piece which requires a technical judgment. I don't know any of the economics people here, or I'd get a reading on it.

Schuman: Yankee Odyssey—this has something, even if it does come from the Coast Guard Academy. I wouldn't mind seeing it published, although I feel that it is rather lax in its construction, that there is a lot of wasted motion in it, etc. How do you all feel about it?

[p. 2] It has occurred to me that with only one story in the current issue, and with the Yeats issue to come up at Christmas, we have to publish a lot of

1. Beach was chairman of the department of English at the University of Minnesota in 1942 when Warren joined that faculty; he recruited several "young, hot" writers to promote the growth of that department. The book to which Warren refers is *American Fiction, 1920–1940*.

fiction in the next two issues, if we are to keep anything like our average. All I know that we have on hand is the Welty piece—and I don't know how you all liked that. I wouldn't mind, as I said, seeing the Schuman piece in. And Fred Brantley's new story, which he is still working on, promises to be fine. Have we anything else?

A letter yesterday from Jean Lowell brings the bad news that she is not well yet. That's tough on everyone concerned. I'm sorry as hell about her, and I'm sorry that it comes at a time when I am not there [to] help relieve the pressure. And I know that it makes it more difficult than ever for you all to indulge me with letters.

When do you go to Princeton, Cleanth? A good trip for you. I'd like mightily to see your paper. Will you send me a copy when you get back home?

No news here. Just more of the same. I'll write again soon.

As ever,
Red

[On April 30, 1941, Tinkum, following Cleanth's instructions as he "hopped on the train," wrote Warren that Brooks agreed "with him about the batch of MS" and that the Brantley story arrived in the morning mail.]

Hotel Nido
Chapala, Jalisco
Mexico
July 17, 1941

Dear Cleanth:

Well, we had a fine time in Austin, though I feel that we only scratched the conversational surface, and that it will have to be a fresh start in September. We greatly enjoyed the Blairs and Thomasons, to whom we hope you will give our warm regards. And will you also let the Blairs know where we are in case they wander this way when they come down. And tell them that we heartily recommend their wandering this way. It's a very nice spot.

We had a pretty dull trip down until we hit the mountains north of Mexico City. And we only spent one night in Mexico City. We shoved on here immediately, and don't regret it. It's a tiny town on a lake, surrounded by mountains, with a fine climate. We have rented a little house, new and verminless, for which we pay six dollars a month, though getting it screened raised the rent several dollars more. A cook is a dollar a week, and food is cheap. The place beautiful and smelly and picture-postcardy. There are some Americans about, including Witter Bynner—who, in fact, *was* about, very much about, with a palatial establishment, but he left yesterday, for Colorado. But we have led a pretty isolated life here. Cinina was pretty busy for a few days getting the domestic machinery into motion, and I've been working and studying Spanish and swimming and going to the can more often than usual. Not that I've got a bug in me yet, but the complaint seems to be usual here upon first arrival.

The war news, in so far as I can figure it out from the local papers, has kept me pretty excited, and I'm getting gloomier and gloomier about it. I wish we had some of the American commentaries—not that they tell you anything but you have the illusion that you are finding out something. We've seen one copy of Time, Latin America edition, but you can't buy it here at Chapala, and we don't go to Guadalajara, thirty miles away, but once a week. And we forgot to get the magazine when we last made the trip.

I'm sticking in the poem I quoted to you in Austin. Hope you like it. I haven't got a copy of the other one which I mentioned and which is coming out in the Va. Quarterly this fall.[1] I've got some ideas for new poems, but haven't done anything on them since arrival. The novel occupies most of my thoughts.

I suppose you are winding up the job in Austin about now. I imagine that things continued to be as pleasant as they obviously were when we were there. I wish we could combine the best features of Baton Rouge, Austin, Iowa City, and the New Jerusalem, and settle down quietly to pipes and beer.

I am anxious to see the paper you will read in New York. I'm sure the trip will be a good one. Best to Wellek when you see him, and to our friends, of older vintage, that is.

Meanwhile, I'd love to have any news from you all. Cinina joins me in this wish and in love to you both.

As ever,
Red

P.S. Did you ever hear from Mizener about the American Prefaces matter? If you do will you drop a card direct to Wilbur Schramm, at Iowa, giving the decision? Thanks.

Chapala
August 5, 1941

Dear Cleanth and John:

You can well imagine my shock this afternoon when I went to the hotel for my mail and found a telegram telling of Pipkin's death. It came from his secretary, and gave no information beyond the statement that he was to be cremated in Memphis this morning. I assume that he died there. The whole thing has been a sad, bitter, nasty business, and I suppose this is the predictable end—at least, it is the one which has been predicted for some time. Heart attack or stroke or suicide or the case of pneumonia. My one-time feelings for him have long since been converted into the feelings which we have shared; and now I only have the thought that he is probably a lot better off than he was.

I may add that the same mail brought the package from the office with the letterheads. But the whole business is too pat.

---

1. "Pursuit," *Virginia Quarterly Review* 18 (January 1942): 57–59.

As for SR business I shall get a batch of MSS off within a day or two with my reports. But several other items of a rather pressing nature have found their way to me. As they come to mind they are:

(1) Sam Monk[1] writes that he fears his piece wasn't satisfactory and was therefore excluded from the summer issue; and also mentions that he had hoped to have the money this summer. I imagine that the expenses occasioned by his wife's death, etc. have something to do with the situation. I can only write him that he ought to know that we are subject to delays and last-minute shifts of publication, and that if anything can be done about the check it will be done. Could you, John, drop him a note or a card, Southwestern College, Memphis? I am writing, but there ought to be a definite word from the office.

(2) Leonard Unger writes that he understands that a new poem by Eliot is to appear in the fall, and asks to do a piece on it {[inserted] & Dry Salvages} incorporating his other stuff on *Burnt Norton,* etc., along the line of his work on *Ash Wednesday* and *East Coker.* He has some corrections to make, you may recall, on the *East Coker* piece we published. {[Handwritten in left margin] Can you, John, let Leonard have a card at 60 University Street, Nashville, Tenn.?}

(3) Shirley Forgotson writes to ask if we can't let him have some reviewing for the fall issue. I had told him that I would take the matter up with you all for some reviewing in the winter (you all may have seen his reviews for *Poetry, American Prefaces,* and the *Nation,* and he is to do some for the *New Republic*), telling him that I was sure we could at least give him a trial piece. Can anything be thrown his way now, as trial anyway? I know he'll need the money badly. I am writing him that he will have a word from the office, that I have written in, etc.

I want to thank you all for the several letters and notes of recent date,[2] and Cinina wishes to thank you all and Tinkum and Jean. She is writing Tinkum and Jean right away, but she is still ailing a little with her shoulder—in bed again today. Tinkum's description, by the way, of the General's call was pretty damned funny.

It's a blow that Jean is leaving us—and a blow that Cal [Robert Lowell] and Peter [Taylor] won't be about. But the Jean business raises an immediate question. You ask for the Bennington girl's address. She is Barbara Deming, 2096 Abington Road, Cleveland, Ohio, but the envelope should be marked with a request for forwarding. I don't know that she types, but she does everything else—has been publisher's assistant, stage manager for Orson Welles, graduate assistant at Western Reserve, a novelist's secretary, and God knows what. And she has a fine record at Bennington. If she types and will take the job she sounds like our best bet. But it should be made clear to her that it will be something like a full-time job, and that she can take little or no graduate work. I say this, because she is applying for a [p. 2] SR scholarship,

---

1. Samuel Holt Monk published *The Sublime* in 1935. In 1930 Warren took a one-year appointment as his replacement at Southwestern College in Memphis (now Rhodes College) while Monk extended a fellowship in England (Blotner, *Robert Penn Warren,* 107).
2. These letters and notes have not been located.

and might get the things confused. If she doesn't take the job, or perhaps even as a first try, it might be worth getting into contact with Mary Jane Forgotson, who is smart as hell and is an expert at short-hand and typing and is very systematic. But she has a secretarial job in Alexandria and might not want to come back to LSU. I don't know. I am simply trying to think of possibilities, for if we don't get a good secretary we'll be in bad shape next year, with the student help lopped off. Another possibility occurs to me. At Iowa there was a very nice girl named Frances Stewart, daughter of a Methodist preacher in Missouri, very intelligent—A's in graduate work with Austin Warren and Wellek—and very, *very* quiet. I am pretty sure that she types, for I seem to remember that she was typing theses last spring. About the short-hand, I don't know, but that, of course, isn't of paramount importance. If she seems desirable, just address her in care of the English department at Iowa, with a request to forward. Sad to relate, the Deming and Forgotson girls probably have better jobs than the SR job. I wouldn't mind trying the Stewart girl at all, if the others—or some other you all have in mind—don't pan out. And it's possible—I really don't know how you all feel about it—that the Forgotson girl might annoy you. She doesn't annoy me, and I've definitely grown to like her and she's smart as hell. But no virtue amounts to a damn if the girl gets in the hair.

Well, that's about all that occurs to me now. Except thoughts about the future. I don't suppose there will be any movement to give us a new editor in Pipkin's place. Or will there be? Unless it's Frey.

Goodbye, and my best and most affectionate greetings to both you gents and all that.

As ever,
Red

P.S. The word sent to Shirley would reach him through the English Department of Iowa, I'm pretty sure. I can't lay hand to his New York address. I am writing him a note to say that he will get a card or a line from the office on the review situation. [Handwritten] Have found Shirley's address: [. . .].

Southern Review
Baton Rouge, Louisiana
[ca. August 1941]

Dear Cleanth

Your letter about the deanship of the Graduate School came today. I don't know anything about the appointee, and so grasp at the straw which you suggest may be there to grasp at.

I mailed the MSS, all of it, back a day or so ago. I was delayed a little after getting it all ready, for I had to send it from Guadalajara, and since I don't have a car, transportation is a problem. But it is off, registered, to the SR. I left the letter of report at home when I went to Guadalajara, and so had to scribble a note there, addressed to Jean, for I wasn't sure when you'd be leaving. I'm keen on the McCarthy, and think some of the other stuff usable—as indicated in the scribbling. Here I'm sticking a page of the report which I had left at home—I can't find the rest of it now. But it doesn't matter, I suppose.

The secretary business is getting grim, isn't it. All I know about Frances Stewart I think I told you before. Very intelligent, quiet, good personality, hard-working (made excellent grades with Austin Warren and Wellek), and, I think, types, and perhaps know shorthand. From Missouri, father a preacher. I like her quite well and we might do worse. The Forgotson girl would be extremely competent, and has had experience. I don't know about the Stewart girl on that score. But here is another possibility. There is a girl named Vivian Dyer, who was a major in Romance languages a year or two ago, who does, I believe, excellent typing and shorthand, is quite agreeable and quiet, and was, at the last report, anxious for a job. She is married to somebody around the campus, a graduate student, assistant, or perhaps instructor, and I don't know her husband's name. But it ought to be able to trace her through the University—Vivian Dyer. You or John or both could actually see her in the flesh and make up your minds more easily perhaps than you could about the Stewart girl. But it's too damned bad about Deming. She would have been perfect.

[p. 2] Well, I haven't got any news, except the predictable. We still like Chapala, but are getting awfully anxious for Baton Rouge. It seems that our car may be ready within a few days—though one can't be too sure. I saw the body work the other day in Guadalajara, and you couldn't even tell that the thing had taken a beating. But it has shore God played hell with what passes for the Warren budget.

The biggest local event for us has been the unexpected arrival of the Albrizios—very much themselves. We enjoyed seeing them a great deal. They didn't know we were here—Cinina just happened to see them on the street at Chapala.

We hope that the New York jaunt turns out beautifully. I know that it will in so far as the paper is concerned, but matters of weather, stubbing toes, catching colds, having hangovers, and such can, I suppose, always stand a few good wishes.

Cinina joins me in love to both Brookses.

As ever,
Red

[Handwritten] P.S. I find that Horrell's MS was left out of the package too. I'm not against using some of his stuff though I've never gotten very [warm] over it. As for the other MS enclosed herewith, no sale.

Monday [ca. 1942]
Dear Cleanth:

Your notes shame me. I haven't a line to show thus far on the text book. But I have read some five books on fiction, trying to warm myself up for the appendix. I hope to be at the actual writing this week, however. Ideally, we should have the body of the book done before I begin writing, but that, I fear, will be impossible. I was thinking of the value of references to examples in the text, and the value of writing in little bits into the analyses to tie them into the appendix. But I suppose that that can be done once the draft of the appendix is prepared and I have a copy of the analyses before me.

The table of contents, which came today, looks good. I don't see that we need the Pit and Pendulum at all. I am fearful, too, about writing a piece on Willie Proudfit[1]—on sober second thought. If, in the end, it seems that the piece will be useful in itself, I can try to do up some exercises, etc., but I'd prefer to see something in its place. As for Mr. Mitty, I believe that that would go best in the character section, probably somewhere toward the end, with special attention in the interpretation, or exercises, to the nature of humor involved. It would seem to call for a pretty extended note in the exercises, or for a short interpretation.

You say in your letter that we should explain the terms about "metaphor" fully or drop them. You are, I am sure, quite right. Can we let that matter stand until we have the other stuff in hand? I am a little afraid that if we start to develop those ideas we shall get into deeper water than our possible buyers will relish. If we use the section headings, etc. you have got a fine start. If we don't use them, we can face the problem after the other work is done. I'll try to push the appendix through soon, and when you have a chance to revise it we can know better what the final layout ought to be. Meanwhile, I'll hold these items of yours and study them a little more.

There's no news here. We've seen Austin W. and one or two other people, but the town is quiet and dull. War has hit this school pretty hard, it seems, except for the navy boys.

We were very happy to know that Tookie is doing nicely. That's the best news in some time.

Best to you all from us both.

As ever,
Red

(over)

P.S. After my departure something occurred to me that should have occurred to me earlier. You recall that the University did not pay Pasinetti[2] for his long story, and that Albert made some arrangement for the money to be held for him. Now that we are winding up the magazine, I suppose we ought to have some definite understanding, if it does not already exist, so that Pasinetti can get his money when the time comes. Can you get the straight of it from Marcus, with some statement that can be put in a safe place for Pasinetti? Or

1. "How Willie Proudfit Came Home," *Southern Review* 4 (autumn 1938): 299–321; it was not included in *Understanding Fiction* (1943).
2. Pier M. Pasinetti, "Family History," *Southern Review* 5 (summer 1939): 69–104.

do you want me to write directly to Marcus and ask for one? I'll be more than happy to do that if you think it the best arrangement.

Also, I've just had a note from Shirley Forgotson who asks that his check be sent to the following address: [. . .].

Also, Prefaces is interested in publishing our Anderson analysis, as in Rocky Mountain Review. What do you think? I don't suppose it could do any harm. Prefaces has first claim, since it spoke first. If you happen to have a copy handy and sent it to me, I'll handle the rest—provided you think the idea a good one. Or did it get off to Hatfield?

821 North Gilbert Street
Iowa City
July 13, 1942

Dear Cleanth:

Don't faint. The little appendix which was to run five thousand words runs, as you see, over fifteen thousand words. I simply couldn't do the trick in less. Of course, if a lot of the illustrations were dropped, it could be reduced, but I kept feeling that everything had to be document[ed] if it was to have any meaning at all. Now please get out your pencil and give this a thorough overhauling. I know that it isn't well written, and there are some points that need clarification. I'm not sure that the business about straight and reversed plots is worth keeping, and I'm not sure that my business about focus of interest, focus of characters, and focus of narration can stand. But I was trying to avoid the ambiguities in the phrase "point of view" and was trying to indicate by making a consistent terminology the relationship among those problems. Perhaps some justification for the length may be found in the fact that much of the Glossary material may be taken care of in this appendix. If this is true, then the Glossary can be on many points simply a kind of index. I am anxious to have your word on this piece.

I am now working on the Hemingway and Porter pieces, and hope to have them to you with[in] five days. But things have been more confused than I had anticipated, and the bad wrist held me up to some extent. I have found myself on six examination committees, and I have had to work over four Ph.D. dissertations, and several theses. But I have these things pretty well behind me.

I got the last SR, and find that on the whole it is a pretty good number, better than a lot of them. I feel that there is quite a bit of excellent poetry in the batch, and the goatherd story stands up for me. Have you had any reactions to our new editorial note? And what is the final set-up with the Kenyon? Did LSU make any concession about your time?

Austin has recently been classified as 1A for the army, and is not very happy about it. He has two dependents, and I don't suppose the buck private's pay will go very far in such a case. He has been trying for some time to get a naval commission, but that is still hanging fire. John McGalliard is also trying for the navy, with no luck as yet. The war news for the past several days has me way down in the ditches with the pismires. God, if the Russians don't hold out this war is going to run on ten years, and maybe more. I've fallen into such a state of the fidgets that everything I do seems perfect[ly] trivial and dull.

Write me how things are going at Michigan. I'm anxious to know.

Our best to you and to Tinkum, and all wishes for a pleasant summer.

As ever,
Red

[Typed at top of page] P.S. Please let me know what French stories I am to translate. I lost my list.

July 19, 1942

Dear Cleanth:

I am enclosing a completely rewritten version of the Porter and of the Hemingway. The Porter especially needed rehandling. I hope that you will find these fairly decent—or at least far enough along so that you can revise them into shape. I shall get at the Kafka tomorrow and shall mail it to you within a day or so. Please let me know immediately what you want me to get at next. I asked you in my last letter to let me know about the translations I'm to do. I'm sorry I lost my list on that point. I wrote some time back to the people who hold the Flaubert copyrights—or rather to two firms, for there are two versions of "A Simple Heart"—but I haven't yet had an answer. You will observe that I have, in the appendix, made some reference to that story, but, of course, they can be deleted if we find at the last minute that we can't use it. Also, how long do you think the appendix on the history of the short story ought to be? Or do you still think that we ought to have it? I've dropped Crofts a note on the point, but as yet no reply. I'm happy to do it, but the library here is not much good for the subject, as I've found out already.

I wish that we could be together for a few days for the mopping-up process—as well as for more enjoyable activities. It sure ain't much fun doing this kind of work by one's self.

There's no news with us. A frightful heat wave almost laid us, and everybody else, low last week, but things have moderated a little in the last twenty-four hours.

I'll close this note. I trust that things are going well with you all—for Tinkum must be with you now. And I've been envying you the cool breezes of Ann Arbor.

Our best to both,
Red

P.S. This is the only copy of this stuff, because of my laziness.

821 North Gilbert Street
Iowa City, Iowa
July 27, 1942

Dear Cleanth:

I am enclosing several items: 1. a copy of the Partisan with the text of "In the Penal Colony," 2. analysis of that story, 3. a translation of "Two Little Soldiers," by de Maupassant, 4. a revision of the exercise on "The Necklace," 5. a revision on the exercise on "Old Mr. Marblehall," 6. a cleaner copy (bound) of the appendix on mechanics of fiction. (I may be able to enclose also a text of Flaubert's "A Simple Heart," and the exercises for it. And I can announce the good news now that we get it from Dutton for nothing except a credit line.)

Please feel absolutely free to work over this stuff according to your best judgment. Particularly, I am worried about the Kafka analysis (my part, not Austin's) and the long appendix. In regard to the appendix, please revise for style (it looks bad to me, but I'm damned fed up with it) and insert at the point which seems most appropriate the excellent little chart which you sent me. I think that the chart, perhaps in an elaborate note with full explanation, would be a great help. You will see that I have cut out the part about straight and reversed plots. Upon second thought, I don't believe that this would do more than confuse the student. It would require a lot more talk to mean anything—if it would mean anything then.

As for the translation, Cinina did it. It occurs to me that it might be a good idea, simply to preclude any question about copyright with publishers who hold translations of the stories we use, to put a footnote telling who translated the story in question, when the translation was made by you or by Cinina. This may be leaning over backward—so use your own judgment. Which stories did you have to do? I have forgotten.

What is the last word about the Thurber and the Saki? I think that it is a good idea to use both if we can afford them and have space. I'm even in favor of squeezing space a little.

I have just received a letter from Florence Gerald of F. S. Crofts and Co. I am also enclosing a carbon [of] my letter to her. All of the permission blanks and letters were left in the file at Baton Rouge, and so I do not have 1. Hemingway, 2. Welty, or 3. Joyce (duplicate blank). I wrote to Frances ten days back on some other matters, but she apparently is not there; anyway, no answer. As for the Thurber and Saki to be used (?), please pick out the ones which strike your fancy. I am writing to Caroline Gordon, Edward Donahoe, and Thomas Thompson, asking them to drop notes to Florence Gerald and release their stories. Caroline will, of course, get a fee—whatever I get from the story Allen is using if it amounts to as much as $25. If my fee doesn't come to that, we can make it up with the $15 we had reserved for that purpose. The Faulkner blank must be in the file at Baton Rouge, too. Do you recall? I am writing to MacDonald at the Partisan and asking him if he can reduce his fee to, say, $30.

[p. 2] This is a scatter-brained letter, but things have grown quite murky around here, with the business of packing, and the last-minute rush of papers.

We leave toward the end of this week, and so you can write me in care of the English Department at Minnesota. We shall be there for two or three days. I haven't yet been able to do the appendix on the history of the short story, but I'll undertake to do it at Minneapolis while Cinina is househunting.

I feel bad about the share of work I've done this summer, but I hope it hasn't left too big a part to you. All I can say by way of apology is that I haven't done a stroke on my novel for more than a month. What time I've had has gone on the text book.

I hope that things go pleasantly for you all. Our best to both.

As ever,
Red

P.S. I've read with admiration the list of questions on stories outside our book. I'm strongly in favor of providing such exercises if Crofts will let us. I know that you must have put in a pile of work on these.

U of M
Minneapolis, Minn
August 5, 1942

Dear Cleanth:

I am wondering if you have received the last batch of stuff I sent you—analysis of Kafka, text of Two Little Soldiers, etc., and if you have yet received a copy of the translation of A Simple Heart, which was to be mailed to you by the typist last Monday from Iowa City? I also sent you a copy of a letter of mine to Florence Gerald of Crofts and her letter to me concerning permissions. I shall say now, while I think of it, that I wrote to Scribners for the blanks on the Hemingway, and to the other firms involved—and to Caroline G. to ask her to drop a line to Florence Gerald releasing Old Red for $25.00. We have fifteen allowed for that story plus what I get from Allen's anthology to make up at least twenty-five. But I am paying the difference, to Crofts I presume. I wrote to Crofts some time back, when we were debating about the length of the appendix, and asked him his view. He wrote back that he was rather against including the appendix on the story. I'll quote: "Being primarily concerned with the growing length of the book, I favor throwing overboard anything that is not absolutely essential. For that reason I should favor an omission of the history of the short story." I don't mind in the least doing the thing along the lines you suggest in your letter on the subject, but I wanted to be sure before embarking on the thing. I would have done it before leaving Iowa City if there had been a moment for it, but I had to get a typist to copy the Flaubert piece as it was. (By the way, I think I wrote you that we get that for nothing, from Dutton.) I have been tinkering lately with the section headings which you sent me earlier, and I think that they are excellent, but that a little expansion might be in order. Also, I'm reporting a conversation which I had with A. Warren. He said that he had been a little worried in *Und.P.* by the use of the term *irony* without adequate explanation of the full structural meaning which we attach to it. He says that in this book he hoped we'll discuss, somewhere, our use of the term in that sense and will be a little more explicit about our basis of evaluation of exhibits—he doesn't mean for us to grade the stories but to indicate that literary judgment isn't to be based merely on a narrow and mechanical notion of structure. He understands us, I think, but he is raising objections which have been raised to him as a defender of the book at the U of I. I feel that, if you think we ought to try to answer these objections, we might do a letter to the teacher, including the following subjects: (1) general intention (2) basis of selection (3) fallacies—as in Letter to *Und.P.* (4) irony, resistance, and structure, as related to form and judgment. If you think this a good idea, I'll undertake to do a preliminary draft of the Letter for your additions and revisions. But what do you think? In any case, the letter could be done after the rest of the book was in the hands of Crofts. Meanwhile, I suppose that next step is for me to send you the section headings with my notes and suggestions. I'll get those to you in a few days.

[p. 2] I've lost the last several days, for we had to hunt an apartment here and do a few chores out at the University. But now I'm free again, and we are leaving in the morning for the country. The first thing I do will be to go over the section heads and get them back to you. Meanwhile, let me hear from you. Just write me in care of the English Department here, for I don't know my exact address in the country.

Just before we left Iowa City, Austin got his orders to go to the Army. He had been trying to get into the Navy, but just discovered that his papers had been lost by the Navy office in Des Moines or in Chicago—a damned nice kettle of fish. The Navy had given him a good deal of encouragement, too, for the Deck Volunteer Specialists. Unless something has turned up in the last few days, this means that he goes in as a private, with two dependents.

Well, I can't think of any more news at the moment. Certainly, I can't think of any very good news. But I would like to have some word about how things are going with you all. Meanwhile our best to both.

As ever,
[Red]

In care of A. A. Secord
Brown's Point
Alexandria, Minnesota
[ca. 1942]

Dear Cleanth:

I am tinkering along with the sections to be put at the head of our divisions, and shall send them to you in a day or two. I really haven't done much but tinker—and scarcely that, for after adding a lot of stuff in a couple of the things you'd prepared, I decided that the points I was making were, after all, pretty well covered in the Introduction and in the first Appendix. I'm hoping to hear from you about the Letter to the Teacher. Shall I push on with a draft of that? If you think so, please indicate any points which you think should be covered.

By the way, a letter from Swearingen called to my attention the fact that his piece, which we had, for all practical purposes, accepted, did not get in our last issue. Actually what happened seems to be that we didn't get together with John for a careful enough check on the contents in those last hectic days in May. We've got to write Swearingen, but I'd like to hear from you before I write the letter to him. Will you speak on this point when you write me? Then I'll send you a copy of my letter to him.

Did you receive the copy of Flaubert's "A Simple Heart"? And did you get the last batch of stuff I sent from Iowa City just at the end of July? And did you get my letter quoting from Croft's letter to me about the second appendix? What do you think of that matter?

It seems that my note is all questions. But there isn't much to say. We've rather pleasantly settled for the next two or three weeks. Use the above address until September 1, in any case. We are not sure that we shall be here much beyond that date for we have a lease coming up in Minneapolis.

I hope that everything has been going well. Cinina joins me in best to you both.

As ever,
Red

Care of A. A. Secord
Alexandria, Minnesota
August 21, 1942

Dear Cleanth:

Thank you for your letter from Michigan. I am sending this to Louisiana, for I imagine, from your letter, that you are bout ready to go home. And if you are not ready to go you are certainly in the last-minute throes of Michigan and would have no time to devote to the enclosed material.

Here is the draft of the letter to the Teacher. I am keenly aware of its shortcomings, and am depending on you to remedy them. Please devote particular attention to the questions of evaluation and irony. And if I have misrepresented your views, please don't hesitate to correct me. Certainly the thing will need some work from you, and I am sure you can clarify my own rather fumbling attempt to lay down in a few well chosen words a whole theory of irony. Or rather to suggest a whole theory, for it certainly could not be developed in the scope permitted here.

You ask me again about the exercises on stories not included in our book. I am strongly for such exercises and feel that we should make a strong appeal to Crofts to include them if he does offer objections on the grounds of size. You see, I have referred to them in the letter. And by the way, I think that the ones you have prepared are excellent. I am sure it took a hell of a lot of time.

No news. Just a moderately pleasant day-to-day existence. But God knows, one can't quarrel with that situation in the midst of the world.

We'll be here until September 1. After that my address will be the Department at Minneapolis. I go there with great perturbation and confusion of spirit; or rather, I should say that I leave LSU with those feelings. My doubts as to my wisdom have grown lately. I hope Frey broils and simmers in the depths for forcing the issue.

Well, goodbye and best to you all. I hope to hear from you soon. Please give my warmest regards to Bob [Heilman] when you see him.

As ever,
Red

3124 West Calhoun Boulevard
Apartment 405
Minneapolis
[early September 1942]

Dear Cleanth:

A cold, which meant a couple of days in bed and a thick head for several days more, and the distress of getting settled in the apartment have delayed my work on the text book. But I am now enclosing the work on the Glossary. I have made, as you see, two copies of the Glossary, one for the printer and one to serve as a key for us when the time comes to put in page references. You will see that I have elaborated several of the items in the glossary, for example POINT OF VIEW (On POINT OF VIEW a query: If we use my Appendix I as it stands, we have there the term focus of narration set up for the mind of the narrator through which the story is given. You see that I have brought the Glossary into line with that usage. But if this stands we should revise the texts of the analyses to be consistent. What about it?) But there are several questions which should be settled on the Glossary sheet before it goes to the printer.

I. As it now stands, when a reference is given to [the] Introduction or to the Letter, we give the full reference—"Letter to the Teacher, p xxi" for example. Wouldn't it be better simply to give the page reference without the title of the section? Then we would be consistent throughout, for we do not give the titles when the reference is to an analysis.

II. As it now stands, when a term in the Glossary is referred to in the Glossary, in the discussion of another term, for example, as we refer to TONE under ATMOSPHERE or as under SIMILE we simply give the reference "See Imagery, p. . . . ." we give the page reference. But wouldn't it be simpler in such cases to drop the page reference because the fact that the item is given in upper case indicates that it appears in the Glossary?

If you think that such a change should be made, a few strokes of the pen would put it right. And, in the same connection, what about the phrases like "for fuller discussion see, etc." Couldn't we simply give the page references?

I hope that the key will be of some use when the time comes to fill in the page numbers. I have indicated in pencil the references which came to mind, but I am sure that you will think of others, and when we get the proofs we shall undoubtedly find additional items to refer to.

I think that Appendix II should be included, and I shudder to think what a lot of work you must have spent on those two pages. I'll do what I can here to fill in the gaps. But I'm pessimistic about getting the date on the Pirandello story. As for Caroline's birth date, I can't help any. By the way, your last letter, which came yesterday, has been mislaid, but I'm sure it'll turn up soon.— I stopped here to hunt, and found the letter with the additional dates. I'm happy to see them, and I'll try to get the others, and soon.

I'll dash off to mail this.

As ever,
Red

[Typed at top of page] P.S. I'm sending the stuff in two envelopes for safety's sake.

3124 West Calhoun Boulevard
Apartment 405
Minneapolis
September 21, 1942

Dear Cleanth:

I've done all I can do here on the dates for the appendix. I found the volume date for "The Kiss" (1888), but couldn't find the date for "The Lament." However, the man who teaches Russian here has kindly agreed to hunt the thing up for me; he thinks that he can find it in the Russian Encyclopedia or in one of his Russian bibliographies. "Filboid Studge," by Saki, appeared in *Chronicles of Clovis* in 1911; so we have only the volume date for that. The *New Yorker* files here in the Library are broken, and despite two afternoons of thumbing through them, I couldn't find "Mr. Mitty." But I did get the date of the volume of *New Yorker* stories in which it was reprinted, 1940. So that will probably have to do. For "The Penal Colony" I have written to Philip Rahv, who is a Kafka specialist. I got the death date of Pirandello without any trouble, 1936, but I can't find the publication date of "War." I don't know what the hell to do about that. I shan't give up right away. Perhaps we might write to the Library of Congress for information. As soon as I can, I'll send Appendix II on to Crofts. Or perhaps I should send it on now, and fill in gaps in the proof?

As for the texts of the stories: The version of "Christ in Flanders" was taken from the old Modern Library edition of Balzac's stories. "A Simple Heart" was taken from the translation by Frederick Whyte, published by Duttons, about 1910.

As for the Faculty Club business, my bill was paid in full a day or two before I left, and I hold a canceled check. So the thing is, on that count, a plain lie. I didn't owe them a penny when I left. Thank you very much for mentioning the matter to me. I suppose the best thing for me to do is to do nothing. The only possible wisp of flame behind all the smoke is the fact that I didn't pay the March and April bill till May, but I imagine that if they started firing members who did that they would have to give the sumptuous halls over to the bats and owls and thereby deprive the jackals and the wild asses of their favorite haunts.

[Red]

3124 West Calhoun Boulevard
Apartment 405
Minneapolis
September 28, 1942

Dear Cleanth:

I received both your letters concerning Bradford, and am heartily in agreement with you. When I saw the article in the Saturday Review I was more disgusted than angry, I guess. It was such a low, snivelling, snotty job—no attempt to meet any issue but just to smear. I'll be more than happy to sign with you. And I think your letter is a clean job. I have made a typed copy so that the thing can go right on in when you get it. You may observe that I have made one small suggestion and am taking the liberty of inserting it. If it seems out of tone, just strike it out.

By the way, I'll take this opportunity of raising another question: Fred Brantley, who is now fall editor of the *American Prefaces,* wants to know if it would be possible to get a list from the SR files which they could circularize? And if it would be possible to get a list of the book stores which handled the magazine? The *Prefaces* would, of course, pay all costs of hunting the stuff up and copying it. I told him I would write to you and get your view, and then he could write direct to the Press. I told him that the permission would have to come formally from Wilkerson, I imagined, but that Wilkerson would probably want your view. I don't think that the *Prefaces* would cut in on the *Kenyon.* By the way, Fred writes me that our Hemingway article caused a considerable flurry of sales, and some letters of congratulations. But to return to the subject, if it strikes you as all right for Fred to have the lists, drop him a card so that he can write Wilkerson.

I have not got the Flaubert (Frederick Whyte translation, Duttons, 1910?). I own the Balzac translation, but most of my books are in crates in a storage basement. —At this point I took time out to hunt, and Praise God! found the book. Pure luck. I am sending it under separate cover.

Goodbye, and best to you all.

Red

. . . .

November 11, 1942

Dear Cleanth:

I have finished the proofs of Understanding Fiction, and am sending them under separate cover. Here, in addition to the things I have marked on the proof itself, are several items of greater importance than punctuation and spelling:

1. Should not the Glossary follow, rather than precede, the Appendixes? Especially since it serves as a sort of index for the book?

2. Should not the Appendixes have titles of some sort? How about this for Appendix I: "Some Technical Problems and Principles in the Composition of Fiction"? It is a little cumbersome, but it is, I guess, fairly accurate. And for Appendix II: "Chronology of Stories in this Volume." You will probably be able to better this attempt, if you accept the idea of the titles.

3. Exercise on "A Simple Heart." I have made out one and have attached it to the proof. Will you revise it, amplify it, or rewrite it according to your views.

4. In the Glossary the word *convention* is not treated, although in our text we give one or two references to the Glossary for this word. Furthermore, although we have the word *conventional* in the Glossary, we simply refer to the head FORM. But under FORM we make not the slightest reference to the idea, much less the word itself. This is a very bad lag, and we ought to do something about it. I propose that we cut out the reference to FORM, and treat the two words *convention* and *conventional* under a separate head from FORM.

5. On galley 107 I have changed "point of view" to "focus of narration" to make the interpretation consistent with the principle laid down in Appendix I. Will you give this a careful look and see what you think?

6. On galley 121 I have questioned a point of style.

7. On galley 178 there may be a piece of bad paragraphing. It should be checked with the original of "Old Mortality." I haven't got a copy (my books are not unpacked yet).

That is about the works as far as I can judge.

By the way, Crofts was just here. He doesn't seem too optimistic about the immediate prospects of the books—the war, etc. But he is talking about revising the Approach before too long. I told him that you and I had signed up with Harcourt for the freshman text. He said that he wished that he had it, but he didn't give the impression that he thought we had betrayed him.

General news with us is thin. We had to stand in a line for three hours at the President's reception for new faculty members and take the beating of our lives. We are filling out gas ration blanks. We are hanging on the radio, as you no doubt are, for news of North Africa and the French fleet. I have just done the last work on my novel [*At Heaven's Gate*], and tried to follow the suggestions you and Bob [Heilman] gave me—changing the lynching scene, for example. Harcourt now has the MS. I've recently done a couple of pieces for the Chicago Tribune's new literary supplement[1]—one short and one long

---

1. "Logic of War Era Leaves Its Mark on Novel," review of *The Valley of Decision* by Marcia Davenport, *Chicago Sunday Tribune of Books*, November 15, 1942, p. 23; and "John Kieran Lives among His Souvenirs," review of *Poems I Remember*, by John Kieran, *Chicago Sunday Tribune of Books*, December 27, 1942, p. 20. Editor's note: Warren told me that he reviewed books for the *Tribune* while he was in Minnesota for "whiskey money"; he was paid five dollars a review.

thing. The long one is on *The Valley of Decision* which affords a perfect example of corrupt patriotism, the debasing effect of war on literature. I got pretty rough (especially for the Chicago Tribune) and rather expect they'll refuse to use the piece. If they do that [p. 2] I'm going to try to have some fun with them. So you see what I said is true—our news is thin. But I have heard from Morton Zabel that he is definitely out of the war. He tried to get into the Navy and was turned down; and now the Army has turned him down, too, for good and all. The last I heard from Austin, he was ready to report to the Army, but was hoping for his Naval commission to come through in time to save him. My status is still unchanged, but I expect a reclassification, as you know.

But what about news with the Brookses? I learned from the Rhodes Scholar magazine that you had been promoted to a professorship. I suppose I should write Hodges and congratulate him on a gleam of intelligence in the administration. And I know, from a letter from Allen, that you were expected in Sewanee on Sewanee Review business. I'd like to know what happened. And I'd like to know the rest about things and your activities.

Speaking of activities, I am inclined to think that we might do well to begin work on two of our projects. First, we've got to give Harcourt some sort of idea about that damned freshman book before too long. They want some statement of plan in December. Second, isn't it possible for us to divide up the reading in terms of periods, and begin to put together an anthology of criticisms of Shakespeare as poet? I think that we could get the stuff together pretty fast, and would have no difficulty in getting a publisher for it. Then, we could do a long introduction, an essay outlining our findings about (1) the state of criticism on the subject, (2) the problems that need investigation, and (3) our views on certain of those problems. I am fearful that if we don't stake out our line by some such preliminary thing we shall wake up and find we have been beaten to the draw. For instance, here is an aspect of the project which might be pretty interesting to you: the critical assumptions underlying eighteenth-century textual emendations. It strikes me that there is a lot of concealed criticism in that field. What do you think? If you are inclined to get on with this, I'll start reading right away and making copies of the excerpts which I think we would use in the book. It won't be much fun doing this in isolation, but I hate to see the thing evaporate. And if we don't get started, it will evaporate.

Well, so long, and all best to you both. Cinina joins me.

As ever,
Red

3124 West Calhoun Blvd.
Minneapolis
[December 1942]

Dear Cleanth:

Crofts's proofs for the first part of the book came yesterday, and I have given them what I hope is a fairly thorough going-over. The man at Crofts pointed out that the letter contains some references to "The Introduction" which has now been merged into Section I. I have rewritten the Letter to cover the present situation, and have picked up one or two other references later to the "The Introduction." You will also observe that I have written in a few lines before the first story, the Kipling, to provide a bridge from the part which was the old Introduction. As far as the page references go, I think that I have located all which are to be found in the copy thus far sent me. But because of the problem of page references, it seems best for me to hold the proof here until I have it all and can check back on the page references. Then I shall send it to you to check by your own proofs. But if you wish me to do the checking this time and to transfer the stuff from one set of proofs to the other, I'll be delighted to do it. I probably ought to, anyway, since you did that rather grim job on the galleys. So send your batch on to me as soon as it is ready.

What did you make of the question about price and number of copies to be printed? In one sense, I don't feel entitled to an opinion, for I don't really know the state of the trade. But in general I would favor the lower price and the gamble for larger sales. I feel that we should stand to gain by that. For instance, I am inclined to believe that I could get the book in here (one of five books to be bought in one term) in my Modern Literature, if the price were low. And that class usually has over a hundred students. Even now it has nearly sixty. But you see that, if the book were expensive, the students could not be asked to add its cost to the cost of the other four books bought in one term. And such a situation probably exists elsewhere. As it is, I shall use it next term in my writing course, which may be pretty fair-sized. But I'll let you take the leap on the question. You let Crofts know how you feel, and incorporate whatever of my opinion seems pertinent.

I was glad to have your last letter, and look forward to another when you get some time. Needless to say, we are anxious to have Baton Rouge news. And I'd like to have your views on our Harcourt text and on the Shakespeare project. I've already put a few things together for the Shakespeare—am starting a folder of copy—from my fall reading. As far as the Harcourt matter is concerned, my mind is damned near a blank. I don't seem to be able to think about the thing—and yet I know that if we were together I could talk my head off. But I've recently got hold of a couple of new books, semantic-y books and such, to inspect. I just haven't had the heart to inspect them though. Instead of inspecting them, I turned in and did a couple of poems, which you can expect in a few days.

The big news with yours truly is that he looks like the boy the Army has been yearning for. The Navy turned me down cold, because of eyes, but it seems that I can pass the Army exam. I know that I can pass it on the eye [p. 2] business, and last spring when I had a very elaborate physical examination the doctor told me that I ought to get by the Army examination without any trouble. I'm not thirty-eight, and so, strictly speaking, the new ruling won't knock me out since my number is up. I've already had my preliminary physical, and expect to be called soon for the induction examination. The thing I chiefly object to is the possibility of getting some nasty like pine desk in Arizona or Omaha with a lot of figures to add and subtract. If I could get into something moderately interesting I wouldn't mind. Except, of course, the private's income makes it a little rough on the lady in the case when there are certain fixed expenses to roll around every month. The University here has asked for my deferment, but they don't sound very optimistic about it. But I ought to know more before long. Meanwhile, this is rather unsettling—after I've just taken one drastic move.

So long, and our best, to both.

As ever,
Red

University of Minnesota
[ca. 1942]

Dear Cleanth:

Thanks for the letter. I'll take up your questions as you number them.

1. I did not doctor the Donahoe story in proof. As I read it, I was under the impression—because of the mildness of the passage—that it must have been doctored in manuscript. But I can't remember actually doing it. Anyway, it didn't seem any stronger than a section of "Old Mortality." But if you still have the proof there, please use your judgment.

2. Hastings: It's a damned good thing that you checked up on the old lad's dates. We would certainly have had a kick-back on that from somebody.

3. I have sent the exercises on "A Simple Heart" to Birch at Crofts. I hope that they are satisfactory, for to save time I didn't pass them on to you.

4. I have not yet been able to get the dates on "A Lament" or "War." The bibliographer here who has promised to help me hasn't been able to find out anything, and I think I've exhausted the resources of the library here in English and Italian. He is a Russian, and hopes to get the Chekhov date from some Russian source. I've written to the Library of Congress about "War" but have had no reply. It begins to look as though we shall have those blanks on the chart.

5. As for the titles for the Appendix, I gave some suggestions in my last letter to you. But the ones you now give in your letter are perfectly satisfactory.

6. I think that Crofts himself is the man to decide on the use of extra exercises—those referring to stories not in the book. I'm personally in favor of the idea.

Crofts was here recently. He was talking up a revision of the Approach, to be launched as soon as the War ends. I told him I'd mention the matter to you, but that I could see no objection to giving the thing an overhauling. He wants to change format, too—but you know this.

MacMurphy of Holts was here last week. He wants to consider doing a version of Understanding Poetry directed to courses in modern poetry. That is, including all our stuff on modern poets, with additions of a good deal more material. Off hand, I didn't know what to think. What is your view?

And what is your view about getting on pretty fast with the book on the Criticism of Shakespeare's poetry—the preliminary one, anthology and introduction? I have begun putting some stuff down and making copies of passages, in the hope that you can see your way to beginning the project. I talked with MacMurphy when he was here, and he seemed to think that Holts would be interested in it as a joint trade and text project.

No, the box of stuff which Frances Stewart was supposed to send never came. I don't know what her address is. Before she left Baton Rouge I wrote to her on several little matters, and reaffirmed my willingness to give her a letter of recommendation if she wanted it. But I had no reply. Also, she apparently did not call up the freight office to pick up the big wooden crates of books of mine which were in the SR [p. 2] office. God knows where they are now.

I've been pretty busy on the James issue of the Kenyon,[1] and have it about lined up. Have you any interest in doing a piece for the thing. I'd love to see you do so, and I know that John and Rice[2] would agree with me. Let me know on this point, for I am holding a space or two open.

There's no news. Except that the radio is claiming a great part of my time now. The Solomons and North Africa haunt my dreams. I can't help but feel that the time has come for Adolf to begin to do his share of the worrying. But my fingers are crossed. Local things are moving pleasantly enough. The fall has been perfect—and unusual, I'm told. The weather is still almost balmy, and we are nearing December.

Goodbye, and our best to you both. Please give my regards to Bob, for whom I keep plotting a long letter. But it looks like I don't get to letters except when I have a practical reason, such as a text book or a James issue.

As ever,
Red

3124 West Calhoun Blvd.
Apt. 405
Minneapolis, Minnesota
January 28, 1943

Dear Cleanth:

I've been trying for days to get at a letter, but this is the first time I could snatch. Things have been pretty busy this month.

Well, my copies of Understanding Fiction have just come. I feel that they did a nice job of book-making on the thing. Don't you? And I was pleased to

1. "The Henry James Number," *Kenyon Review* 5 (autumn 1943): 481–617.
2. Philip Blair Rice was managing editor of the *Kenyon Review* and helped establish the prominence of that newly founded journal. By 1943, John Crowe Ransom considered Rice more of a joint editor than a managing editor (Marian Janssen, *"The Kenyon Review," 1939–1970: A Critical History* [Baton Rouge: Louisiana State University Press, 1990], 91–93).

know that Texas had adopted sight-unseen. You must have hypnotized the boys there or something. But I suppose that in these times such a book will move very slowly. I fear that the new war programs at Yale and Princeton and Dartmouth will knock out those back-log adoptions for Understanding Poetry, too. But there's nothing we can do except hope. I have written to Crofts to give the addresses of Thompson, Donahoe, and Moreau, who should receive copies. I didn't have Hinton's address, but I called their attention to the fact that he should have a copy. We ought to get a copy to Don, too. I'll sign a copy and send it to you so that you can sign it and forward it to him.

Have you had any thoughts on the Harcourt text book? I've been inspecting handbooks, and such, and have read two little books on semantics which are intended for elementary use. I'm trying to cook up some simple way in, but I can't say that my heart is set on the business. And damn it, it would be fun, too, if we could sit down and talk it out. But we've got to give Harcourt something to think about before long. We promised them a statement in January.

As for the Shakespeare project, I've put a few things into a folder—fragments from Henn and Ridley, the essay on metaphor by the husband of Katherine Mansfield (whose blessed name escapes me at the moment),[1] and some odds and ends. Have you any more words on the eighteenth-century emendations?

I am anxious to see the essay you mentioned in your last letter. Could you let me see a copy? I'd send it back.

There's not much news here. We've had flu in the house, and have tossed it back and forth. I've been doing some poems, and shall send copies before long. At Heaven's Gate is announced for April. I was lucky enough to get a split on the Shelley Prize this month. Which was convenient. But that is the best one can say for it.

Well, so long, and my best. Our best to Tinkum.

As ever,
Red

3124 West Calhoun Boulevard
Minneapolis, Minnesota
May 1, 1943

Dear Cleanth:

I had heard indirectly of your father's illness, but your letter was the first word of his death. I can well imagine the strain under which you all have been, and I am very sorry for it. After I had heard about your father's illness I didn't write again simply because I knew that a letter would just be one more thing to distract you. Now since getting your letter a visit from Morton Zabel,

---

1. Mansfield's husband was John Middleton Murry, critic and editor, whose works include *The Problem of Style* (1922) and *Keats and Shakespeare* (1925).

a hellish amount of work, and some aggravating personal complications (of no consequence but time consuming) have conspired to cut me off from my correspondence. Today I have settled down to it.

The outline of the Macbeth essay sounds fine. The child stuff is brilliant! I really feel that you have got something by the tail. And I am anxious to see the essay. Please send it as soon as you conveniently can. I don't see why you let your generosity of spirit carry you to the length of proposing that I collaborate with you on an essay on Macbeth for the Atlantic. Hell, you've got the work done, it seems. If it so falls out that I do have some contribution to make to it, well and good. But otherwise, the idea won't wash. How is the book coming with Bob? I wish that it were out for there might be a chance for me to use it in a course which now promises to be one of my staples. I have inherited Stoll's modern drama—a big course and lots of copies of text books. One of the chief difficulties is getting hold of something which will give them practice in close analysis. The class is so big that it's hard to work the business in the ordinary sort of walky-talky way. The course has been, contrary to my expectations, interesting to me. I've been sunk in Ibsen and Chekhov and such, but it hasn't been entirely chore-work for me.

You mention your situation with the Army. I am encouraged to hope that, since I have not yet been called, you will not be called. The whole matter looks pretty senseless to me, for I don't see what they expect to do with the old crocks. But all the University appeals for my deferment were rejected and lately I've been ordered up for another physical. My thirty-eighth birthday fell last week. But I don't know what difference that makes. Meanwhile I have a gang of soldiers—Air Corps boys, in pre-meteorology—one section. They are nice boys and very respectful, earnest, and comma-conscious.

Life gets along here. I've led a hermit's existence with a bust about every two weeks. Very mild busts, however. Literary arguments around the bottle, with Beach, Brown, Castell (a man in Philosophy whom I like very much) and Stein. The only work of my own I've done for some time is on a long poem, which is now drawing toward a close. It is about the Billie Potts story—you may remember it, the man who killed his son with the tomahawk? It is a sort of ballad with inset stuff in other styles. I'll send it when it's done. The novel was slated for April; then was postponed for May; then for June; now for July. Trouble with printing, etc. But they say that it is out for [p. 2] sure in July.[1] A copy will come wandering in to you some day. The poems are still slated for fall. I wish that I could have the benefit of your judgment in making selections. I may send you a full manuscript and ask you to strike out pieces. There are several new ones which you haven't previously seen, in addition to the Ballad of Billie Potts. Laughlin was inclined to bring out another pamphlet this summer or fall (I have enough new stuff for one), but

---

1. *At Heaven's Gate* was finally published August 19, 1943, though the first impression of 5,000 copies was printed April 23, 1943 (Grimshaw, *Robert Penn Warren: A Descriptive Bibliography, 1922–1979*, A5.a1, n. 1).

Harcourt didn't want a conflict, and didn't want to postpone publication of the book.

Have you heard any word from Crofts lately on the fate of UF? I'm pretty pessimistic about the chances of getting off to a good start. But I was surprised to get the Holt statement the other day. God help it to continue.

I shall look forward to the Macbeth essay, and I would certainly like to see the Pope piece if you have a copy around. I'd send it back. I haven't done anything lately toward the Shakespeare anthology. Do you think that we should try to get that together pretty soon with the introduction? I talked to the Holt man when he was here—the text book editor—and he seemed favorably disposed toward it. Not wildly enthusiastic, of course.

Well, goodbye. I hope that things will go better for you now. I'm damned sorry about the situation you have been through.

Write to me when you can. Cinina joins me in warm regards to you all.

Goodbye,
Red

Louisiana State University
Department of English
Baton Rouge, Louisiana
August 31, 1943

Dear Red,

I have read your book *[At Heaven's Gate]* with great interest—I need not tell you—and I want to say that it is truly fine. For me, Sue's character came over far better this time, and the ending seems to me a great improvement over the first draft, and altogether satisfactory. It is a very rich piece of work— the characters are alive—and the integration of the characters and incidents is remarkable. (I hope that this does not sound like a cheap review—it is altogether candid—the book is a very fine novel, indeed.)

I have been furious for the last week, however, in seeing some of the wooden-headed reviews. That in the Chicago *Tribune* might have been expected, I suppose; but even so, it sets a high of some kind: it sounds like Fulton Oursler in the pulpit at a camp-meeting. But the other reviews are pretty disgraceful. I've seen only one thus far that seemed to have been written by a competent person—that in *The Nation*. In spite of his Communist prejudices, he got the point—or at least some points. And I thought his opening sentences were significant: namely, that with the nationalist hullabaloo in full swing, reviewers were not likely to notice favorably a book which so signally failed to flatter the nationalist ego. (I've put the matter in my own terms—but you've seen a copy of the *Nation* by now.)

You will probably hear from Bob Heilman on the subject soon; he was tremendously impressed with the first draft of your book, you remember.

[p. 2] I wish that you all might have come down here this month, though your letter had warned that it was unlikely. On the 18th, I went down to the Induction Center in New Orleans, and was adjudged 4*F. They looked me over a couple of days before throwing me back. I confirmed there what I had already guessed—that if taken at all, I would get only limited service. As between being a male WAC and teaching my three army sections here, I had just as soon go right on with what I'm doing. I judge that everybody was happy at the decision therefore, except some of my friends and neighbors on the draft board.

I finish up with the army people in the next two or three days and then we are going down to N[ew] O[rleans] for a week's holiday; for term starts again on the 10th of September.

Will there be any chance of you all's coming down this fall or winter? I wish that you could. I need some talk, and I have some special brands of mischief planning that I would like to talk over with you.

By the way, will you be able to look over a fairly short book MS. in the next few weeks? I hope to finish up my new critical book, and I need advice badly. Much of it you've seen, but the essays on *The Rape of the Lock,* "The Ode on a Grecian Urn," "Tears, Idle Tears," and "Among School Children." And I'm especially anxious to get your marginal comments on the last long chapter which is a reply to Pottle[1] in particular—though a respectful and pleasant one—and a sort of summary of the critical position implied by the concrete studies of the earlier chapters. Don't let me impose; but if you can [p. 3] give a quick look at the MS., let me know when it is most convenient and I'll plan to send it up.

There's little news from here. Conrad is still here but is planning to go up to New York soon on a year's leave of absence. The department is mainly teaching army people in the A.S.T.P. program;[2] and the Administration is having the time of their lives. I believe, however, that they are worried a little about the spreading fame of Troy Middleton,[3] who is leading an army in Sicily and who will undoubtedly come back a lieutenant general. You know what B.R. thinks of a military hero, and this one will come back with an ax sharpened for the crooks. And he knows who they are. I've seen some of Middleton's letters to Caffee, Heilman, and Carmichael. Anybody corresponding with radicals like these is obviously up to no good from the standpoint of Frey-Lee-Robert and Co.[4]

I must hurry this off. Do let me have a letter from you when you can. Tinkum sends regards to you and Cinina. All my best,

Cleanth

1. Frederick A. Pottle was a professor at Yale University and a noted scholar; his works include *Idiom of Poetry* (1926) and *Pride and Negligence: The History of the Boswell Papers* (1984). Brooks refers to his work in progress, *The Well Wrought Urn,* which was published in 1947.
2. A.S.T.P. is the Army Specialized Training Program.
3. Troy H. Middleton, Commandant of Cadets at Louisiana State University, 1930–1936, became acting vice president, comptroller, and later president, 1951–1962. The LSU main library bears his name.
4. Brooks is referring to the opposition at LSU.

1715 Logan Avenue South
Minneapolis, Minnesota
December 6, 1943

Dear Cleanth:

Well, it's a bullseye. Or I'm badly mistaken. I think that the business about the daggers is interesting and instructive, and right, but the business about the babes in the play is an eye-opener. It really does something. I have tried your idea on Huntington Brown,[1] who was struck dumb with admiration, and on one of the younger men here in the philosophy department. Hunt, who is a crony of Stoll, doesn't think Stoll would take your line—for reasons which you can surmise; but I'm going to try it on Stoll just to see for myself. I'll report.

Now somewhat haphazardly, let me make some trivial comments on the essay. I'll take them as they come up in the MS.

p. 2. Somehow I can't help but feel that you could handle the Donne-Shakespeare business a little more tactfully. I mean something as simple as this. Why not simply refrain from pitting the metaphysicals against Shakespeare? Why not, at the expense of candor, say that this imagery might cause some qualms among those who retreat to Shakespeare's authority when they seek to urge the claims of "noble simplicity" in poetic style. Then something like this: "But perhaps we have here simply another poetic resource, another type of imagery which, even in terms of its apparent violence and complication, Shakespeare could absorb into his total structure etc." You see what I am up to, too, is to tone down the forensic flavor of the passage—the sense of scoring a point in a debate. Of course, there *is* a debate, but maybe you could trick them.

p. 4. You say "Miss Spurgeon can do little with her discovery." Well, it's a fact. She's like a child with a loaded machine gun, shooting off in all directions and chortling with glee. But again, it might not cost too much to take a milder tone, and say something like this: "Miss S has not, perhaps, fully investigated the implications of her discovery." Or something of the sort. (By the way, last year in PMLA—last year, I think—there was a long article on the limitations of the Spurgeon method, which might be of interest to you.)

p. 5. You have "justification of such mixed metaphors." Again, I think a more neutral word would improve the temper—say "analysis of such mixed metaphors in terms of the premises of Sh's style," or something of the sort. (By the way, I am inclined to feel that the matter can be discussed in terms of the degree of commitment of consistency which the poet makes—but you know that line.)

p. 10. "an attractive possibility not yet seriously entertained." How seriously in the past? This raises the question of the previous status of the subject between M and Lady M—the background of guilty speculation and hope.

1. Brown was a friend of the Warrens in Minnesota.

How much? etc. Perhaps a more qualified statement is in order here, just to cover possible [p. 2] objections.

p. 12. "Laws of cause and effect." I am troubled here a little bit, not by what you mean but by the terms of the statement. Let me see if I can get my feeling straight. As stated, you seem to imply that M would deny the rational order of cause and effect. But he is acting under the tutelage of a "rationalist" who maintains that a certain kind of cause and effect does work. It is a question of what is the margin which man has to go on, and Lady M simply gives him an insufficient margin for him to work on. M wants to break the bank of the future—put it in a metaphor—but he hasn't got enough capital to cover his bets. He reasons without sufficient evidence. Lady M and M suffer from intellectual pride, in one sense. They have the "reasonable" answer and act on it. See on p. 16 toward bottom where you use "irrational" to describe those things which make man more than machine. Are they literal[ly] irrational, or merely do they seem irrational to the stripe of rationalisms advocated by Lady M.? I think this line of thought needs a clearer statement, but I fear I've only muddied the waters.

I think that you might underscore a little more heavily, the very excellent point made on p. 11 about the added dignity achieved by M if we regard him in the light of his metaphysical attempt as contrasted with his personal attempt at a throne. He has undertaken a more than mortal struggle *but a struggle which man must as man forever undertake.* Man must try to predict and plan and control, as his destiny. But he can never be sure that he has arrived at the right premise for the effort. M is trying to follow man's destiny. Man has to try to break the bank of the future. The fact that he cannot does not mean that he must not try. The question is on what terms can he try and with what attitude. Something along that line. I feel that this can be developed. On this general point, I would suggest a comparison with the play Julius Caesar. We have a somewhat parallel philosophical issue. Brutus is a Stoic, therefore a determinist. He does not act because for him action is futile. But Cassius, an Epicurean, who by definition believes in the efficacy of will and reason in relation to the "future," lures Brutus into action. In the end Cassius says "you know I once held Epicurus strong" but has lost his philosophy and now begins to "credit things that do presage"—[in] other words has begun to doubt man's role in relation to the future. Here the set-up is different in that the Fate is not a moral order, shall we say, but a political and historical situation, which has not been adequately analyzed. Etc. But the same basic issue seems to be raised here. Or am I wrong?

Well, all of my remarks are trivial. The paper is damned enlightening, and ought to stir up something. As I read it I was filled with nostalgia for all our old arguments and discussions and collaborations. "Ah Ben, say when—."

As for my own activities: I have been working on a new novel, and have done near two hundred pages. Needs reworking, of course, but I have something. But also I am in an awful stew about the whole thing. The dark night of the soul is what yours truly now is going through. I hope he'll pull out. On the side, I've worked out a new reading of the Ancient Mariner which I hope to commit to paper before too long. Boy, that thing is built like the Swiss watch, I [p. 3] assure you. I've been reading a lot of criticism on it, and the fashionable view (Griggs, for example) that it is a pleasant journey into a realm of imagination which mean[s] nothing makes me want to call for the old granite slop-jar. And on the other hand, there are the allegory boys. But more of this later. Again I wish I could argue the matter out with you.

I suppose you had McMurphy's letter about a revision of Understanding Poetry and about an anthology to compete with Untermeyer. Well, Holt would bear some permission costs, which Scribners would not do, according to our old contract. But if we ever did do such a book, I guess we would be honor bound to go with Scribners. Maybe not. But the whole thing would look so far off. We have that damned Freshman book on the ticket now. And I can't bear to think about it. A passing mood, I trust. By the way, hunt up Robert Graves' Reader Over Your Shoulder and work on it with the freshman book in mind. Very useful for us.

No news. Just dragging on. Vacation next week, praise God. AHG *[At Heaven's Gate]* doing pretty well. Mild winter so far. Small bout with flu.

Goodbye and our best to you all. As ever,

Red

P.S. As for any announcement of our intentions, that would certainly be agreeable to me—but the problems created by distance are great. I envy you this piece and wish that I could have a hand in it.

[Handwritten] I wish when you write a final copy you'd provide me with one?

1715 Logan Avenue South
Minneapolis, Minnesota
December 17, 1943

Dear Cleanth:

Your letter came today to give cheer to a dull morning of correcting exam papers. I'll repeat, I found the Macbeth essay very, very illuminating, and I am anxious to see the whole MS of your book *[The Well Wrought Urn]*. When you have it together I'd like nothing better than to read it; I'm a little too impatient to wait for the book. I think that you are probably doing the right thing to answer your critics head-on. It can certainly be managed in the proper spirit.

By the way, thank you for the kind remark about the Julius Caesar business: the Stoic-Epicurean affair. I worked that business out a while back—by "out" I don't mean with any degree of finality that would convince every reader, God knows—but I've never sent the thing off. Tucker Brooke[1] seemed to think

1. C. F. Tucker Brooke, Shakespearean and Elizabethan drama scholar at Yale, apparently taught Warren in one of his Shakespeare classes and stimulated Warren's interest in Shakespearean drama.

the thing might stick, but he's one of the few people who has seen it. And he's probably forgotten it.

I finished my grades today and turned them in. So I feel pretty good to be a free man again, even if for a little. I do hope to get some work done this month. I've got a review of Welty to do, an article on Faulkner (New York Times "re-evaluations" series), and the novel. In that order. But I don't imagine I'll get to the novel until January again. Welty is an extremely interesting gal. I'm not inclined to think that she has gained ground in her last book, but she has plowed the same ground a little more deeply. I've been trying to define her basic theme. Fumbling in results as yet. Alienation, perhaps. All main characters are "cut-off" characters. Deaf boy. Women sex-starved, to use the tabloid word. Artists afraid of world. Little girl looking across the street at big girl. Or perhaps, not merely alienation, but vicariousness. Well, this is certainly fumbling.

Recently I discovered an old unmailed letter to Bob Heilman about his Sewanee Review piece. God, what he must think of me after all this time. It had slipped down between the walls of my desk and came to light in sorting papers after our moving to our present house. I'll have to recopy and send it. Not that it says anything.

Goodbye, and our best to you both for Christmas.

As ever,
Red

. . . .

Louisiana State University
University, Louisiana
May 14, 1944

Dear Red,

I have heard from you indirectly a half dozen times during the last month, what with friends writing in about their pleasure at seeing you on your trip east. But that's not the same thing as hearing from you direct, and so I am sitting down to a letter of sorts in hopes that it will draw one from you.

I have been working like a dog of late. The Percy-Malone volume of letters has been endless trouble and has taken up countless hours of time. The index, for instance, devolved on me since Tillotson, the special editor, is in the R.A.F.; and the index alone must have taken up sixty hours of working time. Fortunately, the book is just about finished.

Meantime, however, the work on the *Understanding Drama* got slowed down and I have been having to steal time for that. But I have something to show for the last months. The piece on *Macbeth* is to appear in the *American Bookman*—within a short time, I hope. An analysis of Tennyson's "Tears, Idle Tears" is to appear next month in *The American Scholar*. I shall have a copy sent to you.

How does the novel go? What's its setting to be? Etc., etc. By the bye, let me compliment you on the piece on Eudora Welty: it was illuminating and informing—exactly what criticism ought to do for a new and difficult author. I don't think Diana Trilling the worst of reviewers, but I think that she has been a little heavy-handed and even densely ignorant on Southern authors. You were polite and gentle with her, but I think that you definitely set her to rights.

Also, congratulations on the fine volume of poetry.[1] It looks well and reads mighty finely; and I am delighted that so many reviewers have had the good sense to see that it does and to say so with enthusiasm.

There is little real news from here. The University settles deeper into the bog every day. We have just elected a hill-billy yodeling governor[2] who is the abject tool of the bankers, the corporation lawyers, and the big sugar men.

I am enclosing a little skit which is self-explanatory. I should have sent it long ago. The report by Uhler and Bradsher[3] is real—thoroughly genuine. The document enclosed is from the hand of one of them—his own copy. My counter-report was not seen by either of them for a week or so. Then someone reported it to Bradsher—we suspect the estimable John Olive.[4] Bradsher came into Kirby's office and demanded a copy. Kirby refused a copy but allowed him to sit down in his office and read it. Uhler could never summon up the nerve to go through this ordeal, and had to be content with Bradsher's report of it. But I wish that I could show you the letters which they wrote to the General demanding my scalp and Kirby's because he did not discipline me. But the old General was afraid to take the case out of Stevenson's[5] hands; so the upshot was that I was never called up and that Bradsher and Uhler never did get any satisfaction except that of blowing off steam before Kirby in Stevenson's office. The tempest was a very small one in a very small teapot, but [p. 2] perhaps it will waft nostalgic odors from the old miasmic swamp to you and Cinina. Please return the documents when you are through with them—which may include showing them to a friend or so if you like.

Tinkum has been working very hard at her father's plant.[6] She's up at six and usually doesn't get home until about six in the afternoon. We have had no social life to speak of for months. By the weekend we are too tired and

1. *Selected Poems, 1923–1943* was published April 6, 1944.

2. The yodeling governor of Louisiana was Jimmie H. ("You Are My Sunshine") Davis, who served two terms.

3. Earl Lockridge Bradshear wrote western novels under a pseudonym and was a member of the English faculty at LSU and one of the "reactionary right" who, along with Uhler, was on the search committee for a new English department chair headed by Brooks (Cutrer, *Parnassus on the Mississippi*, 175).

4. Professor Olive was another member of the English department committee that was investigating the direction the department should go.

5. Dean Wendell Holmes Stevenson of the College of Arts and Sciences had edited the *Journal of Southern History* until its publication was suspended (Cutrer, *Parnassus on the Mississippi*, 251).

6. Tinkum worked at her father's plant in Baton Rouge during the war (Mark Royden Winchell, *Cleanth Brooks and the Rise of Modern Criticism* [Charlottesville: University Press of Virginia, 1996], 205).

sleepy to do much more than catch up on sleep. It's certainly not a formula for a lifetime. But for the moment it's not bad, and we seem to thrive on it. But it will be good when we can relax again, and get around the country a bit.

Is there any chance of you all's getting down this summer? We ought to have a meeting if we can—for the fun in it, but also to get started on that cursed book.[7] I believe that I could get interested in it if we had some talk together. What are you all's plans?

Also, though I suppose this is even farther in the future, I would like to talk over the Shakespeare studies. We ought to do a little along, if only a little. I've been working on Falstaff recently and I am going to be working on *Lear* in connection with the drama book. I do have the feeling that if we could once get started, some of the stuff would come almost automatically.

Do find time to write. I miss our talks a great deal. If we can't be together, I, for my part, wish that we could write more often, and intend to see to it that I do.

Best regards from both of us to both of you.

Cleanth

[OH]

Louisiana State University
College of Arts and Sciences
Department of English
Baton Rouge, Louisiana
May 26 [1944]

Dear Red—

Mr. Allen S. Wilbur of Crofts has sent in a list of misprints to be corrected in the reprinting of *An Approach to Literature* now imminent.[1] I have returned his list with approvals for all but one. The professor who sent in the list suggested changing (p. 19, second column) "Jonathan Wild" to "Roderick Random" since, as he says, *Jonathan Wild* is not told by the hero in the first place and therefore is not a relevant example.

I'm ashamed to say that I know too little about the matter to know whether he's right or whether Roderick Random would be an appropriate substitute. (I'm not sure he would be appropriate in view of the sentences which follow.)

Anyway, make a revision of some kind, and send it to Wilbur (F. S. Crofts, 101 Fifth Ave.) direct.

I have recently been working on a poem. I hope to send it to you in a few days with the request that you be as severe with it as candor and true friendship demand. I have no business at this day and time of writing and trying to publish third-rate verse.

Love to both of you,
Cleanth

7. Although *Modern Rhetoric* did not appear in print until 1949, it was already their albatross.

1. The ninth printing of *An Approach to Literature* was August 1944.

Louisiana State University
College of Arts and Sciences
Department of English
Baton Rouge, Louisiana
July 27, 1944

Dear Red,

Thanks for the letter! I was afraid that you had indeed become a wraith—perhaps a phantom haunting the roads between Minneapolis and Washington. For various friends wrote of seeing you in the East and in Ohio, and I concluded—after getting a dirty mimeographed form from the Library of Congress saying that a Mr. R. Warren of Minneapolis was applying for a job and asking for comments on his character—that you had taken the Washington post; but I couldn't be sure.

I'm awfully glad that the appointment came and am glad that you decided to accept it. It ought to give you more time for your writing and, for some reason, Washington seems much nearer to us here than does Minneapolis. I hope that you have luck with the housing situation. I understand that it is awful.

We are having here a hot and busy summer. But I dawdle a little with *Understanding Drama* and with the new critical book—chapters of which I will send to you for your comments. When I get tired I tinker with my bookbinding. We are binding the S.R. in half binding (tan buckram and green leather) and, even with our home-made tools, it's going to look mighty nice.

By the way, as to the Nebraska proposition,[1] I have no decided opinions. It seemed a little silly to have such a book issued in Nebraska; yet, perhaps we ought to take her up. If you think we should, that's fine. I haven't really thought about the matter. I remember the letter vaguely, but it must have been sent long ago, and probably about the time of my father's death when I was too worried with a multitude of things to answer my correspondence properly. I'd be glad to join with you in making a selection for her if you would like; or I'll make an alternative proposition: We ought to be able to get somebody in New York to issue a volume of selections with a longish essay giving some comments on the history of the magazine and on its death. And if we wrote with anything like the frankness with which I hope that we would write, the L.S.U. Press would want to be left out of the matter anyway. What do you say?[2]

I am enclosing a MS which I ask you to read carefully—even though I know that you are busy. It's the first piece of verse that I've tried in a long time. Maybe it will be the last, though I've two other poems that I've begun to tinker with.

1. On July 14, 1944, Warren had relayed a request from Emily Schossberger, editor of the University of Nebraska Press, for some *Southern Review* material for an anthology of writing from "little" magazines.
2. That book, *An Anthology of Stories from "The Southern Review"* was published November 23, 1953, by the Louisiana State University Press in a printing of 2,923 copies.

Please be candid. I'm entirely too old to be setting out to be a fourth-rate poet if that is what I fear the level of the performance really is. Give me the honest low-down; and if there is enough to salvage, mark excisions and make suggestions. For if you tell me it's good enough, I shall probably be sending it to Allen or John. And it's better to save me and them embarrassment. As you know, I have preferred to be a critic of competence rather than a botch of a poet; and I've kept away from verse when I felt that there was nothing that I wanted to say in verse, preferring to suppress the motive of wanting in general to be a poet and allowing only the motive of wanting to write this *particular* poem. I wanted to write this particular one—regardless of what I did with it and of whether I did anything with it. So I've already had my reward, and you can afford to be as candid as, in this case, a good friend ought to be.

[p. 2] The verses require no explication beyond the fact that I am retelling the story which Poe tells in his story about the maelstrom,[3] which I know that you have read. I haven't reread the story in years, but my references to it are fairly specific, I believe, including the rainbow in it.

Hatcher *is* president.[4] Stevenson has been fired, though this has not been announced. The enemy are running hog wild. I don't know whether matters can get any worse. I'm not crawling out on any rotten limbs, but I think that it's generally known that I'm just itching to be fired, if I can be fired for the right reasons. That probably won't happen, because the Administration isn't that crazy. (I'm using my own case as a typical one.) But the Administration is crazier than we had thought. The job of Comptroller was offered to Red Heard! who had more wit than the President and refused it. McKnight has been given job after job, and the firing of Stevenson indicates that Hatcher has no sense of shame—Stevenson, you may remember, was Hatcher's major professor just a few years ago. Stevenson's mistake—a typical Quaker mistake—was that he didn't fail the bastard then, and so never have let the problem arise.

There's little more in the way of news. We must get together, but I don't know how either—unless we can lure you and Cinina down for a B.R. visit or a stay on the Gulf Coast or something. We will come East when we can, but that seems quite impossible for the moment.

Do write soon. Best luck to both of you in getting settled. Regards from all the friends here.

Cordially,
Cleanth

3. The poem by Edgar Allan Poe is "A Descent into the Maelström." Brooks's poem was published by Allen Tate in *Sewanee Review* 54 (winter 1946): 116–18.

4. William Bass Hatcher was an associate professor of history at LSU during the 1936–1937 and 1938–1939 academic years, a special lecturer in history in 1937–1938, dean of the College of Arts and Sciences in 1941, and dean of LSU's junior division in 1942. From June 1944 to February 1947, he served as LSU president.

The Library of Congress
Reference Department
Washington
[August 1, 1944]

Dear Cleanth:

First things first: The poem. It is not third-rate or anything like that. It is first-rate. Very original, very beautifully composed. I am delighted with it. Unless I am badly mistaken, it is the berries. No kidding. Damn it, why didn't I think of it myself? You've sure been keeping something under a bushel. Get right down and turn out a lot more of them. Quick. I am truly enthusiastic. I have one small suggestion, but it has nothing to do with the text of the poem. Your remark in your letter about the Poe story set the poem up for me. When I had first read it, I hadn't read the letter. (You had said that your poem was coming, and my interest was so great that I leaped for that first when I opened the envelope.) As soon as I read the Poe stuff the poem took on lots of new force. So I suggest that you put some sort of quotation, perhaps rather full, from the Poe story as a heading for the poem. I think that that would pay its way.

About the SR anthology. It seems logical to me that we should have one of our own, and a damned frank preface. I'm game to try for a New York publisher on this, and quick. AS SOON AS I hear from you I'll write to Lambert[1] (who will say no)—if you think that we ought to do it. Albert might handle the matter in New York, as a matter of fact. It would be easy to select a damned good book out of the mass of stuff.

The news about LSU is pretty terrific. The best we can hope is for the bastard to over-reach himself. Did he simply fire Wendell from the deanship or from the University? Do you still hope for things to blow up when Middleton comes back, or does this new appointment of Hatcher preclude that? By the way, I hear from Iowa that Foerster has resigned. Terrible doings there. It is always the same story. Austin and René Wellek are way down.

Things here are confused. I'm house-hunting, with no luck yet. I am staying with the Cheneys, and greatly enjoying their society. I have seen some other friends, too. I shall see Hugh Cox in the next day or two. Tommy Thompson rolls in from the Pacific today. Leonard Unger was here last week, and I had a long session with him. At the Library I have to spend a lot of time getting acquainted with folks and attending conferences, but I read five books last week. Wonderful stuff. I've been reading books by ex-slaves for some time now, and here I am working over the 37 volumes, in manuscript, of narratives by ex-slaves. The most magnificent collection of stuff you ever saw. Very moving and funny at the same time. As far as the social and historical side

1. Lambert Davis was managing editor and subsequently editor of the *Virginia Quarterly Review*. As an editor at Harcourt Brace he also read the manuscript of *All the King's Men* for Warren and suggested, among other things, that Warren change the protagonist's name from Talos to Stark, according to James A. Perkins, Westminster College (Pennsylvania).

goes, it gives exactly what any sensible man would expect. There was enough human decency to make a bad system tolerable. I wish I could tell you some of the tales.

Do send me the new book stuff. I'm anxious to see it. By the way, I enjoyed the Empson piece in Accent. And the piece in the American Scholar. Write soon.

Best to Bob, Tinkum, and you.

As ever,
Red

[OH]

Louisiana State University
College of Arts and Sciences
Department of English
Baton Rouge, Louisiana
Sept. 14 [1944]

Dear Red—

I should have made a better return to you for your good letter of some weeks ago than this belated note. In particular I should have written to tell you how much I appreciated your good word about "The Maelstrom." But we had examinations, and then, registration, and I am just crawling out of the confusion.

About the poem, by the way: I sent it to Allen, who has accepted it for publication. But I have written to ask him to hold off—for a while at least. The reasons are various. Much as I appreciate your commendation and high as I put your critical judgment, I am not sure that you haven't been moved unconsciously by good nature and friendship in speaking well of it. In the second place, I want to see whether I am going to write other poems or not. (It would be foolish to publish one if it were to be the first and last.) Anyway, I'm going to wait a little and let it mellow and look back at it, and I wish you would do the same for me. In the meantime, I'm going to try another one which I'll send along for your judgment when it's finished.

We hope that you and Cinina are now settled comfortably. It's bound to have been a period of confusion—the move itself and the business of finding a house. May you all have a fine and pleasant fall! The north wind has been blowing here, however, and we're all having an access of energy after the hottest summer in years.

[p. 2] I have just hired a part-time secretary (out of my own funds, of course) and hope that this will be a means of pulling myself out of the confusion into which I've got myself. That is, I hope that with her help I can get certain MSS. finished up and typed up so that they can be sent for your inspection.

Bob and I are supposed to finish up the drama book this month—though perhaps we won't. Then I'm going to try to finish up the critical book, some sections of which I want your word on. The Macbeth piece (with your suggested revisions) was accepted by *The American Bookman* early in the summer for immediate publication. But I've heard nothing from them. Has that outfit folded up?

I am going into this amount of detail about my own projects—not because I think that they are of burning interest, but because I take the *Southern Review* project very seriously, and am trying to see when I can get to work on it. Not before next month, I should think. But I can at almost any time start making a list of nominations as to what pieces we might use. We could compare our lists then and come to agreement, and that would leave as the only big matter the writing of the history. What do you suggest about procedure? Let me know.

Do you ever see Hebert? He's in the Adjutant General's office in Washington. Jean Albrizzio[1] is a WAC—stationed I don't know where. Conrad breezed in the other day from New York and is teaching here again.

There's little further news. I feel very bad to remember that I failed to answer Thomas Thompson's[2] fine letter from the Pacific. [p. 3] It deserved a prompt answer. But it came during the time that I was getting no sleep and was in no shape to answer letters—and having neglected then, it slipped out of sight later when I did have time. If you see [him], express my regards and apologies.

All of which reminds me that Tinkum and I are long overdue on a letter to Katherine Anne. T. gets in every day so tired out that she's rarely in shape to write. But that's no excuse for me. Pass on our regards to her when you see her.

This letter sprawls over three pages but says little. Do write me soon, however, and if the *S.R.* project really interests you, make some specific suggestions.

Again, may you and Cinina have a most pleasant fall. Tinkum joins me in regards to both of you.

Cleanth

1707 Cloverdale Avenue
Baton Rouge, Louisiana
Nov. 5, 1944

Dear Red,

It looks at the moment as if I might get into the East twice next month. Sometime in the middle of the month or perhaps earlier—say around Dec. 5—I am going up to Yale to give a Bergen Lecture. Also I hope to get up to New York for the MLA at the end of December. (The last little matter will depend, however, on whether the University will cough up traveling money.)

Anyway, out of the two chances I ought to get to see you. Best of all, I wish that I could persuade you to go on up with me—on one trip or both.

1. Gene Albrizio, "The Bereft," *Southern Review* 6 (winter 1941): 454–88.
2. Thomas Thompson, a Pulitzer Prize–winning journalist, published three short stories in the *Southern Review* between 1936 and 1938; he was one of Warren's students at LSU.

I've got a subject for the MLA paper—one on which I think I can write rapidly enough. But I've been casting about in vain for a suitable subject for the Yale piece. What do you think of my Macbeth paper (which has not yet been published)? Is it good enough? Will it get too rough a reception? What will Tucker Brooke think of it? etc., etc. Please give me your best advice. I still have time to do another one if the Macbeth piece would not suit.

As soon as I have more definite word about a date, I'll write you again. Meantime start fattening the calf.

I should add—even in this hasty note—that I heard from Fred Crofts recently about a revision of the *Approach*, and sent him a letter making some suggestions [p. 2] which I promised to relay to you. Actually, it may be just as well to save details until we have a chance to talk next month, but the gist of what I suggested was this: retention of copyright material and analyses and introductions; rather drastic revision of the essay and biography section which would involve, among other things, shortening them; expansion of the poetry, short story, and drama sections. I told him that I thought the essay and biography sections were good, but that I was willing to bow to criticism— the essays were undoubtedly hard for the average instructor and the Calhoun had undoubtedly lost us some adoptions. With the space gained by shortening in these sections, we could put special emphasis on the materials which we know from experience have gone well.

I suggested another play and a development of our analysis of A[ntony] and C[leopatra], with a special section dealing with the poetry in the play and thus tying the drama and poetry sections together.

Turn these matters over in your head and when you have time, let Fred have a note on this subject.

I hope that you and Cinina are both thriving. I certainly look forward to seeing you all. T. joins me in cordial regards.

In haste,
Cleanth

The Library of Congress
Reference Department
Washington 25, D.C.
December 7, 1944

Dear Cleanth:
First, for business. That is, the question which you have put to the Reference Department of this institution. I have checked the catalogue in both the main reading room and the Rare Book Room and find that your friend must be misinformed about the card of Rice Vaughan's Coin and Coinage (1675), for Henry Vaughan on those cards is not referred to as "the Silverist"—or even, if I recall correctly, as "the Silurist." In fact, I don't think that Henry is referred to at all. So I haven't yet got information about the authority for the error. I shall pursue the matter and try to find when the error was corrected.

Second, I want to say what a great pleasure your visit gave. Though it was very teasing to get on Macbeth and Henry IV and leave it all in the air after a short evening. I could even enjoy doing that damned H[arcourt] B[race] book if it could be done as the books in the past. But you must get some ideas on that quick and pass them on to me. I'll start trying to work out what you propose. Meanwhile, I am trying to get started on the Approach. I am writing to Scribner's about the Wolfe, and am running over lists of possible novels and novelettes. One trouble is that it is hard to find a novelette which isn't really a long story instead of a short novel. Naturally, if we pair it with Wuthering Heights or Vanity Fair, we want the short novel type—like Old Mortality. But there isn't another of KA's pieces which isn't merely a long story. I toyed with the idea of The Oxbow Incident, which is short and popular, but upon reflection was inclined to drop it. In the first place, even though it is a novel in length, it isn't much more than a story according to its line. And its appeal is pretty special. But you might give this a thought. I have thought, too, of Elizabeth Madox Roberts, but her best book, the Time of Man, is, again, too special.

Well, enough of this. I wish you all success on the Yale expedition. Give my best around in Baton Rouge, but not too liberally. But <save> some for your household.

As ever,
Red

The Library of Congress
Reference Department
Division of General Reference and Bibliography
Washington, 25, D.C.
May 22, 1945

Dear Cleanth:

Long time, no see, no hear. But have heard about. I was up at New Haven, to follow you as a Bergen lecturer, and heard little but the hymn of praise of Brooks. Menner and Pottle especially. What did you do? Give them a love potion? Also I hear that you are probably going to be the editor of the Yale Review. If that comes off, maybe they will have a magazine there. This from Allen, who was here not long ago. I saw Dorothy Bethurum, who is still plugging her idea of a magazine in New England with you and me as editors. I don't know what will come of it. There are some difficult angles to deal with. But I suppose there's no use talking about it until something more positive develops. She says she has a guarantee of $6000 a year now, but that isn't near enough to do the job off brown and it shouldn't be done unless it is done with bells and ribbons. Also? I don't see how the thing could be run at long distance and all that. Without consultations now and then between us, etc. That raises questions about our physical locations.

I am enclosing herewith a study of Coleridge's *AM* for your inspection and that of Bob Heilman.[1] I desperately want your close opinion, for I shall soon want to put the thing into final shape for publication. This isn't exactly a finished job, but it is consecutive and does give the argument fully. I know that the notes will have to be somewhat reduced but I don't know how far I can get them down and keep some of the pertinent quotations. I may have to assume that people will go to the texts—which they won't do, of course, in ninety-nine cases out of a hundred. Well, give the thing the once-over. Write your comments on the margin, and tell Bob to do likewise. Send back to me express collect. And be assured of my undying gratitude. I know it's a dirty trick to dump this into your lap. But here it is.

I go back to the last chapter of my novel, which I hope to finish next month or shortly thereafter.[2] Then I shall revise a paper on Frost which I did in the winter. Then I plunge into a new long poem which I hope to finish in the winter—a companion piece to Billie Potts. The story I have for it is simply marvelous. Of course and alas that doesn't guarantee anything about the poem.[3]

[p. 2] Enough of Billings. Let's have a little Mooney for a change. To quote my old joke. Which you have probably forgotten. What are you up to? Albert told me that R&H[4] hopes to bring out your new book of essays. That is fine, I think, for all concerned. What about the drama book? What about the new text book with Crofts? What about our book with Harcourt? Oh, God. Maybe next year I can get down to Chicago to confer with you, etc. We've got to do that thing quick now. Harcourt says they will make us rich. I don't believe that, of course, but it would be nice to have a little extra pocket money. Wouldn't it?

I wish I could get a long session with you. The visit here was nothing but a teaser. Perhaps we can meet in the fall. It is too bad that you couldn't take the Yale job. We could have seen each other this summer in that case.

Well, so long, and all my best, as usual. I hope that your household flourishes.

As ever,
Red

1. "A Poem of Pure Imagination: An Experiment in Reading," part of which was delivered as the Bergen Foundation Lecture at Yale University in 1945, was published as an introduction to *The Rime of the Ancient Mariner* in 1946 by Reynal and Hitchcock. An excerpt was printed in *Kenyon Review* 8 (summer 1946): 391–427 and collected in *Selected Essays* (1958) and in *New and Selected Essays* (1989).

2. The novel *All the King's Men,* which emerged from the earlier dramatic version entitled *Proud Flesh,* was published by Harcourt on August 17, 1946.

3. Warren did not break his ten-year hiatus in poetry until 1953 with the publication of *Brother to Dragons.*

4. Albert Erskine was an editor for Reynal and Hitchcock Publishers. The book of essays to which Warren refers is *The Well Wrought Urn,* published by Reynal and Hitchcock in 1947.

June 5 [1945]

Dear Red,

I have gone over the A.M. paper several times and with a growing admiration. It is easily the finest thing that has ever been done on that poem—and probably the only essay on it that makes entire sense.

I have made a few quite trivial comments on the margins, but I have nothing of importance to say about it. The brevity of comment is a measure of the extent of my agreement with you. I regret a little that you did not bring in the Industrial Revolution as you did once in conversation with me; but I can see that that would be needless—you've cut beneath it, and it might bring the personal matter to too much focus again, or might put off the reader by making him think that your argument was to prove Coleridge an Agrarian. I think that something might be made of the sexual imagery—the penetration of a virgin world: "We were the first that ever burst / Into that silent sea." I noticed with interest your showing that the bird actually came to church because I thought that that was a discovery of mine; until I reflected that I had probably heard it from you in conversation in Washington, and then forgotten that I had. It's a pretty point, and, if I did come upon it independently, that fact ought to help confirm the interpretation.

I am sure that the Yale audience was delighted. They should have been.

I am not returning the Ms. herewith, because Bob was not able to read it before he went to Cambridge (where he is to do some work in the Harvard Library this summer). He is to send me his Cambridge address, and I promised to send it to him there. He will return it direct to you with comments—and his comments, as you know, are always worth having. Bob's last week here was so crowded with exams and leasing his house, etc., that he simply didn't have time to get through the essay before he left. Should you need the Ms. right away, however, let me know and I'll return it at once.

I am bogged down at the moment with a mass of things. I am trying to finish the Percy-Farmer Letters, the critical book, and a book which Edward Hardy and I are doing on Milton's minor poems.[1] By the way, I wish that we could issue Bob's essay on Marlowe's *Dr. Faustus*—it's very good—my Shakespeare piece, and your A.M. piece as a slim volume entitled *Prolegomena to a Rewriting of the History of English Poetry*. But you doubtless have plans for your piece, and as for mine, perhaps I had better leave it in *The Well-Wrought Urn*, which is nearly finished, or I'll find that I will have to start that book all over again.

I do think it is interesting, however, to compare the light imagery as I have worked it out in "L'Allegro-Il Penseroso" or in "Wordsworth's Intimations Ode" with your brilliant handling of it in the *Ancient Mariner*. (You have seen

1. Brooks's writing projects included vol. 2 of *The Percy Letters*, which was published in 1946; *The Well Wrought Urn*; and the book with John Edward Hardy, *Poems of Mr. John Milton: The 1645 Edition with Essays in Analysis* (New York: Harcourt, Brace and Co., 1951).

the Wordsworth piece, I believe; if you haven't seen the Milton, I would like to send it to you.)

I got a copy of the letter from Reid at Harcourt, and wrote Reid that if we couldn't get together in the near future—perhaps while I am at Chicago—that I would prefer to return my advance. I have committed myself too far, I know, but I simply can't get going on the composition book.[2] Maybe if we can get a few sessions together on it, I could get interested, get some ideas, and go ahead. You were doubtless wise to decline to go into the Crofts book—the survey—though I very much regret that you won't be in. If later, you have a mind to, please let us know. We can [p. 2] always make arrangements.

When do you leave for Connecticut? I want to send you soon my last chapters of *The Well-Wrought Urn* which Albert is taking for Reynal and Hitchcock. If it won't be too much imposition, I would like your comments on the last chapter and the appendix.

I remember that I haven't said anything about the problem of the notes in your Coleridge piece. It's a shame to scrap them. Many are highly interesting in themselves: together they add a great deal of authority to the piece. I suppose that the ideal way to handle the matter would be to publish the lot at the end of the essay; and this plan would be feasible in book form. *The Yale Review* (where I suppose you will publish) raises a special problem. For that, I think that I would kill all the mere references and publish the longer notes as a sort of appendix to the essay. If even that is not feasible, what about publishing at the end of the section a general note indicating basic sources, the problems that you take up in the notes, and as samples, one or two of the longer notes on Coleridge's doctrine of the imagination?

I wish that we could have some talk—more than ever after reading your essay. Give our regards to Cinina. Tinkum has had a little rest, but is back at work again. Have a pleasant summer!

As ever,
Cleanth

The Library of Congress
Reference Department
Washington 25, D.C.
June 8, 1945

Dear Cleanth:

A scream of pain and alarm: you simply can't get out of the freshman text book. I could never do the damned thing by myself and I don't want to do it unless you are my collaborator. Now, you will be in Chicago in the fall. If you will save the time I shall come down there and work with you a while

---

2. The reference is to *Modern Rhetoric*.

to try to get the thing laid down. Then after we have done some work on it I can come back for another huddle. Etc. Meanwhile, let's try to get some thinking done on the subject. I swear that's an assignment for me for the summer. Too, I'll get out books and try to work up a plan to compare with yours. It's too bad you aren't to be at Yale this summer. Then we could really get under way.

Well, you overwhelm me with your remarks on the Ancient Mariner paper. I have read the letter over several times, not because I had to do so to know what [is in it] but because it was a pleasure. It may very well be that the bird-church business was picked up from you in conversation. I just don't recall. I am going to make more of the sexual business in the re-write, I think, and shall acknowledge you[r] silent sea business. I want to get that in in so far as it is objective—not a mere index of Coleridge's disorders, etc. As you see, at the present have left the personal stuff out entirely. I am glad that you have put some comments on the paper itself. And I look forward to Bob's comments. I agree with you that he always has something fruitful to offer. As for your idea of a little book by you, Bob, and me, I should be honored. The only plan I have for the piece is to give it magazine publication, if John or Allen wants it, and then some day to put it in a book of essays. But the book is far off and perhaps less than divine as an event.

The thought of a joint project with you all makes me think of Crofts's book. I simply didn't see how, with my present set of commitments, I could undertake anything else. For the moment. If it hadn't been for the freshman book, perhaps yes. But that couldn't be welshed on. Perhaps things will develop later, and it is touchingly kind of you all to invite me and then, in the face of my refusal, to hold a door still open.

[p. 2] Albert had told me that R&H was to bring out The Well Wrought Urn. You are about to burst into a great blaze. But a blaze not too sudden, I am sure, for there has been fire as well as smoke for a long time. But with the Drama book, the Percy letters, and the essays, plus your incidental productions, God knows what the landscape will look like. Do send me the Milton piece. To New London, Connecticut College—*after* June 20. I certainly want to see it.

Things don't change much here. The time now draws nigh for departure and there is a great piling up of chores and goodbyes, etc. I am trying [to] finish up an introduction to a selected edition of Blake done for the Talking Books. Then the annual report. Then I am a free man. I trust that the revision on my new novel will be finished by the end of July.

Well, so long, and as always, all the best to you all. May prosperity sit on the roof tree of Brookses.

As ever,
Red

Louisiana State University
College of Arts and Sciences
Department of English
Baton Rouge, Louisiana
July 10 [1945]

Dear Red,

I have delayed answering your last good letter because I have been very busy getting off the last revision of the notes to the Percy-Farmer letters to Nichol Smith in England. They take so long to go and come back that everything has to be subordinated to getting them off; but now I have a little extra time.

I despair of getting very far in thinking about the H.B. textbook until we have some talk. If we can arrange to get together some this fall and winter, maybe we can get going. In the meantime, I have started work on the revisions of U.P. and of the poetry section of the Approach. I hope to have something to show you—rather, to send you, in a week or so.

I think that the most intelligent criticism of U.P. was made by Mizener[1] who felt that the exercises were too brief and set problems too hard for the student, particularly in the first sections. My revisions consist of rewriting and expanding the questions in these exercises. Also, I shall suggest a few omissions and a few substitutions.

I am enclosing the "L'Allegro-Il Penseroso" essay. Please make marginal comments. Since it is to be a chapter in *The Well-Wrought Urn* and is not to appear in magazine form or as a lecture as I had once intended, perhaps the style should be revised. Do not hesitate to mark what strike you as repetitions. The material was thinned out originally and now, however, I am so familiar with it that I am no longer a good judge as to what ought to be cut out and what retained. The piece was done in 1942–43. It is interesting that the light imagery should—at least in the emphasis it receives—parallel at some points the importance which you have rightly assigned to the light imagery in the *A.M.*

There is little news to report from here. Mann, our only good psychologist, has left to take a much better post at Tulane. Bob Clark is going to Texas to take over the headship of the department there. The exodus seems to be on. I must say that I think that the administration is getting a little worried.

Who, by the bye, took over your post at the Library of Congress? Did you meet Maynard Mack when you were at Yale? He and his wife are awfully nice. Perhaps you all will see them this summer.

The heat here is sweltering, but T. continues at her work, and I am getting a fair amount of things done.

All our best to both of you,
Cleanth

1. Mizener's review appeared as "Recent Criticism," *Southern Review* 5 (summer 1939–spring 1940): 376–400.

111 Nameaug Avenue
New London, Connecticut
July 31, 1945

Dear Cleanth:

The essay[1] is very finely wrought and subtle. One of your better pieces, certainly. And that is giving it as high praise as it could ask. It really helps me with the poems—gives me a new way of considering them. As for suggestions, I have only one, and that's a matter of strategy. I don't think I'd say, at the top of page 3, that it comes as a relief to "find a scholar who suspends his interest in literary sources long enough to. . . ." It doesn't help the tone any, and in addition, it isn't phrased very tellingly. Anyway, Tillyard[2] is a little better than the average in these matters.

I have tinkered a little with UP—using it in my class here and making notes to myself for revision. In addition to that I have got a lot of suggestions from Rosemund Tuve,[3] who is a very keen lady. And I have a couple of large-scale suggestions of my own. As I may have written you, I worked over the Housman manuscripts at Washington (I even discovered that on the pasted-down backs of the sheets were a large number of earlier versions and had them exposed to the light of day). These manuscripts in many cases give beautiful examples of the approach to a poem, a series of revisions leading up to the finished product. For instance, there is an elaborate lot of revision before the Athlete[4] is finished. I suggest running a photograph of the manuscript, and analyzing the process which Housman went through. Then we might give photographs of a couple of other poems by Housman with exercises. We might even do the same with some other poets. What do you think? I also suggest that I write an analysis of Frost's Apple Picking (I have done an essay on Frost which is to appear in Poetry), and can adapt the stuff from the Ancient Mariner for an analysis—if you think that not too cumbersome. I fear that it may be. But anyway, our questions on the AM are misleading, it seems to me. Here is a thing for us to consider, too. We lost the adoption here (over the protests of Tuve, and I think, Bethurum) because the Thomas book had a livelier selection of poems. The Waste Land, for instance. I suggest that

1. Probably the essay that became chapter 3, "The Light Symbolism in 'L'Allegro-Il Penseroso,'" in *The Well Wrought Urn*.

2. E. M. W. Tillyard, Master of Jesus College, Cambridge, is known for his work in Elizabethan literature; among his publications are *The Elizabethan World Picture*, *Milton*, and three books on Shakespeare's plays.

3. According to Richard D. Altick and John J. Fenstermaker, Rosamond Tuve, author of *A Reading of George Herbert* (London, 1952), "wrote long before the explicit concept of intertextuality appeared, by that name, in literary criticism, but the connection she described between the meanings (plural) that a poem had for its author and the sources he or she drew upon clearly foreshadowed it" (*The Art of Literary Research*, 4th ed. [New York: W. W. Norton, 1993], 109).

4. In the revised edition of *Understanding Poetry* (1950), Brooks and Warren include a facsimile of A. E. Housman's "The Immortal Part," facing p. 617, and an analysis of the poem's development.

we spend a little money to jazz up our selection. We might even make a pass for the Waste Land, and you could adapt your essay. That would knock the Thomas book out completely. I have some other odds and ends I've thought up—perhaps a short analysis of Arnold's Scholar Gipsy—or at least some elaborate exercises on it. Then I think we might dip around into criticism a bit and draw in a few brief bits that are enlightening—for instance, Richards' bit on the word "intrinsicate" in the Antony and Cleopatra business. We need some stuff on ambiguity and depth in imagery and diction. And we need a [p. 2] better discussion of symbol (the massive quality, the nature of its expression and communication—the "unspeakable" etc.), of theme (depth and levels again, "root-idea"). I've got a gang of ideas along this line. Let's do the thing up brown and drive our competitors out.

You ask me who followed me at the L.C. Louise Bogan is the name.

And about Maynard Mack. I want very much to meet him. Dorothy was arranging a dinner and an evening, but ran into the grim fact that the Mack family have the mumps. That chills me off. I have never had the mumps and I don't want it or them or those. But I hope to get to meet him before the summer is over.

I'm looking forward to seeing you in the fall. And damn it, we've got to do the HB book. We've got to get rich.

Things go pleasantly here. I'm not getting as much done as I had hoped, but I get something done. News of your achievements is heartening.

Goodbye, and best from us both to you all.

As ever,
Red

[OH]   The University of Chicago
                                              Department of English
                                              Chicago 37, Illinois
                                              October 28 [1945]

Dear Red—

I enclose some materials which should have gone to you months ago. Indeed the last months for me have been so full that I have had no time to go on with the revision at all. And now it seems that Holt wants me to push on with the larger edition of *Understanding Drama* to get that out of the way before coming back to revising *U.P.*

I heartily endorse your suggestions about revising *U.P.*—those you sent me in a letter months ago which, to my shame, I have not answered. What I am sending you herewith doesn't seem to me to run counter to your suggestions at all, but even if we, in addition to your suggested revisions, rewrite and expand the exercises as I suggest, I am not certain that we will want to go as far in expansion as the enclosed notes would suggest. Let me know what you think.

By the bye, an idea occurs to me (of which Holt would doubtless disapprove) but I pass it on. If we get crowded with poems which we would like to include but all of which we can't, I can see no reason why Holt shouldn't print an A and a B edition, provided the different poems came toward the end. To be specific, some of our readers will want *The Waste Land* as you indicated, but others, as they have indicated to me, will want *The Rape of the Lock* (a poem I have worked out). Include both, if we can; but if we can't, Holt could use the same plates for the first 6 sections and have a somewhat different selection in Section VII of the two versions. (This is intended only as an illustration. I am not pining to include *The Rape*.)

[p. 2] I have never been more busy or confused than since I arrived here. The "Humanities" sections I am teaching turn out to be straight philosophy—which may be all very well, but which have worked the Hell out of me, my philosophy being largely of the non-technical sort and my reading of it, such as it is, a matter of twenty years ago.

The new experience is going to be very good for me. But I have ended each day worn out and [un]fit for anything but letter writing. Meantime, Tinkum has had to go back to Baton Rouge (where she now is) and until she returns I have had all the disadvantages of a bachelor apartment with a little—a very little—light house-keeping thrown in. But she is to return soon.

We must get together on the H.B. book. I still have next to no ideas, but I hope to get some in talk with you. When can you all come down? Let's do some planning ahead. We have an apartment, not yet quite in order, but when T. comes back I think it will soon be straight. Meantime you all think over dates.

I have to go to Cornell for a lecture on Nov. 15—I'm to be away for three or four days. Otherwise, one time will suit me as well as another. (I *hope* soon to be over the worst of getting settled and getting on top of my classes.)

Actually, I've seen little of the city. As for my colleagues they are very nice, but getting on to the various groups and subgroups is almost as complicated as learning the [p. 3] various Islamic heresies and sub-heresies.

I hope that you and Cinina are comfortably settled again in Minneapolis, and that the weather there is as delightful as it has been here for some two weeks past. But since I write so late, you all are now bound to be settled again and well into the year's work.

Is the novel ready? I am anxious to see it. Could you possibly let me have a carbon of your *Ancient M.* piece? I shall need it for some class work in the next months, but probably before it appears in the *Kenyon*.

Best regards to you both,
Cleanth

P.S. I've had little news from B.R., but there is another fierce quarrel going on. Twenty-three doctors at the Medical Center have resigned and there is to be an investigation. But I have little hope that any permanent good will come of it.

You know, of course, that Arthur Mizener has taken the headship of Carlton College which can't be terribly far from you.[1]

---

1. Carleton College is in Northfield, Minnesota, about thirty-eight miles south of Minneapolis.

[OH]

The University of Chicago
Department of English
Chicago 37, Illinois
December 20 [1945]

Dear Red—

I have just heard from Napier Wilt that you are coming to the MLA. As I wrote yesterday, I won't be here. I wonder if you could stay on to Jan. 2 when I will get in? But maybe it's better to plan to see each other for a longer session after Xmas. I'm counting on that.

There are several people here anxious to meet you. Crane, in particular (the department chairman), hopes he will run into you while you are here.

Best regards to both of you,
Cleanth

U of M
Minneapolis, Minnesota
December 22, 1945

Dear Cleanth:

Just a note—belated—to say that I shall be in Chicago for a day or so during the MLA meeting. I owe you a dozen apologies for not answering your fine letter, which was greatly appreciated. The story is predictable. I couldn't shake loose here until I had put the finishing touches on the novel. I sent it in for criticism. Then they asked me to clarify certain scenes, etc. I did that. Then when I was in New York in early December (I went to the Library Fellows' meeting in Washington), I had a two-day session with the HB people. They had some new ideas, and so did I. So I brought the MS back and put in another run with it. This time the final effort I trust. Except that I have one more idea which I shall put into the proof. So the fall has been taken up with that. I must say that the HB criticisms and suggestions were good and helped me crystallize out feelings I myself had had. I wish that I could have the benefit of your criticism, and of Albert's, as in the old days, but I haven't the heart to throw a big chunk at you and demand a long letter. And to write such a letter is like writing an essay. But I am going to ask you to read and give me close comment on the revised version of the Coleridge piece. When I say revised, I don't mean that it is now in final form. I am going over it again from start to finish before publication. That's why I'm going to throw the wad at you. But that will come later, when I've got the thing back from my typist.

Now about the HB book and our session on it. I know that we shan't have much opportunity during the MLA meeting. But we can talk some and set a date for a real pow-wow on it.

Anyway, I am looking forward to seeing you and to getting the news. I hear glamorous rumors from all sides, but each one contradicts the last. But I'll bring a large kit of assorted congratulations to have in readiness.

Meanwhile, Merry Xmas to you all.

As ever,
Red

2740 West Lake of the Isles
Minneapolis, Minnesota
January 29, 1946

Dear Cleanth:

Will it be possible for you all to receive me if I come down on Thursday, February 7, in the morning, to stay until Sunday night or Monday morning? That would give us several days for steady work on the God-damned book. If that time will not suit, will you let me know immediately, please? So that we can set another date.

I have been plugging along pretty steadily on the book for some time. I have nothing spectacular to report, but I do have a lot of odds and ends of ideas, and have written a kind of introduction which will be something for you to shoot at. Before I come, I suggest that you take a careful look at Donald Davidson's American Composition and Rhetoric, and at the Thomas, Manchester, and Scott book, plus one or two other competitors. There's a little book on semantics written for prep school and freshman college work by two teachers at Phillips Exeter or Andover or some place like that which we ought to look at but which I can't find here. Can you get it? I saw it once, but want another look. I do *not* mean the book called *Language in Action*. Anything else you can get together for our purposes will be useful.

No news. Just the same old seven and six. Cinina joins me in the best to you all, and expects to come down with me on the second trip at the end of the month—I have a committee meeting down there about the end of February, but I didn't feel that we could wait that long to start work on the text book.

As ever,
Red

P.S. Keep your mind firmly fixed on the $15,000 which will be your half of the royalty on the text book. That is all that keeps me going.

2740 West Lake of the Isles
Minneapolis, Minnesota
March 15, 1946

Dear Cleanth:

Thanks for the note. It cheered me in the midst of depression which a protracted case of flu has saddled on me. I haven't been laid up much, but I have sure God been dragging.

I am sorry that you aren't going to make it up here. I had hoped to get word from you that you would try, but I know how pressed you have been. As a matter of fact, I haven't accomplished much on the text book. But I have finished the winter term, and have the coming term almost free except for two weeks when I shall be lecturing. I hope to accomplish a lot then.

Now I am making the final revisions on the Coleridge piece, and I am anxious for your comments before I take the last plunge. May I have them now?

I have had to do the proofs and last revision on my novel since my return here. That was a nasty job, for the book has turned out to be about 250,000 words. A publisher's delight in the middle of the paper shortage.

Goodbye, and all the best. I certainly enjoyed our talks. Damn it, I wish there were more.

As ever,
Red

[OH]

Louisiana State University
University, Louisiana
April 30 [1946]

Dear Red—

A letter from Austin Warren the other day said that you and Cinina had been through Iowa City on your way to Tennessee. I am not sure that you are now at Gambier, but I am sending this letter there because I suppose that you will shortly be in Gambier, if you are not already there.

Our best regards to John and Robb. I had a most pleasant visit with John on my way South last month, though I missed seeing Robb. Please tell John that I shall write to him within a few days.

The immediate occasion of this letter is a proposal by Marcus W. that the Press here bring out a collection of *Southern Review* stories. It ought to be done, of course, but whether the L.S.U. Press deserves to be the publisher, I do not know. At any rate, I made it plain that, if it were done, it ought to have a preface by the editors and that you should be consulted about it. In fairness to Marcus, that idea suited him perfectly—he had had that in mind all the time. I suggested that he write to sound you out, and promised that I would write you too.

I find it hard to make up my mind about the matter. From Marcus's standpoint, the collection is a good idea, and it would be idle to tell him that it was not. Our standpoint is [p. 2] a rather different matter. I retain enough bitterness about the whole episode connected with the death of the *S.R.* not to be intrigued by the idea of the volume—though I find it hard to visit very much of my resentment on Marcus personally. But I certainly don't want to urge you into the matter.

On the other hand, I must say that I have no strong feelings *against* issuing such a volume. (If you do not want to do it, we can always plead lack of time and let the thing come out without a Preface.) Anyway, let me know what you think.

I am sorry that I had no more to offer on your *A.M.* essay than the one or two marginal comments. But that fact is a measure of my admiration for the essay. I look forward to seeing it in print. I'm sorry that I can't show great progress on the composition book. But I'm re-acclimatized now, and hard at work. I shall have something substantial by June I think.

I hope that you and Cinina are enjoying the sunshine of the spring on the Kenyon campus. I wish the pair of us were with you all and the Ransoms.

Cordial regards to all,
Cleanth

I go up to Vassar for a brief visit during the middle of next month. I take it that you are not likely to be in N.Y. around the 15th.—But if you are to be, let me know!

2740 West Lake of the Isles
Minneapolis, Minnesota
May 3, 1946

Dear Cleanth:

Your letter sent to Gambier reached me here at Minneapolis today. For we didn't have the time to go to Ohio this trip. We are planning to go there in July.

First, about the SR volume. I guess I feel about as you do. I don't mind making the selection or writing the introduction, but I hate to see LSU now try to make something out of the SR after having thrown it the old piece of meat with the rusty fish-hook and the arsenic in it. But that doesn't apply to Marcus, who, I presume, had nothing to do with the demise or the attendant circumstances. Although Helen Dear apparently shot off her mouth a good deal on the subject—how the money could be better used by the Press, etc. But if the Press is going to do the book—and I assume that there would be no way to stop them if they want to—it is probably best for us to make the selection. As for the preface, here are some thoughts that cross my head:

Date of founding and brutally compressed statement of circumstances.

Editorial policy and intention: relation to "South," new writers versus old, etc. Conception of role of quarterly. Place of fiction in that conception.

Statement of demise. I think that a sinister reticence on this point is probably our line. Perhaps a paragraph composed of two sentences: "In the spring of 1942, the editors of the SR were informed by the officers of the administration of LSU that funds would no longer be available for the magazine. The last issue, concluding volume VII, appeared in June." I don't think it's our job to whitewash the affair.

As for other details. This will cost some money, and I don't think it would be fair to pay some contributors and not pay others. So I propose that the Press set a minimum of $25 per story {[handwritten in margin] (Some stories will cost a good deal more.)}, and that we dicker with publishers for those where we have to dicker. We have one ace in the hole there—we can say that the book is a prestige book and not primarily a commercial project. As for us, I don't suppose it has crossed the head of MW that we should receive anything for our trouble, and I don't care. But we damned well ought to have about ten copies apiece of the book when it appears.

[p. 2] I propose, if you think well of the idea, that we have the Press get Albert to design the volume, at his usual fee. Not because Albert would need or want the fee, but because it would be appropriate for him to design the commercial volume, and because we would be assured of a handsome book. In our introduction we can pay our respects to Albert as an editor, but this would also be appropriate.

Dedication: Why not dedicate the book to our contributors? That will avoid a lot of things which we needn't go into here.

As for the contents, I imagine that we would come mighty close to agreement without discussion. For instance, there are such obvious things as Old Mortality (or Pale Horse), The Bridegroom's Body, Madness in the Heart, one of Caroline's stories, The Face, The Petrified Man (or another of Eudora's), Mary McCarthy's story, Jesse Stuart's story, and one or two other things before we sit down to really picking and choosing. Perhaps Tommy Thompson's Jolly should go in. I am inclined to think so.

Well, as for the whole project, if you think it worth going into, I am satisfied.

Second, about the God damned text book. I have done some more but I haven't done as much as I had hoped would be possible. For one thing I found late that I had to do a new piece for the Grinnell centenary,[1] when I had been planning on using something I had in hand. That lost me some time and energy. But I am back at the thing. Let's push the thing through and make a million dollars and forget the agony.

I assume that you have worked out your Yale arrangements, for the grapevine tells me bits of news, and Austin Warren writes today that he had reluctantly declined an invitation to visit LSU. Write me your news about that and other things.

I am just starting Bob's Lear piece. Goes fine thus far.

Best regards all around.

As ever,
Red

P.S. It seems that we may have one or more very fat fellowships for students interested in writing or in literary criticism. Students pretty well along, with book projects. Can you nominate somebody?

---

1. Editor's note: I have been unable to locate Warren's piece for the Grinnell centenary.

2740 West Lake of the Isles
Minneapolis, Minnesota
May 21, 1946

Dear Cleanth:

I have been back over the SR and have come up with the following stories. Fortunately, we see almost eye to eye on the matter, to judge from your tentative listings. I shall put mine in two groups, musts and desirables, and those I'm not too sure about I'll follow by a question mark.

. . . .

I imagine that our musts would agree pretty completely. On the desirables I should certainly be happy to do some swapping. (By the way, in that group, two stars indicate first choice, one star a second choice, and no star a third choice for the book.)

Right away you can see that the book, to be truly representative, will have to be pretty big. Even my musts run, as you see, to 112,700 words, and I am convinced that we ought to include more stories than the fourteen in that group. My own two-star stories of the desirable will add 36,000 words, making a total of 148,000 words. That is not an enormous book, just a fairly substantial one. And I don't see why we should not hold out for something that size. We could reduce by not including the novelettes, but I think that we should include them. They are all damned good, even Gene's and to leave them out would give a false picture of what we were up to. [p. 2]

As far as the introduction is concerned, if you wish I'll do a rough draft, including what I have in mind. Then you can take that and expand and polish it, returning it to me for a look. Then back to your hands for the last look. Is that all right? If you wish, I can do the first draft in June.

To hold permissions down, we might take the line the Vanderbilt Press took for the Vanderbilt Miscellany. In writing to firms which hold copyright on material we desire, we might point out that this is not a commercial project, that it is really a "prestige" publication for the university and a sort of memorial to the magazine. Or we might put it in slightly different words. But I do feel that we should pay all contributors, not just those who are lucky enough to have a publisher to do the dirty for them. Say $25.00?

You raise the question of omitting some of the novelettes and publishing two short stories instead for some authors. I am against this because it doesn't look well on the contents page. It looks as though we had to do it to fill out a book.

I know that you are not thinking of any fee for editorial work, but I believe that the Press should allot us about ten books each for our pains, especially since we would be able to take the thing to a commercial house and get it done on another basis. And had had the idea in mind for a long time. I also think that the book ought to be designed by Albert, since he had such a hand in making the magazine a success. The Press ought to attend to the actual typing of letters to contributors and publishers who hold copyrights; we can provide a model and one of us can sign. Even commercial firms do that sometimes. R&H is offering to do it for Unger, who is working on a book for them.

Well, this is all that comes to mind at the moment on the matter of the SR book. Let me know how you respond to this. Meanwhile, all the best to you both. Regards to my friends about the place.

As ever,
Red

2740 West Lake of the Isles
Minneapolis, Minnesota
May 26, 1946

Dear Cleanth:

The Crofts man has asked me what stories we would want to add to the back of Understanding Fiction to buck up the selection with some flashy modern items. I told him that I would write to you. Off-hand, I suggest Conrad's Heart of Darkness, Mann's Disorder and Early Sorrow, and Steinbeck's Flight. I am not awfully sold on the last, but it is a pretty good story, about S's best. It just doesn't happen to be in a class with the others. What are your views? Can you make some nominations? And perhaps another short piece or two? These would simply be added at the end of the stories. The only expense would be in renumbering the Appendixes and Glossary.

I have just heard from Albert about designing the SR book for the Louisiana Press. He says that normally the figure for a complete job of designing (including jacket, binding, and insides) would be about $125, but that for the dear old SR he would do it for $75. And he is not exactly anxious to do it, and couldn't do it right away. But he would insure our having a good-looking book.

To come back to *UF*. These stories would not require analyses. I could undertake to draw up leads and questions on Conrad and Mann pretty off-hand, because I've studied those a good deal. There wouldn't be any real editorial work for us. And it might buck up the book. Which, by the way, is getting new ground under its control, I am told.

I am anxious to hear your reaction to my last long letter.

As ever,
Red

[OH]   Louisiana State University
University, Louisiana
June 4 [1946]

Dear Red—

Sorry to have delayed answering your letter of May 21, but I have been delayed in getting to see Marcus, and I have waited to postpone this letter until I had seen him. His reaction to your letter is favorable. He would be glad to have a book of 148,000 words more or less. (I think we could go over that figure somewhat if we had good reason.) He will be glad to let us have, not 10, but 15 or 20 copies apiece if we like. He is willing, I believe, to pay out the royalty fees of $25 apiece to the authors. (He thought we might get some for $10, but I believe that I talked him into seeing that he would probably come out much better in proposing a straight fee and hoping that authors' loyalties can be engaged to hold down the fees of those writers who could command really big ones.)

He is glad to have Albert design the book. The only catch is that he must get machinery moving here for bids, etc., before July 1 in order to "encumber" some money which will otherwise revert to the general fund. Therefore he has made specifications out already. I think that he has a case here. But he seemed quite happy to have Albert design the title-page, cover, jacket—if there is one—and agreed that specifications could be altered later if they needed to be. In short, he is to write Albert at once telling him the situation and asking him to design the book. I think he may get a shock when he finds that Albert will expect a fee—but maybe he knows this. Anyway he will know it soon when he has Albert's reply. [p. 2] I even stipulated that we have the right in our introduction to tell the truth about the killing of the *Review*. (I did indicate, however, that we were not anxious to stir up a fight or pillory anybody—that we would be factual, not provocative.)

As a matter of fact, I suspect that Marcus entered upon the project with the feeling that this book could be a sort of "quicky," done in a hurry and on the cheap side. But if he thought this, he is reacting reasonably as he begins to see what is involved. My reasons for suspecting that M. did not know what he was in for are such matters as these: I had to tell him this morning that we bought only first serial rights—that we did not have the right to use anything we had printed in the *Review* simply because we had printed it, and that we might even run into trouble with some of the publishing houses with regard to stories like "Old Mortality." I assuaged his fears a little by pointing out that the personal appeal of the editors in some quarters and the authors in some might hold these down to nominal sums. Incidentally, do you think that we could get "O.M." or "The Bridegroom's Body," or "The Petrified Man" for $25? I think that M. would be willing to go over this fee in a few cases— perhaps a good deal over it—but I don't know whether he could in many instances. In any case the bad news—if it is bad—ought to be broken to him quickly.

Marcus is willing to furnish all the typing service he can. In the interest of convenience, since I am on the scene, I will write in both our names, if that [p. 3] suits you. But in addition, I want to send some of the letters on to you for you to add a personal note and in one or two, you ought to do the whole letter.

I certainly go along with you on the "musts." I might rate "Family History" in the desirable column rather than in the "musts," but I can't have much quarrel with you there. I do think that "When the Light Gets Green"[1] should go in the "musts." We'll add it, and count that matter settled.

As for the "Desirables," I am willing to settle for your two stars: "Bad Boy from Brooklyn," "Washerwoman's Day," "The Honey House," and "The Bereft." I think that it would be good politics to have the Lumpkin story—but fortunately we don't have to worry about that. I wish that "Mediators to the Goatherd" weren't so long—but it is long and I am willing to strike it. I wish you would look over "William Crane" once more: what it does is very quiet but beautifully done.

I'm working on the chapter on "metaphor." I've got some ideas, but it certainly goes painfully and slowly. I'll write another letter soon about *that* book, however, and about your own materials for it which arrived in good order. By the way, could you send me a copy of our typed plan? My copy is here somewhere, but I've mislaid it and can't put my hands on it now.

I hope you have a good trip. All our best to you both.

Cleanth

P.S. I'm writing Crofts about Unger.

[OH]   Louisiana State University
                                                           University, Louisiana
                                                                June 5 [1946]
Dear Red—

I stupidly omitted in yesterday's letter to answer your letter of the 26th.

I heartily endorse *The Heart of Darkness* and *Disorder and Early Sorrow*. There is against them the fact that they occur in the pocket book of short stories, and that one of them (the Conrad) occurs in Sewell and Short as well. But, on the other hand, maybe that very point is in their favor: it might help our book to compete with the Holt entry.

I am ashamed to say that I do not know Steinbeck's "The Flight." I'll look it up and read it. But in the meantime let me propose another candidate: either Faulkner's "The Bear" or "The Fire and the Hearth." Both are printed in *Go Down, Moses*. Faulkner is a bigger modern name than Steinbeck and the usual objection, that Faulkner is too depressing or gloomy etc., etc., which might hurt sales otherwise simply couldn't be applied to these stories, even by an ignoramus. Indeed, from the frailer brothers and sisters who might be disposed to object to Faulkner, I think we might even get the benefit of disappointed expectations by showing them that even Faulkner is fine in their own terms. But perhaps I rate the stories too high. Let me know what you think. (I have noticed that one recent anthology has already used "The Bear.")

[p. 2] Fred Crofts wishes that we could get together at the English Institute for a meeting on the revision of the *Approach*. Is there any chance? It meets

---

1. Warren's story "When the Light Gets Green" appeared in *Southern Review* 1 (spring 1936): 799–806.

at Columbia U., Sept. 9–13. I mention it because I am to be there, and as a meeting, it certainly is miles ahead of the MLA for pleasure and profit. But the E.I. itself is hardly the temptation for a long trip. The important thing is our own getting together somewhere.

Let me know what you think. T. joins me in cordial regards to you both.

Cleanth

Gambier, Ohio
June 30, 1946

Dear Cleanth:

I'm sorry to have been so slow about answering your letters, but the business of packing up and getting out of Minneapolis, and then of traveling to Kentucky and back up here killed a lot of time and more energy. While I was in Kentucky, I had to put a good deal of time on some work in records there, and that ate into my resources. But I trust that Marcus has gone on to allocate the money he had to have before July 1, and has proceeded with the project.

As for the stories, I am perfectly happy to have "Wm Crane" in the book. It is a very good story indeed. Maybe I think better of Pasinetti's "A Family History" than you do, but if you are willing to count it among the "desirables," I shall feel emboldened to hope that it will go into the book. As for Katherine Anne, I am inclined to feel that we ought not permit the fact that "Old Mortality" has been widely anthologized—and even anthologized by us— to stand in our way here. The present project is very different from text book work, and we ought to put our best foot forward. If not "Old Mortality" then one of her other novelettes, rather than two short stories. For one thing, the stories we have printed by her are not her absolute best, and the novelettes are. Lumpkin will suit me, too. I have the hope that we can get in Gene's novelette, for it is one of our non-professional finds. The fact that Gene hasn't gone on with our writing shouldn't deter us, perhaps. By the way, I have lost my list of stories and word lengths. Can you send me a copy of the one I sent you so that I can have something concrete before me? Thanks.

About the additional stories for *UF*, I am glad that you think that "The Heart of Darkness" and "Disorder and Early Sorrow" will serve. I can undertake to work up leads and questions for the Conrad. Will you do the Mann? I don't suppose that we want analyses—just a lot of leading questions and comments to guide the student in the job. As for the Steinbeck "Flight," I am happy to say that Faulkner is a better bet. But we do have one Faulkner story already in, and have a long analysis of it. There is no question as to where my heart lies, and I am not wild about this particular Steinbeck. But we might beat another Faulkner for our special purposes. Think up something. Meanwhile, do you want me to write for permission costs on the Conrad and Mann? I wish that "Billy Budd" weren't so long. By the way, how do you like the last statement from Crofts—$825?

I'll write again soon. Send me the list of stories etc. for the *SR* book, and your present views, and we'll try to finish that off.

Things go well with us at the moment. Same with you all, I trust. Goodbye, and all the best.

As ever,
Red

Louisiana State University
University, Louisiana
July 13 [1946]

Dear Red,

I have been owing you a letter for some time, and I am the more ashamed because I have also been owing you a comment on your novel—which I stayed up most of the night to finish when it came in some three weeks ago. It is very fine—the best of the three; and, unless I miss my guess completely, as solid as a rock. I feel that the ending is particularly powerful, but I do not find it in any way forced—it is thoroughly inevitable.

It must have been a hard book to write—as it is for the Louisianian a hard book to read—in the sense that one is tempted to impose his own interpretation of events upon the pattern of events in the novel. That is why I am so confident of the book's goodness, for I think that I provide in a way the hardest kind of audience—at least the kind of audience which is subjected most to the temptation to wrest the book away from its own pattern and so misread it.

In particular, I am delighted with your handling of the mistresses—both of them, at the end of the book. You will remember that in the play I was not quite satisfied with the motivation of some of the main characters. (I may very well have been wrong there.) But, in any case, for whatever it's worth, I feel completely convinced by your handling of them in *All the King's Men*.

The story of Cass Mastern was a stroke of genius. It furnishes you with a very powerful lever—which you use admirably. Tinkum too has read the book with intense interest and with great admiration. She joins me [in] congratulations to you. I hope that the book sells like hell—and I imagine that it will—but that is of course something that too often [p. 2] has little to do with merit. I won't write to you what Marvell wrote to Lovelace

> The Ayre's already tainted with the swarms
> Of insects which against you rise in arms.
> Word-peckers, Paper-rats, Book-scorpions . . . .

The air has *been* tainted with them, but I think that even they will be careful in this case. (This is not to say, of course, that some of the Louisiana species of paper-rat will not bristle, and at least one of them is going to be hard put to it to know what to say.)

My schedule through summer school—15 hours—demolishes my mornings, but I am getting a little done in the afternoons: a start on the chapter on Metaphor and a few pages on the chapter on Situation and Tone. But I shall try to have some material to send you soon.

As for the S.R. anthology, I have not been summoned into the presence recently, and so I do not know whether Marcus has heard yet from Albert. But when I last saw him, he was to write to Albert immediately about getting him to design the book, and was in general quite enthusiastic. I must confess that in proposing a long story from Faulkner for U.F. I had quite forgot that we have a Faulkner analyzed. Let me make one more proposal. Would Henry James's *Turn of the Screw* be too long and cost too much? As you know I am not exactly a James fan, and my proposal is put very diffidently. But the story might take advantage of the big boom in James's stock at the moment. But I should be very happy to settle for the Steinbeck. (I shall try to prepare some exercises on the "Disorder and Early Sorrow" and try to send them to you next week.)

I know that you all are having a fine time at Gambier. It's beautiful country and it must be very pleasant seeing the Ransoms regularly. Please give our warm regards to Cinina, Robb, and John. I wish we could be with you all. All our best,

Cleanth

P.S. I enclose on a separate sheet a copy of your list for the S.R. anthology.

. . . .

To recapitulate our further comments (as well as I remember them), I am checking with your Musts, adding your **'s (and "When the Light"), and asking to include "William Crane." This will pretty well push our general limit of 150,000 words. If we can squeeze in "The Treasure" which is short, or some other short one, well and good, but I think that to go further would be to strain it badly. And I don't think we will be able to improve much on this list, even though we may want to meditate it further.

Gambier, Ohio
August 10, 1946

Dear Cleanth:

I'm sorry about the delay in answering your fine letter. I am very happy that you like the novel and am grateful to you for writing to me so fully about it. I have no idea yet as to how it is going. The comments sent to HB by advance readers have been gratifying, but advance readers are rather handpicked in the first place, and they certainly don't represent John Doe or Mrs. John Hokinson Doe. But I'll know in about ten days now.

I have been working very steadily at the text book. I have just finished and sent to the typist a big wad, about 85 pages, on description. It is too long, I know, to stand as it is for the book, but it can be cut and compressed. I found that I had to work it up in that scale. It has very liberal quotations, which can be reduced. The hell of the job was hunting illustrative material. I have spent as much as two days trying to find a good example of one type of descriptive method. That kind of waste of time is heart-breaking. I fear, too, that I have been over-elaborate in my analyses and classifications. For instance, as you will see, I have distinguished ten methods of organizing descriptive detail. Probably all rot. But I'll depend on you to bring a fresh eye to the problem. I shall get it off to you next week, if the typist keeps her promise.

HB wanted a good deal of simplification on the stuff we had done earlier. I don't see much point right now in going back and trying to rewrite that, but I have been over it several times, trying to clear my own mind. They are right. We could have made a more direct approach in the first chapter. Or rather, I could have done it, for that is my composition. I'll undertake to revise it before it comes to you again. While on this point, I may add that I am very dissatisfied with my own style in the chapter on description. It is both clumsy and dull. We've got to try to strike on a really simple and attractive treatment for the book, and I'm certainly fumbling yet. I am anxious to see what you've done on metaphor, etc. You have a gift for simple exposition of rather complicated notions, which I envy.

About the SR anthology: Thank you for sending me a copy of the list. To combine my suggestions and your suggestions, we come out with something like this attached list. I am willing to stand on this if you are. But please don't think that I am trying to nail the matter down now. I'd like to see some additions, but I suppose that we haven't the space. Certainly I want "William Crane" in the book. I have reread it, and find it every bit as good as you say. And naturally I'd like to see Manson represented. I'd also like to see Elma Godchaux in. Can we get one of hers in? It would probably be good tactics, too, to increase the number of stories by unknown writers, or nearly unknown writers. She would be one. Of course, a lot of the people who are well known now, were unknown when we published them. And we must make that point in the introduction.

[p. 2] I have recently had a letter from Wilbur of F. S. Crofts & Co. He wants to know when we can do the revision on the Approach. They are selling vast numbers now, and he writes me that they will have an extremely handsome check for us in January. We ought to get the most out of this since we have the investment of time and energy already sunk in it. But can we do anything on it until we finish the HB book? I shall undertake to have the chapters on description, narration, and argument done this summer. Perhaps I can do exposition, too, but I doubt it. Could we finish by January? God knows, we've got to try. Let me know your views so that I can write Wilbur. He wants to know soon, because the number of copies for their next reprint depends on our promise for the date of delivery of the revised version.

As for the additional stories for UF, I should like to see James' "Screw" included, but it is very long, and I don't think it is really very appealing to most readers except these in the fancy. We might try to get a shorter James piece, and I'll undertake to nominate one. When I proposed Steinbeck I was really thinking of sales, though the "Flight" is about his best. And quite good. Look it up and see what you think. Soon, huh? So we can let Wilbur know.

Things go pleasantly here. Good weather, good conversation, lots of croquet, enough work. Pier Pasinetti is here with us. He goes back to Bennington next week. Andrew Corry comes in then for a few days. I may go to New York about the last of August for a day or two, but hope I shan't have to.

No news.

Best to you all. Pier asks to be remembered.

As ever,
Red

P.S. Fine news about John Palmer and the Sewanee Review, isn't it?

. . . .

[OH]   August 17 [1946]

Dear Red—

I enclose a draft of exercises for "Disorder and Early Sorrow" as a token of the fact that I have not been completely idle. Should it be longer and more detailed? It could easily be made so. Jot down your comments on the margin, please, and I'll rework it.

Let's settle for the Steinbeck "Flight." The James *Turn of the Screw* is rather special, and, come to think of it, we would have to devote pages of commentary and notes. I think that "Flight" with the other two stories will buck up the book powerfully. Will you let Wilbur know?

I've heard no more from Marcus about the *S.R.* anthology, but I'll call on him next week. The revised list [you sent] is excellent and suits me down to the ground. Marcus should have heard from Albert by this time.

As for the Harcourt Brace book, I've got less to report than I had hoped. I too have had trouble finding examples, and the 15 hours of teaching this summer (coupled with an especially hot summer) have certainly slowed me down. But I think that we can promise a MS. by January. I don't believe that I am overconfident in saying this. I found during the summer that by employing a part-time secretary—even though I spent the morning teaching—I could triple my normal output. I intend to use the same plan this fall, and with a lighter schedule and cooler weather I really think that I can come up with my end.

[p. 2] The drama book enlargement is nearly out of the way. (A great deal of time had to go into that this summer.) I simply will refuse all other commitments until the H.B. book is finished.

That leaves the problem of revising the *Approach*. You will remember that I sent you a fair amount of revised exercises for *U.P.* last summer. If that material, you feel, is any good, then I could promise to bring up my part of the *Approach* during the fall, for the material I sent you was done in about three days with a secretary. I know therefore that it goes fast. But you will have to judge its quality. If much rewriting is involved, then that might run into time.

To sum up: I think that I could hope to finish my part of the H.B. book *and* the revisions of the *Approach* together by March. I don't believe I'm oversanguine. Certainly I have learned this lesson: to avoid any more commitments—even the most innocent, until those projects are complete.

The latest item contributing to my education in this matter is a paper which I contracted to do for the *English Institute* for this September's meeting. It looked easy, but it has been sheer hell. I've been trying to make an examination of Marvell's "Horatian Ode" for Mizener's program on the relation of critical to historical method.

I am about to finish up, and I have a proposal to make—for a little book to be done—*after* March 1947. It grows out of your talk last winter about a piece of Marvell you were meditating. When you've published it, couldn't we gather up our point and separate analyses [p. 3] on Marvell to bring out, with little extra work, a really nice small edition of the *Miscellaneous Poems, 1681,* with each poem analyzed, briefly or at length as the case might demand, and with a 10,000 word epilogue on Marvell as a poet?

The Horatian Ode has been hard to do, because, in addition to the complexities of the poem itself, I have had to examine the whole political career of Marvell and I have been surprised to see how complicated the issues are. But don't give an answer until you have seen my piece on the "Horatian Ode." *That* may give a *no* to me as well as you.

By the way, can't you arrange your trip to N.Y. to coincide with the English Institute meetings (Sept. 9–13)? It would be fun to have the meeting with you all, and Fred Crofts has suggested that he would like to have a talk with both of us about some new idea that he has for managing the disposition of the *Approach* and the Purser interest in it.

Give our best to Cinina, Robb, John, and Passinetti.

As ever,
Cleanth

P.S. I enclose a little piece on Corbet's "Fairies Farewell"[1] which you may not have seen, and I shall send another for John.

[OH]   October 31 [1946]
Dear Red—

It was good to see you and Cinina, even for a little while. We wish that the sessions could have been longer. Perhaps in the future they can be.

But this letter is not to that but to let you know that I have not been idle, though my long silence may have given you that impression. Except for ten days that I took out to read proof of *The Well Wrought Urn* (publication early next year, according to Albert), I have been working at the composition book.

1. Richard Corbet's "The Fairies' Farewell" appears in *Understanding Poetry* (1950), 250–52.

I am afraid that in undertaking to do a simplified (or rationalized) section on grammar, I bit off much more than I can comfortably chew. It is the very devil: for it is not merely the job of cutting straight roads through a tangle; you yourself are part of the tangle. I have had a few triumphs: that is, I see a way to eliminate any mention of the subjunctive by giving a couple of simple rules which account for all the "subjunctive" use now still alive. But on many points I am not sure that my simplification actually simplifies. But I have gone so far, that it is easier to try to finish up this draft and let you see what has been accomplished. Then we can retain whatever seems to you of value and drop back on conventional terminology and treatment for the rest.

In brief: the scheme that I have in mind would throw less weight on grammar (the rules governing what is possible in English) and much more on rhetoric (the art governing what is best in a given context) and on idioms and usage (the matters which come under no rule).

[p. 2] I think that I shall enclose my tentative prolegomena and my treatment of the parts of speech with this letter. The rest I shall hope to send on a little later when it is straightened out and typed up.

The other chapters ought to go much, much faster. I shall keep steadily at it. I am still aiming for the January 1 deadline.

And now a few words further on your chapter on logic. There are some passages in Richards' *Interpretation in Teaching* which say very well what I was trying to tell you in New York. I type them for you here:

. . . .

I think that there is a moral in this for us. I know that the passage (and others like it in *Interpretation in Teaching*) will scarcely help you write the chapter on logic. But I think it may serve to justify your treating strict logical prose as a relatively sophisticated and special form.

I have been rereading *All the King's Men* with increased enjoyment and admiration. Bob H. and I are to have a long session on it in preparation for his review of the reviewers of *A. the K. M.* which he is doing for the *Sewanee.*[1] Bob tells me that John Palmer says that I suggested that he arrange for such a piece. I don't remember it, but I think it's a good idea anyway, and John has chosen admirably in getting Heilman to do it.

Yale has announced my appointment and I have notified Kirby. Actually, I think the news has been out to all intents and effects for some time.

Tinkum continues to work much too hard, but joins me in all cordial greetings to you and Cinina.

As ever,
Cleanth

P.S. Remember that the fragment enclosed is tentative and a fragment. I am so uncertain about what I am doing that I don't want to spend time at this point in rewriting. (If adopted, of course, it would imply some changes in Chapter VIII.)

1. Robert Heilman, "Melpomene as Wallflower; or, The Reading of Tragedy," *Sewanee Review* 55 (January–March 1947): 154–66.

1532 Waverly Place
Minneapolis, Minnesota
November 22, 1946

Dear Cleanth:

I have been pretty harried lately, and so am behind on my correspondence. I have studied your revision of English grammar, however, and feel that it is on the right line. Whether it would have to be modified to keep from scaring off too many sales I don't know.

This raises a question. Jimmy Reid was here about ten days ago and I had a long talk with him about the book. You recall that last September something was said by us to him about the possibility of a third collaborator, or perhaps a limited collaborator who might take over, say, the grammar and punctuation sections, and maybe a little more. Nothing was settled at that time, and I have no views on the subject now. But Reid suggests that *if* we want a collaborator Whitehall (John Ransom's friend) at the University of Indiana is the man. He is a language student and all that. I told Reid that I saw no immediate reason for taking on a collaborator but that I would consult with you and be guided by your feeling in the matter. If you want to work with somebody on the whole question of a streamlined grammar, it is OK with yours truly. And I do think that Whitehall is about as good a man as we could find. He is aware of the things which most language people never dream about. I did tell Reid that if we took him on as a collaborator the split would probably not be a third even, for you and I already have a pretty heavy investment in the project. And he agreed to that. He had another suggestion, too. To have Whitehall serve as reader or adviser on the book for a flat fee, which, I assume, HB will pay. This strikes me as perfect sense. I should feel much happier about the book if not one but several very competent people had gone over it with a fine-toothed comb. I know that there are plenty of lapses and lags in my stuff, and a new look by a new man might do a lot to help. Let me hear pretty quick about your feelings on these two propositions, for Reid has asked for a decision.

Marcus wrote me a little time back about this idea of a royalty split for contributors for the SR anthology rather than a flat fee. This would suit me, of course, if it would suit the publishers who control the copyrights. So for a test on the point, I have written to Lambert Davis to find out if HB would accept such a proposal; they are the key firm, for they hold more rights than anybody else. I shall report to you as soon as I hear.

You will find here a copy of my chapter on narration. It may not stink but it certainly does not smell like a Night in Paris, Guilty Secret, Tabu, Indiscretion or any of the more highly advertised cock-teasing lotions. It does not even smell like talcum powder. Like [p. 2] everything else I have written for this book, it looks as though somebody had been trying to make a Swiss cuckoo clock, with a gadget to tell the weather for tomorrow, with a fire-ax as his only tool and lumber from a dismantled privy as his only material. Whenever you get ready sail into it with a pencil and revise and correct, etc. I am trusting you to save me from myself. Meanwhile I have driven on into the chapter on exposition and am approaching the end. My chapters are running so God damned long. The one on description ran about seventy-five pages, and exposition promises to be longer still. I have to write the stuff out pretty full, however, to see what I am doing. Maybe you can see ways to reduce. Or perhaps we should let reduction (not revision) wait for the critic.

By the way, have you seen the following books:

Direct Communication, Written and Spoken. Robert Gorham Davis, F. G. Fassett, William Greene, Frederick Packard, and Mark Schorer—Heath and Company.

Language in Action. S. I. Hayakawa—Harcourt Brace.

The Art of Plain Talk. Rudolph Flesch—Harpers.

A Preface to Logic. Morris Cohen—Holt.

Language Habits in Human Affairs. Irving J. Lee—Harpers.

Some of them might be helpful.

Things go along with us. Nothing to complain about except a dull ache all over and exquisite boredom with this text book. Let's finish the damned thing off and make a fortune and spend all the money on high test bourbon to take the taste of the thing out of the mouth. Why can't we be comfortably collaborating on Willie Shakespeare or just doing nothing? But it ought to be over before too long. By the way, Wilbur told me that the Approach is selling like nobody's business, a vast sum due in royalty in January. Maybe that will cheer you up.

Let us hear how things go with you all. It'll be nice when you all get to New Haven. That has NYC as a common ground with Minneapolis. I can occasionally get an errand in that neighborhood.

So long, and all the best to you both.

As ever,
Red

1532 Waverly Place
Minneapolis, Minnesota
December 4, 1946

Dear Cleanth:

You are going to be surprised when you see the winter *Kenyon Review* to find some of your words appearing there without quotes and not over your name. The story is this. A year or so ago Scribners asked me to do an introduction to an edition of Hemingway's *A Farewell to Arms.*[1] I did the piece and incorporated in it several pages of our piece on Hemingway. I read the piece last summer to a club at Kenyon and John asked me for part of it for the *Kenyon.* I sent it to him this fall as a chunk to let him make some cuts. In the proof I cut the section which came out of our essay, but John has

1. The edition, published in 1949, was part of Scribner's Modern Standard Authors Series.

recently notified me that he restored it—the section on style—and will run it. I had not told him why I made the cut and so he didn't understand that I had other motives than a desire for economy. So it will appear there without acknowledgment. When—and if—the thing appears in the book I want to do the thing differently. Shall I simply run a note to the effect that several pages are the result of our collaboration and get permission from Crofts? I didn't recast the material because I was sure that I couldn't improve it, and a recasting would simply have been a dodge, a mere verbal change. What do you think is the best way to handle it? If you think a recasting is the best thing to do, I shall be happy to undertake it. It wouldn't, of course, be hard to do. As for the general piece, though there are some traces here and there of our original phrasing, other than in the section I refer to, the line of the essay is different for a different occasion. I am concerned for a large part with defining Hemingway's role as a religious writer and in applying this notion to the particular novel. But you will recognize a lot on the business of the typical hero and on the matter of style. The whole piece runs about 13,000 words, and I imagine that altogether about 1,500 words repeat, or stay pretty close to, our original version. But I'll send you the thing when I get a decent copy back. As far as the *Kenyon* is concerned, however, I let the thing slip up and all I can do is crave your indulgence for an old pal.

I wrote Marcus recently that Harcourt Brace is in principle willing to deal with us on the SR anthology on a royalty basis—1% for a story and say about 2% on a novelette. I felt, as I think I wrote you, that we had better get a publisher's reactions before we committed ourselves. I am willing to get down to that whenever you think good.

The text book moves slowly, but moves. I'll have another batch for you when the typist can get at it. What is your feeling on the Whitehall matter?

Best to you all,
Red

[Handwritten up left margin] How do your plans for New Haven go? And what other news do you have? Write when you can.

[Typed at top of page] PS. Tom Kirby recently wrote me about the possibility of returning to LSU. I really appreciate the letter.

[OH]   Louisiana State University
                                                      Department of English
                                                    Baton Rouge, Louisiana
                                                       December 9 [1946]

Dear Red—

This is being written aboard the train taking me up to Memphis to address the Academic Deans of the South—whatever they are!—at their meeting tomorrow. The roadbed is not of the smoothest; but I hope you can make out this scrawl.

Your letter came today. There is not the slightest need for you to be concerned about overlaps on the Hemingway piece—there is no need even of a note. If you have to have a note anyway for the Crofts' acknowledgment, a brief and very simple note will take care of everything. Incidentally, I'm very anxious to see what you will say. As I wrote you, your Faulkner piece was superb.

I hope to have the rest of the grammar section typed soon and the metaphor chapter typed to send you. I am working at it steadily, but it goes very slowly. I think that the time I have put in on the grammar is not wholly wasted—I have at least a much clearer idea of what we can do and can't. I see a number of short-cuts which I think we can incorporate, even if we have to fall back on a much more modest treatment along the lines of the conventional system.

I had thought for some time that we ought to have [p. 2] some specialist read the material. It had occurred to me that Marquardt of Michigan might be the man. He is able—is sympathetic with the attempt to write a functional grammar, etc. But Whitehall suits me fine if he suits you. I knew John's high opinion of him: I did not know that he was a specialist in syntax and grammar, thinking of him as an expert on the history of sounds. But this is simply my ignorance. Suppose we settle for him. I am inclined to argue with you that a flat fee—even if a substantial fee—is the best way to handle matters. I am mortified somewhat that I can't put this section in fine order myself—you have had to carry so much of the load. But as you know, this subject is a life's work in itself. Do try, however, to give me your opinion on some of the grammar section that I have done so that we will be able to indicate to Whitehall what we want and what we are driving at.

A hasty reading of your narration section indicates that it's mighty fine. The detailed reading with marginal notations will have to come later.

I shall have a conference with Marcus later in the week about the S.R. anthology and write you at once minutes on our discussion.

Our plans for Yale are still very hazy. I don't *have* to be there until September 1947. We'll probably be moving sometime during the summer. The news is of course out—and seems to be stirring up some repercussions here.

Tinkum joins me in cordial regards to you both.

Cleanth

[At top of p. 1] Little news: Hatcher has been in the hospital for over two weeks with apparently a serious ailment—we think so, since everything is so elaborately covered up. The buzzards are sailing in close spirals now. But the poor fellow may pull through. Yet the parallel with the General's illness is ominous. I shall not be surprised to be waked up with a simultaneous announcement of H's resignation and the name of the new president. Here, they don't even wait for "The K. is dead" to bellow "Long live the K." It's shortened to "Long live the new King."

[At top of p. 2] I take advantage of this stop for another note in finer writing. The Basso article in *Life*[1] is a pigpen, isn't it? Somebody needs to go over literary Manhattan with a vacuum cleaner.

---

1. Hamilton Basso, "The Huey Long Legend," *Life*, December 9, 1946, pp. 106–8, 110, 112, 115–16, 118–21.

[OH]

Louisiana State University
Department of English
Baton Rouge, Louisiana
January 20 [1947]

Dear Red—

I enclose a rough draft—very rough—of the metaphor chapter. It needs rewriting, I know. But I want to let you see it before I go further with it. Do let me have some general comments on it soon. I hope to send later in the week the rest of what I have on the tentative grammar chapter. The rest of the fragment will allow us to get down to cases on the Whitehall matter.

I hope to have soon the rough draft of the tone chapter which I shall send as soon as I can get a typed draft.

I am sorry to be so abominably slow. But I have been beset from every quarter. The drama book is almost finished—even to texts and final drafts. When Bob and I have that out of the way in the next week or so, I can give unlimited time to this book. That <will> make, for me, a real difference.

[p. 2] Let me praise once more your *A.M.* book. It reads very well indeed—I have reread it. And Albert has done a fine job of bookmaking on it.

The Well Wrought Urn, he tells me, will be ready next month. Naturally I have a copy for you and Cinina.

The wild rice was delightful. We are both of us completely immersed in work. I begin to look forward to next year (academic year) as a release from drudgery rather than as more. No future year could be more tangled than this one has been.

Regards to you both,
In haste,
Cleanth

I have reviewed your (*A.K.M.*) book here twice, and I am told by one of the bookstores, it has had a little effect. At any rate, the B.R. paper reviewed it (very favorably) just two days ago! The ice seems broken here at last. I have no doubt that there was a tacit conspiracy to hold down the sale.

1532 Waverly Place
Minneapolis, Minnesota
February 10, 1947

Dear Cleanth:

I have been very wicked about the text book. I didn't do a stroke on it, at least not enough to mention, during Christmas. I might as well break down and confess that I wrote a novelette in a burst of energy and relief after farting around with the problem of definition and the stages of argument, etc. until I was blue in face and ass. Now I have again turned blue in all parts, and am back at the text book. My typist has some stuff which she promises before too long, but she had to delay me because of work for the department and a thesis she had promised a time back. I am very depressed about the quality of the stuff I am turning out for the book. I am particularly depressed by the quality after rereading your chapter on metaphor. It is very good and clear. And, of course, sound doctrine.

My particular thoughts on the chapter are as follows:

(1) I believe that the writing might be thinned out just a little here and there—that vocabulary might be somewhat simplified in a few cases, not many, just here and there.

(2) It might be good strategy to add some simple cases of metaphorical usage. Stuff based say on slang usage. What do you mean to convey when you say, "The night is dark as a wolf's belly"? That sort of thing, with analyses. As an introduction to your more full-scale and sober analyses. Or the use of terms of endearment, etc. Just some kind of mooring of the discussion more specifically into ordinary usage and needs. You have all of this said; it is just a matter of a simpler set of tactics at one stage in the discussion. Probably before you treat the matter of bad metaphor at length. I don't know about the placing, but I feel that this ought to go into the discussion.

(3) This would mean a closer relating of the chapter to the question of tone. You touch on this, of course, in relation to *Hudibras*, for example, but the tie might be made more effective, etc.

(4) The chapter might be backed up with some exercises, making the student analyze good and ba[d] usage of metaphor in both prose and poetry, single examples, and examples of passages. In the passages, the problem of violations of tone, extension of tone, etc. might arise. Some leading comment on the exercises might be helpful in some cases.

[p. 2] (5) One point of theory preys on my mind a little. Not, I mean to say, that you need instruction in the theory, but merely a matter of presentation. In analyzing some of the cases of bad metaphor, you seem to imply that a metaphor must be extended, or be capable of extension, in connection with other metaphors in a passage to make a coherent picture. You see what I mean. The matter boils down to the question of mixed metaphor. When is metaphor mixed in a bad way? When is it allowable? I suppose it is a question of the kind of commitment the writer makes.

That is all that strikes me offhand. And these aren't fundamental objections, by a long shot. And to adjust the chapter to meet these objections, if they are well grounded, wouldn't mean much work. A matter of last-minute revision.

Well, it is a grim business, and I suppose the only thing is to sustain our courage by keeping our eyes firmly fixed on the dollar mark in the sky. Speaking of dollar marks, wasn't Crofts's last little offering rather encouraging? I suppose you curse me daily for luring you into this project. And I beat my breast. But I can only beat it because we have to do the thing in such isolation with none of the pleasures of conversation to sweeten the brew.

No news. Things rock along pretty well, except that I have a little too much to do and don't get it done well enough to make me happy.

Oh, while I think of it, Pier, who is still here, has about decided to go to Yale next year to finish off his American Ph.D. in Comparative Literature, hoping to get Wellek to supervise his dissertation, a book on the role of the artist-writer figure in 19th-century fiction. You can predict the nature of the study. He has given you as one of his references along with me, Mario Praz, and some others. I have seen the Praz letter, and it is very, very good. I know that you knew Pier only when he was a boy of twenty-one, and cannot speak of the development of the last eleven years. You have your own opinions, of course, but I might give you some facts, if you think they would be relevant. He took his Dottore in Lettere at Padua with first honors. He speaks well Italian, German, Swedish, French, and English, and has studied Latin for nine years and Greek for six. He has had two years of graduate study in this country, the year for the MA in American Literature at LSU, and a year at California after that. The last illness of his father called him back to Italy then, and, as you [know], the war trapped him in Europe. He has been here a year now, and has his first citizenship papers.

I saw Hornberger the other day, who told me that he had seen you in Chicago on your way back from Detroit. And this morning I got the announcement of the lecture. I'd like to see it, of course. And I am looking forward with the greatest interest to the *Well Wrought Urn*. By the way, speaking of our little projects, I just had a very courteous letter from Leslie Griggs, enclosing the ms of a review of my *Ancient Mariner* which he has done [for] the *Virginia Quarterly*.[1] Well, all I can learn from the letter and the review is simply that he and I don't communicate. He welshes a little on his old view that the poem doesn't mean *anything* and takes the position now that it simply can't mean very much. A. Warren says he is a nice guy, and I guess he is to write me so decently after my bad treatment of him, but Jesus, the English language just does serve as a vehicle of communication sometimes.

Best to you both from us both.

As ever,
Red

1532 Waverly Place
Minneapolis, Minnesota
February 24, 1947

Dear Cleanth:

This is a letter which I should have written long back. Last fall Allen and I realized that John Ransom will be sixty in 1948, and thought that it might be a nice thing to get a little literary birthday gift into shape with the help of some of his other friends. John Palmer says that he would be happy to offer the Sewanee for such a purpose. So we are trying to get together some essays on the subject of John's work by various old students and friends. You are a logical man to do a piece on John's criticism, or on some aspect of it. I know

1. Earl Leslie Griggs, "Date Shells and the Eye of the Critic," *Virginia Quarterly Review* 22 (April 1947): 297–301.

that you are snowed under with work, but I also know that you think this is a good occasion. How about aiming for June? Since Allen has secretarial help and a filing system he will receive the manuscripts and see that they are put in order.

The actual list of contributors isn't yet nailed absolutely down, but it will include (God and the contributors willing) Jarrell, Lowell, Peter Taylor, Matthiessen, Lytle, Marianne Moore, Merrill Moore, E. E. Cummings, Robert Graves, Herbert Read, MacLeish, Katherine Anne Porter, Wade, Davidson, Unger, Eliot, Frost, Owsley, Lanier, Bethurum, Beatty. If you have any hot suggestions, let me know. I have only one iron-bound, triple-dyed, brassplated thought: no Edd Winfield Parks.

Your letter about Pier has just come. Thanks very much for speaking your piece. Meanwhile Wellek has written again to say that he will do all possible, and the head of the California English Department has written to say that his letter is in and that he could go all the way, Pier having made two A pluses with him. So it looks pretty good. As far as you can tell about such matters.

I am starting another chapter of the text book, overwhelmed by a sense of my inadequacy. The damned thing can start so many fundamental questions, can't it?

I am going slowly mad. Quite literally. I never had as much to do in my life. If June finds me alive and well, I swear I'll take a rest cure.

Best to you all from us all. If my sabbatical comes through I'll see you in the summer or fall, God again willing.

As ever,
Red

[Typed at top of page] P.S. The Ransom issue is a dark secret. From all the world.

Louisiana State University
Department of English
Baton Rouge, Louisiana
February 28, 1947

Dear Red:

I need not tell you that I shall be happy, very happy indeed, to contribute to the Ransom number. {[Handwritten at bottom of page] My secretary sometimes garbles matters wonderfully. Forgive the many pen corrections.} I may very well take some other aspect of John's work rather than his criticism. But I shall start thinking about it at once and promise to get my piece ready in plenty of time. It ought to be a distinguished group of names, and if they would only come through—or three-quarters of those whom you name in your letter—the tribute ought to be resounding. John, of course, deserves no less than that.

Your next to last paragraph, in which you profess to be going slowly mad under the pressure of work, fairly takes the words out of my mouth. The difference would seem to be that you are getting something done—have something to show for it—whereas I seem to get no where at all. But I faithfully promise to get somewhere from now on with the textbook. Bob and I have finished up our commitment to Holt, I have written and delivered two papers which in a weak moment I contracted, and with the help of a secretary, I hope to have matters rolling steadily hence forward.

With regard to the chapter I sent in: The writing certainly can be, and ought to be, thinned. Examples from colloquial use had occurred to me before I finished up. But I was so anxious to deliver something into your hands that I simply didn't hold the chapter back for any further insertions and rewriting. I forgot to tell you that I had planned to add exercises to be printed at the end of the chapter.

Your point 5—the point of theory—is well taken. With your comment I can see now plainly that some wrong conclusions could well be drawn from the chapter as it stands; i.e., the implication that a metaphor must be extended or capable of extension. That, of course, is not what I mean to imply, and I shall take steps to protect us from that implication. By the bye, it is a very nasty problem here, and I am not satisfied with the treatment of any of [p. 2] us on the subject thus far, including our treatments in *U.P.* I shan't, of course, try to work out the matter fully in this book (though I think somebody ought to work at it soon), but I shall try to work out some comments which will at least not seem to commit us to a position which neither of us holds.

As to Whitehall, let me try to work out a fairly detailed letter on the subject of grammar to go along with those fragmentary actions which I have thus far prepared. In the letter I shall indicate what we would like to have done in such a chapter, and shall send it to you for your comment and suggestion. I take it that we are not *primarily* interested in pioneering toward a simplified grammar in this book, but if there are some simplifications which can be adopted without too much sense of radicalism, we should like to avail ourselves of them.

If the letter (re. Whitehall) which I shall send you seems to make sense, it could be sent on along with your suggestions to Whitehall or to Harcourt and then to Whitehall. It would give Harcourt and Whitehall some idea of what we would want specifically from him.

I am enclosing a copy of a paper which I delivered at Wayne University last month. Goodness knows there isn't much to the paper but the last part does have to do with Mr. Warren and it does have to do with one of Marse Warren's poems, and I should like you to see it even though I am afraid it shows all the earmarks of a hasty job.

I hope that Pier has success at Yale. Tinkum joins me in regards to both of you.

As ever,
CLEANTH

P.S. Next week I shall send you the Whitehall letter and I hope, soon after, the draft of the chapter on Tone.

P.S.S. As John may have told you, Robert Davis, who did the review of your book for the New York *Times*, has sent a very feeble reply for Palmer to print. Bob is answering it very briefly and very powerfully and I decided to put my oar in, not on the matter of the novel, but on the facts concerning the *Southern Review*. When the *Sewanee* appears, I think that you will be able to hear the squeals clear to Minneapolis, for I think that this pig has been caught definitely under the gate.

[OH]   Louisiana State University
                                                   Department of English
                                                   Baton Rouge, Louisiana
                                                   March 17 [1947]

Dear Red—

Here is the letter on the grammar section. Will you add your comments and queries and send it on to Whitehall? Perhaps the grammar sections which I sent to you ought to accompany it—not that I think that much is usable, but it might give him a better idea of what I have been fumbling toward. (If you have misplaced them, let me know and I will send him copies that I have here.)

I think that I am about to break the "tone" chapter open. What has troubled me thus far is the distinction between the writer's attitude toward his reader and his attitude toward his audience. Richards makes this distinction, you remember, and confines the term "tone" to the former. In our textbooks, however, we tended to identify tone with the latter. I believe that I now see why we did it and its justification, but attitude toward the reader has to be dealt with, especially in a book like *Purposive Writing* where much of the emphasis is on *rhetoric* rather than on *poetics*—works of practical persuasion rather than poems and stories. At any rate, I believe that I am beginning to get the tangle straightened out—so that I can make simple what I was afraid would have to remain cloudy or difficult. I shall not try the untangling here, but hope to send you the draft of the chapter soon. (I have most of the illustrations already chosen and individual comments on them done, as well as much of the writing on the [p. 2] chapter itself.)

Your letter of Mar. 14[1] has just come in this morning's mail. I shall send this one, therefore, to North Carolina. I wish that you were to be nearer. Peter has sent me a program and it would be nice to come myself, but it's impossible.

I am glad that you are to see Whitehall personally. Whitehall may conclude that not much simplification of our grammar section is possible—or that a great deal is; he may see it as a rather small task or a very long drawn out one. Any arrangement you make would suit me fine: to have him do the job for a fixed fee or for a percentage.

One thing only I believe is important to have him see: namely that we are not *anxious* to do a big pioneering job in rhetoric and grammar too—

---

1. Editor's note: I have been unable to locate this letter.

particularly if adding the grammar job would delay the book a long time. If we could do both without delaying the book too long or without frightening away too many adoptions, I for my part would like for us to do both.

If he says there's little to be done, I shall be glad to knock out a mechanical job—it would have to be that—or better, to have Whitehall do that for us. Let me repeat, whatever you decide will suit me fine.

I am anxious to see the logic chapter—another nasty job that fell to your share. I hope to have the Tone Chapter to you by that time.

All our best to both of you,
Cleanth

1532 Waverly Place
Minneapolis, Minnesota
April 8, 1947

Dear Cleanth:

Thank you very much for sending the stuff to me to show Whitehall. He is interested (sight unseen) in working on the book if we want him. I told him what you will read in the enclosed carbon of my last letter to him accompanying the manuscript to him. HB wants him as an adviser and critic. Time is getting on so that it would suit me, if it suits you, to bring him in as a collaborator. He took the line with me that he thought that you and I had had a year of grief with the thing already and that he would not expect to come in on an equal basis—that we might estimate his time as against our time and reach some percentage basis. But there is no commitment on either side, either literal or moral. If he can bring a fresh eye to bear on the mountainous chapters I have written and can reduce them and can do the grammar and punctuation sections and help in making selections for the readings with some accompanying exercises and analyses we ought to be through with the damned thing pretty quick. I can't bear the thought of dragging it on past summer. For one thing, I've got a Guggenheim and want to get to work on a new book. And I know that your case is identical with mine: you have projects on foot and are facing the move to New Haven. Lambert Davis, who was just here, says that the book ought to make a vast lot of dough. Which is fine. All I ask is that it make the dough and not quite disgrace us. When I think how pleasant even this chore would be if we could talk it out together and how terrible it is in grim solitude, I gnaw my knuckles. Well, let me hear from you. Meanwhile, you have my <wire> asking that you send copies of all your chapters except the one on metaphor to Whitehall (Indiana University, Bloomington). At the moment I can't lay hand to your other chapters.

In this package, as you see, there is a draft of my chapter on exposition, not quite finished. But I have the rest of it in very rough draft, and am starting on the argument chapter. I have had Castell go over the chapter for logical problems, and he gives it a pretty fair bill of health. Some minor inconsistencies which I can correct. The nominalist position about the nature of definition might be qualified by saying that this is a debatable matter or something of the sort, too. But the chapter is very cumbersome and needs streamlining. Anything you can do or suggest along this line will be welcome.

I am anxiously waiting to see the press on the Well Wrought Urn. The copy I ordered hasn't come yet, but I've had a look at O'Connor's, and it looks fine. The Sewanee has just come with your Marvell piece. I haven't read it, but I almost hate to: I have been projecting a Marvell piece with the Ode as the central fact.

[p. 2] No news that shakes the world. Our summer plans are unsettled. I have a sabbatical this June but haven't thought much beyond saying that I want to go abroad in the fall. With a good harvest this summer things ought to be possible by then, according to best reports.

Let me hear from you when you've had a chance to read this chapter and to think over the Whitehall matter. If you don't want the arrangement, it can be dropped without any embarrassment or ill will. Anyway, give me your thoughts on it.

Best to you all.

As ever,
Red

[OH]   April 21 [1947]
Dear Red—

A hasty note to say that I entirely approve of bringing in Whitehall as a collaborator. Any plan that you can suggest to him and to Harcourt will, I need not tell you, suit me.

I should have sent you this word earlier, but Katherine Anne has been with us for the last several days and I have simply not had time to write. (K.A. came a week ago, lectured last Wednesday, and leaves this Wednesday for Sewanee where she is to lecture. It has been fine to see her—she is radiant and apparently very well indeed these days. We wish that you all had been with us so that we might have renewed old times in Baton Rouge.)

I am anxious to know what you think of the Marvell piece. Even if you feel that it is basically right, it still leaves much to say. Long as it is, you will see that it is finally merely a "reading." What I should like to suggest once more is that when you have done the piece, or pieces, you have in mind, we might bring out a special kind of edition with analyses and a long 10,000 word summary piece on Marvell as a poet. But, as I seem to slip further behind with everything, it's foolish to propose something new. This, for me, has been a most discouragingly crowded year.

A belated copy of the new book [*The Well Wrought Urn*] has been dispatched to you and Cinina. I thought Reynal & H. had sent a copy. Sorry for the delay. T. joins me in cordial regards to you both.

Cleanth

Department of English
Louisiana State University
Baton Rouge, Louisiana
May 14, 1947

Dear Cleanth:

Some days ago I heard from Harold Whitehall. I should have written you immediately, but the last week has been rather confused and busy for me, and I let the time slip past. I am enclosing Whitehall's letter. Since he is prepared to take a good deal of the weight off of us—enough to give us a fighting chance of winding up the book pretty quickly. I am now in the chapter on Argument, but the fact that I have busted a wrist and cannot type is making progress very slow. But I have also been doing a good deal of reading around for material for the Anthology section. I am sending under separate cover copies of some of the stuff I have had typed up and which I submit for your remarks. I shall send other things within a few days.

I have told Whitehall that you would write him directly about his proposal for the part of the book he might do. I think you should make the decision here. Whatever you say is jake with me. Whitehall is a very decent and reasonable guy, and you need have no fear that he will get his back up if his plan does not fit exactly with your ideas.

I have been reading your book and find it engrossing. But more of this later when I have given it more thought and when I am able to type myself and do not have to depend on dictation.

Our best to you both.

As ever,
Red

[OH]   Louisiana State University
Department of English
Baton Rouge, Louisiana
May 16 [1947]

Dear Red—

First, belated congratulations on the Pulitzer! If I am not as thrilled as I might be, it is because I think you confer honor on it rather than the reverse. But it is good to see merit recognized, and I am very, very glad that they were sensible enough to make *A. the K. M.* their choice. The prestige is worth something. (Even though it *adds* no prestige in the circle of your friends, it does serve to introduce you to a much wider circle of readers.) Its repercussion on the sales of *A. the K. M.* ought to be powerful.

And congratulations, too, on the production of the play. Girault wrote in a detailed and lively account, and Arthur Mizener, in a letter a day or so ago, said that he had seen it and that it went over in fine fashion. Tinkum and I hope that you may get a Broadway production out of it.[1] Surely, everything conspires to make that a possibility now: a fine novel, widely read, Huey Long, the Pulitzer, and a brilliant production—even though on a university campus.

You deserve everything that has come to you! It is fine to see some of the things begin to come. Incidentally, the *Reveille*[2] here, which has an able editorship this year, has made certain that none of these items is lost on the L.S.U. audience.

[p. 2] I like Whitehall's plan very much. I would happily, for my part, have Whitehall, as he suggests, take over the language-grammar aspect of the book. I have been certain that a functional treatment of grammar and syntax was possible. I am delighted to see him give a positive statement to that effect in his letter. I do not know how it's to be done. Had I known, I might have finished the chapter on grammar myself. As it was I could only fumble toward a solution, but I have had, from the beginning, confidence that *someone* could do it. His letter is, therefore, for me the most heartening word that I have had.

Naturally, I want to feel free to suggest changes or additions (as I know you do, and as Whitehall himself will want us to do), but I expect I have little to offer. The only question that gives me any worry is the possibly increased size of the book—but that is part of a general problem to which you and I are contributing by the length of our own chapters. And it may well be that Harcourt Brace will decide that the book *has* to be this big. Anyway, that general problem can be settled later.

As for Whitehall's wanting to "confine the grammatical appendix to grammatical errors which actually occur in student writing and to ignore completely those which don't"—that [is] quite all right by me. Indeed it was toward such a goal that I was fumbling in my work on the grammar.

To sum up, all that Whitehall says about his general [p. 3] plan makes good sense to me. It will be a relief to have some one work out such a plan. I found that I had done too little freshman teaching of late and was too far removed from recent developments in linguistic theory to have much confidence in such short cuts as I would propose.

I have a typist at work on the "Situation" and "Tone" chapters and shall send [them] in shortly. Then, on to the next one. I am ashamed to see how I let my year be frittered away by letting myself in for short papers and reviews

1. The world premier for *All the King's Men* was held in 1947 at the University of Minnesota. The many productions that followed included one at the Dramatic Workshop of the New School for Social Research, New York, directed by Erwin Piscator, in 1948; another version, *Willie Stark: His Rise and Fall*, at the Margo Jones Theater, Dallas, Texas, with Aaron Frankel as managing director, in 1958; an off-Broadway production at the East 74th St. Theatre, New York, directed by Mark Schoenberg, in 1959; and a production at the Dallas Theater Center, *Prologue to "All the King's Men"* (chapter 4 of the novel), adapted and directed by Adrian Hall, in 1990.

2. The *Reveille* is the LSU student newspaper.

which each time were to take up "only a day or so" and which actually took up weeks.

I am not teaching this summer (and the regular term is nearly out). Unless the Yale move turns out to be harder than I now expect, I hope to get in lots of time this summer. Among other things I hope to prepare revisions of the *Approach* and *U.P.*—on which, in order to try to balance matters a little, I am planning to do the major portion of the work. (I shall want your revisions, but if I can give you pretty full drafts, your penciled suggestions and additions would not have to take up too much of your time.)

May all go well with your plans for next year. It would be good to see you all before you get away—at least we must plan a good meeting when you all return. We shall be then in the East. T. joins in cordial regards to you both.

Cleanth

Gambier, Ohio
June 30, 1947

Dear Cleanth (and Fritz):

I have studied the chapter on Situation and Tone with lively satisfaction, and have very little to offer in the way of adverse comment. My chief remarks there concern the choice of two examples, that by Thomas Browne and that from Swift (the second, as a matter of fact—Modest Proposal). The first is so far in style from anything which a freshman or sophomore will ever undertake to write that I cannot help but feel that its inclusion will seem pedantic to a good many of our possible customers. The second is good in itself for the purpose suggested, but the occasion is so remote that I feel the need of a more modern piece here or at least a piece with a simpler occasion, one that needs less explanation, etc. I feel fairly strongly on both these points. On a third I do not feel very strongly but I'll mention it anyway, that from Alexander Hamilton. In fact, it is probably good enough. But it might be possible to get a better example of the same thing, one in which you don't have to dig so deep to make the point, one in which the focal bits of "tone" could be more readily identified. I know that hunting examples is the great time-killer and that you finally take things out of weariness or desperation—at least, I do.

I have no doubt that the material on pages 39–40 is extremely valuable for teachers. But I do have some doubt that it is—at least as given—well adapted for our students. I said the "material"—that is wrong. I should have said that this stuff probably needs a little simplification. But not sure.

I also have some suggestions for another section for the chapter and for some exercises.

(1) Why not add a short section on words and phrases which imply a bias of prejudice, etc.—the sort of poison which can be so easily smuggled into a piece of writing to color the whole thing? Such expressions really indicate the tone. In *Understanding English: An Introduction to Semantics*, by F. A. Philbrick

(Macmillan), there is a nice little chapter on "bias words." He does not use them in relation to tone but we might do so with advantage. For instance, he sets up a scheme like this to illustrate:

FAVORABLE	NEUTRAL	UNFAVORABLE
leader of the people	party leader	demagogue
tribune of the people, etc.	ringmaster	rabble-rouser, boss

. . . .

[p. 2] It seems to me that this is grist for our mill, and we might borrow directly from Philbrick. He also has a little bit, just a paragraph or two, on bias words and irony—the favorable word for the unfavorable fact—*aroma* or *perfume* for a stench. Or the reverse, which is, of course, rare, a form of humorous understatement for praise.

The same line of reasoning would give us a bit of the mock heroic in irony, etc. Couldn't this be developed a bit, with brief examples?

(2) What about the area from which imagery is drawn as a means for indicating tone? The famous lobster in Hudibras, for example. Elevation, mock elevation, detachment, denigration and belittlement—all these can be accomplished by means of the area from which imagery is drawn. And all these things are matters of tone. For example, Lamb's old lady and whist is a perfect case of the mock heroic irony based on the choice of an area for the imagery—military imagery, etc.

(3) The use of mixed vocabulary, mixed style, etc. to give comic, ironic, and other effects, some good.

Perhaps these are other things [that] might be treated as separate issues, with examples.

(4) The chapter probably needs some exercises, some brief quotations and some made-up sentences or passages which are to be investigated for key words or phrases indicating tone—bias words, imagery, etc. And further, the student might be sent to certain selections in our anthology section [to] locate other such devices.

I am about through with a chapter on argument which has given me fits. I hope to get copies off to you all within a week or so. If I can get a decent typist here to put it in shape. That means that I have now completed, in addition to the Introduction (I) and Nature of the Modes (II) the chapters on Description, Narration, Exposition (needs some revision), and Argument. Six chapters in all. I have also collected a rather large body of stuff for possible inclusion in the anthology section, and have typed up or clipped out most of it. I shall undertake to get the rest typed very soon for your opinions. This is all provisional, of course, and a lot of my stuff will have to be rejected in the last round-up. You all will have lots of suggestions, I know. But we can pool our stuff at the end. Perhaps Fritz and I can get together for a bit to work over the anthology section and cook up exercises and some analyses.

Now I shall push on to do a chapter on the paragraph, and shall follow that by the Appendix on the Whole Theme, Term Paper, Observation Reports, Book Reports, Outlines, etc. That will give me eight chapters as my contribution. OK, boys?

It is very important for me that you all read my stuff over for all sorts of things, style, organization, logic, and content. I have had one professional logician work through Exposition and I shall get one on Argument, but after you all go through this stuff, HB will probably put it through the hands of a critic. But I'm depending on you all to give it a rigorous examination, and to make revisions.

[p. 3] One of the questions you raise, Cleanth, has me greatly disturbed: that of length. Four of my chapters run up to 75 or 80 pages, and this means that they have to be cut. Several of the chapters are, of course, rather short, but Situation and Tone runs 44 pages, I see by the present count. And we have to have a pretty hefty anthology section. HB will allow us about 750–800 pages, I think, but even so we shall be very crowded. By God, I just can't condense my stuff in the early drafts. But it can probably be cut by a fresh hand.

Who will do the chapter on Rhythm? This could be, and would have to be, rather short. It may not be necessary at all, but it would be a new feature for such books, and could be a very useful one for a good many students. Fritz, I know that you are chock full of stuff on this point. Why don't you do a short chapter, which could be largely a collection of cunningly selected quotations which would almost tell their own story? Then this could be related to the question of tone.

Cleanth, I shall keep your MS around for reference. I presume that you don't need it back.

Well, I'll sign off, for the clock is striking midnight. God bless us one and all and let's finish this damned book and make a million dollars and blow it all on riotous living to recover our souls.

Yours,

Red

P.S. Who is to do the chapter on Style and Personality? For the life of me, I can't remember. My notion is that both of you ought to make contributions to it, and let one put it into final form. I say this because both of you have lots of ideas on that subject. Also, having looked back over the chapter on the Sentence, I am very much worried about it. There must be a simpler way into that.

MORE: Shouldn't the chapter Metaphor and the Word: Problems of Meaning, have a little dash of elementary semantics, as it were? Plus a section on usage, the business of using the dictionary, and that stuff?

And Cleanth: I have just read the new Sewanee, and want to say that your job on the Gregory book[1] is a very nifty performance. I must say that I may

---

1. "Poets as Historians," an unfavorable review of *A History of American Poetry, 1900–1940,* by Horace Gregory and Marya Zaturenska, *Sewanee Review* 55 (1947): 470–77.

not be a fair judge in the matter, for I can't help but be favorably inclined by your stout defense of me.

Things go pleasantly and busily here. Palmer comes up next week for a bit. Wish you were along. But I shall see you in the fall, in any case. Meanwhile, regards to you both.

[OH]   1707 Cloverdale
                                                                [Baton Rouge, La.]
                                                        Saturday [July 5, 1947]

Dear Red—

I suppose that I am snake-bit on this book. Thursday I lost—God knows where—my chapter on "Style and Personality" which was almost complete. Today, however, I have nearly twenty pages of it rewritten, and I expect to send you and Whitehall copies next week. Perhaps the loss of the first draft was a blessing—it was certainly no great shakes. I do think that this new version makes more sense.

At any rate I shall send you the chapter, for suggestions, cuts, additions, etc. It will be shorter than some of the other chapters, but perhaps that's to the good. More about those problems, however, in the letter which will accompany the draft.

What alarms me (rather than heartening me) is the fact that you have done so much and I so little. I can't accept an equal share of the royalties unless I can bring up my end a little better than I have. Fortunately, the first team is back in the game now. By dictating to Tinkum (who is through with her job) I have already tripled my rate of output. I can keep on hitting it at that rate henceforward. So prepare to push off some of the work on me rather than preparing to do the rest yourself.

And now for a few hasty suggestions.

[p. 2] The section on rhythm could easily be made a part of the chapter on style—unless you want a special chapter. In any case, I'll pitch in to it, if you like.

The chapter on the Sentence (VIII) can't really be revived until Whitehall indicates what he will do on grammar. Again I'll undertake (in collaboration with him—or, at least by discussing it with him) to see that this chapter is tidied up.

Your remarks and suggestions on "Tone" are certainly well taken. I'll do a rewrite (once the draft of the Ch. on Style has been mailed to you) incorporating your suggestions for this Chapter, and also those for "Metaphor."

Take a rest; go fishing; play a round of golf. But for God's sake let me pull a little more in the boat, now that I've got the oars going. (I never thought I'd write this: I haven't become suddenly energetic. I prefer Marse Warren's prose to my own. But I do have a lively sense of shame.)

Give our best to Cinina, Robb, and John. We wish that we could join you for a few days. If the new car for which we're angling should miraculously come in, perhaps we would.

I'll write next week when I mail you "Style and Personality."

Regards,
Cleanth

Gambier, Ohio
July 18, 1947

Dear Cleanth:

I have studied the chapter on Style pretty carefully and with general satisfaction. A lot more satisfaction than I felt when I reread my new chapter on argument the other day before taking it to the typist. What I have to say about your chapter is primarily a matter of additions, but I have a few words about revision of what already stands.

Revisions: I feel that there are a good many repetitions which could be eliminated. I know why the repetitions are there. Trying to make things stick. But even so, some of them might be eliminated and the statement here and there might be compressed. This kind of remark doesn't do much good unless documented, and I'll scribble a few things on the margin of the MS. I am inclined to think that the general remarks you make might be reduced to make room for more concrete illustrations and perhaps a closer gearing with the chapter on Tone. Also, some of the actual writing is not aimed at the freshman but at the instructor—for instance, the phrase about Carlyle—"melodramatic diction," which wouldn't convey much to the student.

Additions:

(1) What about starting the chapter with the discussion of the basis of a good workable and working, anonymous style? This would involve questions of clarity, usage and diction, syntax, etc. I am strongly inclined to say that you might look at some of the stuff in Rudolph Flesch's *The Art of Plain Talk* (Harper's, 1946) and some of the stuff in a book I have already mentioned to you (last letter) *Understanding English*. These with such things as the Graves book (which, of course, you use) might give some good leads and examples. The Flesch is especially suggestive, and you might lift some of his examples and rewritings. I don't mean to endorse him as a total job, for he falls into some of the errors of Graves in assuming an absolute ideal of style, but he is pretty cute sometimes and does some nice bits of revision. Also there are some good bits in Herbert Read's book on prose—I recall a passage quoted from Arnold Bennett and Read's analysis of it. Also, there are some touches in Munson's *American Prose Style* which might come in useful in the personality section. But I have got ahead of the game. To return: The first section of the chapter might deal exclusively with the good, clear, anonymous style. It might

discuss usage, the sort of thing one finds in a good handbook like Perrin.[1] It might show bad style revised, a batch of examples illustrating different kinds of badness. On this general subject Fritz Whitehall would probably have a lot of ready suggestions, and might even write the stuff for the first half of the chapter. I had raised the question of his doing the entire chapter, but if he did the first half it would relieve you a lot. And the second half you already have in the bag anyway.

(2) As for the second half (which you now have) it might take less, as I have said, of general discussion, and more concrete examples analyzed. Your stuff about Johnson, the races from Porter and Hemingway, etc. strike me as fine. But a little more of that might be useful, and you might make up some [t]ried cases of people saying the same thing in different styles. And the relation of style to audience as well as to personality might come in. And the whole business might be, as I said, more closely geared to the question of Tone. I found when I was doing a brief (and rather bad) section of Persuasion at the end of the chapter on Argument that I was relying heavily on your chapter on Tone. In the end I just passed the buck to that chapter.

[p. 2] (3) The chapter might carry some exercises. Make the student do some revisions of bad passages, drawn from standard sources or composed for the occasion. Make him find some bad passages in our body of selections and readings or in *our own prose* for criticism and possible revision. Give him a set of facts and ideas in synoptic form and have him embody them in several different kinds of style—loose and informal, humorous, formal, etc. Make him take a passage in one style and put it into another by locating the key words and phrases, the special rhythms, etc. and changing them. This chapter should come after chapters like Tone, Rhythm, etc., and could use all the resources acquired earlier. (I should have said earlier that the chapter on Metaphor and the Word could have embodied some problems of this sort, and could also be drawn now into the chapter on Style as one of the basic considerations.)

I am slamming all this down in a very dogmatic fashion, but you know how to take it. I'm sort of shooting at random hoping to hit on something which will suit you and Fritz. And I am more and more impressed with the danger we run in getting too abstract. Exercises and examples well chosen and tied together will do a lot for us.

By the way, I found a nice piece of rewriting to us[e] perhaps in our Readings, J. W. Beach rewriting some passages from John Dewey. I'll get those copied off and send along with a batch of readings when ready. I have assembled a lot of possible readings. Since we three can't be together, I am having them typed up, although I know that some of them won't be used in

1. Porter G. Perrin, *An Index to English* (Chicago: Scott, Foresman and Co., 1939), was revised with a longer title, *Writer's Guide and Index to English,* in 1942. Perrin was a professor at Colgate University at the time.

the end. This runs into a bit of money, but I'll keep a record (in fact we can all do so) and pool the expense at the end.

What do you think of these general notions?

A section from Ernie Pyle.

A section from William Laurence's *Dawn Over Zero* (official report of the creation of the atomic bomb, etc. Rather good).

A section from John Hersey's *Hiroshima*.

Christian Gauss on the limitations of science.

Two items from the Atlantic on the responsibility of scientists for military research

—should scientists strike?

Froude's account of the execution of Mary of Scots and a Catholic account (a good example of coloring and interpretation of narrative when the basic facts are the same).

Thurber on football.

A section from one of Strachey's Victorians for the poison word and irony.

Norman Angell on Pacifism, and a section from Aldous Huxley's book on the same subject for argument.

This is not a complete list. I have a lot more stuff gathered, but this indicates some lines. Please give me any suggestions you have and make any selections in typescript which you can as things occur to you. Then we can cull, the three of us at the end, and draw up exercises, analyses, and ties. If we sort of do it as we go along it will help a lot. By the way, do you know a good Catholic account of Mary's execution? I haven't found one.

This letter is a frightful hodgepodge. But maybe you all can make sense of it. I am sending a copy of it to Fritz along with your MS. He will no doubt have some comments to add to mine.

Meanwhile, all the best to you both.

Yrs.
Red

Gambier, Ohio
July 19, 1947

Dear Cleanth:

In my last note I forgot to mention that when John Palmer was here we talked over the project of the Ransom issue of the Sewanee. John says that he aims for Spring, 1948, but has to have his stuff in hand in early fall of this year. This is just a gentle jog to you. If the thing is to be done you simply have to be in it, and at length. I know that you are hag-ridden by work, but the occasion, as you know, is special. I am certain that in your case, knowing that the piece would definitely come, John Palmer could stretch the deadline. Forgive me for the jog.

Several pieces are already in, Matthiessen and Wallace Stevens I have seen.

Did I say that my chapter on Argument is in the hands of the typist? But she doesn't promise immediate delivery. The thing is long, about 85 pages, God help us. I am now working on the chapter on the Paragraph. It ought to be pretty short.

Yours in Christ,
Red

Louisiana State University
Department of English
Baton Rouge, Louisiana
July 31 [1947]

Dear Red (and Fritz)—

This note is a brief progress report. I have remodeled the chapter on "Metaphor and Word," more or less in line with Red's suggestions. I've added exercises on the use of the dictionary, as well as rather extensive exercises on metaphor itself at the end of the chapter. I think that I've managed to thin the discussion of a good deal and to make a little plainly the case for "functional metaphor." The opening of the chapter is certainly much easier now and I think maybe I've solved the matter of tying in a discussion of metaphor with that of diction, particularly in so far as the latter calls for exercises on the use of the dictionary. At any rate, the chapter is now being typed and I hope very shortly to have copies off to you. It won't lure old men from the chimney corner, God knows, or freshmen from Joe's Bar; but I think it's much nearer the chapter we want.

I have been reading stuff for a revision of the chapter on Tone, and shall start revising that one right away. I have read Philbrick and Flesch and Hugh Walpole's little book on semantics (which Richards tells me he thinks is the best brief introduction). Do you all know Altick's *Prefaces to Critical Reading* (Henry Holt)? It's much the same sort of thing and rather well done. I think that all of them tend to simplify the problems a little, particularly Flesch, who is a little brash and somewhat the boy with the new gadget. But I intend to use some of his (and the others') suggestions for illustrations involving rewriting passages. And I shall certainly work in some word lists on the order of Philbrick's early in the chapter.

I'll send copies of the revised Metaphor chapter to each of you in the next few days; then shortly after, I hope, revisions of that on Tone. The chapter on Style with both your comments has just come in. I'll save that for a later note.

All my best,
Cleanth

[Handwritten at top of page] Dear Red—I haven't forgotten the matter about which you talked to John Palmer recently. My contribution will certainly get in in time—I simply won't let it get left out. Fortunately I have a topic: a parallel between our friend's fine poetry and that of the young Milton. I think that there are real parallels, as my work on Milton's minor poetry during the last few years makes more and more plain to me. Naturally, I have nothing academic in mind. I would use the Milton, not to claim it as an influence but as a lever to use in order to open up for the reader what I call R's sense of "aesthetic distance." What do you think of this? T. joins me in good wishes to you, C., Robb, and John. We still don't have a car, nor definitely a New Haven house, though we *think* we have an apartment there.

Gambier, Ohio
August 18, 1947

Dear Cleanth and Fritz:

I have read several times the new chapter on Metaphor and the Word, and think that it is about nailed down. Very clear and effective. I have little to suggest by way of revision. What little follows:

(1) Exercises on word meanings might be extended. Why not set up some sentences in which words are used and misused, and ask that the student comment on the particular words underscored? Why not set up some exercises to fill in a blank from a multiple choice? These are pretty silly, maybe, but I think they might find favor with certain instructors, and it probably doesn't matter much how you make a student inspect meanings. Anyway, exercises make things look "practical."

(2) In discussing metaphor (pp. 31–32) as thinking, particularly as "naming" the new thing, why not give a little more example—"eye" o[f] needle, "jaws" of vice, etc. occur elsewhere but, as I seem to recall, not in this connection. And about metaphor as thinking, why not something about Richards's idea that big new ideas and insights frequently come as metaphor—not in the literary sense but because that is the only way they can come. Even scientific thinking may involve this—as well as scientific communication. For example, the discovery of the benzine ring—the dream. Cf. Whitehead and man's relation to nature. Then you could move on to the more literary and local uses which you handle so well (pp. 32 ff.).

(3) On p. 12 you say, "this is not to defend slang." Is slang as such to be defended or not defended. It is like defending trees—something which naturally exists and has its place in the order of things. Rather, isn't the question to understand the proper place of slang—occasion, style, etc. Of course, all of this is implicit in what you say (and may be explicit, but at the moment I don't recall it), and I don't pretend to instruct my old pal. But maybe a little discussion of slang would come in handily.

(4) First paragraph on p. 14: Is the metaphor itself good? Can one become entangled in wraiths? They have no substance, can offer no resistance, cannot restrain. "Entangling" seems to involve solidity.

(5) A matter of style: The repetition of the *id* in *acid* and *vapid* seems to imply some relation not in fact existing.

(6) I'm not sure that the metaphor from Vaughan on p. 37 is well chosen for the present purpose. Maybe not interesting enough for the freshman student. Not sure, however.

(7) Perhaps the relation of metaphor to tone (a direct connection with the chapter on Tone) might be indicated more positively.

(8) This does not have to do with anything in the chapter as it now exists. But what are we to do about a section on usage and diction as such? Idiom? Would it fall into this chapter? Should there be an appendix on the topics? Examples of common errors, explanations of some involving difficulty, etc. A practical section. This strikes me as important. Where should it go?

[p. 2] I have just finished a chapter on the paragraph, a few days ago, and it will be on the way this week; the typist is almost through with it. Meanwhile I have extended Chapter I by some twenty pages to provide a better (I hope) background for the succeeding material. We should all begin to give some thought to the over-all organization of the book, how it is to be used, how it constitutes a "course" or how several different kinds of courses could be set up for it. We ought to have a letter to the teacher explaining the ways to use the book. HB is keen on this. For instance, there is the great problem of the scale of the chapters on the modes. They will be too long for many classes and perhaps too advanced. Can they as they approximately stand be so divided that elementary classes can use the first part, and skip the rest? Some books give an early section on, say, simple exposition, and then later come to another section on advanced exposition. But that strikes me as unduly complicated and confusing. How do you all feel?

Cleanth, I am anxious to have your reactions to the chapter on Argument. HB is going to put the stuff in the hands of readers for new suggestions. Some of that should reach us soon.

Thanks, Fritz, for your letter. Will you go over Cleanth's chapter and send it to him at your earliest convenience? I have already sent him a copy of this letter, so you need not include that.

Best to you all,
Red

[OH]

Yale University
Department of English
231 Hall of Graduate Studies
New Haven, Connecticut
September 18 [1947]

Dear Red—

We got in here on the 13th. I saw Pier yesterday for a minute, and he gave me your present address. We're very anxious to have you all stay with us, and to stay long enough for a real visit. Our van of furniture has not yet got in, but it's overdue—surely, it will be in tomorrow. Once it comes, we shall very shortly be straight. We have a big apartment—really lots of room. We hope you and Cinina will make it headquarters while you're in this area.

We drove right through New York City the other day without stopping. Consequently, I've seen no one, though I have tried to phone Albert from here.

Do plan to stay with us as long as you can. T joins in love to you and Cinina.

In haste,
Cleanth

Hotel Marguery
270 Park Avenue
NYC
[October 1947]

Dear Cleanth:

I have been so pressed with interruptions and with work on my play that I haven't even answered your letter—or anybody else's. But now I begin to see some light. I shall be on the script of the play all next week, but Sunday (October 26) the first reading will occur. After that a few days of tinkering with timing, etc. ought to put me in the clear—unless the thing seems too God-awful in the reading. Casting should be finished by November 1.[1] About that time we should like mighty well to come to N[ew] H[aven] to see you all. We are looking forward to that as the reward for the work of the last few weeks. Does that date look all right for you all? Am sorry that I can't set it absolutely, but it will be another week before I know.

I am enclosing an appendix of the text book for you to consider. And I have picked up a good bit more stuff for possible use in the readings. When I come down there we can have a thorough analysis of our needs. HB now wants the MS by January 1. We ought to be able to make that, don't you think.

There are a thousand and one things to talk over, but I'll save them until we meet face to face. Meanwhile, our very best to you both.

As ever,
Red

Albergo Bel Soggiorno
Taormina, Sicily
Italy
February 21, 1948

Dear Cleanth:

I have already written you a letter air-mail of a more personal nature [February 20, 1948], and so shall confine this to our business. I am, as you see, enclosing the revised copy of the chapter on EXPOSITION. I am definitely not proud of this, but I feel that I have shot my wad on it. I might do better later, but for the moment, it is as good a job as I can do. In an earlier version Castell

---

1. Erwin Piscator had thought that *All the King's Men* would open December 17, 1947, at the Dramatic Workshop of the New School for Social Research; the opening was later changed to January 8, 1948; in a letter dated April 12, 1948, Piscator refers to the success of *All the King's Men* at the President Theatre since its actual opening on April 7, 1948.

gave it an OK, but I feel that it should get a reading by a professional, both from the point of view of howlers and from that of improved and simplified statement. Can you take this matter up with Jimmy Reid at Harcourt, or can you get a local professional to help out? (I know that there are some questions ignored in the chapter. For instance, the use of Mill's rules of determining cause are presented without any of the reservations which they demand, but they seem to be a good practical thing to put in. Or I have not distinguished in discussing cause between the "thing" and the "state of the thing" etc. And I imagine that there are slips and confusions which I know nothing of.) I have not prepared a clean manuscript because I am taking you at your word that your boy will have some time to give to our project. But I think that everything here is legible.

This chapter could do with some revision for style, and I hope that you and Fritz Whitehall will polish it up. Also you will notice on the MS that I have put some questions on the margin about the advisability of keeping in passages. Use your judgment on these matters. In a few cases I have left it up to you to fill in the exercises, and of course you will have to put in references to material in the READINGS. I have here a series of notes to you which I will list:

(1) Be sure to put in first chapter of Mill "On Liberty" and Newman's "Idea of a University" for both are analyzed in this chapter. With these in the READINGS should be one essay showing an extended definition.

(2) Put in an essay which begins with, or uses significantly, the derivation of a word as a step toward definition. See page 28 of this MS and fill in reference.

(3) Get permission to use the sentence quoted on page 33 of this MS from J. S. Huxley, RELIGION WITHOUT REVELATION, p. 137. London, Ernest Benn. I don't know the American publisher, if any.

(4) Rewrite note on page 35 of this MS to give fuller information if you think necessary.

(5) Will you write, if you think necessary, a student theme illustrating use of derivation of a word as a step toward definition[?] We seem to need an example of student theme for definition anyway.

(6) Locate and put in READINGS an essay giving an example of analysis as a dominant intention, and fill in reference on page 39 of this MS. Should there be here a short student theme, written by you? I seem to remember that in the possible selections for READINGS which I had typed up there is an anthropological essay which is a piece of analysis. You might check on this, for READINGS.

(7) Get an essay illustrating functional analysis for READINGS and insert reference at bottom of page 56 of this MS.

(8) I seem to remember that Bryce's "On Democracy" is a good example of the study of cause and effect. You can get the appropriate excerpt from the Freshman text book written and edited by Saidla, published (I think) by Harcourt Brace. Anyway, [p. 2] Jimmy Reid will know the book, even if HB does not publish it.

(9) I am enclosing an excellent little chapter called "The Colors That Animals Can See" from THE PERSONALITY OF ANIMALS, by H. Munro Fox, to be used in READINGS. It strikes me as interesting in itself and it gives a good example of some of Mill's rules of reason being used in a scientific experiment. It might be a good idea to look also in some other good popular scientific work for another selection of this sort.

(10) Fill in the information about Carmel, California, needed at bottom of page 7 of this MS, or write in a similar example to serve the purpose. I'm sorry I neglected to do this before leaving.

(11) I seem to remember that there are some good bits in Robert Graves's GOODBYE TO ALL THAT which might be useful for selections for READINGS, perhaps for autobiography.

That is all I have in my notes about the present chapter. And just before I left NY I read over the copy of the chapters ON DESCRIPTION and NARRATION, and found them long-winded and tedious. Will you undertake to cut them to your taste? For one thing, I am not sure that the summaries and recapitulations really help. Maybe they just complicate matters. And particularly in the chapter on description I may have been too elaborate in discussing combinations of point-of-view, etc. But my eyes were so dulled at the time that I don't trust my judgment. What I am really asking for is a good fresh critical reading by you and a merciless pencil.

I don't suppose there will be proofs for quite a while to come, but when they are ready you can send me a batch. I shall undertake to read them, too. The best address for me is care of Helen Strauss, The William Morris Agency, 1270 Sixth Avenue, New York City. She sends out everything air mail, and I can keep her informed by cable of any changes of address. If you have proofs to send you might send her a covering letter to be sure that they get out. Costs will be charged to my account there, so don't worry about that—about imposing on the agency.

To return to the question of the present chapter: Can you undertake to make the revisions necessary after the reading by the professional logician? For one thing I am without reference books here. For another thing, it would save a lot of time. And for a third, by God's grace, the revisions won't be drastic. Jesus, I have my fingers crossed here!

This is the only copy of the revised version of EXPOSITION. It might be a good idea to get your boy to make a copy before it goes out to a reader. There is some complication in numbering but a little attention will solve the difficulty.

This letter sounds very abrupt and arbitrary, but you know what I mean. I mean for you to use your best judgment and feel free to make any changes that seem good to you. And I hope to God I'm not dumping too much of the stuff on you. If I have, I'll try to make it up on the revision of our other stuff when I get back.

Cinina joins me in all the best to you both.

Red

P.S. Give a close squint at the talk in this chapter about "referent," etc. Is this consistent with our usage elsewhere in the book[?]
[Handwritten at top of p. 1] Cleanth: Check to see if original of Declaration of Independence, referred to on page 1, is parchment or vellum and correct text if necessary.

Albergo Bel Soggiorno
Taormina
March 4, 1948

Dear Cleanth:

In my scatterbrained way I forgot to add one suggested title for our reading section of the text book. As I remember things, you might get a good piece as an example of a special form from Agee's *Let Us Now Praise Famous Men*. Let me hear from you when you get the big batch of MS I sent, for though it was sent registered my mind is not completely at peace about it.

. . . .

Best to you all on all counts. Regards to René and Pier, etc.

Red

[Handwritten] Goodbye to all that.

March 8, 1948

Dear Red,

We were happy to know that you and Cinina arrived safely, for all the reports certainly indicated that it was a stormy season on the Atlantic. Sicily ought to be particularly nice at this time of the year. I was on the island twice, once for nearly a month, and found it as I know you all find it, charming and interesting.

A couple of weeks ago I had a long session with Jimmy Reid. Everything went well. I <made> out for him what was still to be done and what I proposed doing. We set April 1 as the deadline for all stuff to be in at the Harcourt Brace office. A final deadline set at July 1 will give time for whatever adjustments and rewritings are required. Whitehall has sent in two of his chapters which I think are very fine. I eagerly await the third and fourth chapters which he promises shortly, and these will tell the tale—that is, as to whether the functional grammar which he leads up to in his first chapters will actually work for our students.

His second chapter is brilliant but just a little condensed in spots, and I am making detailed rewritings to "thin" the chapter in a few places. I'll put them to him as suggestions, of course. I can't very well rewrite the chapter on the sentence until his chapters are in; and I am holding up the chapter on the paragraph for the same reason. But I have almost licked into shape, I fervently hope, the chapter on style and personality, cutting out a good deal of dead wood and other difficult material, rearranging the chapter radically, and incorporating a short section on prose rhythm.

Meantime I am trying to put the section of selections into shape. Thanks for the reference to the Ullman book and the Hemingway book on the Spanish War. I'll get them out of our library at once. But as I have been afraid, the book has grown on us, and I think that we may end up with more material than we can use. I have got from Jimmy Reid the absolute maximum pages that we can have—800—I am making word counts, and shall certainly try to make the very best disposition possible of the selections, making sure that all the kinds of writing are represented, etc. I'll send you later a table of contents of the selections indicating my final disposition for them, for your OK or suggestions. But don't worry about this matter or anything else connected with the book. I think that you have done more than your share of work and worry with it. Things go well, I am working steadily at it, and I mean to make the deadline without fail.

I shall, however, send you a copy soon of my rewritten style chapter, for I want you to feel satisfied with it before I count it settled.

[p. 2] My job as I see it from now on will be primarily that of pre-press man, adjusting, fitting together, perhaps even suggesting a few cuts—if we have to have them. And my proximity to N.Y. renders that job easier. In any case I shall be keeping in close touch with Jimmy Reid from now on out.

We hope that you all have a fine time in Sicily. Tinkum joins me in cordial regards to you both and in very special thanks for the copy of *The Circus in the Attic*, which came in, pronto.

As ever,
Cleanth

Albergo Bel Soggiorno
Taormina, Sicily
Italy
March 17, 1948

Dear Cleanth:

Another note on our selections section. In looking over some of my papers yesterday I came across a suggestion I had written to myself but not passed on to you. Take a look at Simeon Strunsky's *No Mean City*, and see if you don't think one of his essays on New York City might not give some interesting variety. I read the book two years ago and thought at the time that it offered some possibilities.

I have just had from Jimmie Reid a copy of a letter sent to Fritz Whitehall—I am sure you have seen it—trying to set up a final schedule. I gather from the letter that my stuff to you (the chapter on Exposition) has arrived, for he says that my sections are all in. If it has not arrived, please cable me, for I was beginning to worry. I was also pleased to observe that Reid thinks the book may have a big sale, and that he is not worried, apparently, about the size.

I know that you are busy as hell, and haven't time for idle correspondence, but if you have a moment, let me know how the book progresses and if you can get a fairly clean bill of health from the reader on my stuff.

Things go well here. I am into a new novel, rather different from anything I have previously done in technique, and am a little jittery, etc. After I have a few chapters I'd like to bother you with them. But maybe not until fall when we get back. I am seeing a good bit of the back country around here. I have made some friends of some young men who know this place well and who take rides or walks back into the hills with me to the villages. You get over the first ridge and Taormina and tourism might never have existed.

Cinina joins me in all the best to you both, and to Pier. Please tell Pier that I have written the letter to Yaddo for him, and shall write him soon.

As ever,
Red

Albergo Catullo
Sirmione, Lago di Garda
Italy
July 15, 1948

Dear Cleanth:

I have been remiss about writing, but the last two months have been pretty full of alarms and excursions of one kind and another. We went to Rome around the end of April and stayed until middle June. A great change from our quiet life of Taormina, for I plunged into smoke-filled rooms and wine-soaked trattorie. There were a lot of people I wanted to see in Rome, and I did find most of them in town. We saw a good deal of Mario Praz, who was very helpful and hospitable. Eleanor Clark, whom we knew in Washington and like a lot, was staying in Rome, recovering from a skiing accident of the winter (she almost busted up both legs, but will be all right), and we saw a lot of her, and something of some of the American Academy people. We got to know Alberto Moravia, who, I suppose, is the reigning Italian novelist, and he went around with us all the time. I found him very interesting. He is about forty. Spent most of his boyhood and young manhood in bed with TB of the bone, but he staged a fine recovery, is very vigorous, rather burly, enormously energetic. Only bad result a bum leg. But he can get about without a stick. I suppose the years cut off from the world have made him a little stand-offish, however. He is rather hard to know at first, but after a little turns into fine company, full of humor, loves to sit up all night and drink and argue. He is an extremely interesting writer. Then we had some pleasant times with Alvaro and some others. When the Erskines arrived, I stopped work, and set about with Peggy and Albert on their sightseeing. We had held off on that till they came. An old friend of Hunt Brown, a very learned old gentlem[an], took Peggy on a few tours, and when he didn't act as guide Moravia usually took over, for he and the Erskines seemed to hit it off from the first. About the middle of June we set out on a trip by car, the four of us—Assisi, Florence, Arezzo, Perugia, Bologna, Ravenna, Venice, Padua, Vicenza, Verona. We stayed five or six days in Florence, where Moravia joined us, and two or three days in Venice. We wound up here at Sirmione, where we have been since early July except for one trip to Milan, where the Erskines caught their train for Switzerland. (At Milan I had a session with Vittorini,[1] whose work I like very much and whom we shall visit at a village south of Genoa shortly before we sail.) The Devlins were waiting for us in Sirmione, and are still here, though poised on the brink of departure. Denis has to get back to his legation job in London, and Caren will go down to stay with Eleanor Clark at a village where she has holed up for the summer in the tower of a 16th-century Spanish coast fortress.

Naturally, I didn't get any work done on the trip, but before that time and for the last two weeks, I have been pretty steady at my new book[2] and now approach the half-way mark. The book is pretty crazy, but I can't tell yet whether it is crazy-bad or crazy-good. Albert has done some very helpful editorial and critical work on the early sections, but I've done a lot which he hasn't had a chance to think over. He just read seriously the hundred pages or so done in Sicily, and took a quick look at the other part. I'll probably be dumping some of it on you in the fall. I hope to get the back of the thing broken before we leave Sirmione in the middle of August, and have up enough momentum to carry me through in the midst of my academic obligations. With luck I'll finish the draft in January.

A note from Jimmy Reid told me that our text book was being read and criticized by some of their advisers, and that some cutting and revision would be in order. But I have heard nothing more, and don't even guess how things stand, how drastic must be the additional work, or when it should be done. What is the score there?

[p. 2] I suppose you all are at Gambier in the midst of the pow-wow. I'm damned sorry to miss that, for I'm sure it is pretty exciting. I am counting on you for a report, and the sooner the better. Drop me a note if you find time. We don't leave Sirmione until August 12.

We reach New York September 1. Will you all be in New Haven by that time? If so, we want to see you all, for we shall have a few days in NY before our run back to Minnesota, where I am due to report on September 15. I am beginning to think seriously of leaving after this year. BUT THIS IS UNDER THE HAT. Not because I don't like the place and haven't got the nearly perfect job for my purposes. But the climate is pretty severe for Cinina, as for a lot of people who aren't bred for it. And a couple of propositions have come my way. One is from Bob Heilman at Washington. It is not nailed down; he is

1. Cinina translated Elio Vittorini's novel *Il sempione strizza l'occhio al Frejus* (Blotner, *Robert Penn Warren*, 259).
2. The reference is to *World Enough and Time*, published by Random House on June 20, 1950.

having a problem of working out something with the administration about the part-time business, and it may not get worked out. Even if it is worked out, I can't predict what would happen. I am certainly not trying to screw something out of Minnesota, for they have done beautifully. It would just be a question of how things look some months from now. The West has a strong appeal for me, but there are certain disadvantages in being out there. So I am writing Bob that we can tell better in the fall. I'd certainly consider myself well off to be in a department which he was running. That is an attraction, I must say. But I don't know anything else about the gang there, except that he has just hired my friend Arnold Stein from Ohio State. The general tone of a department means a lot, especially after the hell we had at LSU.

Well, I've given you a good [d]ose of Billings. I hope to have some word about Mooney and his doings, hopes, fears, and aspirations. Write when you can. Cinina joins me in all the best to you both.

As ever,
Red

U of M
October 13, 1948

Dear Cleanth:

This is to report my progress, which has not been sensationally good. We got back about the first of the month, fagged out from the driving, to find, naturally, a great pile of little academic chores, bulging classes (I have 190 students in three classes, since I have inherited Beach's popular technique of the novel class to add to my own chicks), and no place to lay my head. The great Huntington Browns took us off the street, and after desperate effort we got two rooms in a residential hotel for the rest of this month, and the promise of a little apartment on November 1. But all of this hasn't helped my text book work very much.

I have rewritten and reorganized the Description chapter, cutting it drastically and I trust improving it. It seemed so damned dull when I read it over that I felt like taking out the pearl-handled revolver. It is now in the hands of the typist, and should be in the mails to McCallum next Monday for last-minute criticism. I'll try to send you a copy, too. I have about finished the Narration chapter, all but one small section which needs to be added to take care of the fiction objections, and some new examples. I have started the Exposition but am making very slow progress. It is a tough nut to crack. But I'll drive on. I make absolutely no engagements and work from dewy morn to eve, and curse God. I have the constant impression that everything I am doing is making matters worse. I know that you are equally pressed, but I am sure you are having better results.

Heilman has sent me a formal offer. At the moment I am so preoccupied with our little chore that I can't give the subject adequate thought, but I have asked him for a period of grace, say till January 1. I haven't yet had his reply.

The other flirtations are still going on, but I have asked for postponements, too.

By the way, do you by any chance have page 27 of Chapter IV, Narration? It is missing from my copy, as some of the critics noted. It has the last bit and my comments on the Jackson duel from Marquis James.

The weather, praise God, continues too perfect to be true. I suppose some morning soon we'll wake up to a blizzard.

Let me hear how you come. Meanwhile our best to you all.

Yours,
Red

[Typed at top of page] P.S. Later: I neglected to mail this, and can now add that I have finished Narration, except for finding two new examples I need—have extended the chapter somewhat to treat characterization. Had to. Am now well into revision of Exposition, but haven't really solved the problem. By the way, among our selections as now listed there seems to be no example of Analysis. We ought to have at least one good example. Have we such an example among the things we copied out but have not put in the table of contents?

U of M
November 6, 1948

Dear Cleanth:

I wrote you the other day and I thought enclosed a copy of a letter to McCallum about my chapters of the text book. But I have just found the carbon which was supposed to go to you. Here it is. It is largely self-explanatory. Will you examine my letter closely and let me know how you react, especially to the notion of making Exposition first, Argument second, etc. I believe that this may take the curse of being too literary off the book, especially since I have fed into Exposition a lot of examples about radar, electrons, a section from Einstein, and such definitely unliterary things. Then when the little pets come to some Proust or James or Conrad or the Holy Bible later on they won't feel that they have been too profoundly betrayed.

I am enclosing here a copy of an essay which will serve very well for an exercise in Argument, "Have Nations Any Morals?" by W. T. Stace. I don't mean this to take the place of your nomination of Becker's "Marxian Philosophy of History." Both would make very good pieces for Readings, and I propose that both be put in. I have already sent McCallum copies of both, but if you are making up the text on the Reading section, you might include them to make sure. All of this, if you see fit in your wisdom, etc. etc., old collaborator.

Forgive this illiterate note, but the hour is late, we are in the midst of moving, and the snail is definitely not on the thorn.

Our best to you both.

Yours,
Red

U of M
November 9, 1948

Dear Cleanth:

One question: Are we each supposed to secure copyright permissions for the material quoted in our chapters? I am prepared to go on that assumption but at the last minute I recall that you said that your boy would take care of copyrights. Or were you referring to the material in Readings? Or does my mind play me a trick? I have located a pretty good person whom I have hired as a sort of assistant—she has helped me with the revisions and is doing some research for me—who can do most of the permissions work. It is only that I don't want to duplicate anything. Will you let me know right away on this point? And I'll be grateful.

I had a note from McCallum yesterday saying that the stuff he had read looked all right, and I give a sigh of relief.

Best to you both,
Red

1315 Yale Station
New Haven, Conn.
Nov. something, 1948

Dear Red,

I am sorry to have been so slow in answering your good letter, but I am sure that I do not need to tell you why I've written no letters for the last two weeks. It has been nip and tuck, and the end is not yet. But I have sent in six chapters that I was revising and have now only one to go (plus, of course, the final layout of the exercises).

I am not too happy about the revisions; but the chapters are certainly better than they were, and I have reworked them several times. As you will remember, under the new scheme, I was to do a short introductory chapter on Style and follow it with a chapter on Diction, and reworked versions of the three old chapters—Metaphor, Tone and Situation, and "Style," now retitled "The Final Integration." I have carbons of all this revised matter for you, but think that I shall not send them immediately until I find out from Harcourt what our procedure is to be.

I much appreciate your letting me know about your possible plans for the future. Naturally I have been, and shall be, completely discreet, but I was able to get word to Bill DeVane (who is the dean of the College here) that if he had any notion of doing what he told me last fall he would like to do, it would be wise for him to work fast—that I knew you were being sought elsewhere and that my *guess* was that you might be interested. I was delighted to find the other day that he has the matter in his mind and perhaps is hard at work on it. What he can do, obviously, I don't know, but he is a powerful man when he sets his mind to something and I hope that he will be able to make arrangements. *Should* that happen, I need not tell you how much Tinkum and

I hope that you and Cinina would consider coming this way. I hope that you are in your apartment and able to get back to your novel. Tinkum joins me in all our best to you both.

As ever,
Cleanth

P.S. I had a very pleasant meeting with Faulkner in New York last week. He strikes me as a thoroughly fine person *as a person,* some of the legends to the contrary notwithstanding.

. . . .

Hampshire Arms Hotel
Minneapolis, Minnesota
December 2, 1948

Dear Cleanth:

Under considerable difficulties I have about finished all revision[s]—and they turned out to be a lot more complicated than I had anticipated. Once I started I began to see more and more things that needed change. But you know how it is. I am now mailing Description and Narration back to McCallum, and the first of the week shall get off the other chapters.

I have proofread all quotations in these chapters, and have located information about copyright—at least as far as I can go. I am enclosing a sheet for Description and Narration. Where items are crossed out, you can understand that the quotation is out of copyright or the length we use is under 75 or 80 words. McCallum said not to bother for things that short. But you will notice in two or three instances that I have given the English and not the American reference, Proust, for example. That means that only the English edition was available here. I have queried a few items on the left margin—when I was not sure whether copyright still holds.

NB: The section called "How to Detect Propaganda," now incorporated in Exposition, should be taken out and put in the general Readings section under the first group of informative articles. The reason for this switch is that I need to refer to the thing in the chapter on Argument, too. And besides the thing is too long to be incorporated in a chapter; it is a full length essay by itself.

Shall we give this book a dedication? If so, what about David Clay, since he had the original idea, etc., and is a friend of us both? Or is it pretentious to dedicate such a job as this?

No news except the old grind, falling arches, twinges of conscience, and metaphysical despair. I haven't even been able to try to make up my mind on the practical question I have to decide. But I'll try to go off and pray during the vacation.

I know that there are other things that should be said now, but my head is so fuzzy I can't think of them.

Our best to you all,
Red

[OH]   1315 Yale Station
                                                        Dec. 12, 1948

Dear Red—

I haven't written before because I have been putting every minute I could into the book. But a letter is long overdue and some of the matters I have to ask you about are pressing.

(1) By all means, let's dedicate the book to David Clay.

(2) Believe it or not, I haven't been able to find the selection you have in mind for Newman's "Idea of a University." I have the book of that title, but what is the "Discourse" or chapter? Thus far I haven't found one which has the excerpt which you quote in "Exposition."

(3) I enclose some of the exercises which are to be inserted in the chapters on "Tone" (XII), "Metaphor" (XI), and "The Final Integration" (XIII). The new chapter on "Diction" (X) is well equipped with exercises. With these exercises added, the last three chapters will have four or five sets of exercises apiece.

But the new exercises have been done in haste—under the lash, during the last two weeks; and I want you to see them before they are irretrievably in. Copies have been going in to Harcourt; I mailed the last set today. Here are the carbons—the only carbons I have. Do look them over, and save me, or both of us, from myself. It's been the very devil putting in exercises that would make use of the selections, and have some variety, and yet not be too difficult. *Metaphor* and *Tone* both have, of course, their original exercises at the end: many short passages illustrating metaphor and tone, to be discussed by the student.

(4) McCallum's estimate (given at our last meeting with him) on the space for selections totted up to about 110,000 words. We have even with the old list over 150,000 words. We might talk McCallum into more space, but, what with the expansions he has called for (extra exercises, etc.) and a full index, I think we are going to be even more crowded before it's over.

[p. 2] Hence, I submit the following proposed cuts for you to think over. (See enclosed carbons.) I comment specifically on one or two.

The Marquardt piece is good, but we're top-heavy now with [that] sort of material.

The Hickman piece (I have had it typed) is good, but it's 8,640 words. The excerpt from Ullman's book on mountain-climbing is not great prose. But it's exciting to the student, and best of all we can cut out a 3 or 4,000 word slice from the Mt. Everest expedition. That may be a saving worth having.

I can cut the Webb school piece down to 4,000 words—in a pinch.

I can cut the Wingfield account of the execution of Mary Queen of Scots even more if we have to.

If we leave the *Letters* category out, make the cuts I suggest, and manage to get a *short* example of the research piece, we'll still weigh in at around 140,000 words—30,000 more than McCallum allows. What do you think? I'm afraid to do less. We can always put material back in if we find that we have room.

Anyway let me have your best thoughts on the matter.

I hope that you and Cinina have a very merry Xmas. T. and I catch a train south on Thursday (the 16th). You can reach me at my mother's (3250 Carlotta St., Baton Rouge). I'll be back here by the 4th of January.

I've written again to DeVane about the possibility, and the need, for getting you here. So far there's no news. I have utter confidence in DeVane—in his attitude toward both me and you. (He raised the matter to me quite voluntarily.) But evidently the poor fellow has not been able to do much. I hate to see you get farther away. Anyway I still hope for something to break, though I know you must make your decision soon. I don't envy you that. I do hope that you make the best decision for yourself. Meantime, all my best,

Cleanth

[At top of p. 1] P.S. The permissions are coming in steadily with most of them *gratis.*

Hampshire Arms Hotel
Minneapolis, Minnesota
December 15, 1948

Dear Cleanth:

Your letter about the Readings and the set of questions and exercises has just come today. First, the exercises look all right to me, with one exception. Look at page XIII-51, on Gauss, section 3. You ask does Gauss possess "maturity and wisdom"? I don't know what your reader would make of this. Why not cut it entirely? Just this one question, I mean.

As for the Readings, I scarcely know what to say. I am inclined to say, at the moment, that we should keep the Hickman piece by Martin, and perhaps drop Ernie Pyle. My thinking would run like this. We have two other war pieces, Hersey and Laurence. Pyle may not be so hot after all, and he may not provide much for exercises that we couldn't get at in other ways. Martin is very good, and is the only piece of social reporting we have. Furthermore, it gives a very good exercise for the analysis of causes, as I have found out. (Who was responsible for the murder? Etc.) Against this is the popularity of Pyle. His piece may be good salesmanship for us.

It may cheer you to know that the first section—Article of Information and Observation—will not look too bare even with the Marquardt and Audubon cut, for I have shifted another item from Exposition to Readings—"The Causes of War," by Durant. It was too big a chunk to put in the chapter and has enough general interest to merit inclusion in the Readings. This does *not* increase our wordage. But I have increased the wordage to some extent in Exposition, by addition of new examples. They will have to make an estimate to find out exactly how much. To balance that, I cut some of my own text, but not enough.

The Letter section might just as well be out.

As for the research paper, I have made some effort to find a suitable one, and it is damned hard. Usually, the subject matter is so deadly for a freshman.

But I have observed that the best ones in other anthologies seem to come from historical journals—articles on incidents in American history. Why not take a crack at the Southwestern Historical Quarterly, Journal of Southern History, or one of the other journals of that type. Even the Southwest Review used to carry documented articles, didn't it? And God knows, some of those would be at the freshman level. Or what about an episode from one of Stanley Vestal's books? Doesn't he sometimes give citations, etc.?

Looking back over our list of contents, I spot only one piece which might get the axe, "A Lark's Flight," by Smith. I think that this has a certain value for our collection, but it is long, and that section of essay formal and informal is pretty full. Or could it be reduced? I haven't read it in so long I don't know that cuts are possible.

Let's aim at 140,000 and see if we can make McCallum swallow the bitter tea.

Needless to say, life has been hell lately. But you can testify to that fact under your own power. I have just sealed up the exposition chapter. It is greatly improved—I had to rewrite the whole thing once I got to tinkering with it. It [p. 2] was just too damned awful. I'm distressed about it yet, but I can't do more and remain sane. It got so I simply stared at the blank sheet and whimpered like a puppy with bugs in the brain. And meanwhile McCallum was wiring me in desperation. I am enclosing a carbon of my letter to McCallum which will indicate some of my bigger changes.

I'm disturbed that you wrote to DeVane on my account. Please don't push the thing. I'm truly embarrassed that you've done it. I'd hate to think that you had let friendship muddy the academic waters.

Well, I hope you all have a good Christmas, and I imagine that you will. We have about decided to stick here for the holidays, though we almost lit out for California. They are filming AKM now, and the director asked me out, but even my morbid curiosity isn't quite enough to stir us. And I've hell's own amount of work, courses for next term, to take care of.

Our best to you both. Let me have a note when you can.

Yours,
Red

[December 15, 1948]
[The following note is typed on the bottom and back of a letter from M. L. Stevens, Permissions Department, D. C. Heath and Company, dated December 14, 1948.]
[Handwritten] Red—Can you write them details—I don't have your quote on this.

Red, also—we're mixed on the Overstreet quotes: you say "H. A. Overstreet: from A Declaration of Interdependence, W. W. Norton, 12 paragraphs beginning 'How the masters, etc.' "
McCallum says:

1. *We Move in New Directions,* Overstreet, Norton, 1933
2. *A Declaration of Independence   "   "   1937

He does not give the length of either. Are there two? If so, how long is the first? Is it *Interdependence or Independence* for the second? Write me in Baton Rouge, 3250 Carlotta St. Leaving here tomorrow (16) back here Jan 4.

[On back of letter] Just can't find in this library the Einstein: Science, Philosophy and Religion, 1944. So can't write publisher. Will you do so and direct the reply here? (1315 Yale Station)

If I'd known this note would stretch out so, I would have indulged myself with a clean piece of paper.

[Handwritten] *Hiroshima* is out—no excerpts allowed at any price. This is the first blow.

Cleanth

Saturday, January 8, 1949

Dear Red,

We spent yesterday in New York, much of the time at Harcourt Brace where I addressed an embattled phalanx of Harcourt salesmen on the subject of the rhetoric—with good results, I think. McCallum, at any rate, exudes confidence and says he's bet good money that it will sell 20,000 copies in the first year.[1]

The permissions have been coming along very well with the usual delays and being sent from pillow to post and tracking some down. Thus far we've been refused only two—the Hiroshima you know about, and a bit of a New Yorker Profile in which I had fashioned an exercise. The fees have been decent, I think, and most of the short stuff has come free. But there are a few things hanging fire:

1. I have not been able to find Brownell's *Indian Races of North and South America* in the Yale Library. Will you send me at once publisher, description of piece, etc., or apply yourself at once.

2. Who published Einstein's *Science, Philosophy and Religion*? I take it that it is a book; but if the Yale Lib. has it, I can't find it. Will you handle this as above.

3. What is the address of the Institute of Propaganda Analysis? We wrote to them at Princeton on a guess; it was referred to Gallup,[2] who disclaims it.

---

1. McCallum may have won that bet. *Modern Rhetoric* was published April 28, 1949, with a first printing of 9,294 copies and subsequent impressions of 10,000 in July 1949, 10,600 in August 1949, and 15,450 in March 1950—a total first-year printing of 45,344 copies.
2. Donald C. Gallup was offered a position in the cataloging department at Yale in 1939. After an interruption to serve in the army in World War II and a brief return to teach at Southern Methodist University, he was appointed curator of the American Literature Collection and assistant professor of bibliography at Yale on July 1, 1947. From his work in Army Intelligence and his bibliographical work, he may have been a most logical choice to examine a document. See his memoirs, *Pigeons on the Granite* (1985).

4. You have a quote from Tolstoy's *War and Peace*, Book 3, Ch. 1. Who is the translator and who the publisher? Please give me info or handle it yourself.

5. We are in correspondence with Norton about the *Declaration of Interdependence*, but seem not to have asked them for Overstreet's *We Move in New Directions*. They require close identification of passage. Please send me identification material on this so we can complete correspondence with them.

6. Will Durant's "The Causes of War," from *Why Men Fight*, is unavailable here. Will you send all the dope on it, or write to his publisher directly. (You say it appeared in *Sat. Eve. Post*, but has it been collected?)

Everything else seems to be in hand or soon likely to be. We are having Harcourt phone some of the slow people in New York and will get out, what I hope will be a last batch of applications, today.

Two other points have come up. I have worked with the short headings that we had planned for the selections. I enclose the fruits of my labor, which smell like the cargo of a banana boat too long at sea. Having worked at them hard I have decided that they are worse than useless, and that to be made useful, they would have to be extended far beyond 500 words apiece. McCallum agrees with me and I plan to omit them, but I don't want to make this decision [p. 2] final until you have looked them over. The crux is this: there's no point in saying, for example, that a biography is the life of a man. That's too elementary even for our audience, but if you're going to do something useful then we have to go much further than the limit we have set. But run over them and if you feel as McC and I, do throw these in the wastebasket. They need not be returned. {[Handwritten in left margin] We need the space.}

There is a further point about the selections. I wonder whether it would not be wise to omit the Stevenson "Technical Elements of Style." Some of the stuff on rhythm and vowel effects is, I think, highly questionable, from the point of view of phonetics. For example, in his analysis of the passage from Milton's *Areopagitica*, he makes much of the use of *s* and *r*, though by my count, *t* is much more prominent. Worst of all, I think, that he is counting in *r* by the appearance of the letter when an *r* sound actually does not occur at all—e.g., vi*r*tue, une*r*cised, adve*r*sary. (Of course, Stevenson as a Scotsman, may have rolled these *r*'s, but then that introduces another complication. Our freshmen are not Scots.) On the other hand your references to the juggler's keeping the balls in the air may demand the retention of the essay. Anyway, it is ready to do in unless I hear otherwise from you.

I favor retaining "A Lark's Flight" because (1) selfishly, I don't want to have to rewrite one or two exercises that refer to it, and (2) we need a sample of the more formal and literary essay. The Hickman story stays in, as you have suggested. Note that I am putting in a little scrap from Ullman's Assault on Mt. Everest (from *High Conquest*) to help out the Reportage section—now that Baldwin's Titanic piece is out. With *Hiroshima* out I think we definitely need to retain the Ernie Pyle.

This is a hell of a time to raise such questions and the selections add up to such a total that I expect thunder from McC, but what else are we to do? I am searching for a short research paper to add as a final item. If you can find one or have found one, for goodness sake let me know.

Gauss has given permission for his "Threat of Science" which is excellent. Do you think we dare simply drop the fourth section of it? It would save 2 or 3,000 words and I don't think would affect the argument at all.

We hope you and Cinina had a fine Christmas. We are groggy from working on the permissions but have survived.

As ever,
Cleanth

Hampshire Arms Hotel
Minneapolis, Minnesota
January 15, 1949

Dear Cleanth:

First, here is the copy of the "Letter" with my suggestions. I have nothing very important in the way of revisions, simply some little cuts and verbal changes to make for simplicity—at least, that is my hope. I do feel that the paragraph on page 5 might go. I believe that it distracts from the main line, and everything it says is already implied above. And notice on page 6 that the last paragraph on the page may be brought up above. Further, I notice that sometimes "the authors" is used and sometimes "we." So I have made it consistent with "the authors." If you like the other tone better, it suits me, but perhaps it should be consistent. Also I suggest cutting out the "you" stuff on page 3. It struck me as a little out of tone. Perhaps not.

Second, would it be a good idea, before we start reading proof, to have an understanding on some questions of stylistic consistency? I tend—I think—to use the relative *that* as a restrictive. I say *tend,* because I am probably inconsistent as all hell. I notice in the "Letter" that you consistently use *which.* I notice that you do not put a comma after the *b,* in the *a, b,* and *c* series. I usually do. Those are two examples. And what shall we do about punctuation after introductory phrases and clauses? There is a good deal of inconsistency in our practice. What about keeping English spelling in quotes from English authors? I have no commitments in my own mind, but I do think that we ought to settle a few obvious matters like these and try to stick to them. If you will provide me with a list of items according to your practice, I shall endeavor to conform. You know, just the most obvious things.

And do you think it would be possible for me to read your proofs and you mine—after we have finished with our own. Or it might be simpler for HB to send each of us a complete set. I should certainly feel happier if I knew that your expert glance had wandered over my pages. Not merely to track down inconsistencies, but to catch lapses of style, etc.

Third, some copyright questions:

1. Do not worry about Brownell's *Indian Races*—pub. 1854.

2. I have written Will Durant direct about "Causes of War."

3. Tolstoy: my quotation is drawn from the translation by Louise and Aylmer Maude, Oxford University Press, as reprinted by Simon and Schuster and acknowledged by them. But the hell of it is that I don't know which quotation we finally used—in the text I have several marked—and none from Bk III, Ch. 1. Will you look at the Simon and Schuster text, page 919 or page 1320? It must be one of those quotations. Or send me a copy of the quote and I shall locate it and write Oxford.

[p. 2] 4. The Hale on Rommel is so short that we do not need a permission. Not more than seventy-five or a hundred words. But I am writing anyway.

5. Propaganda: I owned the little book this was drawn from, but several days of frantic search have not turned it up. I shall check the library Monday. Meanwhile, I have found another quote from the same book in another anthology, and observe that their acknowledgment only says "Institute for Propaganda Analysis" with no indication of place or author.

6. Einstein: I lifted this quotation from another anthology and a lot of looking has not turned up the book from which I originally got it so that I could check their acknowledgment. I have certainly dropped a stitch there. I'll do the best I can to locate and God help us. It might not be a bad idea to send me, if possible, the text of the Einstein quote so that I can have something definite to check by. Now I have to trust my memory.

Fourth, I agree with you about the little heads for the reading sections. They ought to go. There is no way to make them really useful in the space available. And that gives the dull instructor something to talk about, anyway.

Fifth, I agree with the cut of Stevenson's essay on style.

Sixth, I have hunted around a lot for a short research paper, and only just now have had a brilliant inspiration—to go to one of the historical journals for an account of some episode in American history. If you have one already wire me; if not I'll go ahead with my prowl.

Seventh, cut the Gauss if necessary—but I made an elaborate outline for this essay in the appendix on outline, and if the thing is cut the outline must be made consistent.

The only ray of cheer is your remark that McCallum expects to unload 20,000 copies the first year. He damned well better do that and continue to do that until we are old and gray or it won't be worth it. I got you into this. Can you ever forgive me?

I hope that this brings us up to date. I'm sorry to have created the trouble about the permissions. I'll do what I can.

No news, just existence. Our best to you both.

Red

P.S. I have been hunting desperately for a little example of an extended definition which wor[k]s from the derivation of a word, say something from a long paragraph to several paragraphs. Can you think of one? There is a gap in the text waiting for it.

[OH]   Yale University
                                                       Department of English
                                                          1315 Yale Station
                                                   New Haven, Connecticut
                                                            [January 1949]

Dear Red—

Here is the copy of the Becker piece which I suggested might be useful for illustrations in your Argument chapter. I've started work—though God knows that it's with groaning—and I hope to have the last four chapters in order soon. Then I shall attack the chapters on Paragraph and Sentence, and the Selections.

I wish that we had had more time for visiting and for general talk. It's a shame to get a mere glimpse of you and Cinina when there are so many things to ask you all about and to talk over. But perhaps we'll have better luck with visiting this year. At any rate, it was good to see you even briefly. T. joins me in all cordial regards to you both.

                                                                    Cleanth

[At top of page] P.S. I've just seen Bob Heilman's *Lear* book. It's handsomely printed and starts in fine fashion—I've had opportunity to do no more than look into it.

                                                     Hampshire Arms Hotel
                                                   Minneapolis, Minnesota
                                                          January 18, 1949

Dear Cleanth:

Since I wrote you I have been swatting away at historical journals in the hope of finding a research article for our readings. I covered the Journal of Southern History, Mississippi Valley Historical Review, and journals complete of several of the state societies. I am arranging in order of preference the items I dished up:

1. Manners and Humors of the American Frontier, by Thomas D. Clark, Missouri Historical Review, vol. 35, p. 3.

2. Amusements in the Republic of Texas, by William Ransom Hogan, Journal of Southern History, vol. 3, p. 397.

3. Life of the Common Soldier in the Union Army, 1861–65, by Fred B. Shannon, Mississippi Valley Historical Review, vol. 13, p. 463.

4. Humor of the Backwoods, by Philip D. Jordan, Mississippi Valley Historical Review, vol. 25, p. 25.

5. Frontiersman and Planter in the Formation of Kentucky, by John D. Barnhart, Journal of Southern History, vol. 7, p. 19.

6. Influence of Slavery upon the Methodist Church, by Walter Brownlow Posey, Mississippi Valley Historical Review, vol. 17, p. 530.

When I say that I have arranged these in order of preference, I refer merely to the intrinsic interest of the subject and readability, not to deeper matters. Number 1 is the best all around for our purposes, it strikes me. Probably number 5 is to be preferred to number 2—if I may change my mind at this date—though neither is written very well. (In fact, a survey of the writing in the historical journals is enough to chill the blood.) There is one problem in all of these—length. But any of them can be cut and the footnotes renumbered to take up slack. I know Thomas D. Clark (number 1) very well and am sure that he would let us tinker [with] his material in a good cause. I think we could cut him to about 3500 words or a little less.

I have made no headway with the Einstein or the Propaganda Analysis. More on this tomorrow.

So long and the best,
Red

Hampshire Arms
Minneapolis, Minnesota
January 18, 1949

Dear Cleanth:

Your wire came this morning. I'm sorry to be such a problem child, but I have been working at these references. After another session at the library I come up with the following results:

1. The quotation about propaganda, the essay rather, is drawn from *The Fine Art of Propaganda,* no author, issued by the Institute for Propaganda Analysis, 1939. The joke is on us—unless my information is faulty—for Harcourt Brace published the little book for the Institute. I am writing McCallum at this same time to ask him to instruct you about copyright, in case HB does not hold the copyright. Just [to] be sure, if I can be sure, I have dug up an old address for the Institute: 130 Morningside Drive, NYC. But this is ten years old or more. I should have written myself for the permission, but I do not have the text, do not know exactly what finally went into the book.

2. Einstein: I am not sure, but I think that the paragraph in question comes from an article by Einstein called "Personal God Concept Causes Science-Religion Conflict," in the *Science News Letter,* September 21, 1940. p. 181. You see, I do not have the text of the quotation and have to rely on my memory. If this is not right, will you please send me a copy of the text we are using so that I can try again. God knows, I buggered this business up, and I am abject. I have tried every Einstein reference I can get hands on, and this seems to be the one.

Goodbye. and all the best,
Red

[Handwritten beside each paragraph in left margin]: H.B. [followed by a check mark]

January 21, 1949

Dear Red,

I am sorry to have kept you so stirred up with telegrams recently, but I seem to live with urgency these days.

I'm sorry also to have put you to trouble about the research paper. I find that I looked over the same area that you have, and finally came up with one called "Spanish Horses among the Plains Tribes" by E. D. Worcester, in the *Pacific Historical Review*, XIV, 1945. It is not too long, it has lots of footnotes, and the style is simple but decent—decent at least as these things go. After several days of frantic searching, I simply got Tinkum to type it and sent it on in, since McCallum was calling loudly for a piece. I've written airmail for permission (which I assume will be forthcoming). Should it not be, I'll grab for the Clark piece, No. 1 on your list. I'm amused that your No. 1 and the piece I sent in are so much alike in scope, and so close also to the piece which Don Davidson has in his book. Anyway I'm sorry for the duplication of our effort, but I was afraid that I just wasn't going to find anything. I wanted to use a fine piece on the Drake plate found in California a few years ago, but it was 8400 words, and I feared couldn't well be cut.

As for other matters, we'll keep the fourth section of Gauss—have them set up the whole essay, but will cut out the Stevenson essay on style.

You're quite right about our needing a style sheet of a sort. Tinkum has questioned my use of the relative *which* and I have corrected it to *that* when it is restrictive in much of the material that I have sent in over the last months. But I am sure that I have not caught all the inconsistent uses, and when you read my proof, watch out for these. I'll count on your correcting them to your usage. Tinkum in her typing does not put a comma after B in the A, B, and C series. But I have caught and corrected all of these lapses, I believe, for my usage conforms with yours. Accordingly all the MS. I have turned in to Harcourt conforms. Let's agree on it at any rate, and we'll both watch for deviations when we read proof.

As for punctuation after introductory phrases and clauses, I tend to use commas pretty regularly. I probably use too many commas. I have no deep conviction on the point except that in expository prose of the sort we are writing, I am inclined to think that a heavy use of commas may promote clarity. As you think best on this. We might ask the style editor at Harcourt to help out here, and to try to pull the various chapters into some sort of consistency. I shall try in the next few days to get down a list of my usages and will send it to you.

[p. 2] You are perfectly right in thinking that each of us ought to read proof on the other's work. Some of my stuff I am not sure that you have seen at all, and I have not seen some of your last revisions. Any way I'll ask Harcourt to send each of us a complete set. I shall be free in making comments on your sections, and for God's sake use the sand-block on mine.

Thanks a lot for your corrections on the Letter to the Instructor. I am taking them to Harcourt in the morning. You've done a great deal to simplify the letter and I agree heartily in cutting out the paragraphs you suggest on p. 5. It is possible that Harcourt will argue that it should stay in, for they are very anxious to get in all the sales points possible. By the way, to indicate that last point and also the rush now going on, McCallum wrote himself two paragraphs dealing with the Selections and sent them to me the other day, asking that I OK them or rewrite them, and allow him to put them in the *Letter to the Instructor*. I had to tell him that he wrote better prose than I did, and rushed them back to him with minor alterations. But you can note them in proof and cut them out at that point if you think that they ought not go in.

You have asked me to check several of your quoted passages, and it may be that I can do that tomorrow at Harcourt, but I have no copy of your late stuff, and it is likely to be at the printer's now, so may not be available to me.

About the Beerbohm—Curtis Brown said we would have to deal with him directly, and supplied the address of their London branch who would forward a letter. They forwarded it to an address in England—Dorking something—but at that point it started back west, and was returned to me with a penciled notation, "Rapallo?" scrawled on it. Then I remembered that you had seen the old bird in Italy last summer, and so thought that you might be able to remember just where you saw him, and so write him. Hope this was clear enough for you to act on.

What with the work that we have done in separation during the last month, I feel like one head of a two headed monster, and that head wracked with a splitting headache. But we'll pray that it is all for best and rewrite the book in proof in so far as we have to. I'll send in the style sheet of my usages in a few days, and will expect a similar list from you. Meantime, Tinkum joins me in all best wishes to you and Cinina.

Cleanth

P.S. We got on to the radio broadcast of *All the King's Men* by accident but heard it all and enjoyed it immensely.[1]

Hampshire Arms Hotel
Minneapolis, Minnesota
January 26, 1949

Dear Cleanth:

I am enclosing the permission from Will Durant for our section, "The Causes of War," from his article "Why Men Fight"—in the Saturday Evening Post. I have written to the Post to clear it with them, though if Durant is the copyright holder I don't see where the Post enters.

---

1. Claris A. Ross, NBC Script Department, wrote Warren about broadcasting a one-hour adaptation of *All the King's Men*, based on the play script, in January 1949.

A letter is out to Norton about the Overstreet quotation. I had hell's own time getting the passage located. Like an idiot I had let the source escape me.

The first batch of proofs have just come, and I am digging in tomorrow with them. I have already looked at my first two or three galleys, and am appalled by the dull style. Please catch anything you can in the way of poor phrasing, etc. in my sections.

Best to you both,
Red

January 27, 1949

Dear Red,

There are still a couple of permissions matters that I'm fuzzy on:

1. *How We Think* by John Dewey. All I have on this is my original letter to D.C. Heath, 285 Columbus Ave., Boston, 16, Mass. written Dec. 13, asking for ten unidentified paragraphs. Though I can find nothing else on this, I have the strong feeling that they replied asking for identifying material and I then asked you about it. Did this happen, or did I dream it? Will you, in any case, identify the passage (p. numbers) and let me know, so I can expedite this?

2. Also, can we get this Overstreet business straight? I'm so confused myself, that I don't know that I can make it clear to you just what is wanted, but something like this:

> Harcourt sent me what was presumed to be a master sheet of your quotes, giving title, author, publisher, date, and the place where they appear in the MSS. The page numbers mean nothing to me, as they refer to Harcourt's numbering of the MSS pages. However, they appear near the end of the list, so presumably these quotes are in your later chapters. At any rate they listed
>
> > MSS p. 283 Overstreet "Long Train of Abuses," Norton, 1937. This I identify as being the same as something you sent me, A DECLARATION OF INTERDEPENDENCE, Norton, 1937, and I have all I need on that.
>
> But Harcourt also lists (MSS p. 410) Overstreet's WE MOVE IN NEW DIRECTIONS, Norton, 1933, and *that* is what I can't identify. Can you check this quote, giving extent and page numbers, beginning and ending words—Norton is quite firm about this. Send me the info. and I will pass it on, as I've already been in touch with them.

The first proof is in, and looks good. I've done no more than look at it, as I'm in the middle of grading examinations, but it reads well—better than I had remembered. I'll be writing you about it in a day or two, as soon as I plow through these 70 blue books.

Cleanth

Hampshire Arms Hotel
Minneapolis, Minnesota
February 1, 1949

Dear Cleanth:

I am enclosing a letter from W. W. Norton giving permission without fee to quote from Overstreet's *Declaration of Interdependence.* As you see they cannot give permission to re-quote what Overstreet quoted from Brandeis, and so I have already written to Lippincott to clear that.

I sent you Will Durant's permission and statement of fee, did I not?

I am deep in the proofs. I have been over them carefully once, and have located several sections that need some revision. I hope to finish that within a few days. I suppose that you have also spotted some lags in my writing—the stuff to be revised is mine. If you find such sections, just plunge in and make the revision. I hope to get Castell to give one more look at several passages in Exposition and Argument.

So long and the best to you both.

Red

Hampshire Arms Hotel
Minneapolis, Minnesota
February 4, 1949

Dear Cleanth:

I am sorry to raise the question at this late date—and I am not at all sure that it deserves to be raised—but I am a little disturbed about some things on galleys 11 and 12.

Galley 11: I fear that the first several paragraphs plunge the student too rapidly into difficult business. My very humble suggestion is to cut the first five paragraphs, substituting the new opening that you will find on attached sheet headed "Galley 11."

Galley 12: The head "Artistic Intention" covers only about half of the material under it—down to the paragraph beginning, "We have presented the scientific and artistic intentions in their extreme forms." I propose that we end the section "Artistic Intention" at that point, then cut the paragraph just mentioned (beginning, "We have presented the scientific and . . .") and insert the material attached marked "Galley 12." Substantially, this brings over your introductory material at the top of galley 11 to this point on galley 12.

I want to emphasize two things: I am not sure that this is a good idea, and I am not at all sure that my rewriting isn't heinous. I devoutly hope that you will revise my suggested paragraphs, and I am not being polite. This will be a very tough section for most students, and for some instructors, and I fear that we may scare off some takers. But the toughness is in the material, and I am not sure that we can dodge the issue.

By the way, I shall attach a note to my proof when I return it saying that the final version of galleys 11 and 12 will be the one you send in.

I have had a hell of a time with some of my exposition chapter. I found some frightfully bad writing in it, and some very confused and confusing formulations. I have had to rewrite quite a bit. But I won't bother you with this. I'll have it checked again by some of our professional logicians here, and let it go at that.

Yours in Christ,
Red

Hampshire Arms Hotel
Minneapolis, Minnesota
February 18, 1949

Dear Cleanth:

Yesterday I received galleys 102 to 126 inclusive. This includes the last part of Narration, and then several chapters of your stuff. Here are my remarks on the parts for which you have the first copy of proof:

. . . .

For God's sake don't take any of this too seriously. My head is so fuzzy that I don't know cow patties from porridge right now.

McCallum telephoned in great excitement yesterday to say that my corrections are running into a fortune. I couldn't settle anything on the phone, and so he is bringing the baby to you. I think we have to keep the new formulations about cause and condition, etc., and all other new formulations except the rewrite of the stuff on science and art at the end of chapter II. But Unger, who very kindly read over the first fifty galleys, also got bogged down on that part—said it would never be understood by freshmen. As for the that-which business, it doesn't really matter, of course. It certainly isn't worth thirty cents a change.

By the way, I have just reread your essay on Marvell's ode to Cromwell. Am using the poem in a class. I had forgotten how damned good the essay is. Had you noticed how "plot" in line 31 charges the passage from line 47 to 52? And the "green" in line 94 is a neat little stroke. And do lines 21–22 have a hint of the disturbance at the time of the Crucifixion? Temple rent, etc.

Goodbye and all our best to you both.

Red

Hampshire Arms Hotel
Minneapolis, Minnesota
February 22, 1949

Dear Cleanth:

I have just received your note with the corrections up to galley 102. I presume that you have by this time received my corrections for your stuff running from galley 106 to 144. Here are my few remarks on the section from galley 144 to galley 161, the last batch to come to me.

. . . .

[p. 2] This is a very clean section from all points of view, and God be praised, for McCallum tells me that every correction costs thirty cents. If the whole thing were in the condition of my galleys, we could sell 100,000 copies and still be in the hole. By the way, the chapter on Tone is really excellent.

I have not been able to wind up the permission about the Einstein quote. But here is the letter from Science News Letter for our files. I have heard from Einstein's secretary, who wanted a copy of the quotation, not just a reference. The copy is now out to her, and we should have final word in a few days.

On the *that-which* business, our previous practice is perfectly correct, if we take Fowler as a guide. We never use that as a non-restrictive. So I have canceled all corrections in late proofs on this point of substitution of *that* for *which,* and am letting our old practice ride—which, as a matter of fact, I did not know was my practice, at least to this extent.

I have just seen the London Times review of your book. Properly respectful, I am glad to note. Any other repercussions from England?

Best <regards>,
Red

P.S. I have just found that the second half of the comments which I had thought already sent are still here. I am enclosing them.

. . . .

Hampshire Arms Hotel
Minneapolis, Minnesota
February 26, 1949

Dear Cleanth:

I am enclosing the permission from Einstein for his quote. No fee, you see. Helen Strauss has received permission from Max Beerbohm for his essay, with a fee of fifty bucks. I am writing her to send you the proper information for your files on this.

I have received no more copies of your proofs since the last batch I wrote you about. What has happened? Are they falling behind schedule? When I do get some more I'll undertake to write you within a day or two with my suggestions and corrections. {[Handwritten] Just curious—I am enclosing my comments [on] galleys 162–198.}

Index: How shall we manage? Can you take half and I half? If it can be broken up this way, will you please let me know what method you think we ought to pursue? Will you settle this with McCallum and then let me know what you want me to do?

I have been thinking some more about Marvell's Ode. Why is it called Horatian? Is this notion too fantastic? Marvell is a poet in a time of civil war. He has a very divided mind, etc. Horace was a poet, in time of civil war. He served with Brutus as a military tribune, etc. Had to come to terms with the new regime. Appeals to Necessity to justify and glory of the state, etc. Can Marvell mean a personal and historical parallel in addition to a literary parallel? You see my line? What do you think? Does it make sense? Of course, you and I are in no condition to discuss such matters now, with an index staring us in the face.

By the way, I saw the review of your book in the London Times. Or did I mention this in my last letter?

Goodbye, and our best to you both.

Red

Hampshire Arms Hotel
Minneapolis, Minnesota
March 17, 1949

Dear Cleanth:

I have read proof twice on the following items:

Fox, T. H. Huxley, Propaganda, Durant, Pyle, Lawrence, Martin, Ullman, Stace, Wiener, Gauss, Mill, Thurber, Williamson, Beach, Santayana, A. Huxley, Marquis, James, Gibbon, Mitchell, Yeats, Steffens, Rice, Sheean.

I don't promise that you have the most perfect proof-reading job in the world, but you have, I hope, a fairly decent one. On the last check I discovered some very bad errors in text, whole phrases dropped and stuff like that. But not too much, and I do think that I have caught the really bad errors. There was a problem about Gibbon and Mill—the text to use. I used for Gibbon the Bury text as reprinted in the Heritage Club edition. It differs slightly from that in our text, and I don't know whether because of typographical errors. For Mill I used an old Oxford text which again differed slightly from what we had. I'm sorry to leave you with the Mary Stuart stuff, all three, the Becker, and the other, I forget what it is. But the books weren't available, except Froude and Ridenour. Those represent my falling by the wayside when my exams came in.

I have written McCallum that he should transfer my markings to your master galleys, and that you will provide all permission notes. Is that OK? The actual proofs will be in the mails to McCallum tomorrow morning.

I am swamped by exam papers now. Forgive this haste. Best to you both.

Yours,
Red

2034 La Mesa Drive
Santa Monica, California
April 18, 1949

Dear Cleanth:

At last, after about two weeks of scouting around, we have a house and are settled into it. A very satisfactory place for our purposes, and so I'm glad that we didn't jump into something else. We had the great good luck to be put up with the Beaches and to have a chance therefore to look about with some leisure.

A bit of business: Shall we plunge in now and try to drive through the revision of the Approach? I suggest that we hit that first because there will be less work than for UP and because it is the more profitable project. Also I have been doing some thinking about it.

If this suits you, shall we have Wilber write to Purser, saying that a revision is in progress and asking him to send any suggestions to one of us and indicating that it might be nice for him to do the proof on the new selections? Or shall we ignore him, and go ahead?

How shall we divide our labors? What about my doing the story section, with a new analysis or two, and a rewrite on the General Introduction. Then you do the poetry section and overhaul the drama. We can talk later about division of essay and other stuff. Meanwhile, I'll be assembling notions and suggestions for your sections and you be assembling them for mine. This is all tentative. Just a starting point for discussion. Will you let me know how you feel?

How about trying for The Great Gatsby for a new novel. That with Scarlet Letter would make a nice pair, perhaps, if we can afford the space.

Goodbye, and forgive this haste. Best to you both.

Red

1315 Davenport College
Yale University
New Haven, Connecticut
Monday, [April 1949]

Dear Red,

We finally got the proof read and checked and in, though Harcourt had to send their Miss Kennedy out here a couple of times to speed up matters and save time in the mails. I must say that the firm really worked hard to get a spring publication, for the book is to be out April 29, only two weeks past the announced date, and considering everything, that is a remarkable feat.

In rereading, it shows itself a better book than I had thought it to be, and I am at long last timidly beginning to hope for sales.

John McCallum called up this morning to lay a proposition before us about which he is writing you. I have given him no answer as yet, and of course shall not until I hear from you. The book ran to nine hundred pages instead of the 700 they had expected.[1] Actually if you took 200 pages away, the readings section (which they expect also to market as a separate item) would of course be wrecked. The over size resulted from our own lengthy work, and my sense

---

1. The pagination of *Modern Rhetoric* (1st ed.) was xxxii + 928, or 960 pages, a hefty textbook by any standard.

of what was happening accounts in part for the rather thin chapters which I at first submitted. But that is neither here nor there; I must say that McCallum took the extra 200 pages like a lamb. At any rate the book is now so large that it can't be sold for the $3.00 which they had expected to set as a price, and must go for $3.75, which is too high. McC wants to set the price at no higher than $3.50, which is already pretty steep if we hope for mass sales.

The proposal is that we take a reduced royalty on the first 25,000 copies; that is, 15% rather than 18%. This would take about 10¢ off the cost of the book and Harcourt would absorb the other 15¢. This would mean, according to McC's figures, that we would get between us $2600 less on 25,000 copies, but Harcourt would also undertake to absorb the extra printing bill which we ran up for proof corrections beyond the free amount. He says that between us we are $900 over the line. This would mean (subtracting $900 from $2600) that we would contribute only $1900 toward the reduced price. Actually I see that McC's figures are wrong. As I make it, we stand to lose on the difference between 15% and 18%, not $2600 but $1972. Subtracting the $900 from this, we cut ourselves out of only a little over $1000 on 25,000 copies, and not $1900. Of course the arrangement proposed is only for the first 25,000 copies. After that we revert to the original contract. And it is this last fact which makes me think that we ought [p. 2] to consider very seriously accepting the proposal. I honestly think that we stand to get more money in the long run if the book sells for $3.50 than for $3.75, and I don't believe that Harcourt will set it at the lower price unless we make the proposed concession. After all, the condition is rather special. We are way over the book size originally stipulated. Moreover, there would be no solution in setting the book at $3.75 and then cutting back the price to $3.50 later. That would look as if the book were being partially remaindered, and probably hurt sales. (This last point is my own, and was not mentioned by McC.)

To sum up, the proposition means that on the first 25,000 copies of the book each one of us forgoes a net of $500 royalty in order to get the lower price. Think it over and let me know what seems best. I frankly don't know, but must say that at the moment the McC offer seems to have merit.

We hope that you and Cinina are having a pleasant stay in California. Our best to both of you.

Cleanth

2034 La Mesa Drive
Santa Monica, California
May 4, 1949

Dear Cleanth:

I have just heard from Giroux about a trade edition of the Rhetoric. As you know, he wants me to do an introduction and you to do a "Postlude." I certainly have no objection to a trade edition, and any dough to be picked up that way would be nice. But what am I supposed to say in an introduction, and isn't there a good chance that you and I would be repeating each other if we wrote separate things? Why not a joint introduction? I might make some rough notes and send them to you, and you make some rough notes and send them to me. Then one of us might make a draft and submit it to the other for rewrite. Something like that. Or as I've suggested to Bob Giroux, they might find some writer who would do an introduction to our book. Or you might do the introduction and take a cash settlement out of royalty for the job. But oh, God, don't leave me alone in the arms of fire.

Write me your full views on this and the UP thing.

In haste,
Red

[OH]

1315 Davenport College
Yale University
New Haven, Connecticut
May 14 [1949]

Dear Red—

I'm sorry to be so late with replies; but I muddled my schedule and have just got through three successive out of town lectures during the last three weeks. Moreover, it's at the busiest time of the year for me.

Now to business: You evidently see the revision as a more thorough job than I had seen it. I expect you are right. I expect that if we are to revise at all, we ought to do the job pretty fully, and thoroughly. What worries the devil out of me is space. Holt wants (or wanted) a book of about the same size. How we are to get in "lots more modern poems" is therefore the question.

I quite agree that we are going to have to solve the problem in part by cutting: especially in the first section (and I would add) in the metrics section. Would you make such cuts and additions on the tentative table of contents sent to you and return it to me? I'll send it back with my comments.

Here's another partial solution: I have got Holt to agree that they ought to print up a pamphlet of suggestions for the teacher, condensed analyses, and bibliography to be *given* to the teacher. I've said I'd do it. I would count on you only to read and blue pencil it. I had thought of it as a way of winning over the teacher by giving him special materials not available to the student. But we might fudge here a bit and put some of our expansion into this pamphlet, making it a somewhat larger pamphlet and filling it with materials that the *teacher* ought to have but not necessarily the student. Someone here has suggested that the exercises might all go here, not in the text. That struck me as somewhat radical, but it may bear thinking about. Anyway, the [p. 2] pamphlet could take up some slack—or rather make room for what I predict will be a real overflow.

I'm all for the section on "how poems are written" and had counted on you for that all along. If you have the Housman stuff in hand, that's fine.

Can you give me more details on (b) "Studies of the work of two or three poets"? This sounds fine—would seem to meet a real objection. But I am thinking again about space. Moreover, would it be as an appendix? Would it be a brief or considerable essay? Would it take off from a particular poem as a kind of analysis? Or what?

Also, can you give more detail about (c) "A piece on poetic language"? Would we develop it as a kind of analysis? Or as a separate essay—in the body of the book? Or as an appendix?

4. and 5 (clarification of term *irony* and of attitude toward romantic poetry) could be done *passim*, of course: Letter to student, exercises, analyses, glossary. The rewritten analysis of "Ode to a Nightingale" and the backed up Wordsworth selections would help here.

I know that you are tied up, and I have told Holt that I expected to bear a lot of the load (that the matter of "divying" up was between ourselves and that since you had carried the load on the last book, I expected to do it here). But I want (and certainly they will want) your general check and OK on the stuff and any suggestions you can give.

If you can return the tentative table of contents with suggestions and queries and will develop a little further what you have in mind of b and c above, I'll try to get down to work. I declined teaching jobs for the summer and hope (D.V.) to get a big hunk done.

Love to both,
Cleanth

[On back of p. 2] I was about to forget the trade edition of *Modern Rhetoric*. Hope I haven't got us into anything here. What happened was this: in facing their embattled salesman early in the year, I had talked about the general impact of such studies as cultural anthropology, semantics, Freudian psychology, symbolic logic, etc., pointing out that the revival of interest in rhetoric was part of a large cultural pattern and had indeed been forced by the breakup of institutions and by the beating that language had taken of late from advertisers, the mass-produced arts, the propagandists, etc. They seemed to like it, and I suggested that if you were agreeable, I might get that into the book—as a postlude, or something to that effect. Actually I was trying to leave the introduction open to you. But I suggested it as only one option, giving as another an introduction by you, or a joint introduction.

It doesn't matter: what I think is important is that your name be prominent in the introduction or preferably the only name. This simply makes good business sense for the trade book. But I'm glad to help with the writing, and in any case I'm anxious for the actual work of writing to be as easy on you as possible. We might well go about it in the way you suggest: jot down some notes, I'll do a draft, and send it to you for a rewrite.

The postlude idea may be not so good at that: it was designed to take the curse off the rather elaborate machinery that the young lay writer might feel that he was getting even in the stripped down *Rhetoric*. It would be a justification for the closer conscious attention to symbols that he's being forced to give in the book. But I'm willing to drop the idea, or if we think it works out at all, it ought to be done as part of the other piece (wherever we put it in the book) and done perhaps in the same [way] that the introduction is to be done.

By the way, when is *All the King's Men* to come out as a movie?[1] T. and I are looking eagerly.

2034 La Mesa Drive
Santa Monica, California
May 16, 1949

Dear Cleanth:

First, I want to ask you a great favor: Several days ago I had a letter from a student of the Yale Drama School, asking to see copies of my AKM plays with the idea of producing a version there next year. I am quite happy to have him read the manuscripts, and am now having one prepared for him. But— and here is where you come in—I lost his letter and do not have his name. He told me that he had talked with you about the matter, and so I gather that you know him. Do you mind having him write me again, or will you write me his name and address? There is some pressure of time on this, by the way. Now don't damn me to hell for putting another chore on your poor shoulders.

I have your letter about the text book, Holt's that is. What I wrote you did not represent deep-seated convictions as to what ought to be done in revision. It was merely suggestion. But I'll describe my ideas a little more fully.

(1) The new stuff should not be in appendixes, but should be on the same level as our present "Sections."

(2) Suggested new sections: How a poem is made; Reading the Poet not the Poem; Poetry and Language. (This is not the order; the last should probably come first in the book.)

(3) The new sections would tend to be essays, with more than essay amount of illustrative material, followed by poems with special exercises when such material is relevant. For instance, in your piece on reading the whole poet, you would do a study of Eliot, with reference to several poems, key pieces, and wind up, say, with an exegesis of the Wasteland, showing how it relates to his general position, etc. The same for Wordsworth, with certain key poems, etc., in these sections. In the introductory discussion (before taking up Eliot or Wordsworth) you could explain how historical information is important, and the[n] illustrate in the discussion of the individual poets. In my piece on

---

1. Columbia Pictures Corporation released *All the King's Men* in late fall 1949; the screenplay was by Robert Rossen. "*All the King's Men:* The Prize Novel about a Demagog Makes Year's Most Exciting Movie," *Life,* November 28, 1949, pp. 111–12, 114, 116–17, 121.

how poems are made, I would give a general theoretical discussion, then a study of some poems by Housman and by somebody else, who I don't know at the moment (any suggestions here?), and then follow up with some poems in various conditions with exercises.

(4) Length: as soon as I get a copy of UP, I'll make a check for things for the axe. I'll also accumulate a lot of suggestions for our modern stuff. Then we can estimate the over-all length of the revised edition. But it will have to be a little longer than the current one.

(5) Language and poetry. In this I had in mind a brief survey of problems of suggestion, ambiguity, depth, etc. Some of this has already been touched on in our analyses, especially in Tone, but it should be brought together, perhaps—a good feature for us. You know—all the wrenchings of language that differentiate poetic from prose use. Lots of little examples, and a few big ones. Big ones to show how the use is not sporadic, etc. but must be consistent with a general style.

To turn to the Approach, I have heard from Scribners that they will *not* let us use Gatsby. So I'm casting around again for a novel or novelette for that. I'm also fiddling with some short story selections. [Subsequent pages of this letter are missing.]

2034 La Mesa Drive
Santa Monica, California
September 12, 1949

Dear Cleanth:

Forgive my terrible delay. I've been driven hard on the work here for one thing, and for another I postponed from day to day in the hope that I would have some decided progress on the revision to report to you. Actually I've done very little, damned little. There simply wasn't the time. I finished the draft of the play only this week—this past week—and the revision of the novel isn't finished yet. But I hope to be hard at the text book in early October. It is barely possible that I could have my share done by the middle of November. That's the best I could hope for. I'll drive hard for that, but we poor creatures rest in God's hand and are also prey to the weakness of the flesh.

Albert was out here for two or three weeks. He and I worked hard at the revision of the novel. I had always known that Albert was about the perfect editor, but I didn't really understand how good he is until I was the subject being worked on. He did a truly remarkable job for yours truly. The best thing is that he can propose simple remedies for complicated diseases—remedies that really work. We had a little fun on the side, but we did get the job done in so far as he and I could do it together. Now it's a matter of my doing the private sweating.

The play looks pretty promising, if I do say it myself. Or perhaps I've caught Rossen's enthusiasm for it. Anyway, he is getting down to business on it right away with his stage designer, and he claims that the dough is available for the production. We couldn't possibly get it on before March, and so, rather than risk that bad season, we'll wait until late summer to put it on the road, and aim for October in NY. We'll be doing the revision in the spring, after he has finished the picture Brave Bulls and I have finished up the text book revisions, etc. AKM is sealed up. It is a superior picture! There are two superlative performances in it, Broderick Crawford and a woman named McCambridge, and several good performances. Very intelligent directing. I may be kidding myself, but I've tried to lean over backward to be critical of it. The previews have been very successful, both in California and NY. It will be released in the middle fall, probably opening simultaneously in NY and Hollywood.

You've let your good nature reassert itself after my bad behavior. Will you let me hear from you at Minnesota? I hope that all things have gone well this summer with you and Tink. We'd love to see you. There's a chance that we'll get East in the late fall. If so, wait for the knock on the door and the gravel on the window pane.

As ever,
Red

Hampshire Arms Hotel
Minneapolis, Minnesota
October 13, 1949

Dear Cleanth:

I've been very remiss in writing, and to make matters worse, I've lost the tentative table of contents which you sent me earlier. I've been doing things toward the revision, but have relatively little to show for it at the present moment, just scribblings and notes for the things I'm to write and some text. The novel had to have a lot of last-minute work, and that couldn't be postponed, and so I've been carrying water on both shoulders and balancing a billiard cue on my nose at the same time. But now the novel is in the mails and I'm devoting all energy to the poetry revision. I'll try to have a draft of the {[typed in left margin] including some analyses of revisions of poems} how-poems-are-made section before long. Then what next for me? In my depleted condition I forget my other chore[s]—except, of course, the analysis of Apple Picking. And I think that we ought to do the following things:

1. clarify our use of the term irony
2. revise our treatment of imagery to make clear the business of pervasive imagery, atmosphere, etc., as compared with imagery that works in a stricter metaphorical way.

Other things, too—but those are much on my mind. From now on I'll be strictly on the job, but I fear that we can't make a delivery by early November. When?

Pardon this haste. Best to you both.

Red

P.S. SOS. what cases can you remember of poets giving an account of the way poems were written—particular poems or poems in general?

[OH]   1315 Davenport College
                                                                        Yale University
                                                                     New Haven, Conn.
                                                                     October 18 [1949]
Dear Red—

A brief note to acknowledge your letter of the 13th. I'll mail the tentative table of contents to you tomorrow or next day. You'll see the problem: how much to cut down the early sections to make room for the added sections and for the addition of modern poetry. The book will have to be bigger—but Holt is sure to buck if we make it a great deal bigger.

I repeat one very tentative suggestion: that in extremity we could shift some of the exercises to the pamphlet to be given away to the teacher. But I'm not sure that we ought to rob the book too heavily of exercises. The present exercises are too thin: they ought to be fattened—perhaps greatly. Anyway, I'll send you the t. of contents and a few samples of the kind of exercises I have been writing. Please return them soon—they constitute my only copy.

Holt will be glad to get this MS. whenever they can—and Alden Clark indicates that a MS. by Nov. 15 or Dec. 1 would have them joyful. I don't think that we can do that, however, not even the Dec. 1 deadline.

I won't write more at this time except to say that we saw Peggy and Albert Sunday and that Albert reports mighty good things of the new novel. I am anxious to see it. T. joins in all cordial regards to you both.

                                                                                  Cleanth

P.S. You know—and Hart Crane, of course—Spender's essay on composing a poem (in Stallman's *Critique*) and you know *Poets at Work* (Introduction by Charles D. Abbott, Harcourt, 1948). You know Allen [Tate]'s *Narcissus as Narcissus*. Aside from these I can't recall offhand other pieces except Coleridge and the man from <Poland> and a few bits in Keats. But Wordsworth and the other Romantics have left lots of brief notes, of course, on some of their poems. I wish I could help more. When I recall others, I'll send them in.

                                                                     Hampshire Arms Hotel
                                                                     Minneapolis, Minnesota
                                                                       November 19, 1949
Dear Cleanth:

It was fine to see you all in New York—even if I could do little more than verify your continued existence at first hand. I felt sort of bad that you all should have taken the trouble to come to NY just for an evening, and know that I appreciate the gesture of friendship. I hope that the next day wasn't too dreary for you before the seminar finished and you could get home and crawl in.

I have to report that since my return here I've got nearly nothing done on the UP work. I had midterms given while I was away, then Cinina got carted off to the hospital for a week, then I had to make up some conference time lost by my absence. (As for Cinina she is now all right. She had not been well for months and so they decided to give a whole series of tests and get at the cause. It turned out to be nothing very serious and can be corrected within a relatively short time by diet and medicine—not even necessary to stay in bed.) Now Albert writes that proofs are coming this week. Well, I'll try to keep at the text book, but it seems that I'm lagging far behind. I hate to slow things up, and I'll do all I can, but I don't see how I can get my share done very soon.

I haven't yet taken any steps about Berkeley except to send some material they requested, bibliography, etc. I don't know when they'll demand a decision. Not right away, I guess, because they are revising their original proposition.

There's the bare chance that we'll get East for Christmas. In that case you and I might get some time together on the revision, and try to settle some questions now dangling. For instance, would there be a use for a special discussion of poetic language, etc.?

I am enclosing a carbon of a letter I've just sent to Harcourt Brace. It is self-explanatory, but for one matter. Mrs. Boardman, who is mentioned in the letter, wants a letter from you, following exactly the same questions as the letter to be written by HB to her. PLEASE do not make any reference to the armed forces in your answer. And be sure to write on a Yale letterhead, for that will impress the Army board. Quicker the better.

Goodbye and best to you both.

As ever,
Red

[OH]   Department of English
                                              Yale University
                                   New Haven, Connecticut
                                        December 9 [1949]

Dear Red—

I am at fault for not having written earlier; but I have had a very mixed up and confused last several weeks. The result is that I've got very little done on the revision of *U.P.* I hope, however, that I'm now out of the woods. I mean to work henceforward steadily on the matter, putting in most of the vacation on it.

If I do this, I believe that we might turn in a MS. by the end of the winter—quite possibly by Feb. 1. I've got to complete my draughts of the new sections and finish the revision of the exercises. There's always a lot more that you have to do, I know. Even so, I hope to be able to finish up in the time mentioned—unless all sorts of troubles and distractions develop—as they have a habit of doing.

MacMurphy is very anxious to pin us down to a specific date. Would you write to him direct, modifying what I report here by your own situation. He thinks there is a good chance of a Manitoba high school (really junior college adoption) of about 5000 copies if he can firmly promise to deliver books by the end of the summer. I'd like to accommodate him—and ourselves—[p. 2] if it can be done. Maybe it can't; if it can't there's no need of our making a promise that we are unlikely to be able to perform.

Anyway, cast up your accounts and write him what you think best on the basis of my report to you.

This is a hell of a way to be wishing you a happy Xmas season—the proposal that we cut into it with work on the revisions! A merry Xmas to you and Cinina, anyway.

T. joins in all regards,
Cleanth

P.S. This note is not an attempt to stir *you* up: it's my ox that has been in the ditch for the last several weeks—I've done nothing, though looking back, I can't see how I could have acted otherwise. Do let me know, however, of suggestions that you may have—and call for any sections that I am working on that you want to see.

The Hotel Marguery
270 Park Avenue at 47th Street
New York
December 27, 1949

Dear Cleanth:

First, I want to thank you for the lavish hospitality and to say how fine it was to get a taste of old times, even if most of the taste of old times had to do with work. Well, work is not so bad if you can do it under the proper circumstances.

Second, I've just had a session with Dr. Madison and Mr. Clark at Henry Holt. They say that they will be happy to allow an extra hundred pages or so for the book. In other words, our estimate of 60 to 70 pages of new poems in the anthology section, 63 new poems in the study section, 120 pages of new prose material, and 25 pages of exercises is acceptable—if we make the cut of 163 pages now indicated from the old material, etc. They want to hold the book down in price, but they also want to make a decent format and to accommodate our new features. They will work out some format they say that will suit our purposes. Also they don't want to stint us on photographic material in the section on manuscript revisions.

In general I feel much encouraged, and I'll start slugging away as soon as I get back to Minneapolis. March 1 will allow them to make delivery in Canada, but we can't break that deadline and stay friends. By the way, I got them to agree to have their proof reader responsible for the text of poems if we deliver a manuscript that we guarantee. There are, I know, a few typographical errors in our present text of poems, or rather, errors in punctuation. For instance in Flammonde there is an error.[1] And we must be sure in the Waste Land to get the most recent text. There are some small changes in that from the first edition—one about the carious teeth. How shall we manage this? Shall I take half the book and get a responsible person to check text back? This I mean in the old stuff in the book. And I'll certainly undertake to guarantee the text of the new poems for the anthology section, etc. I'll start making additions to that for your veto, but I wish that you would jot down any titles etc. that occur to you. I think that we ought to make an effort to incorporate some fresh material from older poets—stuff like [John] Clare that doesn't get into ordinary anthologies. Madison thinks that that would be a talking point. This of course along with a good spread of modern poets.

I'm sorry that I didn't see Tinkum. I hope that she is having a fine time in Louisiana. Best to you both.

Red

---

1. In *Understanding Poetry,* 134, in the last stanza of E. A. Robinson's "Flammonde" (line 92), a period is omitted after the word *been.*

1950s

[OH]
176 Dwight St.
[New Haven, Conn.]
February 2, 1950

Dear Red—

I enclose some material for the revision of U.P. for your suggestions and correction.

I am trying to get the first four {(in the new numbering)} sections laid out in proper form so that I can send them on to Holt by or before the middle of the month.

Here are the changes I suggest on the questions that I have to ask:

(1) You suggested that John Ransom's bird poem might be inserted right after "The Three Ravens." "Husband Betrayed"? [Insert in the left margin illegible] Is that the one? I'm not sure that it isn't, for all its simplicity, going to seem a bit sophisticated for the student at this point, but maybe not. Anyway confirm the title, and I will append a brief exercise.

(2) Unless you disagree, I am cutting out Robinson's "Flammonde" (Gen. Section) and Browning's "Serenade at a Villa" from this 1st section. They can go in easily, but the pressure on space is going to be terrific. The section on seeing the poet in wider perspective (Wordsworth-Eliot-Marvell) is simply, in spite of all that I can do, long as hell.

Section II: Descriptive Poems

(3) Have you readied your analysis of "After Apple-Picking"? If so let me have it to include.

(4) I enclose my revision of the exercises for Shakespeare's "Winter-Spring" and "To a Waterfowl" to see whether I have removed the objections we discussed when we went over them. I'm assuming that the other exercises are OK, but I can send the whole MS. if you want it and have time to go over it once more. (But I can well imagine—from my present state—how busy you must be.)

(5) I am adding a brief note on the Philomela legend to the Bridges' "Nightingale" analysis. Students could look it up for [themselves], but they don't, and this is preparation for *The Waste Land* job. [Subsequent pages of this letter are missing.]

[Cleanth]

Hampshire Arms Hotel
Minneapolis, Minnesota
February 21, 1950

Dear Cleanth:

I didn't get this stuff off yesterday as I had planned, and I yet haven't got my own piece ready to send. The typist hasn't finished yet, but promises it tomorrow. You can count on it this week, however. Things go badly as far as my time is concerned. I've got to lose two days this week with the medical profession—they're taking another set of X-rays etc. about my innards—but I do have the new Prufrock finished and in the hands of a typist, and I have the Frost about ready. The permission letters for the pile of new stuff for the new general anthology section are going out this week. I've sorted the stuff and have two girls doing the letters, etc. I hope to get the new Introduction done this week-end or shortly after.

As for the enclosed stuff, I have scribbled comments on the text. I suppose that most of them will be legible. Many of them (the things in brackets) are indicated cuts or reductions to pick up a bit of slack here and there. For others I go through now.

. . . .

This is very crude as comment, but it may make some sense to you. I'm greatly impressed by the fact that you have got so much into such little space and make it make fluent sense. I have only one suggestion of any size. It strikes me that at the beginning of the Waste Land discussion that you might tell the student a little about what the general method of the WL is before you begin the exegesis—about the hero, the voices, the lack of transition and why—just a recognition of some of the difficulties that he has confronted in his first reading. Let him go back and think of Prufrock, etc.

Well, goodbye and all the best.

Red

Hampshire Arms Hotel
Minneapolis, Minnesota
February 25, 1950

Dear Cleanth:

Here at last is something: (1) New "Prufrock"; (2) essay on "How Poems Come About" with photograph of Housman MS and a typed copy of MS, all attached; (3) your essay on "Ambiguity" with my scribblings. Tomorrow I shall mail my analysis of "After Apple-Picking," which the typist has held up, and some other material. I am now working on a new introduction, which is not coming at all well. I have got out all permission letters, and am arranging the new poetry section of sixty pages. This should be ready by end of week.

As for my essay on "How Poems Come About," I am depending heavily on you to make stylistic changes and to head off any egregious nonsense. I am not sure that I make my point about Keats' "Ode to Indolence"—so give this a very close squint. Also I am very worried about the organization of the whole thing. Does it follow along? If not, what could be done to help matters? I have sweated blood over this, Goddamn it, and it still looks bad. Same goes for "Prufrock." Look carefully at it for style and other things.

Attention: We must have Keats' "Ode to Indolence" in the book to support my essay. Also all the Yeats poems "Upon a Dying Lady," and Housman's "Immortal Part." Also place of "After Apple-Picking" must be changed, for it now is too complicated for its present position. In it I begin the notion of the poem and the poet's whole work, etc. You can put a back reference in your Wordsworth to it.

I found your piece on ambiguity very good indeed. My only thought is that it needs some talk about how one word charges another sometimes in a complicated context, the sort of thing that Richards does in his comparison of Dryden and Donne—elegies. You might also use some fine examples from *Antony and Cleopatra*—"strong toil of grace"—"knot intrinsicate"—etc. As for exercises, I think it would be fine if we could set up some examples for them to analyze, some new and some by reference to poems in the text. Other comments are scribbled on your manuscript. But look carefully at the note on page 22 about the "daughters of the swan"—this would be a reference, wouldn't it, to Leda's daughter Helen, and not to Leda herself. Unless I've gone crazy, it was Helen, wasn't it? I am doing this in haste and haven't time to check. Also on the reference to irony here you might give a back reference to the analysis of "Prufrock."

Goodbye and all the best. I'll come along with stuff as fast as possible. To make matters worse, I almost had a nervous breakdown when my typist lost a whole batch of stuff, my only copy, and had trouble in finding it.

Best to you both—ever yours,
Red

[Typed at top of page] The epigraph of Prufrock should be printed with poem. Eliot uses a version which ignores accents, etc., but I suppose that we should follow his text.

[OH]   February 28 [1950]
Dear Cleanth:

I wasn't kidding when I said to Eisenman that he and I sure knew how to pick our friends. Thank you.

Here is the new poem. I'll take you at your word, but please, please, remember that the book of poems doesn't come out until next January, that there is plenty of time to get your mind on my troubles, and that I am going to fling the whole MS at you when pressures let up on you a little.

I have just had two pieces of news about our little recording project. One bad, one good. Bad first: Roethke is in the clink, and there is no prospect of his being out any time soon. For the present at least we'll have to count him out. I suggest that we proceed without him, then if he is available later, we can splice him into the record.

Good news: John Ransom is enthusiastic about doing the thing. He is beginning a book for Random House, an anthology for metrical-and-such analysis. This will be right down the line of his present concerns. He will be here in April, on a lecture trip, so all is well. We can set up [a] recording date in NY. Meanwhile we should start fixing our frame for the interviews and give him a copy to revise for us, etc.

Who shall we get for Roethke's place? Shall we try Cal? Or Shapiro? Cal is readily available, that's one advantage. And I apologize for not getting Eliot's address. Plain forgot it. Will you proceed through Gallup? Will you ask I. A. Richards, too?

I hope you like the poem. It isn't polished, and that chigger is merely filler. But you know the horrid word that is the option. I find it horrid myself, in itself, but here it is right—it belongs to the mean little slick bastard, sliding in, cocky and adroit and contemptuous.

Goodbye. Tell Tinkie to get well quick and tell her we'd love to have her here Tuesday night and we'll promise to keep the thundering herd of loving buffalo off her bed.

Yrs,
Red

Minneapolis
March 12, 1950

Dear Cleanth:

I am enclosing the following items:

(1) Material for the General Anthology section, with a guide to contents.

(2) A suggested version of contents for Tone and Attitude, with copies of the new poems to go in it.

(3) A suggested version of contents for Imagery, with copies of the new poems to go in it.

(4) A batch of material for the Metrics section clipped together and self-explanatory.

(5) Some scribbled comment on your exercises for Shakespeare's "Spring" and "Winter" and Bryant's "To a Waterfowl."

(6) Certain corrections of text.

(7) A translation of the epigraph of The Ancient Mariner to be used as a note. THE EPIGRAPH SHOULD BE PRINTED WITH POEM.

(8) A copy of "Rocky Acres" by Robert Graves, to go in section of Description.

(9) A continuation of the analysis of Donne's "If Poisonous Minerals." I felt that we needed to say more and tie things to the technical aspects of the poem.

In the General Anthology section I have broken up the poems into several groups—miscellaneous, love, elegies, social protest, society and collapse of values, philosophical, war, irony and satire. I do not mean for these titles to be printed. They are merely guides to us for possible use in making up exercises, etc., for our jack to the teacher for this section. The order I have put the poems in seemed to have some utility to me at the time, for purpose of comparison and contrast in possible exercises. I have indicated the poems I think are *musts*, those I think are highly desirable, etc. You will see my code symbols.

I am clearing all copyrights for new material. I haven't yet made up a cost sheet, but you can guess how things run. Most poems are fifteen to twenty-five dollars.

I presume that you have already in hand my (1) "How Poems Come About" (2) Analysis of "Prufrock," (3) Analysis of "After Apple-Picking."

I have not yet done a new Introduction to the book, but am working on it now. With little success. My head is thick, I got gas on my stommick, this is exam week, I have a million students, and God is on the thorn and the snail's in heaven. I'll try to get to you in a day or so. God help Henry Holt. Maybe they can still make the deadline. But I truly done my best.

On the Approach I'll undertake to bear the brunt to try to even things with you.

As ever,
Red

[OH]   1315 Yale Station
New Haven, Connecticut
Thursday, March 16 [1950]
Dear Red—

Your big packet came in, and now, at my first opportunity, I hurry off this letter. I'm afraid that I have caused you useless trouble, by not having made perfectly clear what I was doing. I sent in to Holt all the sections within a few days after March 1, thinking that you knew that I was doing this. I prepared—too hastily, I know, but as well as I could—exercises for the sections—all save VII, which we agreed Xmas was not to have exercises.

Now that I have your materials, I shall try to see what *can* be done and what ought to be done. I'll try to get into New York early in the week and make what changes I can, if the stuff has not already gone to the printer. Fortunately, the more important changes can—if necessary—easily be made in galley proof. I am thinking of such matters as substituting some of the exercises you submit for some that I turned in, and such matters as rearranging some of the sections. For instance, it would be a rather simple matter to rearrange the poems in Section IV in the order you suggest by merely shifting type. (After it has gone into *page* proof, of course, that would be a different matter.)

I enclose a table of contents for the book as it went in, with the shifts that would be involved in your arrangement marked in ink so that you can see precisely what would have to be done. I expect that some of the rearrangements (e.g., whether "Departmental" precedes or follows "Ode to Duty," Section IV) you will regard as quite immaterial. On the other hand, other shifts may well be worth making (e.g., "The Rape of the Lock" placed at the end of Section IV rather than leaving it where it is now placed). A few, I should want to question: shouldn't we keep "Go, Lovely Rose" and Pound's "Envoi" together (as now) since Pound's "Envoi" leans so heavily on Waller's poem, making explicit reference to it?

I wish that you would give special attention to the placing of "Desert Places," and "After Apple-Picking." I agree with you that your excellent analysis of "A A-P" is too difficult for Section II. Therefore, since I had to make a decision at once—you can imagine that Holt has been putting pressure on the one close at hand—I made [p. 2] the arrangement you see. (It isn't irrevocable: we can change it in galley proof.) Anyway here it is: I wanted to keep the poem in II to match with "Autumn," and "Autumn" ought to stay here, because exercises in III (metrics) refer to it—and to "A A-P," for that matter. So I left "A A-P" in II with an exercise only. Needing an analysis at this point in II, however, I brought up "Desert Places" from IV (tone). (We originally had "D.P." in II, you remember.) Then I put "A A-P" in VI (Statement and Idea) because it seems a beautiful example of one very important way in which idea gets into a poem. (I really think that it serves this purpose better than it does in V [Imagery].) Is it proper, however, to use a poem twice? I think we can justify it. Incidentally, we need not repeat the *text*—simply send the reader back to II, if we like, and then follow with the analysis, and with "Birches." By taking up the poem in two connections, we dramatize an important point: that a poem can be read at different levels. But let me have your candid opinion—here and elsewhere. I haven't meant to be high-handed. I thought that we had agreed on an order for the poems this Xmas, and I thought that you knew that I was sending the stuff on in. God knows, you have had enough to do—and I can imagine— with illness—with what difficulties you have done what you have done.

But let us definitely decide here and now to adopt your arrangement for Section VII. Mine is largely haphazard and I set no store by it. Yours has a principle which we ought to try to follow. The real trouble is going to be to get in even a part of the further modern poems that you suggest adding. Taking just the poems you marked [X] I count 37 that are not included. (Some of your "musts" are to be found in other sections, particularly in VI, and I have checked on the enclosed copy those that occur in the present Section VII.) But if you study the contents for VII, you will see the problem: "To the Memory of Oldham," I need for a reference in the Ambiguity section; "When Lovely Woman" and "Prothalamion," for the *Waste Land*. You felt, wisely I think, that we simply couldn't drop "Lee in the Mountains." The same would hold true for "Ode to the Confederate Dead." We could drop "John Anderson" and "Intellectual Beauty"; we could also drop "The Hawk o' the Autumn" and "When first I came here"—though they're both nice. If you go back to VI, it's the [p. 3] same problem. "Prospice" is about all that's left of Browning. Emerson's "Brahma," if dropped, would gain us just 12 lines. We could substitute another Jarrell for "Losses," but do we want to? Gray's "Elegy" or Johnson's "Vanity of H[uman] W[ishes]" would gain some space; but our representation of the whole latter half of the 18th century rests upon those two poems. We've got to keep one; I'm not sure that we won't gain adoptions by having both. I know some people who will be disposed to adopt the book because Johnson's "Vanity" is there. It indicates to them that we are not inexorably opposed to what they think of as "didactic," solid, moralistic poetry.

I'm going to try to get Holt to let me add in all of the new modern poems that they will possibly take. (Since these poems are not to be accompanied by exercises, they can go in at the last minute.) But in view of Madison's last letter, I don't think that they will get in a half of the "musts." But we'll see.

I am grateful that you are at work on the Introduction—and ashamed that I've let you do so much. I'll try to send you soon a draft of the revised "Letter to the Teacher." And I'll take the principal load of preparing the teacher's manual.

Incidentally, thanks for the extension of the analysis of Donne's "If Poisonous Minerals"—which is excellent.

I do hope that Cinina is recovering—and you, too, remembering your report that you were to go *back* to the hospital. T. and I hope that both of you are definitely now on the mend.

In haste,
Cleanth

Tinkum slipped on the ice and chipped a bone in her wrist. She now sports a little cast on it, but is hoping to have it removed in a couple of weeks. Fortunately, as she says, most of the typing she was doing for me was finished when it happened.

Hampshire Arms Hotel
Minneapolis, Minnesota
March 17, 1950

Dear Cleanth:

I presume that by this time you have received the large packet of poems, etc., which I sent registered at the first of the week, by air. I have sent direct to Charles Madison some additional stuff for "How Poems Come About": a letter from Frost about his methods of composition—very neatly designed for our general purpose and certainly a useful item; and a short analysis by Shapiro of his composition of the poem "The Minute," to be included in the same section. I am sending the stuff direct to him and passing your judgment by, because the stuff seems pretty essential and will certainly be useful as a sales argument. I have not yet had Eliot's clearance on the letter to you, though I wrote him long back. I'll wait a bit longer and then jog him.

Two things:

(1) In going over our metrical analysis I am wavering on our treatment of Meredith's "Lucifer" (page 497 present edition). We give the first line:

$$/ \quad / \qquad / \quad / \quad /$$
On a starred night Prince Lucifer uprose

On second thought I suggest:

$$/ \qquad /\backslash \quad / \qquad /\backslash \quad //\,/\backslash \quad /$$
On a starred night Prince Lucifer uprose

For the first foot, even if we do treat it as an anapest, the syllable "On" gets a secondary accent and we'd have a balanced anapest. And considering the temper of the whole, I feel the thing as a trochee followed by a foot with a hovering accent or a spondee, and not as an anapest followed by a monosyllabic foot.

(2) The sonnet by Shakespeare "No More Be Grieved," which is printed on page 292, is *not* entered in the index under Shakespeare on page 667, though it does appear in other appropriate places in the index.

Then there is the problem of "Essex Heights," which, someone tells me, we define as a survival of Old English alliterative verse. But I can't find the spot where we say so—if we do. But the real question is, do you think that an adequate description of the poem's metrics. What about a six (running) against a seven? Give this some thought, and let me hear from you. And try it on somebody else, too, will you?

I am now writing the Letter to the Teacher thing. I have decided to [p. 2] try it as an elaborate postscript to the old Letter. Then they can see before them the whole thing. Bob MacMurphy, who is here now, thinks this a pretty good, or at least acceptable, idea. How do you feel?

I'll leave all the questions here to you to settle and to correct in the text if you think good. If the text is still with you. Anyway, let me hear how things seem to you. I know you're driven to death.

Love to you both,
Red

[OH]

Department of English
Yale University
New Haven, Connecticut
March 24 [1950]

Dear Red—

By th[is] time you will have received from Holt a copy of the revised Section VII. I managed to squeeze in 13 more of your poems marked "must." In doing so, I cut Burns' "John Anderson" and Shelley's "Intellectual Beauty" and substituted Robert Lowell's suite "The Quaker Graveyard" for the one short poem I had from him. I also tried to arrange the poems somewhat in the order that you suggested—though whole categories were cut out or trimmed down. (W. C. Williams' "poem" is "On the Way to the Contagious Hospital.")

I also managed to get in the poems you had suggested for the other sections like Lawrence's "Piano," Crane's "Voyages II and VI," Fearing's "Portrait," etc. Counting in your "must" poems that occur in earlier sections and especially in Section VI which you did not mention, we have now got in a great many of the "musts," but not many that you had marked "0." If, by some odd chance, the book is *not* loaded to the gourds when we see galley proof, we might try to get in more [p. 2] poems still. But I shoved in all that I felt I could. The book is bursting at the seams now. Holt estimates that it runs to around 750 pages in the new format and with the extra poems I put in, it ought to run to 800.[1] That—according to Madison—is about the limit they can go and still keep the price down to around $3.00.

I hope that you will approve of the proposed shorter edition which Holt seems willing to do.[2] (I proposed it in part to try to get us more leeway with the full edition.) I can't see where we can lose. Anyone who really wants *U.P.* will take the longer edition, but I think that we stand to pick up many adoptions for the shorter—people who give 6 weeks to poetry—adoptions which we would otherwise lose with a $3.00 book. (And the paper cover copies will go to pieces mighty fast: mighty few second-hand sales out of those!)

One more item: I have not yet put in Shapiro's "University" (in Section IV). It can be put in in galley proof (and several other adjustments are going to have to be handled in galley proof). My reasons for wanting you to think it over once more before we put it in are these: Tuesday at Holt's office I found that the poem was in competition with thirty or forty others. Only a few could go in. It wasn't a case of do we want this, but [p. 3] do we prefer this to this poem and that poem and that? All can't go in. Moreover, the poem has to be the U. of Virginia or nothing. It's incomprehensible otherwise. The exercise would simply evade a problem if it failed to indicate that the person alluded to on the mountain was Jefferson. I don't balk at the poem, but I do balk a little at the note or the exercise. If we do insert it, let's put it in in Section VII where exercises are not required. (The U. of Va. which uses *U.P.* would probably continue to use it—the poem notwithstanding. That's not my real worry.)

I hope you are sending in soon the Introduction and the P.S. for the "Letter to the Teacher"—though I blush to think that I've let you do so much and I don't see, with your illness and Cinina's, how you've done what you have. I am at work on the manual for the teacher. I can at least take the brunt of the proof reading—and shall gladly.

I do hope that you and Cinina are now out of the woods. I hope that you will be able to make the Bollingen Com. meeting. That would be wonderful.

Cordially,
Cleanth

1. Pagination in the 1950 revised edition runs lvi + 728, or 784 pages.
2. The shorter revised edition was copyrighted July 31, 1950, four days after the revised edition, and published in paperback.

Hampshire Arms Hotel
Minneapolis, Minnesota
March 28, 1950

Dear Cleanth:

I've been sick again, about ten days of it. That accounts for my long silence and the fact that I haven't yet done the new stuff for the front of the book. But I'll get at it now and whip out something.

Meanwhile, I've been looking over your table of contents, etc. You've been anything but high-handed. You have to cut what you have to cut, and after all, my suggested order was just a suggestion. I now have only two thoughts that strike me as important:

(1) A Fine Old Ballad, by Clare, should be kept and paired with As I Walked Out One Evening, by Auden. They make a wonderful pair for the study of tone, and probably ought to be in that section.

(2) Why not let me tie the Apple-Picking analysis to Birches, so that it won't float in the air? Or, better, let's move Two Tramps in Mud-Time back to the section where Birches is, tie the Apple-Picking analysis to Two Tramps, and follow with Birches with a set of exercises. I think that will solve all our problems, and give a kind of pre-view of the treatment of a poet as a whole.

(3) I think you are right about not doing an exercise on Shapiro's University.

I saw MacMurphy when he came through. He looked at the Rinehart book for format and was much impressed with it, seemed encouraged about our book, and said he would discuss with Madison.

We expect to leave here for Sewanee about April 9, and shall be there until about May 8 or 9. Can the proof be had during that period? I can arrange for the indexing if we have page proofs in early May. What about this? Or I can have it done afterwards, for Mrs. Morgan Blum is extremely intelligent and understands such matters.

Our present plan is to sail on May 18, but things may change. I hope to wind up my obligations to you and Henry Holt by that time, and to have something done toward Approach to Literature.

Too damned bad about Tinkum's fall. The Warrens are in the proper mood to give sympathy on that score after Cinina's busted spine and all the grief that has flowed from that episode on the ice. But she is fine now. Really recovered, it seems.

Goodbye. I'll try to write soon.

As ever,
Red

[OH]

Department of English
Yale University
New Haven, Connecticut
April 7 [1950]

Dear Red—

Sorry I'm behind again with an answer to your last letter.

For your specific queries, here's the dope: Clare's "Fine Old Ballad" and Auden's "As I Walked Out One Evening" *are* paired and are in the tone section. (Do you have a copy of the current Table of Contents? If you don't, write or wire and I'll get you one post-haste.)

At present your fine "After Apple-Picking" analysis is in Section VI (Theme and Idea) and is followed immediately by "Birches" with an exercise. "Two Tramps in Mud Time" is in VII (General Anthology). "A A-P" doesn't "float in air" now, but if you want to tie it in with "Two Tramps," fine. The trouble is that that means more work for you, and I am trying to save you that. (Adjustments could be made, of course, in galley proof.)

The real ox that is in the ditch is the "Introduction" and the "Letter to the Teacher." They are what Holt is yowling for. If I can lend a hand here, wire me at once. Meantime, I stand by for the Glossary, and the Indexes. It's good to know that we can count on [p. 2] Mary Evelyn Blum for Indexes: but, I don't know whether we'll have page proof by early May, and the nature of the material is such—stanza, indexes, etc., that I'm not sure that the work could be delegated. Anyway, I'm prepared to handle that.

I'm also prepared to handle all proof reading on the texts of the poems. You will want to read (and I'll want your check, of course, on) what we say in our own stuff, including the exercises.

If you have any time—though God knows I don't see when you'll find it—I had rather you put it in on plans for the *Approach*—contents, etc. Crofts & Co. have found out about the revision of *U.P.* and are hollering for theirs. They would love a MS. by Sept. 1 if it can be done. (If we don't plan elaborate alterations, I dare say it could be.) The substitution of materials would not require a great deal of time. But it's foolish to promise what we can't deliver. What do you say? What shall I write them?

We had a most pleasant brief visit with John Palmer, and envy you and Cinina your visit with him. Sewanee ought to be delightful during this early spring period.

Tinkum has shed the cast on her arm and joins me in all cordial regards to you and Cinina.

In haste,
Cleanth

Hampshire Arms Hotel
Minneapolis, Minnesota
April 9, 1950

Dear Cleanth:

I am sorry to have been so long with the new front material, but I'm not really back on my pegs yet, and my brain is fuzzy. I've had dinner out of bed only three times in three weeks. I usually crack up in the afternoon, and I usually get my breakfast abed. I rather enjoy this system, but it doesn't make for work. But I'm better now.

I am enclosing a "Postscript" to be appended to the old "Letter to the Teacher." I'm inclined to say that we should reprint the old Letter just as it was, except for adding a date to the title, and then in the Postscript make our new comments. I'm not happy about it, and I expect you to do some drastic rewriting. For one thing, I'm not sure about the tone. Is it too pretentious, too much the tone of an "occasion"? Well, rework it, and fix it up in any way that comes to mind. Then will you send this on to Madison?

Since we are leaving in two days for Sewanee, there are a few questions to be tucked in.

(1) I am leaving my permissions material in the hands of Mrs. Morgan Blum [. . .], who will make up a final permission sheet as soon as she is provided with a final table of contents. Will you send her a table of contents as soon as it is definite? Then she will send the list on to me for another check, and I'll return it to you or to Madison.

(2) Madison has written to me about index. Mrs. Blum is quite capable of making the index, too, if that seems desirable rather than a professional indexer in NY. She has made them before and knows the tricks. And the indexer before made some errors. If Mrs. Blum is to make the index, she can't do the job until she has page proofs. So Madison should send her a set as soon as possible. Or better: he should send her galley proofs, so that she can set up the index except for the page numbers, and then send the page proof immediately after. You all decide whether you want Mary Evelyn to do the job. As for payment, I am paying her personally for the assistance on permissions, but the indexing should perhaps be charged against us at Holts as it would be if a professional indexer did the job.

(3) On page 497 of the old edition we scan "Lucifer in Starlight," by Meredith. I'm not happy about our job. Did I send you a revision on this for your criticism? I mean a new metrical marking? If not, let me know.

(4) Do you have any notion of dates on proof? I'll be at Sewanee (care John Palmer) from April 18 to May 8. If I had proof during that time I could do a good job. Proof at a later date is going to cause some trouble.

[p. 2] I'm sorry I've been such a problem as a collaborator. Everything has worked against the business. But I'll try to make it up on the next round.

Best to you and Tinkum.

As ever,
Red

Sewanee, Tennessee
April 24, 1950

Dear Cleanth:

Here is the proof, from galley 1 to galley 173. I have checked pretty carefully the prose material (that is, I've been over it twice), and have read the poetry. But I don't give the poetry an OK. I simply have made some corrections that I could get at. And sometimes, I haven't had good texts to work from. Below you will see some questions bearing on this point.

I am greatly relieved by our conversation of yesterday. I hope that you will make whatever changes seem good in my "Postscript," and I feel pretty sure that there ought to be an addition to it saying that we know the book to be too advanced for some classes, but have aimed to give a lot of latitude for the teacher, etc. We might also say why we haven't put exercises in the last section of poems. I forgot this. As far as the Introduction is concerned, I didn't see that it needed much. The only point that might have been treated there (or in the Postscript) was our use of the term *irony*. I hesitated, because we had given a pretty full discussion in two or three places. But perhaps it should be in the Introduction. I don't know.

Here are some questions about the enclosed proof. The numbers refer to galleys.

. . . .

I am not at all certain that we are consistent throughout with use of italic and quotes for certain titles of poems. I've tried to be sure. But damn it, what do we want for the Wasteland? And if that is italic, why not Ancient Mariner? Etc.? Can you settle this problem?

Meanwhile the next batch of proof has come and I have given it a first reading. I hadn't realized in manuscript how very good and useful your discussion of ambiguity, etc., actually is.

Best to you both.

Red

P.S. About index. I have written to Mary Evelyn to do the author-title index and the index of first lines (if we had an index of first lines in the original edition—I don't recall off-hand). Will you see that Holt sends her galleys now and page proofs when possible? Her address is Mrs. Morgan Blum, [. . .].

Sewanee, Tennessee
May 3, 1950

Dear Cleanth:

I sent the proofs off to you Air Mail Special Delivery, and hope that they are already in your hands. Before I sent them I did not have available a reference as needed. If you will look on the galley of my essay "How Poems Come About" you will see, just after the quotation about Oughtred, an insertion in pencil, a quotation from Henry D. Smythe about the "Guess Word" method of mathematicians. The citation on this should be: "Address delivered before Amherst College, March 23, 1950."

We are leaving Sewanee in two days, and shall be at Hotel Marguery late on the afternoon of Friday, May 12. I am somewhat worried about not having received the last few galleys of proof, and the proof for the "Letter to the Teacher" and the "Postscript." I am writing to Holt today to try to get this sent to the Marguery.

All the best———hastily———

Red

[Handwritten] P.S. Is there any chance of having restored the poem "Goat Paths," by James Stephens? I have always found this damned useful in class—tone or imagery section.

[postmarked May 21, 1950]
Sunday

Dear Red,

First page proofs (up to p. 185, galley 60) came in Friday with Madison's urging that it be returned at once. I am getting it off to him in the morning. I had thought to send it to you first to get the benefit of your final judgment, but on second thought, I believe that this is unnecessary, and might simply entail your making a call on Holt which at this time you may not have planned to do.

We check so closely together on minor changes that I think there is nothing of consequence there. On your added questions for the exercises: I have inserted these with the proviso that they be inserted if elaborate repaging would not be entailed. I am sure that most can be got in without that. There are only two major suggestions of yours that I have not put down on the page proof. One involves the shift of Graves' "Rocky Acres" from its present position before Bridges' "Nightingales" to a position just after it. Since I had already supplied a couple of questions for "Rocky Acres" (they don't show on the galley but got in on page proof) and since very elaborate repaging would be required by the change, I think you'll agree that the shift is not worth it.

The other major item is the long sixth question which you proposed for the "Hell Gate" exercise. It is good but it involves a very subtle point, and I wonder whether it isn't much too subtle for so early a place in the book. I enclose a copy of it, and since there *may* be space for it, send it over to Holt at once if you still feel that it should be inserted. Otherwise we might put it in the Manual for the Teacher.

We are looking forward to seeing you Wednesday, and for as long as you can stay. Tinkum joins me in best to Cinina, and hope that she is feeling better.

As ever
Cleanth

[OH]   Saturday, [June 1950]
Dear Red—

I am sending to you, c/o of Albert at Random House, a copy of *World Enough and Time*.[1] Please sign it and send it on to Tinkum at 4721 Perrier St., New Orleans, La. (It's not for us—we'll get you to autograph ours this

1. *World Enough and Time* was published June 20, 1950, with a first printing of 37,000 copies; a special, limited edition for presentation to the Booksellers of America and another special, limited Kentucky edition were published simultaneously.

fall—but it is a copy we are giving someone.) I hope this is not too much trouble to you or Albert; we simply forgot to get it done while you were here.

I saw Norman Pearson this morning. He says that he can arrange to have you take out all the books you need, and to tell you that it will be arranged pronto. Norman is a member of the Department, but has an official connection with the Library. He says that he will be here nearly all summer, and to call on him for any help in this matter or anything else. (He has an office in the Library and in the Hall of Graduate Studies, one block away.)

I hope I haven't got you into anything in taking this up with Norman. We are not close, but he wants to help, is genuinely interested in meeting you, and I know will count it a *very real pleasure* to be of service.

It was good to see you and the Erskines. It's a shame that we are having to leave just at this time. You'll be hearing from me soon.

T. joins in regards,
Cleanth

P.S. The Holt proof came in and I am returning it to them today.

[OH]   1871 Mignon St.
                                                               Memphis, Tenn.
                                                               July 1 [1950]

Dear Red—

My apologies for not having reported earlier. We had a pleasant enough trip down; and now I am temporarily settled and ready to go to work.

I mean to attack first the poetry section of the *Approach*, revising it along the lines of our last discussion. I won't make any promises at the moment as to a definite date, but I shall hope soon to have some MS. on this section for your correction, amplification, etc. It ought to go rapidly—though I know from old experience that it actually never does. Anyway, I've got to work.

Tell Albert that I have been going over Milton for the last several days and hope to have some of my Foreword on paper soon. (I have brought along with me all the Milton materials that I think that I shall need for that purpose.) But I shall be writing to Albert about that direct.

I was disappointed in *Time*'s review of *World Enough and Time*.[1] It was a favorable review, certainly; but it was niggling and captious in a way that *Time* can be—and usually has been since its book department went to pieces some years ago. I've just finished reading a long and extremely enthusiastic review in one of the Dallas papers (*Morning News*) by one Lon Finkle. If it is anything like a fair sample of what the book is getting in the way of reviews, then the book is *in*—and very properly so. I do hope that it will have something like the sale that it deserves. It's a fine book—easily your best.

Let me know what I ought to be doing on the *Approach* (aside from the immediate work on the Poetry section). I expect to be going to New Orleans

---

1. "The Web of Politics," *Time*, June 26, 1950, p. 98.

later in the month, but this address will catch me for a good part of the summer (and mail will be [p. 2] forwarded promptly if I happen to be away).

It's a shame not to be in New Haven while you are so near, but I take heart from your statement that you would be at Westport when we got back. I hope we can manage to get back very early in September.

With best regards,
Cordially,
Cleanth

Box 54
Saugatuck, Connecticut
July 21, 1950

Dear Cleanth:

I'm sorry to be so slow in answering your letter, but I'm dull and slow these days, I don't seem to be making any progress on the work, and I was a little ashamed to confess it. I have been reading stories, but I don't seem to be able to make up my mind. And I haven't any notion of what novelettes to use. Maybe we'll have to come back to KAP's Old Mortality for one that has the problems of a novel. Most so-called novelettes are just long stories in structure. But how about one of Gertrude Stein's Three Lives, along with KAP's OM? Please think up some titles here. I can't start writing the introduction to fiction until the selection is made, for the references must be to things in the book.

I'm delighted that you think WEAT my best book. You want your last to be best, you want to feel that you're going somewhere, getting better. The press, you know, has been very bitterly divided, with, thank God, some of the best reviews in places that would do the most good. On the practical side, the thing is doing well, for two weeks number three on the national list and next week number two. But the trouble is that it's all for matches, for the war has ruined the book trade or just about.

Cinina improves, but our plans are still indefinite. I'm certain that we'll be around here when you all come back to your new house, or old house, however you choose to regard it. By the way, the more I remember the house the better I like it.

No news. The Erskines and I drift along here without any great doings. They stay out here when the heat is too bad, otherwise just on weekends. I hope that things go well with you all, that you are happy and well adjusted and sleek as cats. Damn it, it is too bad that you all are off there the only time in years I've been about this neighborhood.

Best to both,
Red

[Handwritten] P.S. Holt is asking for the Teacher's Manual. What about this? When I can do it?

228 East 71, NYC
November 6, 1950

Dear Cleanth:

I hope you didn't call me up this afternoon after all, for my business downtown, which I had thought would be over by three, kept me on much later. And it was of such a kind that it couldn't be postponed. Anyway, here are the last comments for the Teacher's Manual. I'm not happy about them, God knows, but maybe they'll do. Especially if you will give a last touch of wit and elegance to them. I'm especially dissatisfied with the comment on Webster's Dirge. But when I came to write it, I decided that if you really did much about the context in the play you'd have to do an analysis of the play, of the Elizabethan view of nature in tragedy, etc., the role of the villain, etc. So I gave a kind of lead, I hope, and let it go at that. It may be enough for those who have some knowledge of Elizabethan tragedy. And books wouldn't be enough for those who don't. But please add to it if you can make things simpler for the instructor.

I'll be seeing you all Thursday. As always I was overwhelmed by your hospitality, and grateful, last week.

Best to you both,
Red

228 East 71
NYC
Wednesday, March 28, 1951

Dear Cleanth:

I have been dickering with Viking for the Death of a Salesman. They want five cents a copy of each book sold. I talked with Wilber, who suggested making them an offer of $1000 cash, for all rights, which is high, but if the sale of the revision does as well as the sale of the old book [that] will bring the price down to about a cent and a fourth a copy. I made this offer today, but don't get word until tomorrow. I'm sorry to have acted without consultation, but Wilber said that that was probably the best we could do, and I thought I'd better go ahead. If I've done gone and done a crime forgive me. Anyway, they may turn us down.

After weeks and a jogging letter a few days ago, still no word from Harcourt about Murder in the Cathedral. Apparently, they have written to Eliot, who controls his reprint policy. And so it will be tomorrow before I'll get hold of Miss McCarthy and hear her story. I'll get her to cable if there's no word in a day or two.

In the last few days I've been working over Hedda Gabler, and instead of doing Shakespeare, as I was supposed to do, I have done a long piece on the Ibsen to supplement what we already have. What we already have should stay in, it seems to me, but it deals primarily with the mechanics of the structure and not enough with the interpretation. I've been carrying around some notions about this play for some time, and so I took this occasion to air them. I'll send you a copy of my analysis soon. If the Salesman rights are cleared tomorrow, I'll get right on with that.

Meanwhile, will you find out if the names Lovborg and Thea Elvsted have any meaning in themselves, in Norwegian. Also I need to know about the translation of one line. At the end of Act III, when Hedda is burning the manuscript, she says: " . . . I am burning—I am burning your child." In English this might, of course, have a double meaning, in the beginning: I myself am burning, am on fire; and a mere intensifying interruption of I am burning your child. But is the verb to burn in Norwegian such that it can carry this double burden? Can you find out about this? From Helga or Konstantin. Don't think I've gone crazy, but suddenly the play is opening up in lots of new directions.

Goodbye, and my very best to you both.

Red

228 East 71
NYC
April 12, 1951

Dear Cleanth:

Here are two items:

(1) a sheet giving the exact form of permission acknowledgment required for each item in the fiction and drama section.

(2) a sheet giving the price of each item and the name of the payee.

I assume that these are the master lists and will be put with the basic manuscript.

You will see that the Circle and Murder are not yet cleared for Canadian rights, and that the Lagoon is yet blank. There is some complication on all these points but letters are out that should settle the various problems one way or another. I am holding the permission forms and shall bring them with me when I come on Saturday morning.

So long and the best,
Red

care Helen Strauss
William Morris Agency
1740 Broadway
New York City
May 11, 1951

Dear Cleanth:

I am, and have been, in Iowa (now at Grinnell) for two weeks. Cause: plans began to blow up in all directions, leaving me stranded here without destination, etc. But today things seem to be taking a little shape, and I'll probably get on West Tuesday. Among the things that blew up was the movie of WEAT, oh, happy thought! Rossen is named a Commie and is in Mexico, but may be saved from the burning. But I shan't continue the catalogue, for it would fill the sheet.

Today, in the first mail to reach me since I left NYC, I had the carbon of Wilber's letter to you about bulk of our book. I don't know what to say. I suppose there's nothing to say until he gets the official count on the size of the whole thing and we can go to mat. Meanwhile I'll try to get hold of an old College Omnibus and count it carefully.

I am enclosing the letter from Jack Purser. You were right. I'm dropping him a note to say to stand by for proofs when and if we get the bulk question settled.

As soon as I know what and where I be, to echo the wor[d]s of the immortal Tennyson, I'll let you all know. Meanwhile it pleases my fancy to see you and Tinkum on Wind Hill. Wish I were too, right now.

Love to both,
Red

P.S. Will you have Wilber let Jack know possible date of proof as soon as they have a forecast?

Donner Trail Ranch
Box 100
Verdi, Nevada
May 29, 1951

Dear Cleanth:

I am enclosing two items which have to do with permissions for the APPROACH, a letter from MCA Management, Ltd., which is self-explanatory, and a letter from S. P. Watt & Son, of London, concerning Canadian rights for Maugham's Circle. But since we don't want Canadian rights, this is just for the file.

Naturally I am very grateful to you for your trouble about the grades. The papers to make up the work for Robert S. Fitzgerald reached me the day after I talked with you. They had been at the Morris Agency since late April. I also have the make-up papers for C. H. Matthews. P. N. Gillingham, who, however, is not a senior, did not complete his work. My record shows some blank for W. J. Hunt, who is a senior. Therefore I have been trying to get him on the phone today to settle the matter. I suppose I'll nail him later in the day. I have meanwhile sent in the grades for Fitzgerald and Matthews.

There's no telling when I'll get back East. Probably I'll stay on here a while and then go into California. My vague notion of going abroad is sort of petering out. By the time I get back your house ought to be absolutely finished and you two sitting preening in the middle in a most loathsome complacency. But I don't blame you. It is a wonderful place.

Goodbye, and best to you both.

As ever,
Red

[OH]   1315 Yale Station
                                                          New Haven, Conn.
                                                       September 26 [1951]

Dear Red—

Greetings! A hasty note to put a question which I should have put some time ago. A lecture series is being prepared, with people on it ranging through all the humanities departments, on the subject of drama. Some one from Greek is to lecture on Aeschylus; Peyre of the French department is to lecture on Racine, etc.

What is wanted is something not technical but general, and a critical rather than merely a scholarly bent. Six lectures have been laid out, running through the first semester. The committee is very anxious to secure you for the last of the series with the suggestion that you deal with modern drama. The lecture would be scheduled for sometime in January or February, I believe. Anyway, if you can see your way to accept, I hope that you will. The best foot of the university is being put forward and you are (quite properly!) regarded as one of the best feet.

This doesn't pretend to be a real letter. It is written in great haste. Katherine Anne has been with us for the last two weeks—she's just returned to N.Y., but promises to return a little later. Not much more has been done on the house, but we are comfortably settled in it. Your books are in your apartment in Silliman.

I hope you have had a good summer. We are eagerly looking forward to seeing you—though we shan't blame you if you postpone your return to New Haven until you have to be here.

                                           Tinkum joins in all cordial regards,
                                                                      Cleanth

P.S. The Crofts book seems to go ahead nicely. I go in to N.Y. tomorrow to talk to a meeting of Crofts salesmen.[1]

                                                                    London
                                                           October 4, 1951

Dear Cleanth:

I'll have to say no to the invitation to do the drama lecture. It's pure selfishness. At last I'm deep in the middle of my long poem, and since it has been postponed so long I don't want to let anything fall across the process of composition. Most of the summer it's been moving. I don't know what I've got but I'll have to play out my hand. I am terribly anxious to read it to you all and to get some reaction and comment. That, by the way, will not be too long off. I shall be home [within a matter] of days or weeks. I had started to Rome, got down at Macon, but my arm began causing trouble again, and

---

1. The third edition of *An Approach to Literature* was printed in 10,000 copies in September 1951; the copyright date is March 18, 1952.

so I decided to come on back and get the thing fixed. So I'm waiting here now for the first transportation out that isn't prohibitively expensive. You can always get a suite, first class, but I want something a trifle more modest, shall we say.

I shan't go into my not very exciting narrative until I see you all. Which prospect fills me with pleasure. And I'm anxious to see the house.

Soon, and meanwhile all good things to you both.

Red

[Perhaps for reasons mostly personal, letters seem to have been scarce in 1952. As of 1995, no letters from 1952 had been discovered.]

223 East 75
NYC
March 19, 1953

Dear Cleanth:

We had hoped to get up to see you all tomorrow, but now it doesn't look too probable. Too much crowds in. But I am sending you herewith a carbon of the SR tentative preface, with Albert's comments and corrections. You can incorporate them when you revise the thing and make it literate and celeritous. Anyway, we can have a session about it when we do get up there before long.

I have also sent you the latest version of Brother to Dragons. I know how busy you are, and I don't want to make too much of a claim on you. But you will add to my already considerable burden of gratitude if you will look with prayerful attention at the new sections between Lucy, Jefferson, and Meriwether, and then at the entire last section beginning with the line of RPW:

> The actual body of Lilburn, or what remains etc.

You will see a rather long and very explicit statement of some of the themes of the poem. Should this be in? Etc.

Allen come by yesterday afternoon for drinks. So we have had at least that much of his society. He won't be able to have dinner with us Sunday, as had been scheduled. He's off to Washington for an extra lecture.

No news. The house continues to be absorbing, for better and for worse, conferences, etc. etc. I'm stuck on several very short jobs, an introduction to a bibliography of KAP, which is to be published as a little book by the NY Public Library, an introduction to a Modern Library All the King's Men, and a few odds and ends like that. Plus more revision of the poem. But soon I hope for a more consecutive life.

Goodbye and best love to you both.

Red

Paradise Farm
Third Beach Road
Newport, R.I.
May 20, 1953

Dear Cleanth:

I have just learned that the Guggenheims have been announced, and I'm anxious, of course, to know if justice got done. How was it? And I'm anxious, too, for any news of you all, as is Eleanor.

As for us, we stumbled into a fine situation, a big old studio, with a modern kitchen, a study (in addition to the big room), a bed room, guest space (balcony—but no guests so far), fireplace and free firewood delivered to door, fine views of the sea, beach in easy walking distance—and, believe it, in the middle of a bird sanctuary. An old lady left the place for the birds, and our rent, apparently, goes to buy sunflower seed. But birds are very businesslike, and so the place is very cheap. We are truly enjoying the solitude, the fine walks and beach, and lots of work and conversation. We have even begun to dispute the species of birds.

Write when there's an idle moment—if there ever is one with you all. Anyway, we'll be seeing you before we stumble to the grave.

Eleanor joins me in love to you both,
Red

[OH]

1315 Yale Station
New Haven, Conn.
May 31 [1953]

Dear Red—

It was good to hear from you, and my apologies for the delay.

The Guggenheim came through all right, as—thanks to my delay—you have doubtless already seen from the papers.

But the avalanche of papers and examinations was a heavy one. I am just crawling out from under it. I had *four* dissertations to read, and it finally got to the point that every waking hour had to be put into the reading.

Now I've had two days outdoors working on the yard and I am coming back to normal.

I hope that all goes well with you and Eleanor. The place you are in sounds delightful—and I hope that it lives up to its name.

No news from here. The L.S.U. Press had been informed by one of the men in the business office that we already owned the stories published in the *S.R.,* and needed only to write for courtesy permissions. I think that I have set them straight on that, and presumably the permission letters have gone out—or will soon.

Mrs. Smylie at the Press caught on as soon as I informed [p. 2] her. But she had made the mistake of asking the advice of Melvin Dakin, a nice guy, but a man who is a better accountant than a literary agent or lawyer. (It seems that poor L.S.U. either errs on the side of corruption, or in reaction to that, goes into the other extreme of being so careful to save the university money that it demands five forms typewritten in order to buy a lead pencil.) It doesn't deserve a quarterly—either in its corrupt phase or in its phase of pettifogging honesty.

But my tirade is really just blowing off steam. The letters asking permission that Mrs. Smylie is actually sending out are quite proper. I checked one of them (to authors), and rewrote the other (that to publishers).

We wish that we could see you. Drop in when you can.

T. joins in all love to you both.

Cleanth

P.S. Tinkum will certainly be here until July 15. I *may* be here until the last week in June (when I leave for Bloomington and the School of Letters)—but I may have to go South earlier.

[OH]   426 South Greer St.
Memphis, Tenn.
July 14 [1953]

Dear Red—

A brief note, principally about the *S.R. Anthology*. Miss Joan Doyle (L.S.U. Press) writes me that Scribner's wants more than $25 for the Caroline Gordan story and Doubleday more than $25 for the Nelson Algren story. Apparently she is trying to haggle them down.

Could you try to expedite these? In any case would you write to Miss Doyle direct to tell her whether we want to drop the stories—if we cannot get them for the fee we propose—or whether to go higher?

I hate to drop this burden on you, but you are nearer the publishers and perhaps could explain matters in person or by phone. Whatever you decide will be quite all right with me.

Indiana was pretty hot, but pleasant enough, with much talk with the Partisan Contingent and with Cal Lowell. Now I am here in Memphis and should be for some time until I join Tinkum in New Orleans sometime in August (but not past the middle of August).

. . . .

In haste,
Cleanth

[At top of page] P.S. *Re S.R. Anthology* proof: hold any that you have until the L.S.U. Press sends us theirs—onto which we will transfer our corrections. Anyway, don't bother to return it to the Colonial Press. I think we will probably both want to depend on the L.S.U. proofreaders for most of it. The Introduction was the only part that I wanted to make sure that you saw and corrected.

[OH]   426 S. Greer St.
                                                                       Memphis
                                                                 July 20 [1953]

Dear Red—

A hurried note in answer to your letter that has just come in. I am honored that you want me to serve with Albert as your literary executor. I am assuming that you know so fully how I feel about the matter that you will have proceeded with the will without waiting for any response from me. But I hurry off a reply anyway: of course, I shall be glad to.

The mail that brought your letter also brought an offprint from Amos Wilder (Thornton's theological brother). It has to do with the *Kenyon* excerpt of *Brother to Dragons*.[1] It is brief, but thoroughly discerning. I'll save it for you.

I didn't see John while I was an Indiana: he was to come over later, for, as he wrote me, Helen and her husband were with them at that time. I did get a good deal of talk with Rahv, Kazin, and Howe (as well as with Cal Lowell). It was all very pleasant and amicable. But I got another good indication of how far the New York liberal and leftist-liberal mind is from the mind of mid-continent America. Several weeks ago I pointed out to them that McCarthy (because of the J. B. Matthews *Mercury* article) had placed himself in jeopardy and was probably going to suffer some sharp reverses with the general public and in the Senate. Even Rahv couldn't see it. I am delighted to see the prediction made good. May they lay it on now, hot and heavy.

[p. 2] I hope that the reconstruction job is going ahead without too many headaches. (It would be folly to hope that there would be *none*.) At any rate, when we return toward the end of the summer, I hope that you and Eleanor will have much to show us. Give Eleanor my love.

                                                                     In haste,
                                                                      Cleanth

P.S. Tinkum was to have got to New Orleans (driving with Virginia) on Saturday. I shall join them sometime next month. Meantime, Dick Bruvjes, Ken's young architect, is occupying our home. Phone him if there are timbers, etc., that we may supply.

                                                                 care Carleton
                                                             Hoyden's Hill Road
                                                           Fairfield, Connecticut
                                                                 August 1, 1953

Dear Cleanth:

Just to say that Rosanna Phelps Warren arrived Monday night, without much warning, and very melodramatically, in the middle of the living room

---

1. The *Brother to Dragons* excerpt appeared in *Kenyon Review* 15 (winter 1953): 1–103; A[mos] W[ilder], "Revising the American Dream," *Christianity and Crisis*, July 20, 1953, pp. 97–98.

floor. No doctor for twenty-five minutes, with a neighbor holding Eleanor and me receiving the baby. Very gory and scary, but all has worked out well. Despite the fact that Eleanor had a brutal time afterwards with about a hundred stitches, and the baby nearly died. But after several days in an incubator, she is now fine and hungry. And very beautiful. Eleanor has to be abed a while longer, but is feeling good, and mighty pleased with herself. She has [a] right to be. She really was the calmest person in our little huddled group on the floor.

House goes along. No other news. I hope that all things are working out happily with you all. Eleanor sends her best. And please remember me to your mother.

Yours,
Red

P.S. I have just received a copy of BTD. As soon as another comes in I'll send it on to you all.

I write to Doubleday and Scribners. Hope to hear Monday at the latest.

[OH]   426 South Greer St.
Memphis, Tenn.
Monday, [August 1953]

Dear Red—

Your letter of August 1 has just come in, and I hasten to reply with hearty congratulations and a fervent thank God! For Eleanor, a croix de guerre seems even more appropriate than congratulations. It must have been a fearful time: quite terrible for her and almost as terrible for you.

. . . .

I'm sorry that you have had to bother with permission troubles—of all times, just this last week. Miss Doyle has written to ask whether we had thought of someone to dedicate the anthology to, and suggests Marcus Wilkerson. Actually we hadn't thought of anyone—certainly, *I* hadn't thought of Marcus. I don't mind doing so, however, and his death may make such a dedication a courteous gesture—though in what direction, I don't know. I feel no special tug of heartstrings toward Helen. Anyway, do let me know what you think—or let Miss Doyle know direct—if you opt for Marcus or for nobody.

Again, love to Eleanor and little Rosanna,
Cleanth

[At top of page] P.S. My mother asks me to tell you that she is sure that your next work will be a piece of very *sensational* fiction indeed—what with hair-raising events on your own hearthstone. She, too, joins in best wishes to you both.

Redding Road
Fairfield, Connecticut
May 26, 1954

Dear Cleanth:

A bit of business: Helen Strauss tells me that she has had an offer from Harpers for our little "writer" project, and that they are very keen on it. This sounded fine until she explained that they wanted to issue it as a text as well as a trade and soft-cover book. I felt that this would conflict with our Harcourt Brace text book agreement for the Rhetoric and Fundamentals, and so explained that to her. She agreed. But she says that she thinks she will eventually pick up some substantial change from it, and is still working on it.

I know that you all have had a good time. Maybe it was your last card [from Italy] that swung the balance for us, but we suddenly decided to go to Italy for the summer. We are about ready to stop painting and gardening and carpentering and try to finish our books. So we'll hole up at Eleanor's place for the entire time except for a few days with the Devlins. We fly on June 1, back here middle September. We only wish that we could have over-lapped some time with you all there. A jaunt together would have been nice.

No great news with us. Tell Ole Tinkie that the leg mends rapidly, the cast off last week, and that whenever pain became almost unendurable the thought of her sympathy gave me courage. I hope I can do as much for her some time. Rosanna is bulging out of her clothes and increases in beauty and wit if not in moral stature. Eleanor is fine, but has been a little too much inclined to lay flagstones and plant hollyhocks at the expense of her spiritual development at the typewriter. We have seen very few people since you left. Home most of the time.

Well, goodbye and our best to you both. Can't wait for next fall and your report. Don't forget anything.

Ever yours,
Red

[Handwritten] I'm sending a note to John Palmer in your care.
[Typed at top of page] P.S. The note to John is to tell him that Jack Jessup would like to see him to make his acquaintance when convenient. Why don't you act as introducer? Jack hasn't anything on his mind, just wants to show interest, etc.

Redding Road
Fairfield, Connecticut
May 29, 1954

Dear Cleanth:

I have talked with John Cheever about doing the piece for Understanding Fiction on the growth of one of his stories, and he has agreed to do it. I told him that he should pick the story—certainly he'd have to pick it to insure one that he could write adequately about. But I also told him that we had to have something that would pass the orals test of college classes. One of his very best, for instance, would not—even though published in the New Yorker, which has a very rigid code ordinarily. He replied that he would like to have an agreement with us on the story. Which means with you, since I shall be out of pocket. So will you write him and ask for his nomination, and ask him where you can read it—either in his recent book (Enormous Radio) or in subsequent stories in the New Yorker. His address is [. . .].

Katherine Ann[e] says that her piece is in process and she will send it to you. But a jog there wouldn't hurt. Her address for the next two months is [. . .].

She had a bad heart business this spring, and for a time it seemed that her Fulbright might fall through, but now, apparently, she is OK and the appointment is confirmed.

I am writing to jog Eudora, but don't have much hope that she will do it before fall—unless it's done already. For she is going to lecture at the American Seminar at Cambridge University this summer, and is writing her lectures.

Well, again a good summer to you all.

And all of our best.
Red

426 South Greer St.
Memphis, Tenn.
July 4 [1954]

Dear Red,

. . . .

Cheever's piece has just come in. I'll drop a note to him, and I'll write KAP at once. Harcourt Brace is having [Richard M.] Weaver (who has used *Modern Rhetoric* every year) to give MR a reading and his set of suggestions for the revision. Gallagher arranged it before he knew that we were good friends of Weaver's. He wants a meeting with us when Weaver's report is in in the fall. By the bye, Weaver's *Ethics of Rhetoric* is a very able book with the first really sensible thing ever [p. 3] written on the Scopes trial.

I am so glad that you give the news about the reviews that BTD is getting in England. I saw one excellent review of it while I was there, but we have been so busy chipping weeds and mowing grass from June 1 until we started south, and so far from magazines and libraries since, that I have been completely out of touch. I am interested in C. S. Lewis's review, which I shall look up. I have my quarrels with CSL but on the basic issues he has proved to be a stout fellow. He at least has the basic perceptions that would allow him to read BTD. The curious thing about that fine poem, and the only thing about it that ever shocked me, was its ability to short-circuit so many otherwise fine critical intelligences. I could not have predicted it, but I think that I am now beginning slowly to discern why. I am tempted to say that it is the first really "new" poem since the *Waste Land*. (I am not trying to praise it in calling it "new": I am simply calling attention to what I am convinced is a historical fact. Allen's reaction is a nice case in point: he has been utterly frank with you and with me in indicating his dislike for it. But I am convinced now that what is involved is more than a particular blind spot in Allen: It is something that Allen shares with others—it is a blind spot in the age.) {[Handwritten in the margin] (Not all the age, thank God!)}

I see that a little later on I am going to have to write a piece for myself on this whole matter, dealing with WET and BTD. I hope that it will not disgrace you when I do. Time enough then to see whether it will be worth publishing.

I am now still struggling with the critical book. But things are slowly beginning to connect up—to arrange themselves in a perspective. I am beginning to feel that soon I may be able to rewrite my chapters so that they will form, with Bill's[1] chapters, a continuity. My head is beginning to clear, but it has been a stubbornly foggy head. Still, if it will clear now, the effort will have been worth making.

[p. 4] During the last few days, at work on the tragedy chapter, a number of notions about Nietzsche have begun to coalesce. My notion—held for the past several years—that Yeats and Joyce were full of Nietzsche is rapidly hardening to a conviction. At the moment I am not concerned with how much they derived from him—they knew him certainly, but how well they knew him, I don't know. What impresses me is the fact that whether they derived much from him directly or whether they did not, still Nietzsche embodies, in a high degree of purity, a strand of ideas that run all through Yeats and are central to *Ulysses*. The fact has been obscured, I dare say, by the journalistic caricatures of Nietzsche that abounded the time of the first World War.

All of which is not to say that Nietzsche is *my boy*. I imagine that he was a thoroughly unpleasant person, and in any case a difficult and cross-grained person. What interests me is the sharpness of his perception of certain aspects of the modern world and the way in which he related these perceptions to the problem of the artist.

But these are matters better discussed over a long drink this fall than now. I repeat: I wish that T. and I could be coming up the goat-path this afternoon to see Rosey-Posey and Eleanor and you. I'm sending your letter on to Tink. She joins me in all good wishes to all of you three.

As ever,
Cleanth

1. William K. Wimsatt, Jr., a Yale colleague of Brooks and Warren's, was Brooks's coauthor for *Literary Criticism: A Short History* (New York: Alfred A. Knopf, 1957). His other books included *The Prose Style of Samuel Johnson* (1941), *Philosophic Words* (1948), and *The Verbal Icon* (1954).

Fairfield
February 25, 1955

Dear Cleanth:

We had a card yesterday from KAP saying that she is having to resign her job and return here for an operation. No details, except that she arrives on the Andrea Doria March 1. We hope to find out today where she will go from the boat. We want to get her up here for a bit if that is feasible.

I am sending today the extra copy of Modern Rhetoric for Tinkum to kindly mark up. I should be through with the novel revisions in another ten days and ready to settle down to that. When that time comes we can set up a preliminary session to guide me.

Yours,
Red

Forest Road
Northford, Conn.
November 15, 1955

Dear Red

The Librarian of Congress, Mr. L. Q. Mumford, sent the fellows a letter dated August 31, 1955, of which I presume you have a copy. A number of us are disturbed not only at what is being done but also at the way in which it is being done. I enclose copies of Conrad Aiken's letter to Mumford of April 23, 1955, and Mumford's reply of May 13. I think that these letters will help to give a little more background for Mumford's letter of August 31.[1]

Some of us are trying to prepare some kind of statement for circulation among the Fellows in the hope that we may be able to revise it into a joint pronouncement. It will help very much if you will let me know your sentiments as soon as possible. Should we urge the Librarian to retain the Fellows—though of course not necessarily the present members, ourselves? If so on what grounds? Should we resign at once? If so, on what terms? Neither Conrad Aiken nor I think that for us to die quietly on the vine will be either dignified or helpful to the cause of Letters.

There is some cause for haste. It seems that one of the Washington papers will soon be breaking a story on this matter of the failure to appoint a new consultant and the failure to call the Fellows together. Do let me have your counsel, even if the counsel is that we should do nothing and say nothing. If

---

1. Essentially, Aiken expressed on behalf of the fellows a concern about the lack of meetings between the librarians and the fellows, about the lack of funds for such meetings, about the general status of the group of fellows, and about the future of the chair of poetry. Mumford's reply was less than encouraging. He said that funds could not be used for other than their designated purpose and suggested that the fellows might have to pay their own expenses.

that should turn out to be our sentiment, at least that ought to be ascertained, no[t] arrived at by default.

Sincerely yours,
Cleanth Brooks

[Handwritten] Copies of this have been sent to the other fellows. I know you are busy, but can you do me *soon* that letter that you promised?

Forest Road
Northford, Conn.
July 9, 1956

Dear Red,

Your card has just come in, asking me how it goes; and I hasten to give a brief report. I am working steadily now and have been for some days. I hope to have some things to send to you, questions to put to you, etc., soon. I go into New York tomorrow for a conference with Miss Boxill.[1] I will postpone a real letter to you until I have talked with her.

I'm sorry to have got down to business so late. Things conspired, as they always do. The worst blow to my plans, however, was when my mother, on a trip to California, decided to stay out there with my younger brothers. That was fine except it meant that somebody had to go to Memphis to close the house, sell heavier furniture, pack the things to be sent, arrange to rent the house, etc. I was glad to do it—it was a burden that my mother should not have been allowed to assume—but it knocked out ten days of working time.

Anyway, here I am facing the typewriter steadily, and if the results are not so high in quality, or so abundant in quantity, as I should like them, maybe things will go better as I warm up.

Tinkum got away to New Orleans last week. I have the house to myself and the typewriter facing me and constantly reproaching me if I do not sit down to it. It's a proper situation in which to get caught up.

For the last several days I have been pounding away on the handbook. I find that I can't redo the chapters on the paragraph and sentence (to be combined in one chapter) until I get the handbook shaped up. It is not hard work, but it is certainly tedious. But I believe that I am going to be able to shape up something that will be not too radical and yet that will avoid the stuffiness of most grammar handbooks. Anyway, pray for me.

Your chapters seem admirable to me. I have gone over them with great care and find little to quarrel with. But I'll leave this screed at note's length and save the letter until I have come back from the New York conference.

[p. 2] No news from here. K.A.P. called this morning and seems to be cheerful and well. I shall drive over to her place for luncheon on Saturday.

1. Mildred Boxill was an associate editor at Harcourt.

I've literally seen nobody here since I came back from Memphis. I hope that I can remain a hermit until I have got something accomplished.

Tinkum writes that all her family in New Orleans are well. She joins me in all cordial regards, to you, to Eleanor, to Rosey-Posey and to Gabriel. We hope that all of you are having a fine summer!

Cleanth

P.S. The radio reported this morning that the keynote speaker at the Democratic Convention is to be the young governor of Tennessee. I suppose that Lon is elated, as he may well be. And certainly he now has a writing chore on *his* hands.

The current *Life* has your fine segregation article in it.[2]

La Rocca, Porto Ercole
pr. di Grosseto, Italy
September 3, 1956

Dear Cleanth:

It has been long since I wrote, and I apologize. But I have been far from idle, and part of my work has been on the textbook. I know from a letter some time back from Mildred Boxill that you have been slugging away very nobly. Well, here is how it stands from this side.

I am enclosing what I hope is substantially the final draft, revised and re-revised, of Argument. I am enclosing Ernest Nagel's report, which I have studied and which, with the exception to be indicated, I have acted on for this chapter. In addition to trying to patch up in the light of his remarks, I have done a lot of incidental fiddling and reordering. Anyway, now I'm stale on this chapter.

But not for staleness, for lack of some reference books, I am passing on back to you some of Nagel's remarks for action.

First, in Argument I am passing back to you the work for pages 74–76—the disjunctive syllogism, though we don't call it that anymore. I see his point, and could patch it up, but I think the best thing to do is for you to check back by a conversation with say, Paul Weiss, and restate the business. If we keep the "inclusive" sense, we certainly have to revise anyway. If I patched, the thing would still be subject to a professional check, and there we'd be.

Second, my chapter on Exposition is lost. And anyway, if it were here, the revision on pages 45 and 55, requested by Nagel, would again need a professional check. I think what we need for the page 45 thing is not so much a cover for the professional reader as an indication in clear language, with a short example, made up if necessary, of some of the processes by which you can block off a definition, by exclusion and by induction. This would apply, too, to the question of the negative on p. 55.

---

2. "Divided South Searches Its Soul," *Life*, July 9, 1959, pp. 98–99, 101–2, 105–6, 108, 111–12, 114. This was an excerpt from *Segregation: The Inner Conflict in the South* (New York: Random House), published August 31, 1956.

I shall have Narrative and Description on their way in a day or two, prayerfully hoping that this will be the last revision of them. There will be no buck passing to you for those chapters. I hate it here, but I don't see how it can be fruitfully helped.

I shall expect your own revised chapters soon, for me to give my going-over to. When will they come? I shall act on them immediately upon their arrival, so as not to delay publication more than necessary.

. . . .

I vaguely thought of going to Germany briefly. My play AKM goes on in Frankfurt in the middle of October, and on live, full-length TV—assuming the rights can be cleared. Fischer has just issued there a theater edition of a translation, and another edition of a regular sort is announced by another firm and will be out in a matter of weeks, I hear. There will be some kind of a general TV introduction, and theater, but I am afraid that the political emphasis might not be to my liking. Therefore, I shall stay away, though invited and paid for. If you don't know what's at stake in such a situation I think you ought to steer clear. A play is one thing, but your presence is quite another. You can only plead dumbness if things go wrong, which is a sad defense. Anyway, I wouldn't want to go alone, and E doesn't want to leave babies. By the way, reporting my concerns, the segregation thing is being translated here and in Germany.

. . . .

Our love, all around,
[Red]

Forest Road
Northford
Sept. 20, 1956

Dear Red,

I am ashamed to have been so poor a correspondent, but I have put every free moment into the revision, including those that should have gone into writing letters to you. Since Mildred Boxill has been sending you reports on my activities, and by this time will have sent you the handbook and the revised chapters that I have done, I don't suppose that we are really too far out of touch on the book. Your Exposition and Argument chapters have arrived and I will undertake the patching that you spoke of, eventually getting an OK on the matters from Paul Weiss. (But if you have any further thoughts on these passages do let me have them.)

I undertook to conflate parts of the Letter to the Student and the first two chapters, simply because Mildred Boxill thought that if we could finish up the whole of the first part of the book, it could be set while the later part was being finished up—provided that we are pressed for time at the end. Otherwise I should have much preferred to have you do the job. When

Mildred sends you this retyped new "Chapter I" you will find that I have cut ruthlessly (and regretfully) some of the good stuff that you had in these earlier sections. But the aim was to shorten the book and to get the student engaged in writing without too much preliminary doctrine. But go over and indicate your changes as candidly as you can. If this new Chapter I is acceptable, then with your four revised chapters—very excellently revised, I think—we have five in hand. Add to these a chapter VI which will be the Paragraph and Sentence compressed and turned into one chapter. (A retyped version of this is on its way to you from Harcourt.) The short chapter on Style will be junked and the chapter on Diction will follow on naturally after the Paragraph-Sentence chapter. I am not to do much in the way of revision of the Diction chapter except to cut out some distinctions and to thin out a few passages that Richard Weaver thought too complicated. I will mail Diction to Harcourt this week and Harcourt will send you a retyped copy shortly.

My next job will be to shorten and simplify Metaphor—I hope to have it done next week. That leaves, then, the chapter on Situation and Tone and the chapter called Final Integration. Situation and Tone will be cut drastically, but then what to do with it? Combine it with a little material salvaged from The Final Integration to a concluding chapter? Or make it a short separate chapter, or what? I am not forgetting that Harcourt wants the last chapter to be a summary of the entire book. See the conference report that I enclose. Anyway, let me have your best thoughts about what to do with the end of the book. Meantime I shall finish up the revision of Diction and Metaphor and make a start myself on the last problem.

[p. 2] Tinkum is helping with the revision of the Reader, but more about the problems connected with the Reader in a later letter. Classes have started here. I keep running into people who are asking about "Red" and sending regards to you. We have just had a big pond scooped out, and Tinkum is planning to take ice skating lessons; so we hope for a hard winter. Maybe you all will be back in time to skate with us. Best love to Eleanor and the children.

In haste,
Cleanth

La Rocca, Porto Ercole
pr. di Grosseto, Italy
Sept. 27 [1956]

Dear Cleanth:

The handbook and the chapter on paragraph and sentence are here. I have studied them, and enclose the result. For the handbook I have here two sheets of comment and bits of trivial nagging. Don't take this at face value, just as an indication of where I was forced to pause a moment or two along the way. For the chapter I am enclosing sheets with suggested revisions or queries, and a re-done sheet for 37 and 38. Regard this with friendly charity. I want to say that I think the handbook very handsomely done, very compact and clear, and the chapter is a great improvement over what we had before.

On my sheet of comment[s] on the handbook, I make a remark about indicating in the book how this material is to be used. I want to emphasize that again, and emphasize the need for mechanical devices to make the stuff handy for marking papers and for locating sections in the book itself. Tabs, indentations, colored sheets—something—or all.

It was nice to have your letter, and the bits of news. We hope to be home in time to let Eleanor and Roposie enjoy your skating. In fact, we'd settle for some Brooks society with or without a pond.

I just now have a cable from Mildred saying that *Narration* has not arrived. I have a carbon here, of the version Mildred sent me, but like an idiot I did *not* make carbons of my revisions of the chapter. God damn it! I suppose I ought to start over, but it breaks my heart. No, I guess I'll hold off a day or two, and hope that Mildred or somebody at HB will cable that it has arrived. Or perhaps it was addressed to you. If you get it, will you cable, or see that they do, and accept thanks.

No news here. We did break our routine, after more than 3 months, by playing hooky day before yesterday, just Eleanor and I, and tearing off to Siena. It was a lovely day, Tuscan hills, two bang-up meals, first-rate Chianti, white for lunch, red for dinner, both meals on the piazza, some pictures that I like very much, especially Simone Martini's big fresco Riccio, the condottieri of Siena, and just plain idleness. We enjoyed the idleness so much that we find it hard to get back to work. The weather remains fine, except for a burst of wind and rain now and then. We hope for two more weeks. Chi sa?

[p. 2] I am sticking in my most recent poem, as a tribute to your learning in theology. I wish I could get some sessions with you on the whole business. I have a raft of new ones, and they keep coming.

Well, write when you can. We love news. Roposie was—is—delighted with Tinkie's illustrated letter. We read it over and over, and admire the pictures. Roposie regards the pictures with a professional's eye. She has begun doing pictures herself.

Goodbye, and love to the Brooks,
Red

. . . .

Academia Americana, Roma
October 26, 1956

Dear Cleanth:

Yesterday the revised chapter on Exposition was sent to Mildred, with a carbon to you of the covering letter.

Now I have a second thought, which would need to be put against the text of the chapter, which, of course, I do not have. It strikes me that we have the method of Identification in the book only for some sort of schematic completeness, and to move from "pointing" in space and time to "pointing" of the chart of genus, etc. But does this serve any useful purpose to a student? I am inclined now to think not. It may simply muddy the waters a little. If you and Mildred agree on this, the remedy is simple. Strike out the little section headed identification, strike out the few subsequent references to identification, and begin the section of Definition by saying that definition is a way to answer the question, "What is it?" A one-sentence lead will set it all up. I am inclined to think that the use of Identification as a method may be sometimes a source of confusion rather than an aid.

I have just seen the morning paper. Gosh, doesn't it look as though Soviet Europe may be cracking up! Today it seems that it's not street fighting and brawling in Hungary but organized war.

No news with us. Albert gets in today. Blackmur has just arrived. Elizabeth Spencer has arrived, newly married to a very county-county Britisher whom we haven't met. (Have you seen her new book? I found it eminently worth attention. And did you see the fatuous, irrelevant caption under her picture in Time? It seems to presume to some dark wit, but what?) We see the Devlins tonight, our first night out in some time, for we have been baby sitting for a week, Isabelle off on a vacation to Venice, and boy, did she come back hopped up. I have been able to work while here, but Eleanor has been housebound. She will start tomorrow, I hope.

Goodbye, and our best to you both,
Red

[Typed up left margin] <I'm having it sent> to you all, it having been sent by the Academia by some method they use for air MS. If it doesn't come in five days have Mildred cable and start new copy to me.

Forest Rd.
Northford
Nov. 11, 1956

Dear Red,

That I have not written you has simply meant that I have been trying to answer the call of duty for the book, putting in every minute that I can spare from the class routine. But I have been reading your letters with delight and profit, and as you will find have adopted nearly all of your suggestions. They have been good as they always are, and they have enabled me to tighten up some awfully loose passages. I am thinking particularly of your very useful comments on the new Paragraph and Sentence chapters.

Even so, I should have acknowledged a long time back the fine new poems which simply bowled me over. I hope that that particular spring continues to flow and that you will send us more copies when you can. One of the things that gives me a bad conscience about this whole book is my acute realization that your time ought to be going for something better than a rhetoric. It has been a case of Pegasus at the plow indeed.

Now for a very brief progress report. I have taken into account your fine suggestions on Diction. I have redone Metaphor and sent it on to Mildred, and I have just finished a remodeled chapter to be entitled "Tone and Other Aspects of Style." It goes to her tomorrow. Now I am starting on the wind-up chapter which is supposed to be a kind of review and recapitulation of the book with opportunities for the student to do a research paper and suggestions for his revision. This is mostly a Harcourt-Brace idea. In any case I have nothing better to offer. The core of the chapter will be a printing of a paper by Geo. Kittredge on the Old Yankee School which will serve as a research paper, and then one or two student papers which will be presented from their origins in the card catalogue on up through outlines, writing, and revision. (The <idea> will be that opportunities will be sprung on the student to be doing likewise with a paper of his own.) I have hired a couple of students to do such research papers for me. I am picking them up this afternoon and look with interest to see what they have done. I hope that the plan works. At any rate it proposes to tell the student how to work up a research paper and how to revise his own work.

In the next hour or so I am catching the train for Notre Dame, not to be scouting the football team for Yale—though Yale ought to be playing them this year—N.D. has lost about 5 games already—but to give 5 lectures. As you may guess, this project was cooked up last winter when I was more innocent and optimistic about what the ghastly future would hold. But the 5 lectures were written two years ago and with my mornings free I probably will get more work done on our book there than I would in New Haven. At any rate, I hope so. I hope to break the back of the last chapter, as well as clean up many an odd and end.

For that reason I shall not go into more detail in this letter about your last suggestions with regard to Exposition, Argument, etc. Obviously I intend to adopt them, or as nearly as I can. But I think it best for me to get the last of my own composition finished before I try to help tidy up the last details [p. 2] of the book. One or two miscellaneous comments, however. We will keep Thurber's "The Dog That Bit People," certainly. Mildred has dug up 3 or 4 short items on Mary Todd Lincoln that will replace the Mary Queen of Scots pieces. I have, by the way, got a copy of Clarence Randall's address so that can be quoted directly in our first chapter rather than indirectly.

No time for anything else at present, but I shall be writing to you as soon as I get a little further along with the last chapter. In the meantime, don't let this wretched thing spoil your and Eleanor's stay in Rome.

Best of love to you all and the children from both us both,
Cleanth (by old Tinkie)

. . . .

Fairfield
November 13, 1957

Dear Cleanth:

A favor, please, even if you are working your head off already.

I am enclosing a first draft of a preface to my Selected Essays which Random House is issuing.[1] Will you please give a careful look and a candid

---

1. *Selected Essays* was published June 25, 1958.

criticism—criticism on all counts, including tone and style, etc. Not to mention content.

I called Mildred at HB, and got our revisions on record. She says that we ought to add a list of acknowledgments, people who have helped with criticism of the book, etc. This seems natural. She will call you to get the names of the Yale people who gave you advice on logic, etc.

Tomorrow morning I head off to Kentucky to go on a jaunt with my brother. Back early next week. See you then. Meanwhile, love to you both. And thanks for this chore.

Red

P.S. Albert wants to get his text ready this month for the essays—so! If I had the nerve I'd ask you to give the manuscript a reading. By the way, I have been doing more in your and Bill's book. It is damned impressive, and very well written. Now be nice, will you?

Sunday, Nov. 17, 1957

Dear Red,

I would certainly love to read the MS of your essays, though I think I would have little to contribute, and if I get too far behind I may have to read more hurriedly than I like. But it would be a pure favor *to me* if you or Albert would let me have a copy.

I like the Preface. I think that it ought to be brief and you have made the main points that ought to be made. I am enclosing a scrappy note on the first few lines. It isn't successful as a re-writing, but it will at least show you what bothers me a bit in the paragraph as it stands. So I'll simply send this yellow sheet along. In the first sentence of the third paragraph I was at first inclined to suggest some such insertion as "though we are not to make a virtue of fragmentation as such," but I was not satisfied with this phrase and besides I didn't see a graceful way to work it into the sentence. Actually you do make the qualification a little later in the second sentence of the last paragraph. Maybe it is just as well to put the qualification here rather than earlier. (I am probably over sensitive on this point anyway, what with the current celebration of the partial and the eccentric as amiable "amateur" virtues.)

I like your suggestion of the different kinds of criticism in the 4th paragraph. I think it might even get a little expansion, with maybe a hint at the kinds of criticism which are to be found in your own essays. In general I think that the tone is good, but you may be *too* modest. You might just possibly consider cutting the very last sentence or softening it a bit.

One trouble in trying to advise you is that I find that I want to read my own indignations, reservations, and assertions into your Preface, and what might be a necessary preface for a collection of my essays certainly needn't be the proper one for yours. So make all the proper discounts when you read this parcel of suggestions.

I hope you've had a good trip to Kentucky. Tink and I look forward to seeing you all very soon.

Cleanth

[p.2] There is an awkwardness in the parallelism in your first few sentences. I would rearrange thus:

For some years I was a teacher, or part-time teacher, and most of my attempts at criticism were tied, in the form of text books or notes, to my teaching, and were directed straight at the classroom. Yet my greatest concern was always to write fiction and poetry, and when I left the classroom, and the obligations of the classroom, most of my energy for writing anything went into poems and stories and novels. But now and then, etc.

[Handwritten] Yet at the same time, my deep abiding desire was to write poetry, fiction, & even though I feel no <immediate> competition between this desire & the profession I enjoyed, I turned most of my energy, when I left the classroom, <and the discipline>, toward writing poems & stories & novels. [A draft of the preface is attached.]

1315 Davenport College
Yale University
New Haven, Connecticut
Tuesday [1958]

Dear Red,

Thanks for the telephone call this morning and the trouble you are taking in making these weekly visits to Holt. I enclose herewith the text of "Yew-trees" and an exercise that I worked out some time ago for "After Great Pain." I will get onto the other exercises this afternoon and I will make a rewriting and a retyping of the analysis of "As I Walked Out One Evening."

Regards,
Cleanth

[OH]
1315 Davenport College
Yale University
New Haven, Connecticut
May 26, 1958

Dear Red—

We were happy to have, the other day, your joint card. I do hope that all goes well now that you all are settled. I hope that France will not create too many alarms and excursions, what with the De Gaulle business up. You both deserve a serene stretch of time both for work and play.

Re: *Understanding Fiction.* Nothing to report at the moment. But I give my last examination today and I hope by the end of the week to get back to it and to serious work. (As you can guess, May has been a steady rush of term papers, dissertations, committee meetings, etc.; but I am now nearly caught up.)

I am asked to sound you out as to whether you would consider teaching a course at Yale—something other than creative writing (since I know you are tired out with that)—on a semester basis (or through the year)—and presumably on some very flexible program. It may be that your answer to this question will have to be a resounding *no*. But Louis Martz is extremely anxious for me to put the question to you and hopes very much that you will say *yes* or at least *maybe*.

This business, I hesitate to say, is none of my doing—though I applaud it. But you must not think that *I* have been putting ideas in anyone's head. Several months ago, Bill Wimsatt was wondering whether you might be induced to give a course, if only occasionally, of your own choosing. Others have made the same inquiry, including Louis Martz (our present chairman). Louis was asking me about it before you told me that Harvard was sounding you out.

[p. 2] When I told Louis that Harvard was also interested, that did nothing to decrease his interest—but I ought to emphasize the fact that it probably did not do anything to intensify his interest either, for Louis was already as hot on the idea as I have ever seen anybody.

It may well be that you have decided that you just don't have the time and energy for teaching. (I couldn't blame you.) But if there are courses that you *would like* to do, regularly or irregularly, I know that the department will want to know, and to judge from conversations with Louis, flexible schemes could be worked out to suit, I would hope, your convenience.

Anyway, don't hesitate to say what you would like on this subject, to me, or directly to Louis. It hasn't been a question of competing with Harvard. Rather, as he and Bill W. have put it: it's a shame to see so great an opportunity go to waste if Red is at all interested in teaching—anything.

No news to report from here. The rains have kept up, and here at the end of May, we have had very little sunshine. But T. and I have had one or two days of mowing in the river meadow and in front of the house. The dogwood and wild strawberries and wild violets were never before so abundant. But I'd like some sunshine now for a change.

I will be writing soon. Love to Eleanor and to Rosie-Posie and to Gabriel.

Cleanth

P.S. We expect to be here until at least the end of June, and if we have to go away, to be back for most of August. But plans are still somewhat fluid. In any case, I expect to be hitting the fiction book soon.

[OH]   533 West Elm St.
                                                              Inglewood, Calif.
                                                              Thursday [1958]

Dear Red—

Your material on Description came in yesterday. I have gone over it hastily and find little that I am tempted to change or expand. It makes a fine opening of the second section. I want to meditate the comment and note on "Pippa" a little further—but I dare say that I shall have little or nothing to suggest here, in the long run.

Your energy puts me to shame. But I am at work and have nearly finished a longish analysis of "Mariana." You remember that we have talked of putting it in the Tone section. But I mean to use it as connective tissue by pointing how that it might have been [p. 2] studied in either the Description or the Imagery sections. Since my books came in several days ago, I have been "soaking" in the Coleridge poem and in Wordsworth's "Yew-Trees." I think that I am about ready to write on them too. (The Coleridge poem is beautiful but devilishly difficult. But I now think I know what I want to say.)

The difficulty is that I have no typewriter and don't want to inflict badly scribbled MS on you. But I shall be starting home soon—on the 8th to be exact, and Tinkie will rapidly type up the analysis as soon as I get in. "Mariana" is quite a poem. There are lots of problems in it, too, a number of which I shall not try to settle in the analysis but shall put into exercises for the student.

"So you agree with what I say? Well, what did I say?" is quite a poem too, though it would have shocked Alfred.[1] The title, by the bye, is excellent. I am not sure that I could "say" what the poem says, but I am much moved by it—and I *think* that I know what it says: at least I have an inkling.

Love to Eleanor and the Children. Don't work too hard.

Cleanth

P.S. I hope that the play negotiations go forward. My mother is well and appreciates your inquiries about her.

[OH]   1315 Davenport College
                                                             Yale University
                                                    New Haven, Connecticut
                                                            August 3 [1958]

Dear Red—

Just a note to say that your analyses of "Hell Gate" and "Mr. Flood's Party" have come in. Very good going. The Hell Gate account is particularly interesting. I want to chew over one aspect of that one—maybe suggest a minor qualification—maybe not. Your account is most persuasive and surely on the aspect of monotony and isolation it is dead right.

I have finished "Mariana" and am over half through with Coleridge's "Constancy to an Ideal Object." With luck, I may also finish W's "Yew-Trees" (which I have already made a start on) before I return.

[p. 2] I am distressed to hear of complications with the play. All my fervent hope that the snarl will untangle.

---

1. The poem appeared in *Delta* (LSU) 14 (1960): 1; and in *You, Emperors, and Others: Poems 1957–1960* (New York: Random House, 1960), 56–57. Brooks may have meant Albert rather than Alfred.

Love to Eleanor and the children. I will be heading east at the end of the week.

Regards,
Cleanth

La Rocca, Porto Ercole
pr. di Grosseto, Italy
August 16, 1958

Dear Cleanth:

I am deep into the text book, and am making progress. I don't know that what I am doing is worth anything, but I am getting ahead. But I need a word:

Didn't you say you would do Hemingway's "Snows of K" for Plot section? I vaguely remember that you said you had some notions on it, had taught it, or something?

Now, if you had not intended to do this interpretation I can do it, though I don't think I'll shine on this particular one, if on any. But if you do not do it, please send me

1. Any thoughts you have on the thing, and general comments about its relation to the section etc.

2. A chopped-out text, for I can not get one here—or a typed copy.

And by Air Mail.

We are down under plot for a Maugham thing, a well-made conventional story. I have only "Rain" here, and don't know that that will do. Perhaps it will. Shall we wait on that till I get back?

Some queries: Naturally as I do things I wonder about correlation with what you have done in earlier sections. For instance, do you have a key treatment of tone under your new "Walter Mitty"? I need it for "De Mortuis," but am assuming that it is already in.

Again, I find that we have no adequate treatment of the term symbol anywhere in our old text. The Glossary gives ref under Titanic, but that is woefully inadequate. As are other refs. Needed for Necklace.

[p. 2] There are, of course, bound to be a lot of loose ends to tuck in when we get together. Let's try at least to record those that we think of along the way.

. . . .

Goodbye and all the best,
R

P.S. I think I can soberly promise you to have my promised part of the book done on time. God helping. The stuff you sent me is fine.

By the way, a note from HB says that Modern Rhetoric has passed [the] 20,000 mark in July.

I'm pleased with your comment on the poems.

[Handwritten up left margin and across top of p. 1]: *NB* I sorely need a copy of Welty's piece on her story (Va. Quarterly—1956 or 7) & a copy of the story.

Also Cheever's story "Goodbye My Brother," which his essay is about—you may have to get information about it from him.

La Rocca, Porto Ercole
pr. di Grosseto, Italy
August 23, 1958

Dear Cleanth:

I am enclosing:

1. Lead on plot section
2. Interpretation and questions on Girls in Their Summer Dresses
3. Interpretation and questions on De Mortuis
4. Addition to interpretation etc. for The Necklace
5. Addition to interpretation, and added questions for A Piece of News
6. Questions for I See You Never
7. Notes for treatment of Snows of K.

{[Handwritten in left margin] All in the rough—please suggest changes & rewrite—or better DO THEM}

I now propose the following lay out for the section:

Lead

1. Girls in Their Summer Dresses—I. Shaw
2. Furnished Room—O'Henry
3. De Mortuis—John Collier
4. Necklace—de Maupassant
5. A Piece of News—Welty
6. I See You Never—Bradbury
7. War—Pirandello
8. Snows—Hemingway
9. ?

Of the first 7 stories 6 (leaving out I See You Never) are very heavily discussed, in either formal analysis or in comment in the form of questions etc. I think this has to be so at this stage. BUT—should we buck up the section by adding maybe a couple of very short pieces for the students to work on, and the teacher to show off on, somewhere before #7? Then give a concealed analysis of Snows (hidden in comment with the exercises), then a fairly sizable story, which will be without any guides from us except questions, and which will give a basis for a review of the section? I have no nominations, however. I suggest all this because I am thinking in terms of what the reduced edition will look like.

I am getting close to being stymied for material. I need the stuff I have already mentioned, and if I haven't mentioned it, The Two Gallants. I shall go on now with my piece on Blackberry Winter—if you still think it useful.

To repeat: I need Uncle Wiggly in Conn

The Two Gallants

Welty's discussion of her story *and* her story.

Love by Jesse Stuart
Love by de Maupassant
Cheever's story—BUT have written him directly for it.

I'm sorry to give you extra fits, but some of the stuff assembled didn't get properly packed, and God forgive me.

I begin to think I see the light on this book, however, and begin to think it might be pretty good. Anyway I'll promise you that it will be better than the competitors, after my survey of them.

No news. Love to you both. All well here. Good weather. Eleanor whacking along on her book.[1]

Yrs,
R

La Rocca, Porto Ercole
pr. di Grosseto, Italy
August 25, 1958

Dear Cleanth:

I have been working on the little piece about Blackberry Winter, and I begin to have grave doubts about using it—doubts having nothing to do with coyness.

First, the piece is long, I mean the story, some 10,500 words—I have just counted it—and we are going to be pushed for space anyway. I honestly think that the thing will not justify itself as a sales attraction, with that length.

Second, I have just read over KAP's piece and Cheever's, and as I mull over what mine will be like I don't think my account of the origins of BW will be different enough. The similarities will perhaps give a false impression of the way fiction is written. One trouble is that KAP's story and my story would be both fairly firmly grounded in a lot of autobiographical material, directly autobiographical, and I, like KAP, would have to do a good bit about setting up that material in the account of the origins of the story. My story, like hers, is a false-and-true memory. Etc. Mine, like hers, had a rather spontaneous growth, etc. What makes my account different, or would make it different if it were to be written, would be the reason I happened to get at that particular story at that particular time, but that would bring on a lot more autobiography, which would have nothing in the world to do with story writing as such. Now, I can think of other stories I have written, say The Circus, which had a very different kind of genesis, as have all my novels. But I can't think of a story of mine suitable for the book that would give us the excuse for the kind of account we need, something that deals with the <objective>, logical problems of fiction in relation to story meaning *and* the background in personal feeling.

So I'm just up a tree. I hate to put a week into writing an account of BW and then find it isn't suitable. Maybe we should leave this to the very last and

1. Eleanor's book was either *Baldur's Gate* (New York: Pantheon Books, 1970), portions of which had appeared in the *Yale Review* and the *Kenyon Review,* or *Oysters of Locmariaquer* (New York: Pantheon Books, 1964), an excerpt of which appeared in 1959.

talk it out when I get back. God knows, though, we'll have enough work to do to make the deadline anyway.

[p. 2] Changing the subject, when I sent you a list of stories for the Plot section I did not include Owl Creek Bridge. But the more I think of the matter, the more I am inclined to think that the story might be kept but that the Interpretation might come to grips directly with the "case history" business—mere psychological realism is not fiction, has no comment, etc. None of the other pieces in the Plot section gives a good excuse for that. This would not require more than a few more lines of space in the Interpretation than we already have. The story itself is a little long, perhaps, but not too long—3,600 words. We do have the problem, however, which I mentioned in my last letter—space—if we intend to add a couple of stories to the section for students to work on.

Do you mind writing me at your early convenience?

Yours,

R

August 29 [1958]

Dear Red,

Your letter of the 25th got in this morning and I make haste to reply. I have finished two paragraphs on tone which will fit into the Mitty analysis and a long footnote on symbol which will be attached to the Lottery analysis. As soon as Tinkum can type these off, I shall send them to you. They are routine, but I think that they will set up the terms for your uses of them in "De Mortuis" etc. I am at work on the lead into the section on character. The lead that I had done is now far out of scale with those that you have done on Plot and theme. I shall do a comparable job, if I can, and send it on to you. By the way, I see the point of the longer leads (in view of our proposed short edition) and I admire what you have done. My criticisms will be of trivia—some little matters of style and phrasing. They are all right in substance as they stand.

I see your problem with "Blackberry Winter" though I hate to give up your account of it. Perhaps we can think of another one of your stories to be so used. But I agree that the thing to do at this time is to wait rather than use up a week perhaps needlessly. We can talk about it when you return.

I am for keeping the "Owl Creek Bridge" story in the plot section. (Among other things it will be useful in helping set up a discussion of Hemingway's "Snows of K.") shall I try my hand at adding a bit to the analysis of Owl Creek in the matter of psychological case study, etc.? We do need such a note somewhere: I find that I had jotted it down already as something to do.

I agree that we need in the plot section some story (after first six) that would be less fully analyzed—or no analysis—for the student to do. I am now looking through Maugham and hope to come up with a nomination. I don't think that "Rain" is really a very good story and there are other things against it. I've read several Maugham things in the last few days—none of which seems clearly right—but I will keep looking. Or, maybe we can find something from some other author.

In the Theme section, I see that you have retained Saki's Filboid Studge. Since I think that I was largely responsible for the nomination of that story for the present text, let me speak out to say that I am confident that we can do better. I'll look through Saki again in the next few days with a substitute in mind.

On Monday I shall plan to send you a copy of the Welty story, Jesse Stuart's "Love," and whatever other pieces that I have ready of those that you have called for. The rest will follow as rapidly as I can get them ready. Don't work too hard. The weather is beautiful here today—Hurricane Daisy has made off to sea—we are finishing painting our house, and the gutters are on, and the chimney repaired. We are soon to be ready for the fall storms.

Give our best love to Eleanor and the children. No real news here except about Missy and the immediate place, for we have not seen the university crowd yet.

All my best,
Cleanth

[Handwritten] I will try to develop the exercise on the "Snows."

La Rocca
September 4, 1958

Dear Cleanth:

When the next to the last of your letters said you thought I ought to go ahead with the BW piece I thought that to be your final word, and so plunged in. I had already done a good deal of thinking about it and preliminary work, and so it went fairly fast. Your last letter, thinking that the thing might be left out, after all, hit me just as I was getting into the last little bit. So I went on to the end anyway. And here it is—a first draft, or nearly that. Now we can think the thing over in the light of what is actually here or potentially here. One small thing—which doesn't alter the views I had against using the story or my comment—is that not KAP, Welty, or Cheever talks about the way there is some oscillation between the undirected ideas and associations and the conscious attempt to get at a pattern, and none of them gives any sense of how a story finds its logic in the actual process of composition. I don't think less of their pieces for that, for they are all splendid and KAP's is important and beautiful. But I do think that for pedagogical purposes something else has to be there, too. That is why I tried to write in and tie it to the personal. I had also hoped that we might get a story for this purpose based, say, on an objective anecdote and not on memory, for this resembles KAP's and the other pieces a little in that regard. But the cold fact is that, with one exception, I couldn't sit down and write about another story of mine without faking too much. (I could about novels, but not about stories.) BUT—I can't do the lead to the section with these comments until I know whether or not mine will be used. If not, I have to work things a little differently from the way I could with my piece in. Not to rush you—for we might let it slide until my return—but be thinking about this. The thing can be cut some, and certainly needs some rewriting. Put your critical attention on revision, if you begin to think we might use it. What kind of question might be taken up? Assuming I can remember the answers.

I shall now get back to the theme section and tidy up exercises and questions. I agree that Filboid Studge is not ideal. I don't think we need a Saki [p. 2] necessarily but that one fills a useful niche—a story light in tone with thematic emphasis and the focus on a satirical generalization. I have a notion where we might find one, though I don't have a particular story in mind. Marcel Ayme, who has several volumes of stories already translated and who has a collection forthcoming with Harpers, might fill the bill to a T and give us a little choice, too. I can't get the books here. Do you want to take a look? I will do comment etc. I have, by the way, written to Buzzati,[1] without waiting for your OK, I am so sure that this story is both good and useful. As I said, if it doesn't have a translation (his stuff may have come out in England) I shall undertake to do one. But I haven't heard from him.

. . . .

Goodbye, and our affectionate greetings, regards, and thoughts, yrs.

R

La Rocca, Porto Ercole
pr. di Grosseto, Italy
September 9, 1958

. . . .

Dear Cleanth

An item I had forgotten: I agree with you that the U of K Library got a poor estimate. It may be just, but it doesn't, in itself, warrant much effort on our part. BUT—from now on we shall make our own estimates. I have some suggestions from Thompson as a guide-line. If you have in hand the MS and stuff of Understanding Poetry, I think we might well claim $1200 maybe more. It is very different from the revision of the Rhetoric—a revision and a book of less general interest and reputation. And I guess that $1200 is worth our trouble. Same for UF. Do you happen to have the original stuff magpied away?

Here I am enclosing two items—the lead for the section on how fiction is written, and an *addition* to the note on Owl Creek Bridge. I am not proud of either, and know that both are rough. But I'll send them on. We can revise later, and I depend heavily on you in that department.

I am now, in odd moments, trying to make up actual MS and clippings for the printers, section by section. I am doing Plot, Theme, and How to Write

---

1. Dino Buzzati was an Italian writer of short fiction. He received the prestigious Strega Prize in Italy for one of his collections.

Stories. A few things I haven't got, like Snows, but we can fill in when I get back.

Remarks: I notice a few mannerisms that crept into the old text of UF. For example—"perhaps the best way to approach this question"—things like that. Let's look out for such on the way. It is easier now than later. ALSO in Character section we ought to have some kind of comment of the use of dialogue and characterization. ALSO somewhere—in Character?—a story that gives us a springboard for a basic discussion of point of view. Man Who, Miss Emily, Uncle Wiggly, and Want to Know Why are all good for this purpose, and can all be used in their places with some reference, but one is too early, and the other three too late. What do you think? I'm happy to write a piece on the topic if we can get the story settled. {[Handwritten in left margin] Please—will you jot down topics that seem to be <scanted> so that we can catch them on revision.}

I am going to make some exercises to put on the four stories under How To Write—primarily on how to understand the stories. I said on the four stories. I have no copy of Noon Wine, so if you get some notions for exercises, jot them down. I'll do what I can from memory.

No news, except that we jog along, which I consider good news. John Palmer is using a new section from E's novel for winter, which pleases her, and me, and which seems to please John. Weather is still good. We cross our fingers as the 22nd comes on.

Our best,
Red

[Handwritten] You have certainly been taking the rap very nobly in getting stuff to me. I can't repair your nervous system from the strain, but at least you can keep counting all the money. When do your classes start?

La Rocca, Port Ercole
pr. di Grosseto, Italy
September 11, 1958

Dear Cleanth:

I am enclosing a section using Lardner's "Haircut" as a springboard for possible use in Plot section. But let me postpone discussion of this until I have summarized the situation in regard to this section.

Tentatively I now have this table of contents for the section:

. . . .

[p. 2] With additions indicated we might run up 60,000 [words] altogether. Thinking of the short edition, this would give us . . . [225,000 words].

This shorter edition would have toward 40 stories, many of them very short but still a very useful layout. The longer edition would have to include the big batch of material in How Written section (67,500, actual count), the appendix on technical questions, (14,000 in present version, to be slightly revised upward), and what new stories to go in under Study and Special

Problems. They will allow us for the big edition around 550,000 words (if my memory doesn't trick me), which after we discount How Written section and technical appendix would leave upward of 225,000 for Study and Special Problems, with such comment as we chose to make. That looks pretty good to me, how about you?

In the light of that situation perhaps we should put into the plot section another very short piece or so for student work?

But to come back to Plot in general. On going over the thing, I began to feel that we had to have a discussion of point of view in that section—after all the actual plot is conditioned by that. I know that Haircut is an old chestnut, but it is damned useful, and L's name is good. Also it gave me a good tie-back to Man Who, and will give a splendid one forward to Blue Hotel. We have to have a Crane, and though this one is often anthologized I have never seen what I consider a decent discussion of it. My present notion is to do a very full set of guiding questions (almost answering themselves) which will give the illusion that it is merely for student work. Then follow that by a story with non-guiding questions. Since we can't confer at this distance I am bulling ahead, with the full knowledge that when we do confer we'll have to do some changing, and perhaps throw out some of my work. But there's no help for it.

In thinking over the two editions, I now feel that we shall have to do an independent Glossary for the short edition, to accommodate the differences in page references, etc. But the Glossary is short and this would not be expensive. I also begin to feel that with the shorter edition we shan't need the technical appendix—feed in the stuff along the way. But with the longer edition it might be useful as a place where topics could be assembled and correlated, in connection with the Glossary—or perhaps for writing courses, as a special feature.

NOW—for your grief and pain, I have the suggestion that you take up point of view in relation [to] one story in the Character section, with special reference to problems of characterization, not a full account but something to develop [my] remarks under Haircut. Then in Theme section I'll develop the discussion a little of I Want to Know Why, to round out the topic, and the discussion under Miss Emily and perhaps Killers. I also think that some of the exercises under Snows ought to touch on point of view.

[Red]

1315 Davenport College
Yale University
New Haven, Connecticut
Sept. 12, 1958

Dear Red,

Your piece on "Blackberry Winter" is very, very fine—in your best vein, I think. I immediately had to show it to Tinkum, who agrees with me as to its usefulness in our text, but also as to its intrinsic interest and its goodness as a piece of sensitive prose. My only regret is that it may be wasted in UF. (It won't be wasted on the best students, however, and not on the teachers. But you should plan to publish it separately before it goes into our book.)

You may well wonder why I have waited so long to write you this—if I am indeed so enthusiastic. There is reason. On Tuesday, Tinkum cracked a bone in her ankle. She doesn't know how she did it nor do I. I was watching her—it was in the house. But the ankle had been badly sprained long before and more than once.

[p. 2] Anyway, it was, as you may guess, very painful. I got her to the doctor quickly and after x-rays, he put on a cast. The worst is now over—the pain is subsiding, and she is beginning, cheerfully as usual, to reorganize procedures in the house to get through the next four or five weeks.

Since it is Tinkum, things will return to normal soon, but the accident has stopped my work on the book, and delayed my writing to you. But I shall soon be back at work, and T. will be typing for me again. My lead in to the character stories is nearly finished, and will soon be typed out and on the way to you. So will the other things I owe you, including the two stories on "love."

No time to write more for the moment. Give our love to Rosieposie, Gabriel, and Eleanor. We do look forward to your return—*all* of you.

Cordially,
Cleanth

P.S. K.A.P. has written to us from Charlottesville, where she is now settled and likes it. Haven't seen John Palmer recently, but we will soon see him. I've stayed away from the University, but classes start the middle of next week. I hope the Great White Father will have some sensible thoughts on Matzu and Quemoy. He leaves me very unhappy on that subject.

. . . .

La Rocca
September 17, 1958

Dear Cleanth:

I have been working away at the Theme section and come up with this tentative table of contents for it—representing some changes, for which I'll give the arguments in a minute:

. . . .

I have kept Christ in Flanders because it is too pedagogically perfect to throw away—right between parable and a modern symbolic story, like the Dragon. Stuart and de Maupassant come next both being rather illustrative treatments of a theme, simply done. The Killers moves over to realistic surface with complicated thematic insides, with good start for point of view discussion again. I Want to Know Why allows some new development of p[oint of] v[iew] in contrast with Killers. Ditto Uncle Wiggly, with considerations again of style and theme. We had postponed Emily, but we can't. We need it here so it will be in the short edition—two reasons, we need a Faulkner and the interpretation is one of our best. A Good Man pairs perfectly with Emily, pathology on surface, serious theme, etc.

This makes a rather long section, but it strikes me that for the short edition we might strike off Mann and Camus, which are both rather advanced any-way, and then follow with our glossary. And perhaps in long edition transfer Mann and Camus to *Special Problems*, etc. {[Handwritten in left margin] Strike off Mann & Camus only if space makes it necessary?}

Another thought: With KAP in the How Written section, we have no example of her in the short edition. How about slipping one of her shorter ones into the Character Section, and dropping Old Mortality for the present from UF? Then when we revise the Approach, we will drop Noon Wine (because here) and slip in Old Mortality with our present interpretation, perhaps slightly simplified? I honestly don't see how we can publish two novelettes by KAP in UF, and this would mean (in Approach) that we could use our old interpretation. The real question now is whether or not to use a short story in the short edition of UF. And if so, where? Would He be useful for character? It would certainly raise some questions about sentimentality and style and tone. And isn't it rather short?

So long, and all the best to all—

Red

[Handwritten] P.S. I have done some odds and ends for the section but they aren't impressive enough to send.

[Handwritten in top right margin] P.S. The copies of *Love* by de M. and *Love* by J. Stuart have not arrived. [I] mention this because in your last letter you said you were mailing them in a day or two. Lastly, we leave here by *Sept. 30.* Address thru October 10: % Lawrence Roberts, Vella Aurelia. Porta San Pancrazio, *Rome*.

Sept. 20, 1958

Dear Red,

Accept herewith some of the delayed items that should have gone to you 10 days ago. They are copies of DeMaupassant's "Love" and Jesse Stuart's "Love," and a rather rough draft of the lead-in to the Character section. You are forging ahead in such fine fashion that I find that recent enclosures from you make obsolete some of the things that I have been working on. See, for example, the patch on p. 7 of the lead-in to the Character stories. But there may be advantages in our duplicating if we are able to neaten the book up later, for the student won't be hurt by repeated tie-ins and tie-ups.

Tinkum is still hobbling in a cast, but she can sit up with[out] discomfort {[handwritten in margin] Freudian error, T.} now and has resumed the type-writer. I am still something of a cook and bottlewasher. Anyway, we're coming along and I hope to keep up my end of UF from now on. School has started, but I am going to budget my time so as to keep on this job. Let me know of other story materials that you may need. The bursary boy will be in action soon and with him and the photostat machine and Tinkum I can supply you without trouble.

Now a brief summary of the substance of your last letters. I agree with all the proposals you make. Your calculation of the number of words we can spare does make our project look most promising. We will have room enough to turn around in in the short version and ought to be able to prepare a really formidable long version. Specifically I like very much your projected section on plot (I'll try to work out a character section in something like the same proportion and along similar lines). Do you still think we should have a Maugham story (a plotted story of conventional shape) in this section or is that example sufficiently now taken care of? I have wasted some time reading a good deal of Maugham but have found two or three that might do in a pinch.

The stuff that you have been sending in is fine. But it is so full and discerning that our problem may be to seem to have left enough for the student and the instructor to do. We must at least give them the illusion of having something to do, particularly the instructor. I haven't any answer to this problem but let's keep it in mind.

Carl Van Ness of Crofts has written to ask whether we can still make the late October deadline with our MS of UF. I am writing him that we are hard at work and still hope to make it, but October 31 already begins to look difficult to me and you may want to give him a later date after you receive this.

In the next day or so I hope to send you some further exercises on Hemingway's "Snows" and an analysis of "Disorder and Early Sorrow." I shall also hope fairly soon to send you a projected outline of the Character section.

I must stop if I am to hope to make the Saturday morning mail from this country post office. Our best to all of you.

C

La Rocca
September 25, 1958

Dear Cleanth:

. . . .

As for UF, I think the lead to Character what the doctor orders. Like my leads, it may need a little tightening when we get everything laid out, to avoid repetitions, etc. But it is fine. We can stand on it.

I have finally heard from Buzzati on "The Killing of the Dragon," and I have closed with him for $125 (17-page story), with the translation our responsibility. I shall use the time on the boat doing that—though I may get stuck. I won't get stuck as far as sense is concerned, but I may very well get stuck in trying [to] get a decent style for it. I am well pleased to have this piece—fresh meat and perfectly adapted to our needs. I hope you like it.

As for date, I propose that we tell Van Ness that we can very probably give him the MS by November 15. That would give you and me 3 weeks to go over everything and revise what we now have. We'll need that much time, I guess. I will put every minute on it during that period, so even if you do have your classes I imagine we can make that date. We could probably give him substantial parts earlier, for that matter, to have his people making ready.

I sent the Blackberry Winter thing to the NY Times, and they are using it—that is, if I cut it down to their standard length. I have just done that, so I guess it is a deal. The cutting will help, too, for the text book—parts were slackly written. But don't be too sure that we have to use it. I am being paid for my trouble anyway.

My next step, after doing exercises for the "Love" stories, will be to overhaul the section of Technique and see if it needs much. I hope not. There will, of course, have to be changes to accommodate new stories and to omit references to our discards. Ditto for Glossary.

Then, except for a new preface, aren't we through? EXCEPT FOR final selection of additional stories for long edition and exercises on them. But we could do that in two days, face to face.

. . . .

Love to you both. We want to see you. Yrs,

Red

P.S. We go to Rome October 2. Address there: Care Laurance Roberts, Villa Aurelia, Porta San Pancrazio. We leave there the morning of October 10. Sail October 11. *Saturnia.*

La Rocca
September 28, 1958

Dear Cleanth:

I have some thoughts to put on record for your consideration. I have begun to be concerned about the nature of our Stories for Study and Special Problems section. As we have it in the old edition, we analyze Tallow Ball, Araby, Miss Emily, Old Mortality, and Penal Colony. These stories did raise in more positive form than in earlier sections certain special problems. BUT now, in our present lay-out, we are touching on most such things in the Plot, Character, and Theme sections. So what I propose is this:

1. Put Araby back into Character section in place of Two Gallants, keeping the old analysis, but revising the questions to relate it to Character more sharply.

2. Put Two Gallants in Stories for Study section.

3. Kill Tallow Ball.

4. Kill Old Mortality (for we'll have Noon Wine in How Written section).

5. Put Miss Emily, with analysis, in Theme section, as already indicated to you in earlier letter.

6. Put Penal colony, with analysis, at END of Theme section, with perhaps an allegorical story to follow for exercise. Then we can cut off the section either before Mann or after Camus, for the Short Edition, with no harm, but for the Long Edition we would have a more tidy arrangement. IN THIS WAY— all our analyses would be grouped under our early heads: Introduction, Plot, Character, Theme. Then would follow [the] section Stories for Study, with leading questions but no analyses, and with refs back into earlier analyses. Then would come the How Written section. Then Technique section. Then Glossary.

Does this make sense to you? If we don't do this, or something like this, we shall have a very funny business in the Stories for Study section, with one or two stray analyses inconsistent with the treatment of other stories. And we simply can't settle in and do a new batch of analyses for that section. It wouldn't be desirable, in the first place.

I am now working on Techniques section and feel that it doesn't need much more than mechanical adjustment. That is, I can't make it much better myself.

Yrs,

Red

Oct. 5, 1958

Dear Red,

Your letters of Sept. 25 and 28th are in, and if I am to reply to them in time for you to receive the letter while you are still in Italy, I must be able to mail the letter today. I picked up a virus infection last week, and though I have not been in bed, my efficiency has been cut. But I should be over it very soon, and since Tink sheds her cast on this Friday, maybe business around here will pick up.

I agree completely with your latest proposals about UF, and for fear that you are not making carbons, let me run over what those proposals were.

. . . .

This all makes sense to me. I particularly like the feature of no analyses in the last section since I have been worried lest the instructor would feel that we had left him nothing to do. The eager beaver ought to plump for the longer version.

I'm glad that you think that the lead-in to the Character section will do (with revisions and polishing, of course). My main job now will be to put the Character section in order against your return and to be on the look-out for stories for the last, unanalyzed section.

The Character section at the moment looks like this:

Tennessee's Partner	Bret Harte
Araby	James Joyce
The Drunkard	Frank O'Connor
The Lament	Anton Chekhov

[p. 2]	Tickets, Please	D. H. Lawrence
	Eventide	James Purdy
	Old Red	Caroline Gordon
	? Disorder and Early Sorrow	Thomas Mann

If we are to provide a full-dress analysis for "Disorder" as you suggested some time ago (my job—I can do it rather quickly), then the story ought to go in this section, I suppose. With an analysis, it ought not to go in Stories for Study (though it might go in Theme).

I haven't counted up the words in these eight stories. Since several are long, the total might be not too far short of the 36,000 that you totted up for the eleven stories in "plot." But I do think that if I can find at least one more short one for this section, it would be well. Maybe you will have a nomination.

Anyway, I will try in the next week or so to put this Character section in order, modifying analyses where required, etc., and if I can find one or two short pieces of fiction that will add variety, or make points that require to be made, I shall have them ready for you to see. I also am going to have my Bursary boy type us up a good copy of some of the earlier material—the introductory part of the book at which we worked last spring.

Our weather holds good: it is perfectly gorgeous today, though I have been inside through the early afternoon watching the Braves beat the Yankees 3 to 0 in a very pretty pitchers' duel. We hope that you all have a fine last few weeks in Italy and a pleasant return voyage. We are very anxious to see you all. Tinkie joins in love to Gabriel, Rosanna, Eleanor, and you.

[Cleanth]

P.S. Tink says to tell you all that she can definitely meet your boat, and that she will be at the dock with her stationwagon unless you tell her not to be.

August 1, 1959

Dear Cleanth:

Here are two more analyses—rough but ready—Hell Gate and Mr. Flood. Hell Gate is for Narrative, toward the end of the section, and the other for Tone, near the beginning. I may have chosen poorly here, but the poem is extraordinarily teachable, and maybe it will be all right here to back up Channel Firing.

I have about lined up Narrative, but have not yet found a good contemporary example. But shall. Next week I shall be on the Tone section, for which I have several new and fresh items to submit to you—poems not ordinarily found in text books. I think I'll try to do an analysis of Campion's Blame Not My Cheeks for this section, with some reference to "tradition" as a background for it. I have been looking over the old Ulalume analysis, and I believe that now I vote to keep it, with some reduction, perhaps. For one thing, the quotation from Huxley at the end is so useful.

I still have no word from the lawyers about the rights on my Cass Mastern play. God damn it, if a mere technicality of that sort now blows up the thing I quit. But I should have word next week.

Albert, Marissa, John, and an old Italian friend Gianturco, who rivals René for learning and Groucho for fun, are here for dinner tonight. So I may forget some of my troubles. Eleanor has had a rough week with Mamma, God help us. But she is now in a sanitarium, and we draw breath.

Speaking of Italian friends, last summer I read the Italian MS of Pier's big novel, and liked it very much. Albert gave him a payment for him to do his own translating, and I have begun that. It is a stupendous job of something— not translation. It is very effective as English prose, scarcely ever the slightest unnaturalness. The book has just come out in Italy as the first selection of the Italian Book of the Month.

Goodbye. All the best.

Red

P.S. I enclose a letter from Appleton Century. I have written them that when you get back we'll cook up the short edition pronto. I would do it now, except for the need for some consultation.

1960s

1315 Davenport College
Yale University
New Haven, Connecticut
April 23, 1960

Dear Red,

I have been awarded a Guggenheim and I make no doubt that I know whom to thank in this matter. Your sponsorship of my case must have carried great weight with the Committee. I am indeed most grateful to you.

Yesterday, in my modern poetry class I took the liberty of reading—we were studying your poetry in the normal course of things—three or four poems from your new book. The effect was sensational! The class really was moved and excited.

Thanks again to you, and love to Eleanor and the children.

Cleanth

[OH]

1315 Davenport College
Yale University
New Haven, Connecticut
July 1 [1960]

Dear Red—

I forward as rapidly as I can—though with apologies that I must be so roundabout—the enclosed carbon of Mildred Boxill's letter. I have not had time to *study* the proposals, but my first reactions are as follows:

1. Mildred's specific recommendations make sense.

2. I hate to face the labor involved either this summer or this fall, with all that I have to do. (And I am sure that you are in like plight.)

3. If we do it soon, I think that we will need help.

4. If it were possible to get someone—of Mildred's choosing or a Yale instructor—to do the work for a flat fee, [p. 2] that would be the most desirable thing. But the person who did the job would want his name on the title-page and a share of the royalties. Still, we might try to find someone who would work for a fee—a good one.

5. It would be nice if we could get Mildred herself to do the job—but since she is already on Harcourt's payroll, that is out of the question, I suppose. We will have much help from her gratis.

Write me what you think. My mother seems surprisingly well and sends her fondest regards. I expect to be back in Northford on July 21. Until July 18, write me (by air, of course):

533 West Elm St.

Inglewood, California.

Give my love to Eleanor, Gabriel, and Rosanna. I hope that you are all having a wonderful summer.

All my best,
Cleanth

[OH]   1315 Davenport College
                                         Yale University
                                     New Haven, Connecticut
                                          July 17 [1960]

Dear Red—

Your letter of July 10 (mailed July 12) called for an answer more prompt than this one. But here in never-never land, I am too much inclined to let things slide. Anyway, here is a brief scrawl.

I'm glad to see that you agree with me that it would not be sensible to have a third name on the title page. If we should get Mildred to do the whole job on a fee basis, that would be my first choice. But I doubt that she will feel that she could keep her *own* time separate from her Harcourt-Brace time in working on a project such as ours. Would you mind putting the proposal to Mildred, however, if you do feel that there is a chance of getting her to do it? In any case we are obviously going to have to lean on her hard—and of course she has already made a sizable beginning in the plan that she has submitted to us.

If we cannot get Mildred to do the work on her own time, then I think the next thing is to check at Yale. If you think well of it (and if Mildred has in the meantime said no), I will canvass the situation at Yale. I expect to be back at Northford on the evening of July 21—that is, this Thursday. (I shall make it, by the way, my first business when I return to get my library friends to find that pre-1859 song book for you. Sorry I missed on that.)

Your "Elijah on Mount Carmel" is a knock-out.[1] It's the last section that brings it off. Daring, yes. But absolutely necessary if the [p. 2] tone is to come right. It does—magnificently. You and Tinkum are going to have me reading the Old Testament soon. I am ordering for you, by the way, a copy of Voegelin's

1. "Elijah on Mount Carmel" appeared in *New Leader*, September 26, 1960, p. 10, and then in *Selected Poems: New and Old, 1923–1966*, 67–68.

Israel and Revelation.[2] Since you are reading the O.T. these days, the Voegelin ought to be by your bedside.

Don't let me, by the way, push us both into an acceptance of Mildred's proposal for a shortened *M. Rhetoric. If* we can do it with really a minimum of work, fine. The money would be useful. But time is so short. I will be eating into my precious year off, in no time. And you, I know, are even harder pressed. But I do hope that you can manage the Lee's <decision> piece. You are right: that shouldn't fall into the wrong hands. I don't want to see a Lee throwing in his lot with the Confederacy because of an Oedipus complex, for instance. This is the way it might come out.

My mother—very proud to be remembered by you—sends fond greetings. To hers, I add my own. I hope that all goes well with the Vermont establishment and that you and Eleanor are having fun but are also getting a lot done. I am sure that Rosanna and Gabriel are having a wonderful time.

Love to all,
Cleanth

P.S. The story about the honey-mooners and the bear is very funny.

Northford
August 2, 1960

Dear Red,

I have let myself get sidetracked into a Percy Letters[1] operation and have been working on it so intensively that I have let other and more important things slip. A letter from Mildred Boxill today calls me back to pressing matters. She says that she has not heard from us about her proposals (July 25th) for editorial help on the condensation of *Modern Rhetoric.* I must say that the fee of $500 for which she thinks she could get the job done seems reasonable to me. And I must say that I think there is some advantage in taking her advice about the man who is to do the job—particularly since she promises to supervise it. You will remember that she wrote that she has a particular young man in mind who has taught English and that she will sound him out. This sounds attractive to me. What do you think? If you like the idea, will you—in order to save time—write to Mildred direct? Otherwise, let me know what you think. I am writing to Mildred today that she will hear from one or the other of us quite soon.

I am ashamed to say that I have not found your song yet, but I do have out of the library *The Liberty Minstrel*, 1844, which seems to be an abolitionist

2. Eric Voegelin, *Order and History,* vol. 1, *Israel and Revelation* (Baton Rouge: Louisiana State University Press, 1956). Voegelin was Boyd Professor of Political Science at LSU before moving to Stanford University.

1. Brooks along with David Nichol Smith, served as general editor for *The Percy Letters.* Vol. 6, *The Correspondence of Thomas Percy and George Paton,* edited by A. F. Falconer, was published by Yale University Press in 1961.

songbook; *The American Minstrel*, also 1844; and *The Washington Songster* (date uncertain) which seems to be a mishmash of everything.[2] I am told that the Music School library has a very extensive collection. If there is no great hurry I should like to explore this matter. Don't tell me not to go to trouble. It is no trouble at all, rather fun to do, except that it is a field that I don't know much about.

You ask me in your letter of July 21st for my meditations on Lee's decision to stay with Virginia and its fundamental appeal to American imagination. I have nothing useful to offer at the moment except that I have been re-reading in the last week Faulkner's *Intruder in the Dust* and remember the same problem arises there. Against the more abstract claims of liberty, justice, etc., there is the concrete claim of the region, the community, the family. I don't know that Faulkner's Gavin Stevens argues those competing claims very well, but surely he is right in arguing that there must be a reconciliation, a true reconciliation, not simply an ironing out of the local claim under the pressures of abstraction. Rereading Faulkner's book and listening to the two platforms via TV have certainly convinced me that the problem of Lee's decision is a very live problem today. If one had to depend on a conception of the United States from the platforms—thank goodness we don't have to—one would certainly conclude that America was a congeries of competing minorities and classes setting up ground rules to keep from jostling each other. The conception of a living, concrete community simply does not emerge—and maybe for a good many parts of this country it does not exist. Anyway, I hope you will yourself meditate the Lee piece and do it.

We hope that all goes will with the whole family at Vermont. Tink joins me in love to you, Eleanor, and the children.

Cleanth

[Handwritten at top of page] What about "Darling Nelly Gray"? It has a pleasant tune—it is about a girl sold "down the river"—"I'm sitting by the river and I'm weeping all the day, for you've gone from the old Kentucky shore." It is of the same period as "Listen to the Mocking Bird." It was sung by both Confederate and Union soldiers during the Civil War. I'll try to *check* the start date. Do you know it? Or would you like a copy?

1315 Davenport College
Yale University
New Haven, Connecticut
August 23, 1960

Dear Red,

It was good to have your letter and the very handsome copy of *You, Emperors and Others*, for which Tink and I are very grateful. It is a fine volume.

2. This discussion may have come up in relation to Warren's work on *The Legacy of the Civil War* and on his novel *Wilderness*, both of which were published in 1961.

Mention of it brings up the main matter of this communication. Louis Martz is very anxious for us to get your record out as soon as possible. He had hoped for next month, but I suppose that is impossible. Anyway, I am now trying to choose the poems that are to go on the record and get ready to write the jacket piece.[1] I am sorry that "Two Studies in Idealism" didn't get recorded on the tape, and it may be that others should have been recorded, including the wonderful ballad "Between the Boxcars." I intend to listen to more of the tapes this week. Though Lee Anderson thought your voice tended to play out toward the end, it may be that we have plenty on tape to provide the record. If we do, however, need to have more poems recorded or re-recorded, what are the possibilities of your getting down for a day to New Haven? Is it at all possible, and if not, when are you counting on returning to Fairfield? It might just be possible to send someone up with a portable recording rig to Brattleboro, but about that I am not certain.

If some re-recording has to be done, I am much inclined to have you do "Original Sin" and "Dragon Country"—at least the latter—not only for their own sakes but as a kind of bridge to the poems in your new volume. On the other hand, you may think it best to confine the recordings to poems in a present volume. What I have chosen very tentatively and without any real check on the amount of time they would take up are "Clearly About You," "The Letter about Money, Love, and Other Comfort, If Any," "Arrogant Law," all five pieces from the "Mortmain" group, "The Well House," and "Two Studies in Idealism," if we can get these last recorded. But I may be choosing poorly and I would very much like to have your suggestions.

Last week the photographer for our recording series indicated that he needed, of course, to get a picture for the jacket. I told him that I would get in touch with him after I had heard from you. I take it there is no hurry about the picture—at least no more hurry than about the making of the record in general.

I have not heard from Mildred Boxill for some time, but I telephoned her promptly after getting the go-ahead from you some ten days ago and she was to put the young man to work on the shortening of *Modern Rhetoric*. As soon as she had some samples of his work Mildred was to send them on to us.

This is a wonderful season for us, the weather cool enough, no classes to bother about, and nothing to do except work away on the Faulkner project and various other matters. I wish we might have some talk. I am afraid I don't have much to contribute with regard to the Lee piece, but I do have a great many things I would like to ask you about with reference to Faulkner. I hope I can count on your reading some of my MS at a later date. Tink joins me in cordial regards to you all.

Cleanth

---

1. *Robert Penn Warren Reads from His Own Works,* Yale Series of Recorded Poets (YP 313), Phonodisc, Carillon Records, 1961; revised under Decca (DL 9148) label [1975].

P.S. Your sentiments with regard to the political campaign are very close to my own. I suppose that I shall end up by voting for Kennedy, but I have very little enthusiasm for either choice.

1315 Davenport College
Yale University
New Haven, Connecticut
September 2, 1960

Dear Red,

Thanks for your letter—which I should have answered earlier. But I got immersed in a hurry-up job that had to be done for a Yale Press book and time got away from me. (I find that the last weeks have been almost the perfect life—work and play merging into each other, no pressures or little to meet deadlines, no classes to keep up with. The drawback is that I lose touch with reality. I don't know whether this is an argument for the doctrine of original sin or simply points to my own depravity. Anyway, since life is a little too good to be true it all becomes a little unreal.)

I am very glad to get your notions on the poems for the record. I hope that you will be perfectly frank about them—not only which you might prefer would not be picked but which ones you would really like to have on the record. My notion about including one or two fine ones from previous books amounts to this: the poems are good in themselves; to include them is to suggest a bridge back to your earlier poetry—a consideration of some consequence for the jacket piece. But most of all, I made the suggestion because, the more I think about it, the less certain I am that Random House is going to approve of all the recorded poems coming from the current book—especially since we shall have to include with the record a text of those poems.

You are right to remind me that the matter has not been cleared with Random House. I wrote Albert a letter the other day and have his reply. He is taking the matter up with your agent and asks me to send agreement forms to him when we have settled upon the particular poems to be put on the record. (Albert also includes the useful tip that we had better use the term "sheet" rather than "pamphlet" of poems to be included with the record.) Albert doesn't suggest that Random House is likely to refuse if all the poems come from the current book, but I think that they may very well be unhappy about it. It is all very well for Yale to say that the record will not compete with the book but will actually advertise it—I think that this is true—but the permissions editor may not agree.

Lee Anderson was here the other day and I had a brief talk with him, but could not reach him yesterday and am afraid that he has now returned to Penna. I had wanted to get his opinion of the quality of the recording in the last two tapes. I shall write to him and think that he will be back here shortly.

There is really no great haste about this matter. Louis, on whom the burden principally falls, is very anxious to keep things moving and he quite understandably wants to get one or two real names into his series of records soon. Yours is an obvious choice. But things will have to wait and indeed probably will have to wait anyway until mid-September—or later. I will mull over the selection of poems, listen to some of those already recorded, and time them, and get going on the rough sketch of the jacket copy. I'll get in touch later on when you are in Fairfield if there have to be additional recordings.

Did Mildred Boxill send you samples of the proposed condensation of *Modern Rhetoric*? I have gone over the samples that she sent me and am very well satisfied. My question is whether so little cutting as he has done will suffice. But Mildred's observant eye is surely on that point. And if Harcourt can market a book with the cutting as light as Coombs is doing, so much the better. I suppose that the big gain in pages will be in discarding the Handbook and the Reader.

The new research paper on Baretti does not strike me as a particularly exciting paper for freshmen. But maybe it is. I think that the principal value of the paper that we now have on jazz is that it illustrates in some detail the need for rewriting and the ways in which one does it. Maybe the Baretti paper—if it is otherwise good and interesting—might be handled in the same way. That is, deliberately mangled if necessary so that we can show the student concretely how the process of rewriting is achieved. What are your notions on this point? On the present paper? On the kind of topic? On the matter of providing revision and correction?

And in general what do you think of Coombs' notions for condensation and of the samples that he has submitted?

We hope that all goes well with you all in Vermont. Tinkum is outside with Mike and Missy, happily sanding on doors from which we are, at long last, trying to remove the last flecks of white paint. She joins in regards to Eleanor, Rosiposie and Gabriel.

Cleanth

Northford
Sept. 23, 1960

Dear Red,

I wrote to Lee Anderson yesterday telling him that you were saving the mornings of October 4 and 5 for recordings. Since I hope this weekend to listen to the tapes already recorded, I ought soon to know more about what has to be done by way of further recordings.

The real occasion for this note, however, is some comment on Mildred Boxill's letter of September 22 and the Baretti paper, a copy of which she enclosed. It is a good paper for the purpose, though I do not think so well of it as she does. I am a little concerned about the number of references to Italian works, though perhaps this makes no difference. What bothers me most about it is a concern as to whether it can be used to show the necessity for and advantages of rewriting. Some rewriting could be done, pretty obviously—and maybe only a little rewriting will be sufficient. The paper on jazz in the present edition may be over-elaborate. Perhaps all we need to do is to illustrate a few improvements in sentence structure, perhaps Coombs could do this, or Mildred—or in a pinch, I could do it myself. (You do agree with me, do you not, that some illustration of what one does in a rewrite job is required for our book?)

Though I am far from enamored of our present paper on jazz, I am not sure that a paper on an obscure eighteenth-century figure is going to be much more exciting to the American freshman. What do you think? The paper is interesting to me, but then I am a working scholar in the period. Since there is such a demand for haste, however, I am certainly tempted to accept the Baretti paper. Let me know what you think.

Cordially,
Cleanth

1315 Davenport College
Yale University
New Haven, Connecticut
October 12 [1960]

Dear Red,

I am working on the jacket copy for your record. The poems that I have chosen tentatively are as follows (though not necessarily to be used in this order):

The Garden
Original Sin
Dragon Country
Two Studies in Idealism
Mortmain (all 5 parts)
Clearly about You
The Letter about Money, etc.
Arrogant Law
Debate: Question, Quarry, Dream
Country Burying
Tiberius on Capri
Founding Fathers

I am glad to find "Founding Fathers" on the list that you recorded the other day, and gladly add it to my selections. I wish that I had remembered to ask you to record "Walk by Moonlight in Small Town," a special favorite of mine.[1]

---

1. "Walking by Moonlight in Small Town" first appeared in *Yale Review* 46 (spring 1957): 328–30, in the subsequence, "Man in Moonlight."

The poems that I have listed above will, according to my calculation, take up about 50 minutes, the allotted time. When I make a final check, we may have time for one more—maybe not. Anyway, give me your opinion of what I have put down. Please be candid. I am trying to get some variety, to spread a little over your career—though it is proper that we represent the last two books heavily, and I would represent the last one even more heavily except that I am afraid that Random House would not like to grant so many permissions from a current volume.

But do let me have your own opinions. I am leaving out many fine poems that I like. I am far from confident of these choices. For goodness' sake, let us try to satisfy your notions too while we are at it.

I may ask you in a few days to go over my jacket copy. It is very hard to say anything in 900 words. I don't want to make a fool of myself—and I don't want to simply talk around in circles. Where some of my comments on a poem lead away from it or miss the point, please say so. But my draft won't be ready to send you for several days yet.

I am to get a couple of student papers tomorrow to look at as possible substitutions for the research paper in *Modern Rhetoric*. From their titles, these don't seem too promising, but maybe one of them can be doctored into something. I am promised more to come. But I am out of touch with the students this year and it has proved harder to come by a good student paper than I had thought. If worst comes to worst, however, we can redo the Baretti paper or keep the one we have on jazz. But I may be able to turn up with something better.

I have been checking over Mildred's sheaves of revised copy as they come in. Thus far there have been few problems—indeed very little cutting except in references to essays now in the Reader.

As soon as I get the material for your record set up, I shall turn seriously to rereading the metrics transcripts for *Understanding Poetry*.

I am at last writing on the Faulkner.[2] One of these days I am going to ask you to look at some portions of it for me. T. joins me in all best wishes to Eleanor, Roposy, and Gabriel.

Cordially,
Cleanth

P.S. I am tempted to take the fine series "Sweet Dream of Peace," but the series needs all or most of the parts to make its full sense and yet the whole series would be quite long. I am glad to know that the "Box Cars" is on tape. It is a fine poem. The word that our records are probably going to come in for wide sale and use by the high school libraries makes me wonder a little about the effect of its fine refrain—"flat on his ass beneath the box-cars"—something that is absolutely necessary for the poem—but something about which the high school instructors might be squeamish. Or am I being squeamish? There

2. The first of two volumes on Faulkner, *William Faulkner: The Yoknapatawpha Country* (New Haven: Yale University Press), was published in 1963.

are plenty of references to the facts of life in the poems that I have chosen, of course; but I think that the impact is a little different.

[Brooks enclosed a copy of his first and second drafts for the jacket of the Yale Series of Recorded Poets.]

1315 Davenport College
Yale University
New Haven, Connecticut
Nov. 9, 1960

Dear Red,

I enclose copy for M.R. What I send picks up with page 429 of the present version of the book and breaks off on p. 446. I had meant to get further, but I am afraid that unless I get this into the mail within the next hour, you will not get it tomorrow.

Please look at pp. 446–53 of the present text. I do not think that we need to do anything with this paper so elaborate as we did there. But I hope to put in a little more material on rewriting and revisions of this sample student paper. Maybe, if we could give another four or five instances of revision for the sake of clarity or removing dead metaphor or getting rid of fuzziness or even introducing a nice metaphor—here is where you come in—it would help. And it would be well to introduce the problem of tone—just briefly and lightly, [p. 2] if we could. This last business might not be easy, however, and might give the student something pretty complicated to handle. But maybe a way will occur to you.

I shall go on myself with some revisions and send them on to you tomorrow.

If other matters occur to you, let me know. If, for example, I have polished the student theme too much—it looks to my present eye *anything but polished*— let me know.

In great haste, cordially,
Cleanth

Nov. 10, 1960

Dear Red,

I worked at this batch of stuff in order to get it into the mails for you but didn't quite finish in time. It doesn't matter since I now remember that it wouldn't have been delivered to you on the 11th anyway. Please go over this carefully and don't spare the rod in correcting, eliminating, and adding. As you will see, the material I have here covers pp. 446–453 in the last version of *Modern Rhetoric*. But it does so on a much reduced scale. Some of the revisions that I have made for the student may seem niggling. I hope that you have more substantial ones.

Do look particularly at what I have to say about tone and metaphor. In the "Jazz" essay the revisions for the sake of tone I think were made to stand up—so also the one or two that had to do with metaphor.

Our new student paper offers less opportunity for taking up the matter of metaphor or tone. But I think that these topics should not be allowed to go by default. Anyway maybe you can come up with something including a fine metaphor to be inserted in the last paragraph of the student paper— something that will cap his argument and bring it all to a neat head!

I am sorry that this batch of stuff bears all the marks of haste, including the messy typing, but my jaded steeds have had to feel the lash all the way through and I am afraid the prose I have written shows it.

Cordial regards,
Cleanth

[Handwritten] P.S. I also enclose the student's maps. We can use the map lettered by himself or have Mildred have someone with more professional skill letter the other map which he has thoughtfully provided for this purpose.

C.B.

[OH]
1315 Davenport College
Yale University
New Haven, Connecticut
July 26 [1961]

Dear Red—

I'm ashamed to have waited so long to write. Eleanor's letter arrived just after we had got back to Northford (late in July) and Tinkum was promising herself to reply right away. I hope that she did. (From my putting it this way, you will surmise that we are now separated on our annual family visits, T. in New Orleans and I here in California. But we return to Connecticut next week.)

. . . .

Charles Madison wrote some time ago to ask permission to use the first 10 pages of the Introduction of *U. Poetry* in a book for engineers being edited by two people under Holt contract. I wrote that I had no objection, if you had none, and [p. 3] that I assumed that, as a friend and an editor of Holt's, he would propose nothing likely to injure the sale of *U.P.* But I suggested that he write you specifically for your permission, giving him your address in Brittany. But Charles wrote back that there was no need of troubling you about such a small matter, and there the matter rests—unless you have heard from him.

The big news for us when we reached New Haven was that you had accepted a professorship in the English department. I trust that Yale met your stipulations or came close to doing so—at any rate, made a thoroughly satisfactory arrangement as to hours, courses, time off, etc., as well as salary. Your appointment this time had to be voted by the Board of Permanent Officers of Yale College (i.e., the full professors.) Louis M[artz] told me that he had rarely seen so much enthusiasm expressed over a proposed appointment. I do not need to tell you of my personal pleasure or Tink's.

I have been back from Europe such a short time (and for part of that time, [p. 4] in effect, dropped down a well here in this backwater of Los Angeles), that I am completely out of touch. I do not even know whether your new novel has been published and have seen only one notice of your Civil War book.[1] (It was a fine and lengthy one by Van[n] Woodward, the leading article in the last Yale Review.)

I hope that you and Eleanor and the children are having a fine summer in Brittany. I am sure that you are. When do you all mean to come home? Perhaps not before winter? Anyway, if you can make out this scrawl—I have no typewriter at my disposal—do let me hear from you.

Love to Eleanor and to Rosanna and Gabriel,
Cleanth

P.S. I've had recently two exuberant letters from Katherine Anne. She seems in fine fettle. And no wonder! The book is finished—as she reports; and *Newsweek* (in this week's issue) says that it is scheduled for spring publication.[2]

1315 Davenport College
Yale University
New Haven, Connecticut
March 13 [1962]

Dear Red,

First, a word about your preface to Eversole's book.[1] I think that it is not sad at all. I think that it is just right: well said, admirably fitting the occasion, and presented in what I think is a most suitable form. I like the idea of Notes.

In Note 2, bottom of p. 2. you write: "It is even conceivable that salvation of the man might be the damnation of the artist." Yeats feared so in his own case. Remember his poem ("Vacillations," I believe the title is. Anyway, the section in question involves a dialogue between the Self and the Soul and Von Hugel is mentioned). {[Handwritten in left margin] It is in *The Winding Stair* volume.}

Incidentally, I agree with your sentiments whole-heartedly. And from what I have seen and sensed of the book, it is just as well that these things that you say be said emphatically at the beginning. (But in note 4, what is the meaning of *acud-vath?* Typing error? Or one of the many terms that I simply don't know?)

I also enclose a request to reprint the "Trees" analysis. I have signed it on the assumption that it will save time for me to have done so in case you want

1. *The Legacy of the Civil War: Meditations on the Centennial* was published February 27, 1961; the novel, *Wilderness,* was published November 15, 1961.
2. *Ship of Fools* (Boston: Little, Brown and Co., 1962).

1. Foreword to *Faith and the Contemporary Arts,* ed. Finley Eversole (New York: Abingdon Press, 1962).

to give permission. What do you think? I suppose that we ought to let him reprint it, though I think he might be asked to print a note saying that this analysis has been revised and somewhat modified in later editions. But as you [p. 2] think best.

Back to the Eversole volume. I am sorry that I did not send you the letters from him to me that I had promised. But you evidently did not need them: I repeat that I think your preface is very fine. And as I now look at the Eversole letters, I am not sure that they would have done much good anyway.

Have a good vacation. We enjoyed the glimpse of Eleanor the other day and the visit from Rosanna and Gabriel.

Cleanth

3/14/62

Dear Red,

"Fiction: Why We Read It"[1] is really a superb job. Both of us know how slippery and difficult the topic is. I think that you have handled it with admirable lucidity. Best of all, you have given one of the few really *concrete* accounts of the matter, and an account tilted over toward the place of fiction in the human economy, without vulgarizing it or blunting and distorting the other issues. Those issues usually do get distorted if someone wants to write about what fiction can do for us and the kind of pleasure that it gives but not in your account. In terms of theory—if I have any right to speak of this matter—your essay seems excellent. I should think that someone like René or Bill Wimsatt would find nothing in it to quibble about at all.

In terms of its concreteness and its simplicity of language—but *simple* in the best sense—it is really a little masterpiece. It would be a wonderful essay for *Understanding Fiction* or *The Approach* if with a proper permissions fee to you, and you deserve a good one—it could be included in either of those books.

I have set down (on the next page) a few very tiny suggestions and queries. None of them amount to much and I shan't mind if you pass over them all.

Now let me turn to another matter. I mean to do a good deal more tinkering with the lecture on you for my little book on *Literature and the post-Christ-Christian World*.[2] There are several repetitions that I mean to clear out. Of course, you may prefer not to tell me anything at all about this discussion of you, but don't hesitate to let me know if there is something that ought to be cut out, or if I strike a note anywhere that troubles you. The Yale Press, by the way, has just told me that they are going to take the book. I am glad and sorry at the same time, since I owe a book to Holt and had hoped that maybe this

1. "Fiction: Why We Read It"—more commonly printed as "Why Do We Read Fiction?"—appeared first in *Saturday Evening Post*, October 20, 1962, pp. 82–84. It is reprinted in the fourth edition of *An Approach to Literature*.
2. Brooks's "little book" was published as *The Hidden God: Studies in Hemingway, Faulkner, Yeats, Eliot, and Warren* by Yale University Press in 1963.

one would be available. At any rate, Yale now plans to publish it probably next January.

[p. 2] notes on Red's article, "Fiction: Why We Read It":

On p. 1, the sanctified term, I believe, is "rain forest," not "rain jungle." On p. 3, last sentence of last paragraph, you might say "We turn to fiction finally because we hope to see in it an image of ourselves." This is probably not right but I believe you need something more *concrete* than the sentence that you have.

On p. 4, last sentence of the long paragraph, don't you need an adjective before "day dream," something like "to the shimmering day dream" or "to Miss Windsor's day dream"?

On p. 5, first sentence of the new paragraph, "makes up for the defects of reality" might be closer to your audience's way of putting it than "Fiction repairs the imperfections of reality."

p. 6, will your readers know Walter Mitty? I suppose so, but you might consider adding a phrase that would identify him or recall his significance in this context.

p. 8, near the top of the page, you might think of giving your reader a little guidance here, making the paragraph open this way: "Some people, especially those who fancy themselves hard headed and realistic, make the mistake of confusing this business of role-taking with the idle irresponsibility of indulging a day dream."

On p. 10, "oblates" fits nicely but I wonder whether your special audience will know it. Maybe "secret dungeons" would be better on this account.

On p. 11, I doubt whether it is really worthwhile going to the trouble to drop the term "mulatto" as applied to Joe Christmas. Probably here it doesn't matter, but if you think it does, you might try something like "The overturned table behind which Joe Christmas, possibly a Negro and certainly a social pariah, cowered."

On p. 20 I am still pedant enough to prefer "human beings" rather than "humans." In any case I think that "human beings" gives you a better rhythm in this sentence.

On p. 23 the second sentence of the long paragraph beginning "All we have to do" [p. 3] trips me a bit. I see what you mean but only after I have first stumbled. You may want to remodel this sentence.

On p. 24, middle of the page, I'm not sure that "We" is rhetorically right. Maybe "We as grown up people" maybe just "The grown-up reader" or "The mature reader." The second "We" is all right and I think could stand.

P. 25, I tend to be too grudging with John Dewey, as I well know, but I do wonder whether the passage you quote from him is half as good as what you yourself are saying. The last part of his sentence "To deepen and intensify its own qualities" seems to me a little lame when what you are saying is that something more than its own qualities is being conveyed—a movement toward vision and significance. But whether you use the Dewey quotation or not, your paragraph makes a fine ending.

[Handwritten] Do you want your copy back? If so drop me a note or telephone me, and I will mail it to you.

Love to the children and Eleanor,
T joins in regards,
Cleanth

[OH]

1315 Davenport College
Yale University
New Haven, Connecticut
Dec. 14 [1962]

Dear Red,

Something has just reminded me that I have done nothing to sound out Edmund Wilson about being with us this spring. Would you do so? And could you right away.

I would say $2000 for 3 weeks, or thereabouts. Perhaps two formal lectures and a good deal of talk with small classes and informal seminars.

Any time between the end of January and the first week in May except that March 16 to April 1 is the spring holiday.

If he should be interested, details could be negotiated.

See you all Sunday
Cleanth

[Handwritten at top of page] P.S. Do you know Albee's "Who's Afraid of Va. Woolf"? We have talked of making a try for him. When I talked to Lillian Hellman some weeks ago, she indicated that she might be available this spring. I telephoned her right after our Dept. meeting, but she was even then packing for Europe.

Elkhorn "Ranch
Bozeman, Montana
June 26, 1963

Dear Cleanth:

I am enclosing a revision of the General Introduction for your attention. Rewrite at will, etc. This certainly is not a finished form. And I am not at all certain, for one thing, that we shouldn't tone down the end a little, and put in a few bows to the historical, etc. We are so open to idiotic attack on that point. Consider this prayerfully. Or perhaps it can be stated more tactfully. You are great on tact: RESTATE.

Another thought: It occurs to me that we might add the Rotary story by George Milburn to our function section, not because the story is such great shakes, but because it gives a perfect little schematic example of irony by point of view of narrator.[1] And we have no other instance. They are hard to

---

1. George Milburn, "The Apostate," in *An Approach to Literature,* 4th ed. (1964), 216–19.

come by. If you agree will you paste up the story and insert it, so we won't forget, then when I am back I'll write a comment, etc.

Things have gone well here. The place is marvelous, and the people ditto. Quite remarkable. Some of the other guests are very attractive, and Gabriel and Rosanna are enjoying people as well as horses. They often ride twice a day, but Eleanor and I have been working in the mornings, riding in afternoons. There are a great number of different trails, beautiful views, snowy mountains, deep woods, streams, elk, moose, etc. Tomorrow, now that we have seasoned our bottoms a bit, we leave on a pack trip. Then on July 3 we ride 20 miles to a rodeo. Our bottoms better be seasoned.

Good-bye and our love to you both.

As ever,
Red

[Handwritten at top of page] P.S. I know we count on "windows" but I'll re-set these later, when I get another copy of the textbook to <edit>.

Breadloaf School of English
Breadloaf, Vermont
July 8, 1963

Dear Red,

Welcome back home—to your Vermont home, that is, for I am assuming that you will be in West Wardsboro by Wednesday. We hope that all of you have had a wonderful time in Montana and that you are not too tired and not too sorry to be back in the East again.

Now to business: I have gone over your fiction section, which is admirable, and have only a few minor revisions to suggest. Ditto for your rewrite of the General Introduction, which came here in good order soon after my arrival at Breadloaf.

I have the poetry section ready to show you. (I am still looking for Cal Lowell's Col. Shaw poem, which I had understood was in the *Partisan,* but with better directions from you, I can locate it here or have Stewart Baker get it and send it up.) I also have a good lot of Xeroxed material for the essay section, and a lot of letters out for permission to use this material and other material including some plays.

I hesitate to mail any of this to you, though I *can* send it by mail or, I suppose, by express. It might be easier to bring it myself—even if I just delivered it and did not plan to stay for much talk just at this time. You all may not be ready for company for some days yet. Anyway let me know, by letter or telephone, and we can make plans. T. joins in love to all four of you.

Cleanth

[Typed at top of page] P.S. We are here in two cars. Tinkie has to go back to Northford for the 16th, when her mother and Liz are coming. But I shall keep my V.W. here and will thus be mobile. If I come to your place at any time my best route will be through Rutland via 11 and 30. Or am I wrong? Anyway: before I come, give me directions from this approach.

West Wardsboro, Vermont
July 23, 1963

Dear Cleanth:

I guess I bobbled it about the poetry, and should have held stuff here until your letter came. But I was anxious to get what I had done to you for your further inspection, and revision. Here I enclose the stuff you sent me. But I'm not sure we couldn't get a rounder piece for Whitman—even quite a bit longer if necessary.

I have been doing nothing but the text book, and have now finished the Essay Section. I shall hold it until I hear from you—which, time being what it is, I hope will be immediately.

I am enlarging the table of contents as it looks. Here are my problems:

1. What letters of permission have been written? I shall happily write any necessary, but I don't want to duplicate, etc. If you will let me know I'll act immediately on this.

2. There are some difficulties about material. I do not think that the Krutch will do. Not because of ideas, but because it is obviously an extract, and hashes up our question of form. As I looked over our content (you see I have put Stevenson back in because it did seem to give the best general starting point for the section, but I am open to conviction here), I began to feel that lots of people, in one way or another, were taking side-swipes at the point of view represented by Skinner. A bright teacher would hunt up Krutch and CS Lewis and such. Maybe we could just leave out Krutch and not put anything in his place. Or perhaps we could add an exercise under Skinner referring to Krutch and Lewis and sending the kids to the library—or sending the teacher. Unless we turn up an *essay* at the right level stating the opposite view. If the exercise is the thing, I nominate you to do it.

3. You will see that I have re-thought and re-entered this general section giving it a new over-all title, etc. Please give this careful thought. I'm not sold on what I have done.

4. I can't get typing done here. Can you? If so, I shall send my stuff on to you and you can get a local typist to do clean copy of my sections that require recopying.

NB. I have just read Krutch again. I still feel that it will not stand as an essay, but if we cut in at the bottom of page 2 and stop near the top of page 14 we have a good section which, with a lead in, might be put [in] the discussion of Skinner, and serve as a kick-off spot for the exercises. How does that strike you?

What you say about permission on WC Williams, and Emily Dickinson, sounds OK. I hope that we can get SKIN, for exercises on that would give some fine ties back to the essay sections.

{[Typed at upper right corner] You were to add a little to the Boswell?}

[p. 2] I am returning the Tennyson, which you can slip in after say Bugle Song—or somewhere—with one sentence referring to the occasion of the grief and asking the little bastard of a student to work the thing out on his own.

I don't feel sure that Robert Shaw actually got a degree from Harvard.

Yes, we have the right to use old permissions if we don't revise more than a certain percentage of the book. I hope we are under that. But we should ask Stanford to have the permissions files checked to see what the minimum percentage is. Doesn't he have the files? If I remember correctly—which I probably don't—this percentage varies with different permission forms.

At last the work has begun on our foundation! But trouble, trouble, trouble. I hope we survive this. Never again.

Good-bye.

As ever,
Red

P.S. NEXT DAY. I have been back over the Krutch thing, and have extracted pages 3–14 and tied it into the last exercise on Skinner. This is the only way I can figure out. It is somewhat awkward, but not as awkward as setting up the unmoored Krutch thing as an independent essay. If this doesn't seem good, squawk! Also I am sending on to you under separate cover the whole essay section. This on the assumption that you can get a typist to redo the pages that need it. *As for permissions,* send me a list on the essays for which you have *not* written (with whatever information you have, plus addresses, about ownership) and I'll take over.

[OH]
1315 Davenport College
Yale University
New Haven, Connecticut
July 25 [1963]

Dear Red,

Bad news about a couple of permissions. I enclose the letters. Perhaps you can put some personal pressure on Wilson, though I suppose he is adamant. Since you have the Xerox copy of the Bronowski, you will know better than I whether a cutting will do us any good. Maybe ten pages would.

No news from here except that I am keeping busy.

Love to all,
Cleanth

[Brooks attached copies of the permission letters: Edmund Wilson did not want the Lincoln chapter reprinted out of context of the book; Jacob Bronowski's publisher, Julian Messner, Inc., declined on the basis that the requested excerpt of *Science and Human Value* constituted too much of the entire book.]

Breadloaf School of English
Breadloaf, Vermont
August 5, 1963

Dear Red,

Your introduction for *All the King's Men* is really excellent.[1] It represents your writing at its very best. It is spirited but clear and concise and makes what I think is the basic point.

Your picture of Louisiana in 1934 and 1935 answers perfectly to my memories of the place, and I think that the tone in which you describe matters is just right. If I haven't any substantial changes to suggest it's because I don't see that they are necessary. It goes just a little against the grain to see young Doctor Weiss called an "assassin" because of the usual associations of that term, but I suppose that the term is technically now a neutral one. Anyway, I have suggested in the margin, with great hesitation, an alternate phrasing. Don't take it seriously. I have also noted in pencil in the margins a number of trivial matters, various notations on punctuation, occasionally a shifting of a phrase for clarity or better rhythm, and a few other trifling matters of that sort. If my suggestions are so few it is not because I haven't read the piece with some care—now four or five times. It is really very fine.

I am enclosing two possible sections from Boswell's *London Journal* along with the pages from Boswell's *Life* to which they are keyed. I must say that I am not terribly happy with either one of them. For one thing since we had cut the *Life* so heavily in trying to get it down to a proper length, I find that I have limited for myself the number of passages from the *Journal* which can be used. Moreover there is necessarily a good deal of repetition between the *Journal* and what Boswell did to it in expanding and reshaping it for publication in the *Life*. I think that this repetition is unavoidable and indeed is part of what the student will have to observe: namely, how Boswell reworked much the same material in getting it ready for the *Life*. But I have tried in the two passages that I enclose to get sections in which interesting things in the *Journal* got left out of the *Life*, for one reason or another.

If you think that we can get by with the second selection, that is the one that I would prefer to use, not only because it is shorter, but because of the mention of Boswell's encounter with the "fine fresh little lass." It will bring home to the student the fact that while Boswell was imbibing moral wisdom from Johnson, he had not stopped cavorting around the streets. What do you think about this matter? Surely the entry for Wednesday 3 August isn't very lurid: compared with some of the other passages in the *London Journal* it isn't anything at all.

It's possible of course that either one of these selections will be too long to be worth the trouble, and yet I think that we are almost compelled to reprint

1. The introduction was for the Time Reading Program Special Edition (New York: Time Incorporated, 1963).

all that is given for the days in question, if a comparison of what Boswell put down in his *Journal* with what he put in the *Life* is to make any sense. [p. 2] Otherwise we will be reduced to simply quoting a few details and instances that are mentioned in the *Journal* that *didn't* get into the *Life*. This we could do, but that pretty well destroys the comparison and simply leaves us with a few editorial notes.

Don and I sent the three very pleasant Italians on toward West Wardsboro this morning. I hope they got in in good time.

Now I turn back to the poetry section which is almost ready. I lost valuable working time this last week, what with our visitors and with preparing examinations. But I hope to get in two or three good days here this week and then back hard at it next week when I land in Northford.

Cordial regards,
Cleanth

P.S. Royce Smith, on his way from Dartmouth to New Haven, passed by here and stopped in for a moment. He was in Europe this spring and summer and was telling me that apparently all the American visitors to Rome knew Eleanor's *Rome and a Villa* and that references to it were what he heard again and again as he himself walked around Hadrian's villa. [Handwritten] Since Royce is a book man (Yale Co-op) he keeps his ear tuned to what people are reading and talking about.

[Handwritten across top of p. 1] Your Introduction (with comments) is coming in this mail under separate cover.

West Wardsboro, Vermont
August 7, 1963

Dear Cleanth:

I'm sorry to be late in catching up with you, but I shan't apologize or as Othello said, extenuate.

(1) Whitman: After some prayerful thought I have come up with this suggestion. Begin *with* Section 14 (page 14) of Song of Myself and continue to the middle of Section 33 (end with "I am the man, I suffered, I was there"—middle of page 40). If this entire excerpt is set in single column in the Approach, we save, by my calculation, about 120 lines—which now spill over to make two. This would mean 15 pages of the Approach for Whitman. But there are certain cuts that can be made: Section 18, Section 23, Section 28, Section 29—a reduction of about 60 lines more. {[Handwritten in left margin] 528 lines of Whitman.} Since we are tying this to Jarrell's piece, and since this excerpt I indicate has something of its own continuity, we may be able to afford this space. What do you think?—By the way, I did this, as opposed to your suggestion, because I thought that this selection gets more continuity, and gives the climax of "I am the man etc." Which, by the way, Whitman muffed. I am returning the edition of W under separate cover.

(2) Permissions on Plays: If we take Saint Joan, I don't see how we can load up too much more on these heavy pro-rata deals. I figure that Glass Menagerie will take up about 35 pages. This would be about 4½ % of the whole book, in other words an annual "loss" of approximately 2¼% {[handwritten in right margin] 2½%}. If, for example, we got $5000 a year, that would be about {[handwritten in left margin] $337.50} to the copyright holder for Glass Menagerie. Is this figuring right? I suppose we could afford this and *Joan* if we don't get into any more trouble of the same sort. But we need *Skin of our Teeth* worse than we need *Glass Menagerie*—if we can call *Skin* a comedy. I suppose we should wait until we get a figure on that play—if it is available. And then make a decision.

But it is clear that we should make a decision about any Knopf-RH play in the light of the fact that if we break the 10% of quantity ceiling we go into that pro-rata arrangement.

And this raised other questions: We don't now know how the Knopf-RH copyrights relate to the bulk of the book. We may have some lee-way. Nor do we know whether they calculate old copyrights, which we have had for years, in making their 10% ceiling. Nor do we know whether they take the "quantity" of the book to be merely the quantity of anthologized material, or whether they calculate their 10% against the total bulk of the book, including our commentary, etc. This might make all the difference. Perhaps we should get a ruling on this immediately. Then we could make a count on what we already have from Knopf-RH. Then make a decision on *Glass Menagerie*. Or does this make sense[?]

As to what Miss Daniels means by "pro-rata share of royalties" [p. 2] it would seem to me (as I have indicated calculating the cost of the Glass Menagerie) that you would take the percentage of the total book occupied by the play in question. Then ½ of this percentage (against the earning of the book for any one year) would be paid to copyright holder. But there remain the questions raised above as to how the "quantity" of the book is to be calculated.

(3) Permissions: You have done a great work on the essays. I have, by the way, written to RH for the Auden piece on Frost, but as yet no reply. I have my own permission letters to go over and shall shortly report. Peter Taylor is clear—his own control.

(4) Plays: I hate to pay a lot of money for an Albee. I am damned sorry we can't get *Godot*. Do you want to take a look at *End Game* and see how you think it would go for sophomores? Or an *Ionesc[o]*? Albee does have the advantage of an American setting.

Now we have definitely:

Oedipus

A&C

Murder in Cathedral

Saint Joan

If we can get only *Skin of Our Teeth* we have a very fine line-up. If no *Skin* then *Glass M*, plus, perhaps, an Albee?

I don't see how Crofts can kick about delivery. We are about at the end and they have plenty to do. They could wait, if necessary, an extra month on the last play? As for Lincoln, I do not feel that I can tackle Edmund personally. He makes up his mind and isn't a man to think that he was wrong in an original decision. I have written to Vann Woodward asking for a suggestion, but he says it's damned hard to fill the slot, and his suggestions aren't very thrilling (as he says). The best one is David Donald in *Lincoln Reconsidered*. Perhaps the essay called "A. Lincoln, Politician." But our use of it might be misunderstood. Take a look, though. He has one other notion: Some section from Lincoln's own autobiographical writings, to be found in a volume called (he thinks) *Autobiography*. Can you send me a copy from the Library if you think anything in it useful?

I am anxious to see your stuff on the plays. Not to get the book done—to know what you have to say. Also anxious to see what you do about my little introduction to AKM. Slash at it. I've got to get the copy in next week, so I am a little pressed.

Our house problems mount. Par for the course, I guess. But it is definite now that our man Samson who was hoping to build for us is out, so we've had to go to a contractor and spend a lot more than had been allocated. Oh, dear.

Love to you both. Rosanna caught a trout and ate him.

Yrs,
Red

Northford, Conn.
August 29, 1963

Dear Red,

I've had some sort of message from the Fulbright people to the effect that they might do something nice for me if I would only apply. The idea of a year in France with just a little lecturing on American literature to go along with my work on Faulkner and the million dollar American Lit. book is irresistible. Of course it may all come to nothing, but on the off chance of its working out, would you say your usual kind words about me on the enclosed form?

Your letter, etc., came in yesterday, but I have given it only the hastiest of glances, thinking it best to go ahead with the drama section, which is nearly finished, before plunging again into the wordage problem. I'll get at it later today or tomorrow.

As ever,
Cleanth

. . . .

[On October 8, 1963, Brooks responded to Martin S. Stanford's queries about the revisions for the 4th edition of *An Approach to Literature*. Most of Stanford's questions dealt with permissions, and Brooks set about justifying their choices. Stanford's reply of October 15 apparently asked them to secure new permissions from Andrew Lytle and Peter Taylor, a task Brooks agreed to do in his October 18 reply.]

Nov. 29, 1964

Dear Red,

I am ashamed to have let so much time elapse without writing to you, but this last five months has been life on the high seas: exhilarating, but a gale blowing steadily, and what with mounting the rigging, battening down the hatches, and such matters, I haven't done any writing except countless business letters and a couple of lectures. The luxury of writing to my friends and important things like that, I simply haven't allowed myself. But maybe there is going to be a change in the weather now. I hope so.

The job is not so bad,[1] or rather it won't be so bad if I can find ways to get through the paper work more speedily and cut down on seeing so many people including the time-wasters, the narcissi, and occasionally the clinically insane. (I talked an hour with an Indian gentleman of this sort last week.) Fortunately, I have a fine secretary who knows the red tape. The deputy C.A.—a friend of Dick Lewis's—is really superb as an officer as well as being a very fine human being. I couldn't manage at all if he were not in the opposite office. And the other members of our section are first-rate people. That helps a lot.

Part of my problem has been the predicament of the man who is being killed with kindness—genuine kindness but also genuine killing—too many luncheons that knock out the middle of the day—too many dinners and cocktail parties. But the worst of that appears to be over. Some of it has been very pleasant and I have met a great many very interesting people. These have been largely writers and artists, university people, editors and publishers, but along with them a fair number of people from the Department of Education and Science and the Foreign Office, with an occasional M.P.

We have seen also—especially in the first several months—an amazing number of Americans, and if there has been a single Yale person that we have missed, I don't know who it can be: half of Yale has been here. Again, this has been very nice but it has carved hours off my working week.

We have finally settled down in an apartment in Mayfair, not ideal though it has some pleasant features. It is brand new with a modern kitchen and a couple of bathrooms, and it is only four minutes walk from my office. It's too small, however, and it's pretty noisy. Now that the windows are shut, that doesn't matter so much. It may be more than we can put up with, come

---

1. Brooks served as cultural attaché to the American Embassy in London, 1964–1966.

summer. I ought to add that it is warm—really warm, and that in a London fall and winter is worth a lot.

Now that we have got into a flat that is more or less permanent, we have been able to unpack—for four months and more we literally lived out of suitcases. I have my books and papers at my disposal again, and my tape recorder. The result is that I have actually got back to writing, and hope that I am going to be able to peck along at some things from now on.

I am scheduled to give lectures all over Great Britain during the next months, most of them, though not all, at universities. Since most people expect me to speak on American literature, I can steer some of this activity into work on our American literature book.[2] Have you or Dick made any further move on it? What I hope to do is to get out my very rough sketch for a beginning and begin to elaborate and explore some of the possibilities there. Out of that work, I can put questions or suggestions to you and Dick. But it may be that you and he are well beyond that and can now begin to put some to me. I had lunch last week, by the way, with a Mr. Upjohn of St. Martin's Press, who knew about the project and seemed very much interested in it.

[p. 2] I'm sorry that you and Eleanor did not get to the Berlin conference. I had not really expected you to be there, and though your presence would have added a lot, I'm not sure that the conference would have been worth the time of either one of you—though there were some very interesting people in Berlin for it.

We were in Rome for a week, two weeks ago. Washington suddenly called a conference of the cultural affairs officers of western Europe and we had a good week in brilliant sunshine and saw a good deal—Tink more than I, since four days they worked us full hours at the conference table. This was our first visit to Rome since 1954. I have been thus far to Oxford three times, to Cambridge once, and last week we went up to the University of Leeds in Yorkshire. But on the whole we stay pretty close. We have not seen many plays and haven't thought too much of what we have seen—nothing world-shaking, though beautifully acted and a pleasure to go to. We have recently seen Olivier's *Othello*. The Iago was fine and so were some of the other characters, but I thought that Olivier made a mess of the title role. We have seen a good deal of ballet and early in the fall we saw all four of Wagner's Ring operas in proper order. (This I had always wanted to do and decided that this was probably my only chance in a lifetime to do so.)

The Heilmans are in town and it is good to see them. The Trillings are at Oxford and we have had thus far a very pleasant meeting with them.

We hope that Vermont was pleasant for all of you this summer and that all of you thrive. Our love to Eleanor and to Rosanna and to Gabriel. Is there

2. *American Literature: The Makers and the Making,* which R. W. B. (Dick) Lewis edited with Brooks and Warren, was begun in 1963. St. Martin's Press published it in May (vol. 1) and June (vol. 2) 1973.

any chance that you all will be on this side of the Atlantic before 1965 is out? T. joins in best love to you all.

Cleanth

[OH]
United States Information Service
American Embassy
London, W.1.
May 17, 1965

Dear Red,

Oxford Press is bringing out *Modern Poetry and the Tradition* as a paperback. A ghost from the past, and probably not worth the resurrection, though I have written a new introduction that attempts to fill in gaps and update matters a bit.

Miss Catherine Linnet (of OUP) has been having her troubles with permissions. The William Morris people have been helpful and cooperative, she tells me, but I write anyway to solicit your good word in the matter.

Tinkie is recuperating nicely. She still has to take it easy but is coming along fast. We spent a strenuous day Friday, much of it at the Runnymede ceremonies, without ill effects. Tomorrow we expect to take off for Greece—lectures and some sightseeing. We return to London on June 1.

When do the Warrens come to Europe? Soon, I hope. T. joins in love to Eleanor, Rosanna, Gabriel and RPW.

In haste,
Cleanth

Fairfield
May 20, 1965

Dear Cleanth:

. . . .

Speaking of work, Dick and I are settling down seriously to the book. I saw him a few days ago, and he remarked that we (he and I) ought to take the view that the burden of the first volume is basically [ours] for we know that you would more than take up any slack in the second. We are having a meeting next week, and shall draw up a program and tentative chart for division of labor. Then you can decide what you think you can reasonably do—and we'll do the rest. I have been on Hawthorne, have reread him almost entire, and a lot of stuff about him. Now I shall do that section as a trial balloon. I'll send a copy for criticism and revision. We must get this done now, for the market, as you notice from your royalty statements, is in the up-swing—we trust.

As for the happy little project of the Oxford Press paper back reissue of your book, William Morris has written me. Helen's view is that they should charge .25 a line. She said that if I insisted they would waive the fee, but would much prefer to make what she calls a minimal one, for technical reasons. I told her to do what she wanted. This has to do with the whole new paper-back business of the last couple of [p. 2] years. I know you couldn't care less. I tell all this, just to say that it has been cleared.

My book on Negro leaders is done and about to come out. It broke my back, but it's done. Nobody knows how it will go. Vann has done a review, very gratifying, in the NR. Only thing yet. There was a fine one done as a commission for LIFE, but they turned it down—on the grounds that the book has been associated with LOOK, and they wouldn't promote a competitor. Review by a Negro named Albert Murray—he himself told me this. I am sending you a copy.[1]

I have done a few new poems, which I shall send soon. They're the only fun I've had in writing in two years. Now I want to do that for the summer a couple of hours of nothing, before settling down to Amer. Lit. I am planning a Selected or Collected Poems for next year. I wish I could talk with you about inclusions, etc. In fact, there are a thousand things I need to talk to you about. I actually hadn't realized how much I was depending on our conversations, for things big and little. I don't have much talk with anybody this year, that kind of talk. Albert is so damned busy, or I see him under the wrong circumstances for that kind of conversation.

I made a Texas trip a few weeks ago, readings and a couple of lectures, driven by greed and need. Eleanor was doing a thing in Phoenix, a big luncheon mob scene with the Southeast Book Publishers and Authors organization. So we met out at Tucson and had a few days on a ranch, riding all day, swimming, wonderful country, the desert and mountains covered with spring bloom. Now it seems like a dream.

. . . .

Good-bye. My love to you both. Take care of yourselves.

As ever,
Red

American Embassy, Box 40
FPO NY 09510
July 11, 1965

Dear Red,

A much over-due letter, especially in view of the fact that I have your good letter of May 25 to answer, plus a subsequent one, plus your fine book on the Negro leadership to comment upon. I won't make elaborate apologies except to say that the whole first half of this year has been terribly trying,

---

1. *Who Speaks for the Negro?* was published by Random House May 27, 1965. C. Vann Woodward's review was "Warren's Challenge to Race Dogma," *New Republic,* May 22, 1965, pp. 21–23. Albert Murray's review appeared in the *New Leader,* June 21, 1965, pp. 25–27.

and June worst of all, with lectures before the British society of Aesthetics, a Shakespeare lecture for Stratford, a lecture for the Friends of the Bodleian, plus three other shorter pieces to prepare and do. July and August are not going to be nearly so rugged, and I am trying to hold down my speaking engagements henceforward.

. . . .

I like your book on the Negro Leadership, very much. At this point, I have not read every word of it, but I have sampled it vigorously, and have read the concluding pages. I wonder, however, whether you will be thanked for it—eventually, yes, but I expect that a good number of people are a little puzzled at a book which does not easily fall into one or the other of the two well-rubbed slots reserved for this topic. I am thinking, for example, of the review in *Newsweek*, in which the reviewer wanted to like the book, and had to admit to its force, but was afraid to give it any final accolade.[1]

In my personal opinion we have well bitched our whole presentation of the Negro problem. With the best will in the world, we've made something of a mess of it. I am calling your book to the attention of some of our people in the London Post, and I think that those who are working closest to the problem will welcome it. But as for USIA generally—I wonder. By the way, the three top people in USIA in Washington have now within a few months all resigned, including Rowan. I wonder what it means.

Did you ever have your talk with [Joe] Roland last month [about taking a post as resident artist in Rome for a year] and did you work out anything with him—either for France or Italy? I have great confidence in Roland, but make anyone in Washington spell out in great detail just what you will be expected to do. Otherwise, don't sign your name to anything.

Later in the day, I shall set down in a letter for you and Dick Lewis my comments on the detailed minutes of your June 13 meeting with Dick on *Understanding American Literature*. In general, it looks very fine, but I am troubled with how little I may be able to help with the first volume, and I wonder whether I shouldn't quietly pull out, so that you and Dick will have a chance to get somebody else into the project at once who can lend a hand. It is not modesty or politeness that dictates this comment. I'm dead serious. I hope that you and Dick will think it over very carefully and give me a very candid and honest answer.

We wish that we could have heard Eleanor's talk at the National Book Award[2] and at Phoenix. Tinkie joins me in all good wishes and love to her and Rosanna and Gabriel.

As ever,
Cleanth

1. "Faces of Change," *Newsweek*, June 7, 1965, pp. 84–86; Warren's reply was published in the July 5, 1965 issue, p. 2.
2. In 1965, Eleanor Clark received the National Book Award for *The Oysters of Locmariaquer*.

United States Information Service
American Embassy
Grosvenor Square, W.1.
July 14, 1965

Dear Red:

The State Department had asked Randall Jarrell to come to read at the Edinburgh Festival, August 24–28. He now writes that because of illness he cannot come. Is there any chance that you (preferably with Eleanor) could fly over for the Festival?

How nice it would be for us and how useful for the cause. (Otherwise, we shall end up with a handful of second or third-rate American poets. I know: I have a good idea who they will be.) Since the State Department has allocated the funds, I think the matter will be open and shut *if* you can simply pick up for four or five days—better still for ten—and come over. But I don't want to mention the possibility to the State Department unless you are available.

As a lame second choice: who else would you suggest?

In haste,
Cordially,
Cleanth Brooks
Cultural Attaché

P.S. Allen Tate was to be in Ireland and since he was to be so near, I had suggested that he come too. He said he would: he actually came to England, but has flown back to Tennessee, and I assume will not be coming to Edinburgh.

West Wardsboro, Vermont
August 18, 1965

Dear Cleanth:

Here is a rough copy of Hawthorne, with a carbon of letter to Dick. No haste, but some day you must give it the works. I shan't fool more with it now, shall move on to Melville's poems, Dick doing the prose. He is now deep in Emerson, and hopes to have that done by October. Don't get panicked. Do what you can. It'll all even out. But we DO need your thoughts about general format and method. I KNOW that the method I have here is wrong. Have you read the stuff in the big Harcourt book (2 vols) with a different man for each author? Dick and Wilbur have good sections, some of the others, Hawthorne for instance, are awful. One thing, we've got to find a level.

Rosanna loved Tinkie's letter.

Best to Both,
Red

I keep getting poem fits, have some new ones going, just take two or three hours first thing in the morning, and later get to honest work. Wish I could see you. Lots of things to talk about.

United States Information Service
American Embassy
Grosvenor Square, W.1.
August 25, 1965

Dear Red:

Your long poem "By way of Solution" is very fine, one of your best, I think.[1] I took it with me to Ireland last week hoping to find the leisure there to write you something about it. Instead we bustled about too much to have time for anything but the driving about in a hired car and the people that I had to talk to at Sligo. But in the next few days I shall set down a few negligible comments about one or two sections—not because I think that the comments will be of any real help to you but as evidence of my interest in the detail of the poem.

I look forward to the arrival of your section on Hawthorne and hope before long to set down some thoughts on Thoreau and Poe. By the way, your piece on Faulkner and the Negro is very fine indeed. Someone who heard you give it at Texas had told me about it, and the published version in *The Southern Review* more than lives up to his praise of it.[2]

We have just been reading Rosanna's charming letter to Tinkie. Love to her, to Gabriel, and to you and Eleanor. I shall be writing to you sometime next week.

Sincerely,
Cleanth Brooks
Cultural Attaché

American Embassy, Box 40
FPO NY 09510
December 26, 1965

Dear Red,

. . . .

Now some comments about the American literature book: I have used this Christmas lull to go back to your Hawthorne, re-read it, and I am much impressed. It seems to me the best thing that has ever been written on Hawthorne—the best that I know of, at any rate. I think that it thoroughly vindicates the general method of presentation about which we talked a year and a half ago. That is, your long essay demonstrates how much can be

1. "By Way of Solution" was a subsequence in the sequence "Tale of Time." The title of the subsequence was changed to "The Interim" in *Selected Poems: New and Old, 1923–1966,* which was published October 7, 1966. This subsequence appeared earlier in *Encounter* 26 (March 1966): 18–20.

2. "Faulkner: The South, the Negro, and Time," *Southern Review,* n.s. 1 (summer 1965): 501–29. The *Southern Review* was revived under the capable editorship of Lewis P. Simpson and Donald E. Stanford in 1965.

woven together of biography and criticism—how much sense can be made of Hawthorne's career by discussing some texts rather fully and alluding to others and bringing in the relevant parts of his life as a man and as an artist— and how all of this material can be pointed toward the study of the history of American Literature.

The only problem, and it is a problem of which you, of course, are perfectly aware, is that the scale on which you have written, if applied to our other authors, would make this book far, far too large. It is going to be very difficult to cut this down without wasting a great deal of valuable material. But obviously, unless we change completely the plan and scale of the book, it will have to be reduced a good deal. My own suggestion, off the top of my head, is this: that you ought to plan to publish this brilliant long essay some time in full, or even perhaps a little further expanded, perhaps as an introduction to a selection of Hawthorne's fiction, and that for the moment neither you nor Dick nor I should try to scale it down until somewhat more of the book is in hand. In any case, I am personally very grateful for your having put the energy and time that has gone into this piece as a way of showing more fully and therefore more convincingly what can be done for an individual author.

Some of the material in this long essay, of course, could be used elsewhere or can justify itself as a treatment of general considerations that would otherwise have to be treated somewhere else. I am thinking, for example, of your remarks on the difference between [p. 2] allegory and symbol that occupy pages 112– 21. The distinction is an important one, generally useful for the book, and I would hate to see it go or even be too much reduced. But I think that any suggestion that I might have about how best to use it or where best to use it can wait upon seeing more of the book in draft.

Common sense—if not shame—in any case suggests to me that I ought to be very careful about recommendations about revision of your Hawthorne piece until I have got something down on the Thoreau and the Poe. In spite of the difficult last four or five months, I am now much more hopeful about catching up. The prospect here is much more encouraging: I can at least see light at the end of the tunnel, and it now looks as if I shall be able to put off my undergraduate course for the first term, which means that the second half of the summer and the months running on up to February 1967 ought to allow a great deal of time for concerted effort. On the other hand, you and Dick have been pulling at the oars so long that unless I can get mine into the water, I hope you will have no compunction in dropping me out of the boat.

Tink and I hope that you and Eleanor and the children have a fine Christ-mas. We did not go to the continent as we had once thought we might, but have stayed in London for the season. We've seen a ballet or so, a couple of plays— the first in months—and we both feel much more relaxed and therefore much more cheerful than we had for a good while now.

Love to all four of you,
Cleanth

American Embassy, Box 40
FPO NY 09510
Dec. 26, 1965

Dear Red,

I am writing this second letter in order to make some comments on your poem "By Way of Solution." It's easier to do it this way, for I can send a carbon of the first letter to Dick and make this a special letter to you.

I like the poem very much, as indeed I like so many of your poems in this general mood and on themes of this general kind. I am thinking of poems like the group entitled "Some Quiet, Plain Poems," or some of those in the "Mortmain" series, or the "Dark Woods" series from *Promises*.

Sections of the poem seem to me to come through beautifully and even at a rapid first reading. The death of the old Negro woman is such a section and so is section VI. I find the vision of the mother as a little girl entirely convincing, and a gnomic passage such as "Know now at long last that the living remember the day only / Because we cannot bear the thought that they / Might forget us" dramatically justified, with the resonance of the whole context behind it. But I am troubled in one or two places by the problem of tone. In section IV, no more may be involved than my natural prudishness. Still, fucking and fuck seem to me over-emphatic—at least at this place in the poem—further along they might be justified. It's not the idea that such thoughts would occur—and indeed they do—but whether the reader, who has so little of the context of the total poem to go on, can manage the jump from the first three sections to the fourth.

My other problem of tone I think may be a little more important, though goodness knows I am hesitant enough in putting it at all. It has to do with the dry, unemphatic questions and statements that end IV a and IV b and IV e or IV g. I think that I see the terms of the debate—the need for the speaker to say "I do not want to have to repeat the question" or after the concreteness of the scene depicted in IV e, the need for the abstract "These are factors that [must] be considered in making any final estimate." But your readers are so chuckle-headed—they miss so much in your fiction and in your poetry too, that I wonder whether they don't need a little more help here. Or is it simply I who am chuckle-headed so that in failing to get all, I myself then worry about the obtuseness of other readers?

Let me try to make one thing clear, however: I am not worried in this poem about the tension or the need for tension—the necessity for contrast. This is the ground plan of everything you have ever written, poetry and prose. My hesitancy is over only a matter of execution, not the master strategy. One passage, however, that may trouble your reader, I would not think of changing. Here the reader will simply have to take his chances and either get the point from his understanding of the total poem or fail to get it if he cannot. That is a passage in IV h, "But the solutions: you / Must eat the dead. / You must eat them completely, . . . etc." This is just and it has the power of great poetry.

I am heartily ashamed to be so late with these paltry comments. If I thought for a moment that they really mattered or were of any consequence, I suppose that I would have made an effort to give them to you more quickly. You have doubtless come to your own terms with this fine long poem, and my comments now claim to be no more than an evidence of my interest in everything that you do.

We saw and liked extremely the poem that the *New Yorker* recently printed.[1] I am sure it's about the man that we met at your house in Vermont. I think even then you told us that he was mortally ill.

[p. 2] I think that I told you earlier that I have been reading some of your poems to various groups in England. I have been delighted—though not at all surprised—at how well they go with an English audience, even when it is hearing the poem for the first time. "Dragon Country," "School Lesson Based on Word of Tragic Death of Entire Gillum Family," and "Ballad: Between the Boxcars" go tremendously well.

Again, all cordial regards from both of us to all of you.

Cleanth

Fairfield
March 18, 1966

Dear Cleanth:

Your letter about the stuff to Kentucky has come. I don't know what the stuff is worth. Maybe they should send us a description—no, I guess not, they'd hate that, and it wouldn't mean anything. But I'd hate to put much of an evaluation on it, we've already drawn on that book. Maybe we should just give it as a logical addition to the previous gift. BUT let's enter that fact—or have it entered—in the gift letter this coming fall. Assuming we have anything else to give.

A matter of Approach business. Stanford thinks it very important to do an alternate edition, which will omit the discursive prose, but will add two features (1) two plays from the theater of the absurd, and (2) an appendix on how to write critical papers. He says that they have a big ready-made sale for this in junior colleges. I said, OK, that I would do the critical appendix (this because I'll be away from libraries this summer) and that I hoped you'd select two plays (he has a list made out) and write a short commentary on one, with exercises on the other. He agreed that he would arrange permissions, etc. to lighten the burden. I hope this is OK, nothing elaborate, just a few hundred words. By the way, the sale as of this accounting is over 99,000 copies, with the prognosis good.[1]

---

1. "Fall Comes in Back-Country Vermont" (a sequence with four sections), *New Yorker,* October 23, 1965, pp. 56–57.

1. Through February 1970 a total of 209,500 copies were printed of the fourth edition of *An Approach to Literature* and 76,500 of the alternate fourth edition.

I have just finished a section on Longfellow, with selections and notes finished. I am embarking on Whittier, with what feelings you may well imagine. Dick is apparently going to stay in the US for the summer and fall—which is fine for our book, for you and he can tie each other down and talk about a plan. I hope to leave you Hawthorne, Melville (poems), Longfellow, Whittier, and one other. And I shall take things with me to do this summer and fall, not yet worked out with Dick which ones. We could make a million out of that book if it's ever finished.

My new book of poems is now in the hands of the printer: Selected Poems, New and Old. I cut hard into old stuff, the first five volumes, and have a big new section. About a quarter or third of the whole, poems of the last five years. (I wish I had had your aid in making it up. One more thing you have been missed for. I feel sorry for the kids, they are very downcast about missing you all for another year. Eleanor and I feel sorry for ourselves, too.) I am enclosing my most recent poem, finished last week. It's wonderful to ride with them, and I hope they keep coming for a while longer. The kind of prose I'm writing on dull days is dull anyway, so I don't mind interrupting it.

No great news around the Department, as far as I know. Or around here. All are well. Tomorrow we go to Vermont for two weeks, if the snow holds.

[p. 2] I am putting the Twentieth Century Views Faulkner together now, having written a draft of my introduction, and revised my Negro piece for inclusion—not a final revision, for I want you to look sharply at it before it goes in.[2] This brings me to my favors, other favors, to ask of you. I can't make up my mind about what of yours would do the book most good. The trouble is, honestly, that several chapters from your book—the whole damned book—tower so much above the field that the choosing is difficult. I assume that you will let me have one—if you don't I'll slay you. But I'd be ashamed to slay you for not letting me have what I am about to ask. In fact, I'm even ashamed to ask it. Can you give an honest answer? Would it hurt your book if I reprinted the genealogies for, of course, a separate fee? You see, I intend, as of the moment, to break the pattern of those books in Maynard's series, and run a section of small excerpts, brief notices (such as some from the Harvard Advocate F. issue), things that have one useful idea or interesting opinion or useful fact. The genealogies would be in this section.

Have you seen Millgate's new book on F.?[3] If so, what do you think of it? In general I am quite depressed by the general level of the Faulkner criticism. By and large, in a certain way, the French stack up better than we do. DO YOU KNOW of any good pieces done in England—or even interestingly wrong-headed? Particularly if by somebody whose name is of interest. PLEASE PLEASE!

2. *Faulkner: A Collection of Critical Essays*, Twentieth-Century Views Series (Englewood Cliffs, N.J.: Prentice-Hall, 1966), was copyrighted November 23, 1966. The genealogies are included in appendix 2.

3. Michael Millgate, *The Achievement of William Faulkner* (London: Constable, 1966) is, perhaps as Brooks infers in his response, better than Warren implies.

As for travel, we sail May 27, Le Havre June 8. What are your plans? Any chance for a meeting, at either end, or in midocean?

Love to you both, from our crew!

R

United States Information Service
American Embassy
P.O. Box 444
London, W.1.
March 24, 1966

Dear Red:

It's good to have your letter of March 18—and the new poems. First, to business: Tink went to the bookstore to-day to start acquiring the texts of the plays I shall read. (I'll read them during our little vacation next month.) I hope to get my commentaries and questions done well before September 1.

I won't take up the American literature book now, but we do intend to come to France for a couple of weeks in September and by that time I hope that I shall be far enough along with my share to be able to talk with you to some purpose.

Of course, you are welcome to anything in my Faulkner volume that you like—including the genealogies. Other people, by the way, are printing genealogies, though most that I have seen include errors, some of them ridiculous. There is a serious error, by the way, in my McCaslin genealogy. *So* when you consult the Yale Press about these, be sure to use the corrected McCaslin genealogy that I sent in some weeks ago.

You are probably a better judge than I of what are the best chapters in my book—and the matter of length has to be taken into account too. I shan't make suggestions therefore.

Millgate has sent me his new Faulkner and I expect to find it very good, but the wheels spin too fast now—and will until we sail on May 26—to allow me to read it.

"Homage to Emerson" seems to me very fine indeed though I have just glanced at it. But I'm taking it home tonight to read at leisure. (We were out last night and the night before.) Your volume of *Selected Poems* is going to be a knockout. Don't cut back too hard, however, on the earlier poems. There are some beauties among them that stand up well in comparison with the splendid new crop that you are just harvesting.

······· [p. 2]

In great haste,
Sincerely,
Cleanth Brooks
Cultural Attaché

· · · · · · ·

Northford, Conn.
as of June 11, 1966

Dear Red,

I am sorry that we couldn't reach you by wireless as our ships passed in the Atlantic two weeks ago, but we were thinking of you all, and Rosanna's letter to Tinkie was doubly welcome since it told us among other things that you all had arrived safely.

We have been living out of suitcases and pretty much on the run since May 19, when we moved out of our flat into a London hotel. We have been briefly in Northford, then in Houston, Baton Rouge, and I am writing at the moment from New Orleans. I fly to Washington tomorrow for several days of what the government insists on calling debriefing. Then we hope to get on back to Northford and into our house by the end of next week.

I left England, however, with a set of paperback plays in my suitcase, and have some notions now about what plays to use and even some vague notions of what to say about them. Since I would like to have the benefit of your comments and suggestions, let me set down the following possibilities. (1) Beckett's *End Game.* Ionesco's *The Chairs,* and Albee's *The American Dream.* An alternate possibility would be (2) *End Game, The Chairs,* and Camus's *The Misunderstanding.* Another would be (3) *End Game, The Chairs,* and Pinter's *The Birthday Party.*

I am not really wedded to any of these, but I am trying to provide some connections and contrasts and to choose plays—two of them at least—which clearly fall into the Theater of the Absurd. *The Misunderstanding* is scarcely a characteristic case, but it is related to the genre and Camus is a fine name. Besides, I have a vague notion of running some parallels between this play and the "Ballad of Billy Potts" and other such stories of father killing son and brother killing brother. Anouilh's *Poor Bitos* and *The Rehearsal* are plays somewhat more to my liking, but they are not quite pure examples of the Theater of the Absurd—maybe that's why I like them—and they are rather longer than the plays that I've chosen. (If we are to have three plays, perhaps we'll have to stick to fairly short ones.)

Pinter's *The Birthday Party* is, again, not a pure example of the Theater of the Absurd, but it is surely related to the genre and it may be a better bet than the Albee or the Camus.

I don't want to throw this baby into your lap: I am perfectly willing to pitch right in and work up comments and questions on one of the sets I've mentioned. But if you do have any preferences, I'd certainly like to have them.

In part, of course, my choice has been influenced by what I can work with for a book of this sort and not the absolute merit of the plays. Thus, I am not sure that *The Zoo Story* may not be a better play than *The American Dream.* But I think I had rather try to tackle the latter. I am sending a carbon of this to Martin Stanford since I would like to have his suggestions also, and particularly with regard to how many plays we shall have room for.

In haste and with all cordial regards,
Cleanth

[Handwritten] T. joins in love to Eleanor, Rosanna, and Gabriel. We hope that you all are rapidly getting settled.

[OH]   Forest Rd.
                                               Northford, Conn. 06472
                                                       July 6, 1966
[Handwritten at the bottom of a typed letter to Martin Stanford about the selection of plays to represent the Theater of the Absurd.]
Dear Red,

I send this off to keep you up to date on the revisions for the *Approach*. If you have any second thoughts about my selection, let me know. I hope to send you a draft of my discussions and exercises very shortly and these will suggest why I have chosen as I have. I don't mean to rush matters too much on these plays but I am anxious to get on to the Thoreau and Poe sections for the American literature book.

We thrive here—though our furniture hasn't come in from England yet and won't for some time to come. But it's wonderful to be at home and this is a fine place in which to work—I'm getting a great deal done and some exercise too!

T. joins me in love to Eleanor, Rosanna, and Gabriel.

                                                      All the best,
                                                        Cleanth

                                                       Northford
                                                  August 13 [1966]
Dear Red,

I hasten to answer your letter of August 9. The first edition of *Light in August* does indeed have Joanna calling out "Negro! Negro!" But of course you are right in claiming that she would have said "nigger." Faulkner's earlier novels were so badly handled by the press people, and for all I know, by the editors, that I don't put it past some copyeditor's silently making the change. But to prove this one would have to look into the Virginia MSS. and in the short time that you have, this is obviously impossible to do.

Here is the reference to the Kubie article: Kubie, Lawrence S., "William Faulkner's 'Sanctuary': An Analysis," *Saturday Review of Literature*, Vol. 11 (October 20, 1934), pp. 218, 224–26.

I enclose herewith a Xerox copy of my note on it.

I am sending to the Prentice-Hall editor corrected proofs—the strips that you enclosed in your letter of August 7. I thoroughly approve of the cuts that you have made in my *Absalom* chapter, but I am glad that I got a chance to see the proof, for it has enabled me to correct a bad error in my own text of this chapter. (The correction is being made in the paperback edition of *W.F.: the Y. Country*, which Yale will soon be issuing.)[1]

1. *William Faulkner: The Yoknapatawpha Country* was first printed in a paperbound edition in July 1966.

I am also sending to Green at P-H a corrected genealogical note and a genealogical table for the McCaslins. The Yale Press, damn it, apparently failed to send to P-H the corrected table. Anyway, I'm glad that you sent me the proofs so that these mistakes—embarrassing ones to me—can be cleared up, not only in my paperback edition but in your P-H book.

Martin Stanford's information that the three plays I had written on are not available for the *Approach* was, as I wrote you, a body blow. I am now trying to choose three more—though this time making sure that Martin has the permissions in hand before I write a word—and to get back to work. He tells me that if I can get my material in by mid October, he can still get the *Approach* out in the spring. But I shall have to stretch myself to manage that, and something else will have to give: presumably, work on the American literature book. The news from Stanford thus deals the final blow to any hopes of our coming to France for a couple of weeks next month. It would have been difficult enough in any case, what with the delays in delivering our furniture. (It arrived on August 2.) We are still trying to get our bridge repaired and our road back in condition—all of which have taken numerous telephone calls and conferences. Anyway, we have sadly concluded that it just can't be done, and though there would be much for you and me to talk about with reference to detailed planning for the Am. Lit. book, such conferences would be much more useful once we were a good deal further along—once *I* was further long, at any rate. But we are truly sorry. It's a shame to further postpone a meeting. Perhaps two weeks could be arranged later in the year. We'll see. T. joins in love to you all.

In haste,
Cleanth

[Handwritten] P.S. Send your introduction along. I'd love to see it.
[Handwritten at top of p. 1] P.S.S. I'm at work on your essay on how to write a piece of criticism. In spite of your deprecation and in spite of some marks of haste, it is excellent. Some of the tinkerings that I am doing are probably just niggling but I know that you want me to go over it carefully. I've been delayed by a flood of company during this week, but the house is again clear. C.

1315 Davenport College
Yale University
New Haven, Connecticut
August 30 [1966]

Dear Red,

I am sending this letter to your new address. I hope that when it reaches you, you and Eleanor and the children will have made the transition easily and will soon be settled again.

I finished today my additions and suggestions for your long essay on how to write a critical paper. It is really very good, with excellent ideas and some acute and apt phrasings. (Incidentally, I thank my God that I didn't have to do it. What a chore—maybe simply because you and I have been over so much of this territory before!) As soon as I can get my corrected and amended draft typed up, I'll send it along. Please go over it very carefully.

Some of my rewritings are perhaps simply so much nit-picking—a habit that I've got into in rewriting the stuff that comes from my Stenorette. I have to do so much of it on my dictated drafts, and perhaps the habit is catching and I go on to do it to excess and with other people's drafts. Anyway, if I've made us sound too pedantic—if I've messed up the tone—restore what you had. The other kind of change I hope you will also look hard at, though for another reason. These changes—there are not many—have to do with more substantive issues. They turn largely on the matter of the primacy of the text and the matter of the intent of the author. I hope that I have kept matters in a persuasive way—and in a nontechnical way. My concern is not so much to keep us in the good graces of certain theoreticians as to set forth what I think makes basic sense in what some of the theoreticians have had to say. Anyway, see what you think of my revised footnote on the matter of the "author's intentions." There is one technical term that I would have us walk around. You will see that I have qualified "contextual" to make it plain that [it] is the social and historical and other such contexts that we have in mind, for "contextual" has in certain quarters taken on a technical meaning: the insistence that the meaning of any part of [a] literary work must be examined in the light of the full literary context in which it operates. We mean *that*—our whole book is based on it—but our point (on the page [in] question) is to bring in a *larger* context and this I have sought to make plain.

Look carefully also at some paragraphs that I have added with reference to choosing a topic. I have tried to bring in at the point the author-work-reader business, not only because it may provide a useful little grid to help the student make his choice, but because it seems to me to give the perfect occasion for our putting in quietly a justification for the form that most of our "analyses" take and for indicating, in spite of this form and emphasis, our entire approval of the kind of liberty used by Bishop, MacDonald, Jarrell, and Auden in their critical essays. But see what you think. (Maybe part of this material might be relegated to the footnote.)

I'm sorry that we had to give up our trip. But I am just going to make the mid-October deadline, if all goes well, and could not possibly have done so if we had tried to come to France. Indeed, except for the reading I've been doing on Thoreau and Poe, I'm nowhere yet on the Am. Lit. book. If I can soon dispose of the jobs for the *Approach,* I shall hope to start actual writing right away, and hope to come up with some ideas about arrangement. Maybe *later,* we will have a lot that is profitable to talk about with reference to the Am. Lit. book. Meanwhile the Brookses will keep themselves as little committed as possible for the future months. Let's keep in touch. Maybe we can come over for a brief visit later in the year—if your plans easily and comfortably permit it. At least, we can see.

[p. 2] In many ways, it is certainly proving expedient that we did not try to make the trip at this time. A few days ago, we got our bridge rebuilt—very tidily—in six hours, once the workmen got started. But the preparation for it took weeks of telephone calls and conferences. At the end of this week we hope to have our roads regraded and surfaced and some work done on the river. This house has to be prepared for painting and then actually painted this fall, for it is peeling badly. Moreover, the war with Kendall has broken out again, though this time I have some hope that it will be the war to end wars—at least any more with him—and I think that I have good hopes of winning this one.[1] Anyhow never a dull moment.

No casualties yet in our summer campaign, except that Tink came down last week with a bad summer cold brought on, I am convinced, by simple exhaustion, but she is now happily recovered, and both of us are thriving once more.

. . . .

Cleanth

"La Moutonne"
Magagnose (A.M.), France
September 3, 1966

Dear Dick and Cleanth:

Here are a few meditations on the AL book which I'll put on the record for what they are worth. They have to do with how we work in background material, literary, social, historical.

One way is, of course, to have some interchapters on periods and in them develop all we need of such stuff, then refer to it in treating special authors and works, as need appears. We have talked a bit about this, and it may be that this is the only and the right way.

But, here is my question. Might it not be better (or would it?) to use interchapters for guidelines rather than for development of such background material and then develop such material when we come to treat the author from whom a special topic is most relevant? For example, in Longfellow, which you now have in hand, I tried a little bit of this, on two points, rather three. I tried to give a brief notion of fireside-ism in the historical setting; of the technical ineptitude which made L in criticism seem so good in the beginning; of the use of American, particularly Indian, materials. (Maybe I should have done a little more with the last, but I didn't know but that it should have been done earlier, certainly Hawthorne touches on the question, and Cooper will.)

1. Willmoore Kindall, political philosopher, was, according to Winchell, "Cleanth's closest friend" at LSU (*Cleanth Brooks and the Rise of Modern Criticism*, 134). Apparently, speculation about the 1966 "war" involved Kendall's plan to use Brooks and Warren in psychological warfare against North Korea (360).

If we adopt this compromise procedure, then two things now in process or about to be in process are affected. I am going to do Whittier. Whittier brings in the whole background of Abolitionism and the slave question. Though directed at Whittier, this might give a chance to touch on Garrison (famous Liberator editorial—he was a man not without a certain literary skill), quotes from The Black Book of Slavery as straight propaganda, H B Stowe, with a little section, after Whittier, using the Whittier stuff as background, Frederick Douglass and a few others could be touched on and quoted from. Here we might also get ready [for] the Gilded Age, etc. The Southern riposte to the Abolitionists was of course the attack on the new industrialism—the exploitation of hired labor—and things like Cannibals All can well come in for a bit of quoting. Ditto for Calhoun and Stephens. This stuff would give a necessary background for Melville in a direct way, as well as for Brooks and Henry Adams. More indirectly for people like William and Henry James, Twain, and later, J. R. Lowell.

The other thing now in process would be Thoreau. Perhaps here the emphasis might not be on the abolitionist thing (not developed, just referred to for the special instance), but on the whole reformist temper of the pre-CW period, Graham bread, bloomers, and all the rest. For this ties in with your stuff, Dick, the New Eden, New Jerusalem, New Harmony, etc. It also ties in with attitudes toward nature (and Nature), quite clearly, at one level, more murkily and interestingly at another. What did Thoreau make of nature in the bed? Also a side glance at David Donald's "class" [p. 2] explanation of transcendentalism and Abolitionism (cf. book of essays *Lincoln* etc.).

Another thing on my mind is the relation of the essay thing at the head of an author and the headnotes on particular selections. Maybe it's too early to worry too much about this. After we get a lot of sections done we can lay them side by side and reach an almost automatic solution transferring stuff back and forth. For instance, since you saw the very early draft of my thing on Melville's poems, I have rewritten it almost completely, and have wound up with a long treatment of Billy in the Darbies. You haven't seen my stuff, so I'm not asking for an opinion, just giving an illustration. This might be in the main essay thing, or a long headnote—say 1000 words. Lots of problems like this.

I am simply struggling for some notion of a shape for the book, something to keep me from fumbling too much as I write a section. Whittier is a big test case. Not that I'm writing. I can't till I've done a lot more background reading. But that brings up the other question of my helper, etc., which I have written about earlier.

No haste for an answer. Just putting this on record. But write when you can conveniently get to it. No—that would be at year 2000. Sooner.

Best to you both, as ever, your fellow sufferer,

Red

Dear Cleanth:

I'll continue with you on a topic or two. I have just found a letter from Holt & Winston about two months old, asking us to prepare a revised UP for the 30th anniversary year, etc. Didn't you get one? They want it by the summer of 1967, clearly out of the question, unless we jettison the AL thing. But mightn't we begin to jot down notes and night-thoughts for one, so we can whip it through when I get back? They are impressed by the luck of the Approach, and think they can do a lot better now.

You no doubt have had a note from Martin about Jack Purser; I mentioned this lately to you. I have set myself down to do a trial letter to him, and enclose a copy. One to Martin, too. This in the first person, and very probably it should be a joint letter. No doubt much needs changing. But you and Martin might chat on the phone, for instance, to revise this, and decide what to do. One thing: it is a cinch Jack will never accept a reduction on grounds of ethics or decency. But if he thinks that we might tire of building up his old age annuity then he might talk turkey. I have hinted threat here—not that I want to cut off my (or your) nose to spite Jack's face. Anyway, here is the draft, let me have reactions, and instructions.

I have your letter to Magagnosc. You are heroic about the drama thing, and I might add about pulling the chestnuts out of the [p. 3] fire in my criticism section. I agree with everything you have in your letter, and shall undertake a rewrite as soon as your criticisms come.

Luck in your war-to-end-war with Kendall.

All here send love to Tinkie and to you.

As ever,
Red

October 4, 1966

Dear Red,

Thank you for your good letter of Sept. 22. I am again woefully behind in answering, but things have been moving at a brisk pace for us for the last couple of weeks. The pressure is still on and therefore I shall not try to do much in this note other than attend to a few matters of current business. I must delay no longer, however, our very warm thanks for the volume of *Selected Poems*. It makes a handsome volume and it is a most impressive one, not only in terms of the new poems but the splendid collection from past volumes. The total impact is really terrific.

I go to Atlanta this morning to give some lectures, and I am taking the *Selected Poems* with me to read, re-read, mull over, and enjoy. I have a further motive, too, however, though one that does not contradict but simply extends the former. I mean to read from your poetry on October 12, when I return. (Mine will be in the series here at Yale that Maynard [Mack] set up, I believe last year. I believe someone had told me that you have been one of the readers in the series.)

Your revision of the analysis of "My Last Duchess" is excellent—in your best manner—and throws some new light on the artistry of the poem. I have sent it on to Martin with only a few quite trivial suggestions for changes.

I believe that the analysis of this poem was the only thing that Jack ever contributed—beyond proof-reading, etc.—to the *Approach,* and I remember that you told me that you had helped him some with it. I suppose that [it] is not odd, then, that this one should contain a howler and have to be rewritten—though in fairness to Jack I must admit that through carelessness or stupidity I had let it slip past me too.

In writing to Martin Stanford today I am telling him that my suggested paragraph in your proposed letter to Jack is intended to put pressure on Jack and does not mean that you and I are seriously preparing to abandon the *Approach.* I'm sure that Martin doesn't need that reassurance, but it won't hurt to give it to him.

I mailed to Martin, by the way, a few days ago all the material that I have done in the way of discussion and exercises for our new section on the Theater of the Absurd. I've asked him, since he has better facilities, to be responsible for making copies and sending them off promptly to you. I hope that you will be quite ruthless in suggesting changes, additions, or compressions. I have no pride of authorship in any of it. In fact, I have begrudged a bit the time that had to be given to it—and what a deal of time it took!

I have supplied a brief note on *Poor Bitos* (it is written but still needs to be copied). I shall send it on to Martin and then to you. It occurred to me that since the various characters in this play are attending a "wig party" in which they play the parts of notables from the French Revolution, we ought to give at least a brief note on the relationships of people like Robespierre, Saint-Just, Danton, et al. (Why, then if such a note is necessary, did I choose this play of Anouilh's? Because I came to the conclusion that this was the best play of his for us to use—at least in this particular context. It is a nice instance of the "theatricality" which characterizes the Theater of the Absurd, and I find it a highly interesting play, much more interesting than some of the others.) Anyway, I think that the note which could be put at the bottom of the page at the beginning of the play would take care of any real difficulty: the play, as a matter of fact, is not obscure or difficult.

[p. 2] Now that this job for the *Approach* is finally drafted, I am eagerly turning back to the Thoreau job. Fortunately when I had to leave it for the Approach section, already I had done a great deal of reading for the Thoreau and had taken some rather elaborate notes. I have now actually begun writing and hope soon to be able to show you something. As soon as I have a reasonable draft, Dick Lewis and I will have a session on it and then I'll send you a copy with our comments and suggestions for a way to organize this material.

I'm glad that Rosanna has been admitted to the Lycee. I hope that she likes it and I'm sure that she will. With Rosanna and Gabriel both now in school, the whole family can plan to settle down for the autumn and winter work. We indeed thrive, though problems do keep arising. We learned the other day that we need a new roof! Ah well, things aren't too bad and on this most beautiful autumn day no one could feel depressed about anything. Tinkie joins me in best greetings to you, Eleanor, Rosanna, and Gabriel.

Cleanth

P.S. I heard the other day from Martin's secretary that he was away on a short vacation. This may account for some delay in copies of various things getting to you, but I take it that he is now back and I am urging him to get mss to you at once.

October 11, 1966

Dear Red,

Your letter of October 5 came in promptly. I like the arrangement that you suggest—that is, "Appendix on Criticism and the Writing of Papers," I, "How to write a critical paper," followed by II, "Critical Essays," with the five in the order that you list. I think it's a good arrangement, and as matters have developed makes thorough sense. I appreciate your scruple about not wanting to sign item I as an essay; it doesn't matter, however, but as you like. But your essay "Why Do We Read Fiction?" ought, of course, to be signed again, just as it is in the present 4th edition.

By the way, let me say that I had not realized—through some failure of long distance communication and because of my own hurry and confusion— that "Why Do We Read Fiction?" was to be included among the five essays. (It ought to be, of course, and it would have been silly to have left it out.) Anyway, this explains why I made no special reference to it when I was adding material on the particular emphases used by Bishop, MacDonald, Jarrell, and Auden. You are quite right therefore (on p. 20) to add "—a topic that is discussed in the essay Why Do We Read Fiction? (p.)." But in the interest of gentle tidiness I think it wise also on p. 22 to put your name in the list after Bishop, MacDonald, etc., and to add on p. 23, after the reference to the stresses made by Bishop, MacDonald, and Auden, the following sentence: "Warren's essay, as its title makes evident, centers its attention on the reader and concerns itself with the various interests to which fiction appeals and with the basic human needs that it satisfies." Then we can go on, making the next sentence start a new paragraph, "Of the five, Randall Jarrell's essay" etc.

As a matter of fact, this sentence is, I believe, the only change that I have suggested. I am quite satisfied with the essay as it now stands and I am sending it in to Martin so that he can begin setting it up. Nothing further remains to be done, I believe, except to drop a few references here and there in the exercises that refer to material which will *not* appear in the alternate edition. Cutting out such references will of course entail also remodeling our "Preface" to the fourth edition. I'll try to get down to that today.

The most welcome item included in your last packet, of course, is the sheaf of new poems "Ile de Port Cros: What Happened."[1] They seem to me very fine. If I can get to know them a little better before tomorrow afternoon, I may use one or two in my reading at the Hall of Graduate Studies. But the *Selected Poems* has so much brilliant and interesting stuff in it that I shall have no trouble finding *plenty* of wonderful poems to read.

I was in Atlanta most of last week. It was pleasant, though I hated to take out four days just at this time. That's the trouble when you make dates a year ahead. Anyway, I hope to stay pretty steadily at it from now on, though the wonderful weather makes it awfully hard to stay inside, plugging away at the Thoreau and other such matters.

Tinkie joins in affectionate greetings to all four of you,

Cleanth

P.S. I enclosed a scrap of telegram that got enclosed by mistake in your last letter. You probably don't need it now, but I shall return it just to be sure.

P.P.S Do be candid and thorough in suggesting revisions in my Discussions and Exercises on the new plays that we are adding.

[Warren wrote Jack Purser on October 26, 1966, suggesting a change in Purser's royalty from 4% to 2.5% for the alternate fourth edition of *An Approach to Literature* and from 2.5% to 1.5% on the fifth edition.]

1315 Davenport College
Yale University
New Haven, Connecticut
November 3, 1966

Dear Red,

I have put off writing to you about the fine suite of poems entitled "Ile de Port Cros" until I have time to do a little rereading and meditation. Anyway, though they can stand a great deal more reading and I am far from having digested them, I mustn't put off any longer telling you that I think they are magnificent. I have at the moment my favorites among the individual pieces, of course, but there is not a weak link in the chain, and what really bowls me over is the impact of the whole group taken as one beautifully interlaced and very rich, massive, long poem.

I have just said that the different parts are beautifully and intricately laced together, but the reader doesn't have any sense of studied design: the effect is that of natural growth, richness, and vitality. Still, let me allow myself a few incidental comments on some of the parts. Your "Venus Anodyomeme" is

1. "Ile de Port Cros: What Happened," a sequence of six poems, was published October 16, 1968, as the "Island of Summer" sequence in *Incarnations: Poems, 1960–1968*.

really quite wonderful in its shattering way—and your Venus clearly belongs in this suite of poems, all right. I like the "Red Mullet" very much. "The Ivy" is a kind of distillation of what preoccupied the Romantic poets. It would be interesting to watch the faces of Messrs. Wordsworth, Coleridge, Shelley, and Keats as the poem was read to them. Coleridge would understand it, I think, but might resist it. I'm not sure that Wordsworth would understand it, though he is a surprising man, and he might very well comprehend it thoroughly. Keats, I am sure, would like it very much. Anyway, *I* like all these poems very much indeed, and am most grateful to have had a chance to see them in ms.

You mentioned in your last letter my reading from your poems at Yale. There was a good crowd. A number of people, including several students, came up to talk to me later about the reading, and there was at least one fervent fan letter. Since the response couldn't have been due to my dulcet tones or histrionic gestures, there is only one explanation for the response, and a perfectly obvious one. Why shouldn't the poems register powerfully: they are simply the best that are being written today in English.

Now down to more poky and prosaic topics. I think your letter to Jack Purser is excellent. It is certainly tactful, but it makes the case very firmly and I find it hard to believe that Jack won't see the value of making a graceful capitulation, even if he wants to haggle a bit over the percentage suggested. Anyway, we'll hope for the best.

I have nearly finished my draft of Thoreau and I hope that you and Dick will like it. If all goes well, I hope to have it typed up by the end of the week. Then Dick and I will go over it and have some talk about it and I'll get a copy off to you right away.

One reason why the thing is taking so long is that I am trying to get even this rough draft down to something like the scale that we will probably have to use, and I am trying to experiment a little with format and arrangement.

[p.2] At a party the other night, I ran into [Jacques] Guicharnaud and sounded him out about looking over the Theater of the Absurd discussion. (I don't know him well, but we have met a number of times and his wife, of course, was copy editor for my Faulkner book.)[1] I told Guicharnaud that we had been making some use of his book on the Theater of the Absurd and that therefore we were particularly eager to have his check against howlers that we might have made, or omissions of important points that should have been noted. Guicharnaud seemed agreeable enough, but I may decide to have Martin Stanford put the formal request to him, suggesting some fee. (The editors will probably have to pay the fee, but it wouldn't be a large one and the fee might come with better grace ostensibly from the publisher rather than obviously out of our pockets. What do you think?)

1. Jacques Guicharnaud, in collaboration with June Beckelman, wrote *Modern French Theatre from Giraudoux to Beckett* (New Haven: Yale University Press, 1961); by the time they updated it in 1967, Beckelman had become Mrs. Guicharnaud.

As I write this letter, the roofers are on top of the house putting on new shingles. It's the first of November and I hope that they can beat the bad weather. They are late. Our painter has failed on his promises and I expect we are going to have to wait until spring to have the house painted. Still, we are gradually getting things back into shape. How nice it would be if we could have a meeting—a family meeting—for we are longing to see and have some talk with Eleanor and the children as well as with you.

Yours,
Cleanth

P.S. One of Bob Heilman's friends has suggested that I nominate Bob Heilman for membership in the American Academy of Arts and Sciences. The friend is seconding the nomination, and I wonder whether you too would be willing to do so. (Four names are needed.) I don't want to press the issue at all, but if you would like to endorse the nomination, could you send a brief note saying so, at once, to the Committee of Membership, American Academy of Arts and Sciences, 280 Newton St., Boston, Mass. I say "at once" only because, through my negligence, the nomination got in fairly late, indeed just before the November 1 deadline. (I am assured, however, that if seconding endorsements come in fairly soon, the fact that they are technically too late will not stand in the way.) Bob's middle initial is B.

1315 Davenport College
Yale University
New Haven, Connecticut
January 13, 1967

Dear Red,

Your letter of January 4 and your copy of the *Approach* proof arrived the other day. I got down to the proofs at once, telephoned Miss Camp at Appleton-Century-Crofts, found that there was time to get your corrections in, and at once dispatched the proofs to her. I think that all is in order now and we are still on schedule.

I knew that you all were in Switzerland and that the proofs would undoubtedly reach you late. They reached me late, for that matter, since I, no more than you, had [not] been forewarned that they were coming. Consequently, they were sent here to Northford and then had to be forwarded to New Orleans, losing five or six days' time in the process. Anyway, knowing all this, I proceeded to make cuts in the "My Last Duchess" analysis and tried to tidy up a few matters. But I was delighted and relieved to have your own recommendations get in in time to be used and, of course, you have caught some matters here and there that escaped me.

The whole of the last edition must have been given a very sloppy proofreading. I was appalled to find some of the misprints that had ridden through in other parts of the book. Catherine Barkley, the heroine of *A Farewell to Arms,* had become Catherine Baker! Did Jack Purser do the proof-reading for this edition? I can't remember.

By the way, it is wonderful news that Jack did capitulate. I think he was sensible to do so, but he has certainly saved us a good deal of bother by throwing in the sponge. Your letter to him was a good one and must have been effective. I think what we proposed was eminently fair. I suppose that even Jack saw that.

We had a good session with the Lewises just before Dick took off for Europe. I told him at the time that I hoped that you and he in your conference would make sure to assign further work on this first volume to me. The original assignment, you remember, was based upon the supposition that you and he would be far ahead and that I would make up my part by seeing the book through the press. Now, though you are ahead of both Dick and me, the gap is not so wide, especially as between me and Dick, and so I am happy to take on another two or three authors for whom I would be primarily responsible.

I appreciate your good word about my Theater-of-the-Absurd section and about my Thoreau discussion. I do hope you are right in thinking that my tone with regard to the Theater of the Absurd is about right. The problem was a tricky one for me, for I am not enthusiastic about these dramatists. But I did want to be fair not to queer the pitch for the student.

The present version of the Thoreau section, of course, is very rough. Let me have any suggestions. I know I can make it read much more smoothly when I rewrite it.

Tink and I last year were in Switzerland in the winter time, and in the mountains for a wonderful thirty-six hours. We had just enough of a glimpse of them to make us envy the stay that the Warrens have just had there.

[p. 2] I am delighted to hear about your prospective visit to Cairo. Our trip to Egypt (part of our Cook's tour of the near East) was very brief, but rewarding. The museums at Cairo are perfectly fabulous. We know that all of you are going to enjoy this visit very much indeed.

I have just written to Helsinki to accept an invitation to give a paper there in late June. How much time we can take to knock around Europe afterwards remains to be seen. But we hope we may possibly get a glimpse of you before we return.

Our little barn is nearly finished. We hope soon to have books and papers sorted and put in some sort of order so that I can find them. I have now got a regular part-time secretarial service and even a little research service and so hope to be able to get more done—especially more on paper—from now on. In spite of the clutter of our lives, we both thrive. Tinkum joins me in cordial regards to all four of you. She promises a letter soon.

Sincerely,
Cleanth Brooks

1315 Davenport College
Yale University
New Haven, Connecticut
March 3, 1967

Dear Red,

You should not be the one apologizing for having been "very poor about writing." The fact of the matter is that I owe you a letter and, in any case, I should have written soon after my talk with Dick Lewis on his return from Europe. He reported a fine visit with you and Eleanor and was full of talk about our book. Apparently the meeting that you and he had about it was very successful and Dick has returned, not only with a lot of ideas about it, but also with a lot of enthusiasm.

I have had a rough winter as far as getting time for writing. Work on the alternate edition of the *Approach* absorbed too much of the summer and early fall, and since then a lot of the time has gone to teaching and to finishing articles for a *Festschrift* here and a *Festschrift* there. Fortunately I think I have cleared out that thicket and I now hope to push on with my share of our American literature book. Indeed, I hope to get to writing on Poe within the next day or so. A great deal of my reading for the Poe introduction has been done. I am well content with my additional assignment of authors. They seem perfectly obvious choices and I am glad to take them on.

The week that has just closed has been a horror. Some entertaining that we had planned began the week; then there were two trips into New York that I found I had to take; and then, an unexpected, though very pleasant visit, from friends just in from Europe. These things have pretty well knocked the week out. But as I look into March, things do seem to be thinning out.

Because of the cluttered week past, I have just picked up your Whittier material and will be getting into it during this weekend. Once I have done that, I can write to better purpose about our book. But I don't want to delay this letter any further. In any case, my conversation with Dick and what Dick had to report about his conversation with you make me feel certain that we are in agreement in principle—very much so, and since that is true, I don't worry too much about our being able to get together rather easily on some of the questions of detail.

I am quite with you about the need to have some comments in our Introduction (or elsewhere) about the relation of American literature to the world outside. Our minds are in thorough agreement here. Shakespeare *is* the greatest American writer because he is, as you put it, just as much American as he is English. These, and related, points need to be made explicitly.

. . . .

Tinkum joins in all cordial greetings to you and Eleanor and Rosanna and Gabriel. I do hope that Eleanor is by this time feeling much better.

Sincerely,
Cleanth Brooks

[Handwritten at bottom of p. 2] P.S. The Bollingen Prize was due—has long been overdue. The honor is a real one, an honor that I coveted for you even though you don't *need* it. But I shall therefore be *base* about the whole thing: how nice that the sum is $5,000! That *is* a useful sum. I hope it's tax-free.

[OH]
Hotel Codan
St. Anne Plads 21
København, K.
July 7 [1967]

Dear Red,

A letter long overdue! But we have been hopping about Northern Europe so fast and I have been so exhausted by nightfall every evening that I have let my correspondence go. Now, in Copenhagen, we are on our last lap and by Sunday evening (two days hence) hope to be home in Northford.

The conference in Helsinki was, I believe, very successful and our trip—London, Oslo, Stockholm, Helsinki, Leningrad, and Copenhagen—has been very pleasant. Best of all, we have had wonderful luck with the weather: only one or two mornings of rain in the whole of the four weeks!

The occasion of this little note, however, is not to chat about our trip but to remind you that I shall be back in touch henceforward and that I see no reason to think that I cannot meet our November deadline. This is what I told Dick L. at our last meeting about the book and this is what I want to say to you. The book gets top priority with me, beginning July 10. I have roughed out the Poe section—thirty pages or so of typescript. That, I must rewrite and also revise my Thoreau section, which you have seen. The three shorter pieces I am to do ought not to take too long, even though I am aware that one always [p. 2] underestimates these matters. But I shall keep the deadline, never fear.

As far as our second volume is concerned, the prospects for me are also good. I have a light teaching load next year (1967–68) and the year after that (1968–69) is a sabbatical!

We are both of us looking forward to greeting you and Eleanor and Rosanna and Gabriel this September. We have much to talk about. After all, it will be three years and a half since we've seen each other! Much too long!

T. joins me in fond love to all four of you.

Cleanth

Port Cros
July 27, 1967

Dear Cleanth:

I am enclosing a copy of the suggested poems to be put in the Lowell section. Mrs. Callahan will get the prose material to you in due course, after the critical section which I have written. All of this is, of course, to be cut back.

Please hold this list of poems for enclosure. I have sent a copy to Peter Conn, who is doing help for me, asking him to get 3 sets of xeroxes made, and to get one to you and one to Dick, and hold one for me. But he may not be around, and my list to him may get lost. So play anchor man, will you?

I woke up early this morning with one of my seizures of poetry and rewrote a section of the new string before I got up. So I'm rather groggy at Lowell, bad cess to him.

Today is Rosanna's birthday. She's not here, off at the Carteron place in Touraine, but we expect her at the end of the week, when there's to be a joint birthday for her and Eleanor. That is our big news.

Love to you both,
Red

P.S. I forgot to say that I haven't quite finished headnotes for the Lowell poems. In fact, I now think that a good bit of the stuff in the general introduction to Lowell will be better transferred to headnotes, somewhat reduced.

1315 Davenport College
Yale University
New Haven, Connecticut
August 3, 1967

Dear Red,

It was fine having the long letter from you the other day and now again a note this morning with its list of poems for the Lowell section. I'll hold on to them. We expect to see the Lewises tomorrow evening and I'll find out from him whether Peter Conn is in town at this time or not. I'll also talk with Dick about two or three other matters connected with our book.

I am just finishing up drafting the Poe instructions, headnotes, and selections. I hope that I have some useful things to say about Poe and I have found, I believe, at least one fresh slant on his grotesque tales. What I am rejoicing over at the moment, however, is simply the fact that I *believe* that my section is just going to fit into the 55,000 words provisionally allotted for the commentary, notes, and selections from Poe. I hope that I haven't miscounted!

My next step is to review the Thoreau material and redistribute it between commentary and headnotes, with some rethinking and rewriting of the material. I am reading Jefferson now and hope to start doing a brief commentary on him, perhaps next week.

I am much interested in what you have to tell me about your new poem. If you have a carbon, please let [me] have a look at it—even if you haven't yet put it in final form.

Tink and I go out to Arizona next week to spend a few days at my eldest brother's ranch. In order to save time we'll fly out and back. We saw Catherine Coffin and the Wilders last night at dinner. Thornton's novel got mauled a bit by the critics but has been selling very well for weeks. I must say that I like it very much.[1]

We are looking forward very eagerly to the Warrens' return to these shores. We'll certainly have a lot to talk about. How proud both of you must be of Rosanna and Gabriel. What a wonderful fifteen months their stay has been for them.

Cordially,
Cleanth Brooks

[Handwritten] P.S. Conn called after this letter had been typed and brought me the xeroxed material.

Northford, Conn. 06472
June 21, 1968

Dear Red,

. . . .

I've just looked over notes of the conversation that we had on the subject of revising U.P. Apparently we do have some ideas and even some fairly definite ones, but I suppose that here, as with some of the other books, much is going to turn on whether we can find eventually—when we're ready to work on it—somebody who can do a great deal of legwork and assembly for us.

I had a note yesterday from one of my MAT students, Miss Raquel Dow, in which she said that Ed Gordon had mentioned to her that we are looking for someone to help with *Modern Rhetoric*. She writes: "he mentioned that you were looking for a reader in connection with revising your book *Modern Rhetoric*. I am very interested in working for you if the position is still open. My summer is completely free, and I can think of nothing I would enjoy more than researching essays and articles for you."

Last fall Miss Dow got off to a fairly slow start in my English 160 but she ended with a mark of honors and all of her papers during the last several months were of honors quality. It's possible that she could do a good job for us. I'll try to talk further with Ed about it and I'll have a long talk with her about the details of the job and try to find out what her conception of it is.

The fact that Ed has evidently suggested that she get directly in touch would seem to indicate that he thinks she is our best bet. Anyway, I'll try to find out more and unless I discover some reason to think we can do better, plan to sign her up. If you have any other thoughts about this matter, however, please give me a ring.

No more at present. Tinkie joins me in affectionate greetings to each of you.

Cleanth

[Handwritten] P.S. I've now talked further with Ed and with Miss Dow. She and I are to have a meeting Monday. I've told her that the first two weeks will be provisional—that we'll see how much she can accomplish in that time,

---

1. Thornton Wilder, *The Eighth Day* (New York: Harper and Row, 1967).

how well she takes to the work, etc., before we sign her on permanently. She is willing to take the going rate—$2.00 per hour. I'll give you a report on her at the end of next week.

[OH]   Forest Road
                                                 Northford, Connecticut 06472
                                                               June 28 [1968]
Dear Red,
. . . .

I am posting to you today under separate cover:
  The Sketchbook (paper)
  Conquest of Granada (second-hand, .95)
  and *Tales of the Traveler* from the Yale Library, checked out in the name of Miss Raquel Dow—
  plus Xerox copies of the four articles for which you asked.
I telephoned Miss Dow after I got your letter and she bought or checked out the books and located and xeroxed the articles: a great time saver! I hope that she can be as helpful in collecting materials for *Modern Rhetoric.*
Greetings to all of you from both of us here.

                                                                  In haste,
                                                                  Cleanth
P.S. I am working on the H. B. Stowe and think I have tightened up the Introduction to Poe.

                                                            early July, 1968
Dear Cleanth:
Here is the sheet for xeroxing Hawthorne. We may have to drop a couple of items from this list, but it is better to have them on hand than to do them up at the last minute. Please note instructions about the texts to use.
As for my progress, I have just finished a long headnote on The Scarlet Letter (5500 words), and this has taken a long time. But I decided (had to decide without consultation) that if we are to do any novel this is one of the "musts," and an interpretation of this is crucial for Hawthorne. The note took me a long time to do (I had done nothing on SL in my previous Hawthorne stuff); had to reread, etc. But I am not too unhappy about the result. Still rough. It goes to the typist today and you should have a copy soon.
By the way, I have just heard from her explaining the delay in the Irving. She was moving to a new house, etc. But she promises to have that out soon.
The final draft of the other Hawthorne stuff goes off this week to her, about 16,000 words, and I hope that won't be too long in coming to you. Some cutting back will have to be done, but I can't do it now. Better in consultation.

Once the Hawthorne is over, things will move fast for me, for it will be only cutting then, I trust.

The weather is good at last, and we are well. Tomorrow, however, I go to Boston to put Rosanna on a plane for France, where she will be visiting for three weeks.

Love to you both!

Yrs
Red

[Handwritten in left margin] Irving has come in *before* 6 July 1968.

West Wardsboro, Vermont
July 9, 1968

Dear Cleanth and Dick:

I am here including:

    (1) Headnotes for Hawthorne selections

    (2) Reading list for Hawthorne

Mrs. Callahan will be sending you:

    (1) A completely redone Hawthorne essay

    (2) A big headnote for *The Scarlet Letter*

As for my general progress, you should now have in hand, from Mrs. C., the Irving and the Melville. But you will note that I have not as yet tried to reduce the Melville. You will notice, too, that the headnotes for Irving are not there. I am now putting those into shape, and they should be in your hands in a couple of days after this letter.

I should explain the long delay about the Hawthorne. When I got down to the nitty gritty, I found that I had little more in the old MS than very elaborate notes, and so I had to settle down to a complete rewrite and re-think job. It is now 15,500 words by something close to an actual count, and—I think, hope—a much better piece of writing than before. As for *The Scarlet Letter*, I decided that, since we had used parts of novels for Cooper, we'd have to do the same for Hawthorne. So I undertook to choose the key chapters and fill enough in headnotes to give a coherent picture of the whole, plus the interpretations and critical comments. (You, Cleanth, have known this from my request for xeroxing, of course.) I had to reread and rethink the novel— and a very thrilling business this was—I began to feel that I had [not] *read* the book before—but I could have wished that the experience came at another time. The headnote for the SL runs 5,000 words, but I have a format idea which will take some of the curse off this. And, of course, you all may make some suggestions for cuts. But it can't be just a little thing.

This has all taken a lot longer than I had expected. I have worked everyday except the weekend of July 4, sometimes up to nine hours a day. From now on, however, things ought to go faster. All the other essays are in a much better shape, and are much shorter to begin with. I think they present merely a matter of cutting and splicing. But now what I need from you is a guide on lengths. I have lost my guide sheet, and don't know what my allowances are on Longfellow, Whittier, Lowell, and the "non-literary" thing—Irving, too, which needs reducing.

Dick, your letter of June 7 has just this morning come, and I am grateful for it. Your remarks about the Melville make me very happy. As a matter of fact, the elaborate notes on individual poems at times run to little essays— for instance after the "Pleasure Party" which I have found more and more interesting, and on some of the Battle Pieces. There I did a lot of work in comparing [p. 2] Melville pieces with the God-awful poems in the Rebellion Record, for example. Anyway, you can't dodge these other notes. Later on, in the fall, I am going to make you read them hard and censoriously. Meanwhile, I am depending on you to try to make connections between my stuff and yours on Melville. But ruthlessly, you'll have to. I look forward to your general Melville piece. By the way, you will notice big traces of your Adam book[1] in my new stuff on Hawthorne, but I hope that you will do some rewriting—and new thinking—on this part of my contribution. Please DO THIS!

Cleanth, more trouble for you. Under separate cover, I am sending you my copy of the book *The Hawthorne Question*, by Agnes Donohue. Will you please have our girl get xeroxes (3 sets) for pages 324–333? One set for each of us. And when convenient return the book to me *here*. I may need it in rewrites, etc.

One question to you both about Reading Lists. Shall we ever put in stuff from periodicals? I know that if we make a practice of this we'll never end, but what about things of special interest?

And what about the biographical summaries? I have done some. Aren't they really useful to the student?

. . . .

Good-bye. I must have forgotten some business—oh yes, I did. I am happy to come down July 19, but wouldn't the session be better after your return, Dick. I have the big job of cutting on my own stuff which will run another month, until you get back. Now *if* my coming will be really useful to you all, OK. Do some thinking about this and let me know. I want to do what will really help the project, you know that. I hesitate only because the thing will not mean much for my work for the next period.

Good-bye, again. Let me hear from you. Love to your ladies, etc.

Ever yours, your fellow sufferer,
Red

[p. 3] PS—You will notice that there are not some headnotes for some of the Hawthorne stories on my list ordered for xeroxing. This does *not* mean that I have discarded stories, etc., which have no headnotes. It means only that some of the stories will have no headnotes. BUT I am far from sure that we can use all the stories I have asked to be xeroxed. That must be settled later.

1. R. W. B. Lewis, *The American Adam* (1955). Warren was godfather to the Lewises' daughter, Emma.

West Wardsboro
July 10, 1968

Dear Cleanth:

Here is another set of things to be xeroxed, readings for Irving:

. . . .

This amounts to more than we'll use, but what I have decided to do is take these chapters from the *History* and make excerpts, bringing us down to about 30,000 altogether.

I suppose you now have my Irving piece? I have been trying to cut back, but without much success. I enclose the biographical summary, and headnotes on Rip and legend. I can't do [the] headnote on *History* until I have text.

Love to you both,
Red

July 11, 1968

Dear Cleanth:

Here are three sheets to be inserted, as numbered, in the Longfellow. I have been cutting it back, but it is in such bits, here and there, that my copy is the only one unless the whole is retyped, and I don't think that is worth that. We can transfer the stuff later, if necessary. The thing now comes down to 6000 words, and I don't see much chance of more sweating-down.

Hastily,
Red

July 12, 1968

Dear Red,

Your letter of July 9 with its enclosures and your letter of the 10th with its list of Irving materials to be xeroxed came in this morning. I hasten to reply.

I hope to pick up some of the Hawthorne materials when I go into town this afternoon. Two books were out (in the editions we needed) and have had to be recalled. As soon as they come in I'll get on to xeroxing the rest of the Hawthorne and the Irving pieces.

The girl who has been working with us, Miss Raquel Dow—has had to go back to California—family illness—though she hopes to be back here by the first of August. She plans to go on ahead assembling essays for our reader since she will have ready access to a good library in California, but her departure makes more difficult our present xeroxing activity. I have already set about, however, trying to hire someone to do just xeroxing jobs for us.

Your Irving reads well—very well indeed, and I hope it won't have to be cut. If it does, I hope that I can be spared the job of cutting it, for it is all so useful in what it says and hangs together so well that it will be difficult to cut it without serious loss.

I have rewritten the Stowe introduction and the headnotes for the Selections in order to give more space to *Uncle Tom's Cabin* and to the millennial ideas in it. This has been retyped and as soon as I can xerox it I'll get copies to you. I have xeroxed two chapters from Uncle Tom and a chapter from Poganuc People and will get copies next week to you and Dick so that you can see whether these are the best to use or make other nominations.

In reworking my Poe material for the short article (of which I told you), which is to appear in the Yale grad. school magazine Ventures, I think I succeeded in tightening up the argument considerably. In the light of this and of a few suggestions from you and Dick, I will do some rewriting on the Poe introduction.

I've been reading William Gilmore Simms in the hope of finding a short story from his The Wigwam and the Cabin that might deserve our reprinting. I'm not sure that I can find anything good enough and short enough at the same time. Still I need to continue the reading long enough to write up the paragraph or so on Simms that at our last meeting we said ought to go into the Holmes introduction (contrasts between Boston and Charleston as different kinds of cultural capitals).

Last week I took off a few days to work at a chapter on Faulkner's poetry and had a good time in the process and may even have a chapter for my second volume. But I'll keep on steadily pointing to our American lit. book until we can get our stuff assembled and laced together.

Now for a few questions. My notes—such as they are—taken at the last conference that you and Dick and I had together, show 9,000 (?) for the Longfellow introduction, 13,000 for Whittier (with a query: cut to 9,000?) and query 14,000 for Cooper. For the "non-literature," my note puts down 12,000 words commentary. But I set no store by these notes. Dick may have ampler notations and at the same time, of course, all of us were simply guessing and we'll have to keep changing our estimates as we go along.

[p. 2] I note your suggestion that it might be better for us to have a conference not on the 19th of this month but after Dick's return. I can't judge of this. We'd like to see you both and have room for you both if either or both of you can come for this meeting. I have no feeling one way or another about it except for the fact that I always enjoy the pleasure of your company.

No further news from here except that we both thrive with lots of mowing, lots of reading, and—I am happy to say—lots of writing on my part, though I sometimes look back at the writing and wish that it were a great deal better than it is. Anyway, it's thus far been a good summer.

In the next few minutes I go into New Haven to pick up Tinkum's mother who will be with us for a visit, but our plans for the writing factory take this into account and won't be disturbed by it at all.

Tinkum joins me in affectionate greetings to Eleanor and Gabriel and we are certain that Rosanna is having a splendid visit in France.

I shall be writing to you early in the week.

Cleanth

P.S. Could you send me in your next note Dick's summer address? I know I put it down somewhere, but I can't now locate it anywhere.

[In a July 12, 1968, letter to Brooks, Warren, and Lewis, Edward F. Earley, the director of St. Martin's Press, suggests an October 1, 1968, delivery date for the first draft of the first volume of *Understanding American Literature*. The title was changed to *American Literature: The Makers and the Making* by the time the book was published in 1973.]

July 17, 1968

Dear Red,

I have found a new xerox agent for us—a pleasant graduate student named Maddox, to whom I have given a big batch of work. It includes the Longfellow selections, which I had simply forgotten about. (I have looked up your letter which lists the poems that we need to have xeroxed. The letter had been mislaid and so I am glad that you asked where the Longfellow material was.) Apparently Maddox is to be here all summer. When we meet in the next day or so I'll give him the material to xerox from the Donahue Hawthorne book and then will return the book to you.

I will soon have a xerox copy for you of the new Stowe introduction and headnotes that I have rewritten. I've got in now an adequate reference—or so I think—to the millennial hope and fear out of which *Uncle Tom's Cabin* came.

Yesterday and today I am working hard over Dick's stuff, for he phoned on Sunday that he will be here on Friday. I'm sorry that you won't be here with us for Friday night and Saturday morning, but I'm sure you have made the right decision. We'll all get together later.

I've just had a phone call from Mrs. Elizabeth Brinton in the State Dept. who is concerned to get one of us to come, if possible, for three weeks of lecturing in South America next month. The place would be Montevideo, Uruguay (though they are thinking of splitting the three weeks and making it ten days in Uruguay and ten days in Chile). I told her that I simply couldn't think of it this time and when she raised the question about you, told her that I expected that you too would find it impossible to go, but that since she had not been able to reach you by phone, I would raise the question with you when I got off a letter to you later this morning.

If you are interested, you might call her at the following address: State Dept., CU/AS 4332 Bureau of Educational and Cultural Affairs, Washington D.C. She seems a pleasant woman; is, I believe, a cousin of a sort of Crane Brinton; and elaborately apologized for so late a notice. Anyway, I keep my promise to her by sending on this information to you.

I'm also enclosing a carbon of a letter from St. Martin's Press, which I assume has been posted to you, but since they sent *two* copies to me, I am relaying one to you. I'm also enclosing a list of essays (for our Reader in M.R.) which Miss Dow has got up for us. My instructions to her were that if she had a good deal of confidence that the article in question was one that we might seriously consider, she was to xerox it forthwith, but with reference to those about which she had more doubt, she was to simply list it with notes. This is the list to date. You might put it in a separate file and when you have the time, look over and scratch off items that you are *sure* we wouldn't want to look at. If other titles seem possibilities, we can then ask Miss Dow to xerox.

In the meantime, I have accumulated a fair-sized set of xerox copies. In the next day or so I'll send you a list of these and the xerox copies themselves any time you'd like to look over them.

No more time for news on this hot and humid day except to relay affectionate greetings to you all.

Cleanth

{[Handwritten] p. 2}
Dear Red,

I forgot to comment on your suggestions for some comments on method in an Introduction to our *Am. Lit.* book. This is an *excellent* suggestion. I'll have more to say about it later.

C.

July 20, 1968

Dear Red,

Dick and I had what I think was a good conference last night in which he made suggestions about my stuff and I about his. What pleased me most was the fact that apparently we are not going to have any real difficulty in fitting our materials together and that there was a much wider range of agreement than I had sometimes thought there might be. Perhaps most satisfactory of all was the fact that Dick seemed to be most optimistic about the future of the book after our session. He seemed genuinely pleased with our interview, and certainly I am.

Maddox, the student who is doing xeroxing for us, hasn't reported yet. If I haven't heard from him over the weekend, I'll give him a nudge on Monday and get some of the newly xeroxed material on to you.

I have the new version of Whittier, but I've not yet had time to look at it. I've the old old version out and will send it on up to you with the next batch of stuff.

I have not very much more to report except that I've done some cutting and tightening on my Thoreau piece: it's down to about 8100 words and I shall shortly be doing the same with the Poe. As soon as I can get back the xerox of the rewritten Stowe, I'll send that on to you. With reference to the Holmes piece, I'm still wrestling with paragraphs which will mention William Gilmore Simms.

Now to turn to *Modern Rhetoric*. I've heard from Miss Dow again. She is finding and xeroxing more articles for us. She has now put in 96 hours (at

$2 an hour); she has used up $30 for xeroxing expenses and I've sent her an additional $20 for xeroxing. This adds up to $242 so far, or $121 each. (Of the $50 you sent me last summer, I believe only $14 was spent, so your share of the bill so far is actually only $85.) I mention the figures not because there is any need of your paying at this time, but simply so that you will know what the job is costing us and so that you can help me calculate whether it is worth keeping up and for how long.

Now that I have finished pointing and preparing for the conference with Dick and now that the conference is over, I mean to take a couple of days and go over Miss Dow's list for possible xeroxing and the articles she has actually xeroxed, and try to make some estimate of what I think may be really usable, and perhaps suggest to her other areas in which to look for materials. If you have any ideas on this subject, or, after looking over the lists that I have sent you, want to relay any ideas of the sort to her, let me have them.

No more news, really. We had last week a most hot and humid spell, finally broken with showers last night, and it now feels like a new world here. But things have not gone too badly. I feel that I'm getting a great deal done on one job and another, and for the first time I'm really beginning to feel happier about the Am. Lit. book. Let's hope that nothing will happen to change our minds on this subject. Tink joins in all cordial greetings to you and Eleanor and Gabriel.

Cleanth

[p. 2]

[Handwritten] These are already xeroxed for *Modern Rhetoric*

C The Graduated Response Fallacy (Dominick Graham) Yale Review, Autumn 1967

B+ The Romantic Rebel on the Campus (James Hitchcock) Yale Review, Autumn 1967

A The Age of Overkill (Benjamin DeMott) New York Times Magazine, May 19, 1968

B "Letter from Anguilla" (John Updike) New Yorker, June 22, 1968

B The American Challenge (Servan-Schrieber) Harper's, p. 31

C Intelligence, the University and Society (Kenneth B. Clark) The American Scholar, Winter 66–67

A The Reach of Imagination (J. Bronowski) American Scholar, Spring 1967
The Scholar in a Nowhere World (August Heckscher) Yale Review, Autumn 1967
Making It: The Brutal Bargain (Norman Podhoretz) Harper's, Dec. 1967
The Scandal of Literary Scholarship (Louis Kampf) Harper's, Dec. 1967
On the Contemporary Apocalyptic Imagination (Earl Rovit) American Scholar
Where Graduate Schools Fair (Christopher Jencks & David Reisman) Atlantic Monthly, Feb. 1968
An American Looks at British Television (Diana Trilling) Atlantic Monthly, Feb. 1968

[Handwritten at bottom of p. 2]
Dear Red—
   Would you like to see all of these or only some and if only some, which, and when?
   I'm assigning a rating of A, B, or C to the ones I've read: A = worth very serious consideration on down to C = probably not for us.

West Wardsboro, Vermont
July 21, 1968

Dear Cleanth and Dick,
   In reviewing the sections on Poe and Emerson, I come up with a notion which I'll lay before you. It strikes me that we might (when material warrants) run a little section with the Selections on an author, with quotes as to what he said about other authors we treat. We have some of this in our text, but only some, and that way, too, it tends to get lost. For instance, under Poe, we could have a long list of quotes from reviews—on Hawthorne, Lowell, Longfellow, etc. Under Thoreau, for example, we could have his bitter late remarks about the friendship with Emerson. Under Whittier, his letter about Thoreau, for example. Etc. It would give some juice and tension to the book, make our people seem more alive. This would work in conjunction, too, with full scale selections on other writers, such as Emerson on Thoreau and Lowell on Thoreau. And we might give, too, a better show of Poe as a reviewer. And more of Emerson's journals.

Best to you both,
Red

July 31 [1968]

Dear Red,
   Our xerox man turned up yesterday with everything done except Irving's Knickerbocker History chapter. These are being done by the Beinecke since the 1809 volume is lodged there and I shall plan to pick up these chapters tomorrow or next day. In the meantime I plan to get off right away the consignment of stuff to you. (Was posted to you on 30 July, yesterday.)
   In the first place, there will be a *Modern Rhetoric* item: Miss Dow's notes on possible articles, pages 6 to 11. The starred items, she is planning to xerox. On the rest she will have our comments before she goes ahead.
   As for the American Lit. book, I am sending some selections from Harriet Beecher Stowe with the proper headnotes; a swatch of stuff for Longfellow; a couple of editorials from William Cullen Bryant. I suggest that we use the two checked, and I am working on headnotes for them. For Poe, I am including his review of Hawthorne's *Mosses from an Old Manse*—to buck up the representation of Poe's criticism. (We may want to use something else.) I'm also enclosing the "Masque of the Red Death," for which Dick has expressed

some preference. We might add it to our Poe selections or else substitute it for something else. For Irving I am including all the material you asked for except the *Knickerbocker History* which is still to come. I also include a copy of the selections from the American notebooks of Hawthorne and chapters from his *Scarlet Letter.* (The library was so dilatory in recalling the Charvat edition that I simply bought a copy. I can use it in my own library.) I enclose also the Holmes selections, though I will still have to supply headnotes for the *Autocrat* and for "The Brahmin Caste." I also enclose the Hawthorne stories you'd asked to have xeroxed and the old copy of Whittier which you wanted returned, plus the Donahue book.

The other day your secretary sent in the revised Hawthorne introduction and, today, the revised introductions for Longfellow and Lowell. When I've had a chance to go over them, I'll make any comments that I think are worth making. In preparation for the meeting with Dick, I did go over *his* material pretty carefully. I'll now plan to review your revised material in much the same way though I think that I shall have little to suggest except an occasional cross reference. You've worked very hard and the high quality of your writing is evident.

Now about several matters that you've mentioned in recent letters. In the first place, I do like your suggestions about our having something to say about our methods in our introduction. I think that this is worth doing for every reason. And I don't anticipate any real difficulty among the three of us in agreeing on methods. We've already shown this in our various talks. As I [p. 2] told you earlier, I more and more see this book as a literary history—though a rather lavishly illustrated *history.* This means, to use my terminology, that we are not primarily interested in simply the *poem,* the *story,* or the *essay,* but also in the author and his personal and intellectual background; and further, in the twentieth-century reader, taking into account, where we can, his interests and blind spots. All that we really need to do to keep our methodology "clean" from *my* standpoint, is to be aware of what we are doing in our various roles as scholars and literary historians and not to make illegitimate transfers from one area to another. To take a perfectly obvious instance: we are interested in *Uncle Tom's Cabin* because of its political, social, and general cultural importance, whether or not we think it a terribly good work of art. Moreover, we are not claiming that it is a great work of art simply because it engaged the minds of its readers powerfully or had powerful repercussions on the national history. If we *do* think it a great work of art in its own right, then we must find our warrant for the assertion that it is so in the makeup of the work itself. That is, we won't say that a novel that was produced by a woman of the character of Harriet Beecher Stowe who believed herself God's amanuensis was bound to be a good work of art nor do we say that three million or five million or ten million Americans can't be wrong; that any book that appeals to so many readers is bound to be a great work of art. (This kind of popularity certainly means *something* and anybody will look very hard at the merits of any work that appeals to so many people, but since there are such things as fads, special topical interests, and extra-literary interests, the proof of worth has to be grounded on the work itself, eventually, if merit is going to be claimed for the work.)

It seems to me that our introductions and headnotes quite consistently imply such a methodology. I am actually not worried about our having to correct what we have already written in our actual introductions. But in view of the present state of critical confusion, we ought to help the young reader, and even some of our more petulant older readers, by stating briefly what we are up to and what our principles are.

I like your suggestion (in your note of July 21) that we include a little block of the comments made by a particular author about his contemporaries. I've already started to collect some of these. I'm not sure just where we'd put them: maybe you have a notion about the format. But the idea is a good one and I propose that we adopt it.

Your letter of July 16 makes some good specific suggestions about some tie-ups and cross references that I might make in my Thoreau piece. Incidentally, I just located the other day a paragraph on Thoreau's view of civil disobedience in a lecture given at Tulane by the present Attorney General of the U.S. (the former dean of Harvard Law School, Griswold). I will incorporate it in my rewritten Thoreau piece.

I don't think I sent you a copy of my somewhat rewritten and tightened-up Poe introduction. I'll get it typed up and a copy off to you shortly.

[p. 3] I'll also send in this letter as an enclosure—or if it doesn't get done in time, in a following letter—a couple of paragraphs touching on Simms that I want to put into the brief reference to Charleston and its society as contrasting with Boston (in my Holmes piece). Who is the critic who talks about certain work not having any "insides"? I THOUGHT THAT I remembered it was I. A. Richards, but I can't find it in his volumes. Do you have any ideas? And where does Allen Tate discuss the two modes of the Southern imagination? I thought I knew all of his critical stuff, backwards and forwards, but this particular reference eludes me.

I mustn't go on forever. If this letter is more illegible than usual, it's because we're trying out a new electric typewriter and haven't yet beat it into submission.

Greetings to all
Cleanth

West Wardsboro, Vermont
August 9, 1968

Dear Dick and Cleanth:

I'll write this to you both.

First, about Dick's Melville. Fine, first rate. One thought: I am not certain but I think that we should run, with some local commentary and analysis, a chapter or two of *Moby-Dick*, even if we have to drop one of the selections now listed. I know we can't give an impression of the whole but I imagine the context for one selection might be adequately set.

Second, about Cleanth's letter to me. Yes, Cleanth, we are writing, as you say, a kind of history of American literature with very full examples, and trying to give various dimensions. This had become more and more apparent to me. My question now is about the dimensions. We are doing very well, I think, on the biographical and psychological, pretty well (with certain gaps to be filled) on the social-historical background, and even some bits (others easily filled) on minor literary characters and issues). But I feel that we need more on two matters:

(1) philosophical background. For example, the sort of thing that Norman Foerster does very well for the 18th century in his big anthology. I don't mean that we should use his method, but I do think that we could build into Franklin and Jefferson an adequate amount of the philosophical stuff, more than is given now. On the same line we might consider adding to the selections from Jefferson some more letters, on religion, etc. And something, maybe incorporated in the Jefferson, of Paine, with a brief selection or two.

(2) problem of schools and movements, Romantic, etc. Let's be sure to review this whole question when we meet soon. I am not happy with any of my own thoughts here.

All for the moment. I'll be telephoning tomorrow to know about time for our conference.

Ever yours,
R

West Wardsboro, Vermont
August 30, 1968

Dear Dick and Cleanth:

I presume that you both have copies of my little things on Kennedy and Simms, which Mrs. Callahan was to send you. They need touching up, for one thing Simms should have some stuff from Cleanth's section on Simms, where the statement of his social views is more pungently put, ref. to Yeats, etc. But this can be done later.

I have been at work on Byrd (finished and sent to Callahan), and on Julia Ward Howe. The notes are short, but have entailed a lot of reading. I am sending marked book to Cleanth for xeroxing stuff for Byrd, but have more to do when we get back, from the Diaries, of which I do not have copies here. Also Swallow Barn on way, with marking for xerox.

Cleanth's Poe, Bryant, Holmes, and Jefferson (new versions) are in hand, and I have read them carefully. Great gains here, it strikes me. Here are some random comments:

Jefferson: Close to ideal, I should say. Maybe we should make a ref to the fact that, once in power, J. had to act against own theory, sometimes. For instance, in regard to Louisiana.

Bryant: Splendid handling of romanticism, etc. In this connection of nature, remind me to give you a quote from Goethe on Holbach's *Nature*, which might well be used, a very fine statement of romantic position. On page 27, the remarks about recesses of human nature imply a lot of the pre-Freudian insights in these poets. Also see Coleridge on dreams. Not to develop, just to indicate. I am inclined to think that the critical discussions of Thanatopsis and Hymn of the City might be put in headnotes. One reason: it reduces the big general chunk, and puts the criticism right with the poem, to be read along with the poem, etc. We can't make a system here, but we might incline in that direction. To cut back a bit, I think we might quote Bozzaris, which is short and has its own kind of force, ditto for elegy "Green grow etc." Maybe some ref. re. romanticism to poetry on the defensive against science.

Poe: Fine. Page 3, footnote on fact Kennedy got him job on [p. 2] *Southern Lit. Mes.*, or ref. to my passage re. Kennedy. Page 10, in connection with deviousness of human spirit, The Black Cat gives most striking example, and most famous; add. Page 22, the ref. to Poe as forecasting psychoanalysis, leads to ref. to same in Hawthorne. I said I would supply this, and here it is:

House of Seven Gables: "Modern psychology, it may be, will endeavor to reduce these alleged necromancers within a system, instead of rejecting them as altogether fabulous." In general, I begin to feel that the thing can be shortened a little, without sacrificing ideas. Maybe this should be tried by Dick or me first, just to see how it looks. (The same principle applies all around. I'd welcome some such service for several of my things, a fresh eye.) Further, here as in regard to Bryant's poems, some of the comment may be put in headnotes, things not quite at the same level of generalization as that of the essay, even though supporting the drift of the essay. This a last minute operation, perhaps.

This has been slam-bang, and forgive me. But I want to restate what I said: great gain here, about final, I should say.

Best to all!
[Red]

West Wardsboro, Vermont
August 30, 1968

Dear Cleanth:

I am sending under separate cover the xerox copies of the magazine articles for the MR. The following ones I think should have serious consideration (as marked, too, on copies):

Albee: Virginia Woolf—very good and useful—if not too advanced for fresh-men, but they will have seen the movie. But how close is movie to play?

Moynihan: Nirvana—heavily written and many of the references are pretty difficult for freshmen but has a splendid point. We should certainly hang on to this for serious consideration.

Mumford: Prehistory—very clear, and has the great value of giving a logic lesson in disguise, nature of evidence, etc. Almost certain to be useful for us.

Clark: University—as a counterpoise to Kennan, et al. Also incidental value of being by a Negro. Very possible.

Updike: Anguilla—how interesting would this be to freshmen? I believe we could beat this for its type. (Here I see I have included an item I don't think useful.)

Hitchcock—possible, but do we need this if we have Moynihan, et al? But an open question.

DeMott: Overkill—very good, almost certain.

Kennan—serious consideration—if balanced against opposite view.

Lipset: Students—very heavily done, and needs some cutting (which we could do), and is somewhat timid. Probably can beat it, but hold on to it for the moment.

Bellow: Skepticism—starts fine, but wanders, rather. Are refs too special for freshmen? Serious consideration, in last stage.

[p. 2] Didion: Bethlehem—very useful, with some cuts.

Podhoretz: Making—almost certainly.

Russell: Auto—I suggest going to the books and trying for a better example.

Riesman: Grad Schools—possible but seems too special, too heavily written perhaps.

Bronowski: Imagination—almost certain. We might go to his books, too, I have read one, and it would be very good on science and poetry.

This is a useful batch to read, gives me some perspective on the problem we face.

Yrs,
Red

West Wardsboro, Vermont
August 31, 1968

Dear Dick and Cleanth:

I have finished a first draft of a note on Julia Ward Howe, for the "Literature of the Non-Literary World" section, where the Battle Hymn will appear. The note has run rather long, probably too long, but the more I went into the matter the more I saw chances to get in certain things not otherwise readily available. It is the perfect—or is it?—chance to nail the apocalyptic strain in our psychology, which has been hinted at here and there. It gives a chance to give a little social history, as it were, to back up Holmes, Lowell, and a few other items, and to prepare for the Gilded Age. It gives a laboratory case of dream composition, a manageable one—I hope. Anyway, here it is, I ask you two to look it over and criticize. I have only one copy. I am sorry.

We are coming back next Saturday, and I'll be telephoning very soon thereafter.

All the best to you both,
Red

[Handwritten] Cleanth—please pass on to Dick!

West Wardsboro, Vermont
September 3, 1968

Dear Cleanth:

Thank you for your letter of August 29, which has just arrived. Your remarks on Simms, etc., are well taken. You spot the problem about Simms. But we have done exactly that—comment without example—with reference to the novelists before Cooper, rather, for some of them, the early ladies, and we may have to cut back on Charles Brockden Brown. As for the lack of insides in Simms, I want to transfer what you say on him, quoting from Yeats, in your reference in Holmes, which is a better statement than mine. I know that this isn't your point, but on the celebratory and polemical aspect of others, I am with you. I shall look back over and try to make the point, perhaps pointedly in a footnote to Simms. I have already made the point most emphatically elsewhere, especially in my remarks on Whitman versus Melville in my piece on Melville's poetry.

Your Stowe piece is here (one sheet missing), and is splendid. Without going in for compliment swapping, I am very happy about the way contributions in general now shape up. I begin to think that we will have a lively, readable, provocative and original book. As for Stowe, my only thoughts are as follows:

page 4: Footnote to my selection from Frederick Olmsted's *Travels* (in non-literary section) in which he describes the hawking of copies of UTC in Louisiana. And reference to Swallow Barn, from [p. 2] which I suggest the chapter on "The Quarters," which Kennedy regarded as an answer to UTC, and about which he had some correspondence with Simms. The version to be used is the revised of 1852 (date?).

page 9. In connection with New Englanders as the "consecrated race," a note to the sermon in *The Scarlet Letter*, on exactly this topic—the Election Day sermon.

page 9-A In connection with the apocalyptic religion, reference to my discussion of "The Battle Hymn of the Republic."

page 13: In the non-literary section I have a section on Seba Smith, with selections. Maybe a footnote ref. See also my Lowell.

These, of course, are merely ways of keeping the interconnections in the foreground, not important in themselves.

We come back next Saturday, and look forward to seeing you all!

Yrs,
Red

I'll say again that the Jefferson is splendid.

September 4, 1968

Dear Red,

Thank you for your good word about my revised pieces. I hope you're not being too kind in the interest of encouraging this rather jaded horse to put his neck into the collar again. I'm assuming that you're not and if you do like what I've done, this is high praise indeed and very sweet to my ears. I think your suggestions are excellent. I'll set about working them into the text or in one or two instances into footnotes. The quotation you send me from Hawthorne from the House of Seven Gables is really a honey. My experience is that concrete pointed statements of this sort are worth whole paragraphs of generalized comment. And the quotation that I make from Poe's "The Black Cat" via Marie Bonaparte matches with this Hawthorne quotation in a fashion almost too good to be true.

As for cutting and compression; I think I'll take you up on your suggestion that perhaps you or Dick could help here. I have got too involved now in the Thoreau piece and the Poe piece to trust my judgment. I can wait a good while and cool off and get detachment a little more, if this is not too much of an imposition on your time. If you or Dick could make some suggestions for cuts and compressions that would be fine.

Your piece on Byrd has arrived. It is meaty and juicy. It fixes his character very well indeed.

Xerox copies of essays for [the] Modern Rhetoric reader have arrived safely too. I am glad to see that we are so nearly of a mind about which ones are usable and which are not. I'll go back over the Kenneth Clark piece, though [I hope] that before we go to press we can find something else of this sort, by a Negro, that is not quite so heavily written.

I have already got something that will beat the Updike account of Anguilla. Thanks to Tinkum's rooting around, I have Gwen Raverat's account of her Cambridge (England) childhood and [it] is witty and very funny and would be a good sample of this kind of writing. I'll make one or two selections from it and let you have a look. Tink has also located one or two other travel books—a special hobby of hers—and we might find something in one of them.

Again at Tink's suggestion I have been looking over John Chadwick's The Decipherment of Linear B, which is an account of how Fentriss broke the language code and proved that the Minoan tablets were written in Greek. It's fascinating stuff and I think would be even for freshmen and sophomores, provided I can find a section that isn't too complicated. Another possibility is a piece that came out in the New Yorker a couple of years ago about the new excavations on the eastern coast of Crete; another great Minoan city is being dug up and this New Yorker piece properly cut would give us something worth using.

I shan't try to go any further with this M.R. material at the moment, but I shall plan this weekend to write a letter to you about it putting in some kind of order what seem to be prime possibilities and letting us see where we stand at the moment.

The moment of truth has arrived: Tink and I have to decide today or tomorrow whether we will dash over to Austria and north Italy for three weeks or not. We are not sure that we will and certainly not sure that we won't. Anyway, I'll let you know and will be back in working harness at the latest by the middle of October.

With all cordial regards,
[Cleanth]

[Handwritten at top left corner]   6 Sept.

Dear Red—Your last letter and your Julia Ward Howe piece have come in since I dictated this letter. I'll write you about them this weekend.

C.

Northford
10 Sept. 68

Dear Red,

I enclose the missing page (p. 10) of the Stowe Introduction. I am also sending this morning, under separate cover, some material for the *Modern Rhetoric* Reader: (1) a proposed selection from the Didion piece (for Reportage section); (2) "Air, Art, and the Civilians"—Viet Nam—which I suggest you look at for the Reportage section; (3) two chapters of Raverat's *Period Piece: A Cambridge Childhood,* for possible use in our Biography section; and (4) an essay on American cities by Camus. No. 2 seems to me well written; it is very short, and whereas it doesn't [take] away from the horror, it is in the best sense non-partisan and untendentious.

No. 3 may not suit you at all, but I find the book amusing and I can think of a number of ways to use it: a brief introduction by us pointing out that the author was Charles Darwin's granddaughter and then most of Chapter 1 or most of Chapter 5. In any case we might include the bit about Queen Victoria on p. 14. What do you think? I can send you the book if you would like to browse for yourself. {[Handwritten] I think that the boys would find it interesting. But certainly it would be something for the girls.}

As for No. 1: it could be cut in various ways. My selection is concerned largely to get in the beginning and the end, filling in with a representative lot of the material that Didion presents. But you may remember better bits to use. I can send the whole thing to you for you to look at again if you like.

I shall send you more xeroxed essays for the Reader, perhaps tomorrow with a very tentative list of a table of contents—including stuff we may want to retain and essays that we may want to add.

T. is typing up additions and corrections for the Bryant, Poe, and other chapters. I'll send these to you as they are readied. I hope to have all this stuff in more-or-less finished shape before we take off for Vienna. (We now have our reservations: we leave on Sept. 19 and are scheduled to return on Oct. 10.)

Best regards.
[Cleanth]

[Handwritten in upper left margin] Also herewith: 2 footnotes (Stowe, 9) and (Indigenes, 26) + handouts for Bryant's "Thanatopsis" and "Hymn of the City."

[OH]   [September 10, 1968]
Dear Red—
    A brief covering note. What worries me in a few passages in Dick's Whitman piece is a smack of something akin to Harold Bloom's propensity to make all poems poems about poetry—i.e., about the [access] to poetic energy or the loss of it. Perhaps I am over vigilant but I hope that I have made clear to both of you what seems to me a certain circularity in the argument which holds that what the poet says doesn't matter—all that matters is his display of "poetic energy." I.e., what matters is the presence of poetic energy. But what is *poetic* energy? It is poetic *activity* that creates a poem. But what is a poem? It is the manifestation of poetic energy, etc.

                                                                              [Cleanth]

[R. W. B. Lewis was not left out of the information loop on these discussions; regarding the above concerns, Brooks wrote Lewis a letter dated September 11, 1968, in which he shared his thoughts about the Whitman piece.]

                                                                2495 Redding Road
                                                                Fairfield, Connecticut
                                                                September 12, 1968
Dear Dick and Cleanth:
    I have been rereading the Whitman, and now dash off a few remarks—for what they may be worth. The remarks are not in order—merely as they come to me.
    (1) I think that here—or in some headnotes to Whitman (and maybe some other critical remarks here) might be [put] in headnotes anyway—we might talk a little about the nature of free verse, just to place Whitman. For one thing we ought to stomp out the idea that good free verse is easy—and explain why not, in so far as we can. We might also point out some of the deleterious influences in this respect that have stemmed from Whitman— such deleterious things always stemming from the work of powerful poets. And this influence has been associated generally with the <codmis> and patriotic Whitman. Explain.
    (2) Some comment on the fact that Whitman might have been a wonderful novelist. Of his powers of narration in John Paul Jones, and Goliad. And in suggestions elsewhere. Relation, in fact, to later fiction in America.
    (3) A useful reference would be to Jarrell's essay "Walt Whitman, He Had His Nerve"—with some quotes etc. Also to Santayana, who is actually saying something about the seamy side of Whitman which must be considered. I

have used Santayana—as sort of a revelation—in my talk about Melville and Whitman as Unionists, and I do think that Santayana does say some things that are related to the formlessness of Whitman's poorer poems. The "form" we admire in his work is not universally achieved.

(4) See page 2: I am not certain I see what is meant by the second sentence of the second paragraph about "values" shaping the "textures and patterns of his verse"—I tend to want specific detail in a statement like this.

(5) See page 2: Why not footnote reminding readers that Emerson's "Scholar" was the end of a long series of such things?

(6) See page 6: Why not say "Paul Fussell" and not "Mr. Fussell"?

(7) Why not a word or so about the nature of mysticism, etc.?

(8) As in all our stuff, I think that this could stand a little cutting, not so much of ideas as of rhetorical repetitions, here and there—not much, but a little.

(9) I don't think that now I take a backseat to anybody in admiring Whitman, but I think that here we might make a sharper distinction (it is made, but not sharply enough, I should say) between Whitman's best and his worst. Always that problem with any poet, of course.

[p. 2] (10) I'm not sure we can just accept W. C. Williams' remark about pentameter. For example, let us not forget Yeats, Eliot, and even Whitman's most renowned follower, Crane, who have done some splendid pentameters—and add Auden. Not to mention others.

Let me emphasize that I think this is a splendid introduction, and what I have said must be taken with that sentiment as a backdrop. I wish I could think that all our book will be at this level.

Yrs,
Red

Fairfield
November 15, 1968

Dear Dick and Cleanth:

In making what I hope is a last round-up, I find several loose-ends—or rather, don't find them. The most important is that the selections for Whittier are not in my hands.

My recollection is (in fact, I know) that I mailed the pasted-up selections from Grasse to one of you, who then had them xeroxed in triplicate. {[Handwritten in left margin] Also 2 copies of Whittier Introduction. I have 2 xeroxed copies of selections and 1 copy of their headnotes.} But—now this *is* mere recollection—the stuff was to be held until I came back, there being no reason to send it back to France. Does anybody have the stuff?

Don't get excited if you haven't. I know pretty well what the selections were and can reconstruct—but it does take a little time.

And Cleanth—this to you: You very kindly had the helper do some xeroxing for me when I was in Vermont—the selections from Irving. What I need to know is, were the selections of Knickerbocker History from the 1809 edition? That is the one we should have. What I am worried about is that the helper may not have followed your instructions. Do you have an assurance on this? It will save a hell of a lot of collation (samples) if you have. {[Handwritten in left margin] My memories are that he did. But we might have to spot check to be absolutely sure.}

Sorry to nag dear friends.

Yrs,

R

Later: The stuff I brought last night [November 15 is] a duplicate of the whole Cooper thing (I wasn't sure you had one), and a copy of the *revised* Lowell. I am now pasting up Lowell, and a copy of the selections will be with you soon.

Nov. 22, 1968

Dear Red,

Some of the matters that are contained in your recent note that came in this morning, I believe, were settled over the telephone yesterday. But I'll go over them again here just in case.

1. As I told you, I don't have any xerox sheets from the works of Frederick Douglass.

2. Here is the quotation from Julia Ward Howe as quoted in Furnas's *Road to Harper's Ferry:*

After visiting Nassau, Cuba and South Carolina the summer before Harpers Ferry she published her opinion that the Dixie Negro was "ugly as Caliban, lazy as the laziest of brutes, chiefly ambitious to be of no use to anybody" and "suggested . . . the unwelcome question whether compulsory labor be not better than none . . . Moral justice dissents from the habitual sneer, denunciation, and malediction, which have become consecrated forms of piety in speaking of the South."[1]

[Note from Tink] Red, I am typing this from the dictating machine and C. is now out of town. I don't trust the accuracy of what I think I hear, can't find the book, and in any case probably couldn't find the passage since no page number is given. Dammit.

3. I believe that I told you that I do have one copy of the Whittier selections in xerox form and two copies of the headnotes.

4. As for the meeting arranged for next Wednesday, the 27th: Though I had understood you to say on the telephone that this will have to be changed,

1. J. C. Furnas's *The Road to Harper's Ferry* was published by William Sloane Associates in 1959.

your note this morning makes me wonder whether I understood you correctly. Anyway, as Eleanor will have told you, I telephoned her so that you could call Tink *if I had misunderstood.* If the meeting on Wednesday is off, then except for Monday I can make a luncheon meeting from here on out.

Yours,
Cleanth

1287 North Foster Drive
Baton Rouge, La. 70806
Feb. 5, 1969

Dear Red,

It's good to hear from you and high time that I get back in touch. First, a word about ourselves. We are well settled in a pleasant apartment which is quiet and usefully located and big enough (actually enormous) for us to have plenty of room to turn around, lay out books and papers, the dictating machines, and the electric typewriter. As a matter of fact, I think it's going to prove to be a good place to work—very good thus far, and I've been able to hit some solid licks, including work on the M.R. revision.

The burden of the settling in has fallen, of course, on Tinkie, who has been rounding up those 500 little things that it's hardly worth shipping but which you find you must have in order to run a house. She's done it very cheerfully and efficiently and we are in excellent shape. The weather has been delightful. We arrived in really spring-like weather, and the present coolness that has come back is no more than that. Japonicas are in full bloom, spring flowers appearing untimely, trees budding, and I can't think we'll have any more really cold weather here.

My work at LSU has started well and I think it will be indeed quite measurably light. For one thing, I've got it organized in advance, thank God, and believe it will not eat seriously into my working time or into such time as we shall set aside for pleasure. Baton Rouge has changed beyond belief. So has the university, really, but there are enough people left that I remember—all of whom remember you—to weigh me down with greetings to you. Your memory is still very green.

Now for some comments on M.R. Thanks for the xerox material. I am sending in the envelope a xerox copy of Hook's "War Against the Democratic Process," which appeared in the February *Atlantic Monthly.* Unless I've miscounted, it's under 4,000 words, and at a fairly hasty reading it seems to me to make nearly all the points that are in the longer essay, which is close to 10,000. Please look this one over and if you feel that it does manage to preserve the gist and force of the longer essay, a xerox copy of which you sent me; we might use it and thus let Sidney Hook do his own cutting for us. My vote is for using the Feuer "Conflict of Generations." It's timely, it makes a lot of sense to me, and I think that the students will find it highly interesting and possibly persuasive.

I wish the style were a little lighter. I wish, too, he wouldn't write such sentences as "Perhaps, in the psychoanalytical [p. 2] metaphor, this identification with the lower class assuages the castrational fears aroused by the students' revolt against their father." This strikes me as over-done Freud, but most people these days prefer well done to rare, and I don't think we'll find any objections on this score.

As for the Peter De Vries piece, let's hold up long enough for me to try it out on one or two of the LSU seniors. I don't mean that they ought to be allowed the casting of a vote, but I do have some doubts as to whether students over the country, somewhat less hep than those in Connecticut, will get all the Freudian implications and, lacking them, they certainly won't find it as funny as those who do.

By the end of the week, I shall type up for you a very tentative table of contents for the Reader, listing the pieces that we have pretty well agreed we are going to use, and putting them under the proper categories, and including also those pieces already in the Reader that we are pretty well agreed we want to retain. By comparing this list with the Table of Contents in the present edition, you and I can see at a glance about where we stand and be in better position to hunt for further pieces that we will need to fill out certain sections and to make improvements on what we now have.

I've made a start on rewriting the chapter on the paragraph and the sentence. I think I can condense it and at the same time make it a little simpler and clearer to read. I'll try to work in more exercises, though I'll have to leave some of the exercises blank until the front part of the book that you are working on has been finished; for I think it important to tie this chapter more tightly to the early chapters which have already been read, noting the paragraph and sentence as elements of the larger units of composition.

Let's not forget the DeMott essay on "Overkill." It can serve to buck up our discussion of propaganda and allied modes of writing, and I want to take some illustrations from it to put into the revised chapter on Diction.

I am making Xerox copies of bits of writing from Gimpel for our gallery of short portraits for the Reader. T. has also found for us some promising portraits in Bower's memoirs, in V S Pritchett's autobiography, and in a new life of Tolstoy.

Tinkum joins me in cordial greetings to all the Warrens. We hope Eleanor and Gabriel are getting in lots of skiing and that you have good word from Rosanna at Milton.

Yours,

Cleanth

P.S. I ran into Ferarra on the campus yesterday. You may remember him from the LSU Music School. He asked that I send you [his] very special greetings.

1287 N. Foster Drive
Baton Rouge, La. 70806
Feb. 27, 1969

Dear Red,

Here is a xerox of a rewriting of Chapter 9. It's still pretty rough, but in this form it has the merit of showing you at a glance where the principal revisions occur.

I do believe that I've clarified some matters (including the relation of *grammar* to *rhetoric*) and I believe that I've made more sense of the terms *unity, coherence,* and *emphasis* as applied to the sentence.

No time for chat on this busy morning except to say that all goes well here and that T. joins me in affectionate greetings to you all.

[Cleanth]

March 6, 1969

Dear Cleanth:

Today I am mailing a big bundle of "Non-literary" stuff—of my part. You will observe that a few small selections are missing. They are caught up in the batch that is today going out to Earley. You will see here my letter to Earley about the delay. The xerox people went crazy.

I am enclosing here some more possible stuff for the Rhetoric readings—an interview with Margaret Meade, which will attract student attention, and a piece on the retirement of a racehorse. (The latter is long, but we can cut it some.)

Here, also, is the greater part of Exposition. I'll have to hunt up the first few pages, which somehow did not get xeroxed, and send later. But here are the guts, anyway. I have finished, except for a few pages, Argument, which will be with you soon. I have done a lot of reordering and rewriting, but it is far from right, and you must slash in hard. And PLEASE look at the themes and selections. Whenever you think wise get some student themes done, but they MUST illustrate the problems—the particular ones—we are concerned with.

I am also enclosing a new long—longish—poem, for your attention and criticism—if you ever have time. I began this poem some twenty years ago and have nursed it along, off and on, and last summer began to get hot on it. I have only recently finished it. I am toying with the idea of making it a little book by itself. Which means that I am partial to it—now, at least. Maybe I'll be ashamed of it tomorrow.[1]

Now news. We go to Vermont on the 14th, back April 3. Our address there is West Wardsboro. Telephone (not listed) [. . .]. I don't recall code.

Love to you both,
Red

1. *Audubon: A Vision* was published by Random House November 20, 1969, in a printing of 6,300 copies, 300 of which were issued simultaneously in a special limited, signed edition.

March 16, 1969

Dear Red,

Your package of "non-literary" stuff came in in good shape. So also did a *second* copy of your chapter on Exposition from page 44 to the end on page 124 (with a notation that the first few pages were lacking). This makes *two* copies of this material that you have now sent me, plus *two* copies of "How to Retire Successfully after [a] Twenty-eight Month Career" and *two* copies of Schlesinger's "On the Inscrutability of History." But no copy of *Argument* has come in. Tink and I have searched carefully and it just isn't here.

I'm putting down all of these details and also sending back to you your letter of March 6 in the hope that this information and the letter will provide some clues to you—jog your memory perhaps—about what happened to your revised chapter on Argument. (Obviously, it would seem you mistakenly sent me a second copy of Exposition when you were really intending to send a copy of Argument.) It is so exasperating and frustrating to do a job of work and then mislay it somewhere. I hope it has by now turned up. Perhaps you'll find that two copies of Argument went to Harcourt instead of one each of Argument and Exposition.

I've gone through your revision of Exposition, carefully marking such corrections and small suggestions as I can make. They are very few. I'm delighted to see that your notion of what we ought to do by way of revision corresponds pretty well to mine. You've done a fine job on Exposition. At your convenience, give me your comments, suggestions, and addition to my revision of Chapter 9. I'm back at work on a rewrite of Chapter 10 and hope to send it to you soon.

I write "back to work" because I took out the better part of last week in drafting the section on Imagism-Pound-Eliot for the Am. Lit. book. It's all very rough at the moment and will need rearranging and rewriting, but I believe I've found how to get in, clearly and even neatly, a great deal that at first glance I'd thought I'd be unable to do. At the moment I am rather high on it. But it will be some time before I'll have a copy of it ready to send you and Dick.

Just a word about your Audubon poem. It's a stunning job. But it's too big, rich, and ambitious for me to say anything about it now off the top of my head. I mean to reread it a number of times and live with it for a few days before I sit down to try to tell you what I really think of it.

Everything still goes happily here. Enough fun, lots of uninterrupted work. Tinkie joins in affectionate greetings to you all.

Cleanth

[Handwritten] P.S. By the way, did I mention that a couple of weeks ago, we saw Oakley and Miss Pierries's portrait about which Audubon speaks. Oakley comes closer to being my favorite of all the old plantation houses.

1287 N. Foster Drive
Baton Rouge, La. 70806
April 29, 1969

Dear Red,

I've been losing my mind again. Today I got back from Willie Wisdom, a New Orleans Faulkner collector, a xeroxed copy of my Diction chapter for *Modern Rhetoric*! He was puzzled but tactful and returned with it a 2-line letter, dated April 3, signed by me addressed to "Dear Red."[1] I suppose that I sent you on the same date a xerox of a rough draft of my chapter on Faulkner's poetry instead of the Diction chapter. I enclose the Diction chapter now. I suppose that the Metaphor chapter has reached you. Faulkner is now laid aside temporarily and so is "Tone" for M.R. while I am feeling rather hot on the MacLeish and W. C. Williams material for the Am. Lit. book.

We are near the wind-up here now. My last class will be met the middle of May. Soon after that we'll go to N.O. for a few days, then back here to give an exam and as soon as it's graded head for home. We should be there by June 1, if not before. Will you all be in Fairfield then—or already in Vermont? We are eager for a big family visit with you all, and want to catch up on all the news of big and little Warrens.

Cleanth

[OH]

Forest Road
Northford, Connecticut 06472
Dec. 17, 1969

Dear Red,

The rest of the marked galleys plus the typescript (including the appendices and finishing up the book) was sent to me. I have gone over it all (taking into account the galleys that you had marked and sent to me). I am mailing it all back to Miss Rothstein in the morning.

I think that I have settled satisfactorily all the queries to the author including those on the appendices for which you were responsible. Only three seemed to me to raise any question at all. I enclose herewith fragments from the three galleys in question. If you don't want Susan's two changes to stand (Galleys 424 and 429) you can communicate with her directly. The third item has to do with the title of Maupassant's story. I believe you told me that the title in French was simply "The Necklace." I've deleted "Diamond" therefore and have added "Celebrated" to help pad out the line.

It's a great relief for both of us to get all the galley proof returned at last. The page proof ought to be a simpler matter.

I have not yet had any further communication from Corbett. I had hoped by this time to have received the amended contract. Have you heard anything?

1. Judge William Wisdom was a well-known bibliophile in New Orleans.

We hope to fly to N.O. Friday afternoon. Our address there will be [. . .]. The telephone number is [. . .]. (In Denver I can be reached at Holiday Inn Central—Dec. 27–30.) I'll be back in N.O. briefly Jan 1–3. But T. will be there right through to handle urgent messages if they are necessary.

We wish a very merry Xmas to all the Warrens.

In haste,
Cleanth

1970s

May 27 [1970]

Dear Cleanth:

I've just read your good rewrite of Thoreau. Have only a couple of minor notions. In connection with his relation to Emerson, you imply that platonism was a point of distinction. But sometimes not. See my quote in section 1826–61 from Thoreau, who was quite capable of jumping through "nature" into eternity like the poodle through the hoop in a dog-and-pony show.

Why not refer to Hawthorne's estimate of Thoreau—see journal—and Lowell's in Fable.

By the way, you do not have a reading list attached. Though there is a bio sheet.

Ever yours,
Red

It just occurs to me that your preface to the new book, which I sat up to read at last night, is a fine start for some of the things we should have in our Introduction to the Am. Lit. textbook. I head on into some of the essays; Housman, for instance, is a very fine thing.

West Wardsboro, Vermont 05355
[June 1970]

Dear Dick and Cleanth:

I have been having some random thoughts about our title. What about American Literature: The Makers, the Making, the *Made*? I know it's not good, but you see what I'm fumbling at. We certainly don't want an "understanding title." I fear that we had better begin to fumble, for a title isn't what comes to you at will at the last minute.

More immediate: I report that Twain is about finished by the typist, who promises copies to me by day after tomorrow. I shall then correct one and get it to Popp to have it xeroxed for you and St. M's. He already has in hand the readings on Twain and headnotes, including a rather massive one for Huck. He will hold all Twain until it is properly assembled. My typist also has in hand Henry Adams (and Popp has some of the readings, but will hold till the whole thing, including xeroxes of text on Adams, is in one piece). I am today

310

mailing off my William James to my typist. It is rather longer than I had hoped, but he gives a good excuse to sketch some intellectual background in for the period, and to cast forward into the next century, 20th. I have for instance done a note here on Hemingway as pragmatist, and some other things of the sort. Cleanth, I suggest that you take a glance at Jay Martin's *Harvest of Change* on Frost and James, if you haven't done so. It is skimpy but may start up some thoughts of a more original sort with you for Frost. In *Harvest*, the page ref. is 159 ff.

I hope to have Holmes ready within five days. It will be shorter, and easier, I hope. At least I know more about him than I often do about a topic.

I am having my typist send you direct an imperfect copy of my piece on James. I want you both to take a look at it before I put the finishing touches on it—if, of course, you have the time. I will get Sidney Hook to read it too, he being the philosophical grandson of WJ. If he is around this August.

Nothing but work and an occasional swim. I'll be glad to be a free man some day. BUT keep your minds on DOUGH!

All the best to all!
Red

West Wardsboro, Vermont 05355
July 16, 1970

Dear Dick and Cleanth:

Thank you, Dick, for your report on progress, and a very encouraging report it is. I look forward with pleasure to seeing what you both have on hand.

My situation is not so bad, maybe—and not so good. I have finished Mark Twain. The general text (35,000 words) is in the hands of my typist, now for over a week. Today I am mailing off the headnotes and the text of the readings to Mr. Popp to get xeroxed. He will get a copy to each of you, and will send two copies off to St. Martin's. Dick, will you give him the name and address of our lady editor? I forget both. Mr. Popp should have the typescript of the Twain in hand soon to make the xeroxes for you and S[t.] M[artin's]. I have also finished Henry Adams and sent it to the typist. It got long, out of scale perhaps, for the Background of Ideas section, but he is interesting and has the secondary value of a kind of culture hero who enacted an important role, perhaps more important than his actual writing. Anyway you all can cut it. I am now deep in William James, and should have him done in a week, Santayana by the end of the month. Do you think that John Dewey should be there? After all, he was publishing in the 1880's. Or is he too much an offshoot of James? Maybe. What about John Jay Chapman? I am, of course, doing Holmes. Have a good bit done, but not assembled. Who else in this section? What about Bourne? Or is he too late?

I forgot to say that I have assembled for the Twain Readings 135,000 words. I cut Huck down to 80,000, and in the headnote explained the omissions as an adjunct to the analysis of the form, or tried to. I put in "To a Person Sitting in Darkness," because it gives in a very effective form Twain's political views—and they would fit today. Anyway, think seriously about the choices and the possible cuts.

Things go well enough here except for too much rain.

Let me have word that all goes well with all.

Yours,
Red

Cleanth, I forgot to say that I am sending you under separate cover an advance copy of Monroe Spears' book on modernism, *Dionysus in the City*. You might want to use it in your modern poetry section, or at least put it in the reading list. After you have looked at it, will you please send it back to Oxford, in the enclosed envelope. But not necessarily right off.

Northford
July 24 [1970]

Dear Red,

Hearty congratulations on your National Book Award.[1] This is very fine news—a much deserved honor—and the $5,000 check will be very useful. You and Eleanor are burning up the track this summer.

The morning mail brought the copy of Spears' *Dionysus and the City*. I read a chapter of it in *Shenandoah* last month and it seems very interesting. Next time I'm in the Co-op I'll put in an order for a copy. I've already assembled 2 or 3 other books that I hope will prove useful for the intellectual history 1914–45.

At the moment I'm trying to wind up a draft of the Southern section. I've now written a fairly brief introduction and quite long headnotes for all the Faulkner except *Light in August*. The other day I talked to Albert on the telephone and he tells me that he's met resistance from his people to our use of *L. in A.* But he promises to talk further with the permissions people and thinks that there is a chance that we might be able to get less than the 30% of the novel that I'm asking for. Anyway, we'll see. Meantime, I want to go on with Ransom and Tate, and the immediate reason for writing you now is that, as you may remember, you once suggested that you would do the Ransom piece, letting me incorporate it in my section.

We would get a better piece, undoubtedly, if we did it that way. On the other hand, you are just as hard-pressed as I am—perhaps harder—and if you would rather I went on and drafted something now, I'll try. In that case, however, I'd appreciate even hastily jotted notes on what you think ought to be said and if you have any unpublished or just recently published material on John, let me know at once so that I can read it.

1. In 1970 Warren received the National Medal of Literature. See, for example, "National Medal for Literature Awarded Warren," *Baton Rouge State Times*, July 22, 1970, p. 14-A. He received the National Book Award for poetry for *Promises* in 1958.

The Southern section has been fun to do, but it is much too long, I fear, and certainly will need a great deal of tightening up at the joints. I hope, however, to be able to get a finished draft to you and Dick during the next ten days. I certainly am going to need some hard reading by you two on it. On the other hand, if you have no hope of reading it shortly, I am tempted to keep whittling on it and smoothing it a bit before I get a copy to you.

The New American Poetry section has long been finished save for some notes on Pound and Eliot. Perhaps I ought to go on and write these up so that xerox copies can be made and got to you.

I look forward to seeing your Mark Twain stuff, but the figures that you give scare me. (The figures for my stuff scare me too.) I believe that at our last conference we said that we could allow about a million words in each volume, but if the Twain readings amount to 135,000 words, plus commentary, that's way over 10% of the volume now. Much as I hate to say it, I am more and more [p. 2] coming to think that we're going to have to leave even reduced novels out, making reference to paperback editions that can be bought as extras. Otherwise, our book will go into 3 volumes.

As for the questions that you put jointly to me and Dick about who should go into the History of Ideas section, I am afraid that I don't have much to offer at this point. Use your best judgment as you will, anyway, of course. When I can buckle down to my equivalent section (1914–45) I'll be in much better position to offer advice. The same goes for Dick's question of July 14 about where to put the Marxist critics. I'm inclined to take his suggestion #2, that they should be treated along with Dos Passos, but these things may have to be settled only by trial and error.

God help us all. We *must* finish by early fall, but can we?

Yours,
Cleanth

P.S. I enclose a letter (which please return) that provided me with sudden inspiration: Leonard Conversi may be *just* the man to help us with the *Understating Poetry* revision. I know him well and think very highly of him, as apparently a good many others do. His sound academic training and brilliant record, his real interest in modern poetry, his experience at the Yale Press (and I believe at the Harvard Press) and his possible *availability* make him appear heaven-sent to me. What do you think? Should I sound him out? I'll do nothing until you think it over.

. . . .

West Wardsboro, Vermont 05355
July 28, 1970

Dear Cleanth:

Your letter is here, and thank you for it. I dash off an inadequate reply.

(1) We talked, once—or did we?—about your using something of Mary

Chesnut's journal early in the southern section. This is a reminder. Wouldn't it help set up lots of stuff that gets into discussions of fiction?

(2) Re: Ransom. What I would say about him and his poetry I have already spelled out in my essay in The Kenyon for his 80th birthday.[1] I have the feeling (really not as a dodge to get out of work) that if you simply excerpted what you thought relevant and wrote in a few bridges *and*, most importantly, added whatever you feel like adding, it would be better than for me to recast the thing. This would give a view with more perspective, and would allow better for reduction. Plus, as I insist, your own valuable thoughts, and phrasings.

(3) Let's don't worry too much about the cutting. We can do that when the whole thing is laid out before us and we can make dependable counts. But I vow from now on to pull in sail. It's not fun writing that way, for in my poor old head I have to sort of push things on out to know what I really think, and, everything being relative, I come on my best ideas that way. But to hell with my best ideas. I am slamming things down from now on. Speaking of length, I have just been looking at the great wad of stuff from Dick. His James is not as sprawling as my Twain or Dreiser, but it *is* long. I want to add, however, that the stuff of his I have read thus far, in James and the other things, is damned fine!

(4) About Conversi. By all means snag him and put him to work, if you know he is good. He can start thinking and reading in the fall and get down to brass tacks after we nail the *AL* book. Here I should add that we hope to go abroad for 15 months, leaving next summer. I have a leave, and the time is right for both children. Rosanna wants to take a free year before going to college, and Gabe wants to do another year in a French school, and has Andover's consent to go and to get credit there. In my paternal pride, I must tell you that Gabe, despite all the angst and anger (I really thought he might simply walk out or bust his exams), came out with Honors for the whole year's work.

(5) Today I finish Holmes.

I wish I could come for the week-end, but I *must* keep the nose to the grindstone.

Love to you both,
R

West Wardsboro, Vermont 05355
July 28, 1970

Dear Cleanth:

Another reminder—or is it a reminder?—maybe I never got around to mentioning it to you:

In dealing with the elder Homes, with his notion of the Brahmin, you might underscore his treatment of money. The Brahmin is superior to money, but

1. "Notes on the Poetry of John Crowe Ransom at His Eightieth Birthday," *Kenyon Review* 30 (June 1968): 319–49.

should, of course, always have some—like a Hemingway hero. This severing of the nexus between caste and money has several aspects. For one thing, you might look at David Donald's little book on Lincoln (I forget the exact title—no, I remember—*Lincoln Revised*), at the essay on the transcendentalist *et al.*, as to how their "idealism" was a reflex of resentment at losing their role in society to the lords of the loom, and State Street bankers. For another thing, you might give a passing word forecasting Santayana's theory of the "genteel tradition" in relation to the hard realities of economic life. That, if I remember Santayana.

Sorry to keep nagging. But I have to slam things down before they blow out of my drafty old head.

Yours,
Red

[Handwritten] Also get out F. M. Ford's *Provence*.

August 1, 1970

Dear Cleanth:

Two tiny notes for your Imagism section.

1. P. 1. I suggest exploiting the paradox that "the new {[handwritten] see new page 1} American poetry" was to some extent part of a development in *England,* and spurred on by English theorist like Hulme. You might even (tho this isn't necessary) allude to the other American development in the mid-west. The first notable poems by Masters etc. were 1913–15.

2. Somewhere between p. 11 and 15: a sentence, or even a footnote, referring to the periodic American effort to cut through to a spare, direct style. The Puritan stress on the "plain" (or "purified") {[handwritten] see footnote on p. 4} style, as against the ornate, bookish, Greek-quoting style. Emerson's insistence on making "the word one with the thing," and on using words that "are vascular and alive." Don't spend much time or thought on this. If you want to glance at it, Matthiessen's American Renaissance pp. 30 ff. has what you need (at least for Emerson).

3. For myself, as much as for you. We'll eventually have to coordinate your opening pages on Imagism with mine on E. A. Robinson.

See you tonight!

Best—
[Red]

August 29, 1970

Dear Cleanth:

I have just finished the Southern section, and am happy about it. I have notes on a few small matters that can wait until we are face to face, but I'll dash off something now at another level.

In the work I have done, and I think in the work previously done by you and Dick, haven't we always (for people who have selections offered) given a Chronology—a sort of synoptic biography *and* also a list of suggested readings, by and about. I know that I have always done this and I thought this was an arrangement we had agreed on. Whatever the case, we now have two different systems going, and should, presumably, get together on matters. Off hand, I don't remember what Dick has been doing. By the way, I may say that I don't feel that this is a matter to be done one way one time and another next time. But maybe I'm wrong here.

Next, in the group of women writers, what about Elizabeth Madox Roberts?[1] I reread her several years ago, and at least *The Time of Man* is very impressive—for me, at least. And this is the one novel about the white tenantry that stands out. I don't know that she should be given a selection— but I certainly would not be opposed to it. I suppose that Flannery O'Connor is not mentioned because of her dates. Is that right? But if she is not to be considered, as being post–World War II in reputation, I feel that maybe she should be referred to in a footnote, or somehow, to explain the omission. Maybe, too, we should think of putting in one or two of Jesse Stuart's stories. There's nothing quite like him.[2]

Have you ever read *The End of American Innocence* by Henry B. May? He has some rather good things to say about the relation of Southern, Middlewestern, and other "provincial" writing to the N.E. hegemony in the post Civil War period (also about the rise of Negro writing later). I won't outline his views here, but let's try to remember to talk those over, all three of us. It will come up again, too, in the black section.

We'll be back September 8. Meanwhile I'll be finishing Crane and starting Hemingway. Crane is a tough one, and is demanding more space than I had imagined.

What I have done this summer is:

Mark Twain

Bret Harte (plus some background for Twain)

Section on intellectual background:

Introduction (including Veblen and Sumner)

W. James

Holmes

H. Adams

Santayana

Crane

Short of what I had hoped, but I've been steady at it. We loved seeing you all!

Yrs, Red

1. Warren's "Elizabeth Madox Roberts: Life Is from Within" was first published in *Saturday Review*, March 2, 1963, pp. 20–21, 38; it was reprinted as the introduction to Roberts's *The Time of Man*, published by Viking in 1963.

2. Warren wrote a foreword to the reissue of Stuart's *Head o' W-Hollow* (Lexington: University of Kentucky Press) in 1979.

2495 Redding Road
Fairfield, Conn. 06430
Friday, September 18, 1970

Dear Cleanth:

Last night I sat up with the poetry section, and I think it is absolute first rate. My remarks are to be taken in that context.

I don't think that we ought to try to make everything match up into the same frame, but I do feel here, especially in Pound and Eliot, that we need more biography. For one thing the personal histories would seem to have something to do with their being expatriates. In what sense are they American writers, too? Etc. And Eliot's marriage has some importance. And his line of studies. His relation to the tone of Cambridge life, and Boston, when he was a youth, etc. Not a massive lot, but something in the way of biography.

Am I wrong in thinking that Aiken ought to come in here? He has suffered in reputation from the very bulk of his production, but I have found more and more in him on looking back. We might make a mark by some selecting here.[1] And by trying to say wherein a good Aiken poem differs from a bad one. I don't see him as inferior to WCW or M[arianne] M[oore]. Certainly he is better than Fletcher or HD, who get a play here—I understand the historical factor here, but even so.

To return to the section. One thing that strikes me is the happy tone of the presentation, many complicated ideas put cleanly and simply. A fine piece of exposition. Also lots of new, fresh commentary.

Best,
Red

September 21 [1970]

Dear Red,

Your letter of Friday came in today and has given me a great deal of satisfaction. I value your opinions and nowhere more than on the subject on which I've been writing. I particularly appreciate your comment on the tone of the presentation. I truly hope you're right about it. The material I've sent you is frankly a draft, to be completed and reworked. It is far from finished and I'm glad to have your suggestions about what further should be done.

You may have noticed that I've left a gap with reference to the development of *The Waste Land*. I've been hoping that Mrs. Eliot's edition of the original ms. of the W.L. would appear in time for us to make use of it. Don Gallup tells me that it won't be out for a while—though it was promised for publication last November. He still thinks that it will get out in time for me to make reference to it—a quite detailed reference, if that seems justified.

In any case, I'm sure you're right in suggesting that I ought to develop further the personal histories of Pound and Eliot. I shall do so. The materials

1. Warren wrote the introduction for the 1982 Schocken Books publication of *The Collected Short Stories of Conrad Aiken*.

are to hand. Oscar Cargill has sent me an offprint of a long article in which he has tried to work out the relation of *The Waste Land* to Eliot's marriage and to his personal life. Parts of his article are strained and I think questionable, but Cargill has worked over the material very carefully and I shall make some use of it. I also have Howarth's book, which though not a formal biography, is the nearest thing to it that we now have.

I found, by the way, some time back, a beautiful short quotation from one of Eliot's letters in which he gives, half jokingly, half seriously, the reason for his expatriation. It is worth quoting.

I take your suggestion about Aiken very seriously. I've found him a charming man but could never get excited about his poetry. Yet I dare say you're right in suggesting that we ought not simply leave him out of account in a book of this sort. I have never been terribly excited about Williams' poetry either, but yielded to the fact that many people were interested in him—including many able people—and that such interest and praise warranted our giving a good deal of attention to him. I'll go back, therefore, to review Aiken's work. If you have any particular poems that you especially like I'd appreciate your pointing them out.

You are right in your surmise that H.D. is so fully represented because of the historical situation, but I've now got too much of her work in and have intended, for some time, to cut it back—especially the long poem on Lais and his mirror.

[p. 2] Since our last talk I've been pondering a way to use a slice of *Light in August.* I now have a passage in mind and at the first opportunity will see what I can do with it. I already have out a collection of Jesse Stuart's work and am looking over it for something that we might use. Does Andrew Lytle have a collection of stories? If not, do you have a nomination or so?

Classes have started, department meetings, visiting Japanese, etc., but I am to have two assistants to help with my undergraduate class and my schedule, as to hours and times of week, is the best I've ever had. I shall be badly disappointed if I can't get in a solid half-week's work right on through the autumn.

Yours,
Cleanth

P.S. Monroe Spears' book is uneven but much of it is very good indeed. It is not only brilliant in some of its insights but it seems to me eminently sane in dealing with some of the issues having to do with recent literary criticism.

2495 Redding Rd
Fairfield, Conn. 06430
October 1, 1970

Dear Cleanth,

First, I have just been talking with Brower at Harvard about the I. A. Richards volume. He is worried that his note to you about it may have gone astray, but he hesitates to nag you. I volunteered to nag you. Have you had his invitation to contribute? Without you, he says, there will be a big hole.

Your Frost piece is here, and is fine. I have only one remark. On page 2 you refer to Frost as a culmination of the farm-village tradition, etc. Why not mention here, not merely Emerson and Thoreau, but Mark Twain and Faulkner, with appropriate reservations and explanations, this to establish the national aspect of the matter. You do come back to Faulkner later, but some of the impact may be lost by that time. Anyway, you might mention him and others, Hawthorne too for example, just to break out of the Emerson-Thoreau box, and then come back to the question later in reference to Faulkner. But there is some shock value in putting F and Twain on page 2.

I am boring myself <cheapless> now writing on James Weldon Johnson.

Best to you both,
Red

March 18, 1971

Dear Red and Dick,

I enclose xerox copies of the General Introduction to "An Emergent Nationalism," the general note to Section 2 of volume 1. I also enclose the introduction to "Thomas Jefferson and Two Contemporaries (Thomas Paine and St. Jean Crevecoeur)."

As you may remember, Paine and Crevecoeur are embedded with short selections in the Jefferson intro. in order to get over ground and save precious space. It occurs to me, however, that if you all do not feel this to be satisfactory, the sections on Paine and Creve. could possibly be moved up into the Gen Intro to the section. Yet, if we did that, it would leave Freneau rather anomalously tucked into the Jefferson intro. by himself.

Both of these introductions can certainly stand some smoothing, tightening up, and perhaps some excisions. I would welcome your suggestions. More seriously, since Dick's intro. to Franklin must now come after this General Intro. to the section—immediately after it, I should say—the Franklin intro. needs to be reworded a bit. Dick's intro. to Franklin is excellent, but some of the more general ideas in it have now been treated in that Gen Intro. and therefore there are overlaps and repetitions that need to be attended to. I think this ought to be done by Dick and not by me.

My suggestion would be that Dick would retain in his introduction nearly everything that pertains to Franklin himself in his individual career. His material on the way in which Franklin retained certain elements of Puritanism, including the Covenant theology, certainly ought to be kept, or just possibly, if Dick prefers, moved back into an appropriate place in the Gen. Intro to Section 2. For there, in talking about Deism, I have made only a brief reference to the way in which the older 17th-century Puritanism moved into Deism and Unitarianism. The main problem in reworking the Franklin intro. will be to eliminate minor repetitions or to make simple adjustments of style—e.g., "as we have said earlier," or "as has been remarked in the Gen. "Intro." etc.

In this Section 2, we now have a subsection 1 on the "non-literary world," which is divided into A and B. A includes "Political and Philosophical Writing" under which we will have the Franklin and then the Jefferson sections; and B, "The Natural Setting, Travel Writing." I plan to put most of the Jeff. selections under A, but we'll put one bit from his *Notes on Virginia* into B: vis., his account of the Natural Bridge.

After these will naturally follow the excerpts from the Lewis and Clark expedition. Do we need any further materials of this sort? If you think so, I would nominate a brief selection from Zebulon Pike's *Account of an Expedition to the Sources of the Mississippi, 1810*, and a brief selection from Wm. Bartram's *Travels through North and South Carolina* etc. 1791. I suppose that we [p. 2] could put here also a bit of Audubon's Journal of 1819–20, but I am assuming that all the Audubon would, because of its dates, fall into Section 3.

What do you think? I do not press for inclusion of any Pike or Bartram. The book is going to be too big anyway. But we now have so little material under II, 1, B that perhaps we need to add one or two more items of this sort.

Except for a little more tinkering with notes for the Jefferson, and making the Pike and Bartram selections—if we use them—I shall have finished working on Section 2 until I hear further from both of you. I'll go on with rewriting the Poe introduction.

Yours
[Cleanth]

P.S. You may not have heard that John Popp's wife, Jean, died suddenly of a stroke. She was stricken, apparently massively, on Saturday evening and died on Monday morning. We went to a memorial service for her this afternoon at the chapel in the Divinity School—hugely attended, most beautiful flowers, and old Sidney Lovett doing his best which was very good indeed. They had sold their big house and were to move into a biggish apartment within a week. I believe that John will still move there—his son and daughter are staying on to help him settle in.

2495 Redding Road
Fairfield, Conn. 06430
April 26, 1971

Dear Cleanth,

It strikes me that you might—if it seems good to you—do a little bit in your Poe to set him a little more sharply in the background of Jacksonian democracy, science, and the industrial revolution that I am trying to develop in my Intro. 1826–61. I am trying to sketch the relation there of the transcendentalists, etc. And if you came in with Poe right afterwards it might complete the picture. But I may be wrong.

All the best!
Red

[Handwritten] On p. 2 (p. 10 revulsion from democracy) you could append a paragraph on Poe's distrust of democracy.

April 28, 1971

Dear Red and Dick,

I am sending under separate cover today a xerox copy of the section of Vol 2 that gives the "intellectual background of the U.S. from 1914 to 1945."

The brief preliminary note was written before I had received from Red his long similar note on the period 1861–1914. He has done, by the way, a brilliant job and I *heartily* endorse it. Because so many of the important matters that affected America's development were issues that were settled by the Civil War, I think that my own note can remain as brief as it is now and that what is principally needed is for me to make some back references to Red's. This, it will not be hard to do, unless one of you thinks of additional material that I should get into my own note. I hope that you don't feel it is necessary, for the book is already bulging at the seams.

I present my group of essayists with a great deal of hesitation. Please feel free, both of you, to suggest additions and especially excisions. One way that we can shorten the section, if it is deemed necessary, would be to omit figures like Mencken and Babbitt entirely or else to discuss them but submit only brief excerpts—a few consecutive paragraphs—to illustrate what I've said about them by way of introduction.

After talking with Red, I've decided to represent Edmund Wilson by a couple of passages from *Patriotic Gore*. Perhaps we ought to reduce these to one, omitting what Wilson says about the Battle Hymn. If we do keep the Hymn, however, then Red may want to readjust a bit his references in Vol I to the Battle Hymn.

I hope you'll agree that the Tourgee selection is a good one. I think that it is on its merit, and that it shows Wilson's gift at its best. But I have another reason for wanting to use it: it will back up powerfully what I have to say in my Southern section about Northerners who observed the Civil War in the South as soldiers and proceeded to write about it. If we use Wilson's piece, then I shall cut out about a page or so of my comments on Tourgee and simply make reference to the Wilson essay.

Please scrutinize carefully the Donald Davidson piece. I think it is a good example to illustrate the resurgence of regionalism in this country and, with its fine section on Vermont, it is not confined to the *Southern* regions. In fact, if it is deemed too long, we could cut it back to what Davidson says about the Vermont Yankee and omit altogether what he says about Georgia. If we are to represent Davidson at all, I think with the exception of a few of his lyrics this is the best way in which we can do it.

I have some misgivings about my choice of an essay of Ransom's. I think that the one I've chosen is a good one; it represents Ransom [p. 2] at his best, and will beautifully back up what we are saying about Imagism and on the need to rethink in our time the whole relation of poetry to discursive prose.

If, however, either of you is unhappy about it, please make your nominations. I might mention two alternates myself. There is "The Concrete Universal," which Ransom apparently likes, and for which I have already written a headnote. But this essay is devilishly difficult and even with my explanations in the headnote, the references to Hegelianism and the Kantian philosophy will, I think, make the essay too difficult for most of our readers. I am also strongly tempted to use a chapter from Ransom's *God Without Thunder,* the one entitled "Satan as Science." It would provide a nice occasion for a headnote on the new interest in myth. It represents Ransom doing his most skillful and interesting writing; and it would point up, from another direction, the crisis in culture about which we shall be talking in the New Poetry.

You will notice furthermore that Allen Tate is not represented in this group. I could easily put Tate in. But hasn't it been decided that we will use "A Southern Mode of the Imagination" as one of his most celebrated and useful essays? If we are to use it, then I propose putting it in the Southern section where it might stand either early in the section or—my preference—at the end as a kind of summation of what has been represented earlier.

At the end of this section, I have supplied what amounts to a little epilogue on the varieties of criticism that we have exhibited in these essays, in which epilogue I make some simple distinctions between the generic, the formal, and affective criticism.

My motive has been designed not only to help out the student as he gets into the kind of critical niceties that he will find in Ransom and Eliot, but also to help out our own book by taking the curse of the New Criticism off it. Yet, maybe the way I have put it is not the best way. I solicit your suggestions and possible rewriting. Moreover, perhaps the end of this section is not the best place to put this material or at least all of it. Red had talked about having a preface which would say something about our methodology—or rather, lack of any tendentious methodology. Maybe that's the place that my little epilogue, or part of it, should go. Anyway, let me have your best notions on this matter.

Yours,
Cleanth

[Handwritten] P.S. I hope to send you soon the missing items: Burke, Davidson's "Still Rebels, Still Yankees," and the two Eliot essays—which need some annotation to be fully intelligible, and which I am supplying.

April 30, 1971

Dear Dick and Cleanth:

Some meditations:

On the Historians which I have been rereading. This is fine, but I have a general idea for the addition—only a few sentences—of their political significance. Bancroft scandalized his proper Bostonian friends by being a rabid Jacksonian. In his address at Williams College, in 1835, he said:

> There is a spirit in man: not in the privileged few: not in those of us only who by the favor of Providence has been nursed in public schools: *It is in man:* it is the attribute of the race. The spirit, which is the guide to truth, is the gracious gift to each member of the human family.
> "The Office of the People in Art, Government, and Religion"

This at the very moment of Jackson's attack on the Bank, etc. B was also nominated on the ticket of the new Workingmen's Party in Mass., but turned it down, hoping for a general coalition of the disgruntled with the Democrats. B was an early Phd. from Germany and a student of Hegel. His history is Hegelian in assumption, apparently, plus German romanticism of the "folk"— i.e., American—plus the fact that his history was, according to the wit of the time, "a vote for Jackson"—all this plus a streak of American Eden, plus millennialism. BUT, if I have read the right books, he made a solid contribution to the development of scientific history in his use of documents.

What about the political ramifications of Parkman, *et al*? Theodore Parker attacked Motley because he was too aristocratic—TP held that history should project the idea of liberty (but feared the tyranny of the majority).

On to Intellectual History 1914–1945. Again fine. A few little additions.

The role of Van Wyck Brooks might give us a way into particular people. He stems from Santanaya's a "Genteel Tradition" theme and the castrating of American writers, in his early stuff on Twain and James, etc. Later goes rather "genteel," of course. This gives us a hinge with my section 1861–1914. What about some reference, too, to the pre-1914 radicalism, such as Randolph Bourne? If space, we might put some Bourne in my selections.

Back to the general idea: The new world of sex, the effect of war on race question with ref to my black stuff and [Joel Chandler] Harris, Renaissance.

Re: Humanists. What works, specifically, did they attack and especially hate? Dreiser for instance, etc. What did they like and applaud? More context.

With Mencken we might add that he helped make Dreiser from the start— though he didn't applaud A[merican] T[ragedy]. But admired trivial poets. Mencken picks up from Santayana a "Genteel Tradition" too.

[p. 2] Cowley: to play fair with him, we might mention that as editor of NR he went South and lived in the country for a while to find out for himself. His long hassle with Faulkner is an important little tale in literature of the period. In each successive review he tried harder to understand what was really at stake, until his Portable. Etc.

Burke: in early work he had direct influence on young writers. He did have a sense of the insides of literature—less as time went on.

[Edmund] Wilson: a "writer," a stylist; always weak on poetry and sociological about fiction, but did have the air of literature, a passion for it, and a sense of the human issues that go into it.

In general, early perhaps, we might remark on indigenous elements in the print against industrialism and against the capitalism of the Depression.

Cleanth, I have a few little nagging nothings we might look at when together, expansions usually.

WHEN you all are ready I'll take my medicine on my sections.

BEST
Red

June 2 [1971]

Dear Red,

The Introduction and selections came in the morning mail. But I think you must have failed to put into the packet the concluding page or so of the Byrd introduction. What I have breaks off abruptly at the bottom of page 4.

The Byrd selections you have chosen are very interesting and ought to make a hit with our students as well as revealing the quality of the man. Let me ask, however, whether we don't need footnotes? Footnote indications are given in the selection and these footnotes ought to be supplied or else the footnote indications removed from the text. It's just possible that we would do well to add a few notes of our own. What do you think? It's the sort of job that might be delegated to somebody.

I am returning herewith the suggested readings for the Meriwether Lewis. You had forgotten that you had sent me a copy earlier. Maybe it's just as well to have the two copies in separate places in case one of us lost his copy.

As soon as I get the Pike introduction written up and one or two niggling notes on Jefferson's account of the American Indian finished, I'll get these sections xeroxed and sent to you.

A few days ago Dick said that he was at work on the Franklin intro and expected to finish it right up. When it comes in, Section Two will be complete.

I forgot to tell you that I decided to substitute for the text of the Dec. of Independence which I had originally put in a text that gives Jefferson's original document with an indication of the changes made in it by the committee. Actually this would cost us very few words extra and I think it may be well worth doing.

In haste,
Cleanth

July 1, 1971

Dear Red,

We put together Vol. I in Dick's rooms in Calhoun and after a certain amount of revision, retyping, and xeroxing, David[1] took the typescript in to St. Martin's yesterday. I haven't heard from him but have a relayed message and the mission was accomplished.

1. David Milch, of Yale University, is acknowledged for his assistance in the preface of *Understanding Fiction*, 3d ed.

There was simply no time for me to revise your discussion of the period from 1826–1861. I wouldn't have felt it proper to insert my own suggested changes anyway. So we sent in your own revised copy—the St. Martin's editor can count wordage and get a sense of what was being said.

Now I have finished up my re-reading and am getting it off to you.

As you will see, I have taken very seriously your request that I look through your typescript. I have done so, though you'll see that most of the changes that I suggest involve the substitution of a word or the transposition of a prepositional phrase or an adverbial clause.

I am far from sure that my positive suggestions are worth adopting but, like Mildred Tackett, I have preferred to give something concrete so as to indicate more clearly what my problem with the sentence or paragraph is. Adopt any that you think proper and forget most of the rest. I am convinced too much revision can take all the juice out of an essay and yours is so lively and pungent that I don't want it to be drained of energy by too much tidying up.

If you decide to use any of the suggestions, I'm sure there is plenty of time at St. Martin's for you to substitute revised pages for the typescript they now have in hand.

I am dictating this morning a start toward our preface for the book. I hope to get some kind of draft to Dick by Friday or Sat. and a copy on its way to you. But the draft will be provisional and preliminary.

We much enjoyed Rosanna's visit.

to you all,
[Cleanth]

[OH]   Forest Road
Northford, Connecticut 06472
July 8, 1971

Dear Red,

Thanks for your two recent notes. I've filed that on Jay Martin and Lanier in my Southern section, on which I get back to work tomorrow. By the way, I hope to dot every i and cross every t in it this weekend.

I've just finished the Conrad Aiken section and, a few minutes ago, the Hart Crane. That just about ties up the section "From Image to Symbol: The Crisis of Cultures." You'll be seeing these soon—and the whole of the section almost as soon as you like. Milch has the Aiken and Crane to xerox.

He is also posting to you today from New Haven (after he has xeroxed it) my start on a Preface for the book. Dick wanted me to do it soon since he was getting ready to start on his second part of it. A copy went to him several days ago. I had meant to send you your copy at the same time.

I've worked hard on the Preface but it has been done under the lash and it is subject—obviously—to being cut, rewritten, or expanded. I'm counting on you and Dick to rework it thoroughly, and particularly you, since you will be primarily responsible for winding the whole thing up.

We can easily come up to Vermont on Tuesday, July 20, and I've talked to Milch today and he tells me he can arrive on Wednesday, the 21st. I'll see that Dick gets the plan promptly—or rather confirm that he has.

Milch tells me that he has already got out of the library a lot of books from the 1945–70 period. He and I will talk about his list in greater detail tomorrow.

I've prepared the Jesse Stuart section and tomorrow mean to finish the rewrite of the Stuart, touch up Lytle, and put the finishing touches on the Faulkner. With this kind of touch-up the Southern section will be almost complete.

That leaves plenty still to do but I take heart now in feeling that the package [p. 2] is beginning to be tied up at last.

No time for more talk on paper. Back to work. But do give our love to Eleanor, Rosanna, and Gabriel.

Cleanth

West Wardsboro, Vermont 05355
August 9, 1971

Dear Cleanth:

I have just sent back, by a passing friend, the Intellectual History section (H. Adams et al.) to be delivered tonight to David M. A few sections are to be added, but he has the list. Certain books never reached me.

This note is to make a remark on O'Hara. For what it is worth. He was a disciple of (1) Fitzgerald and (2) Hemingway. But he lacks what both had—a "view," a philosophy. He admired Fitz for his picture of an age and of social types, missing the fact that what makes F in the end any good is a view. Gatsby fits into a deep American issue and into a deep philosophical issue. Ditto for H. O'Hara set out to be a social historian, without having an instinct for the difference between history and poetry. He has an irony and it often works very well in a generalized way. He had talent, a great talent for a special kind of ironic reportage, but no final center.

I slam these things down to be knocked off the page and I don't feel that they'll be much use. But here they are.

Have you seen an old essay by Trilling (admiring) in the Nation about 1945? NOT the same as his intro later. At least, that is my recollection.

See you all soon!

Yrs
Red

[38 Claix]
At Sea,
August 30, 1971

Dear Cleanth:

I am enclosing (in a big envelope to David, along with other stuff for him to distribute) the sheets I have drawn from Volume I written by you—those on which I have any comment. There aren't many, and I trust that you can make out my rather trifling criticisms.

As for general comment, I want to say—as I am saying to Dick—that after reading the whole volume, I am much happier about it than I had been able to predict. [Volume] I *does* seem to hang together as a book, and looking carefully at the stuff you two have done, I never detect a sense of strain, of fatigue, of boredom (on your parts)—nothing merely perfunctory. It does feel fresh and freshly considered. And various.

On the mechanical side, there are a few little problems. (1) The bio summaries are not consistently handled. David, or somebody, ought to work through them all, in both volumes, and see that they have the same method and format. Otherwise they will look sloppy. And they are not now on the same scale. Furthermore, in most instances a minor figure like Crevecoeur does not have a summary. This needs a thorough overhauling. (2) There is an inconsistency in the Suggested Readings. For example, Dick has a reading list attached to his general intro for the Puritans, etc. In corresponding sections that I have done—1826–61, for example—I do not have reading lists. I don't know which is the best procedure, but I do think that we ought to be consistent. But I do know that making a reading list for the period from 1826–61 would be one hell of a job.

A matter of content: The essay by David Donald in *Lincoln Revisited* on the social background of abolitionists gets referred to four times in Volume I, once by Dick, twice by you, and once by me (without name, I think). To some readers this would suggest that we set special store by this piece, and might let us in for some misinterpretations. Especially in the light of the fact that the essay has been severely attacked. I had meant to go into the attacks, but life got too thick, and all I have to go on is an answer Vann gave me when I asked him about it; just that it had been attacked on statistical grounds. But we were interrupted and never got back to the subject. If Vann is around, he might be able to give you the facts in a short conversation. In any case, I am inclined to think that you might use one reference to the piece and not two. I am pretty sure that Donald has hold of a truth, but it would apply more widely than to abolitionists. More accurately I think to transcendentalists, who were displaced intellectually as well as socially—i.e., by science, of which they hadn't the slightest notion.

I have rewritten my own stuff rather drastically. Much reduced the Hawthorne and, I trust, improved it. Ditto Cooper. I am holding my own rewrites until I get the criticism from you and Dick. Then I'll try to put my stuff into final shape, and send it in.

The voyage is proving very pleasant. Good food, fine weather, pleasant companions, on schedule. Gibraltar today. Also I'm getting lots of work done.

Don't think that the efforts of the Brookses to speed our departure [p. 2] were not appreciated. They were.

All the best to both from the W's!

In haste
[Red]

96 Pivot
Furonniere-Stendhal
38 Claix, France
September 27, 1971

Dear YOU-ALL:

I am sending under separate cover (registered) my revisions of the section on the novel, now, as you have suggested, "The Novel: The Beginnings to Irving and Cooper." This is certainly the best arrangement; it is a proper unit. But I don't have a table of contents here, alas, and I leave it to you all to fit it into the whole scheme. In my revisions I have drawn on David's revised sheets and the notes from Cleanth and Dick.

A general comment: Observe that some pages are missing. Those are pages that require no changes whatsoever, as far as I can determine. Simply insert proper items from your MS. Numbering is [the] old way.

Beginnings: page 1. Smollet's novel: I have followed Dick's suggestion of [a] footnote on Jeff's letter to daughter on fiction. But I do not have text and do not know whether it is in the Jeff section. If it is in Jeff section, insert page ref. If not, quote letter in my footnote. Page 14. I do not have that page here, so please correct Court of St. James to C of St. *James's.*

Irving: Page 15. I have written a long note as Dick suggests on the "past" of America and inserted it as 15-*A.* Page 21. Please fill in first name of explorer Bonneville.

Kennedy: Page 32. After quote from Kennedy's journal on death of Poe, can you, Cleanth, add note—if required—on the "facts" given by Kennedy. I am rusty on Poe's bio, but feel that this is wrong in some details. If it is, it should be corrected in a note.

[p. 2] Cooper: Page 1. Somebody please add context of indicated footnote on Cherry Valley Massacre. I don't have reference books here. Page 50–51. Here you, Cleanth, raise the question of the placement of Jeff's note on the case against Cresap. I don't know that it {(the position)} really matters. I leave it in your hands. Please observe a new note, or rather an extension of an old one, on page 52. I'm sorry to be passing the buck so much.

A rather important, if small, matter occurs to me. Dixon Wecter, in *The Hero in America* (New York, 1941), has some items that should be in our Suggested Readings. His Franklin bio, "Poor Richard: The Boy Who Made Good," and his "Lincoln: The Democrat as Hero," are especially good. "Jefferson, the Gentle Radical" is also worth mentioning. I am adding the Lincoln to my piece on him.

Observe that on my enclosed work, I have flagged with a red arrow on left margin all changes—or I hope all.

Please let me have word of the arrival of the Ms. I'll be worrying until I am sure it's safe. Just a card.

I have NOT renumbered in any way, the section here enclosed, but it is in proper sequence now.

I'll start the 1826–61 section tomorrow, prayerfully. I'm not too happy about it now.

David, tell Broadbent we'd love to put him up here. Tell him, too, that there are two two-star restaurants in the neighborhood and that I hope his expense account is in running order and well-oiled. You can't afford not to keep hens, cows, and writers in anything but the pink of condition.

Affectionate greetings to all. Yrs in Mammon,

Red

96 Pivot
Furonniere-Stendhal
38 Claix
France
October 5, 1971

Dear Guys:

I am mailing by air today, under separate cover, the Whittier. The chief problem has been, of course, the cutting. As it now stands I have reduced it by 2500 words, bringing it down to 14,000. I tried to work out a way of putting the analysis of *Snow-Bound* into a headnote, but I found, or seemed to find, that the meaning of the poem was so tied up with the discussion of structure and "perspectives" that, with the time at my disposal (even though I had been tinkering, off and on, with this problem for some days), I couldn't work it out. BUT this is not to say that it couldn't be worked out without making *SB* seem, in the running text, [to be] given less serious treatment than other pieces. On this matter I point out that originally I *did* have a lot of this in a head note on *SB*. I don't have a copy of that version here, but you all should have—it was the first version—and you may, with that, be able to get [the] substantial part into the headnote. I have, however, cut the stuff about *SB* and Cooper, Hawthorne, Faulkner, etc. A good suggestion, Dick. I have also reduced the stuff about his love affairs. If you all find other things for the axe, please chop without consultation.

Now for some details: Dick, I hope I have answered you on the matter of treating "Ichabod" in two places (see new lead to second entry). You see, the first treatment won't accommodate the "nostalgia" theme—there is no background for it at that point. (See p. 29) David, would you please get my Whittier book[1] and on page 20 of book transfer section on Woolman to page 12 of my present textbook version? This is a suggestion from Dick, and a good one. AND give footnote ref to Woolman, whom Dick treats elsewhere.

You will see that I have returned only the sheets of Selections that have changes indicated. The others I have junked. BUT there is a question of inclusions. The full table of contents of poems as now given is 1982 lines. The

---

1. *John Greenleaf Whittier's Poetry: An Appraisal and a Selection,* which Warren edited, was published by the University of Minnesota Press, June 2, 1971.

problem in cutting is that some of the weaker poems have some importance for my discussion of themes (cf "Maud Muller" in relation to lost girl theme, etc.) and these tend to be long. For instance "To My Old Schoolmasters" is 196 lines. It is a poem leading to *SB*, but the critical text could be easily adapted to allow dropping the poem. The poem does have a certain kind of realism that is worth noting—i.e., the drunk wife berating her husband in the room adjoining the school room, etc. "School Days" is an American classic, <ditto> for "Barbara A." It's pure junk, but somehow should be in the record. We *can* cut: "First Day Thoughts," "The Hive at G," "The Gentian," and perhaps "Holmes"—164 lines. "Mass to Va" is pure junk, but illustrative. Pray and do what you must.

EVER YOURS,
Red

October 6, 1971

Dear Cleanth:

I have been studying your 1914–71, and find it splendid, really a great job of synthesis and survey with a constant grip on ideas and relations among ideas. What the doctor ordered. My remarks to follow are matters of mere detail.

(1) p. 1. The C[ivil] W[ar] did "commit" the US to centralization etc., was a "turning" point; but it strikes me as very important to distinguish between the "symbolic" importance of this and the "literal." As symbolic—as the enactment of ideas—it is focal for our history, it seems to me, a definition of issues, etc. AND of the issues in a marination of ironies of all sorts. But some of these ironies, those that would put the Southern values into other perspectives, did not function because defeat raised those values into another dimension: they were spared the test of the future-become-history. The Northern values were, God knows, put to this test with a vengeance and are still being put to it with pollution, Attica, etc. What I am getting at is this: I feel that there is a very strong probability that if the South had won, they would have embarked socially and economically on much the same course. First they would have learned that you have to industrialize. They were at the moment trying their best to industrialize, to catch up, in order to win a war. If they had won, in one way, or another, they would never have settled for the plantation team—and many defenders of the Southern system were already aware of the industrial needs. Fitzhugh. Furthermore, there was a strong imperialistic, expansionist psychology in the South, which was expressing itself, of course, in terms of expanding the plantation system. Cuba, Central America, etc.—but it wouldn't have confined itself to that; it would have been soon geared to a new psychology. But you see the line I indicate without further detail. It's my guess, too, that the South and North would have found it mutually profitable to reunite. NOT I am not saying that such a reunion might not [p. 2] have given a healthier and morally better country. BUT I am

saying that it would have given us something recognizably similar to what we have now, with the same tensions. And how much better is anybody's guess. Of course, this is all a guess. For present purposes, what I am thinking is that we have to avoid the suspicion of simplistic thinking—of being thought to "think" that a Southern victory would have avoided—literally—many of the ills we are now heir to. So I proposed some indication of this distinction in the first two paragraphs. OR am I off base?

(2) p. 2. line 2, do you want to add William James to Twain and Dubois?

(3) p. 5. In connection with new intellectual influences. Marx is a special problem but might be put into context here, preparing for later. There had been Marxism in the country before [World War I] but with the Russian Revolution it took on an entirely new meaning.

(4) p. 6. Footnote. Make Dreiser representative not merely of "poor"—but *immigrant poor.*

(5) p. 9. Second para. There was a visible movement toward "homogeneity" —perhaps slower than some had feared, but there, and it is still in process, accelerated. You seem more optimistic than I think you really are. Just a touch to put the process in the perspective of the present.

(6) p. 10. Bottom second para. "Muck-rakers" NOT "mud-rakers." Further, I think what we have is not merely the muck-raking spirit. With Garland, anyway, there was the shattering discovery, after the time of loneliness and dreaming back on boyhood in the West, this while living a tough life in Boston, of the cramp and meanness of life in what had become the dream world. Also, the reality, suddenly seen in contrast to the overarching "American dream of the West." Not simply muck-raking. Maybe ref. to section of Garland, etc.

(7) p. 17. Early socialists as heirs of Whitman, etc.: But Whitman, for example, had been [p. 3] much hit by Fanny Wright and the gospel of the class struggle. See my 1826–61, etc. The idea of class struggle emerged, too, in the late 19th-century social troubles. What you say is true, I think, but needs a little context, maybe. Anyway, you know more about this than I, I am sure. But another item. Emma Goldman was functioning in Greenwich Village and elsewhere in the period of 1914 on. Dreiser knew her there. Ditto, Henry Miller—in California.

(8) p. 36. Second para. " . . . truly grateful." But fade something like this. "And grateful, too, for the powerful tonic effect that the pull of the future, like the pull of the great spaces of the continent, exerted on American energies and will to act."

(9) p. 38. Top of page, ref. Sighting in good "cause." There are two versions of the "Star-Spangled Banner" on this point: "*when* our cause, it is just" and "*For* our cause, it is just." Maybe a footnote ref to this in my "SSB" in American folk song section.

(10) p. 40. To "our Hawthornes and Melvilles" might be added "Twain, Dreiser, and Faulkner." If you think good. It's still going on, though.

That's all. The piece is fine. PLEASE review my new version much reworked —of 1826–61. And please watch style closely. I did it mighty fast.

I am now beginning Non-Lit section, the last I have to do with Vol. I. I have already given it (on boat) a full work-over, so this should be fast. In the mails today I am putting Longfellow, Whittier, Lowell, and Melville's poems. Your remarks on all have been absorbed. Fine.

. . . .

But this spot is gloriously beautiful to look at. And I am happy to have some time of solitude. We haven't been seeking life, avoiding it rather, to try to regroup after a period of pressure for many months. E. has a study fixed up now in the old caretaker's house of the place, and begins to get that brooding look. But she got together a marvelous dinner last night.

Our best to you both.

Yrs,
Red

96 Pivot
Furonniere-Stendhal
38 Claix
France
October 13, 1971

Dear Cleanth:

I have just finished a review of all vol. ii, and I feel good—present company excepted. The modern poetry section is GREAT. Wonderful ease in handling complicated ideas, meaty with information, fluent in expression, judicious, fine selections. One book St. Martin's ought [to] draw out is poetry Emily D. to H. Crane. It would sweep the field.

But I didn't start this note to say all that. Something more immediate. Do you realize that Peter Taylor does NOT belong before 1945? He was publishing a few stories only, and it wasn't until after 1945 he did his first little collection—in 1947 I think. It seems that we must change his location. Otherwise there is no logic to putting Flannery O'C and me—a more glaring example—after 1945. (Don't misunderstand me, that is where I want to be!) But this change of Peter's place would make a small cut, too—the commentary on him.

I am now getting on with typing up notes to you and Dick. Nothing important. Nagging.

Best to both!

Yrs
Red

Oct. 15, 1971

Dear Red,

Five letters within a week—it's high time that I make some kind of response.

Bless your heart for putting in your letter of Oct. 3 that wonderfully succinct sketch of your beliefs about the South, slavery, the dialectic history, the validation of value, and other basic things. It's not only admirable: I derive a very special personal satisfaction from it—for obvious reasons and reasons that I shall not take time to elaborate on this occasion except to say that I always find great satisfaction in discovering that our ideas about the essential things are not too far apart.

[p. 2] About one matter in particular, however, I shall say something a bit more. Whether we call it millennialism or use some other term, [we] evidently both fear and perhaps even detest that oversimplified and reductionist theory which insists on over-riding the human condition and the nature of history and claims a privileged insight into the universe which may finally be essential as a matter of faith but is certainly not "proved" in the sense that it is immune to the test of history. But enough of this, except that I couldn't refrain from this little joyful outburst of approval.

[Following five paragraphs handwritten] Last Wednesday, Dick, David and I had a conference on Vol. I. (David is taking the first and corrected copy into N.Y. today.) I came expecting that we would have a long hassle over "1826–1861" because of the way in which you had treated Emerson, the Abolitionists, and the Transcendentalists. In fact I had made rather elaborate notes on how to make some accommodations between the 1826–61 Prelim. Note and Dick's Intro. to Emerson and yet avoid taking the bite out of the Prelim. Note.

As it turned out, to my surprise and relief, no such revision was asked for. Two main points were made: (1) that the discussion of the Transcendentalists shall be given a more historical reference rather than having the issues treated historically and on their merits and (2) that the discussion of the Abolitionists should precede that of the Transcendentalists. I find merit in both proposals: the abstract and often harebrained notions of the inner light people are just as completely exposed when [p. 3] one treats it as an aberration conditioned by and consummate with the times, and the transposition of the Ab. Trans. blocks makes good rhetorical sense: then we take up first the obvious and outward political manifestation, then go on to look at the underlying philosophic ideas, and thence on to the literature in which these notions [are] reflected.

What I would have worried about (and would have sought to prevent) would have been the watering down of your fine, and to my mind, quite accurate and certainly not too severe account of the meaning of these inner light, antinomian interests. I gather that Dick regards his letter to you on the subject as just teasing—"go a little farther, Brother Warren and you'll be maintaining that the South ought to have won the War," etc. He remarked that he couldn't fault you on any of the things that you'd said about Emerson even if he could wish that some didn't have to be exposed.

Naturally, I was happy enough to leave good enough alone and I certainly have no hint that Dick's attitude is not one of perfectly cheerful acceptance of the Prelim. Note as it stands—with of course the two revisions proposed by David, but revisions that make no substantial difference. It was a good and happy-spirited conference in which all three of us felt confidence in the shape of the Vol. as it stands and sanguine about its success.

Day before yesterday I started rereading Vol. I. I shall try to put every available moment on that until I have finished and you may expect to be receiving next week such notes as I may have on your own stuff. Surely this, as you have suggested, is the economical way to work. Then eager as I am to get on to a final revision of my own work, I'll postpone [p. 4] that until I've read your stuff and Dick's. Nevertheless, I want to set down here a few remarks on your comments (in your Oct. 6 letter) on my Prelim. Note. 1914–71.

How useful it is to have another person go over a piece of work like this. For example, it had not occurred to me that anybody might infer from what I'd said about the Civil War that there was intimation that with Southern victory things would have been quite different. But having read what you have to say, I see at once that this just might be inferred by the reader, and could be most damaging to us if that inference were drawn. My own view is that a Southern victory would have only slowed down the movement toward centralization, urbanization, and industrialization. But that slowing might have been generally beneficial. If it had delayed our becoming a super power—<pawn> to *Time, Inc.*—I would rejoice. A Southern victory might also have helped us preserve certain traditional views about life—at least have kept them alive longer. But I quite agree that in any case the South would have eventually become industrialized.

[p. 5] (Even France and Italy are at last rather rapidly becoming industrialized.) I agree with you that in all likelihood the South would have worked out economic and perhaps political accommodations on the order of those now between the U.S. and Canada—or closer.

I also agree that the plantation system had already been weighed and found wanting. I think that there is good reason to believe that slavery itself would have in time died a natural death and that the trend in the South would have been toward smaller land holdings, a larger yeoman class, though certainly some—perhaps a great deal of industrialization.

These are all mere speculations. I put them down simply to indicate the depth of our basic agreements about substantive issues. Now I'll go through the rest of your suggestions with equal care. Very grateful for the time that you've taken with this piece of mine, which I confess I have found very hard to write.

{[Handwritten up right margin] Your long letter of comments on "From Imagism to Symbolism" arrived this morning. A hasty glance indicated that they are pertinent and will prove extremely helpful. I'll save further comment until my next letter.}

I hope that you received the other sheets for Vol. I—I sent two pages that show considerable rewriting. If what I've done seems to have turned the trick, well and good. Otherwise, be candid.

. . . .

All best regards,
[Cleanth]

[Handwritten at top of page] P.S. You've probably seen the very favorable review of *Meet Me in the Green Glen* in the *Washington Post.*[1]
[Handwritten] P.S. The mail this morning brings me your handsome comments on my poetry piece. Naturally I'm highly gratified.

December 2, 1971

Dear Cleanth:

There are two enclosures, the carbon of the relevant part of a letter to Lewis Simpson (self-explanatory) and a memorandum on your revision of the Letter to the Teacher. But to go on with the general question you raise in regard to the Letter, I am inclined to think that the stuff about the use of the novels and the references to the drama are very important to have in the letter and probably in the advertising brochures to boot. Anyway the brochures won't be handy when the teacher faces the hard facts of the case. Most of them won't, in fact, have read the brochure. A committee often does that and makes the adoptions. If our words on the novel are worthwhile, they are worthwhile here. But Tom is right—it gets off the main line of interest. Maybe—only maybe—we might recognize this in the text.

. . . .

[p. 2] Some random observations: (1) It strikes me that we might do ourselves some good if we could get one example of a piece of black writing post 1945, from somebody younger than Ralph [Ellison] and Baldwin (and Malcolm X) who are of ripening middle age. Somebody who would correspond to Pynchon in age, say. I refer above for prose fiction. I am uncertain how we stand on poetry, for the sheet I have in hand shows only one black, Leroi Jones. I remember that there were one or two others, but can't off hand say who. Back to prose: I was disappointed in the piece by Coover that David sent me, "J's Story." If we can't beat that, let's drop him. I do like a novel of his, however: short of idolatry. (2) I enclose a letter from New Directions about F's Crack-up, etc. Note matter of hard-and-soft covers. Please get this to David if he is keeping a file on such letters as I have sent him in this connection. (3) Has David sent me the NYC address of World Publishing Company so that I can negotiate with them for *A[n] A[pproach] T[o Literature]*? If not, jog him, please. (4) Back to # 1 above: It strikes me that I might get from Ralph, confidentially, a nomination or two for young Negroes (born by 1935)—I have read quite a few but haven't the books here, and anyway he would have covered the field, I imagine.

That's all I think of at the moment, but know I have forgotten something important.

But about our interview. Can't we be sort of thinking of topics and approaches, etc. It's hard to do a good off-hand. AND is it true you and Tinkum are coming over?

1. See also John W. Aldridge, "The Enormous Spider Web of Warren's World," *Saturday Review,* October 9, 1971, pp. 31–32, 35–37.

Eleanor and Gabe are off on the mountains, this being Thursday afternoon. Rosanna writes that the Academia is going fine for her, also other things. No news.

Best from Warrens!

Red

[Handwritten] Do you have an English address for I. A. Richards?

Furonniere-Stendhal

38 Claix

France

December 4, 1971

Dear Cleanth:

I don't want to bombard you with letters, and I think I wrote you about the general matter of revising the *Approach* some days ago, when I first had a feeler from Miss Lumsden whom we were first acquainted with, very briefly, at Harcourt, and who has, apparently, taken Martin Stanford's place. In reply to the earlier letter from her, I said yes sure, we'd try to get something going and I would write you. The hell is, I really can't be sure I did.

I presume that you have had something equivalent for her enclosed letter to me, but if you haven't, here it is. If we can get a good helper at Yale, I see nothing against our having a revision ready (a six-week job of our mop-up work maybe) in time for the date she has in mind—and I see nothing against our using their research people, etc., especially their MS preparation services, with the clear understanding that we are in the saddle. I don't think it's even worth discussing that side with her—except to say yes (if we decide yes)— this sentence on second thought: we'll just write what we want anyway. And we'll have to get it done when we can.

If we can get some good hints out of the survey people, OK; if not, OK.

Let me hear your thoughts. I'll write her a note meanwhile, saying that we are thinking things over.

In haste—as usual these days!

Best to both,

Red

[p. 2] P.S. I have been meaning to write you and Dick for some time on what I am about to say, but it hasn't worked out and so I'll raise the question with you to discuss with him. It has been on my mind for some time that we might take a look at John Hollander's poetry. I don't think we're open to the charge of playing personal likings in the book, and I don't want to do anything here that we can't justify on general grounds. But I do hope that you all will take a look and see how you really feel. In the new book (in which some very good poems are ruined by wordiness, just aren't drawn up in tight enough rein) I find several to propose to your consideration: "Under Cancer," "Crossing a Bare Common" (which I take to be a ref. to the famous passage in Emerson), "Ad Musam" (in spite, I think, of origins in Sylvia Plath), "The

Moon at Noon" (a little slack in the middle, but good I think), "Alaska Brown Bear," and "Adam's Task." The book is uneven, should have been cut, but look at these. I do not mean to disqualify earlier poems, but these are all I have here.

I say don't use any unless we want them. But because of the personal equation, I do want us to be sure that we have given a hard look.

Furonniere-Stendhal
38 Claix
France
December 15, 1971
[Handwritten] Letter #1

Dear Cleanth:

This morning the letter of December 9 from Lumsden reached me. I flew into a rage, and am enclosing the typed result. I have *not* sent this to her. I did it to relieve my feelings, and to send it to you, with the suggestion that you revise, adapt, or scuttle as seems best. If you decide to adapt some into a joint letter—which I urge you to do—urge you not to take any of this but to write a letter—then go ahead and sign my name with yours. DO not feel committed to any of this.

But looking ahead a bit, what happens next? They have been good at selling and no doubt will continue to be. But maybe if we do send a letter somewhat resembling this, we may be hunting a home. This would mean finding some firm that would buy us out. But I suppose what comes next is to communicate with L and wait for consequences.

I guess you are about off the hook about American Literature, and for your sake, I hope so. I have read the sheets of rewrites you sent me. The long section pp. 108–108G is *splendid,* maybe could be compressed a bit, but *splendid.* Nothing better on the subject. What is as good? Two tiny remarks. p. 108-Ce: perhaps a footnote to page on Santayana where I talk about poetry as religion and religion as poetry. p. 108-F: Russell in his Autobiography is rather mean about [p. 2] E's bride, etc.: "[common]" E also said somewhere that R would have been first-rate if he had had a classical education.

Back to Lumsden. I've had time to cool off a little. Please defang what I have said and read it in that light. Anyway, make it more polite, etc. I have just reread her letter of November 16 to you (which I return now). The real question is what do they do in the way of hurting us, really reprinting criticisms and market if we do not take the 25% cut in royalty.

. . . .

Write me what you think about Lumsden. I'm glad I've cooled off a little. Our very, very best to you both!

Ever yours,
Red

[OH]   Dec. 16, 1971
Dear Red,

I enclose a draft of my Wilder piece which has been looked over by Dick and David and has received their suggested additions and alterations. I've tried to keep it short and to keep it focused on *Our Town.* At your convenience let me know what you think of it.

I have now incorporated your (and Dick's) suggested additions and alterations in the "Letter to the Teacher," "From Imagism to Symbolism," and "The Southern Section." Having done these, along with "Preliminary Note: 1914–1971" (which has already long gone in), I have only one more section to turn in: "Intellectual Background." I have your notes and Dick's and David's for this section, and mean to get at it right away. As you will recall, this last section is really last: it comes at the very end of Vol. II. So I am far ahead of the hounds. But I want to finish it soon and get it out of the way.

You are a good editor. How sharp your eye is! I value your suggestions too much to treat them cavalierly. I've really tried to meet the problem you spot, clear up the possible ambiguity, etc. There are very few of your suggestions that I have not adopted or at least taken into special account.

I am enclosing a sheaf of some of the more important instances in which I have attempted to restate a point. If you still have your copy of "From Imagism to Symbolism," you'll be able to see whether these pages fit in and what they replace.

We've been promised copy-read text to begin checking over, answering queries, etc., but thus far none has come in. But we expect it any day and we have resolved to read and return it as fast as St. Martin's [p. 2] sends it to us. David says that this work will not take long.

My undergraduate classes ended yesterday. I have a few more graduate classes in January and there will be final papers to read and an undergraduate examination to give and read. But the worst is now over. What an autumn! I want my free semester to begin (Jan. 25) so bad that I can taste it. I'll try to write a real letter—and a legible one, properly typed—next week. Meanwhile, our affectionate regards to all the Warrens.

                                                                        Cleanth

                                                      December 17, 1971 *Letter #2*
Dear Cleanth:

Enclosed you will find a letter to you written two days ago and a draft of a letter to Lumsden marked *Version 1* and one marked *Version 2.*[1] Version 1 was written in the heat of passion. I have cooled down by today and have tried

---

1. In version 1, Warren emphatically rejects the proposed reduction in royalties and then discusses their relationship with Appleton-Century-Crofts and their relationship with other publishers who offer better incentives. In version 2, Warren reverses his rhetorical strategy and begins by reviewing their "meditations" on the proposal and concludes by suggesting a face-to-face meeting.

to do a more tactful thing. All for your inspection. NOTHING has been sent to Lumsden.

In regard to this whole business, I wish we knew what percentage of profit a publisher expects on a text book? If we get 13% from *An Approach,* what does ACC get? Also if we feel that the going might get rough with ACC, then I wonder if another firm might buy out the rights on the book? But this is unwieldy. Forget it. For now, anyway.

BUT it would be good if we could see a sample of one of the surveys made on some book to help us decide what would be useful for us.

Here I'm just wandering. I guess all we can do is to wait for another move from L. So will you, with what you want to use from my Version 2, write her? You are the guy to be both firm and tactful. God, I'm furious at the whole cheesy ad-man, come-on tone of L's letters.

. . . .

Goodbye, all our best!

Red

Furonniere-Stendhal
38 Claix
France
Christmas Day, 1971

Dear Cleanth:

Merry Christmas! It is now 2 PM, and ours was quite jolly, with some nice guests in the house, skiing companions, a late breakfast (Christmas dinner was last night in the local custom) and the present giving, and then everybody but yours truly tearing off to the slopes for the afternoon. You see what I am doing.

I have been reading your Wilder piece, and find it excellent. I have only a few, very few, and trivial remarks.

P. 4 and 4A: It strikes me that there is some sense of overlap and repetition between the paragraph beginning "This willingness to innovate . . ." and the following one. I see the line of logic you are following, but the sense of reduplication remains. Let me try to fuse them. (See below)

P. 9: para. 2, line 6: "well" should be "will."

P.10: para 1, line 5: "sains" should be "saints"

P.11: para 3, next to last line: "film of familiarity." This echo of the usual phrase of W's is disturbing because it is an echo and not an unquoted quote. Why not use "veil of familiarity" and be done with it?

P.12: para 1, lines 5 and 6: Change to : " . . . stress on the essential normality of his people . . ."

Imagism, p. 318, bottom of page. I don't seem to remember that Thomas is characteristically descriptive, at least not in the poems that stuck in my mind. Some of his work has a lot of emotional power, it strikes me. Often not unlike

Frost's. What about Blunden, who does strike me as more atmospheric and descriptive. Or W. S. Blunt? But check these, I haven't read them in years.

Here's my try to revise the stuff on Wilder pp. 4 and 4A:[1]

[p. 2] Forgive this vile typing, and ignore anything here that doesn't strike your fancy.

I have just mailed, yesterday, a long letter to David Milch in answer to various questions he had just raised. All my remarks are directed to you and Dick, and I have asked David to xerox the letter for your deliberations. So I won't repeat myself here.

GOODBYE, and all the best to you both,

Red

[OH]   Forest Road
                                          Northford, Connecticut 06472
                                                       Jan. 4, 1972

Dear Red,

A very brief note to accompany material that should have gone to you weeks ago: I enclose pages giving the *major* charges and additions of the Southern Section and the Intellectual Background Section. I'm not troubling you with the less important ones.

If you've saved your copy of the originals, you can fit these replacement sheets in. I hope you will approve of what I've done by way of rewriting. I finished my revisions some time back. We are ahead of the game with the publishers. (I saw and talked with two [Latimer and Miss Green] of the St. Martin's people last week in Chicago when I went out for three days to the MLA. They are both enthusiastic about the book and our prospects.)

I also had a brief chat with Miss Lumsden (of A-C-Crofts) at Chicago. I've tried to be agreeable with her but firm. I've promised her to come into New York a little later and let her show me her bag of tricks. But I am quite as [p. 2] much annoyed as you are. Her very first letter put my back up. But in our brief talk in Chicago I said nothing to offend her and we parted company on amicable terms.

No time for a real letter, though I shall write you within the next few days in detail about a number of matters.

I already feel like a new man. By the end of the month, I will have finished the first semester and can begin to pick up the pieces of my life. But enough of these scattered remarks for this writing.

T. joins me in affectionate New Year's greetings to all the Warrens.

Cleanth

P.S. That was a most handsome comment you made on my effort to deal in more detail with Wordsworth and Eliot on the subject of science and poetry. Most *gratifying* to your old comrade in arms.

---

1. Editor's note: Warren's revision was not found with his correspondence.

Jan. 26, 1972

Dear Red,

This is to bring you up to date on the Harcourt negotiations. Did you get the Jan. 12 letter from Walter Holden, saying that he was leaving Harcourt as of that day? He gave a home address, somewhere in N.Y. state. He did not give reasons, but the tone of the brief letter I took to be somewhat bitter. His successor is Bryan Bunch, whom I will never be able to think of as other than Faulkner's Byron Bunch.

After my letter of Jan. 17 to Miss Wile (of which you have a copy) I got a phone call from Bunch saying in effect that they thought surely they had mentioned the royalty rate from the start but could find no proof of this. They had phoned Walter Holden, who was no help, but I guess his memory too was that the 8% rate had been told us. Bunch had got out the 1969 contract for the Third College edition and was perfectly agreeable as to our adding such clauses to the proposed contract as were added to that one. I asked him to put all this in writing and he has done so. A xerox of his letter is enclosed.

Now I am mailing a letter to Bunch (copy to Corbett, copy to you) but frankly I do not expect it to have any result in raising the royalty rate—it's just a last ditch effort before we sign, to my way of thinking. But I shall certainly not sign anything until I get the complete go-ahead from you.

This is of interest: My business manager (and spouse) phoned Ed Gordon, who has done several high-school textbooks, and asked for information which he was very willing to impart. Ed says that 8% is quite normal for high-school texts. These books have to be sold very cheaply. One of his, which he says looks very elegant, with lots of color plates, etc., sells for 4 dollars. This means that the publisher expects and must have an enormous sale to make anything on it. So on a very large sale, the smaller royalty rate may be as profitable to the author as a higher rate on a smaller sale. Some royalties are even lower—4 or 6 percent. Tink can't remember whether Ed said this usually applied to books for the lower grades or upper grades—apparently the grade level makes a difference. Ed is now doing a book for 11th grade on which he does get a higher royalty—thinks 10%—but it is a book on tragedy, with limited sale possibilities, and this has been taken into account. He agrees that even though 8% is routine, it is not much of a royalty to be split 3 ways.

It looks to me like we are stuck. I genuinely want to make sure that Corbett thinks the over-all view of *Modern Rhetoric* is not being ignored, and I suppose there's a slim chance that he will say "O.K., boys, take 9," but I cannot see that there will be any rosy surprise coming to us—unless they sell a million copies.

I go to N.Y. on Feb. 2 for meeting with Appleton and on to an evening at the Institute. Will take my business manager with me. (It worries me that maybe they *did* tell me 8% and I just didn't take it in.)

I've just finished grading (with help, I admit) 84 final exams and about that many long papers. Now I'll attend to any little loose ends in Am Lit., and try to work through a huge backlog of commitments—letters, *Festschrifts* and reviews.[1]

[p. 2] We're planning a trip in April, but not to Greece. We hope for 10 days in London and 2 weeks in Persia. Persepolis or bust! It would be grand if you all could come to London while we're there. I fear there's no chance of our getting to France. The complications of this trip are already formidable.

Yours,
Cleanth

[In a January 24, 1972, letter, John P. Lindhorst, Staff Producer/Director of "The American Experience," USIA, asked Warren's permission to produce a segment on Warren's work as representative of southern values. Brooks served as the go-between with Warren, who was still in France.]

Furonniere-Stendhal
38 Claix, France
February 4, 1972

Dear Dick and Cleanth:

It has just occurred to me that perhaps the USIA people might be persuaded to get interested in our book. At the least they might republish in some of their various magazines for foreign parts some sections, but I should hope they might make a certain number of bound copies—hard-cover, I mean—for libraries or for distribution among professors or institutions in various countries. Cleanth, you would know something about this and I don't, but is it worth exploring with Broadbent? He, of course, would have to carry the ball. But I can't help but feel that there may be some useful angle here. At a minimum, getting some copies, even promotion copies, in a few European and English hands, a highly selected list. But the big idea is, of course, to get the USIA to do something. Or is this all moon shine—as it may very well be?

Naturally, I am anxious for news—when there is hard news—about how things go. When do we get proofs, etc.? Any change in schedule? All those things? As for availability, I am here until March 25. Then I am out of pocket until the night of April 10—that being spring vacation and the Warrens, presumably, off doing North Italy art and more Venice.

April 10 is the day when *GG* [*Meet Me in the Green Glen*] comes out in England. Rosenthal, my new guide, philosopher, and friend at Secker and Warburg, had set up a sort of apparatus of TV, radio, readings, etc. in London, and just yesterday I decided it really wasn't possible—five days of that—that

1. These would have included "Dionysus and the City," review of *Dionysus and the City* by Monroe K. Spears, *Sewanee Review* 80 (1972): 371–76; "Faulkner and History," *Mississippi Quarterly* 25 (spring 1972): 3–14; "The Tradition of Romantic Love and *The Wild Palms*," *Mississippi Quarterly* 25 (winter 1971–fall 1972): 265–87; and "I. A. Richards and the Concept of Tension," in *I. A. Richards: Essays in His Honor,* ed. Reuben Brown, Helen Vendler, and John Hollander (New York: Oxford University Press, 1973), 135–56.

is the time where we had planned our family vacation in Italy. First things come first, and I don't want to go alone, and I don't know what good this sort of thing does anyway, and suddenly, what I want most is friendly conversation among friends or family, or quiet work. Maybe my bones are getting older. Anyway, I can't believe *GG* is English meat, Mr. R, to the contrary.

Back to real business: You all talk about the USIA thing and if it seems a good deal with Broadbent. I can't be sure about the idea, of course.

Best to you both and your houses,
As ever,
Red

[OH]

Forest Road
Northford, Connecticut 06472
Feb. 4, 1972

Dear Red,

T. and I had a long session with the Appleton-C-C people on Wednesday (Feb. 2) with what I believe were good results. I didn't lose my temper but kept pressing our position steadily. I think they are now ready to call off "Option 2" in favor of a regular revision. Our meeting—with Lumsden and her superior Jourard—ended amicably and with no one's feelings hurt—at least visibly. But I shall write a play-by-play account of what happened when I can get more time this weekend. I told the A-C-C people that I would do that and that our *final* decision would come only after you had had an opportunity to review matters. You'll be hearing shortly.

The present occasion is to forward the enclosed letter to you as I should have done some days ago.

I don't know whether you will be in the least interested but you might possibly be. The Frank O'Donnell mentioned came up last week from Washington. He is not a member of USIA but does work on commission from them and chafes, I think, from time to time under their restrictions and what he regards as their sometimes stupid guidelines.

[p. 2] O'Donnell is no fool. He is genuinely interested in your work and before I said a word on the subject, he showed that he already saw that for a half hour show of the sort proposed, the emphasis ought to be on your work, not your life, and on your sense of the Southern scene.

If you should be interested at all, I believe that O'Donnell could come up with something quite interesting. USIA, he tells me, would steer him away from the darker problems with which you have been concerned and the more tragic aspects of Southern history, but I think O'Donnell would avoid mere sugar-coating or tepid gentility.

I'll be sending you an account of the A-C-C Conference—typed, not in this scrawl—soon.

Love to Eleanor and Gabe.

Cleanth

P.S. We were writing about the atmosphere of Miss Lumsden's letters. The whole joint fairly stank of promotion and the advertising agency's lingo.

February 10, 1972

Dear Red,

Here is a delayed report on the mission to Appleton-Century-Crofts. I had hoped to get it to you earlier, but things intervened and my last note to you did indicate at least what the basic outcome was.

We sat down (Tinkum was with me) with Miss Lumsden, and she set out to sell us a bale of goods. She made a great play of what their new market research would do for our book, under the Second Option. They would have men in the field finding out why people didn't adopt the last edition, what they wanted changed, what they didn't, etc. We would save time, for we would have to give them only a "core book," which their special people would work up for us—to our own taste, of course; we would retain absolute veto powers, etc. They would do an index, bibliography, provide summaries, etc., pay up to perhaps $8,000 for permissions, obtain the permissions. I kept pressing her about what these services would really cost, pointing out that though we as authors might make an absolutely larger sum of money if the book were immensely successful in this rejuvenated form, we would be paying proportionately much more for the revision than would Appleton. She was vague and defensive about figures but I finally got out of her these approximate costs: It might cost $5000 to 6000 for market research, $2500 for a project editor (this is the person who turns a "core book" into a "product"); $2500 for a typist; an undetermined amount for a permissions arranger.

I asked her to show me samples of the kind of production she was talking about, and it turns out they have not done any literature books in this way. All she could produce were books in sociology and psychology; for instance, one done by an economist who admitted he could not write English but had some fine ideas. They have not yet started to work on any book which already exists and is to be revised. Ours would have been the first.

We were joined for lunch by a senior editor, Julian Jourard, and the conversation continued. I pointed out that our book was different from the kind they had been processing under Second Option conditions—that in a book on literature the ideas and the way you stated them were inseparable. I would want to have some of her re-write people to take some of our exercises, analyses, etc., and prepare the kind of questions and comments that the new market research dictated, and to have a look at these first. At first I got the reply that they could furnish such samples. Later, it became evident that they didn't really have any such people at work, but they would hire someone to work specially with us. Jourard said that in the present market position there were plenty of bright young PhDs who would be available. I said that we had our pick here, and that we would have to know the person well enough to decide whether he could actually be of help to us in this kind of enterprise.

In the course of the later conversation I managed to get over the idea—civilly, of course—that what they were proposing probably would work much better for social science books where there was a big name to exploit and where the writer in question couldn't write very well, but that we didn't want to see our book cheapened to the point of embarrassment and were not out to sell our names.

We asked for a list of the management, since the people we had formerly known there, Mr. Crofts, Martin Stanford, etc. were no longer around. Alan Ferren is president of Meredith, of which Appleton is the Educational Division. Charles Walter, a Vice Pres. of Meredith, is in [p. 2] charge of Appleton. Tim Adam (not Adams) is manager of the College Division of Appleton. Jourard is, on his card, Executive Editor. He indicated that Adam is in charge of Development and Jourard is in charge of—? Production? I forget. Or maybe it's the other way around. There is a Mrs. Somebody, Projects Coordinator, who was supposed to join us after lunch but we didn't go on after lunch. Project is one of their main words, and a Project results in a Product. (Tink at one point innocently asked why Miss L kept calling it a Product instead of a book. She explained that she meant not just the content, but the cover, the index, the illustrations, etc.—the whole package.)

After getting the rundown of who is who in management, I asked Jourard who was the person who decided to approach Warren and Brooks with this scheme. That was when Jourard said firmly "I am." And at exactly that point, he gave us up as a lost cause. We had now been going on for 3 hours. He no longer pressed the issue of Second Option. Perhaps it would really not be the one we should take. In any case, he wanted us happy. He was glad we were willing to undertake the revision and hoped we could make the deadline of March, 1973, that they had proposed. He himself suggests that we not make a radical revision. If changed too much, there might be permissions arrangements to make over and perhaps buy again. In any case, the fact that a book was a new edition, no matter how little revision there had been, made it sell better at once. He assured us that all the usual services that Appleton had accorded us in the past would be ours—the letters and cards from users of the book, comments and suggestions from salesmen in the field, etc. I had earlier pressed this last part pretty hard, pointing out that we had always got, from all our publishers, editorial help, comments from the field; had always hired indexers, were now getting from other publishers permissions assistance, etc.—all these things they were making a big deal of (and for which our royalties were to be cut) were not exactly earth-shatteringly new.

I have my doubts that much help will be forthcoming with enthusiasm even though they say it will. But we never got too much anyway in the past, and with the new team in I don't think we'll get much in the future. There seems no question that a new team is in. Miss L hinted that the firm had been on the verge of going broke (not certain whether it still is) and had needed a shakeup. Former salesmen had been getting their friends among the college teachers to write books, admirable enough as books, but not money-makers.

My guess about the background of this occasion is this: I think that Jourard and Miss L dreamed up the idea that if they could take an established book like ours, gimmick it up, make a big push toward places like the community colleges and the open-enrollment universities, they might make a killing out of the book. I surmise further that the top management wouldn't let them get by with this special investment of money, special advertisement, etc., unless they could take it out of the author's hides. So Miss L was told to sell the package to us and when Jourard saw it was no go, he finally gave up and became pleasantly understanding and agreeable.

Incidentally, their "discount" is 27%, i.e., author's royalty is figured on 73% of retail price. When I suggested that in the event of a really large sale there would be an upward scaling of author's royalty rate, Jourard was quick to say "Absolutely not." That arrangement had always been unfair to the publisher, it seems, because a book normally sells best its second year, perhaps well enough to run up the author's percentage, then the sales slow down and the publisher is stuck with a high royalty to the [p. 3] author on a book which is now in decline.

I suppose that by turning down Option Two we *could* lose a good deal of money. These bandits may know what they are up to and may make a lot of money for the book—a lot even for the authors with reduced royalty. And they would pay permissions up to $8000. But I think we are being used. I don't trust them, and since I don't, I think we might spend as much time correcting and rewriting the suggestions of our Appleton "helpers"— the Project department—as we would spend in revision by ourselves, or by actually hiring someone like Conversi or Milch as a helper, paying him out of our own pockets. Since we don't have the time to both revise this book and do all the other things we are committed to or would just plain like to do, it is tempting to think that somebody would be told to do not only the fetch-and-carry and leg work, but some intelligent rewriting or additional writing for us to oversee or revise. But my guess is that no Mildred Boxills will be forthcoming from the Appleton stable, and very frankly I think that to work the book down to the point that it would appeal to [the] level they have in mind would debase the book. Jourard had mentioned earlier that the open-enrollment universities formed 80% of the future market, and remarked further that by test, those students had an average reading ability of 9th grade. When questioned, he backed off from the idea that our book would be aimed at that market. I certainly don't despise the more humble places that have adopted the *Approach* in the past, and told Jourard that for years I had noticed on the sales list how many such places there were, but that neither one of us, I was sure, wanted to write a book for real illiterates—or at least without some balancing attraction, and that didn't seem to be offered.

I told L and J that I would try to report the facts fairly to you, giving both sides, and I encouraged them to write you directly, presenting their case to you. I don't think they will, for I have indicated earlier, I think, that Jourard has hauled down the flag for keeps.

If you agree with me that it has to be the First Option, we are stuck with re-doing that book in the next 12 months. Shall I look around for a possible helper? Let me have your thoughts.

[A few additional impressions from Tinkie] The atmosphere of Appleton's office is that of a firm enduring hard times, and Miss L is frank to support, indeed suggest, that is the case. She said that the firm had been going down for 10 years because of its lavish policy with authors. Their salesmen had been, in effect, acting as editors as well, soliciting books, chatting with professors about their projected work, etc. All changed. Now a salesman is a salesman and an editor is an editor and they don't overlap.

Mr. Jourard is hard to place. He said he had lived in N.Y. for only the past 10 months. Came there from Boston. But he has a very odd accent, not French as his name would indicate, plus a lisp. He made no reference to his former occupation, although Miss Lumsden was always eager to remind us that she used to work for Harcourt and knew everyone in the N.Y. publishing field. Mr. Jourard didn't say whom he knew. He seemed uninformed about us. Referred, for instance, not to "An Approach," or the "Approach," but to "Approaches." He gives me the definite impression of a man who has moved in from the "Communications Industry"—advertising, television?

[p. 4]   Modern Rhetoric:

With regard to the school edition of MR., as you know from the copy of my last letter of "Byron" Bunch, I told him I was sending a copy also to Paul Corbett. Corbett's brief reply (which you may have, but I'll repeat) says:

> We will not, I assure you, move ahead with a yet shorter version of MR., to be distributed by the School department, without having convinced ourselves—and you and Mr. Warren—that there will be a *net* benefit to all parties as a result of it. We are studying the matter closely.

This would seem to mean "We would not move ahead . . . and therefore are not moving ahead . . . and will study the matter closely and let you know what we think" or does it mean "We would not have moved ahead had we not convinced ourselves . . . but we have convinced ourselves, and are of course keeping a sharp eye"? All I'm hoping to get out of the sad letter I wrote to Harcourt is a very small percentage of increase in royalty over their proposition, and am doubtful we'll get that. But in any case it's almost a pleasure to be victimized by people who write ordinary (though perhaps ambiguous) English after undergoing the jargon interview with Appleton.

I hope Corbett will write soon to say that he has gone over the case and thinks that the proposed school edition will not undermine our shorter college edition. (Or that, if the risk exists, there is some good hard reason to believe that we will make more money even at the reduced royalty they propose for the school edition.) I'll send him a note and ask whether, having investigated, he can satisfy our qualms on this point. If he can, then I suppose the thing to do is accept the 8 percent royalty they propose and let them go ahead. O.K.?

American Literature

I reported to Milch some weeks ago our interest in looking over Hollander's poems for inclusion in the 1945 supplement. When I heard from you the other day I took up the matter with him again and found that something had gone amiss. He had lost my note or something. But he is on the job to get out Hollander's new book and other materials and will take a look. Since he may have forgotten also—or I have failed to communicate—the *et al.*, please, in your next note, jot down the names of some of the other younger poets that we ought to consider. I'll follow up the matter.

I've read the copy editor's last batch, going up through Holmes, Lowell, and Stowe, and turned it back to David the other day. There are not many problems. The copy editor seems to be doing a good job but the work goes slowly and they are now somewhat behind. {[Handwritten] But still claim they can publish in November.}

When you have time, give us a more detailed account of Gabe's adventures on the mountain.

I must turn back to other matters now and mustn't lengthen this already too-long letter.

Best love to all,
Cleanth

[Handwritten at top of p. 1] P.S. Your letter of Feb. 4 to me and Dick has just come in. The idea sounds good. I'll talk over matters with Dick and I'll get in touch with a couple of friends of mine in USIA. They can advise and may be able to help. I'm delighted to know that Secker and Warburg mean to do something about the novel. Send news!

Furonniere-Stendhal
38 Claix, France
February 14, 1972

Dear Cleanth:

Your letter of February 10 made record time, getting here this morning. You have gone far beyond the call of duty—or friendship, to be more exact— in your detailed report of the A-C-C meeting. I am quite sure that we had better leave their scheme alone. The nail in the coffin is, of course, the idea that hired editors, Ph.D's or no, can write for us on the basis of some scheme. I am perfectly willing to try to go ahead and revise the best we can. Especially if we can get a really good assistant for this *and* for *Understanding Poetry.* In fact, *UP* might well be our number one project here. It has more prestige and with the revision, if the Holt editor is talking sense, will make a lot of money. We could start them both, with assistants. I imagine that Milch would do well with the *Approach.* Maybe he would be fine with the UP, but I don't know how acute he is about poetry. Maybe just fine. But you know your other man is fine in the poetry business. BUT is he available to us? He has left New Haven, hasn't he?

As for Hollander, I named some poems, I think, in the letter to Milch: "Under Cancer," "Crossing a Bare Common," "Power Failure," "The Night Mirror," "Ad Musam," "The Moon at Noon," "Alaska Brown Bear," "Adam's Task," and "As the Sparks Fly Upward." All from *The Night Mirror.* These for a pool. But you all may like others better.

Did David pass on my nominations for Adrienne Rich?

I have a note from H[arcourt] B[race] J[ovanovich] about the MS of *Modern Rhetoric*, Third. The other stuff has gone to Kentucky, hasn't it? If so this has value only in connection with that. If it is there, why not send this on deposit and wait to see if the law is changed? But what do you and Tinkie say? The lady at HBJ [is] Elizabeth H. Hock, in case you've mislaid the note.

About *Modern Rhetoric* high school version. I say go ahead if Corbett now clears it. Many a mickle, and pray.

No news here. Rosanna comes for the short vacation next Friday, much to our joy.

Thank Tinkie for her valiant and valuable part in the A-C-C fray. I'll try to make it up some way to you all.

Love from all to you both,

Yrs,
Red

Feb. 23, 1972

[Typed at the bottom of a copy of a letter from Brooks to Miss Lumsden at Appleton-Century-Crofts]
Dear Red,

I think we've got these crooks on the royalty business, at least. Their contract (Nov. 1963) for the Fourth Edition specifically refers to "and all Subsequent Editions" and Mr. Samuelson's letter (he was V.P. then) of April 28, 1967, when we had it out with Jack before the Alternate Fourth, lists royalty shares for Fifth[1] and Subsequent Editions as follows: You and I each 6¼ of *list*; Jack 1½; LSU Press 2. All of *list*. The dogs wanted us to split 10% of net (wholesale).

C.B.

[OH]   Forest Road
Northford, Connecticut 06472
Feb. 25, 1972
Dear Red,

Re school edition of *Modern Rhetoric*. For some reason U.S. mail between N.Y. and Conn. has recently been very bad. Two copy-edited sections of *Am.*

1. The fifth edition of *An Approach to Literature* was published by Prentice-Hall, copyright March 4, 1975.

Lit took nearly 10 days to reach us. Fortunately they were not lost, but got in safe (Emerson and Thoreau) and David M. is planning on getting future stuff back and forth by personal delivery. {[Handwritten at top of page] St. Martin's is somewhat behind schedule but [they] don't seem worried and apparently remain enthusiastic about the book.}

The delayed mails also explain why I have been so long in hearing from Bryon Bunch of H.C. about the school ed. of *M.R.* He called by phone the other day to explain the delay and to talk about matters.

(1) I take it that he is not enthusiastic about Rodney Smith as a redactor and adapter of our work. I suggested that he send me what Smith has done thus far so that I could see for myself. This time the mails were quick—the packet arrived this morning—registered mail—and I will get at it as soon as I can.

(2) Bunch says that they are having difficulty [p. 2] estimating the market: apparently it's in chaos with little units of this and that. Hence his suggestion that the school ed. of MR should be concentrated on themes of exposition and persuasion—though he admits that some treatment of diction, jargon, etc. might need to be included too.

(3) I suggested that I could come into NY to talk with him in March and this is what I'll plan to do. I simply can't estimate the situation properly from his letter or from a short telephone conversation. Unless Bunch or his superiors are really enthusiastic about this school ed., I am inclined to let it alone. Our royalty will be so meager at best that unless they believe in the book and believe they can sell lots of copies, we can use our time more profitably on other projects.

But I don't mean to *discuss* the present project. I will talk with Ed Gordon about the market generally and I'll try to see what kind of man Bunch is before I sign off for us. (At the moment, I think that Bunch is prepared to sign off.)

I have told him that I can't plan to have a talk with him until almost two weeks hence. Sunday (Feb. 27)—unless there is a big snow storm—T. and I plan [p. 3] to drive south for lectures at Chapel Hill, N.C., Clemson University, S.C., and stop-off at Newberry, S.C., and Charleston. We hope to be back here on March 8. We both need a change of air and scene and a break in the grind. South Carolina in March won't be precisely spring-like, but there may be azaleas in bloom in Charleston.

David Milch will be happy to help us with the 5th edition of the *Approach.*

Leonard Conversi has passed his orals at Harvard—is back at home here in New Haven—and will welcome some work as he works at his dissertation. He'll be glad to pitch in on the revision of *U.P.*

I have got some ideas about what we might do with U.P. Let me revolve them through my mind for a time and then if they still look good, send them on to you. If they do meet my own more considered approval—and of course, yours—they might allow us to make a rather [p. 4] dramatic rearrangement of the book and perhaps a real improvement as well as a freshening of it *without involving any really drastic change of principles or method.* Well, we shall see what we shall see.

We've had a relatively mild winter, but we did get considerable snow the other day and more is threatened. Still, I don't have to get into town for classes and so I can wait for the lane to be plowed—or, if the fall is relatively light, plow it out myself. (I like snow plowing almost as much as mowing.)

Love to all the Warrens in which Tinkie heartily joins me.

Cleanth

P. S. A quick look at the Rodney Smith stuff indicates that it is not very good. But I'll examine it more deeply later on.

Sunday, Mar. 26, '72

Dear Red,

I send under separate cover a rough draft of my proposed sections I and II of *UP*. Section II is not even wholly a draft: my pages are simply notes to be worked up later. But time is catching up with me—we fly to London on April 5—and in any case it is high time to let you see what I'm up to.

The draft speaks for itself and may appear to you to hold possibilities or may mean a dead-end street up which I must travel no further. Yet though it ultimately speaks for itself, let me make a few introductory comments.

If we are to use in Section II a common factor like birds and perhaps in Sec. III poems of varied form and mood about love, and in IV poems—again of the widest variety—about death, then it will be important to introduce the student early to concepts like dramatic structure, imagery, tone, metrical pattern, and theme. Hence the rather fully worked out Sec. I.

Even here, however, there is common factor: Hardy's "Channel Firing," which is brought back for discussion under every one of the rubrics mentioned above. Obviously one can't give a full treatment of tone, for instance, in the two or three poems as discussed in Sec. I, but then, tone will be discussed in all the rest of the book. What I'm trying to devise is something that will not involve any basic change in our principles or our notions of what literary criticism is, but which will allow us to come at these matters indirectly, in connection with other things, making more use of comparison with other poems, etc. etc.

I'm convinced that we can win back many of our former adoptions and lots of the new instructors who have come along if we can catch their eyes with what looks like a fresh and unjaded approach. If my suggestions for a way in have any merit, then we can do a great deal more: give the impression, for instance, that we are aware of past history, intellectual background, bias and special concerns linked to biography, etc., in this way. See for example, the Hardy poems in II, the Housman in I, the Frost-Keats cluster in II, etc.

I must say that I myself have found it interesting to go at poems in the way that I suggest in Sec. II—and maybe that is a good sign. If what I suggest seems to make sense, the general "method" is endless in its possibilities.

You'll notice that in the selection of bird poems I've kept pretty close to what we already have in UP. But Leonard Conversi has promptly turned in ten new possibilities—from Ogden Nash to "The Phoenix and the Turtle." You can probably think, offhand, of a dozen more.

I hope that you also find that you are stimulated to devise questions for exercises—by the constant juxtaposition of poem with poem—themes that look alike but really aren't, analogical devices that go different ways out of the same basic situation, etc.

If, again, there seems to be much possibility in this approach, I am for devising a really good teacher's manual—with stuff for the bonehead instructors to use and also suggestions for our more imaginative brethren. We could provide a whole aviary of bird poems for the instructor to use: some with very simple questions that the bonehead could pass off as his own; and some suggestions that would allow the bright instructor to develop some of his own interests.

Leonard would be, I am confident, very good with this sort of thing. He has got up for me promptly new poems for a narrative section (if we should go back to the old plan) and a very bright and fresh introduction. I think that his introductory section is too difficult (though it might be used as an appendix on abstract-concrete, and on the kind of "authority" that lies behind a poet's "statement"). But I've now set him about a new attempt at an introduction, making use of some very contemporary poetry. We'll have to wait and see. But there's no question about Leonard's value in locating interesting fresh poems—ancient and modern—from which we can choose. And he would also be fine at helping to check everything and put it in final shape.

[p. 2] One or two more ideas: if we did decide to have sections on Birds, Love, and Death, or other special categories, we'd still have plenty of room for special problems—"how poems come about"—a special metrics appendix— and other features that we may be able to think of.

In any case, I believe we need, in order to meet the opposition, a fairly shortish book (paperback?) plus a full-length one. I see the need of a really useful manual with both.

I believe Conversi would be useful if we wanted to assemble other critics' comments on particular poems and perhaps even a special section featuring some of the various fashionable approaches with our own quiet comments on how they are related to each other and what they are finally good for in literary criticism.

Do let me hear your notions when you can. My London address (morning of April 6 to 12, and again April 26–27) will be Old St. James House, 7 Park St. If you can't get word to me here before we leave on April 5, I can receive a letter in London and then write Conversi indicating what he is or is not to go ahead on. His address, by the way, in case you want to write to him, is [. . .]

A long letter, but no help for it. Tinkie joins in love to all the Warrens.

Yours,
Cleanth

[OH]

Forest Road
Northford, Connecticut 06472
March 29, 1972

Dear Red,

I trust all goes well with all the Warrens. We are in the approaching throes of packing and other preparations for our trip to England and Iran. As I've written to you earlier: we fly to London on April 5, stay there almost 8 days; fly to Iran for 2 weeks of conducted sight-seeing; then back to London for a couple of days, and then home. {[Printed in right margin] London Address: Old St. James House, 7 Park St.}

I wish we could take longer. I wish most of all that we could pay a visit to you all. But too much remains to be done here. I must have a productive summer and get several big projects moving or else throw in my hand.

Friday (Mar. 31) Ed Gordon and I will go into Harcourt and talk to Bunch about a high school ed. of M.R. I do hope Ed will be willing to take it over. If we could get that one settled satisfactorily and if you think my start on UP shows any promise, then <reaching> David's promised help on the *Approach,* we might get on with matters. I want to do something more than revise text-books [p. 2] all year and I'm sure that this goes double for you. I have a couple of Percy volumes to finish and another Faulkner volume. You are at work on another novel and I am sure a dozen other things. Let's pray for grace (if it's addressed to Jehovah) or for luck (if our prayer goes up to Tyche). Maybe we'd better take no chances and pray to both.

I'll get off a note before we leave giving you a report on the Harcourt interview. {[In right margin] No recent news from St. Martin's.}

I enclose some sample writings from Mrs. Patricia Staros. She has had two courses with me and I have learned to have a great deal of respect for her mind. She has intelligence and sensitivity—considerable for one so young.

Whether she has any literary flair is another matter. But she's fairly dying to get into your writing course, for she knows your work and knows further that this fall is her last chance. I've held out absolutely no hope to her but I did relent and tell her I would send you the sampler. All that she had was poems. I told her that she had better scratch up a little prose in a hurry. Having looked at it, I'm not sure that it forwards her cause. But I send the batch anyway: the prose bit, an imitation of Spenser, and a couple of poems. I wish that they were better.

Give our best love to Eleanor and Gabe, and when you write to her next, to Rosanna.

As ever,
Cleanth

[Handwritten at the top of p. 1] P.S. Being on leave seems to have made no difference at all to me. I suppose that the backlog of postponed commitments was bigger than I had believe[d]. That logjam, at least, is beginning to loosen.

[OH]

Forest Road
Northford, Connecticut 06472
April 2, 1972

Dear Red,

Happy Easter to all the Warrens.

Friday, Ed Gordon and I went to talk with Bryan Bunch and three members of his staff. We had a frank talk about the high school edition and I shall summarize the conclusion thus:

(1) We all agreed (Ed and I emphatically) that Rodney Smith will not do as a reviser.

(2) Harcourt will disentangle themselves from him and pay him for what he has done.

(3) The original plan (proposed by Holden) for a kind of quickie with simplification and shortening will not work. Miss Wile, who worked through Smith's attempt to do this for the first chapter, is convinced that it wouldn't do because we have woven the book too tightly together. Ed thinks that the key to a good book for high schools [p. 2] on how to write [is that it] must not summarize or get on an abstract plane. So, the book needs to be kept concrete and to detail the individual steps, i.e., what we have done or even more so.

I agreed but argued that we would be satisfied with an "honest" book—one that did not evade issues or slur over matters that needed detailed examination—but would not insist on a book that tried to do everything. Thus, if, as Ed thinks, description is the best place to start, then we may have to leave most of argument out if the book with it became too large and unwieldy. In short, an honest book, but not one necessarily that went from A to Z—maybe just from A to Q.

(4) The crucial decision was this: That Ed would take our shortened 3rd ed. of *MR*, go over it carefully, write [a] report on what he thinks can be done and ought to be done and—most important of all—whether he can understand it. He will not report until I get back at *the end of the month.*

Comment: I think that Ed honestly admires our book and his more special notions of what a high school book on Composition ought to be seem to be in better close agreement with our ideas. Moreover, Ed was frank to say [p. 3] to me on the train going down and to Bunch and Co. at the office that he would rather like to see his name on the title page with ours. But he is fairly heavily committed and is working on two books at the moment for Harcourt.

Thus, I don't know what he will decide. If he says that he would like to do it, I'm for offering him a third royalty and with his name on the title page. If he says no, then we can drop the whole thing or try to find someone else. Before I asked Ed whether he would himself be interested, he had said he could try to find us somebody.

Harcourt's h-s text department seems to me rather demoralized. They are quite at sea about what kind of book they ought to do and frankly say so. Ed told them that the h-s teachers were at sea too—didn't know what they wanted, though the best of them realized that their students weren't being taught to write. Ed's view was that Harcourt ought to supply the proper book and hope that the teachers would find it and use it. With that view I heartily agree, but I'm not sure that the Harcourt staff is convinced of it and I concede, in any case, that this procedure doesn't promise any early [p. 4] killing for us in the text book market.

So we wait at the moment to see what Ed Gordon will say.

We are in the final frantic stage of trying to be ready to catch that plane early Wednesday (5th) morning. Our address in London (5th to 12th) is [. . .].

Love to all the Warrens from us both,
Cleanth

[At top of p. 1] P.S. I hope you can make out this wretched scrawl. No time to hire it typed.

Furonniere-Stendhal
38 Claix, France
April 27, 1972

Dear Cleanth:

. . . .

You must wonder why I've been an even worse correspondent than usual. The very night we got back from Italy I took to my bed with flu, then had a series of relapses, and now have some mysterious ailment, which alas, may be hepatitis, there being an epidemic here. Anyway I'll know by this afternoon, when I get a diagnosis. Anyway I feel rather beat up, and am getting little done that I can't do lying on my back. Lying on my back I have done a lot of reading and rereading your work on *UP*, and every day I've been thinking I'd get up to do a long letter. This won't be that. This is to say that I think every word can be well used, handsomely used, in our revision. I've made only some five or six trivial notes on the content, nothing of consequence; but I am not persuaded that Section I, as now set up, would work. That is, as a section (the stuff could be broken up easily and redistributed, of course). The real problem is that as now presented Section I would, I fear, put more of a load on the teacher. Too many issues, perhaps. The old system had at least the virtue of having a topic for each section to which other things could be related. Now I *definitely* do not have a scheme. I am fumbling. But vaguely I am fumbling toward something. First, I'd have to say that I think your clusters a brilliant notion of teaching. But I think we might try to combine it with another base method. How about thinking along these lines? Redo all we now have *before* "theme," making the sections somewhat shorter and sharper, with some new material, and using material drawn from other people and commented on by us. *Then* for the theme section do an elaborate use of the cluster system. Here we would show how, in many different ways, with different themes, or with the same theme, poetry emerges. Playing this both ways. Say a cluster of the bird sort (subject cluster), or more than one such cluster, set against a cluster (or clusters) using same theme but using different subjects to dramatize theme. You see what I have in mind? This would give us, too, a fine problem for the poems in the pool. To make kinds of clusters and justify them, etc. This as a starter. To cut back on myself: we might postpone for this section, Theme, some of the more elaborate items from each of the earlier sections, for here they'd get fuller play, and in a context of the fuller sense of what a poem is. To cut back some: I have been thinking of the possibility of a new general introduction, before Section I. But I won't try now to describe it. Enough. Write me your response to this and [p. 2] don't take it that what I say is more than tentative. I am *sure*, however, that one way or another the cluster method should be the big show thing of our book. And let's try to get somebody assembling and xeroxing (1) analyses and discussions of poems that we might use to back up [our] own (and sometimes save us work), and (2) competing books for poetry courses. This means out of your hide, but I'll work like ten when I get back.

Best to both,
Red

[Handwritten] Looking back over this mammoth letter, I want to clarify one thing: *kinds* of clusters. (1.) Same subject—different themes, critiquing Bird cluster
(2.) Same theme—different subject. The use of *both* kinds and *variants* might be useful.

[OH]

Forest Road
Northford, Connecticut 06472
May 2, 1972

Dear Red,

We are back—arrived home three days ago—after an exhausting but highly interesting trip to Iran. I'll save an account of it until we can sit down together this fall with a bottle of Bourbon on the sidetable.

The occasion for this note is business: I'm seeing Dick and David this noon for a conference on the *Am. Lit.* book—possible cuts that the publishers want, and other matters. I'll give you a report in the next day or so.

I'm also seeing Leonard Conversi this afternoon to talk about the revision of *Understanding Poetry.* Did you get the sample that I sent you some weeks ago? What do you think of the suggestions for revision that I there proposed? Shall we go ahead on these lines or not? It's possible that you have already flashed the green light in a postcard or brief note [p. 2] that got lost in the shuffle of our frantic preparations to get away at the end of March. Anyway please confirm your OK if it's already been sent or apply the brakes if that application is called for. And do be frank.

We had a very sweet and thoughtful card from Rosanna just before we left. Love to her, to Eleanor, to Gabe, and to yourself—affectionate greetings in which Tinkie fervently joins.

Cleanth

P.S. David told me over the telephone yesterday that you had a bout with the flu. I hope that you have entirely recovered. We got through Persia without a trace of explorer's tummy or any tremors of the big earthquake of mid-April.

West Wardsboro, Vermont 05360
July 12, 1972

Dear Cleanth:

I have just talked to Lewis Simpson about the SR project. The LSU people now want to go directly into a book. Financially, as they figure it, a book would be deprived of a substantial part of its sale if the core essays were published in any magazine before the book. So it boils down to a choice between book and magazine. But they may be forgetting a hard fact of life, contributors to the book get no pay, those to the SR would be paid. I'll go back on this. But I hate to rock the boat. One argument for the book is that they would be happy to have a very long interview, while the magazine would have to be a moderate one, say 6,000 words. But of course the magazine, if it proceeded with the project, could use a reduced version of the interview, with the full one in the book. Anyway, I'll be going back to Simpson. This is, apparently, his project. For one reason, he is on the board of the Press.[1]

I have written a rough version of the introduction to the Fiction in AP-PROACH, and have made some provisional rearrangements of the selections. I'd like to have suggestions here, especially of new and currently fashionable people. One thought. It may be good to drop "Disorder and Early Sorrow" and "The Wife of Nashville." Reasons: I am not at all sure that the Mann piece means very much to present-day students. It is very long, and we might find a more exciting novelette to replace it, or two stories. Peter's piece has much the same arguments against it. But I should suggest getting one of his stories and a story from somebody else to take up the space. I'd hate to drop him as a contributor. I now think, too, of using Hawthorne's "Young Goodman Brown" for thematic purposes. And Bierce's "Chickamauga." I feel that we ought to have some fine older stories mixed in with new stuff (as we have been doing, but perhaps a little more now).

What about length of the revised version? Just drop the prose and see how it counts out? Or do we make it a little longer than that, enlarging both Fiction and Poetry, and adding a play to Drama? We need an idea about this. Maybe you all settled this in the conference. Maybe you even told me and I forget. Anyway, I don't know now.

. . . .

Love to both, from both,
Red

1. *The Possibilities of Order*, ed. Simpson, contains "A Conversation with Cleanth Brooks" (pp. 1–124), compiled by Warren—a record of conversations, or a long conversation, that they had over the period of half a century.

P.S. Am thinking about adding Jean Stafford, Donald Barthelme, Tolstoy (Ivan Illyich in place of Mann, much more teachable—and better). More to come.

West Wardsboro
August 10, 1972

Dear Cleanth:

Thank you for your long letter of August 8, which came yesterday, especially for the quote from Coons.

As for the stories, we see eye to eye on all of them. Let's settle for Barthelme's "Inland Uprising," Malamud's "Magic Barrel," and Borges' "South." On all of them you have given valuable comment that will be incorporated in my remarks. The funny skit-stories are from Perelman. Let's take "I Dreamt I Dwelt." But DeVries has a book of stories out in the fall, and we may get something there. I think we ought to buck up the comic a little, for we have a good start already.

Let's shift from "Clay" to "The Boarding-House," as you suggest. Can you have a xerox sent me so I can begin making my lay-out and comments?

Meanwhile, what do you think of a Tolstoi novelette (Ivan Illyich, for example) in place of Taylor's "Wife of Nashville"? (I am having Rosen send you xeroxes for new possibilities, shorter, by Peter.)

I recognize the difficulties for many students in Barthelme, Borges, and others in our list, but they may carry themselves with some help, and they do freshen things up. I hope you'll keep your eye out for some such items in the New Yorker, and elsewhere that might help us. I am now trying to get a new way in for fiction sections. I don't feel happy with the old.

. . . .

All the best to both.

As ever.
Red

West Wardsboro, Vermont, 05360
August 13, 1972

Dear Cleanth:

Before I get on with stories, I'll report, for the record, that I did decline the Charles Eliot Norton Professorship, even though it was for 1974–75. I just can't see that far ahead, even to the writing of the lectures. I simply haven't any burning idea. I guess I am having the classic reaction of gloom and blankness reported by all victims of my late indisposition. But anyway I don't have the thing hanging over me. So let's get on with the God-damned textbooks, and let the dead Future bury its half dead.

Speaking of such God-damned text books, I am having D. Rosen send you xeroxes of the following: 2 stories by Jean Stafford; 2 by Marcel Ayme; 2 by

Peter Taylor; 1 by Kafka; and 2 by F. O'Connor. {[At bottom of page] And 2 by Dylan Thomas.} I was struck by the mediocrity of most of Jean's stories, far under what I had anticipated. I read the whole book of the collected ones. But these may be useful. Or maybe I'm simply wrong in my literally post-jaundiced view. You may prefer another one by O'Connor (or others). But I think we can certainly use (for my purposes) one of the two by Thomas (see below)—brief, well written, aiming at an "emotion" not a mechanical turn. Very good of a special genre. PLEASE make critical comments on what you read. The things you said in your last letter will be very useful. I have filed the letter with the stories. As soon as I have the xeroxes back from Rose, I'll begin writing head notes and exercises. I think I have a new format for the section, new divisions, etc.

Best to you both,
Red

[OH]   Sept. 3, 1972

Dear Red,

High time that I got a letter to you. First, thanks for your comments on my Thoreau piece. Proof-reading has taken more time and occupied me longer that I had thought it would. {[At bottom of page] Much time was required also to go over the copy for "From Imagism to Symbolism." But it seems now in good shape and we have managed—David and I—to date all the poems—as the copy editor has requested—save one, on which we are still at work.} There were a good many tricky quotations that needed checking and now that the official text of *Walden* (CEAA) is at last out, I thought that I ought to read our selections back against it.

I'll turn over this Am. Lit. material tomorrow to David M. as well as a copy of the newly recovered Dreiser piece so that he can get the one to St. Martin's and the other to you. I'm not assuming that you will want to make any use of " 'I Find the Real American Tragedy' by Theodore Dreiser." But I'm sure that you will be interested in it and would like to have a look. (Please hang on to my magazine—the piece is really too long to xerox—and I'll recover it from you in due time.)

I got a good letter the other day from Jane Ross, of Holt Co. She seems genuinely to like the samples of the revised *U.P.* that I sent her. There is nothing specific that she says, however, worth scribbling down in this long-hand letter. But she has a few suggestions, does promise any help that she can give, etc. When I see David tomorrow I'll have him xerox the letter and send it on to you.

I'm ashamed to say that I have done nothing of late on the U.P. revision. The *Festschrift* articles (and other such matters) have really swallowed my time this summer. Fortunately, the last of them has been dispatched to the proper editor and I can address myself to more pressing matters. I mean to do so.

Tuesday, we drive down to the USIA-State Department meeting called to talk about plans for the 1976 celebration. Since all the other former Cultural Attachés (of university background) who have served at London, Paris, etc., are to be present, I felt that I [p. 2] had to put in an appearance. I have no wisdom to offer them—though I think that I have learned much about our literature from working on *Am. Lit.: The Makers and the Making*. Whether I can convince the official crowd of that fact is, of course, another matter. But I hope for the best and at the least I may learn something useful for the promotion of our book.

T. and I will drive to Washington and then on out to Airlie house, which is about fifty miles away in northern Virginia. It's a brief conference and we probably shall be back here in Northford by Friday evening—by Saturday, at the least.

Dick and his family apparently got away without incident last Friday. I got his back-up reading on Thoreau before he left and got your Melville reading into his hands via David.

I hope all goes well with the Warrens in Vermont. Come to think about it, in almost no time, you'll be headed home. Classes begin on Sept. 14, I am told.

All our best,
Cleanth

[At top of p. 1] P.S. We had intended to go to the meeting of the English Institute this past week-end. (It met this year in Cambridge, Mass.) But I canceled at the last minute. I simply couldn't find the time.

P.S. I was amused by Hugh's note on the trial and appreciate your letting me have notice of it. It has now gone into the waste-basket. No need to risk its being put on record for posterity.

P.S.S. It has occurred to me that at the end of Thoreau's "Civil Disobedience" essay, I have provided (by adding something from Austin Warren) *three* comments on it, two at least of which make some criticism—though filled with praise for Thoreau's zeal and sincerity and for the brilliance of his presentation. I've decided to keep *all* three, but if you have a copy of the Thoreau galleys still at hand, you might look them over. A word to David Milch would, I believe, be in time to cut out one of the three. Tinkie and I will be in Maryland and Virginia until Saturday, the 9th.

July 10, 1973

Dear Red,

Your card of the 3rd arrived yesterday. We were both glad to hear, for we wondered how you all had fared in the Vermont flood. I hope that your house and property took no damage.

I'll have "A Matter of Vocabulary" xeroxed and I'll hold the McPherson volume for your return. I've heard nothing more from the Albee *Zoo Story* permission. If I don't have an answer in the next day or so, I'll jog them.

So much for the *Approach.* Now for some notes on *UP.* I have finished a draft of the section on Metrics (III) and hope to get a copy to you shortly.

I have taken your suggestion on Imagery—namely, that we couldn't really bypass "Description" and get right off into the more difficult problems. So I have just finished remodeling Description and Circumstantial Detail (II) and am beginning work now on Imagery proper (V), which will get into the more intricate problems of metaphor and symbol. In II, I am attempting to move rather slowly from almost pure description up to symbolism and implications of attitude and theme. Section V will treat metaphor and simile and the more specially focused symbolizations with some comment on the relationship between metaphor and symbol and the difference between the two strategies involved.

Here follows a tentative table of contents for the new II.

Two Voices in the Meadow (Wilbur)
Pippa's Song (Browning)
Written in March (Wordsworth)
Cuttings (Roethke)
Cavalry Crossing a Ford (Whitman)
Inversnaid (Hopkins)
Go, Lovely Ros (Waller)
To Autumn (Keats)
Composed upon Westminster Bridge (Wordsworth)
Prelude (Eliot)
{[Handwritten] More poems could be added}

The titles given above will have fairly detailed discussions and analytic comments as well as questions.

Then there is to follow immediately what might be called Part 2 or Part B of II.

from The Place of Art (24 lines or so of descriptions of various landscapes) (Tennyson)
The Woodspurge (Rossetti)
The Geranium (Roethke)
Rocky Acres (Graves)
A Letter from the Caribbean (Howes, Barbara—in the Strand anthology)
The Yew in the Graveyard (Tennyson)
Yew-Trees (Wordsworth)
{[Handwritten] more poems could be added}

[p. 2] This Part 2 or Part B we'll append after each poem *only* 2 or 3 questions as an exercise. Analytic material for the poems now in UP or material to be devised for the fresh poems will be recast for the teacher (along with further questions that he may wish to put to his students) and printed in the Manual. This second part will really recapitulate the problems and discussions in Part 1, but it will put the student much more on his own and it will deal the big cards under the table to the instructor—if he wants to use them. This arrangement will actually allow the instructor eager to hurry on or whose class does not need extra exercises on the problems encountered at this point to choose only one or two poems from this part—or none at all.

I'll try to get on with a rough draft of the Manual material for this Section as remodeled so that you can see in some detail what I am attempting to do. If you feel it won't work or that it needs serious modification, you can then say so, knowing that I will not have made a serious investment of time in the experiment.

To summarize: I'll try to get you soon (a) a copy of this remodeled Section II (with the Manual material that applies to it); and (b) a draft of Section III (Metrics). Section IV (Tone), VI (Theme), and VII ("the Birds") can wait until I have heard from you or we can perhaps get together for a conference. For the immediate future I will have plenty to keep me busy with reworking I (along the lines of the remodeled II,—unless you have serious modifications to propose) and Section V (Imagery).

All the best to all three of you. I hope the summer goes well and that you can get some time for your own work. I regret the time you are having to spend on this UP revision.

Regards
Cleanth

P. S. We had dinner with the Wilders last night. He looks in much better health, and says he is. I gave him a copy of *Am. Lit.* in both our names.

West Wardsboro, Vermont 05360
August 16, 1973

NOTE: on page 1716 (Lanier) we give the date of the Centennial as 1886 not 1876. Are you in a position to catch this?

Dear Cleanth:

I have now read, with marked satisfaction, the batch of stuff you sent me on Eliot and the Southern section. A very few and very trivial comments are indicated on the enclosed sheets. (I have numbered the sheets in red for my comments.)

1. In the sentence for which I suggest a revision, I don't quite get the meaning of the original. Re: footnote: it strikes me [as] tactful to add Cash— whose title I forget—*Mind of the South*?

2. It was not only the Abolitionist attacks as such, it strikes me, that accounted for the Southern attitude—though they dramatized the issue.

3. Revision at top of sheet: go back to whole sentence beginning on sheet 2. It strikes me that the word *though* in the dependent clause is wrong. Is this the meaning? What about something like this: But it was not only by such restrictions that the South, with the economic underpinnings of its old order destroyed, was unable to share in the prosperity of the new national order; the whole cultural orientation that had been associated with the old economic system of the South worked against an easy adaptation to the new world of industrialism and finance capitalism—I see that this isn't quite what you had

meant to say, but thinking of the beginning of the paragraph with "cultural climate" I switch back to pick it up.

Lower down on sheet 3. I suggest a footnote on Sidney Lanier (if we have a base for it in the revised shorter edition), who in his blundering way suggested some such dialectic in the heart-brain nonsense. But this may be superfluous.

4. Check spell

5. line 3 from bottom. It strikes me that *simply* and *mere* repeat the same idea.

6. word missing at bottom

7. In the discussion of Faulkner and black psychology, perhaps Dilsey demands mention. Here, though she is not given inwardly, her place and her attitudes are, in a sense, the moral center of the book.

None of the above strikes me as important. Here it is for what it may be worth.

The family with Rosanna got back from Boston last night. All well.

Yours,
Red

Fairfield
October 23, 1973

Dear Cleanth:

I know it's none of my business, but I'll put the name of James Wright into the pot for teaching poetry at Yale—a term, year, or longer. I think that his best work is very fine and strong, he has had a lot of recognition lately, and he has had much experience in teaching. (Hunter now, I think.) But I do NOT know him, never laid eyes on him, and don't know what he is like personally. That could be learned, though.

Yrs,
Red

I've mentioned his name to Louis Martz, too.

167 Sunset Blvd.
Baton Rouge, La. 70808
[January 19, 1974]

Dear Red,

Tinkum tells me she has written to you all with an account of whatever modest adventures we have had; so I'll just say Greetings, and start right in with business. I'm well enough organized now with my classes, etc., to get down to work on *UP*.

During the past couple of days I've made a careful check through the Metrics section (III) that you turned over to me before I left Northford. It's a fine job, the best and most nearly complete that I know anywhere, and my only concern, which may be yours, is that it is so complete and so detailed that it may be somewhat outsized for a textbook that is to compete with *Sound and Sense*[1] and other such volumes. I am sending separately xerox copies of the pages in which I have attempted any substantial correction, expansion, or rewriting. I think it may be a waste of time to bother you with the more trivial changes that I have made.

I trust that you have by you a xerox copy of the last stage or that, lacking it, there is enough context in these pages that I am sending to make clear what I have done. If not, give me a ring and I'll get a full copy off to you by *3rd class, special handling,* which I have found gets [a] package to its destination almost as fast as airmail.

If you want to indicate changes on the pages I'm sending you, I'd suggest that you use red ink, so that your changes will show up readily. I don't think that the fairly brief changes that I've suggested will take very long for you to approve or revise. As soon as you have them ready, mail them to me here (home, not LSU). In the meantime we'll get started here with a re-typing of the entire Section III. If your pages do not come in before the retyping is finished, it might be best for you to send them to Holt directly; but on second thought, there might be some difficulty in their placing them in sequence since the pagination will be different after retyping.

Because Section III is so full and so coherent, I am strongly tempted to have [Holt] print it complete in the text. If we do so, we can include in the Manual some suggestions and directions about how it may be best used. For example, we may want to tell the instructor that, with some classes, he may want at the first go, to teach only certain sections and to postpone others until need or the proper occasion suggests itself to him. (We could indicate to him what we think some of the proper occasions would be.)

Another possibility would be to relegate a good deal of the material now in the Metrics section to a metrical appendix at the back of the book. Maybe nothing would be gained by this, but we might make the subject of metrics seem a little less formidable by presenting the student only a small dose first. If you decide—and I'm happy to leave the decision to you—that some of the more complicated material should be relegated to a later period of study, and that fact be signaled by putting it in a special Appendix, then you might consider the following parts for such relegation: the special treatment of anapestic, [p. 2] trochaic, and dactylic poems (pages 21 New–27 New); the discussion of the French forms, like the villanelle (pp. 49 New–49B New); perhaps some of the material under "The Music of Verse" (56 New—and on to the end of the whole section, including the long sections on stress verse and free verse). A less drastic cutting might simply remove one or two of these sections plus some of the poems embedded in Section III for discussion or exercises.

1. Laurence Perrine, a Southern Methodist University professor, was the author of the very successful *Literature: Structure, Sound, and Sense,* which Harcourt first published in 1956. Two textbooks that dominated the market in the 1960s were Perrine's anthology and James M. McCrimmon's *Writing with a Purpose.*

Yet with so thorough and complete a job done on metrics, and in view of the fact that Holt means to print a short version of our book later, it may be well to print the whole Section in the long version and trim it down *only in the shortened version*. In the short version, we would have several options: we might see that a copy of the long version of the book was given to the instructor on the occasion of his adoption of the short version for classroom use. We might also, in the Manual, suggest to the teacher a number of poems out of copyright that he could, at his discretion, mimeograph for class distribution in order to illustrate more special points.

Next week, I will be sending in more material to Holt. Miss Nolte there is apparently eager to see what the book is like, or may be like, and I shall send her a xerox of Section III, including such changes and modifications as I have made. I'll make it plain, however, that she is to regard that copy as merely provisional until you have communicated with her, indicating any further cuts or changes.

Now for some bad news. I was appalled to discover last night that after all the careful packing that I had tried to do, I failed to bring with me the comments and suggestions that you made, I believe on Dec. 19., on Sections IV and V. Notes on the Table of Contents of Sec. IV, I have now recovered, and will get right on to work at this. (I include these notes herewith.) I shall hope to send you within a week's time a copy of Sec. IV which will take into account the poems we decided to cut from my original draft of IV and the poems we decided to add, plus discussions and exercises.

The real disaster is with Section V. I well remember that you reorganized the whole beginning of V, moving from poems of mere description on up through indications of attitude and then of idea. But I cannot undertake to reproduce from memory what you had worked out with such careful articulation. The question that I want to put to you, therefore, is whether you have a copy of this material, or lacking that, notes on it—light or elaborate. If you do, please xerox them and send them and send me a copy at once.

If you don't have a copy of what you showed me on Dec. 19, the plan may be so clear in your mind as not to require too much time for you to name the poems in the opening sequence and indicate the main points to be made with reference to each poem. If you could do that, I believe I could make a fair reconstruction, filling out the scheme and rewriting it, and then sending it to you for your correction and retouching. I am indeed horrified at this lapse on my part and want to penalize you just as little as possible for something which was my fault. But I know that you are well aware that mishaps [p. 3] of this sort can occur when one is moving books and papers.

Unless you have preserved a copy of your reworking of the beginnings of V, or unless you could readily set down for me a scheme of what you did, then there seems only one other possibility, though that one is very hard on you, I fear. It would be for you to go to Northford (after getting in touch with our house-sitter, Wayne Harvey, so that he could open the book room for you) and make a search yourself for the missing mss. I hate to ask you to do this, and there may be an easier way—my phoning Harvey, for instance, telling him what to look for. But then I have visions of his failing to recognize the missing papers or of his getting the wrong version after all, and more consequent delay. David Milch might be able to do the search, but that would require your briefing him thoroughly. He is at least familiar with our modus operandi, our hand-writings, etc. There is a lot of paper stored in the various cartons in the bookroom. Perhaps the team of Warren and Milch would be the most efficient, if it were possible for you both to spare the time.

If you are willing to conduct the search, then the way to alert Wayne Harvey is to phone him at 484–2189. (Our telephone number has been put on a standby basis, so is of no use. His number was to be transferred to our house—whether it actually worked out that way, I'm not sure—in case of difficulty, information would have his.)

The bookroom is a mess, I fear. I remember using it for a general storage dump at the end. It's possible that the mss. are in clear sight on a table. Perhaps they are in one of the cartons on the floor. Certainly not in the big bookcases; just possibly in the small bookcases to your right as you enter. Bad as it is, I am presuming that you would rather make a search of the bookroom than start all over making revisions for Sec. V. I am truly sorry.

My work week here is short and class preparation is on the whole light. I hope therefore to push *UP* right ahead and send in sections of it to Holt during the next 2 or 3 weeks. They are obviously eager to see the book even in sections. But I shall make it plain that these submissions are provisional and that Miss Nolte must hear from you and take into account your corrections and comments before she accepts the text as final.

Has Leonard Conversi been in touch with you? Has he turned over to you the copies of the two poetry textbooks that I had asked him to buy for us? I haven't seen them. His telephone number is [. . .] his address, [. . .]. (I put down these numbers because you may not have them handy and they are hard to track down, since the phone is not in his name.)

I won't undertake to make any comments here on your new, long poem except to say that it is a very fine work indeed. Detailed comments on it will be coming in my next letter.

Tinkum joins in affection[ate] greeting to you and Eleanor and the children. At the moment Louisiana is not very inviting—fog, rain, unseasonably warm weather. But our yard is full of camellias. Wish you all could come see them.

Yours,
[Cleanth]

P.S. Most of the material in cartons in the bookroom is labeled, but there is, of course, the possibility that the missing material has been put in the wrong carton. No need of looking in file cabinets or drawers. However, there is nothing in the bookroom that is in any way confidential, so anyone is free to poke away.

February 26, 1974

Dear Cleanth:

First a report: I took our contract to Robert Morris, a lawyer, who has done work for me before, and whose specialty is literary law (he is a kinsman of the Wm. Morris of the old agency, and his firm was the legal branch of the Morris Agency for many years). He gave a quick report, which in substance is this: The one vol. edition must have a new contract (unless of course SM gives us what we want without it); this legal position hinges on the distinction between "edition" and "revision." For revision our contract is clear; for edition, no. But for the four-way split, the contract is not legally clear, and if we find need to fight here, we probably end up in arbitration. On the practical side the situation, as we now see it, is this: The sales are for the moment good, something around 13,000 *sets*, this as of January 31. SM expects something around or over 15,000 by the end of February. This, given the late start, is very good, about $14,000 each gross, that is before deduction for advances (different in each case) and permission costs. The one vol. comes out in the late spring, in hard cover, over $12 the vol., with a much higher take per vol. than either in the first edition. THIS is the important thing: the costs for both the one vol. and the 4-vol. split of the big edition come to only $16,000 with SM, by their old ratio paying 28%. There would be no use in having a fight for a gain of a few hundred dollars each, to push their ratio up to, say, 35%. BUT in our conference next week with TOM we'll make it clear that we aren't establishing a precedent for the future. The only thing good about the work of your amateur friends is that Tom B is an amateur too. What we hope for is this: to stand firm and final on the notion that the 2 vol. must be calculated for royalty as a unit, that the 1 vol. payments cannot be held up to clear the 2 vol. and so on with the 4 vol. Each a unit for royalty calculation.

Now to UP. I have been going over and over Section IV and find it splendid. You will see my sparse comments, for what they are worth. NOTE that I have stuck in a poem by Gwendolyn Brooks (black, female) in this section. (I am putting in floating poems by Bogan and Rukeyser to be placed where you think best to beef up the womanly stuff.) I am also sending in a day or two a beautiful poem by John Wheelwright to be placed somewhere—a novelty— (he's never anthologized).

Enclosed here is the Section (number?) on poets in this past decade, that is, those who have made their basic contributions of fame tally. (John Berryman is here, but you might think best to push him back earlier; the fame is latterly but he is rather in the years and dead. Use your judgment here.) Without him in this section we have 30 poets, and I'm rather pleased with the general quality. I hope you are. Anyway, I did break my back on this, not the kind of backbreaking you are engaged in, but I did my best.

I have a few new pieces to stick in the Approach too. But this is provisional. Next week David M has a list of all permission costs and I'll send you the info then.

Nothing yet definite about the contract with P[rentice-]H[all]. But any squeak from them and back I go to Robert Morris.

Eleanor's play at the Cabaret was fine!

Love to both,
Red

[OH]   167 Sunset Blvd.
                                                Baton Rouge, La. 70808
                                                          March 29, 1974

Dear Red,

I hope that I have timed this letter right so as to catch you in Fairfield before you all depart for Rome.

I hope that all goes well with your Jefferson lectures.[1] I have utter confidence that it will though I can imagine that the last months have been harried ones—what with all the other things that you have had to do including the problems of the *Approach* that you have had to work out for both of us. My last letters from Prentice-Hall would suppose that there never was any intention of discarding the *Approach*. The letters sent to me indicate that the book has all along been scheduled for next year and that its production goes on apace.

The one report of a reader that I have seen is laudatory but not very impressive with regard to positive suggestions. But I'll go over it more leisurely this week—with special reference to the drama section.

I did get all the UP suggestions, additions, and corrections that you sent in. After checking they have all gone in now to Holt: the Introduction, Sections I–VII, and this morning, the appendix on Parodies. I shall hope to get in VIII and the last sections on Poems for Study next week. I shall have questions about the latter items but no need to worry you about them now. Plenty of time for discussion about just what will be added and [p. 2] whether to have two sections of Poems for Study or only one when the Jefferson lectures are past. (Remember that these Poems for Study have no Exercises or Discussions [except for what we may put in the manual].) Therefore, my indication to Holt of about how many poems will be involved and an estimate of the number of pages required will be sufficient at this time to enable them to speculate about the length of the full edition.

The handsome invitation to the Jefferson lectures has arrived and we have been much tempted. It would be fun and we would like to be present on so fine an occasion. But practicality has raised its ugly head—as it usually does. The L.S.U. term has been—through no fault of L.S.U.—more of a ratrace than a frolic. I shall be hard pressed to get everything finished and to return to Northford—as we hope to do—fairly early in May. In fact, the Lectures come just on the eve of the examination period here. So we've reluctantly sent in our

1. Warren delivered the Third Annual Jefferson Lectures in the Humanities in May 1974. His lectures were published as *Democracy and Poetry* by Harvard University Press in July 1975.

regrets, conscious that the loss is ours and that we will have missed something very fine.

I had a recent letter from a very old woman (Roman Catholic) that contains a heart-felt appreciation of your poetry. She writes: "I suppose poetry has been almost forced into becoming a religion by the defection of religion. What bothers me is that there's far more 'transcendence' (and that's a dicey word to use) in almost any of Warren's poems than in the trash we now have in the ICEL [the recently translated into English] Mass and other messed-about services. Take 'Walk by Moonlight' or that spooky new one about Christmas."[2]

Coming from me, you will not feel that there the grim wolf with piety paw is after you. Anyway, I pass it on to you as a real tribute to the power of your poetry and what it gives to people who are indeed the hungry sheep who are cornfed and look up to the kind of junk that my own church and the R.C.C. are handing out—synthetic fodder.

T. joins in love to all the Warrens. Have a good time in Rome.

Cleanth

Baton Rouge
May 9, 1974

Dear Red,

I hope that the letter I wrote hoping to catch you in Fairfield before you left for Italy did so. It conveyed little news, but mostly our confidence in the success of your big lectures and our deep regret that we decided it was simply impractical for us to try to be present. But it must have been a great event, one that filled all of your friends with pride, and I am eager to see the text of the lectures.

We are in the course of preparation for leaving. I have given my last examination, and if all goes well we hope to set out for Conn. on Monday (May 13) or Tuesday; and expect to make it back to Northford in about 4 days, though driving regulations, gas, etc. may slow us down. I hope we'll be able to get together very shortly, for we have many things to talk with you and Eleanor about, and of course there will be the nagging business of *U.P.*, with a number of problems still to be settled.

When this letter reaches you Harriet Nolte will have either the last sections of the book in complete text, or at least indications of what will be in them.

. . . .

She has also been told that we are retaining Sec. XI (How Poems come about) which is to be taken pretty well as it stands from the 3rd edition; an Appendix of parodies, which she already has; and the Glossary—basically as it stands, but with certain modifications entailed by our new plan and with the page references changed.

2. Possibly a reference to "The Natural History of a Vision," *Atlantic Monthly*, December 1973, pp. 84–90, published as "I Am Dreaming of a White Christmas: The Natural History of a Vision" in *Selected Poems, 1923–1975* (January 1977).

I am sending you under separate cover the Readers' Reports sent by my Miss Nolte a few days ago. You will note that they cover only Sections I through IV. They seem to me unusually stupid and of not much help to us. One of the readers spends most of his time pointing out typographical errors—a task not very useful for us at this juncture. He also—unless I have mixed him with another Reader—begins by confessing that he doesn't like the Brooks-Warren approach anyway. The second Reader takes the first four sections to be the entire book, etc. This is not to say, of course, that even stupid reports can't be helpful to us. They can at least show what some of the problems are, and brace us to prepare a counter-offensive against some of the recurrent prejudices and misunderstandings. One bright [p. 2] spot in the reports is that they seem to like the sample of the Manual and its tone.

I hope before I get away to be able to write up a brief comment on the reports, which I shall send to you for your inspection and correction before it goes on to Miss N. I intend to be tactful and civil, but it may be just as well that you know exactly what I am writing to her on the subject. You can either absorb my report into your own or, if you prefer, send it in along with your own report.

A couple of days ago Miss Mary Klein of Holt telephoned to ask that I send in the Author's Questionnaire. I reminded her that this is the fourth edition of a book long published by Holt and that there is abundant material on us in the Holt office, and that *Who's Who in America* was pretty well up to date on both of us. But I took occasion to tell her that I was much concerned about the problem of salesmanship for this edition. I indicated that I was well aware that a great many stereotypes had been built up about *U.P.* and that there were prejudgments that would have to be overcome or circumvented. In short, I suggested that this edition might require a rather special presentation. I even suggested that our fourth edition might have marketing problems of its own that were just as special as those for our first edition back in 1938.

I promised her some notes on this problem within the next 2 or 3 days and indicated that I would be happy to come in to N.Y. to talk to salesmen if this would be helpful. I told her in any case I would be back in Conn. by the end of next week and that you and I, both well aware of the special problems concerning this edition, would certainly be happy to cooperate in helping Holt market the book.

She seemed to be an intelligent enough woman to catch the point. Incidentally, the Readers' Reports, which I had fresh in my mind as I talked to her, will indicate to you some of the things that we should need to do if the book is to get a fair reading by the young instructors. I am really quite sanguine about what can be done if Holt can be given a little direction. I told Miss Klein that this was the best textbook that you and I had ever put together.

We look forward to seeing all the Warrens in the next few days.

Yours,
Cleanth

. . . .

West Wardsboro, Vermont 05360
July 13, 1974

Dear Cleanth:

Action on the *Approach* Front. Robb Reavill has just been here with the various reports from the cast-off, printers, etc. We must cut, they say, 128,000 words to be competitive. Otherwise we can't compete in price with—guess who!—the Perrine book recently out which sells for $11.00. But this is not as bad—128,000 words—as it sounds. First, after sitting down with her and actually working through the fiction section, I convinced her that we can't cut under 52,000 words there. Since they think the poetry section is fine and can take very little cutting, very little that would mean anything in space, that leaves drama. The only thing that can, it seems offhand, be cut is the Camus play, and some of the discussion (reduced) of Ionesco; we would stand around 60,000 over all. But it is not certain that the need for 128,000 to be cut is made before or after the dropping of the second story by Flannery O'Connor and "The Boarding House." So the 60,000 may be actually 70,000. Even if those items had already been discounted we could still do enough sorting of our discussions to come easily down to 64,000. But I say 64,000 because they have to deal in units of 64,000 words—i.e., 64 pages, as the thing is now set up. Robb R is going back to NYC and try to work out a 64,000 cut with the PH people, and a price at $11.95—for she argues that though the Perrine is out at less, they will have to go up right away with the next printing on account of booming paper costs and that with their 1400 pages they are stuck, while we with approximately 900 will have a little flexibility and will probably underset them a little after the first batch of theirs is sold out.

If 64,000 words out will not do (I hadn't said that their new format calls for a little over 1000 words per page and is good-looking), *maybe* they can get a press that will deal in units of 32,000 sheets in conjunction with 64,000-sheet units. In that case, we could by a lot of sweating make 96,000 words. But since they have a deal with an English company to do the printing she can't yet be sure of the 96,000 words cut as feasible. The English press is the only one, she says that will *guarantee* to give books March 1. (What about English labor, though? It's a nest of strikes, etc.)

That's the way it stands.

For the copy-editing, especially of poetry, they have hired a man who, on the stuff I have seen, seems very good and intelligent. He lives two hours from here, over in NY. The idea is to proceed, win lose or draw, with the cuts I now give in fiction, which provides enough material to get the presses rolling (the copy editor has already done final work on the fiction). This will give us time to think about other cuts if needed. This coming yesterday I'll have final and hard word on the cuts, so we can know exactly where we stand. But we are supposed to have a meeting with the copy editor the first of August to fix the next batch of material for delivery. Robb proposes that the editor come from NY (state) and that you come from Connecticut to meet here to harden up the thing in one long session that might, of course, spill over into a second day. I hear in a day or two from copy editor with proposed dates. Then I'll submit them to you. By the way, the copy editor is an old Vanderbilt product and apparently very bright. You and I presumably met him at the Fugitive reunion in 1956.[1]

Here are the stories I cut today: Hardy, Caroline Gordon (or we may cut [p. 2.] Powers if that seems a better bet—the argument for it is that we have a discussion of it all worked out), Ring Lardner, Bunin, de Maupassant (La Mere), Borges, George Milburn, Bellow, O'Connor (a Good Man). I am stuck here with balancing several considerations (what place does a story have pedagogically? What is ethnic value? What is advertising value of name? What is merit of story?). All I can say is under pressure I have done the best I could. But, as I suggest above, one option may be left open until I hear from you: would you prefer to cut Bowers and keep Gordon even with the work on a discussion? And, again, would you prefer to cut Pirandello (Jar) and keep Lardner? Now I am about to swing back to keeping Haircut. It does give a beautiful, simple example of irony in point of view, and it is possible that The Jar does have rather little appeal for the ordinary student—too foreign. Also we do have a useful (I hope) discussion of Haircut. Let me hear from you right away on these points.

The copy editor has raised some points with Drama. In the first section of Drama, our title is Tragedy and Comedy. There are no comedies. We have some time for study here. So I leave this question with you. Meanwhile, I'll be thinking about it too. Also, the copy editor says that as now set up the section seems to suggest that the only kinds of drama in the world are the standard "tragedies" of the first part, and then the "Absurd."

Enough for now. But I want to say that I begin to feel that these people are at least serious about making money. They have schedules and work at them, and Robb seems very able, ditto copy editor. I have just heard from Brauer. I did send the lawyer's letter, and she reports that she has sent it to their legal department and has as yet no response. I also wrote her that we'd better settle the contract for Understanding Fiction now rather than later. Ditto for that.

I have asked for a copy of the Perrine book. Maybe some hint there about the drama section.

Love to both,
Red

[OH]   Lieber College
                                               U of South Carolina
                                               Columbia, S.C. 29208
                                                   Feb. 2 [1975]

Dear Red,

I enclose a copy of a fan letter and some suggestions from the fan for addition or corrections. We had noticed already the *Thanatopsis* <garbling>.

---

1. For more on that reunion see Rob Roy Purdy, *Fugitives' Reunion: Conversations at Vanderbilt, May 3–5, 1956* (Nashville: Vanderbilt University Press, 1959).

I thought that it had been corrected. At any rate I'll check to see that it has been.[1]

I've sent a copy of the enclosed letter to Dick to see whether anything needs doing about Franklin's *Autobiography*. Since I haven't a copy of *Am. Lit* by me, I don't know whether the Emerson question is one cited by you or Dick, but you'd probably like to see the letter anyhow.

T. and I have finished the B-W interview and we shall be sending a copy to Lewis Simpson on Tuesday. I owe you many thanks for the hours you put in on it.

T. has checked through the *U.P.* material as far as [p. 2] we can go at this point. When Miss Nolte sends the "reviewers'" suggested revisions, we'll get right at them and get them off to you, probably section by section so that you won't be delayed.

T. joins me in affectionate greetings to
you and Eleanor,
Cleanth

2495 Redding Road
Fairfield, Connecticut 06430
February 12, 1975

Dear Cleanth:

Just to assure you that I live, breathe, move, move eyeballs, and have my being, and am busy with UP. I am up to date on my reading of your stuff. All to the good. I am making little nagging changes here and there—very few—and am adding a few poems, mostly for tactical reasons.

The only thing now is to be sure that when you come to Metrics you insert in proper place your stuff on Danny Deever etc. and dipodic verse.

No news, we were on the way to NYC today for a 2-day stay for Eleanor's massed interviews about her books, and got snowed out on the road, six inches now.[1] We limped home, and had to abandon ship at a filling station two miles from home and get carried on by gas station's Jeep. We try again tomorrow, the storm now being over. Have a nice warm blossomy time in SC!

Love to both,
Red

2495 Redding Road
Fairfield, Connecticut 06430
[March 1975]

Dear Cleanth:

Just a word to say that I have just this afternoon finished my first review and work for the UP. I take it in Friday morning to Nolte.

1. The "fan" letter was from Hugh J. Dawson of the University of San Francisco, dated December 26, 1974. He also complimented Brooks on his Housman lecture at the Library of Congress in the spring of 1959.

1. The reference is to Eleanor Clark's *Dr. Heart: A Novella and Other Stories* (New York: Pantheon Books, 1974).

I enclose my letter to Bly, the shit-heel. I hope I have puzzled him a little bit.[1]

Love to both!

In haste
Red

West Wardsboro, Vermont 05360
March 25, 1975

Dear Cleanth:

Long silence—at least from this end.

I have talked today with Miss (Ms?) Pamela Forcey, of Holt, who will be doing our book from the mechanical side. You have had her letter (a copy of which came to me), and know what that says. Here are a few things not in her letter;

(1) The design and cast-off will be ready before April 15, time enough to let us cut or adapt as required.

(2) Proofs by early August, all by end of September—galleys, that is.

(3) I am seeing that Milch gets the permissions to her now. A letter out in this mail.

These dates work out well enough for me. I'll be in Fairfield until June 20, then Vermont, and available. But we half-way plan to go to Europe (perhaps Poland, then Italy) in October. Gabe has worked out his arrangements for admission to the school in Rome that will allow him junior credit at Amherst (or so it seems now) and has been accepted, too, by the sculptor whom we admire so much with whom he wants to do some private work. We won't be in Rome hanging over him, but in Venice, in striking distance for visits, and for a Christmas vacation in the Alps (I wonder why) together. Presumably back home in January.

Immediate pressures are off me. That is, I have my Harvard Press stuff done, and now am only concerned with my private whimsies, which I can adjust to the UP schedule. Since Christmas I have had a little burst of poems, the last of which (I've been on it for months) I now enclose—full well knowing that you are so deep in your own work and obligations that you haven't time even to extend a helping. But a finger would be appreciated. I don't know what I've got here, and am still revising a lot. But I feel the need for a human eye. Also, since coming to Vermont, I've been every morning back at my novel. (NO—I'll not bother you with this, now or later, I promise.) I'm two

---

1. Robert Bly had taken offense at David Milch's addressing him as "Mister Bly." Warren's March 5, 1975, letter to Bly offering an explanation and apologies for Milch is a paradigm of manners and courtesy. Brooks and Warren had asked permission to include Bly's poem "Hunting Pheasants in a Cornfield" in their revision of *Understanding Poetry*. Apparently Bly did not give permission to reprint his poem. In a 1978 interview with Wayne Dodd, Bly stated that he had started the magazine *The Fifties* "precisely to attack Allen Tate's and Robert Penn Warren's view of poetry" (*American Poetry: Wildness and Domesticity*, by Robert Bly [New York: Harper and Row, 1990], 308).

thirds through the first draft, and like it so far, but the next chapter makes or breaks it, and I'm very uncertain, blind, and groping there.[1]

My two little reading tours (five days each) are over. Very profitable but tiring, and my God, how the sound of one's own voice gets through to one. All I wanted was silence when I got home. I don't know that I'll do it again— unless the economy gets even worse, or our text books do miserably. Which is possible.

Back to *UP*. Miss Forcey and I will be getting together for some face to face as soon as the cast-off is done, and you [p. 2] have let me know how the xerox you now received looks to you. And this brings up a question: It seems that we have never once taken up the matter of the work of the individual poet in contrast to the individual poem. Even if we don't do a section, as in *An Approach*, we might do something about this? In the book or in the *Manual*? Or something in the book for a base, and a good deal in the *Manual*? Be thinking this over.

When do you all get back here? I am going to be at home almost always till June 20, but am in Cambridge or Boston three times in May, for a night each time.

We have had a fine time up here. Decent weather for skiing and walking, Rosanna here for a week or so, Gabe still here but back to Amherst to do some work before school opens. Both in top shape and very tender with their aged and infirm parents.

We'd love to know how life treats you all.

Our love to both,
Yrs,
Red

PS. I have just heard that Jim Dickey is ill and hospitalized. Let me know about this, please.

[Handwritten beneath P.S.] On my jaunt I was in both S.C. and N.C. People just like Columbia last year. What a joy!

[OH]
Southern Studies Program
Lieber College
University of South Carolina
Columbia, SC 29208
April 3, 1975

Dear Red,

It's pleasant to have your letter of March 25 and the poem. Also: the new number of *The Georgia Review* has just arrived and I am looking forward to a careful reading of your contribution there.[1] First, however, I'll take up the

1. *A Place to Come To*, Warren's tenth and last novel, was published March 1977 in a printing of 50,000 copies.

1. "Ballad of a Sweet Dream of Peace: A Charade for Easter," with music by Alexei Haieff, *Georgia Review* 29 (spring 1975): 5–36.

U.P. stuff. Holt sent me a xerox of the present typescript the other day. It looks good but alarmingly large. I hope that we will not be forced to cut too much— or that as an alternative, Holt will be able to see its way to a complete *and* a reduced edition. I await the results of the cast off with fear and trembling.

As for the matter of a special treatment of the work of one author: I'm in favor for handling this in the manual. I hate to risk delaying the main edition by additions so late in the day and, besides, it is already bursting at the seams. I think I can devise this summer something acceptable for the Manual. I've checked over the table of contents and have added up the number of poems written by one author—not a complete list, to be sure, but one that covers the obvious candidates for this treatment.

The best prospects come out this way: Auden, 5 poems
                           Tennyson, 10 poems (or parts of poems)
                           Hardy, 5 poems
                           Frost, 6 poems
                           Wordsworth, 5 poems

I've checked over the poems that we have by these authors and they are sufficiently representative to allow for the kind of presentation that we are after. The case against using Frost is that we have already treated him in this fashion in [p. 2] the *Approach;* so have we treated Keats in the *Approach,* though he is a good candidate otherwise and we have 5 excellent poems by him in the new *U.P.*

There are still other possibilities. Eliot with 3 items (though one is *The Waste Land*) and Yeats, 4 items (though one of the 4 is a long suite of poems).

What do you think? I could do one, two, or three or more authors in the Manual without, I believe, too much trouble. Let me know, if you approve of such a plan and let me know your choice of the poets—one or more. (One advantage of putting the whole apparatus for the focus on one author in the Manual will be to provide the instructor with a little bag of tricks that he could pass off as his very own.)

We've just come back from two days in Savannah, Ga., where we saw some very fine old houses and a couple of very old plantations. A day or so before the Savannah trip we were on one of the South Carolina sea islands for a day and a night—there is a beautiful unlittered beach that stretches for miles and miles. Now it behooves me to get very hard to work to make up for these two holidays.

I don't view the prospect of getting back to work as a grim one. I'm as lazy as the next man, but what I am doing, both in reading and writing, at the present time is highly interesting. My problem is simply needing a few more hours in the day; but that is a common human failing, I've come to believe.

We expect to come back to Connecticut in early May and stay home the rest of the year. I shall be in Oxford, Miss., for the first week in August. Whether we will get to Europe this fall remains to be seen. At the moment, we have no plans. But we will be again somewhere in the South for the spring term of 1976.

There were notices in the local paper of your reading at <Coker> College. If we had heard in time, we would have been tempted to go. I'm glad that you found the [p. 3] company pleasant. One does get tired of hearing his own voice. (I gave three lectures on one day on my Virginia Circuit riding in February, and so I know.) But I know that your audiences were given great pleasure by your presence and by hearing your voice.

I like very much indeed "Old Nigger" etc. I think the final section is superb. It repeats one of your big themes but does so in its own way and with a special richness of tonality. Indeed, this section represents you at your very best.[2]

The preceding sections of the poem are vintage Warren. I don't quite connect up the first section of the poem with what follows—but that is probably simply my own density—my difficulty in connecting the nameless dancer with the rest of the experience.

I'm very much interested in the news that the novel is going ahead. I do want to see it. God knows I've spent enough time for the last fifty years reading student papers. From now on I want to spend my eyesight on something more rewarding and something that means more to me. So do let me see what you have done, either sending it here or letting me have it when I return, early next month.

I've not seen Jim Dickey yet—no fault of his—dates simply haven't worked out. But Tink has spoken several times over the telephone to Maxine. Both are well and thriving.

T. joins me in love to Eleanor and Rosie-posie and Gabe and you.

Cleanth

2495 Redding Road
Fairfield, Connecticut 06430
April 5, 1975

Dear Cleanth:

It was fine to hear your voice and to know that all goes well with Brookses. We want to see you all, so hurry on.

A little business. I enclose a poem by Thomas Hood, which we may find useful: "Ode: Autumn." My notion is that if this is paired with Keats' poem, that contrast would be pedagogically very useful. Hood presumably (I'll check into this and some other background) rewrote Keats, and did a foul job of it, too. It turns out to be a pretty good lesson in how NOT to write a poem.

But there are problems. We have Keats in Section II (Description, Imagery, etc.) and not enough background has been established to make much of the contrast. The only thing I can think of (assuming you think the thing worth

2. This poem was subsequently published as "Old Nigger on One-Mule Cart Encountered Late at Night When Driving Home from Party in the Back Country," *New Yorker,* December 8, 1975, pp. 46–47.

doing at all) is to insert Hood after Keats, and there give an Exercise going as far as possible under the circumstances (the mere fact of the pairing may be useful for a teacher even); and then, later on, in the big section on Analogical Language, *after* the ref to Meter, etc., has been given, a ref which puts the student on the track of verbal texture, time, etc., and would prepare for a fuller contrast of the two poems. In Supplemental Poems of Section IV, then? As a ref tied to another poem, or even in Meter, Ap. B? Give me your notion on this, and if you think well of the idea, I'll write it up.

It also strikes me that we might add another female or two. Louise Glück (highly admired by [Stanley] Kunitz, [Richard] Howard, et al.) and Eleanor Taylor, who is getting a reputation and is greatly admired by Jarrell. I am enclosing my picks for these two. We might, too, get a couple of little poems by contemporary American Indians, just out of avarice.

I have done more work on "Old Nigger," but your letter and criticism has not yet come. Anyway, I won't bother you again about this until I am surer— if ever—of it. By the way, R[andom] H[ouse] is issuing in 1976 (early) a big Selected of my things, and I'll be at you for some advice, and let you damn my soul for it, too.

My flu is better. I am sitting up today, and moving about.

Our best to both! Yrs,
Red

University of South Carolina
Southern Studies Program
Columbia, S.C. 29208
April 8, 1975

Dear Red,

I've been thinking over the matter of having a section or sections on the poet's work as a whole. My present feeling is that this can be best handled in the Manual, where we can set up for the instructor one, two, or three such sections with suggested exercises and teaching strategies, and even suggest how he may devise a half-dozen more if he likes the idea.

I don't see the need of providing a "base" in the text, though I enclose an effort at providing additional exercises which point toward this kind of study. These that I include (or others like them) wouldn't take up much room and could hardly do any harm. I think the job could be better done in the Manual, however, and would not be at the cost of adding another dozen pages to the text itself—already crammed to the limit.

As for letting people know that our new edition does have this feature, we don't really need a *base* in the text itself. For the promotion of the book could easily make plain to the only people who need to know—i.e., the instructors— that full provision has been made for the study of groups of poems by one author in terms of his characteristic manner and his characteristic themes. But see what you think of the several exercises I enclose.

I also enclose a rewriting of the discussion of Kipling's "Recessional." I hope I've made the account clearer and more compact.

I've nearly got through the xeroxed copy of UP. It looks good to me, though I am making a few minor changes here and there, primarily adjustments required because of our having dropped certain poems. A copy of these changes will be in the mails for you in the next day or so.

All goes well here. The rest of the week will be rather hectic with a Faulkner conference going full blast. When that's over we'll be ready to start preliminary packing for our trip back, which we now expect will begin on the first of May. How time flies!

T. joins me in affectionate greeting to you both.

Cleanth

2495 Redding Road
Fairfield, Connecticut 06430
April 11, 1975

Dear Cleanth:

I have your letter of April 8. I agree with you about the use of the idea of the "whole poet" in the Manual, not in text. Just so it is strongly emphasized in Manual so it can be "promoted."

I have been working at the big xerox of UP, and make some headway. Which brings up a few questions:

(1) Did I send you copies of a poem by Eleanor Ross Taylor and Louise Glück for inclusion in Section VIII. Eleanor Taylor has been getting a good deal of attention lately and she is better than most of the current ladies. Glück, just out, is getting a hand from responsible people. I must have sent these, for carbons of both are missing. Anyway, no immediate harm done. I am sending copies to Nolte to add to the text for the cast-off. We can make final decision later.

(2) I enclose here a very beautiful poem by C. Aiken, which fits perfectly into Section II. I enclose Exercises, too, and page indicated. Of course, this is for final discussion.

(3) I have just seen some very good poems by the only American Indian of any reputation, N. Scott Momaday. I'll get his books Monday and see if something might be useful for Section VIII. It might buck our "minority" group without sacrificing standards.

About the poem. I've been rewriting, and don't yet feel it's final. But about the first stanza: The "nameless" dancer—merely "flesh," merely desire, etc., is supposed to be set against the "name" clutched like a flower or toy in the last few lines. The poem is "namelessness" to "name." But clearly I'm not getting it over. I'll be seeing what I can do.

I have been in bed for almost two weeks with a nasty flu plus antibiotic poisoning. Yesterday the first day really up in NYC for a sort of birthday party. A little groggy today. You and Tinkie were missed, but I don't think you missed much.

Love to both, hurry home—
Red

PS. I also sent you Hood's "Ode: Autumn" with a question about tying it some way to Keats' "Autumn."

2495 Redding Road
Fairfield, Connecticut 06430
April 20, 1975

Dear Cleanth:

I have had a note from Lewis Simpson saying that all is in order for the book about CB. He says he is "high" on the interview, and that others (outsiders) are, too. It does occur to me, however, that one question certain readers are going to look for is what you would make of slavery (and the race question in general) in the context of Christianity. Would you want to speak to this point in the interview?

Or maybe, I have asked this before—my memory is getting so bad.

We look forward to seeing Brookses!

Yours,
Red

July 23, 1975

Dear Cleanth:

Here are the sheets of the new galleys on which I have any comment. I presume that you will send the Master Copy on in to Pam.

Here also are two new poems, contemporary, by Indians (I spotted a new anthology and got a copy, just out); I believe that these are among the best in the book, certainly among the best <short> ones.[1] If there is space, what about using them to buck up our "minority" showing? I am sending copies direct to Forcey to hold.

All the best!

Yrs,
Red

[OH]
West Wardsboro, Vermont 05360
August 28, 1975

Dear Cleanth,

This strikes me as really helpful and beautifully toned for the occasion— really splendid. I am anxious to see the next installment.

---

1. Warren sent copies of Leslie Marmon Silko's "Love Poem" and Charles Ballard's "Sand Creek."

Under separate cover I am sending my blundering and somewhat inflated version of the Preface (& a copy to Pam Forcey, who will return us a critique). I have thought better at this stage not to try to compress matters to the limit but, rather, to offer all the material possible.

Ever yours
[Red]

P.S. I have made various little notes and suggestions, but do look at your page 35 (re "Hell Gate"). I don't believe the "dark conductor" is a demon, but Satan himself. In support of this view, turn to lines 55–58 and 65–86. Here there is no report of Satan's appearing from within. [p. 2] Hell & all the focus of attention is outward toward the approaching pair. In 65–67, Ned is certainly left looking rational (recognizing his friend—& Satan). In the passage 80–86 the scene is of the encounter on the drawbridge, < >. And why not have Satan, the tempter who does, after all, get around a lot & talks to us all, do the escorting? *Well?*

[Twelve pages follow of suggested changes and alterations in Warren's recognizable, but barely legible, scrawl.]

"Fonte ai Frati"
50020 Panzano in Chianti
(Firenze) Italy
December 1, 1975

Dear Cleanth:

Even if this reaches you about Christmas it isn't intended as a Christmas present, just one of my thousands of little and big nags over the years. Perhaps by the [time] I see you—we'll be with you and Tinkie in early January—you'll have some words to utter of helpfulness if not cheer.

John's house is a nice place to be but would be a little better if he had a better plumber or didn't get conned. Certainly he had organized the countryside to ply us with food and drink and English accents. Several of E's old friends turned up in the general neighborhood having wine-making establishments here on their places, and so we have had a good dose of vendemmia as well as of the aged products thereof. The country is beautiful, very wild right here, and we do a certain amount of walking when we aren't over-run by boar hunters, this being open season. {[Handwritten in left margin] Here windows aren't frosted!}

Gabe is deliriously happy at Rome. The sculpture teacher is said to [handwritten from this point on] be one of the best foreign Americans. Gabe says he is a wonderful and imaginative teacher. He is now working in stone and feels more into <cue>. He was here for Thanksgiving, spent most of the term hammering on a 45-pd rock he had brought with him on the train in ropes.

[p. 2] E. is busy at something she won't talk about. I've done one rewrite on my novel but won't touch it again until I've seen Albert's response to this.

We see the Lewises every week or so in Florence, where they are happily situated.[1] He is engaged in the pleasant business of "cooking" up Tuscany—which we have been doing too—seeing some winter spots—sometimes together.

We leave here December 15 for Rome, where I'll give another reading & we'll see two gatherings of friends before going to the mountains to be joined by Rosanna.

Then home.

Our love to you both.

As ever,
Red

West Wardsboro, Vt. 05360
July 25, 1976

Dear Cleanth:

I have finished the MS, ready for xeroxing except for the insertion of the story you suggested—which could be stuck in plot or character—or even theme. But I hear from David that he has another operation tomorrow (two new moles have turned up as malignant). So I hold the MS here until I hear whether he can take charge of the very onerous job of getting five copies made and checked. This is a matter of a day or two of delay. If he can't do it, I think we ought to hire somebody (very responsible—David might know such a guy) to take over for that particular task. As for us, we badly need a general discussion with the publishers at this stage. I'll write Marilyn and bring her up to date.

It was great to see you, and I can't tell you how much it really meant to Gabriel. He keeps coming back to the topic—even a boy as close-mouthed as he generally is.

I stick in a poem I've been working at for several weeks. Cross your heart you'll speak the truth.

Love to you both.

As ever,
Red

[OH]   Forest Road
Northford, Connecticut 06472
3 August 1976

Dear Red,

I like your poem, "Dreams of a Dream," very much indeed.[1] The theme is one that is very congenial to you these days but, more than usually, here you

---

1. R. W. B. Lewis writes about the Warrens in Italy in *The City of Florence: Historical Vistas & Personal Sightings* (New York: Farrar, Straus and Giroux, 1995), 73–75.

1. "Dream of a Dream" was printed as a Christmas card by G. K. Hall of Boston in 1976.

have found the images to give it clarity and carrying power. The theme, of course, is the great theme from the Romantics on—the fact of the rift between the subjective world of value that sometimes seems as empty as smoke and the beautiful unconscious world outside us. The theme comes on down to *us*, but how much better some of the moderns—and I think of *you* emphatically in this connection—handle it better than most of the Romantics did. But why should I be saying all this to you—maybe just in the hope that I will indicate how deeply I am involved in what you are saying here and in many of your later poems.

I telephoned David yesterday. His troubles are not over—more of the black moles have appeared and have been removed, and [p. 2] he indicated that still more surgery was probably ahead. Poor fellow. How sad it is and how grave and calm he is. He had not yet received the U.F. ms to xerox, but was to call me when it got in. I have not heard from him yet today (2:00 p.m.) {I have told David that I didn't want him to worry himself with our problems if he is not up to it physically or mentally. I've urged him to call me if he needs help or wants me to try to find someone else to take over. I hope I made it clear to him that we don't want to burden him at this most difficult period.}

As soon as I get the xerox, I'll get to work. (I've reread the recently published Updike story and will get it xeroxed and sent to you to see what you think.)

All goes well with us. We lead a quiet and monotonous life but we are happy in it and I am getting a great deal of work done. The Faulkner book is now moving right along.[2] I am becoming hopeful of it.

It was fine seeing all the Warrens on our recent trip to Vermont. T. joins me in affectionate greetings to Eleanor, Rosanna, Gabriel, and yourself.

Cleanth

West Wardsboro, Vt. 05360
August 9, 1976

Dear Cleanth:

When you are so pressed, I don't see how you got around to doing the letter. But I assure you that no letter was ever more appreciated, or heartening. And I am grateful.

What good news it is that the Faulkner moves well. I hope you can drive on now to the end, and a glorious end it will be. It will undoubtedly be one of the monumental American studies of our time.

Ever as I hope that you drive on to the end, I send you another poem, one I've been at for quite a time. Don't bother to write. If you have some views or criticisms, tell me face to face when we get back (September 14).

. . . .

2. The second and final volume of Brooks's Faulkner study, *William Faulkner: Toward Yoknapatawpha and Beyond* (New Haven: Yale University Press), was published in 1978.

Well, I hope all goes well there, even the weather.
Love to you both, from us all!

Ever Yours,
Red

PS. I just learned today, definitely, that a movie producer has taken a very heavy option on my forthcoming novel and that the book is already in the hands of script writers. We'll see. If it goes into the next phase, I'll go on a binge.[1]

[OH]   Forest Road
                                                    Northford, Connecticut 06472
                                                                 18 August 1976

Dear Red,

Thanks for your recent letter and for the long poem.[1] It is—to use the language that Faulkner used in telling someone about one of his finest novels— it's a real son of a bitch. I found it so fascinating that I couldn't put it down. In a few days I want to go over it more meditatively and if I have any thoughts worth conveying to you then, I'll send them along. It is really a remarkable poem.

The special occasion for this note is to send along with it a suggested reworking of "The Furnished Room." As you will see the brief comments and the 7 questions are all that would be printed in the text. Everything else (including nearly the whole of the present analysis) would be reserved for the manual. It would not be denied to the student—simply mediated to him through the instructor. If the student has a bone-headed instructor [p. 2] the student is in bad luck, but if he has a really bone-headed instructor, the student will probably not see our book anyway. (I have, however, as you will see, tried to include one or two questions at the end that would give some clues to the brighter student—clues that might stimulate him to ask the instructor what about certain things—and thus make the instructor divulge what we've put in the manual.)

The Faulkner book continues to go well and I stay busy with one thing and another. If you can correct or confirm, however, some of my notions about the size and shape and quality of the manual, I'll forge ahead with providing more questions for the text and copy for the manual. I can find the time and I rather enjoy doing this sort of thing. You've already done the hard part.

1. A copy of the screenplay for *A Place to Come To*, by Julian Barry, is in the Robert Penn Warren Collection (YCAL MS 51) at the Beinecke Rare Book and Manuscript Library, Yale University. It is marked "First Draft / 13 June 1977" with the following note in Warren's handwriting: "This is the original draft by Barry with which Barry, Robert Redford, and I worked with the director. . . . His [Barry's] new draft refused & another writer called in on 1 Nov. 1977 . . . . 26 Nov. 1978." To date, no movie has been produced.

1. The poem is possibly "American Portrait: Old Style," *New Yorker*, August 23, 1976, pp. 26–27.

I really think, provided I have the right idea, that I could draft a manual rapidly.

. . . .

T. joins in affectionate greetings to you all,
Cleanth

P.S. I hope that the Hollywood business pans out!

2495 Redding Road
Fairfield, Connecticut 06430
March 29, 1977

Dear Cleanth:

Thank God, you are such a bad correspondent that I didn't have to apologize to you for being one. But at last business drives me to it.

You have no doubt seen the (on the whole) glowing reports Prentice-Hall has for Understanding Fiction, but realize that some substantial cutting has to be done and a manual concocted from the waste pile. Now dates.

I go to Nashville on May 5 and return May 9 (after a little visit to my brother). On May 17 we leave for Greece (a little knock-about sailing tour of the islands), with the Vann Woodwards, and Kirstin and his lady friend, not a tour, just doing a knock-about according to whim on a 70-footer that George has leased, he being the expert seaman on the lot (with a crew of four and a cook). Back home May 27. Then here until June 19, then Vermont.

I have finished my book on poor KAP.[1] (I suppose you've heard the news, two strokes, right side pretty well paralyzed, but a minimum impairment of head, except for groping for words now and then. She may be allowed to go home where she will be well taken care of by her Marine. We saw her in Baltimore and could have some conversation with her, but it's all very sad.)

But back to business, do you suppose that we (with David, I trust) can finish the Understanding Fiction in the month before we go to Vermont. Then we can divide up stuff to do for the HB *Rhetoric*, and maybe get by on one summer meeting—though we'd regard it as a privilege to have you for more. As for the order, it seems that we are so close to the money on UF that we ought to drive that on through first.

I suppose you got the copy I sent of Selected Poems, which has had a fine reception, and new printing on the paperback. The Novel, except for the NY Times (which had crowned me with laurel for the poems), didn't have much laurel left for the novel. But the general [p. 2] press reception has been quite good, and there have been three orders to reprint, I am told, since the original 50,000 copies, these of 5,000 each. But with books returnable, you never know exactly where you stand. The Movie man, who comes around now and then,

---

1. *Katherine Anne Porter: A Collection of Critical Essays*, Twentieth-Century Views Series (Englewood Cliffs, N.J.: Prentice-Hall) was published January 23, 1979. Porter died September 18, 1980, in Silver Springs, Maryland.

is very intelligent and attractive, and has certainly done his lesson on the book. He has some sixty-odd pages of script done and is pushing on. We'll see. Anyway, I'm in the comfortable position with the Lit[erary] G[uild] and the paperback contract of not worrying too much about the movie. But we are all greedy.

. . . .

Spring slow. And we miss you. Non sequitur. Hurry back.

LISTEN! We've just heard the awful rumor that you are selling your place here. Is that true? You simply can't upset us that way. It is not Christian. It is not even Episcopalian. It's not human.

Tell us, for God's sake, it's a foul libel on decent people.

Love from all,
Red

[OH]   Northford, Conn.
                                                                   23 June, 1977

Dear Red

Your letter of June 20 came in this morning's mail and I hasten to reply. Eudora's address is [. . .]

As for KAP's "The Grave" my impulse is to say you may have it for nothing. I'd like to be in the book because of my affection for you and KAP. But if a price is to be named, I'll say $25.00.

I am putting in mornings working at the revision of MR. I hope to put into the mails tomorrow a suggested rearrangement and rewriting of the section beginning at the bottom of p. 28. (This is the section that we had agreed that I should do at once.) Please reject, add, or modify as you see fit.

I am picking away at my other assignments in our plan of revision. I expect to have more to report shortly. I'm at work now on the essay on literature—and on the paragraph-sentence chapter.

. . . .

Love to Eleanor—in which Tinkum joins.

Cleanth

West Wardsboro, Vermont 05360
July 10, 1977

Dear Cleanth:

By breaking the Sabbath all day long and some days before, I have a version of Chapter IX herewith, plus some Manual sheets, or sheets to be adapted. I simply couldn't reduce this more. I felt we had to have some good examples (these are pretty good, I think) and I thought we needed the business of George and his dog, etc., to show, concretely, how a piece of fiction might be built. God knows it's not world shaking but I can't beat it—could merely do more of the same—or something just about like it. PLEASE revise or rewrite as the Lord guideth.

I don't know what to turn to next. To make a check, I have now mailed you revisions (remounted on separate sheets, and Manual sheets) for Chapters 1, 2, 3, 4, 8, and 9. Is that right? What do you propose that I do now?

Beautiful weather now, Gabe's boat flourishes. I have managed to write two poems despite all. Eleanor plugs away in her cabin at some secret project. Rosanna is enjoying Crete, and has done some beautiful poetry. Painting again, too.

We can't wait to see you all.

Meanwhile, love from all,
Red

[OH]   Forest Road
                                             Northford, Connecticut 06472
                                                            12 July 77
Dear Red,

Here's a brief report on what is going on at this end.

I've called Marilyn Brown at Prentice-Hall. She is on vacation, not to return until July 18. I'll telephone her then, but will in the meantime write her a note to be held for her return.

Your two packages are in. I have gone over the material. It's all to the good. I am conflating my rewriting of pp. 28–29 with yours, using my basic rearrangement (as you suggested) but retaining most of your incidental changes.

I've finished a draft of the new material on writing essays and reviews of poems, stories, etc. This new material will replace pp. 395–421. It is now being typed up and will be xeroxed and sent to you a little later in the week.

I hope that you will approve of it and I trust that it is not too lengthy. It will give samples of *how not to write* about a story and a poem but also samples of acceptable writing. It's all very concrete, quite simple, and I hope practical. At worst it will be something to begin altering and revising.

I am at work now on some of the chapters I promised to revise including that on the paragraph and on the sentence. I'll go on to work on Diction, Argument, and Persuasion.

All goes well here. The weather has not been too bad. Indeed we've had decently cool nights.

Love to Eleanor and yourself.

Cleanth

[OH]   Northford
                                                           August 5, 1977
Dear Red,

The briefest of notes to say that I have reworked your draft of the letter to Pullin and sent it to David for his own suggestions. He'll send it on to you for you to reduce to its final version.

As you will see, when you receive the revised version, I've taken you at your word and done a good deal of rewriting. I hope that I haven't introduced a lot of hot air into it. If I have, simply let it out.

It was nice having the visit to Vermont—truly pleasurable—and I do think that we got a great deal accomplished.

Love to Eleanor and Gabe.

Cleanth

P.S. I look forward with much eagerness to seeing your new version of *Brother to Dragons.*[1]

[OH]   Forest Road
                                             Northford, Connecticut 06472
                                                              Nov. 4, 1977

Dear Red,

By this time you will have received Anthony McClellon's letter about the Hilton Head project. It would be fun to see you and Eleanor there and I confess that it is a place that I would like to visit, at least once. T. and I have been on nearby Kiowah Island a couple of times but Kiowah is still private and woodsy, though now that the <Order> has purchased it, it will too become rich and glamorous. But I will like to see what the glamour looks like once, anyway, though I am by nature the other sort of person.

Anyway, I won't press you to say yes. There is no honorarium, as McClellon has told you, just expenses. Besides you have so many activities and projects that you may be already booked.

I've been reading *Brother to Dragons* with great satisfaction and enjoyment. It is a magnificent poem. I do have one or two cautious suggestions to make; I am not at all confident that they will, if acted upon, constitute improvements. But when we next get together, let's set aside a little time to chat about them.

That meeting, however, can't occur right away. Tinkie is having to make a fourth trip to New Orleans to go through her mother's papers, make plans to distribute and dispose generally of her effects, etc. We plan to fly down together on Sunday morning (Nov. 6), for I am to be picked up on Monday to be driven to Hattiesburg, Miss., [p. 2] where I am down for a lecture. Then on the 10th I shall be driven to Oxford for the Eudora Welty three-day festival. I expect to get home on the evening of the 13th (Sunday). T. doesn't know when she can get home—just possibly as soon as I do, but maybe not until the middle of the week of the 13th.

I go to West Point to talk to some of the cadets on Nov. 17 but return to Northford the next day.

I've received your pages for the *Modern Rhetoric* revision—those mailed to me Nov. 2—and having looked them over cursorily will go over them the more

---

1. *Brother to Dragons: A Tale in Verse and Voices (A New Version)* was published in September 1979. A collection of essays that discuss the two versions, *Robert Penn Warren's* Brother to Dragons: *A Discussion*, ed. James A. Grimshaw, Jr., was published in 1983 by Louisiana State University Press as part of its Southern Literary Studies Series.

carefully tomorrow. (Thank goodness I finished my Faulkner page proofs last Wednesday and have turned them in to the Yale Press.) I am handicapped, however, by not yet having a copy of the xerox of our last version. I telephoned Pullin last week to ask for a copy and it should have got here days ago. I've written to him today asking him to send it on. But I can't get it now until November 14 when I return.

In the meantime, however, I have been working away at some of the matters that had troubled <Swets>—what I meant about dead metaphor awaking from the dead to spoil the discourse, the too-sketchy treatment of the nature of the sentence, and so on. Some of my new stuff will go into the text but some also into the manual as suggestions to the instructor as how to handle these problems.

I hope all goes well with *all* the Warrens. Our special love to Eleanor and we are looking forward especially to seeing Rosanna after this long, long interval.

All the best,
Cleanth

[Written at top of p. 1] P.S. Should you need to get in touch with me from Nov. 10 to 12, I will receive a letter sent to me c/o Professor Louis Dollarhide (yes, that's the name—Eudora uses it in one of her novels), English Dept., U. of Miss., University, Miss. 38677.

West Wardsboro, Vt. 05360
June 22 [1978]

Dear Cleanth:

First matters first: I can't say how much we enjoyed the stopover in all ways. It was a life-saver—and a delight. Thanks, as always.

Now to grim business. Today I mail a box of MS to you, containing (1) the MS, numbered to all pages as they now exist, with pink slips still attached for you to look at too, each section introduced by a yellow numbered sheet and in a rubber band, but with the whole of the MS as it now stands held together by heavy red rubber bands in one big packet; (2) in the bottom of the box, all the rejected material, just in case, now or later, we need it; (3) the technical material, introduced by yellow sheet to be added to Manual; (4) odds and ends, including an analyzed contents sheet from PH.

You notice that I have xeroxed and inserted in place of "The Lottery" the Hawthorne story, along with a discussion. I am not happy with the discussion and hope that you will give it your closest attention.

Bad news: I didn't realize until just now that one sheet of Tolstoi's *Ivan Ilich* is a bad xerox and must be redone. {I have now made a new xerox for Tolstoi and inserted it.} The sheet is numbered 573 in the most recent red marking (my most recent addition of pagination). I hate to throw this rock at you, but getting that done here. Hurrah! I have just learned that I can get a copy made in the town hall—a xerox machine has just arrived!

I suppose you are to send this to Robb Reavill as soon as possible. If we have to make one more cut I suggest "The Sojourner" by Carson McCullers. But not unless it is demanded.

I guess this is all, and fervently hope so. The ZIP code for P-H, Inc, in case you don't have it, is *07632*. It may speed matters to know that Robb is College Book Editorial-Production Department.

Weather good, brook singing, the schooner looming tall, no porcupines yet. Love to both!

As ever,
Red

[OH]   Forest Road
                                  Northford, Connecticut 06472
                                                   July 1, 1978

Dear Red,

We trust that you and Eleanor and Frodo had an easy and comfortable trip back to Vermont. Your box of UF ms got in several days ago and I have nearly finished going through it. I expect to mail it back to Robb on Monday.

All seems to be in order and I have made very few additions or changes. I have been taking notes for the manual as I've gone along. It's a good book and I am satisfied with it. If a decent and useful manual can be written, I think that we are all set.

There are, however, these few further matters to be dealt with or at least to be talked about.

As you may have learned already, Bellow has refused permission for our use of his "Father to Be" on the grounds that he doesn't want that story printed anywhere again. Shall we try to substitute another Bellow story or simply let it go?

On p. 340 in the discussion of "29 Inventions" you write: "And like 'In the Heart of the Country,' it ["29 Inventions"] calls attention to what is artificial in its organization" etc. Since "In the Heart" has been dropped, do you have any suggestions for a substitute title?

On p. 375, in Question 1 on "The Balloon," you write: "Contrast the Satiric techniques in 'The Balloon' with those in 'The Lottery.' " Since "The Lottery" has been dropped, have you any suggestions for a substitute reference?

I see that Section 8 is to be put in the Manual. I won't therefore send it to Robb Reavill with the other material on Monday. It needs a good deal of working over anyway because of its several references to stories that have now been dropped from the present book. In fact, I expect that [p. 2] it may have to go back to you eventually before it goes back to P-H. In the meantime, I will see what I can do with it.

In looking over Section 7 ("Stories for Reading") I have had some second thoughts about Malamud's "Black Is My Favorite Color." It's an interesting story and I am glad to have us use it on its merits. But I wonder whether it won't offend the blacks. There is a great deal of black prejudice in this story, prejudice with reference to all whites and especially Jews and there are plenty of black thugs using switch-knives. Doubtless, you've already considered this matter and if you see no special problem, I'll be happy to put away my own concerns. We are not going to get many adoptions by black colleges anyway.

As I said, I hope to pack up the MS and send it off to P-H on Monday, all that is except the rejected material and the material to be put in the manual. I can't do much with that manual immediately, however. For every extra minute for the next weeks must go to preparation of the manual for *Modern Rhetoric*. See below.

Now for some comments on MR. Andrea Haight wants the new preface by early August and earlier if she can get it. I include herewith a draft of that preface—quite short, like that of the preceding edition. Add, revise, or rewrite as seems good to you. We are to start receiving galley proofs on MR early next week. You will be primarily responsible for Chapters 1–9; I, for the rest. I'll send you corrections for chapter 1–9 and having added these to your own (or having modified or rejected them), you'll send them on to Harcourt. We'll reverse the process for chapter 10 to the and.

Andrea also wants that Manual ready by December. I don't know whether it can be done, but I must try. I've already made a start and I'll get back to the job at once.

Tinkum joins me in affectionate greetings to you, Eleanor, and Gabe.

[Cleanth]

2495 Redding Road
Fairfield, Connecticut 06430
January 13, 1979

Dear Cleanth:

It was such a pleasure to see you all! We still feel deprived, but comfort ourselves a little with the thought of Charleston.

A favor, please. For the Franklin Library I am to do an introduction to *The Sound and the Fury*, in a series they are projecting of, it seems, something like "seminal books." Or something of the sort. Nothing ambitious. Just 1000 words, at an intelligent but sub-technical level.

I am way behind with the Faulkner criticism and I'd appreciate any suggestions of reading worthwhile of late years, and, best of all, any late thoughts of your own. The thing will focus on two points: 1. Original intuition and background, and 2. key interpretation.

Love to Tinkum and you, from us both!

As ever,
Red

. . . .

[Handwritten] *Regards to Lewis.* Got a new poem, to my surprise!

[OH]   The University of North Carolina at Chapel Hill
Greenlaw Bldg. 066 A
Chapel Hill, N.C. 27514
January 18, 1979

Dear Red,

It was pleasant to hear from you the other day and I got busy at once on a short *Sound and the Fury* bibliography. I didn't bring any of my Faulkner library here with me but a run through the Faulkner titles in the University library here has refreshed my mind.

In the first place, however, I would trust, if I were you, what you *already have in your head* to provide the basic ideas for your introduction. Your basic insights into that book have always seemed right to me and they still seem so. In the second place, not a great deal of valuable work on the *S and F* has been published during the last decade and the best of that has been highly speculative—too subjective and speculative to trust very far. Yet I will mention a few books and indicate where you can find up-to-date bibliographies for the rest.

One of the most interesting of the new books on the *S and F* is by a young Frenchman who teaches at the U. of Strasbourg, André Bleikasten. The title is *The Most Splendid Failure: The Sound and the Fury,* Bloomington: U. of Indiana Press, 1976. It appeared first in French. I have not read the book carefully and I expect that it is too "psychological" and too "structuralist" for our taste. But Bleikasten is an intelligent man and his book is recent enough to gather up most of the more recent scholarship.

John T. Irwin has published recently an extremely interesting [p. 2] book on the Quentin Compson of the *S and F* and of *Absalom, Absalom!* I think that at best it tells us what *may just possibly* have gone on in Faulkner's unconscious mind as he developed the character of Quentin and at its weakest it represents what kind of speculation an ingenious mind that is soaked in Freud and Neitzsche gives off when it encounters the creation of Quentin. But Irwin is bright as hell and a nice guy. His book is called *Doubling and Incest, Repetition and Revenge: A Speculative Reading . . . ,* Johns Hopkins Press, 1975.

Albert Guerard, Jr.'s *Triumph of the Novel* has a big section on Faulkner and specifically on the *S and F.* (New York: Oxford U. Press, 1976). I think that he makes entirely too much of Faulkner's fear and hatred of women, but the book is well written and represents a point of view.

Most of the articles that I have read on the *S and F* are trivial or just plain wrong—such as an attempt to rehabilitate the character of Jason Compson.

A useful bibliography is John Bassett's, *William Faulkner: An Annotated Checklist.* New York: D. Levis, 1972. He gives brief descriptions of what the book or article contains and, often, a very sensible evaluation. He has a whole section on books and articles specifically on *The S and F*—but it takes you down, of course, no further than 1971–72.

For later articles on the *S and F* you might look at the last 4 or 5 *summer* numbers of the *Mississippi Quarterly.* These summer numbers are devoted exclusively to Faulkner and either mention or actually print articles on Faulkner. One of them prints Faulkner's hitherto unpublished introduction to the *S and F,* which was discovered a few years ago in the box of papers in Faulkner's Oxford, Miss., house.

[p. 3] These Faulkner numbers are edited by James B. Meriwether, Albert E's *bete noir.* But he knows a great deal about Faulkner and I found these *Miss. Quarterly* Faulkner numbers invaluable in working up *Toward Yoknapatawpha.*

On the tangled Benjy section of *the S and F*, let me recommend Edmund Volpe's *A Reader's Guide to William Faulkner*, New York: Farrar and Straus, 1964, and an article by George R. Stewart and Joseph M. Backus in *American Literature*, vol. 29 (Jan., 1958), 440–56. They, in slightly different arrangements, sort out the various items in Benjy's long stream-of-consciousness flow and they have done it convincingly. Mind you, I have little respect for the literary insights of Stewart and Volpe; and Backus, in at least one place elsewhere, has shown himself to be a real dunce! But these decodings are thorough and they do reveal something about the quality of Faulkner's mind. (Whether you need to go into the structure of the Benjy section, or want to, is, of course, a matter for you to decide.)

I hope that this hastily gathered bibliography material will be of some help and that you can make out *this slovenly scrawl*.

I like the poems you let me take away with me, "Part of a Short Story" and "Antinomies of Time."[1] I'll be sending them (along with Moss's letter) back to you within the next day or so. Whether I shall have any suggestions to pencil in on the poems, I doubt. They seem finished to me. But if I do have any ideas, I promise to set them [p. 4] down.

We are now pretty well settled in our house. It is pleasant. It does not, as we feared it might, look awesomely grand, but it sprawls on and on in its nooks and crannies and little sitting rooms and extra side rooms. But thus far it works well and we feel that the labyrinth itself is becoming less fearsomely labyrinthine. I feel now like a B+ white rat who is finally becoming to be at home in the maze. But I still don't negotiate it very rapidly.

I've started work on the Manual and it goes well—or so it seems to me. I mean to keep at it until it is sufficiently finished to send to you.

T. joins in affectionate greetings to you and Eleanor. What a nice evening we had together on Jan. 6! We look forward to seeing you all in Charleston. Congratulations to Gabe on selling one of his works even before his show began. We are sure that the show will be a great success.

All our best,
Cleanth

The University of North Carolina at Chapel Hill
Greenlaw Bldg. 066 A
Chapel Hill, N.C. 27514
February 24, 1979

Dear Red,

. . . .

I enclose a copy of a letter to Robb Reavill. It will more or less bring you up to date on the state of the Manual for *UF*. When my revised draft begins to

1. "Part of a Short Story" appeared in *Georgia Review* 33 (spring 1979): 86–88; "Antinomy: Time and Identity" sequence was published in *Yale Review* 68 (summer 1979): 540–41.

reach you please use the blue pencil right along and mark at least provisional cuts, for I may have gone beyond reasonable length.

I'm not eager to cut for cutting's sake. My experience with the two manuals done thus far is that being truly helpful with reference to a story or a poem requires a certain amount of space in which to turn around. If you are curt and abrupt, you spoil the tone. In talking to the instructor as an equal, you have to put your discussion on the level of general discussion, suggestion, an alternate approach, etc. To do this requires extra space. But if we can reduce the text without real loss to either courtesy or intelligibility, of course we want to do it. Besides, Prentice-Hall may balk at an extended Manual. Holt did, though it was finally persuaded to use all the copy we submitted.

I hope that you will approve of the way I have handled "The New Fiction," i.e., Section 5. It gave me considerable trouble. Thus far I have done nothing about Section 7 ("Stories for Reading"). I'll be glad to attempt something, but I prefer to wait to see whether we shall have room for it. In the Manual for *UP* we had to leave out any consideration of Sections 6, 7, and 8 because it would have made the Manual too long.

I finally got hold of *Trousered Apes* and like a great deal that I see, but you are right in making reservations about it. Williams is indiscriminate in finding allies and supporters. I am now reading Christopher Lasch's *The Culture of Narcissus*. It's quite a brilliant performance and as compared with Williams' scatter gun, Lasch is using a very powerful precision rifle.

Tinkum sends affectionate greetings to you both, along with mine.

Cleanth

[Typed at top of page] All mail goes to office. Home telephone is [. . .].

April 27, 1979

Dear Cleanth:

I have done you wrong by not getting at the work on the Manual—the chief reason being that I cannot find my copy, God knows why. Do you have an extra, and do you wish (if you have it) to bring or send it? I'll get right on it.

I am sure that you have a copy of the letter and other material (instruction for preparation of copy for Manual). The cost to us for preparation of MS (if they do it) will be $250. I'll call my typist right now and see if she would undertake it. It might be cheaper that way, but it might be less certain. If the whole fee to us is $250 we know where we stand, and $125 each wouldn't ruin us. What I fear is that my typist might be working at a job strange to her and might take excessive time. She has a full-time job anyway.

But the main thing now is for me to get—with all grief and apologies—a copy of the manual and/or more importantly, specific directions on what I should do. God knows, give me any suggestions you can.

You raise the question of the appearance in the text of [the] Manual of the titles of stories that are not now included. I propose that once I have the text in hand I try to find stories we *do* print that might be substituted for our old standbys, or to get principles stated without example, or with improvised examples.

Maybe the best thing is to wait till we are face to face (you come in less than 3 weeks) and then try to lay out the work for me. This would save you the trouble of writing, mailing the MS, etc. For instance, if you have only one copy, I could xerox it here for my use. In any case (is this right?), the copy for Manual is not pressing is it? The book is out, summer is coming on, and it seems doubtful that much would hinge on the three-week delay. What about it?

Eleanor has been having a grievous time with lenses and lights trying to do the proof of her new novel. But she has valorously finished—that being something on which nobody could help her. It is a very impressive book—by far her best piece of fiction.[1]

. . . .

It was great to catch the glimpse of you all in S.C. Hurry and come to see us. Our love to both!

As ever,
Red

---

1. The reference is to *Gloria Mundi* (New York: Pantheon Books, 1979).

1980s

2495 Redding Road
Fairfield, Connecticut 06430
March 17, 1980

Dear Cleanth:

How kind you are—you and Tinkie! It makes me feel awful good to think you liked the Davis piece, even if I have to make some allowance for your generosity to an old friend.[1] But I hate to think of you so wore out and Tinkie reading that to you when [she] could have been reading you *Alice in Wonderland*. Thin as the little book is, the U of K Press is publishing it. I've got to do a little retouching. I wrote it with very little in the way of reference books in Vermont (in the afternoons, mornings trying to go for poetry) and when I got back from here, my sheets were full of question marks. So I had to put in a lot of days grubbing to check or correct matter of fact at Yale. One thing may have crossed your mind. It was often said in Nashville in the 1930's that the Ganymede on the Parthenon had the little boy Randall Jarrell as a model. Of course that would not have been chronologically possible with the Centennial opening in 1897. Except for the fact that the original Parthenon was a temporary structure and the permanent structure wasn't begun until 1920 or the next year. I remember seeing some of the pediment panels propped on scaffolding in, I think, 1921. But I must explain this in the piece. I've already had one mildly abusive letter.

. . . .

Eleanor is hard into something she won't tell me about. I'm at poems, and how much good you did me with your comments in the book and on the new things. I've now done the proofs. New title: *Being Here*.[2] Not so damned pontifical. By the way, all contracts signed, major casting done, on the opera being made of *AKM*. Which is finished. It was the idea of Kennedy Center, but will open with the Houston Opera Company, a week's run. Then on to Kennedy if there aren't too many rotten eggs, I guess, in Houston. Anyway,

---

1. *Jefferson Davis Gets His Citizenship Back* (Lexington: University Press of Kentucky) was published December 6, 1980; it first appeared in the *New Yorker*, February 25, 1980, beginning on p. 44.
2. Random House published *Being Here: Poetry, 1977–1980* in July 1980.

they got a very hot director and claim they have a cast to suit him. We'll see. That's one more opera I guess I'll have to see.[3]

We miss you all. The visit to Knoxville was fine, but fine in its own way. Our love to both!

As ever,
Red

[Handwritten at top of p. 1] Thanks for the offer of the book. It sounds damned interesting. But let me get it from the library!
[Handwritten at bottom of p. 2] We go to Arizona the second half of April for <ten days or> two weeks, winding up on the ranch we love down on the Mexican border.

2495 Redding Road
Fairfield, Connecticut 06430
November 21, 1980

Dear Cleanth:

What a joy even the glimpse of you and Tinkie was for us. And I am happy that North Carolina is turning comfortably. You don't know how much you are missed here. We forget how much even your presence in the state means, much less more immediate contact. You all are something to turn to, which is a comfort even when there's no reason to turn except idle conversation.

Cleanth—and Tinkie, you bet your bottom dollar—I can't say how much I appreciated your coming to Kentucky and all that the fact meant.[1] I'm not talking now about what the fact clearly meant to a lot of other people, but what it most deeply meant to me. There is no end to your generosity, and I can't wait for you to be 75 so I can return the compliment, even if not with your inimitable grace. To save embarrassment—whose I don't know, yours or mine, or both—I was jerked away from your paper or whatever it was. You have been so generous, so embarrassingly so, in the past, I hope you didn't further imperil your integrity just because I am old and defenseless.

I'm not as defenseless as I was, however. I still go five days a week to get my shoulder worked on, but I'm gaining ground. If only I had had a week of proper attention in the summer this would have been cured immediately—as it was 13 years ago at Harvard. But Vermont is a safe place only for the sniffles.

. . . .

3. Carlisle Floyd opened his opera, *Willie Stark*, on April 24, 1981—Warren's seventy-sixth birthday—at the Houston Grand Opera. It opened at Washington, D.C.'s Kennedy Center on May 4.

1. The University of Kentucky held the "Robert Penn Warren 75th Birthday Symposium" in Lexington on October 29–30, 1980; *Kentucky Review* 2.3 (1981) published some of the papers presented on that occasion. The symposium was followed by a fifty-year reunion at Vanderbilt University in Nashville on October 30–November 1, 1980, of the four Agrarians still living: Lyle Lanier, Andrew Lytle, Robert Penn Warren, and Cleanth Brooks.

Eleanor is at one of her secret occupations. I have finished a draft of a book of poems, and now for the tough part of rewriting and discarding. I wish I had the nerve to bother you some. But I really haven't the nerve any time soon.

I can't close this inadequate letter without ending where I began. We miss you all most terribly, and I can't say how deeply I felt your visit to Kentucky.

Eleanor joins me in all love,

Red

[Handwritten at top of p. 1] P.S. Dear Cleanth: I have just seen the poems in *Ky Poetry* and take serious pleasure in them.[2] They make me wonder again—what I have often wondered—why that was a path not taken. Though the one you did take has led to the greatest distinction.

[OH]   [1981]

Dear Red,

Congratulations on your handsome Common Wealth prize. We might have missed notice of it except that Tom Sebeok, the semioticist and one of [the] Fellows at the Center here, was telling me about it, mentioning that there was a pleasant account of it in "Talk of the Town" in the last *New Yorker* in December. Our *New Yorkers* had piled up here while we were away on a twelve day trip to Texas and Louisiana. Again, hearty congratulations.

We spent some five or six days at the ranch owned by Tinkum's younger sister at Brenham, some hundred miles north of Houston, and saw Houston only on the night of our arrival in Texas and on the last night and day we were in Texas.

We were fortunate enough to find Rosanna free and Jake, Eleanor's husband, bid her to dinner with us and other friends. I had dreaded the MLA experience for her, but she seemed to be happy, finding friends everywhere, and apparently cutting a wide swath through a half dozen or more job interviews.

My own appearance at the MLA was a matter of less than three hours. I spoke my little piece at the meeting of the Society for the Study of Southern Literature and then T. and I headed for the airport.

We had three nice days in New Orleans (where among others we saw the Manson Redfords) and two in Baton Rouge before we boarded the plane for North Carolina.

By chance at the airport we ran into John Hollander and Sandy McClotchy, and from them derived that you [p. 2] had been awarded the Hubbell Medal. How the honors continue to rain down upon you.

2. *Kentucky Poetry Review* 16.2–3 (autumn/fall 1980) included two poems by Brooks, "Tennessee Landscape" (1932) and "Mystery on the Brentford Road" (1932), pp. 6–8; and two by Warren, "English Cocker: Old and Blind" (1980) and "Prophecy" (1922), his first published poem, pp. 4–5.

This particular one is overdue you in view of the service that through the years you have rendered the study of American letters—quite apart from your contributions to American letters by way of creating some memorable examples of them.

We seem to thrive here at the Center. The 1980–81 set of Fellows are particularly congenial. We have lots of good talk at our lunches and from time to time at the dinner parties that we give each other.

When we read the weather reports we worry about you and Eleanor and our other New Haven friends. New England does seem to have had a frigid first months of winter. It has even been nippy in North Carolina though we've thus far had no snow.

T. joins me in affectionate greetings to you both.

[Cleanth]

2495 Redding Road
Fairfield, Connecticut
March 2, 1981

Dear Cleanth:

We miss you all most dismally, and it doesn't get any better. We can't wait to see the tops'l break the horizon. Head here, of course, for your first landfall, and let's get acquainted.

I'm doing a vile thing to you right here, and I hope it doesn't break up 56 years of our friendship and my dependence on you in so many ways. The Book of the Month Club, to my astonishment, is issuing a deluxe edition of *AKM* on the 35th anniversary of its publication, and wants me to do an introduction. I had sort of written myself out on the subject, long back. But here is my try. I undertook to relate how certain things flowed into the background of the writing, this in a running sketch of Louisiana. I want you two to take a look, and see (1) if the thing is OK in my memory of Louisiana, (2) if it isn't a little overlong (please indicate what seems expendable), and (3) anything else that crosses the astute minds of Brookses. Just scribble on the MS. I enclose an envelope self addressed. I've depended on memory about Louisiana.

No great news. Except that Rosanna apparently wowed 'em at Vanderbilt. They looked no further, and signed her on as assistant professor (courses she wanted), and said to hell with the Ph.D. She really liked the faculty, especially the middle and younger brackets, and [Walter] Sullivan, who personally is a very fine guy I know.

Albert and I have finished going over the book of poems due out in October. Is this title too fancy: *Have You Ever Eaten Stars?* I am using it for a poem, but as a book title it might not do so well.[1]

. . . .

1. Preliminary ads carried that title, but Eleanor objected strongly to it. Random House published the volume as *Rumor Verified: Poems, 1979–1980* in April 1981.

Eleanor joins me in all love to you all.
Thanks!

Ever yours,
Red

[postcard]
2495 Redding Road
Fairfield, Connecticut 06430
[postmarked September 28, 1981]

Dear Cleanth:

Your note fill[s] my heart with joy, not only as a general matter, but as a matter of choices of poems. I must say that in the midst of your hurlyburly (with which the W's now thoroughly sympathize), it was heroic to get off the comforting lines. Things are hell here, nothing yet in its right place. And on October 9, I head for Montana to stand on the spot where Chief Joseph surrendered to wait for a mystic vision.[1] In late October E[leanor] and I, with Gabe and wife, head for North Africa to ride camels with the Berbers for a couple of weeks, then E. and I, to Jerusalem to read poems, etc. and follow Clarel's pilgrimage. Back home about end of month, and the thing we yearn most to see is the faces of a couple of Brookses. Meanwhile, be nice to them while we are gone. Our love to both!

Yours,
Red

West Wardsboro, Vermont 05360
July 16, 1982

Dear Cleanth:

Your most kind letter and sheaf of comments has just come, and I am very grateful—not grateful enough, no doubt, when I remind myself of the burden you always lay on yourself. Even if I make what I hope approximates the right discount due because of your kindness and old friendship, I still take pleasure in your kind opinion. I must say that I am glad you like the last section most. It ought to be that way—to lay the muzzle on the target. But I honestly say that I don't know exactly how I feel myself about what I have, the thing in hand. Some days I feel good, some bad, and I suppose I'll be doing a certain amount of rewriting in proof. When that will be, I can't yet say. One thing I know. When I lay the proof out, your notes will be beside them. For the time being, I let the whole matter lie—except for a couple of remarks that seemed to demand immediate attention.

1. *Chief Joseph of the Nez Perce*, published in March 1983 by Random House, was privately printed in 1982 by the Palaemon Press, Winston-Salem, N.C.

I'm delighted to hear that you and Tinkie are finding pleasure in the Ogden Street house. Why shouldn't you. I think you lucky to find a place so closely designed to your needs and tastes.

Life goes along here pleasantly enough. I get my prebreakfast kilometer, and Eleanor has had quite a bit of tennis. It's quite wonderful to see how she bears up with the vision business, and how hard she works at it. Our big event, so far, has been the July birthday party—Eleanor, Gabe, and Rosanna all in a huddle, with wife, husband, and a few of their friends.

Rosanna has done a couple of new poems, one which strikes me as fine and original. But most of her time is taken up with a new course she has devised. She is taking certain passages from Homer, a chorus or two from Greek tragedies, some *Aeneid*, bits of Dante, Petrarch, the poets of 17th-century France, some of the 19th century, some modern Italian. Then she pairs each with several translations in English, and sees what each translator has really done. She goes back to 16th-century English (Wyatt, Surrey, Sidney, Jonson, etc.) on up to Robert and other contemporaries of ours. It aims, she says, to be a course in poetics, with a new slant, a new focus. I wonder where she'll get the students. Lit. Comp. I guess. She's not attached to a department for the first two years, quaintly what is called a "Presidential" prof. In the third year she goes back to the English Department. It all sounds crazy. Gabe is boat-and-sculpture as usual, chiefly boat right now, for after having had a lot of new interior work, she goes back into the briny next week. Otherwise, he's inspecting oyster boats or reading Mary Renault.

Speaking of reading, I'm deep for the summer into F. Braudel's 2 vol. *Mediterranean*. A fascinating book, which I highly recommend.

No news. All thanks again. And all love to you and Tinkie. How could we ever live without you all!

Ever yours,
Red

[Handwritten] I've done three poems, but am shaky about them.

2495 Redding Road
Fairfield, Connecticut 06430
January 15, 1983

Dear Cleanth:

Thinking that the fact might have some bearing on our decision to revise the Rhetoric, I asked them for the royalty statement thus far. Marland Agriesti writes that it now amounts to $18,895.90 each. {[Handwritten] This is for the 4th edition only.}

But I don't see how we can do anything apart—that is, lay out an apparently different plan, etc. Agriesti is agreeable to getting a secretary or somebody to help.

I hope all goes well and happily. Do you see Eudora much?

No news with us, I guess. Except the trifling thing that my *Chief Joseph* has been taken as one of their secondary things by the BOM Club. No fortune here.

All love from us to you both.

As ever
Red

2495 Redding Road
Fairfield, CT 06430
January 28, 1983

Dear Cleanth:

Do not faint at the size of this MS! In fact, I hope you will take all time possible—six months, or more. Reading at odd moments, taking time to think things over bit by bit, not rushing, letting feelings and opinions. Don't just sit down and make a protracted chore.

You will notice also that I have not numbered sheets. Even if I do give a provisional guide list in sections, this order, in all ways, is subject to your feelings. You can shuffle around poems according to your feelings. (Many of my groups simply grew as poems came along.) There is plenty of space on the sheets for you to make notes—curses—improvements, remarks on revision (or rejection) of individual poems, etc.

These represent the work of about two years, after I have cut out false starts and failures. I have left some doubtful in for your better judgment.

Be honest with yourself and with me. As far as placement of poems is concerned, please shuffle them about as instinct dictates.

Let me now explain the larger plan of which this is a part. Albert talks of bringing out in late 1984 or early 1985 (eightieth birthday as it were) another New and Selected Poems. Size (as well as other things) suggests deletions from earlier books (though the chronology of past books will be preserved) making these "new" poems the first in the book, with own title page epigraph, dedication, etc.[1]

When the choice and order of these poems are at least provisionally settled, then comes the job of making cuts from earlier volume. The first date there would of course be the first date on new title for the selected *volume*.

So don't think you are home free when you finish this job. I'll be on your neck for a review of all previous books—face to face I hope. But maybe not "face to face" is the best way to handle this; you take all the time you need. Don't forget to scribble large or small notes on sheets.

Take all the time you need. This in the hope that you will feel it less of a burden, and also give you a chance to reconsider judgment.

1. The new section is "Altitudes and Extensions, 1980–1984"; Random House published it in *New and Selected Poems, 1923–1985* in March 1985. Editor's note: Erskine told me in conversation that he was holding some of Warren's manuscripts and releasing only one a year for a better distribution of Warren's work.

I won't belabor the fact of gratitude for this. I owe you so much already in so many ways, even a chunk as big as this seems small.

The news from Jacksonville is welcome. Sorry about the conference. You, [anyway], know all I've got to say.

Tell Tinkie how much she is missed. Eleanor squawks often. Me too.

Love to Eudora. And to you grand pair as always.

Red

2495 Redding Road
Fairfield, Connecticut
April 23, 1983

Dear Cleanth:

I am sure that you have received a copy of the vast batch of letters and material sent by Marland Agriesti, of Harcourt Brace Jovanovich. What do you make of this? Life is short, and I know that you, like I, know the pressure of time. Have you any idea of what to do? Whatever we did, it would have to be something that wouldn't take more than a week out of our lives. I don't even remember what the annual take on this book is, and the only reason I would touch it is if the financial prospects were exciting. It seems to have paid for itself many times over. God, but the boredom of it.

I suppose they want some sort of answer soon, but I (we) wouldn't be back in New Haven until mid-fall, at the earliest.

I hope the floods have spared you. They didn't spare our cellar.

Love to all,
Red

West Wardsboro, Vermont 05360
September 16, 1983

Dear Cleanth:

I hear that you all have been returned to us in safety and, I trust, in happiness. We look forward to seeing you all next week—if we can ever do the mop-up here.

I want to thank you devoutly for the pains you took with the poetry manuscript. It was very useful to me, and surprising in a few instances. You upgraded poems I was not at all sure about. I only fear that you were too easy on the book—which is like you. But this leads to a broader thought, which I have thought for a long time. You must—you plural—must have known of the dimension of our attachment to Brookses and admiration. I can look back longer than Eleanor, but with no more feeling. But I want to say something more special now. You can't imagine how much I owe you about poetry—on two counts. Our long collaborations always brought something new and eye-opening to me, seminal notions, for me, often couched in some seemingly incidental or casual remark. One of the happiest recollections I have, is that of the long sessions of work on *UP*—not to mention all earlier and later conversations. The other count has to do with the confidence you gave me about my own efforts. I'm sure that you were often over-generous, but even allowing for that, it still meant something fundamental to me. I have often wanted to say something like this to you, but I know how you'd give an embarrassed shrug and disclaimer. Anyway now I can say it without your interruption.

{[Handwritten in left margin] This does not cover so many other indebtednesses.}

The present MS has grown some since you saw it, in number of possible poems, clearly not all. But I won't come at you about that. That much mercy in me.

Give our love to Tinkie. We'll see you—and soon.

As ever,
Red

[Handwritten] No answer, please.

[OH]   March 19, 1985
Dear Red,

I've gone over your brief essay on poetry with real interest. I found nothing to quarrel with in it and a great deal to admire: specifically, your insights, your good sense, and your choice of illustrations. You do a great deal in a few words, and that's much better than most of us do.

I've checked and corrected the text for "Western Wind"—"Christ, that" rather than "Christ, if." Our text in the 4th ed. of *U.P.* is wrong there and I think that the note on "rain, can down rain" in that edition is faulty.[1] I've thought it over and looked at the OED again and I think your original interpretation, "can" as meaning "may," is better. The small rain that the poet has in mind is the gentle warm rain [p. 2] that the west wind brings off the Atlantic to England, not the harsh dreaded east wind off the North Sea. (But I'm not suggesting that you mention this point in your account: I mention it only in confirmation of "may rain." The blowing of the Western wind makes for the possibility that such a gentle and soothing rain may begin to fall.)

In "Go Lovely Rose," line 15, reads "And not blush so to be admired."

Your brief account is a wise exposition of the coalescence (amounting to identity) of the structure of the poem and its meaning—it "says" what it "says" by being what it is. I thought of suggesting a reference to MacLeish's "A poem shall not mean / But be." But such a citation is not necessary and will, for most readers, be distracting and confusing. You have [p. 3] set forth the kernel of truth in what he writes far more simply and certainly far more persuasively than his little poem did.

You have evidently been so harried and hard-pressed that your typing has sometimes left me baffled. Most of the red marks I have scratched on your

---

1. The line in *Understanding Poetry* (4th ed.) is "rain, down can rain?" (p. 138). In their note they interpret "can" as "can begin to."

text simply mean that I didn't understand the word or the phrase. But when you write in a hurry you usually manage to make so much more sense than the rest of us.

Around here, we are beginning to get in something of a hurry ourselves, there is so much to see about and arrange for, but the major problems are beginning to get solved and I think we will be ready to fly, come the morning of March 28!

See you all come a month hence.

Cleanth

West Wardsboro, Vt. 05360
June 20, 1985

Dear Cleanth:

I don't remember your exact dates for England, but I suppose that you and Tinkie will be back soon. And I am sure that you all must have enjoyed the gala. I hope that [Nevill] Coghill was still around so that you could shake his hand. By the way, he invited me to Table at Exeter once—my only experience in such grandeur until 53 years later.

We are now in Vermont, where our heroic son and his girl drove us on June 20, and where he arrived just in time to find a little flood in our utility room from a leaking tank. Well, he, being a man of various talents, drained the tank, found the tiny rust hole, managed to plug it with a screw of some kind, and all was well long before the plumber arrived with a new tank. Speaking of Gabe, we did stop to see the exhibit. Gabe had three big new pieces, the result of their period in the Southwest. These just knocked [us] down. And did the same to a collector, who casually dropped by and immediately bought one of the big ones. Forgive me if I sound too fondly paternal.

I come to my business of this letter. A man whom I had never seen or heard about, a prof, I gather, at University of Florida, had written a letter to an unknown "Bill" in answer to a question about the founding of the old *SR*, and the letter, I am glad to say, wound up in my hands, God moving in His mysterious ways. First, read the letter from Frank Taylor. Second, read my letter to Frank Taylor, who claimed to have the gospel from Andrew Lytle's mouth. Then read my letter to Andrew Lytle. I simply cannot believe that Andrew told such a tale as gospel. Well, you know him. By the way, I have sent him xeroxes of the business. Rather, I have put the stuff in an envelope but it won't get off until next trip to P.O.

Let us hear how the trip went.

Eleanor joins me in old affection to the Brookses.

Yours,
Red

[Handwritten] I never have learned to type or write either.
[Handwritten] Since you are involved in the Frank Taylor narrative, I trouble you with this stuff. God, the lies that do [get] around!

West Wardsboro, Vt. 05360
June 30, 1985

Dear Cleanth:

Just a little nag. I have done several poems since putting the last book together, but I don't like them. That is, really, though I have put two into magazines. But I'd never put them in a book. Too self-imitative. The worst kind of imitation. Since getting here I have done two more, which I enclose.

I don't know what they are like. I want your considered opinion, when you get a chance. I don't totally trust you in such a matter, but do try to overcome your natural impulse to kindness and friendship, and speak the truth as it is vouchsafed to you.

All thanks.

And love to you all from us both.

Yours,
Red

[Handwritten at top of page] June 30, "Maple Leaves"

West Wardsboro, Vermont 05360
July 9, 1985

Dear Cleanth:

Just a piece of nuisance for you: I think (but am not sure) that I sent you a copy of my letter to William Miller, the friend Bill, to whom that Frank Taylor guy had written the letter about how you and I took Huey for $100,000.00. If you have it, may I have it back to copy for that Miller. I did not have his address when I wrote you and now that I have it, I have mislaid my letter to him. I'll make a copy to send him, and return yours for your invaluable records—or to throw into the wastebasket.

By the way, today have a letter from Andrew saying that he never had said any such thing. He says that the only thing he remembers ever having said was a joke about Huey having wound up with LSU, a football team, and a tiger, and a magazine. But he says he can't be sure that Taylor was even present when he made the joke.

Love to Tinkie. Ever yours,
As ever,
Red

Eleanor says your voice sounds terrible!
[Handwritten] Andrew says that he is writing Taylor—

West Wardsboro, Vt 05360
July 11, 1985

Dear Cleanth:

I can see your expression of outraged modesty, but I want to say that every man should, in the long view of things, be as modest as humanly possible. But this letter concerns only the very short view. So stop that outraged squawk.

Here is the short view. Malcolm Cowley and I have been in correspondence about the nomination of C. Brooks for the Academy of A & L. It is now settled that I am to write the nomination and Malcolm is to second it. I can't get some facts accurately here and so I ask your help. (1) A bibliography, including books of Percy-Farmer letters, etc., and the general collaboration with N. Smith. (This is not a direct requirement for the Academy, but it bears on the case, and I seem to agree.) (2) Account of your period at the embassy, dates etc. and activities. Subsequent appointments by State Dept. (3) Now—and for God's sake, be helpful, and to hell with your blushes—relevant quotes about your general work. Here the dates of certain essays would be helpful. I know how old-standing is your interest in Faulkner, but I'd like to have any relevant dates. For other things too. (4) Anything about works in progress or projected. It is helpful to have a notion of what is now happening, etc., and has happened since the Institute. (5) Anything you think might be useful. When I get a draft of the nomination, I'd like for you to see it and check.

There are now only two spots in the Academy now, and we want to get the nomination in as soon as possible. September 1 is, I think, the deadline, but we want to beat that by as much as possible.

Malcolm points out that the majority of voters are non-literary, other arts, and that most of them know only candidates who make a splash in fiction, and so novelists have always the pull there, with poets and critics always last. So we are really aiming for 1986. But—who knows?

Love to you all.

As ever,
Red

West Wardsboro, Vt. 05360
July 13, 1985

Dear Cleanth and Tinkie:

I am enclosing the xerox of a "tribute" sent to my brother's widow after the funeral back in January. It was written, you can see, how painfully printed, by Thomas' yard man, always just a shadowy figure, Negro, with a lawn mower or clippers or such. Well, Thomas deserved this. Some day I want to tell you all about him. Since I never lived at home after age 15, and he was 6 years younger than I, he was for years thereafter only a little nuisance to be put up with. We didn't get to know each other until after our mother's death in 1931.

Ever yours,
Red

[OH]   [July 1985]

Dear Red,

I am just beginning to feel like a human being again—not completely, but nearly enough to try to write you a decent letter.

First things, first: the poem you sent to me. I believe you undervalue it. It has (or may have) a place after all among your fine meditations on nature and its mystery. I see what the military jet is doing in the poem: the second pilot who is not contemplating the mystery of nature is not being brushed off; he is acting honestly and normally and may well be the stuff of heroes—even if he is thinking of food and a game of billiards at the end of his flight—not of the impenetrable beauty of the world through which he flies.

By the way I like the furrow his plane seems to plow through the sky better than the notion of his plane being pulled along by an invisible thread. Drop the thread and concentrate on the furrow as fresher and more intense?

The closing reference to "that path and where it leads" may need amplification—or maybe just preparation leading up to it. It has to bear a great deal of emotional intellectual weight and [p. 2] perhaps cannot really do it. Think about it.[1]

The tribute from your brother's yardman to him is truly moving. I am glad to have a copy of it.

I hope that you will someday talk to me about your brother Thomas. You have on one occasion or another in the past, told me various things about him. I am eager to hear you out on the whole subject.

Your relation to him has some odd parallels with my relation to my elder brother, but in my case it was he who left home while I was still small and it was not until our later years that I got to know him. I wish I had known him earlier. He was an unusual person. Our paths widely diverged but we felt at the end a very special relation to each other.

I enclose a xerox from *The New Criterion* to which I now subscribe but which I believe you do not see regularly. I don't agree with all of Richman's judgments but I am impressed by his general conclusion. He has the wit to [p. 3] perceive and value your poetry and to set it in just perspective for the century. I note too, with satisfaction, that he singles out Rosanna in the younger generations of poets.

How is the poor brave girl doing. We trust she has by now made a complete recovery from her ordeal.

Finally, Red, I ought to scold you for your efforts in my behalf. It is a hopeless task, Red, for the reasons that Malcolm mentions as well as deeper and more important ones: I'm not of Academy grade.

But it is characteristic of you to make the effort and, urged on by a lurking personal vanity, I'll send you right away the material you ask for. But neither you or Malcolm ought to exert yourselves: I'll be fully satisfied by the knowledge of your good will and friendship.

I'll phone John Walsh, who is working on my bibliography, [and] ask for a partial copy of his list. I'll then tick off what I think are the stronger and more attractive items.

1. The poem is possibly "New Dawn," which was published in *Hiroshima* by John Hersey (New York: Limited Editions Club), in 1983.

My Jefferson lecture notices turned out to be good.[2] The NEH obviously worked hard to get all the publicity it could for me, and, of course, for itself.

[p. 4] Three of them sound to me particularly thoughtful and perceptive accounts: those in the Washington *Post*, the Chicago *Tribune*, and Boston *Christian Science Monitor*.

I enclose a copy of the last one. It is scarcely appropriate for use in the matter in hand, but I'd like for you and Eleanor to see it.

I still haven't quite shaken off my cold though Tinkie, the hardier soul, has either come close to it or else—as usual—keeps up a good front.

I hope that the summer is proving enjoyable to both of you. I really must get back my energy: I have some articles to write before the summer is over.

With fond greetings from us both,
Cleanth

P.S. The England trip was moderately successful. We saw a few old friends. The weather ranged from fair to good. We saw a few plays—none of them particularly good. Oxford looked beautiful in the sunshine.

West Wardsboro, Vt. 05360
July 23, 1985

Dear Cleanth:

Last night Eleanor and I were settling down for her music and my reading when the radio announced, for 10 P.M., a recording of your Jefferson Lecture. So we caught it at 10. I had read it before, but I had had no idea how it would sound to an audience. But Eleanor simply jumped up, literally, with delight. So deep, so available, so astute. I simply had not caught—certainly not fully—the effectiveness. Both E and I were really hit by the way the Yeats was handled. A deep and fundamental reading of Yeats, but made so clear and available. Well, there it is. Later E. remarked that a few generations back "Cleanth would have been a great theologian and preacher." Well, I am glad he was saved for our time. When he is more sorely needed. How effective the take-off is, too.

Now, the last of this Frank Taylor business. I return to you the letter of xerox which you sent me. I enclose, too, Taylor's *second* letter to me, my final letter to Taylor (delayed by grandbaby etc.) and my letter to Taylor's correspondent Miller. Also, and most important—if anything here can be called important— is Taylor's second letter to me, in which his refreshed memory (what a hen-roost that memory must be!) tells him that it was not Lytle who told him the juicy news but some government employees in Washington—also thirty years ago. Miller is supposed to be a "distinguished journalist." God, what a dependable reporter he is, always heads right to key sources. Do with this stuff what you will. It may reappear, and we are stuck together in the damned business.

2. Brooks gave the Jefferson Lecture in the Humanities in 1985.

News continues good from Rosanna, and I'm getting jealous, of course. Reviews begin, months late, of her poems. One (Peter Stitt) extremely favorable, and I think, thought about. The other favorable but stupid in the Sunday Book section of the Times.

I have just seen a big anthology of "younger American poets." You can't imagine what a dreary crew it is, with a few exceptions. [p. 2] Everybody writes reams of free verse, or almost everybody, and what they think is free verse is usually a vapid bit of narrative that sounds like a newspaper item with lines chopped up. No sense of rhythmic integrity or build. Dull imagery, always predictable or strained. They are almost all exactly alike. If this is a couple of generations—up to 45—God help the future.

Well, love to you all.

As ever,
Red

[OH]   [July 1985]
Dear Red,

Here is the material you requested. I could not be as prompt as I would have liked, for I had to wait until I heard from John Walsh. He has kindly run off a compendious list of my publications from the beginning to 1984. He has provided you with far more material than you need, but that is, of course, because he is attempting a detailed bibliography and, as you know, they have to get in everything.

I have tried to simplify your task by checking a lot I regard as the more interesting articles, but I've checked far more than you need.

I'll forget about parts II and III as of no importance. But they are short and since Walsh sent them along, I've included them.

So much for the articles. I've done my own listing of the books, for I have them here at hand and I thought that by doing them myself, I might organize them for your purpose better than Walsh has.

As you will see, I've separated off in special sections the text-books and the Percy Letters series.

I used to keep a list of my [p. 2] lectures, but I let it lapse many years back. You don't need them for your purposes anyway, but I do have a list of those I gave in 1964–66 while I was at our London Embassy. It came to 132, most of them given in Great Britain though a few were delivered in Germany, Switzerland, and Greece while I was "on loan" from the London Embassy.

The word I value most about my service at London came from the Ambassador, David Bruce, who sent me the following note:

> Dear Cleanth,
>   I greatly regret not having seen Mrs. Brooks and you to say a last good-bye after my return from Washington.

I do want to report how grateful I am for the truly wonderful work you did here for the U.S. Government. I hear nothing but expressions of profound sorrow over your leaving—the best are from three Britishers, Roger Sheffield, Harold Carrio, and David Perth who politely told me you were "irreplaceable."

[p. 3] This is not the kind of note that one feels very comfortable to have passed around. But I don't mind you and Eleanor seeing it nor Malcolm C., for that matter. But you will know best whether to mention it at all and, if so, to whom.

We have pretty well shaken off our summer colds and I have got back most of my energy. Tinkum, that hardy soul, apparently never lost hers.

I am getting down to work again, and goodness knows I find enough unfinished business lying all about me. We trust that you are both well and that you are enjoying the best of a Vermont summer.

Cleanth

. . . .

[OH]   Boston
                                                            August 7, 1985
Dear Cleanth:

Your package of information came a few days ago, and splendid it is for the purpose at hand. I have done a crude draft, but a typing job for M's scrutiny got delayed by Boston, where I am back for a few days, in the hospital. Don't give it a thought. I should be out in a few days & back home. I'll let you know when I get back.

Meanwhile we have been able to cuddle and deeply admire the new granddaughter. She is a splendid specimen of this [p. 2] race of squallers. When she [is] not trying to exhibit her tonsils, she is beautiful.

My love to you and Tinkie. In this, Eleanor would join me, if she had not just gone to Rosanna's house. After installing me here.

Red

Rosanna is torn between bliss and sleepiness—the beautiful squall-er—but thinks that she will survive both experiences.

[OH]   70 Ogden Street
                                          New Haven, Connecticut 06511
                                                          16 August 1985
Dear Red,

It was good to hear your always cheerful voice on the telephone the other morning. I do take heart from that but you must expect your friends, all of us, to be much concerned about anything that threatens your health in any wise. Do let us know from time to time how you are doing and, most of all, by all means let us know if there is anything that we can do to be of service. We can so easily get into the car and drive up to give you and Eleanor a helping hand.

What a fine poem, "John's Birches" is![1] It got deeper and more resonant with each rereading. We have enjoyed it very much. You achieve in it—without any sense of strain—the clean, grave beauty of your best later poems. {[Handwritten in left margin] If Wordsworth were alive, he would envy—or ought to envy—your handling of a theme that was obviously dear to him.}

I am heartened by your remarks in a [p. 2] recent letter on the subject of the great mass of contemporary poetry. I have been worried of late by my own grudging to indifferent response to it and have been tempted to put it down to my hardening arteries and aging taste in poetry. But apparently I am not alone. Sure, we both know that some good poetry is being written. But the game has become so easy to play and it is rapidly becoming simply a game—as empty as just that.

I have nothing very interesting to report about myself. I've just finished drafting a lecture on Faulkner's religion. If it looks good enough when trimmed and pruned and polished, I'll send you a copy. There are one or two things to do before the summer is out. Among them is writing a final chapter to my 17th-century book. What I am really eager to get back to work on is my study of the Southern dialect. I'll have a foretaste of what I am up to in my Lamar Lectures which should be off the press and ready for publication this fall.[2] I'll get you and Eleanor a copy when it comes out.

Meantime we have no unbreakable or un-postponable engagements between now and October. If we can help, pick up the telephone and let us know. Tinkie joins in affectionate greeting to you both.

[Cleanth]

West Wardsboro, Vt.
August 22, 1985

Dear Cleanth:

Here, in a rough form, is the draft of the "citation" sent to Malcolm and Maggie Mills for comment. For the same I now send it to you. There is haste, this month, and so please [send it] right back as soon as possible. And no foolishness out of you. Reduction may be necessary, so any mere reductions might be useful. But don't let idiocy get the upper hand of you. Maggie is corralling the seconders after Malcolm and De Vries.

All the best of everything to you two, who deserve it most.

Yours,
Red

1. "John Birches," *New Yorker*, August 12, 1985, p. 26.
2. *The Language of the American South*, Mercer University Lamar Memorial Lectures, no. 28 (Athens: University of Georgia Press, 1985).

West Wardsboro, Vt 05360
August 25, 1985

Dear Cleanth:

The letter and enclosure [Cleanth's nomination for membership in the American Academy of Arts and Letters] to you is being mailed today. That means that it will be in the mail Monday morning. All these damned delays. I expected to hear from Malcolm and Maggie yesterday, but no word. Tomorrow almost certainly.

But what started this letter was reading again your letter with the generous offer (what a tame word this seems—"generous") to help us. We have never had, or even heard of, any friendship beyond this—and rarely anything to match it. Hug Tinkie for us. Don't thank her. Just give her a hug for us.

Ever yours,
Red

2495 Redding Road
Fairfield, Connecticut 06430
December 2, 1985

Dear Brookses:

Thanksgiving was, as usual, a splendid matter. On table and from bottle. But that is not all. Even more importantly was the whole feeling of the occasion. I can't tell you what it means to me—and to us—to see the faces of those who have for so many years meant so much. That is all I want to say, but I may add "thanks."

Our love to you both. And all the best to the boys.

Eleanor joins me in love.

Red

[Handwritten] This is not, God damn it, a "thank you note"!!

[OH]   2495 Redding Road
Fairfield, Connecticut 06430
February 4, 1986

Dear Cleanth and Tinkie:

This morning, on a little holiday from chores, I have been sitting & reading the "Ancient Mariner"—and looking at Doré's pictures. So I feel the impulse to write you two for making this possible. It is not the first time that book has been on my knee.

God, the poem seems better—deeper—than ever. And it strikes me that all poetry is, in some deep way, an attempt to bless the water snakes. All poetry that is very good. Even if a poet doesn't quite realize the fact. Even if a critic does not. I know a few writers who have known—or do know.

All thanks, profound thanks, for the book, to you two.

As ever,
Red

Speaking of Doré, I must have told you all about once seeing a book of my father's father—a translation of Dante, illustrated by Doré. An episode rather fresh to me now, for I've been doing bit by bit a memoir of my father. *Not* & *never* an autobiography.

[OH]   70 Ogden Street
                                         New Haven, Connecticut 06511
                                                            7 April 1988
Dear Red,
    Your recent letters have given me a great deal of pleasure. I too am hoping that something more than old friendship is in your saying that you are satisfied with what I have had to say about *All the King's Men.*
    When I told the audience that the topic had not been chosen by me but by the Levy Committee, I had in mind something like this: because we are old friends and because presumably I know something about the Louisiana scene, it would have been an easy—and even selfish—choice for me to make. I wanted them to know that there were better reasons for choosing it.
    I'm glad that you noted that fact in my paper, but glad for a different reason: your name in Louisiana is well known and your memory fresh and green. They—even in the Cajun Country—are proud of a book so fine that has its setting in Louisiana. They wanted to hear about it.
    My cue I thought, and you must have noticed, was to take the Louisiana setting so much for granted—so obviously there—that I needed only to remind my audience of it, and devote my time to showing how universal the book is, how much it reflects general stresses in the culture of the West, and thus takes its place alongside the work of the other great writers of our century. This last point is so important that I hope that I was at least partially successful in getting it over to my audience.
    On Sunday I fly out to Roswell, New Mexico, to give a lecture and to join with Bo Grimshaw in a seminar on Faulkner's *The Reivers.*[1] About a half hour ago, I had a telephone call from Tommy Thompson. He was inquiring about you and told [p. 2] me that he would soon be sitting down to write a letter to you. He is to be at Roswell. (I think he is an alumnus of the New Mexico Military Institute.) He will drive me back to Amarillo, Texas. I'll spend one night there and fly back to New York from there. Amarillo has a better air service than Roswell.
    I expect to get back to New Haven on the evening of April 14.
    My Lecture at Lafayette, I was told, is to be dedicated to Tinkum in the little pamphlet-sized publication that they will do. I found out also, to my surprise, that they had asked Bob Heilman to do a tribute to her, which is also to be published in the little booklet.

---

    1. The occasion was a colloquium at the New Mexico Military Institute in Roswell, New Mexico, at which Brooks gave the keynote address, "The Role of the Humanities in a Technological Age," on April 12, 1988.

Bob is very good at this sort of thing and has done a nice piece of prose which makes, I think, some very just observations about her. (I am, of course, the last person who could speak as an honest reporter on the tribute.) But it does please me and I think it will please you and Eleanor. I'll get it xeroxed and send it along.

With all good wishes to you both,
Cleanth

P.S. Though I thought I knew *A the K's. M* well, having, among other things taught it on several occasions, I reread it as I prepared for my lecture. How that book stands up to repeated readings. It's truly rich—keeps on giving of itself on later readings!

Afterword
by R. W. B. Lewis

THE NEW ENGLAND PHASE in the lives of Cleanth Brooks and Robert Penn Warren effectively began in 1947, when Brooks left Louisiana State University to take a position at Yale. Warren had departed from the South five years earlier, when LSU authorities behaved shabbily over a salary matter, and had gone to the University of Minnesota. In 1950, Warren also accepted an appointment at Yale, to teach playwriting. He pulled out in 1955; but in 1961, he came back to Yale for keeps, as writer in residence and professor of English. The Yale invitation had been connived at, tactfully, by Brooks, who on July 26 remarked on the exceptional enthusiasm shown by the other English professors at news of the event. In retrospect, the two can be seen collaborating in their lives as well as in their professional activities. And so, having both been born in southern Kentucky, they spent their last decades in Connecticut—Warren in a large and imaginatively remodeled barn, with a summer home in Vermont; Brooks in suburban Northford, and then on an attractive residential street in New Haven.

Their New England surroundings made them both more aware of their southern homeland than ever before. It is a familiar reaction: F. O. Matthiessen, recounting a year in Prague and Salzburg in the postwar 1940s, could say that he had come to Europe to find out what it meant to be an American. It might almost be said that Brooks and Warren came to New England to find out what it meant to be southern.

Warren in particular was conscious of this. Talking with an interviewer in 1974, he mused that as long as he was *living* in Tennessee and Kentucky, "and knew about various kinds of life there," he had no special notions about the region. But "as soon as I *left* that world . . . I began to rethink the meaning of it."

In the case of Cleanth Brooks, the rethinking took the primary form of a long, deep look into the world and the writings of William Faulkner. For a good many years, Brooks's own critical work had dealt almost entirely with English writers, with English poets and poetry. He labored over the multivolume edition of the letters of Thomas Percy, the eighteenth-century compiler of the *Reliques of Ancient English Poetry,* and composed essays like those in his classic 1947 study of poetic structure, *The Well Wrought Urn,* which

417

dealt with Shakespeare, Milton, Gray, Wordsworth, Keats, Tennyson, Yeats. But by midsummer 1960, we were hearing allusions to a close scrutiny of *Intruder in the Dust* and its reflection of the southern temperament; and in 1963, there appeared *William Faulkner: The Yoknapatawpha Country*, the first of Brooks's several Faulkner volumes, a truly magisterial work, steeped in southern history and language and cultural accentuation.

Long before the Yale years, Warren of course had been exploring that southern scene in fiction from *Night Rider* in 1939 to *World Enough and Time* in 1950. What the change of base to Connecticut brought out in Warren, first of all, was a rush of reminiscences: in poems such as "Gold Glade," about "wandering . . . the woods of boyhood"; or "Country Burying (1919)," with its memories from when he was fourteen; or "School Lesson Based on Word of Tragic Death of Entire Gillum Family," with its spine-tingling memory of an eighth-grade experience. (All of these poems are in the 1957 volume *Promises*.) But what is most striking about Warren's response to his new environment is his heightened attention to the double phenomenon of north and south.

In 1956, Warren published the book-length essay *Segregation*, a work vitalized by a sort of intellectual and moral anguish. Its subtitle was *The Inner Conflict of the South*; but within a few years, Warren was meditating rather on the South and the North together, in conjunction and conflict. In the single year 1961 (the year of his reappointment at Yale), there appeared *The Legacy of the Civil War*, an eloquently ironic sketch of the ongoing posture of North and South toward the great collision; *Wilderness*, a novel about the war (from draft riot to battlefield), with characters of incompatible persuasion playing their parts; and the poem "Two Studies in Idealism," which pairs a plain-speaking southern countryman and a high-minded Harvard graduate of the class of 1861, the two meeting fatally at Shiloh. The subtitle of the twelve-stanza work is "Short Survey of American, and Human, History"; for Warren the 1860s war virtually created American history, or the sense of history in the American mind, and as such was a paradigm of all history.

In their correspondence, meanwhile, Brooks and Warren repeatedly touched on matters southern. In the summer of 1960, both were pondering the question of Robert E. Lee's decision (to borrow Brooks's phrase in an August 2 letter) "to stay with Virginia." Brooks felt, and apparently Warren agreed, that as "against the more abstract claims of liberty, justice, etc.," there was for Lee "the concrete claim of the region, the community, the family." At other times, most notably in the fall of 1961, they speculated on what might have happened if the South had won the Civil War.

As to that, both were sure that a southern victory would have affected the pace but not the fact of southern industrialization. "My own view," Brooks wrote on October 15, 1971 (in a letter of considerable and diverse interest), "is that a Southern victory would have only slowed down the movement toward centralization, urbanization, and industrialization." It might also, Brooks added a bit wistfully, "have helped us preserve certain traditional views about life—at least have kept them alive longer." Warren put the matter more strongly. "If the South had won," he wrote on October 6, "they would have embarked socially and economically on much the same course. . . . They would never have settled for the plantation team—and many defenders of the Southern system were already aware of the industrial needs." Although to an obviously different degree, both had moved quite far away from the agrarian anti-industrial doctrine of the collective volume of 1930 (to which Warren had contributed), *I'll Take My Stand.*

This particular exchange bore on the treatment of the Civil War and southern society in the work then in progress, a textbook on American literature that Brooks, Warren, and I were coediting. The immediate concern of the other two was that the book should carry no hint of any editorial belief in a self-perpetuating old-style southern culture if the Confederacy had triumphed.

American Literature was only one of a number of college textbooks that Brooks and Warren were engaged in, and that they meticulously revised throughout the 1960s and 1970s. The letters are crowded with long and detailed discussions of writers and texts and strategies. By 1976, their most famous collaborative work, *Understanding Poetry*, was in its fourth edition. The year before, *An Approach to Literature* entered its fifth edition; *Understanding Fiction* appeared in a third edition in 1970; and *Modern Rhetoric* in its fourth in the same year.

But for a decade, from 1963 to 1973, the chief topic of textbook conversation was the American venture. This had begun when an editor from St. Martin's Press in New York approached Brooks and Warren with the idea of a textbook to be called *Understanding American Literature*. After thinking about it for a while, the two veteran textbook designers decided that they needed a bona fide Americanist to take part; and since I was on hand, a Yale colleague and friend, they invited me to join the team. At a later moment, and after considering alternatives, we changed the title to *American Literature: The Makers and the Making* (the phrases were Warren's).

The Brooks-Warren letters offer a fair enough account of how the textbook came into being, and how it expanded far beyond a New Criticism survey of the chief texts in question (which is what the St. Martin's editor had anticipated) into something like a full-scale account of American cultural history—with literature at the core—from the Puritan origins to the 1970s. There is perhaps less talk in the letters than one would want about some aspects of the expansion process: how the textbook took in what we called "Literature of the Non-Literary World," political writing, nature writing, travel writing; how the concept enlarged to include Indian oratory, folk songs, and the blues (down to "The Big Rock Candy Mountain" and "Empty Bed Blues"), as well as "intellectual writing" (William James, Kenneth Burke, and others) and, beginning in the late nineteenth century, a broad selection of African American writing from Charles Chesnutt and Paul Lawrence Dunbar to Langston Hughes, Richard Wright, and Zora Neale Hurston. But the essential experience is conveyed accurately enough.

As with the other textbooks—Lewis Simpson has noted this in the Fore-word—the procedure was a "social" one. Cleanth Brooks made the point in the Letter to the Reader, which he drew up and which Warren and I endorsed: "Our method was inductive," Brooks said, "and our mode of working was social; that is, we read and we talked." We met and talked for an afternoon or for two and three days at a time—at the Brookses' home in Northford, at the Warrens' home in Vermont, at Calhoun College at Yale (where I was then the Master in residence). Usually, all three of us convened; but occasionally, if either Brooks or Warren was out of the country (Brooks, for example, was in London as the cultural attaché in 1965–1966), only two of us could come together. These latter sessions, and their findings, are carefully summarized by Brooks and Warren in their letters to one another.

We divided the authors and introductions among us as we moved ahead from period to period; and over the ensuing years, the letters speak of some of the individual undertakings—Brooks on poetry and southern writing, Warren on Cooper and Hawthorne, me on Emerson and Henry James. For Warren, it seems to have been an exhilarating voyage of discovery and rediscovery; and, as could later be realized, of self-discovery.

On May 20, 1965, as an example, Warren said he had "been on Hawthorne, have reread him almost entire, and a lot of stuff about him. Now I shall do that section as a trial balloon." Seven months later, Brooks wrote from the American Embassy in London: "I have used this Christmas lull to go back to your Hawthorne, re-read it, and I am much impressed. It seems to me the best thing that has ever been written on Hawthorne—the best that I know of, at any rate." Thirty-odd years later, I would second that judgment. What Brooks admired was the way the essay wove together biography and criticism—"discussing some text rather fully . . . and bringing in the relevant parts of [Hawthorne's] life as a man and an artist." That is exactly right; but my own enjoyment comes also from the sense that in the essay Warren is, so to say, standing shoulder to shoulder with Hawthorne, appraising him not as an academic critic but as a fellow practitioner of the art of fiction. In sizing up Hawthorne, Warren is indeed defining himself:

> He lived in the right ratio—right for the fueling of his genius—between an attachment to his region and a detached assessment of it; between attraction to the past and its repudiation; between attraction to the world and contempt for its gifts; . . . between a fascinated attentiveness to the realistic texture, forms, and characteristics of nature and human nature, and a compulsive flight from that welter of life toward abstract ideas.

There, in perfectly chosen wording, the southern-born resident of New England identifies the supreme New England creative temperament, and in the same wording expresses himself—in his own ambiguous relation to his own region, to the past of that region, to the world of nature and to abstract ideas.

Brooks, in the letter quoted, had only one worry about the Hawthorne piece: its excessive length. Warren did tend to submit massive essays on the major authors he covered. In the early 1970s, he incorporated several of them into separate volumes devoted to Melville's poetry, to Dreiser, and to Whittier; the Hawthorne and Mark Twain introductions were also published separately. But all three of us wrote at generous length; and I once calculated that, before we were through, we had each of us written the equivalent of five hundred typescript pages of headnotes and introductions to authors and selections.

As we worked along together, I became oddly aware of a certain thickening of cultural attitudes. Brooks and Warren, to my view, became more and more southern in their comments and emphases, and I more and more northern—I began, like Emily Dickinson, "to see New Englandly." This was a subject for bursts of laughter rather than for tension. Brooks is referring to this aspect of our work together in his letter of October 15, 1971, when he suspects I might be warning Warren (then absent): "Go a little farther, Brother Warren, and you'll be maintaining that the South ought to have won the War." The occasion here was Warren's choices among Herman Melville's Civil War poems, most of them depicting northern disasters—like "Ball's Bluff," where, in Warren's notation, "four regiments of Federal troops were . . . pinned against the river at Ball's Bluff" in a battle that "became little better than a massacre."

A more troublesome concern was our radically different appraisal of the New England transcendentalists. Brooks and Warren were congenitally hostile to the New England penchant for abstractions and concepts like "the higher law"; and Brooks feared a possible discord between Warren's introduction to the period 1825–1861, where that hostility was apparent, and my introduction to the section on Emerson, where I declared him to be "the *indispensable* figure in American literary history." Brooks remarked in the October 15, 1971, letter that he had "made rather elaborate notes on how to make some accommodations between the 1825–61 Prelim. Note and Dick's Intro. to Emerson and yet avoid taking the bite out of the Prelim. Note." To his relief, the two sections jibed pretty well. If they did not coincide, they worked together dialectically. Warren made reference to the New England habit of abstraction in a fine jaunty little passage of a letter dated May 27, 1970, where he describes Thoreau as "quite capable of jumping through 'nature' into eternity like the poodle through the hoop in a dog-and-pony show." Warren, truth to tell, recognized the abstracting tendency in himself; we can recall his allusion to Hawthorne in this regard.

When it was all over, Brooks, in his Letter to the Reader, and with an air of happy exhaustion, said: "We were aware that we represented divergent personalities, interests, and degrees of specialization, but we hoped to make a virtue of these very differences. Different perspectives on an author might produce a portrait more nearly in the round."

Another major dimension of these letters is the purely personal one. Warren, as family-oriented a human being as one could ever meet (he used regularly to ask solicitously about the health of my wife's brother-in-law), gives constant updates on family affairs: on accidents incurred by wife or daughter while skiing or horseback riding; on the attractive growing-up symptoms of his daughter, Rosanna, and his son, Gabriel; on their marriages and the births of their children. My own very last glimpse of Red Warren, in the Vermont home in West Wardsboro in the late summer of 1989, is of a fading ghost looking with silent heartfelt joy at the newborn child of Gabriel and Ana—welcoming the new life even as his gave out.

Another dimension is Brooks's repeated appreciation of Warren's writing. In November 1966, we find him expressing high admiration for the recently published sequence of poems called "Ile de Port-Cros." (It was named for the island northeast of Toulon on the Riviera where the Warren family had spent some time earlier that year; it appeared in the volume *Incarnations,* suitably retitled "Island of Summer.") Brooks indicated two special favorites in the sequence; and later in the same letter, he reported on his reading of Warren's poems at a Yale gathering. The poems created a remarkable effect on the listeners, Brooks said. "Why shouldn't the poems register powerfully: they are simply the best that are being written today in English."

In March 1969, Brooks found Warren's long poem *Audubon* "a stunning job." It is indeed; all things considered, *Audubon* is the most beautifully realized of Warren's full-length poems. Then, in March 1974, writing from Baton Rouge (he had gone back to their old university for a semester), Brooks quoted from a recent letter sent him by "a very old woman (Roman Catholic)," who told him, "I suppose poetry has been almost forced into becoming a religion by the defection of religion." She went on: "there's far more 'transcendence' (and that's a dicey word to use) in almost any of Warren's poems than in the trash we have now in the ICEL Mass [the New English translation] and other messed-about services. Take 'Walk by Moonlight' or that spooky new one about Christmas."

The second of those references is to Warren's haunting visionary reminiscence, "I Am Dreaming of a White Christmas" (published as "The Natural History of a Vision" in the *Atlantic Monthly* in December 1973). The first poem cited, from the 1957 volume *Promises,* is also a visionary reminiscence in its way. It tells of the poet, on a return visit to his hometown of Guthrie, being awakened by moonlight pouring across his bed. He arises, gets dressed, and goes for a walk. As he wanders along, he remembers things:

> How long ago, at night, up that track,
> I had watched the Pullmans flash and fade,
> Then heard, in new quiet, the beat my heart made.

He glances in the store windows:

> Down Main Street, the window dummies blessed,
> With lifted hands and empty stare,
> The glimmering emptiness of air,

As though lunatically to attest
What hope the daylight heart might reasonably have possessed.

That hope of the daylight heart, thus rhymingly and skeptically described, finds formulation in the final stanza, where the poet strives in the Warren manner for some mode of genuine transcendence:

Might a man but know his Truth, and might
He live so that life, by moon or sun,
In dusk or dawn, would be all one,
Then never on a summer night
Need to stand and shake in that cold blaze of Platonic light.

The old Catholic woman's comment could be the basis of a long and searching essay on the religious impulse in Robert Penn Warren's poetry. Sending it along, Cleanth Brooks, good Anglican that he was, added: "Coming from me, you will not feel that there the grim wolf with piety paw is after you. Anyway, I pass it on to you as a real tribute to the power of your poetry."

In his seventy-ninth year, Warren drew himself together to say something about what Brooks's literary help had meant to him. He had sent Brooks a sheaf of new poems, some of those, presumably, included in the section "Altitudes and Extensions" in Warren's last collection, *New and Selected Poems, 1923–1985*. Warren thanked his friend of more than sixty years "for the pains you took with the poetry manuscript," fearing only that Brooks may have been "too easy on the book—which is like you." This led to a long passage of multitiered gratitude—for the long companionship of Cleanth and Tinkum Brooks; for Brooks's stimulating and educational talk over the decades about poets and poetry in general; and for Brooks's particular contribution to Warren's own work.

It is a small echoing hymn of friendship. The passage was fittingly quoted by James Grimshaw, as the conclusion of his luminous introduction; but it is worth a second slow savoring reading:

But this leads to a broader thought, which I have thought for a long time. You must—you plural—must have known of the dimension of our attachment to Brookses and admiration. I can look back longer than Eleanor, but with no more feeling. But I want to say something more special now. You can't imagine how much I owe you about poetry—on two counts. Our long collaborations always brought something new and eye-opening to me, seminal notions, for me, often couched in some seemingly incidental or casual remark. One of the happiest recollections I have, is that of the long sessions of work on *UP*—not to mention all earlier and later conversations. The other count has to do with the confidence you gave me about my own efforts. I'm sure that you were often over-generous, but even allowing for that, it still meant something fundamental to me. I have often wanted to say something like this to you, but I know how you'd give an embarrassed shrug and disclaimer. Anyhow now I can say it without your interruption.

In the margin Warren added: "This does not cover so many other indebtednesses." At the bottom of the page, following the signature—"As ever, Red"—
and handwritten, is the injunction: "No answer, please." Brooks evidently
obeyed the command.

Index

A.S.T.P., 78

Abbe: Warren on poems submitted to *Southern Review,* 53

Abbott, Charles D., 174

Abolitionism, 272, 333, 362

Academic Deans of the South, 118

Academy of Arts and Letters: nomination of Brooks to, 407, 412, 413

Accent, 88

Account of an Expedition to the Sources of the Mississippi, 320

Achievement of Robert Penn Warren, The, 4

Achievement of William Faulkner, The, 11

Adam, Tim, 345

Adams, Henry, 272, 310, 311, 316

"Adam's Task," 337, 349

"Ad Musam," 336, 349

Aeschylus, 197

"After Apple-Picking," 97, 173, 178, 179, 180, 182, 183, 187, 188

"After Great Pain," 215

Agee, James, 143

"Age of Overkill, The," 291, 297

Agrarian movement, xii

Agriesti, Marland: with Harcourt Brace, 403

Aiken, Conrad, 206, 317, 318, 325, 379

"Air, Art, and the Civilians," 300

"Alaska Brown Bear," 337, 349

Albee, Edward Franklin, 267

Albrizio, Gene, 59, 109

Albrizio, Jean, 89

Alfred A. Knopf, Inc., 253

Algren, Nelson, 200

Alice in Wonderland, 396

"All Is Calm" (Sundgaard), 54

All the King's Men, 80, 92, 115, 128, 414, 415; revisions, 102; Brooks on, 110; advance readers' responses to, 111; Baton Rouge reviews of, 120; filming of, 153, 171; Modern Library edition of, 198; Time Reading Program introduction to, 251, 254; opera of, 396; 35th anniversary edition of, 399; mentioned, xv

All the King's Men (A Play), 140, 172; premiere performance of, 128; radio broadcast of, 161; staged in Germany, 209

Altick, Richard D., 137

"Altitudes and Extensions," 2, 423

Ambiguity: subject of, 179, 180

American Academy of Arts and Sciences, 278

American Adam, The, 286

American Bookman, 82, 88

"American Challenge, The," 291

American Composition and Rhetoric, 101

American Dream, The, 267

American Indian, 324

American Literature, 393

American literature: significance to the world, 280

American Literature: The Makers and the Making, 12, 254, 256, 257, 259, 261, 268, 270, 271, 280, 284–86, 292–93, 298, 301–2, 307, 315, 316, 319, 331, 348, 356, 419; making of, xi; length of, 287, 288, 311–12, 313, 314, 329; proposed delivery date, 289; methods of introductions, 293–94, 310; as history of American literature, 295; nonliterary world section, 299, 320, 332, 419; Southern section, 312–13, 321, 325, 338, 340, 362; new American poetry section, 313; intellectual background section, 313, 316, 321, 323, 326, 340; imagism to symbolism section, 315, 325, 338, 359; biography in, 317; tone of presentation, 317; emergent nationalism section, 319; footnotes in, 324; preface, 325; galleys

425

Gordon, Edward: with Harcourt Brace, 283, 341, 350, 353, 354
"Graduated Response Fallacy, The," 291
Graham, Dominick, 291
Grammar: subject of, 115, 116, 119, 120, 126
Grapes of Wrath, The, 33
"Grave, The," 386
Graves, Robert, 81, 123, 134, 142, 181
Gray, Thomas, 184
Great Gatsby, The, 167, 326
Green: with Prentice-Hall, 269
Green, Miss: with St. Martin's Press, 340
Greene, William, 117
Gregory, Horace, 132
Grieve, Christopher Murray. *See* MacDiarmid, Hugh
Griggs, Earl Leslie, 81, 122
Grimshaw, James A., Jr. (Bo), 414
Griswold, Erwin T., 294
Guerard, Albert, Jr., 392
Guicharnaud, Jacques, 277

H.D., 317, 318
Haight, Andrea, 391
"Hail Fellow, Well Met," 26
Haines, George, 43
"Haircut," 224, 225
Hale, 157
Hamilton, Alexander, 130
Hamlet, 84
Harcourt, Brace and Co., 70, 71, 77, 159, 175, 203, 213, 341, 349, 353
Hardy, Edward, 93
Hardy, Thomas, 24
Harper and Brothers, 203
Harris, Joel Chandler, 323
Harte, Bret, 230, 316
Harvard Advocate: Faulkner issue, 265
Harvard University: interest in Warren, 216; the press, 313, 374
Harvest of Change, 311
Harvey, Wayne, 365
"Hat, The" (Dreyer): Warren on, 53
Hatcher, William Bass, 86; health, 119
Hatfield, 61
"Have Nations Any Morals?" 148
Have You Ever Eaten Stars? See Rumor Verified
"Hawk of Autumn, The," 183
Hawthorne, Nathaniel, xii, 260, 261, 265, 271, 284, 285, 310
Hawthorne Question, The, 286, 289
Hayakawa, S. I., 117

Healy: Brooks on submission to *Southern Review,* 44
Heard, Red, 86
Heart of Darkness, 106, 108, 109
Hebert, Paul M., 23, 31, 34, 38, 45, 49, 89
Hecksher, August, 291
Hedda Gabler, 20, 194–95
Hegel, Georg Wilhelm Friedrich, 322, 323
Heilman, Robert B., xiii, 7, 39, 67, 70, 77, 78, 82, 88, 92, 93, 104, 115, 125, 146, 147, 158, 256, 278, 414
Helen: with L.S.U. Press, 103
"Hell Gate," 191, 217, 231, 381
Helsinki, Finland, 279
Hemingway, Ernest, 8, 135, 219, 144, 311, 316, 326; essay on "The Killers," 54, 61, 62, 69; on Hemingway hero, 315
Henry Holt and Co.: *Understanding Poetry,* 23; permissions, 81; mentioned, 36, 98, 174, 183, 187, 215, 245. *See also* Holt, Rinehart and Winston
"Henry James at Newport" (Kees): Warren on, 54
"Herman Melville" (poem), 42
Hero in America, The, 328
Herrick, Robert, 19
Herron, Edwin, 26
Hersey, John, 136, 152
Heywood: Brooks on submission to *Southern Review,* 43
"Hickman Story, The," 151, 155
Hidden God, The, 245
High Conquest, 155
Hilton Head project, 388
Hinton, James, 75
Hiroshima, 136, 154, 155
Hitchcock, James, 291, 297
"Hive at G, The," 330
Hock, Elizabeth H., 349
Hodges, Gen. Campbell Blankshear, 50
Hogan, William Ransom, 158
Holden, Walter: with Harcourt Brace, 341, 354
Hollander, John, 336, 398
"Holmes," 330
Holmes, Oliver Wendell, 288, 290, 314, 316
Holt, Rinehart and Winston, 273
Holy Bible, 148
"Homage to Emerson . . . ," 266
"Honey House, The," 108
Hood, Thomas, 377
Hook, Sidney, 304, 311
"Horatian Ode," 114
Hornberger, 122
Horrell, Joe, 45